Sixth Edition

Classical Sociological Theory

George Ritzer
University of Maryland

The McGraw-Hill Companies

CLASSICAL SOCIOLOGICAL THEORY, SIXTH EDITION

Published by McGraw-Hill, a business unit of The McGraw-Hill Companies, Inc., 1221 Avenue of the Americas, New York, NY 10020.

Some ancillaries, including electronic and print components, may not be available to customers outside the United States.

This book is printed on acid-free paper.

2 3 4 5 6 7 8 9 0 DOC/DOC 1 0 9 8 7 6 5 4 3 2 1 0

ISBN: 978-0-07-802665-2

MHID: 0-07-802665-2

Vice President & Editor-in-Chief: *Michael Ryan*
Vice President EDP/Central Publishing Services: *Kimberly Meriwether David*
Senior Sponsoring Editor: *Gina Boedeker*
Executive Marketing Manager: *Pamela S. Cooper*
Managing Editor: *Nicole Bridge*
Project Manager: *Erin Melloy*
Design Coordinator: *Margarite Reynolds*
Cover Designer: *Kay Lieberherr*
Lead Photo Editor: *Alexandra Ambrose*
Cover Credit: *Wetzel and Company*
Buyer: *Nicole Baumgartner*
Compositor: *Glyph International*
Typeface: *10/12 Times Roman*
Printer: *R. R. Donnelley*

All credits appearing on page or at the end of the book are considered to be an extension of the copyright page.

Library of Congress Cataloging-in-Publication Data

Ritzer, George.
Classical sociological theory / George Ritzer.—6th ed.
p. cm.
ISBN 978-0-07-802665-2 (pbk. : acid-free paper)
1. Sociology—History. 2. Sociology—Methodology—History.
3. Sociologists—Biography. I. Title.
HM435.R56 2010
301.01—dc22

2010006326

www.mhhe.com

About the Author

George Ritzer is Distinguished University Professor at the University of Maryland, where he has also been a Distinguished Scholar-Teacher and won a Teaching Excellence Award. He was also awarded the 2000 Distinguished Contributions to Teaching Award by the American Sociological Association, and in 2004 he was awarded an honorary doctorate by LaTrobe University, Melbourne, Australia.

He has served as Chair of the American Sociological Association's Sections on Theoretical Sociology and Organizations and Occupations. He held the UNESCO Chair in Social Theory at the Russian Academy of Sciences, a Fulbright-Hays Chair at York University in Canada, and a Fulbright-Hays award to the Netherlands. He has been Scholar-in-Residence at the Netherlands Institute for Advanced Study and the Swedish Collegium for Advanced Study in the Social Sciences.

Dr. Ritzer's main theoretical interests lie in metatheory as well as applied social theory. In metatheory, his contributions include *Metatheorizing in Sociology* (Lexington Books, 1991), *Sociology: A Multiple Paradigm Science* (Allyn and Bacon, 1975, 1980), and *Toward an Integrated Sociological Paradigm* (Allyn and Bacon, 1981).

Professor Ritzer is perhaps best known for *The McDonaldization of Society* (5th edition, 2008; translated into more than a dozen languages) and several related books (also with a number of translations), including *Expressing America: A Critique of the Global Credit Card Society* (1995), *Enchanting a Disenchanted World: Revolutionizing the Means of Consumption* (3rd edition, 2010), *The Globalization of Nothing* (2nd edition, 2007), and the forthcoming (with Craig Lair) *Outsourcing: Globalization and Beyond.* He edited the *Encyclopedia of Social Theory* (2005) and is the founding editor of the *Journal of Consumer Culture.* He edited the eleven-volume *Encyclopedia of Sociology* (2007) and *The Blackwell Companion to Globalization* (2007).

In 2010, McGraw-Hill published the third edition of Professor Ritzer's *Contemporary Sociological Theory and Its Classical Roots: The Basics.* In 2010, McGraw-Hill will publish the eighth edition of *Sociological Theory*. The latter texts, as well as this one, have been translated into a number of languages.

TO MOTHER,
With Appreciation and Love

Brief Contents

Contents

Biographical Sketches

Preface

The publication of the sixth edition of *Classical Sociological Theory* is characterized by both continuity and change. The book continues to do what it has always done—offer a comprehensive overview of classical sociological theory in a single volume. As in previous editions, the in-depth discussion of theories (often enlivened with examples) in the text narrative is accompanied by informative and—I hope—engaging biographical sketches of many of the most important thinkers in the history of sociology.

Classical Sociological Theory continues to include two historical chapters covering the early history of the field (Chapter 1) as well as its most recent developments (Chapter 2). These chapters give students an overview that allows them to put the work of each theorist in its historical, social, and political context. In one convenient volume, this book offers students a handy overview of most of what they need to know about classical sociological theory.

The social world is a complex and difficult subject; so are many of the theories about it. I have striven to make theory interesting, relevant, and as clear and accessible as possible.

The biggest change in the fifth edition of *Classical Sociological Theory* is the addition of Chapter 13 devoted to the work of Joseph Schumpeter. It has been my custom to add a new chapter devoted to a particular classical theorist (previous additions include chapters on Alexis de Tocqueville, W.E.B. Du Bois, Thorstein Veblen, and Karl Mannheim) to each edition of this book. Schumpeter (like Marx, Veblen, and others) is most often thought of as an economist, but there are important sociological ideas in his work. Best known is his thinking on creative destruction, but less well-known is the fact that it is embedded in a broader theory of the dynamics of capitalism in particular and the economy in general (his economic sociology). Of particular interest is the relationship between Schumpeter's theory and that of Marx (especially on socialism) and Weber (especially on rationalization).

At the suggestion of reviewers of the previous edition, two previously deleted sections have been restored to this edition. The first is the restoration of the section entitled "Marx's Economics: A Case Study" to Chapter 6. The second is the return of the Appendix, which deals with metatheory as well as the metatheoretical approach that lies at the base of this book. To make room for the additions, a number of deletions have been made throughout the book. These involved a variety of secondary issues (e.g., Spencer's thoughts on the sources of biases in sociological research) and their elimination does not adversely affect the integrity of the work discussed.

The rest of the text remains largely unchanged, although I have updated references as often as possible.

Acknowledgments

Once again, I want to thank Patricia Lengermann and Gillian Niebrugge for revising their pathbreaking Chapter 10 on classical feminist theory. Their chapter has not only made this book much stronger, but it also has had a strong influence on theorizing independent of the book.

I would like to thank Craig Lair for co-authoring the new chapter on Joseph Schumpeter. I continue to be grateful for the contribution of Doug Goodman to an earlier edition to this book. Thanks to Jillet Sam who provided invaluable assistance in preparing this edition. I would also like to thank various people at McGraw-Hill for their help and encouragement, including Gina Boedeker, Nicole Bridge, and Craig Leonard.

Finally, thanks are due to a panel of reviewers whose comments and suggestions helped to make this edition a better book:

Neil Quisenberry, McKendree University
Andrew Perrin, University of North Carolina, Chapel Hill
Harland Prechel, Texas A & M University
John Clarry, Bloomfield College (and TCNJ)
Echo Fields, Southern Oregon University
Whitney Garcia, Towson University
Michael Klausner, University of Pittsburgh—Bradford
Eleanor LaPointe, Rutgers University
Tom Arcaro, Elon University

George Ritzer

PART I

Introduction to Classical Sociological Theory

CHAPTER 1

A Historical Sketch of Sociological Theory: The Early Years

Chapter Outline

This book is designed as an introduction to the work of the classical sociological theorists, and we begin with one-sentence statements that get to the essence of the theories to be covered in these pages:

- We are headed to an increasingly centralized world with less individual freedom. (*Alexis de Tocqueville*)
- We are evolving in the direction of a world dominated by science. (*Auguste Comte*)
- The world is moving in the direction of increasing order and harmony. (*Herbert Spencer*)
- Capitalism is based on the exploitation of the workers by the capitalists. (*Karl Marx*)

- The modern world offers less moral cohesion than did earlier societies. (*Emile Durkheim*)
- The modern world is an iron cage of rational systems from which there is no escape. (*Max Weber*)
- The city spawns a particular type of person. (*Georg Simmel*)
- Gender inequality explains most of individual experience, the ills in society, and history. (*Charlotte Perkins Gilman*)
- A "veil" rather than a wall separates African Americans and whites. (*W. E. B. Du Bois*)
- People engage in conspicuous consumption. (*Thorstein Veblen*)
- Capitalism is virtually synonymous with "creative destruction." (*Joseph Schumpeter*)
- Knowledge is shaped by the social world. (*Karl Mannheim*)
- People's minds and their conceptions of themselves are shaped by their social experiences. (*George Herbert Mead*)
- In their social relationships, people often rely on tried and true "recipes" for how to handle such relationships. (*Alfred Schutz*)
- Society is an integrated system of social structures and functions. (*Talcott Parsons*)

This book is devoted to helping the reader to better understand these theoretical ideas, as well as the larger theories from which they are drawn, within the context of the lifework of the classical theorists.

Introduction

By classical sociological theory we mean theories of great scope and ambition that either were created during sociology's classical age in Europe (roughly the early 1800s through the early 1900s) or had their roots in that period and culture (see Figure 1.1). The theories of Tocqueville, Comte, Spencer, Marx, Durkheim, Weber, Simmel, and Mannheim were produced during the classical age largely in France, England, and Germany. The theories of Veblen, Du Bois, Mead, Schutz, and Parsons were largely produced later and mainly in the United States, but they had most of their sources in the classical age and in European intellectual traditions.

The work of these theorists is discussed in this book for two basic reasons. First, in all cases their work was important in its time and played a central role in the development of sociology in general and sociological theory in particular. Second, their ideas continue to be relevant to, and read by, contemporary sociologists, although this is less true of the work of Comte and Spencer (who are of more historical significance) than it is of the others.

This book does not deal with all sociological theory but rather with classical theory. However, to better understand the ideas of the classical theorists to be discussed in depth throughout this book, we begin with two chapters that offer an overview of the entire history of sociological theory. Chapter 1 deals with the early years of sociological theory, and Chapter 2 brings that history up to the present day

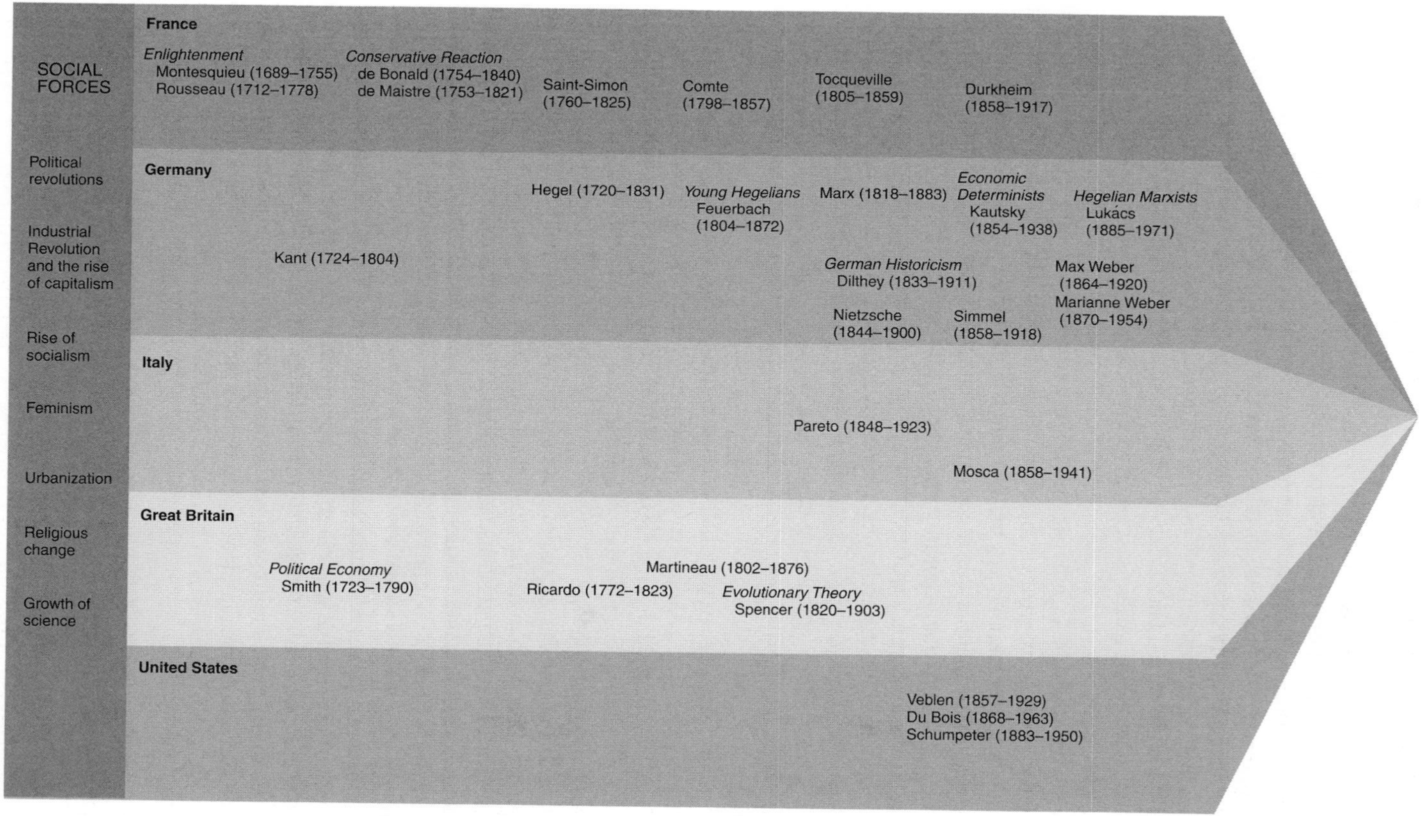

SOCIAL FORCES

Political revolutions

Industrial Revolution and the rise of capitalism

Rise of socialism

Feminism

Urbanization

Religious change

Growth of science

France

Enlightenment
Montesquieu (1689–1755)
Rousseau (1712–1778)

Conservative Reaction
de Bonald (1754–1840)
de Maistre (1753–1821)

Saint-Simon (1760–1825)

Comte (1798–1857)

Tocqueville (1805–1859)

Durkheim (1858–1917)

Germany

Kant (1724–1804)

Hegel (1720–1831)

Young Hegelians
Feuerbach (1804–1872)

Marx (1818–1883)

German Historicism
Dilthey (1833–1911)

Nietzsche (1844–1900)

Economic Determinists
Kautsky (1854–1938)

Simmel (1858–1918)

Hegelian Marxists
Lukács (1885–1971)

Max Weber (1864–1920)

Marianne Weber (1870–1954)

Italy

Pareto (1848–1923)

Mosca (1858–1941)

Great Britain

Political Economy
Smith (1723–1790)

Ricardo (1772–1823)

Martineau (1802–1876)

Evolutionary Theory
Spencer (1820–1903)

United States

Veblen (1857–1929)
Du Bois (1868–1963)
Schumpeter (1883–1950)

FIGURE 1.1 ***Sociological Theory: The Early Years***

and to the most recent developments in sociological theory. Taken together, these two chapters offer the context within which the work of the classical theorists is to be understood. The two introductory chapters are animated by the belief that it is important to understand not only the historical sources of classical theories but also their later impact. More generally, the reader should have a broad sense of sociological theory before turning to a detailed discussion of the classical theorists. The remainder of the body of this book (Chapters 3 through 16) deals with the ideas of the major classical theorists. Thus, the ideas of the major classical theorists will be discussed twice. They will be introduced very briefly in either the first or second chapter in their historical context, and they will be discussed in great depth in the chapter devoted to each of the theorists.

Why focus on these theorists and not the innumerable others whose names and ideas will arise in the course of these first two chapters? The simplest answer to this question is that space limitations make it impossible to deal with all classical theorists. Beyond that, many theorists are not given full-chapter treatment because their theories do not belong to, nor have centrally important roots in, the classical age. Furthermore, to be discussed in depth, theories must meet a series of other criteria. That is, to be included, theories must have a *wide range* of application (Turner and Boyns, 2001), must deal with *centrally important social issues,* and must have stood up well under the *test of time* (that is, they must continue to be read and to be influential).[1] Thus, a number of theorists who are briefly discussed in this chapter (for example, Louis DeBonald) will not be discussed in detail later because their ideas do not meet one or more of the criteria previously listed, especially the fact that their theories have not stood the test of time. A number of the more contemporary theorists discussed in Chapter 2 (for example, Erving Goffman and Harold Garfinkel) are not discussed further later in the book because they are associated more with the modern era than with classical sociological theory.

Our focus is on the important classical theoretical work of sociologists, as well as on work that has been done by those who are often associated with other fields (for example, Karl Marx and his association with the field of economics) but that has come to be defined as important in sociology. To put it succinctly, this is a book about the "big ideas" in the history of sociology, ideas that deal with major social issues and are far-reaching in their scope.

In addition to the theorists previously mentioned, Chapter 10 is devoted to a number of early female theorists—especially Harriet Martineau, Charlotte Perkins Gilman, Jane Addams, Ann Julia Cooper, Ida Wells-Barnett, Marianne Weber, and Beatrice Potter Webb. Because their contributions are only now being recognized, they do not fit fully the profile of classical sociological theory outlined in the preceding few

[1]These three criteria constitute our definition of (classical) sociological theory. Such a definition stands in contrast to the formal, "scientific" definitions (Jasso, 2001) that are often used in theory texts of this type. A scientific definition might be that a theory is a set of interrelated propositions that allows for the systematization of knowledge, explanation, and prediction of social life and the generation of new research hypotheses (Faia, 1986). Although such a definition has a number of attractions, it simply does not fit many of the idea systems to be discussed in this book. In other words, most classical (and contemporary) theories fall short on one or more of the formal components of theory, but they are nonetheless considered theories by most sociologists.

paragraphs. On the one hand, they are clearly classical thinkers who worked in the same time frame as the male theorists previously mentioned. In the main, their theories have a wide range of application and have certainly addressed centrally important issues. They were either sociologists or nonsociologists whose work is coming to be seen as important in sociology. On the other hand, one cannot say that their work has stood the test of time. The fact is that as a result of discrimination against women, they were not widely read or highly influential in their own time, let alone ours. Nevertheless, they are included in this book because of the belief that as their work is rediscovered and read, their influence will grow in future years. As with the male theorists, these female theorists have produced a set of "big ideas."

Presenting a history of sociological theory is an important task (S. Turner, 1998), but because we devote only the first two chapters to it, what we offer is a highly selective historical sketch. The idea is to provide the reader with a scaffolding that should help in putting the later detailed discussions of classical theorists into a larger context. As the reader proceeds through the later chapters, it will prove useful to return to these two overview chapters and place the discussions in that context. (It would be especially useful to glance back occasionally to Figures 1.1 and 2.1, which are schematic representations of the histories covered in those chapters.)

One cannot establish the precise date when sociological theory began. People have been thinking about and developing theories of social life since early in history. But we will not go back to the early historic times of the Greeks or Romans or even to the Middle Ages. We will not even go back to the seventeenth century, although Olson (1993) has traced the sociological tradition to the mid-1600s and the work of James Harrington on the relationship between the economy and the polity. This is not because people in those epochs did not have sociologically relevant ideas, but because the return on our investment in time would be small; we would spend a lot of time getting very few ideas that are relevant to modern sociology. In any case, none of the thinkers associated with those eras thought of themselves, and few are now thought of, as sociologists. (For a discussion of one exception, see the biographical sketch of Ibn-Khaldun.) It is only in the 1800s that we begin to find thinkers who can be clearly identified as sociologists. These are the classical sociological thinkers we shall be interested in (Camic, 1997; for a debate about what makes theory classical, see Connell, 1997; R. Collins, 1997b), and we begin by examining the main social and intellectual forces that shaped their ideas.

Social Forces in the Development of Sociological Theory

All intellectual fields are profoundly shaped by their social settings. This is particularly true of sociology, which not only is derived from that setting but takes the social setting as its basic subject matter. We will focus briefly on a few of the most important social conditions of the nineteenth and early twentieth centuries, conditions that were of the utmost significance in the development of sociology. We also will take the occasion to begin introducing the major figures in the history of sociological theory.

Abdel Rahman Ibn-Khaldun

A Biographical Sketch

There is a tendency to think of sociology as exclusively a comparatively modern, Western phenomenon. In fact, however, scholars were developing sociological ideas and theories long ago and in other parts of the world. One example is Abdel Rahman Ibn-Khaldun.

Ibn-Khaldun was born in Tunis, North Africa, on May 27, 1332 (Faghirzadeh, 1982). Born to an educated family, Ibn-Khaldun was schooled in the Koran (the Muslim holy book), mathematics, and history. In his lifetime, he served a variety of sultans in Tunis, Morocco, Spain, and Algeria as ambassador, chamberlain, and member of the scholars' council. He also spent two years in prison in Morocco for his belief that state rulers were not divine leaders. After approximately two decades of political activity, Ibn-Khaldun returned to North Africa, where he undertook an intensive five-year period of study and writing. Works produced during this period increased his fame and led to a lectureship at the center of Islamic study, Al-Azhar Mosque University in Cairo. In his well-attended lectures on society and sociology, Ibn-Khaldun stressed the importance of linking sociological thought and historical observation.

By the time he died in 1406, Ibn-Khaldun had produced a corpus of work that had many ideas in common with contemporary sociology. He was committed to the scientific study of society, empirical research, and the search for causes of social phenomena. He devoted considerable attention to various social institutions (for example, politics, economy) and their interrelationships. He was interested in comparing primitive and modern societies. Ibn-Khaldun did not have a dramatic impact on classical sociology, but as scholars in general, and Islamic scholars in particular, rediscover his work, he may come to be seen as being of greater historical significance.

Political Revolutions

The long series of political revolutions ushered in by the French Revolution in 1789 and carrying over through the nineteenth century was the most immediate factor in the rise of sociological theorizing. The impact of these revolutions on many societies was enormous, and many positive changes resulted. However, what attracted the attention of many early theorists (especially Tocqueville) was not the positive consequences, but the negative effects of such changes. These writers were particularly disturbed by the resulting chaos and disorder, especially in France. They were united in a desire to restore order to society. Some of the more extreme thinkers of this period literally wanted a return to the peaceful and relatively orderly days of the Middle Ages. The more sophisticated thinkers recognized that social change had made such a return impossible. Thus, they sought instead to find new bases of order in societies that had been overturned by the political revolutions of the eighteenth and nineteenth centuries. This interest in the issue of social order was one of the major concerns of classical sociological theorists, especially Comte, Durkheim, and Parsons.

The Industrial Revolution and the Rise of Capitalism

At least as important as political revolution in the shaping of sociological theory was the Industrial Revolution, which swept through many Western societies, mainly in the nineteenth and early twentieth centuries. The Industrial Revolution was not a single event but many interrelated developments that culminated in the transformation of the Western world from a largely agricultural system to an overwhelmingly industrial one. Large numbers of people left farms and agricultural work for the industrial occupations offered in the burgeoning factories. The factories themselves were transformed by a long series of technological improvements. Large economic bureaucracies arose to provide the many services needed by industry and the emerging capitalist economic system. In this economy, the ideal was a free marketplace where the many products of an industrial system could be exchanged. Within this system, a few profited greatly while the majority worked long hours for low wages. A reaction against the industrial system and against capitalism in general followed and led to the labor movement as well as to various radical movements aimed at overthrowing the capitalist system.

The Industrial Revolution, capitalism, and the reaction against them all involved an enormous upheaval in Western society, an upheaval that affected sociologists greatly. Five major figures in the early history of sociological theory—Karl Marx, Max Weber, Emile Durkheim, Georg Simmel, and Thorstein Veblen—were preoccupied, as were many lesser thinkers, with these changes and the problems they created for society as a whole. They spent their lives studying these problems, and in many cases they endeavored to develop programs that would help solve them.

The Rise of Socialism

One set of changes aimed at coping with the excesses of the industrial system and capitalism can be combined under the heading "socialism" (Beilharz, 2005d). Although some sociologists favored socialism as a solution to industrial problems, most were personally and intellectually opposed to it. On the one side, Karl Marx was an active supporter of the overthrow of the capitalist system and its replacement by a socialist system. Although Marx did not develop a theory of socialism per se, he spent a great deal of time criticizing various aspects of capitalist society. In addition, he engaged in a variety of political activities that he hoped would help bring about the rise of socialist societies.

However, Marx was atypical in the early years of sociological theory. Most of the early theorists, such as Weber and Durkheim, were opposed to socialism (at least as it was envisioned by Marx). Although they recognized the problems within capitalist society, they sought social reform within capitalism rather than the social revolution argued for by Marx. They feared socialism (as did Tocqueville) more than they did capitalism. This fear played a far greater role in shaping sociological theory than did Marx's support of the socialist alternative to capitalism. In fact, as we will see, in many cases sociological theory developed in reaction *against* Marxian and, more generally, socialist theory.

Feminism

In one sense there has always been a feminist perspective. Whenever and wherever women are subordinated—and they have been subordinated almost always and everywhere—they seem to have recognized and protested that situation in some form (Lerner, 1993). Although precursors can be traced to the 1630s, high points of feminist activity and writing occurred in the liberationist moments of modern Western history: a first flurry of productivity in the 1780s and 1790s with the debates surrounding the American and French revolutions; a far more organized, focused effort in the 1850s as part of the mobilization against slavery and for political rights for the middle class; and the massive mobilization for women's suffrage and for industrial and civic reform legislation in the early twentieth century, especially the Progressive Era in the United States.

All of this had an impact on the development of sociology, in particular on the work of a number of women in or associated with the field—Harriet Martineau (Vetter, 2008), Charlotte Perkins Gilman, Jane Addams, Florence Kelley, Anna Julia Cooper, Ida Wells-Barnett, Marianne Weber, and Beatrice Potter Webb, to name just a few. But their creations were, over time, pushed to the periphery of the profession, annexed or discounted or written out of sociology's public record by the men who were organizing sociology as a professional power base. Feminist concerns filtered into sociology only on the margins, in the work of marginal male theorists or of the increasingly marginalized female theorists. The men who assumed centrality in the profession—from Spencer, through Weber and Durkheim—made basically conservative responses to the feminist arguments going on around them, making issues of gender an inconsequential topic to which they responded conventionally rather than critically in what they identified and publicly promoted as sociology. They responded in this way even as women were writing a significant body of sociological theory. The history of this gender politics in the profession, which is also part of the history of male response to feminist claims, is only now being written (for example, see Deegan, 1988; Fitzpatrick, 1990; Gordon, 1994; Lengermann and Niebrugge-Brantley, 1998; Rosenberg, 1982).

Urbanization

Partly as a result of the Industrial Revolution, large numbers of people in the nineteenth and twentieth centuries were uprooted from their rural homes and moved to urban settings. This massive migration was caused, in large part, by the jobs created by the industrial system in the urban areas. But it presented many difficulties for those people who had to adjust to urban life. In addition, the expansion of the cities produced a seemingly endless list of urban problems—overcrowding, pollution, noise, traffic, and so forth. The nature of urban life and its problems attracted the attention of many early sociologists, especially Max Weber and Georg Simmel. In fact, the first major school of American sociology, the Chicago school, was in large part defined by its concern for the city and its interest in using Chicago as a laboratory in which to study urbanization and its problems.

Religious Change

Social changes brought on by political revolutions, the Industrial Revolution, and urbanization had a profound effect on religiosity. Many early sociologists came from religious backgrounds and were actively, and in some cases professionally, involved in religion (Hinkle and Hinkle, 1954). They brought to sociology the same objectives as they had in their religious lives. They wanted to improve people's lives (Vidich and Lyman, 1985). For some (such as Comte), sociology was transformed into a religion. For others, their sociological theories bore an unmistakable religious imprint. Durkheim wrote one of his major works on religion. Morality played a key role not only in Durkheim's sociology but also in the work of Talcott Parsons. A large portion of Weber's work also was devoted to the religions of the world. Marx, too, had an interest in religiosity, but his orientation was far more critical. Spencer discussed religion ("eccelesiastical institutions") as a significant component of society.

The Growth of Science

As sociological theory was being developed, there was an increasing emphasis on science, not only in colleges and universities but in society as a whole. The technological products of science were permeating every sector of life, and science was acquiring enormous prestige. Those associated with the most successful sciences (physics, biology, and chemistry) were accorded honored places in society. Sociologists (especially Comte, Durkheim, Spencer, Mead, and Schutz) from the beginning were preoccupied with science, and many wanted to model sociology after the successful physical and biological sciences. However, a debate soon developed between those who wholeheartedly accepted the scientific model and those (such as Weber) who thought that distinctive characteristics of social life made a wholesale adoption of a scientific model difficult and unwise (Lepenies, 1988). The issue of the relationship between sociology and science is debated to this day, although even a glance at the major journals in the field, at least in the United States, indicates the predominance of those who favor sociology as a science.

Intellectual Forces and the Rise of Sociological Theory

Although social factors are important, the primary focus of this chapter is the intellectual forces that played a central role in shaping sociological theory. In the real world, of course, intellectual factors cannot be separated from social forces. For example, in the discussion of the Enlightenment that follows, we will find that that movement was intimately related to, and in many cases provided the intellectual basis for, the social changes discussed earlier in this chapter.

The many intellectual forces that shaped the development of social theories are discussed within the national context in which their influence was primarily felt (Levine, 1995a; Rundell, 2001). We begin with the Enlightenment and its influences on the development of sociological theory in France.

The Enlightenment

It is the view of many observers that the Enlightenment constitutes a critical development in terms of the later evolution of sociology (Hawthorn, 1976; Hughes, Martin, and Sharrock, 1995; Nisbet, 1967; Zeitlin, 1996). The Enlightenment was a period of remarkable intellectual development and change in philosophical thought.[2] A number of long-standing ideas and beliefs—many of which related to social life—were overthrown and replaced during the Enlightenment. The most prominent thinkers associated with the Enlightenment were the French philosophers Charles Montesquieu (1689–1755) and Jean Jacques Rousseau (1712–1778) (Singer, 2005a, 2005b). The influence of the Enlightenment on sociological theory, however, was more indirect and negative than it was direct and positive. As Irving Zeitlin puts it, "Early sociology developed as a reaction to the Enlightenment" (1996:10).

The thinkers associated with the Enlightenment were influenced, above all, by two intellectual currents—seventeenth-century philosophy and science.

Seventeenth-century philosophy was associated with the work of thinkers such as René Descartes, Thomas Hobbes, and John Locke. The emphasis was on producing grand, general, and very abstract systems of ideas that made rational sense. The later thinkers associated with the Enlightenment did not reject the idea that systems of ideas should be general and should make rational sense, but they did make greater efforts to derive their ideas from the real world and to test them there. In other words, they wanted to combine empirical research with reason (Seidman, 1983:36–37). The model for this was science, especially Newtonian physics. At this point, we see the emergence of the application of the scientific method to social issues. Not only did Enlightenment thinkers want their ideas to be, at least in part, derived from the real world, they also wanted them to be useful to the social world, especially in the critical analysis of that world.

Overall, the Enlightenment was characterized by the belief that people could comprehend and control the universe by means of reason and empirical research. The view was that because the physical world was dominated by natural laws, it was likely that the social world was, too. Thus it was up to the philosopher, using reason and research, to discover these social laws. After they understood how the social world worked, the Enlightenment thinkers had a practical goal—the creation of a "better," more rational world.

With an emphasis on reason, the Enlightenment philosophers were inclined to reject beliefs in traditional authority. When these thinkers examined traditional values and institutions, they often found them to be irrational—that is, contrary to human nature and inhibitive of human growth and development. The mission of the practical and change-oriented philosophers of the Enlightenment was to overcome these irrational systems. The theorists who were most directly and positively influenced by Enlightenment thinking were Alexis de Tocqueville and Karl Marx, although the latter formed his early theoretical ideas in Germany.

---

[2]This section is based on the work of Irving Zeitlin (1996). Although Zeitlin's analysis is presented here for its coherence, it has a number of limitations: there are better analyses of the Enlightenment, there are many other factors involved in shaping the development of sociology, and Zeitlin tends to overstate his case in places (for example, on the impact of Marx). But on the whole, Zeitlin provides us with a useful starting point, given our objectives in this chapter.

The Conservative Reaction to the Enlightenment

On the surface, we might think that French classical sociological theory, like Marx's theory, was directly and positively influenced by the Enlightenment. French sociology became rational, empirical, scientific, and change-oriented, but not before it was also shaped by a set of ideas that developed in reaction to the Enlightenment. In Seidman's view, "The ideology of the counter-Enlightenment represented a virtual inversion of Enlightenment liberalism. In place of modernist premises, we can detect in the Enlightenment critics a strong anti-modernist sentiment" (1983:51). As we will see, sociology in general, and French sociology in particular, has from the beginning been an uncomfortable mix of Enlightenment and counter-Enlightenment ideas.

The most extreme form of opposition to Enlightenment ideas was French Catholic counterrevolutionary philosophy (Reedy, 1994), as represented by the ideas of Louis de Bonald (1754–1840) (Bradley, 2005a) and Joseph de Maistre (1753–1821) (Bradley, 2005b). These men were reacting against not only the Enlightenment but also the French Revolution, which they saw partly as a product of the kind of thinking characteristic of the Enlightenment. De Bonald, for example, was disturbed by the revolutionary changes and yearned for a return to the peace and harmony of the Middle Ages. In this view, God was the source of society; therefore, reason, which was so important to the Enlightenment philosophers, was seen as inferior to traditional religious beliefs. Furthermore, it was believed that because God had created society, people should not tamper with it and should not try to change a holy creation. By extension, de Bonald opposed anything that undermined such traditional institutions as patriarchy, the monogamous family, the monarchy, and the Catholic Church.

Although de Bonald represented a rather extreme form of the conservative reaction, his work constitutes a useful introduction to its general premises. The conservatives turned away from what they considered the "naive" rationalism of the Enlightenment. They not only recognized the irrational aspects of social life but also assigned them positive value. Thus they regarded such phenomena as tradition, imagination, emotionalism, and religion as useful and necessary components of social life. In that they disliked upheaval and sought to retain the existing order, they deplored developments such as the French Revolution and the Industrial Revolution, which they saw as disruptive forces. The conservatives tended to emphasize social order, an emphasis that became one of the central themes of the work of several sociological theorists.

Zeitlin (1996) outlined ten major propositions that he sees as emerging from the conservative reaction and providing the basis for the development of classical French sociological theory.

1. Whereas Enlightenment thinkers tended to emphasize the individual, the conservative reaction led to a major sociological interest in, and emphasis on, society and other large-scale phenomena. Society was viewed as something more than simply an aggregate of individuals. Society was seen as having an existence of its own with its own laws of development and deep roots in the past.
2. Society was the most important unit of analysis; it was seen as more important than the individual. It was society that produced the individual, primarily through the process of socialization.

3. The individual was not even seen as the most basic element within society. A society consisted of such component parts as roles, positions, relationships, structures, and institutions. Individuals were seen as doing little more than filling these units within society.
4. The parts of society were seen as interrelated and interdependent. Indeed, these interrelationships were a major basis of society. This view led to a conservative political orientation. That is, because the parts were held to be interrelated, it followed that tampering with one part could well lead to the undermining of other parts and, ultimately, of the system as a whole. This meant that changes in the social system should be made with extreme care.
5. Change was seen as a threat not only to society and its components but also to the individuals in society. The various components of society were seen as satisfying people's needs. When institutions were disrupted, people were likely to suffer, and their suffering was likely to lead to social disorder.
6. The general tendency was to see the various large-scale components of society as useful for both society and the individuals in it. As a result, there was little desire to look for the negative effects of existing social structures and social institutions.
7. Small units, such as the family, the neighborhood, and religious and occupational groups, also were seen as essential to individuals and society. They provided the intimate, face-to-face environments that people needed in order to survive in modern societies.
8. There was a tendency to see various modern social changes, such as industrialization, urbanization, and bureaucratization, as having disorganizing effects. These changes were viewed with fear and anxiety, and there was an emphasis on developing ways of dealing with their disruptive effects.
9. While most of these feared changes were leading to a more rational society, the conservative reaction led to an emphasis on the importance of nonrational factors (ritual, ceremony, and worship, for example) in social life.
10. Finally, the conservatives supported the existence of a hierarchical system in society. It was seen as important to society that there be a differential system of status and reward.

These ten propositions, derived from the conservative reaction to the Enlightenment, should be seen as the immediate intellectual basis of the development of sociological theory in France. Many of these ideas made their way into early sociological thought, although some of the Enlightenment ideas (empiricism, for example) were also influential.[3]

---

[3]Although we have emphasized the discontinuities between the Enlightenment and the counter-Enlightenment, Seidman makes the point that there also are continuities and linkages. First, the counter-Enlightenment carried on the scientific tradition developed in the Enlightenment. Second, it picked up the Enlightenment emphasis on collectivities (as opposed to individuals) and greatly extended it. Third, both had an interest in the problems of the modern world, especially its negative effects on individuals.

The Development of French Sociology

We turn now to the actual founding of sociology as a distinctive discipline—specifically, to the work of four French thinkers: Alexis de Tocqueville, Claude Saint-Simon, Auguste Comte, and especially Emile Durkheim.

Alexis de Tocqueville (1805–1859)

We begin with Alexis de Tocqueville even though he was born after both Saint-Simon and Comte. We do so because he and his work were such pure products of the Enlightenment discussed earlier (he was strongly and directly influenced by Montesquieu [Singer, 2004]), especially his *The Spirit of the Laws* [1748]) and because his work was not part of the clear line of development in French social theory from Saint-Simon and Comte to the crucially important Durkheim. Tocqueville has long been seen as a political scientist, not a sociologist, and furthermore many have not perceived the existence of a social theory in his work (e.g., Seidman, 1983:306). However, not only is there a social theory in his work, but it is one that deserves a much more significant place in the history of social theory.

Tocqueville is best-known for the legendary, and highly influential, *Democracy in America* (1835–40/1969), especially the first volume that deals, in a very laudatory way, with the early American democratic system and that came to be seen as an early contribution to the development of "political science." However, in the later volumes of that work, as well as in later works, Tocqueville clearly develops a broad social theory that deserves a place in the canon of social theory.

Three interrelated issues lie at the heart of Tocqueville's theory. As a product of the Enlightenment, he is first and foremost a great supporter of, and advocate for, *freedom.* However, he is much more critical of *equality,* which he sees as tending to produce mediocrity in comparison to that produced by the aristocrats (he was, himself, an aristocrat) of a prior, less egalitarian era. More importantly, it is also linked to what most concerns him, and that is the growth of *centralization,* especially in the government, and the threat centralized government poses to freedom. In his view, it was the inequality of the prior age, the power of the aristocrats, which acted to keep government centralization in check. However, with the demise of aristocrats and the rise of greater equality, there were no groups capable of countering the ever-present tendency toward centralization. The mass of largely equal people were too "servile" to oppose this trend. Furthermore, Tocqueville links equality to "individualism" (an important concept he claimed to "invent" and for which he is credited), and the resulting individualists were far less interested in the well-being of the larger "community" than the aristocrats that preceded them.

It is for this reason that Tocqueville is critical of democracy and especially socialism. Democracy's commitment to freedom is ultimately threatened by its parallel commitment to equality and its tendency toward centralized government. Of course, from Tocqueville's point of view the situation would be far worse in socialism because its far greater commitment to equality, and the much greater likelihood of government centralization, poses more of a threat to freedom. The latter view is quite prescient given what transpired in the Soviet Union and other societies that operated, at least in name, under the banner of socialism.

Thus, the strength of Tocqueville's theory lies in the interrelated ideas of freedom, equality, and especially centralization. His "grand narrative" on the increasing control of central governments anticipates other theories, including Weber's work on bureaucracy and, especially, the more contemporary work of Michel Foucault on "governmentality" and its gradual spread, increasing subtlety, and propensity to invade even the "soul" of the people controlled by it. There is a very profound social theory in Tocqueville's work, but it had no influence on the theories and theorists to be discussed in the remainder of this section on French social theory. Its influence was largely restricted to the development to political science and to work on American democracy and the French Revolution (Tocqueville, 1856/1983). There are certainly sociologists (and other social scientists) who recognize his importance, especially those interested in the relationship between individualism and community (Bellah, et al., 1985; Nisbet, 1953; Putnam, 2001; Riesman, 1950), but to this day Tocqueville's theories have not been accorded the place they deserve in social theory in general, and even in French social theory (Gannett, 2003).

Claude Henri Saint-Simon (1760–1825)

Saint-Simon was older than Auguste Comte; in fact, Comte, in his early years, served as Saint-Simon's secretary and disciple. There is a very strong similarity between the ideas of these two thinkers, yet a bitter debate developed between them that led to their eventual split (Pickering, 1993; Thompson, 1975).

The most interesting aspect of Saint-Simon was his significance to the development of *both* conservative (like Comte's) and radical Marxian theory. On the conservative side, Saint-Simon wanted to preserve society as it was, but he did not seek a return to life as it had been in the Middle Ages, as did de Bonald and de Maistre. In addition, he was a *positivist* (Durkheim, 1928/1962:142), which meant that he believed that the study of social phenomena should employ the same scientific techniques as those used in the natural sciences. On the radical side, Saint-Simon saw the need for socialist reforms, especially the centralized planning of the economic system. But Saint-Simon did not go nearly as far as Marx did later. Although he, like Marx, saw the capitalists superseding the feudal nobility, he felt it inconceivable that the working class would come to replace the capitalists. Many of Saint-Simon's ideas are found in Comte's work, but Comte developed them in a more systematic fashion (Pickering, 1997).

Auguste Comte (1798–1857)

Comte (see Chapter 4) was the first to use the term *sociology* (Pickering, 2000; Turner, 2001a).[4] He had an enormous influence on later sociological theorists (especially Herbert

[4]Although he recognizes that Comte created the label "sociology," Eriksson (1993) has challenged the idea that Comte is the progenitor of modern, scientific sociology. Rather, Eriksson sees people such as Adam Smith and more generally the Scottish Moralists, as the true source of modern sociology. See also, L. Hill (1996) on the importance of Adam Ferguson; and Ullmann-Margalit (1997) on Ferguson and Adam Smith (see also Rundell, 2001).

Spencer and Emile Durkheim). And he believed that the study of sociology should be scientific, just as many classical theorists did and most contemporary sociologists do (Lenzer, 1975).

Comte was greatly disturbed by the anarchy that pervaded French society and was critical of those thinkers who had spawned both the Enlightenment and the revolution. He developed his scientific view, "positivism," or "positive philosophy," to combat what he considered to be the negative and destructive philosophy of the Enlightenment. Comte was in line with, and influenced by, the French counterrevolutionary Catholics (especially de Bonald and de Maistre). However, his work can be set apart from theirs on at least two grounds. First, he did not think it possible to return to the Middle Ages; advances in science and industry made that impossible. Second, he developed a much more sophisticated theoretical system than his predecessors, one that was adequate to shape a good portion of early sociology.

Comte developed *social physics,* or what in 1839 he called *sociology* (Pickering, 2000). The use of the term *social physics* made it clear that Comte sought to model sociology after the "hard sciences." This new science, which in his view would ultimately become the dominant science, was to be concerned with social statics (existing social structures) and social dynamics (social change). Although both involved the search for laws of social life, he felt that social dynamics was more important than social statics. This focus on change reflected his interest in social reform, particularly reform of the ills created by the French Revolution and the Enlightenment. Comte did not urge revolutionary change, because he felt the natural evolution of society would make things better. Reforms were needed only to assist the process a bit.

This leads us to the cornerstone of Comte's approach—his evolutionary theory, or the *law of the three stages.* The theory proposes that there are three intellectual stages through which the world has gone throughout its history. According to Comte, not only does the world go through this process, but groups, societies, sciences, individuals, and even minds go through the same three stages. The *theological* stage is the first, and it characterized the world prior to 1300. During this period, the major idea system emphasized the belief that supernatural powers and religious figures, modeled after humankind, are at the root of everything. In particular, the social and physical world is seen as produced by God. The second stage is the *metaphysical* stage, which occurred roughly between 1300 and 1800. This era was characterized by the belief that abstract forces like "nature," rather than personalized gods, explain virtually everything. Finally, in 1800 the world entered the *positivistic* stage, characterized by belief in science. People now tended to give up the search for absolute causes (God or nature) and concentrated instead on observation of the social and physical world in the search for the laws governing them.

It is clear that in his theory of the world, Comte focused on intellectual factors. Indeed, he argued that intellectual disorder is the cause of social disorder. The disorder stemmed from earlier idea systems (theological and metaphysical) that continued to exist in the positivistic (scientific) age. Only when positivism gained total control would social upheavals cease. Because this was an evolutionary process, there was no need to foment social upheaval and revolution. Positivism would come, although perhaps not as quickly as some would like. Here Comte's social reformism and his sociology coincide. Sociology could expedite the arrival of positivism and hence bring order to the social world. Above all, Comte did not want to seem to be espousing revolution. There was, in his view, enough disorder in the world. In any case, from Comte's point of view, it was intellectual change that was needed, so there was little reason for social and political revolution.

We have already encountered several of Comte's positions that were to be of great significance to the development of classical sociology—his basic conservatism, reformism, and scientism and his evolutionary view of the world. Several other aspects of his work deserve mention because they also were to play a major role in the development of sociological theory. For example, his sociology does not focus on the individual but rather takes as its basic unit of analysis larger entities such as the family. He also urged that we look at both social structure and social change. Of great importance to later sociological theory, especially the work of Spencer and Parsons, is Comte's stress on the systematic character of society—the links among and between the various components of society. He also accorded great importance to the role of consensus in society. He saw little merit in the idea that society is characterized by inevitable conflict between workers and capitalists. In addition, Comte emphasized the need to engage in abstract theorizing and to go out and do sociological research. He urged that sociologists use observation, experimentation, and comparative historical analysis. Finally, Comte believed that sociology ultimately would become the dominant scientific force in the world because of its distinctive ability to interpret social laws and to develop reforms aimed at patching up problems within the system.

Comte was in the forefront of the development of positivistic sociology (Bryant, 1985; Halfpenny, 1982). To Jonathan Turner, Comte's positivism emphasized that "the social universe is amenable to the development of abstract laws that can be tested through the careful collection of data," and "these abstract laws will denote the basic and generic properties of the social universe and they will specify their 'natural relations'" (1985:24). As we will see, a number of classical theorists (especially Spencer and Durkheim) shared Comte's interest in the discovery of the laws of social life. While positivism remains important in contemporary sociology, it has come under attack from a number of quarters (Morrow, 1994).

Even though Comte lacked a solid academic base on which to build a school of Comtian sociological theory, he nevertheless laid a basis for the development of a significant stream of sociological theory. But his long-term significance is dwarfed by that of his successor in French sociology and the inheritor of a number of its ideas, Emile Durkheim. (For a debate over the canonization of Durkheim, as well as other classical theorists discussed in this chapter, see Mouzelis, 1997; Parker, 1997.)

Emile Durkheim (1858–1917)

Durkheim's relation to the Enlightenment was much more ambiguous than Comte's. He has been seen as an inheritor of the enlightenment tradition because of his emphasis on science and social reformism. However, Durkheim also has been seen as the inheritor of the conservative tradition, especially as it was manifested in Comte's work. But whereas Comte had remained outside of academia as had Tocqueville, Durkheim developed an increasingly solid academic base as his career progressed. Durkheim legitimized sociology in France, and his work ultimately became a dominant force in the development of sociology in general and of sociological theory in particular (R. Jones, 2000; Rawls, 2007).

Durkheim was politically liberal, but he took a more conservative position intellectually. Like Comte and the Catholic counterrevolutionaries, Durkheim feared and hated social disorder. His work was informed by the disorders produced by the general social changes discussed earlier in this chapter, as well as by others (such as industrial strikes, disruption of the ruling class, church–state discord, the rise of political anti-Semitism) more specific to the France of Durkheim's time (Karady, 1983). In fact, most of his work was devoted to the study of social order. His view was that social disorders are not a necessary part of the modern world and could be reduced by social reforms. Whereas Marx saw the problems of the modern world as inherent in society, Durkheim (along with most other classical theorists) did not. As a result, Marx's ideas on the need for social revolution stood in sharp contrast to the reformism of Durkheim and the others. As classical sociological theory developed, it was the Durkheimian interest on order and reform that came to dominate, while the Marxian position was eclipsed.

Social Facts

Durkheim developed a distinctive conception of the subject matter of sociology and then tested it in an empirical study. In *The Rules of Sociological Method* (1895/1982), Durkheim argued that it is the special task of sociology to study what he called *social facts.* He conceived of social facts as forces (Takla and Pope, 1985) and structures that are external to, and coercive of, the individual. The study of these large-scale structures and forces—for example, institutionalized law and shared moral beliefs—and their impact on people became the concern of many later sociological theorists (Parsons, for example). In *Suicide* (1897/1951), Durkheim reasoned that if he could link an individual behavior such as suicide to social causes (social facts), he would have made a persuasive case for the importance of the discipline of sociology. But Durkheim did not examine why individual *A* or *B* committed suicide; rather, he was interested in the causes of differences in suicide rates among groups, regions, countries, and different categories of people (for example, married and single). His basic argument was that it was the nature of and changes in social facts that led to differences in suicide rates. For example, a war or an economic depression would create a collective mood of depression that would in turn lead to increases in suicide rates. As we will see in Chapter 7, there is much more to be said on this subject, but the key point is that Durkheim developed a distinctive view of sociology and sought to demonstrate its usefulness in a scientific study of suicide.

In *The Rules of Sociological Method,* Durkheim differentiated between two types of social facts—material and nonmaterial. Although he dealt with both in the course of his work, his main focus was on *nonmaterial social facts* (for example, culture, social institutions) rather than *material social facts* (for example, bureaucracy, law). This concern for nonmaterial social facts was already clear in his earliest major work, *The Division of Labor in Society* (1893/1964). His focus there was a comparative analysis of what held society together in the primitive and modern cases. He concluded that earlier societies were held together primarily by nonmaterial social facts, specifically, a strongly held common morality, or what he called a strong *collective conscience*. However, because of the complexities of modern society, there had been a decline in the strength of the collective conscience. The primary bond in the modern world was an intricate division of labor, which tied people to others in dependency relationships. However, Durkheim believed that the modern division of labor brought with it several "pathologies"; it was, in other words, an inadequate method of holding society together. Given his conservative sociology, Durkheim did not feel that revolution was needed to solve these problems. Rather, he suggested a variety of reforms that could "patch up" the modern system and keep it functioning. Although he recognized that there was no going back to the age when a powerful collective conscience predominated, he did think that the common morality could be strengthened in modern society and that people thereby could cope better with the pathologies that they were experiencing.

Religion

In his later work, nonmaterial social facts occupied an even more central position. In fact, he came to focus on perhaps the ultimate form of a nonmaterial social fact—religion—in his last major work, *The Elementary Forms of Religious Life* (1912/1965). Durkheim examined primitive society in order to find the roots of religion. He believed that he would be better able to find those roots in the comparative simplicity of primitive society than in the complexity of the modern world. What he found, he felt, was that the source of religion was society itself. Society comes to define certain things as religious and others as profane. Specifically, in the case he studied, the clan was the source of a primitive kind of religion, *totemism,* in which things such as plants and animals are deified. Totemism, in turn, was seen as a specific type of nonmaterial social fact, a form of the collective conscience. In the end, Durkheim came to argue that society and religion (or, more generally, the collective conscience) were one and the same. Religion was the way society expressed itself in the form of a nonmaterial social fact. In a sense, then, Durkheim came to deify society and its major products. Clearly, in deifying society, Durkheim took a highly conservative stance: one would not want to overturn a deity or its societal source. Because he identified society with God, Durkheim was not inclined to urge social revolution. Instead, he was a social reformer seeking ways of improving the functioning of society. In these and other ways, Durkheim was clearly in line with French conservative sociology. The fact that he avoided many of its excesses helped make him the most significant figure in French sociology.

These books and other important works helped carve out a distinctive domain for sociology in the academic world of turn-of-the-century France, and they earned Durkheim the leading position in that growing field. In 1898, Durkheim set up a scholarly journal devoted to sociology, *L'année sociologique* (Besnard, 1983). It became a powerful force in the development and spread of sociological ideas. Durkheim was intent on fostering the growth of sociology, and he used his journal as a focal point for the development of a group of disciples. They later would extend his ideas and carry them to many other locales and into the study of other aspects of the social world (for example, sociology of law and sociology of the city) (Besnard, 1983:1). By 1910, Durkheim had established a strong center of sociology in France, and the academic institutionalization of sociology was well under way in that nation (Heilbron, 1995).

The Development of German Sociology

Whereas the early history of French sociology is a fairly coherent story of the progression from the Enlightenment and the French Revolution to the conservative reaction and to the increasingly important sociological ideas of Tocqueville, Saint-Simon, Comte, and Durkheim, German sociology was fragmented from the beginning. A split developed between Marx (and his supporters), who remained on the edge of sociology, and the early giants of mainstream German sociology, Max Weber and Georg Simmel.[5] However, although Marxian theory itself was deemed unacceptable, its ideas found their way in a variety of positive and negative ways into mainstream German sociology.

The Roots and Nature of the Theories of Karl Marx (1818–1883)

The dominant intellectual influence on Karl Marx was the German philosopher G. W. F. Hegel (1770–1831).

Hegel

According to Ball, "it is difficult for us to appreciate the degree to which Hegel dominated German thought in the second quarter of the nineteenth century. It was largely within the framework of his philosophy that educated Germans—including the young Marx—discussed history, politics and culture" (1991:25). Marx's education at the University of Berlin was shaped by Hegel's ideas as well as by the split that developed among Hegel's followers after his death. The "Old Hegelians" continued to subscribe to the master's ideas, whereas the "Young Hegelians," although still working in the Hegelian tradition, were critical of many facets of his philosophical system.

Two concepts represent the essence of Hegel's philosophy—the dialectic and idealism (Beamish, 2007; Hegel, 1807/1967, 1821/1967). The *dialectic* is both a way of thinking and an image of the world. On the one hand, it is a way of thinking that stresses the importance of processes, relations, dynamics, conflicts, and contradictions—a dynamic rather than a static way of thinking about the world. On the other hand, it is a view that the world is made up not of static structures but of processes, relationships, dynamics, conflicts, and contradictions. Although the dialectic generally is associated with Hegel, it certainly predates him in philosophy. Marx, trained in the Hegelian tradition, accepted the significance of the dialectic. However, he was critical of some aspects of the way Hegel used it. For example, Hegel tended to apply the dialectic only to ideas, whereas Marx felt that it applied as well to more material aspects of life—for example, the economy.

Hegel is also associated with the philosophy of *idealism* (Kleiner, 2005), which emphasizes the importance of the mind and mental products rather than the material world. It is the social definition of the physical and material worlds that matters most, not those worlds themselves. In its extreme form, idealism asserts that *only* the mind and

[5]For an argument against this and the view of continuity between Marxian and mainstream sociology, see Seidman (1983).

psychological constructs exist. Some idealists believed that their mental processes would remain the same even if the physical and social worlds no longer existed. Idealists emphasize not only mental processes but also the ideas produced by these processes. Hegel paid a great deal of attention to the development of such ideas, especially to what he referred to as the "spirit" of society.

In fact, Hegel offered a kind of evolutionary theory of the world in idealistic terms. At first, people were endowed only with the ability to acquire a sensory understanding of the world around them. They could understand things like the sight, smell, and feel of the social and physical world. Later, people developed the ability to be conscious of, to understand, themselves. With self-knowledge and self-understanding, people began to understand that they could become more than they were. In terms of Hegel's dialectical approach, a contradiction developed between what people were and what they felt they could be. The resolution of this contradiction lay in the development of an individual's awareness of his or her place in the larger spirit of society. Individuals come to realize that their ultimate fulfillment lies in the development and the expansion of the spirit of society as a whole. Thus, individuals in Hegel's scheme evolve from an understanding of things to an understanding of self to an understanding of their place in the larger scheme of things.

Hegel, then, offered a general theory of the evolution of the world. It is a subjective theory in which change is held to occur at the level of consciousness. However, that change occurs largely beyond the control of actors. Actors are reduced to little more than vessels swept along by the inevitable evolution of consciousness.

Feuerbach

Ludwig Feuerbach (1804–1872) was an important bridge between Hegel and Marx. As a Young Hegelian, Feuerbach was critical of Hegel for, among other things, his excessive emphasis on consciousness and the spirit of society. Feuerbach's adoption of a materialist philosophy led him to argue that what was needed was to move from Hegel's subjective idealism to a focus not on ideas but on the material reality of real human beings. In his critique of Hegel, Feuerbach focused on religion. To Feuerbach, God is simply a projection by people of their human essence onto an impersonal force. People set God over and above themselves, with the result that they become alienated from God and project a series of positive characteristics onto God (that He is perfect, almighty, and holy), while they reduce themselves to being imperfect, powerless, and sinful. Feuerbach argued that this kind of religion must be overcome and that its defeat could be aided by a materialist philosophy in which people (not religion) became their own highest object, ends in themselves. Real people, not abstract ideas like religion, are deified by a materialist philosophy.

Marx, Hegel, and Feuerbach

Marx was simultaneously influenced by and critical of *both* Hegel and Feuerbach (Staples, 2007). Marx, following Feuerbach, was critical of Hegel's adherence to an idealist philosophy. Marx took this position not only because of his adoption of a materialist orientation but also because of his interest in practical activities. Social facts such as wealth and the state are treated by Hegel as ideas rather than as real, material entities. Even when he examined a seemingly material process such as labor, Hegel was looking only at abstract mental labor. This is very different from Marx's interest in the labor of real, sentient people. Thus, Hegel was looking at the wrong issues as far as Marx was concerned. In addition, Marx felt that Hegel's idealism led to a very conservative political orientation. To Hegel, the process of evolution was occurring beyond the control of people and their activities. In any case, in that people seemed to be moving toward greater consciousness of the world as it could be, there seemed no need for any revolutionary change; the process was already moving in the "desired" direction. Whatever problems did exist lay in consciousness, and the answer therefore seemed to lie in changing thinking.

Marx took a very different position, arguing that the problems of modern life can be traced to real, material sources (for example, the structures of capitalism) and that the solutions, therefore, can be found only in the overturning of those structures by the collective action of large numbers of people (Marx and Engels, 1845/1956:254). Whereas Hegel "stood the world on its head" (that is, focused on consciousness, not the real, material world), Marx firmly embedded his dialectic in a material base.

Marx applauded Feuerbach's critique of Hegel on a number of counts (for example, its materialism and its rejection of the abstractness of Hegel's theory), but he was far from fully satisfied with Feuerbach's position (Thomson, 1994). For one thing, Feuerbach focused on the religious world, whereas Marx believed that it was the entire social world, and the economy in particular, that had to be analyzed. Although Marx accepted Feuerbach's materialism, he felt that Feuerbach had gone too far in focusing one-sidedly, nondialectically, on the material world. Feuerbach failed to include the most important of Hegel's contributions, the dialectic, in his materialist orientation, particularly the relationship between people and the material world. Finally, Marx argued that Feuerbach, like most philosophers, failed to emphasize *praxis*—practical activity—in particular, revolutionary activity (Wortmann, 2007a). As Marx put it, "The philosophers have only *interpreted* the world, in various ways; the point, however, is to *change* it" (cited in Tucker, 1970:109).

Marx extracted what he considered to be the two most important elements from these two thinkers—Hegel's dialectic and Feuerbach's materialism—and fused them into his own distinctive orientation, *dialectical materialism,*[6] which focuses on dialectical relationships within the material world.

Political Economy

Marx's materialism and his consequent focus on the economic sector led him rather naturally to the work of a group of *political economists* (for example, Adam Smith and David Ricardo [Howard and King, 2005]). Marx was very attracted to a number of their positions. He lauded their basic premise that labor was the source of all wealth. This ultimately led Marx to his *labor theory of value,* in which he argued that the profit of the

[6]Although first used by Joseph Dietzgen in 1857, the term was made central by Georgi Plekhanov in 1891. While he practiced dialectical materialism, Marx himself never used the term (Beamish, 2007).

capitalist was based on the exploitation of the laborer. Capitalists performed the rather simple trick of paying the workers less than they deserved, because they received less pay than the value of what they actually produced in a work period. This *surplus value,* which was retained and reinvested by the capitalist, was the basis of the entire capitalist system. The capitalist system grew by continually increasing the level of exploitation of the workers (and therefore the amount of surplus value) and investing the profits for the expansion of the system.

Marx also was affected by the political economists' depiction of the horrors of the capitalist system and the exploitation of the workers. However, whereas they depicted the evils of capitalism, Marx criticized the political economists for seeing these evils as inevitable components of capitalism. Marx deplored their general acceptance of capitalism and the way they urged people to work for economic success within it. He also was critical of the political economists for failing to see the inherent conflict between capitalists and laborers and for denying the need for a radical change in the economic order. Such conservative economics was hard for Marx to accept, given his commitment to a radical change from capitalism to socialism.

Marx and Sociology

Marx was not a sociologist and did not consider himself one. Although his work is too broad to be encompassed by the term *sociology,* there is a sociological theory to be found in Marx's work. From the beginning, there were those who were heavily influenced by Marx, and there has been a continuous strand of Marxian sociology, primarily in Europe. But for the majority of early sociologists, his work was a negative force, something against which to shape their sociology. Until very recently, sociological theory, especially in America, has been characterized by either hostility to or ignorance of Marxian theory. This has, as we will see in Chapter 2, changed dramatically, but the negative reaction to Marx's work was a major force in the shaping of much of sociological theory (Gurney, 1981).

The basic reason for this rejection of Marx was ideological. Many of the early sociological theorists were inheritors of the conservative reaction to the disruptions of the Enlightenment and the French Revolution. Marx's radical ideas and the radical social changes he foretold and sought to bring to life were clearly feared and hated by such thinkers. Marx was dismissed as an ideologist. It was argued that he was not a serious sociological theorist. However, ideology per se could not have been the real reason for the rejection of Marx, because the work of Comte, Durkheim, and other conservative thinkers also was heavily ideological. It was the nature of the ideology, not the existence of ideology as such, that put off many sociological theorists. They were ready and eager to buy conservative ideology wrapped in a cloak of sociological theory, but not the radical ideology offered by Marx and his followers.

There were, of course, other reasons why Marx was not accepted by many early theorists. He seemed to be more an economist than a sociologist. Although the early sociologists would certainly admit the importance of the economy, they would also argue that it was only one of a number of components of social life.

Another reason for the early rejection of Marx was the nature of his interests. Whereas the early sociologists were reacting to the disorder created by the Enlightenment, the French Revolution, and later the Industrial Revolution, Marx was not upset by these disorders—nor by disorder in general. Rather, what interested and concerned Marx most was the oppressiveness of the capitalist system that was emerging out of the Industrial Revolution. Marx wanted to develop a theory that explained this oppressiveness and that would help overthrow that system. Marx's interest was in revolution, which stood in contrast to the conservative concern for reform and orderly change.

Another difference worth noting is the difference in philosophical roots between Marxian and conservative sociological theory. Most of the conservative theorists were heavily influenced by the philosophy of Immanuel Kant. Among other things, this led them to think in linear, cause-and-effect terms. That is, they tended to argue that a change in *A* (say, the change in ideas during the Enlightenment) leads to a change in *B* (say, the political changes of the French Revolution). In contrast, Marx was most heavily influenced, as we have seen, by Hegel, who thought in dialectical rather than cause-and-effect terms. Among other things, the dialectic attunes us to the ongoing reciprocal effects of social forces. Thus, a dialectician would reconceptualize the preceding example as a continual, ongoing interplay of ideas and politics.

Marx's Theory

To oversimplify enormously (see Chapter 6 for a much more detailed discussion), Marx offered a theory of capitalist society based on his image of the basic nature of human beings. Marx believed that people are basically productive; that is, in order to survive, people need to work in, and with, nature. In so doing, they produce the food, clothing, tools, shelter, and other necessities that permit them to live. Their productivity is a perfectly natural way by which they express basic creative impulses. Furthermore, these impulses are expressed in concert with other people; in other words, people are inherently social. They need to work together to produce what they need to survive.

Throughout history, this natural process has been subverted, at first by the mean conditions of primitive society and later by a variety of structural arrangements erected by societies in the course of history. In various ways, these structures interfered with the natural productive process. However, it is in capitalist society that this breakdown is most acute; the breakdown in the natural productive process reaches its culmination in capitalism.

Basically, capitalism is a structure (or, more accurately, a series of structures) that erects barriers between an individual and the production process, the products of that process, and other people; ultimately, it even divides the individual himself or herself. This is the basic meaning of the concept of *alienation:* it is the breakdown of the natural interconnection among people and between people and what they produce. Alienation occurs because capitalism has evolved into a two-class system in which a few capitalists own the production process, the products, and the labor time of those who work for them. Instead of naturally producing for themselves, people produce unnaturally in capitalist society for a small group of capitalists. Intellectually, Marx was very concerned with the structures of capitalism and their oppressive impact on actors. Politically, he was led to an interest in emancipating people from the oppressive structures of capitalism.

Marx actually spent very little time dreaming about what a utopian socialist state would look like (Lovell, 1992). He was more concerned with helping to bring about the demise of capitalism. He believed that the contradictions and conflicts within capitalism would lead dialectically to its ultimate collapse, but he did not think that the process was inevitable. People had to act at the appropriate times and in the appropriate ways for socialism to come into being. The capitalists had great resources at their disposal to forestall the coming of socialism, but they could be overcome by the concerted action of a class-conscious proletariat. What would the proletariat create in the process? What is socialism? Most basically, it is a society in which, for the first time, people could approach Marx's ideal image of productivity. With the aid of modern technology, people could interact harmoniously with nature and with other people to create what they needed to survive. To put it another way, in socialist society, people would no longer be alienated.

The Roots and Nature of the Theories of Max Weber (1864–1920) and Georg Simmel (1858–1918)

Although Marx and his followers in the late nineteenth and early twentieth centuries remained outside mainstream German sociology, to a considerable extent early German sociology can be seen as developing in opposition to Marxian theory.

Weber and Marx

Albert Salomon, for example, claimed that a large part of the theory of the early giant of German sociology, Max Weber, developed "in a long and intense debate with the ghost of Marx" (1945:596). This is probably an exaggeration, but in many ways Marxian theory did play a negative role in Weberian theory. In other ways, however, Weber was working within the Marxian tradition, trying to "round out" Marx's theory. Also, there were many inputs into Weberian theory other than Marxian theory (Burger, 1976). We can clarify a good deal about the sources of German sociology by outlining each of these views of the relationship between Marx and Weber (Antonio and Glassman, 1985; Schroeter, 1985). Bear in mind that Weber was not intimately familiar with Marx's work (much of it was not published until after Weber's death) and that Weber was reacting more to the work of the Marxists than to Marx's work itself (Antonio, 1985:29; Turner, 1981:19–20).

Weber *did* tend to view Marx and the Marxists of his day as economic determinists who offered single-cause theories of social life. That is, Marxian theory was seen as tracing all historical developments to economic bases and viewing all contemporaneous structures as erected on an economic base. Although this is not true of Marx's own theory (as we will see in Chapter 6), it was the position of many later Marxists.

One of the examples of economic determinism that seemed to rankle Weber most was the view that ideas are simply the reflections of material (especially economic) interests, that material interests determine ideology. From this point of view, Weber was supposed to have "turned Marx on his head" (much as Marx had inverted Hegel). Instead of focusing on economic factors and their effect on ideas, Weber devoted much of his attention to ideas and their effect on the economy. Rather than seeing ideas as simple reflections of economic factors, Weber saw them as fairly autonomous forces capable of profoundly affecting the economic world. Weber certainly devoted a lot of attention to ideas, particularly systems of religious ideas, and he was especially concerned with the impact of religious ideas on the economy. In *The Protestant Ethic and the Spirit of Capitalism* (1904–1905/1958), he was concerned with Protestantism, mainly as a system of ideas, and its impact on the rise of another system of ideas, the "spirit of capitalism," and ultimately on a capitalist economic system. Weber had a similar interest in other world religions, looking at how their nature might have obstructed the development of capitalism in their respective societies. On the basis of this kind of work, some scholars came to the conclusion that Weber developed his ideas in opposition to those of Marx.

A second view of Weber's relationship to Marx, as mentioned earlier, is that he did not so much oppose Marx as try to round out Marx's theoretical perspective. Here Weber is seen as working more within the Marxian tradition than in opposition to it. His work on religion, interpreted from this point of view, was simply an effort to show that not only do material factors affect ideas, but ideas themselves affect material structures.

A good example of the view that Weber was engaged in a process of rounding out Marxian theory is in the area of stratification theory. In this work on stratification, Marx focused on social *class,* the economic dimension of stratification. Although Weber accepted the importance of this factor, he argued that other dimensions of stratification were also important. He argued that the notion of social stratification should be extended to include stratification on the basis of prestige (*status*) and *power*. The inclusion of these other dimensions does not constitute a refutation of Marx but is simply an extension of his ideas.

Both of the preceding views accept the importance of Marxian theory for Weber. There are elements of truth in both positions; at some points Weber was working in opposition to Marx, whereas at other points he was extending Marx's ideas. However, a third view of this issue may best characterize the relationship between Marx and Weber. In this view, Marx is seen simply as only one of many influences on Weber's thought.

Other Influences on Weber

We can identify a number of sources of Weberian theory, including German historians, philosophers, economists, and political theorists. Among those who influenced Weber, the philosopher Immanuel Kant (1724–1804) stands out above all the others. But we must not overlook the impact of Friedrich Nietzsche (1844–1900) (Antonio, 2001)—especially his emphasis on the hero—on Weber's work on the need for individuals to stand up to the impact of bureaucracies and other structures of modern society.

The influence of Immanuel Kant on Weber and on German sociology generally shows that German sociology and Marxism grew from different philosophical roots. As we have seen, it was Hegel, not Kant, who was the important philosophical influence on Marxian theory. Whereas Hegel's philosophy led Marx and the Marxists to look for relations, conflicts, and contradictions, Kantian philosophy led at least some German sociologists to take a more static perspective. To Kant the world was a buzzing confusion of events that could never be known directly. The world could be known only through thought processes that filter, select, and categorize these events. The content of the real world was differentiated by Kant from the forms through which that content can be comprehended. The emphasis on these forms gave the work of those sociologists within the Kantian tradition a more static quality than that of the Marxists within the Hegelian tradition.

Weber's Theory

Whereas Karl Marx offered basically a theory of capitalism, Weber's work was fundamentally a theory of the process of rationalization (Brubaker, 1984; Kalberg, 1980, 1990, 1994). Weber was interested in the general issue of why institutions in the Western world had grown progressively more rational while powerful barriers seemed to prevent a similar development in the rest of the world.

Although rationality is used in many ways in Weber's work, what interests us here is a process involving one of four types identified by Kalberg (1980, 1990, 1994; see also Brubaker, 1984; Levine, 1981a), *formal rationality*. Formal rationality involves, as was usually the case with Weber, a concern for the actor making choices of means and ends. However, in this case, that choice is made in reference to universally applied rules, regulations, and laws. These, in turn, are derived from various large-scale structures, especially bureaucracies and the economy. Weber developed his theories in the context of a large number of comparative historical studies of the West, China, India, and many other regions of the world. In those studies, he sought to delineate the factors that helped bring about or impede the development of rationalization.

Weber saw the bureaucracy (and the historical process of bureaucratization) as the classic example of rationalization, but rationalization is perhaps best illustrated today by the fast-food restaurant (Ritzer, 2008). The fast-food restaurant is a formally rational system in which people (both workers and customers) are led to seek the most rational means to ends. The drive-through window, for example, is a rational means by which workers can dispense and customers can obtain food quickly and efficiently. Speed and efficiency are dictated by the fast-food restaurants and the rules and regulations by which they operate.

Weber embedded his discussion of the process of bureaucratization in a broader discussion of the political institution. He differentiated among three types of authority systems—traditional, charismatic, and rational-legal. Only in the modern Western world can a rational-legal authority system develop, and only within that system does one find the full-scale development of the modern bureaucracy. The rest of the world remains dominated by traditional or charismatic authority systems, which generally impede the development of a rational-legal authority system and modern bureaucracies. Briefly, *traditional* authority stems from a long-lasting system of beliefs. An example would be a leader who comes to power because his or her family or clan has always provided the group's leadership. A *charismatic* leader derives his or her authority from extraordinary abilities or characteristics or, more likely, simply from the belief on the part of followers that the leader has such traits. Although these two types of authority are of historical importance, Weber believed that the trend in the West, and ultimately in the rest of the world, is toward systems of *rational-legal* authority (Bunzel, 2007). In such systems, authority is derived from rules legally and rationally enacted. Thus, the president of the United States derives his authority ultimately from the laws of society. The evolution of rational-legal authority, with its accompanying bureaucracies, is only one part of Weber's general argument on the rationalization of the Western world.

Weber also did detailed and sophisticated analyses of the rationalization of such phenomena as religion, law, the city, and even music. But we can illustrate Weber's mode of thinking with one other example—the rationalization of the economic institution. This discussion is couched in Weber's broader analysis of the relationship between religion and capitalism. In a wide-ranging historical study, Weber sought to understand why a rational economic system (capitalism) had developed in the West and why it had failed to develop in the rest of the world. Weber accorded a central role to religion in this process. At one level, he was engaged in a dialogue with the Marxists in an effort to show that, contrary to what many Marxists of the day believed, religion was not merely an epiphenomenon. Instead, it had played a key role in the rise of capitalism in the West and in its failure to develop elsewhere in the world. Weber argued that it was a distinctively rational religious system (Calvinism) that played the central role in the rise of capitalism in the West. In contrast, in the other parts of the world that he studied, Weber found more irrational religious systems (for example, Confucianism, Taoism, Hinduism), which helped inhibit the development of a rational economic system. However, in the end, one gets the feeling that these religions provided only temporary barriers, for the economic systems—indeed, the entire social structure—of these societies ultimately would become rationalized.

Although rationalization lies at the heart of Weberian theory, it is far from all there is to the theory. But this is not the place to go into that rich body of material. Instead, let us return to the development of sociological theory. A key issue in that development is: Why did Weber's theory prove more attractive to later sociological theorists than Marxian theory?

The Acceptance of Weber's Theory

One reason is that Weber proved to be more acceptable politically. Instead of espousing Marxian radicalism, Weber was more of a liberal on some issues and a conservative on others (for example, the role of the state). Although he was a severe critic of many aspects of modern capitalist society and came to many of the same critical conclusions as did Marx, he was not one to propose radical solutions to problems (Heins, 1993). In fact, he felt that the radical reforms offered by many Marxists and other socialists would do more harm than good.

Later sociological theorists, especially Americans, saw their society under attack by Marxian theory. Largely conservative in orientation, they cast about for theoretical alternatives to Marxism. One of those who proved attractive was Max Weber. (Durkheim and Vilfredo Pareto were others.) After all, rationalization affected not only capitalist but also socialist societies. Indeed, from Weber's point of view, rationalization constituted an even greater problem in socialist than in capitalist societies.

Also in Weber's favor was the form in which he presented his judgments. He spent most of his life doing detailed historical studies, and his political conclusions were often made within the context of his research. Thus they usually sounded very scientific and academic. Marx, although he did much serious research, also wrote a good deal of explicitly polemical material. Even his more academic work is laced with acid political judgments. For example, in *Capital* (1867/1967), he described capitalists as "vampires" and "werewolves." Weber's more academic style helped make him more acceptable to later sociologists.

Another reason for the greater acceptability of Weber was that he operated in a philosophical tradition that also helped shape the work of later sociologists. That is, Weber operated in the Kantian tradition, which meant, as we have seen, that he tended to think in cause-and-effect terms. This kind of thinking was more acceptable to later sociologists, who were largely unfamiliar and uncomfortable with the dialectical logic that informed Marx's work.

Finally, Weber appeared to offer a much more rounded approach to the social world than did Marx. Whereas Marx appeared to be almost totally preoccupied with the economy, Weber was interested in a wide range of social phenomena. This diversity of focus seemed to give later sociologists more to work with than the apparently more single-minded concerns of Marx.

Weber produced most of his major works in the late 1800s and early 1900s. Early in his career Weber was identified more as a historian who was concerned with sociological issues, but in the early 1900s his focus grew more and more sociological. Indeed, he became the dominant sociologist of his time in Germany. In 1910, he founded (with, among others, Georg Simmel, whom we discuss next) the German Sociological Society (Glatzer, 1998). His home in Heidelberg was an intellectual center not only for sociologists but for scholars from many fields. Although his work was broadly influential in Germany, it was to become even more influential in the United States, especially after Talcott Parsons introduced Weber's ideas (and those of other European theorists, especially Durkheim) to a large American audience. Although Marx's ideas did not have a significant positive effect on American sociological theorists until the 1960s, Weber was already highly influential by the late 1930s.

Simmel's Theory

Georg Simmel was Weber's contemporary and a cofounder of the German Sociological Society. Simmel was a somewhat atypical sociological theorist (Frisby, 1981; Levine, Carter, and Gorman, 1976a, 1976b). For one thing, he had an immediate and profound effect on the development of American sociological theory, whereas Marx and Weber were largely ignored for a number of years. Simmel's work helped shape the development of one of the early centers of American sociology—the University of Chicago—and its major theory, symbolic interactionism (Jaworski, 1995; 1997). The Chicago school and symbolic interactionism came, as we will see, to dominate American sociology in the 1920s and early 1930s (Bulmer, 1984). Simmel's ideas were influential at Chicago mainly because the dominant figures in the early years of Chicago, Albion Small and Robert Park, had been exposed to Simmel's theories in Berlin in the late 1800s. Park attended Simmel's lectures in 1899 and 1900, and Small carried on an extensive correspondence with Simmel during the 1890s. They were instrumental in bringing Simmel's ideas to students and faculty at Chicago, in translating some of his work, and in bringing it to the attention of a large-scale American audience (Frisby, 1984:29).

Another atypical aspect of Simmel's work is his "level" of analysis, or at least that level for which he became best known in America. Whereas Weber and Marx were preoccupied with large-scale issues such as the rationalization of society and a capitalist economy, Simmel was best known for his work on smaller-scale issues, especially individual action and interaction. He became famous early for his thinking, derived from Kantian philosophy, on *forms* of interaction (for example, conflict) and *types* of interactants (for example, the stranger). Basically, Simmel saw that understanding interaction among people was one of the major tasks of sociology. However, it was impossible to study the massive number of interactions in social life without some conceptual tools. This is where forms of interaction and types of interactants came in. Simmel felt that he could isolate a limited number of forms of interaction that could be found in a large number of social settings. Thus equipped, one could analyze and understand these different interaction settings. The development of a limited number of types of interactants could be similarly useful in explaining interaction settings. This work had a profound effect on symbolic interactionism, which, as the name suggests, was focally concerned with interaction. One of the ironies, however, is that Simmel also was concerned with large-scale issues similar to those that obsessed Marx and Weber. However, this work was much less influential than his work on interaction, although there are contemporary signs of a growing interest in the large-scale aspects of Simmel's sociology.

It was partly Simmel's style in his work on interaction that made him accessible to early American sociological theorists. Although he wrote heavy tomes like those of Weber and Marx, he also wrote a set of deceptively simple essays on such interesting topics as poverty, the prostitute, the miser and the spendthrift, and the stranger. The brevity of such essays and the high interest level of the material made the dissemination of Simmel's ideas much easier. Unfortunately, the essays had the negative effect of obscuring Simmel's more massive works (for example, *Philosophy of Money,* translated in 1978; see Poggi, 1993), which were potentially as significant to sociology. Nevertheless, it was partly through the short and clever essays that Simmel had a much more significant effect on early American sociological theory than either Marx or Weber did.

We should not leave Simmel without saying something about *Philosophy of Money,* because its English translation made Simmel's work attractive to a whole new set of theorists interested in culture and society. Although a macro orientation is clearer in *Philosophy of Money,* it always existed in Simmel's work. For example, it is clear in his famous work on the dyad and the triad. Simmel thought that some crucial sociological developments take place when a two-person group (or *dyad*) is transformed into a *triad* by the addition of a third party. Social possibilities emerge that simply could not exist in a dyad. For example, in a triad, one of the members can become an arbitrator or mediator of the differences between the other two. More important, two of the members can band together and dominate the other member. This represents on a small scale what can happen with the emergence of large-scale structures that become separate from individuals and begin to dominate them.

This theme lies at the base of *Philosophy of Money.* Simmel was concerned primarily with the emergence in the modern world of a money economy that becomes separate from the individual and predominant. This theme, in turn, is part of an even broader and more pervasive one in Simmel's work: the domination of the culture as a whole over the individual. As Simmel saw it, in the modern world, the larger culture and all its various components (including the money economy) expand, and as they expand, the importance of the individual decreases. Thus, for example, as the industrial technology associated with a modern economy expands and grows more sophisticated, the skills and abilities of the individual worker grow progressively less important. In the end, the worker is confronted with an industrial machine over which he or she can exert little, if any, control. More generally, Simmel thought that in the modern world, the expansion of the larger culture leads to the growing insignificance of the individual.

SIGMUND FREUD

A Biographical Sketch

Another leading figure in German social science in the late 1800s and early 1900s was Sigmund Freud. Although he was not a sociologist, Freud influenced the work of many sociologists (for example, Talcott Parsons and Norbert Elias) and continues to be of relevance to social theorists (Chodorow, 1999; Elliott, 1992; Kaye, 1991, 2003; Kurzweil, 1995; Movahedi, 2007).

Sigmund Freud was born in the Austro-Hungarian city of Freiberg on May 6, 1856. In 1859, his family moved to Vienna, and in 1873, Freud entered the medical school at the University of Vienna. Freud was more interested in science than in medicine and took a position in a physiology laboratory. He completed his degree in medicine, and after leaving the laboratory in 1882, he worked in a hospital and then set up a private medical practice with a specialty in nervous diseases.

Freud at first used hypnosis in an effort to deal with a type of neurosis known as hysteria. He had learned the technique in Paris from Jean Martin Charcot in 1885. Later he adopted a technique, pioneered by a fellow Viennese physician, Joseph Breuer, in which hysterical symptoms disappeared when the patient talked through the circumstances in which the symptoms first arose. By 1895, Freud had published a book with Breuer with a series of revolutionary implications: that the causes of neuroses such as hysteria were psychological (not, as had been believed, physiological) and that the therapy involved talking through the original causes. Thus was born the practical and theoretical field of psychoanalysis. Freud began to part company with Breuer as he came to see sexual factors, or more generally the libido, at the root of neuroses. Over the next several years, Freud refined his therapeutic techniques and wrote a great deal about his new ideas.

By 1902, Freud began to gather a number of disciples around him, and they met weekly at his house. By 1903 or 1904, others (for example, Carl Jung) began to use Freud's ideas in their psychiatric practices. In 1908, the first Psychoanalytic Congress was held, and the next year a periodical for disseminating psychoanalytic knowledge was formed. As quickly as it had formed, the new field of psychoanalysis became splintered as Freud broke with people such as Jung and they went off to develop their own ideas and found their own groups. World War I slowed the development of psychoanalysis, but it expanded and developed greatly in the 1920s. With the rise of Nazism, the center of psychoanalysis shifted to the United States, where it remains to this day. But Freud remained in Vienna until the Nazis took over in 1938, despite the fact that he was Jewish and the Nazis had burned his books as early as 1933. On June 4, 1938, only after a ransom had been paid and President Roosevelt had interceded, Sigmund Freud left Vienna. Freud had suffered from cancer of the jaw since 1923, and he died in London on September 23, 1939.

Although sociologists have become increasingly attuned to the broader implications of Simmel's work, his early influence was primarily through his studies of small-scale social phenomena, such as the forms of interaction and types of interactants.

The Origins of British Sociology

We have been examining the development of sociology in France (Comte, Durkheim) and Germany (Marx, Weber, and Simmel). We turn now to the parallel development of sociology in England. As we will see, Continental ideas had their impact on early British sociology, but more important were native influences.

Political Economy, Ameliorism, and Social Evolution

Philip Abrams (1968) contended that British sociology was shaped in the nineteenth century by three often conflicting sources—political economy, ameliorism, and social evolution.[7] Thus when the Sociological Society of London was founded in 1903, there were strong differences over the definition of sociology. However, few doubted the view that sociology could be a science. It was the differences that gave British sociology its distinctive character, and we will look at each of them briefly.

Political Economy

We have already touched on *political economy,* which was a theory of industrial and capitalist society traceable in part to the work of Adam Smith (1723–1790).[8] As we saw, political economy had a profound effect on Karl Marx. Marx studied political economy closely, and he was critical of it. But that was not the direction taken by British economists and sociologists. They tended to accept Smith's idea that there was an "invisible hand" that shaped the market for labor and goods. The market was seen as an independent reality that stood above individuals and controlled their behavior. The British sociologists, like the political economists and unlike Marx, saw the market as a positive force, as a source of order, harmony, and integration in society. Because they saw the market, and more generally society, in a positive light, the task of the sociologist was not to criticize society but simply to gather data on the laws by which it operated. The goal was to provide the government with the facts it needed to understand the way the system worked and to direct its workings wisely.

The emphasis was on facts, but which facts? Whereas Marx, Weber, Durkheim, and Comte looked to the structures of society for their basic facts, the British thinkers tended to focus on the individuals who made up those structures. In dealing with large-scale structures, they tended to collect individual-level data and then combine them to form a collective portrait. In the mid-1800s it was the statisticians who dominated British social science, and this kind of data collection was deemed to be the major task

---

[7]For more recent developments in British sociology, see Abrams et al. (1981).

[8]Smith is usually included as a leading member of the Scottish Enlightenment (Chitnis, 1976; Styrdom, 2005) and as one of the Scottish Moralists (Schneider, 1967:xi), who were seeking to establish the basis for sociology.

of sociology. The objective was the accumulation of "pure" facts without theorizing or philosophizing. These empirical sociologists were detached from the concerns of social theorists. Instead of general theorizing, the "emphasis settled on the business of producing more exact indicators, better methods of classification and data collection, improved life tables, higher levels of comparability between discrete bodies of data, and the like" (Abrams, 1968:18).

It was almost in spite of themselves that these statistically oriented sociologists came to see some limitations in their approach. A few began to feel the need for broader theorizing. To them, a problem such as poverty pointed to failings in the market system as well as in the society as a whole. But most, focused as they were on individuals, did not question the larger system; they turned instead to more detailed field studies and to the development of more complicated and more exact statistical techniques. To them, the source of the problem had to lie in inadequate research methods, not in the system as a whole. As Philip Abrams noted, "Focusing persistently on the distribution of individual circumstances, the statisticians found it hard to break through to a perception of poverty as a product of social structure. . . . They did not and probably could not achieve the concept of structural victimization" (1968:27). In addition to their theoretical and methodological commitments to the study of individuals, the statisticians worked too closely with government policy makers to arrive at the conclusion that the larger political and economic system was the problem.

Ameliorism

Related to, but separable from, political economy was the second defining characteristic of British sociology—*ameliorism,* or a desire to solve social problems by reforming individuals. Although British scholars began to recognize that there were problems in society (for example, poverty), they still believed in that society and wanted to preserve it. They desired to forestall violence and revolution and to reform the system so that it could continue essentially as it was. Above all, they wanted to prevent the coming of a socialist society. Thus, like French sociology and some branches of German sociology, British sociology was conservatively oriented.

Because the British sociologists could not or would not trace the source of problems such as poverty to the society as a whole, the source had to lie within the individuals themselves. This was an early form of what William Ryan (1971) later called "blaming the victim." Much attention was devoted to a long series of individual problems—"ignorance, spiritual destitution, impurity, bad sanitation, pauperism, crime, and intemperance—above all intemperance" (Abrams, 1968:39). Clearly, there was a tendency to look for a simple cause for all social ills, and the one that suggested itself before all others was alcoholism. What made this perfect to the ameliorist was that this was an individual pathology, not a social pathology. The ameliorists lacked a theory of social structure, a theory of the social causes of such individual problems.

Social Evolution

But a stronger sense of social structure was lurking below the surface of British sociology, and it burst through in the latter part of the nineteenth century with the growth of interest in social evolution (Maryanski, 2005; Sanderson, 2001). One important influence was the work of Auguste Comte, part of which had been translated into English in the 1850s by Harriet Martineau (Hoecker-Drysdale, 2000). Although Comte's work did not inspire immediate interest, by the last quarter of the century, a number of thinkers had been attracted to it and to its concern for the larger structures of society, its scientific (positivistic) orientation, its comparative orientation, and its evolutionary theory. However, a number of British thinkers sharpened their own conception of the world in opposition to some of the excesses of Comtian theory (for example, the tendency to elevate sociology to the status of a religion).

In Abrams's view, the real importance of Comte lay in his providing one of the bases on which opposition could be mounted against the "oppressive genius of Herbert Spencer" (Abrams, 1968:58). In both a positive and a negative sense, Spencer was a dominant figure in British sociological theory, especially evolutionary theory (J. Turner, 2000, 2007).

Herbert Spencer (1820–1903)

In attempting to understand Spencer's ideas (Haines, 2005; J. Turner, 2007; see Chapter 5), it is useful to compare and contrast them with Comtian theory.

Spencer and Comte

Spencer is often categorized with Comte in terms of their influence on the development of sociological theory (J. Turner, 2001a), but there are some important differences between them. For example, it is less easy to categorize Spencer as a conservative. In fact, in his early years, Spencer is better seen as a political liberal, and he retained elements of liberalism throughout his life. However, it is also true that Spencer grew more conservative during the course of his life and that his basic influence, as was true of Comte, was conservative.

One of his liberal views, which coexisted rather uncomfortably with his conservatism, was his acceptance of a laissez-faire doctrine: he felt that the state should not intervene in individual affairs except in the rather passive function of protecting people. This meant that Spencer, unlike Comte, was not interested in social reforms; he wanted social life to evolve free of external control.

This difference points to Spencer as a *Social Darwinist* (G. Jones, 1980; Weiler, 2007a). As such, he held the evolutionary view that the world was growing progressively better. Therefore, it should be left alone; outside interference could only worsen the situation. He adopted the view that social institutions, like plants and animals, adapted progressively and positively to their social environment. He also accepted the Darwinian view that a process of natural selection, "survival of the fittest," occurred in the social world. (Interestingly, it was Spencer who coined the phrase "survival of the fittest" several years before Charles Darwin's work on natural selection.) That is, if unimpeded by external intervention, people who were "fit" would survive and proliferate whereas the "unfit" eventually would die out. Another difference was that Spencer emphasized the individual, whereas Comte focused on larger units such as the family.

Comte and Spencer shared with Durkheim and others a commitment to a science of sociology (Haines, 1992), which was a very attractive perspective to early theorists.

Another influence of Spencer's work, shared with both Comte and Durkheim, was his tendency to see society as an *organism*. In this, Spencer borrowed his perspective and concepts from biology. He was concerned with the overall structure of society, the interrelationship of the *parts* of society, and the *functions* of the parts for each other as well as for the system as a whole.

Most important, Spencer, like Comte, had an evolutionary conception of historical development. However, Spencer was critical of Comte's evolutionary theory on several grounds. Specifically, he rejected Comte's law of the three stages. He argued that Comte was content to deal with evolution in the realm of ideas, in terms of intellectual development. Spencer, however, sought to develop an evolutionary theory in the real, material world.

Evolutionary Theory

It is possible to identify at least two major evolutionary perspectives in Spencer's work (Haines, 1988; Perrin, 1976).

The first of these theories relates primarily to the increasing size of society. Society grows through both the multiplication of individuals and the union of groups (compounding). The increasing size of society brings with it larger and more differentiated social structures, as well as the increasing differentiation of the functions they perform. In addition to their growth in terms of size, societies evolve through compounding, that is, by unifying more and more adjoining groups. Thus, Spencer talks of the evolutionary movement from simple to compound, doubly-compound, and trebly-compound societies.

Spencer also offers a theory of evolution from *militant* to *industrial* societies. Earlier, militant societies are defined by being structured for offensive and defensive warfare. Although Spencer was critical of warfare, he felt that in an earlier stage it was functional in bringing societies together (for example, through military conquest) and in creating the larger aggregates of people necessary for the development of industrial society. However, with the emergence of industrial society, warfare ceases to be functional and serves to impede further evolution. Industrial society is based on friendship, altruism, elaborate specialization, recognition for achievements rather than the characteristics one is born with, and voluntary cooperation among highly disciplined individuals. Such a society is held together by voluntary contractual relations and, more important, by a strong common morality. The government's role is restricted and focuses only on what people ought not to do. Obviously, modern industrial societies are less warlike than their militant predecessors. Although Spencer sees a general evolution in the direction of industrial societies, he also recognizes that it is possible that there will be periodic regressions to warfare and more militant societies.

In his ethical and political writings, Spencer offered other ideas on the evolution of society. For one thing, he saw society as progressing toward an ideal, or perfect, moral state. For another, he argued that the fittest societies survive, and unfit societies should be permitted to die off. The result of this process is adaptive upgrading for the world as a whole.

Thus, Spencer offered a rich and complicated set of ideas on social evolution. As we will see, his ideas first enjoyed great success, then were rejected for many years, and more recently have been revived with the rise of neoevolutionary sociological theories (Buttel, 1990).

The Reaction against Spencer in Britain

Despite his emphasis on the individual, Spencer was best known for his large-scale theory of social evolution. In this, he stood in stark contrast to the sociology that preceded him in Britain. However, the reaction against Spencer was based more on the threat that his idea of survival of the fittest posed to the ameliorism so dear to most early British sociologists. Although Spencer later repudiated some of his more outrageous ideas, he did argue for a survival-of-the-fittest philosophy and against government intervention and social reform:

> Fostering the good-for-nothing at the expense of the good, is an extreme cruelty. It is a deliberate stirring-up of miseries for future generations. There is no greater curse to posterity than that of bequeathing to them an increasing population of imbeciles and idlers and criminals. . . . The whole effort of nature is to get rid of such, to clear the world of them, and make room for better. . . . If they are not sufficiently complete to live, they die, and it is best they should die.
>
> (Spencer, cited in Abrams, 1968:74)

Such sentiments were clearly at odds with the ameliorative orientation of the British reformer-sociologists.

The Key Figure in Early Italian Sociology

We close this sketch of early, primarily conservative, European sociological theory with a brief mention of one Italian sociologist, Vilfredo Pareto (1848–1923). Pareto was influential in his time, but his contemporary relevance is minimal (for one exception, see Powers, 1986). There was a brief outburst of interest in Pareto's (1935) work in the 1930s, when the major American theorist, Talcott Parsons, devoted as much attention to him as he gave to Weber and Durkheim. However, in recent years, except for a few of his major concepts, Pareto also has receded in importance and contemporary relevance (Femia, 1995).

Zeitlin argued that Pareto developed his "major ideas as a refutation of Marx" (1996:171). In fact, Pareto was rejecting not only Marx but also a good portion of Enlightenment philosophy. For example, whereas the Enlightenment philosophers emphasized rationality, Pareto emphasized the role of nonrational factors such as human instincts (Mozetic and Weiler, 2007). This emphasis also was tied to his rejection of Marxian theory. That is, because nonrational, instinctual factors were so important and so unchanging, it was unrealistic to hope to achieve dramatic social changes with an economic revolution.

Pareto also developed a theory of social change that stood in stark contrast to Marxian theory. Whereas Marx's theory focused on the role of the masses, Pareto offered an elite theory of social change, which held that society inevitably is dominated by a small elite that operates on the basis of enlightened self-interest (Adams, 2005). It rules over the masses of people, who are dominated by nonrational forces. Because they lack rational capacities, the masses, in Pareto's system, are unlikely to be a revolutionary force. Social change occurs when the elite begins to degenerate and is replaced by a new elite derived from the nongoverning elite or higher elements of the masses. After the new elite is in power, the process begins anew. Thus, we have a cyclical theory of social change instead of the directional theories offered by Marx, Comte, Spencer, and others. In addition, Pareto's theory of change largely ignores the plight of the masses. Elites come and go, but the lot of the masses remains the same.

This theory, however, was not Pareto's lasting contribution to sociology. That lay in his scientific conception of sociology and the social world: "My wish is to construct a system of sociology on the model of celestial mechanics [astronomy], physics, chemistry" (cited in Hook, 1965:57). Briefly, Pareto conceived of society as a system in equilibrium, a whole consisting of interdependent parts. A change in one part was seen as leading to changes in other parts of the system. Pareto's systemic conception of society was the most important reason Parsons devoted so much attention to Pareto's work in his 1937 book, *The Structure of Social Action,* and it was Pareto's most important influence on Parsons's thinking. Fused with similar views held by those who had an organic image of society (Comte, Durkheim, and Spencer, for example), Pareto's theory played a central role in the development of Parsons's theory and, more generally, in structural functionalism.

Although few modern sociologists now read Pareto's work, it can be seen as a rejection of the Enlightenment and of Marxism and as offering an elite theory of social change that stands in opposition to the Marxian perspective.

Turn-of-the-Century Developments in European Marxism

While many nineteenth-century sociologists were developing their theories in opposition to Marx, there was a simultaneous effort by a number of Marxists to clarify and extend Marxian theory. Between roughly 1875 and 1925, there was little overlap between Marxism (Beilharz, 2005c; Steinmetz, 2007) and sociology. (Weber is an exception to this.) The two schools of thought were developing in parallel fashion with little or no interchange between them.

After the death of Marx, Marxian theory was first dominated by those who saw in his theory scientific and economic determinism (Bakker, 2007). Wallerstein calls this the era of "orthodox Marxism" (1986:1301). Friedrich Engels, Marx's benefactor and collaborator, lived on after Marx's death and can be seen as the first exponent of such a perspective. Basically, this view was that Marx's scientific theory had uncovered the economic laws that ruled the capitalist world. Such laws pointed to the inevitable collapse of the capitalist system. Early Marxian thinkers, like Karl Kautsky, sought to gain a better understanding of the operation of these laws. There were several problems with this perspective. For one thing, it seemed to rule out political action, a cornerstone of Marx's position. That is, there seemed no need for individuals, especially workers, to do anything. In that the system was inevitably crumbling, all they had to do was sit back and wait for its demise. On a theoretical level, deterministic Marxism seemed to rule out the dialectical relationship between individuals and larger social structures.

These problems led to a reaction among Marxian theorists and to the development of "Hegelian Marxism" in the early 1900s. The Hegelian Marxists refused to reduce Marxism to a scientific theory that ignored individual thought and action. They are labeled Hegelian Marxists because they sought to combine Hegel's interest in consciousness (which some, including the author of this text, view Marx as sharing) with the determinists' interest in the economic structures of society. The Hegelian theorists were significant for both theoretical and practical reasons. Theoretically, they reinstated the importance of the individual, consciousness, and the relationship between thought and action. Practically, they emphasized the importance of individual action in bringing about a social revolution.

The major exponent of this point of view was Georg Lukács (Fischer, 1984; Markus, 2005). According to Martin Jay, Lukács was "the founding father of Western Marxism" and his work *Class and Class Consciousness* is "generally acknowledged as the charter document of Hegelian Marxism" (1984:84). Lukács had begun in the early 1900s to integrate Marxism with sociology (in particular, Weberian and Simmelian theory). This integration was soon to accelerate with the development of critical theory in the 1920s and 1930s.

The Contemporary Relevance of Classical Sociological Theory

Classical sociological theories are important not only historically (Camic, 1997), but also because they are living documents with contemporary relevance to both modern theorists and today's social world. Tiryakian (1994) has outlined three criteria for judging a sociological work a classic. First, it is "must reading" for beginners because it demonstrates "the power and imagination of sociological analysis" (Tiryakian, 1994:4). Second, it is useful to both contemporary theorists and researchers. That is, new theories are built on the shoulders of the classic theorists and their work generates hypotheses to be tested empirically by modern researchers. Third, it is of sufficient richness and depth that it is worth rereading at a later point in a sociologist's career.

The works of the theorists discussed at least in some depth in this chapter qualify as classics in terms of these criteria. More specifically, the work of the classic thinkers continues to inspire modern sociologists in a variety of ways. Let us look briefly at just a few examples of this kind of work.

Although Durkheim has usually been seen as a political conservative, some recent commentators have tended to see a more radical, even revolutionary, strand in Durkheimian theory (Gane, 1992; Pearce, 1989). In fact, Pearce's major theme is "that the development of many of Durkheim's concepts can be used to help specify a realistic set of socialist goals" (1989:10). Alexander (1988b) has used some of Durkheim's ideas on culture and religion to analyze the Watergate scandal; for example, the ritualistic aspects of the Watergate hearings, and other aspects of the scandal. Mestrovic (1992:158) has addressed Durkheim's work in light of the contemporary conflict between modern and postmodern thinkers and has concluded that Durkheimian theory provides the seeds of a perspective that is preferable to either of the others: "Durkheim was seeking a new world order that would preserve . . . progress and capitalist efficiency [the modern viewpoint], but that would be balanced with . . . mystic sympathy and a sense of international social solidarity [a more postmodern viewpoint]." Lehmann (1993a) has used a key tool of the postmodernists, "deconstruction," to analyze Durkheim's work. (Lehmann [1993b] has also been in the forefront of studying Durkheim's ideas in light of feminist theory.) Specific aspects of Durkheim's work have also spawned a great deal of contemporary thought and research, but none more than his work on suicide and its various correlates (Skog, 1991).

Similarly, Weinstein and Weinstein (1993) have presented a "postmodernized" version of Simmelian theory to complement the well-known modern side of Simmel's perspective. Ritzer (1995) has used aspects of Simmel's theory to highlight many of the central problems associated with the increasingly global credit card society, especially the "temptation to imprudence," fraud, and threats to privacy.

The challenge in interpreting Marx's theory is the failure of communist nations ostensibly built on his principles. However, many Marxists feel that those nations were highly distorted versions of Marx's communist vision, and with those distortions out of the way it will now be possible to gain a clearer sense of Marx's ideas. As Graham says, "the enterprise of assessing Marx seems to me to be in its infancy" (1992:165). Thus, rather than being a dusty historical figure, Graham contends that "Marx is our contemporary" (1992:165).

On the contemporary relevance of Weber, Goldman argues that "there is continuity between many of Weber's concerns and the concerns of contemporary sociology . . . Weber still has much to contribute to the development of contemporary sociology" (1993:859). Said Collins, "Reading Weber, for some of us, is at least as worthwhile as reading contemporary writers on the same topics, if not more so. Weber is deeper, more analytical, more comprehensive . . . Weber in many respects is still the state of the art" (1993:861). Examinations of the success of the Japanese (Ritzer and LeMoyne, 1991), and more generally a number of Asian (Biggart, 1991), economies have been based on Weberian theory. As mentioned earlier, Ritzer (2008) has used Weber's rationalization theory to analyze the McDonaldization of society and, more specifically, the McDonaldization of credit through the widespread dissemination of credit cards (Ritzer, 1995: Chapter 8). More specifically, Weber's most famous book, *The Protestant Ethic and the Spirit of Capitalism,* has over the years spawned an enormous body of work, and such work continues (Davies, 1992; Silber, 1993).

Of notable interest in this context is the work of the early women sociologists to be discussed in Chapter 10. In many cases their work has been, or is just now being, rediscovered (Rogers, 1998, 2001). Thus, we are at the very early stages of the exploration of the contemporary relevance of the ideas of the classic female sociological thinkers. We can expect the list of contemporary effects to grow exponentially in the coming years.

Summary

This chapter sketches the early history of sociological theory. The first, and much briefer, section deals with the various social forces involved in the development of sociological theory. Although there were many such influences, we focus on how political revolution, the Industrial Revolution, and the rise of capitalism, socialism, feminism, urbanization, religious change, and the growth of science affected sociological theory. The second part of the chapter examines the influence of intellectual forces on the rise of sociological theory in various countries. We begin with France and the role played by the Enlightenment, stressing the conservative and romantic reaction to it. It is out of this interplay that French sociological theory developed. In this context, we examine the major figures in the early years of French sociology—Alexis de Tocqueville, Claude Henri Saint-Simon, Auguste Comte, and Emile Durkheim.

Next, we turn to Germany and the role played by Karl Marx in the development of sociology in that country. We discuss the parallel development of Marxian theory and sociological theory and the ways in which Marxian theory influenced sociology, both positively and negatively. We begin with the roots of Marxian theory in Hegelianism, materialism, and political economy. Marx's theory itself is touched upon briefly. The discussion then shifts to the roots of German sociology. Max Weber's work is examined in order to show the diverse sources of German sociology. Also discussed are some of the reasons why Weber's theory proved more acceptable to later sociologists than did Marx's ideas. This section closes with a brief discussion of Georg Simmel's work.

The rise of sociological theory in Britain is considered next. The major sources of British sociology were political economy, ameliorism, and social evolution. In this context, we touch on the work of Herbert Spencer as well as on some of the controversy that surrounded it.

This discussion is followed by a brief discussion of Italian sociological theory, in particular the work of Vilfredo Pareto, and the turn-of-the-century developments in European Marxian theory, primarily economic determinism and Hegelian Marxism. Finally, there is a brief discussion of the contemporary relevance of classical sociological theory.

This concludes our review of the early history of sociological theory. In this chapter, we have already discussed, in historical context, the work of seven theorists who will later receive full-chapter treatment—Tocqueville, Comte, Spencer, Marx, Durkheim, Weber, and Simmel. We will also touch on these theorists in the next chapter in terms of their influence on later sociological theory. Chapter 2 also includes a brief discussion, within the historical context of more recent theoretical developments, of the work of other theorists defined here as classical thinkers and treated in depth later in the book—Veblen, Schumpeter, Du Bois, Mead, Mannheim, Schutz, and Parsons.

Finally, although we have mentioned feminist theory and the early women sociological theorists in this chapter, we have not had much to say about the nature and impact of their work. That is because, as we will see in Chapter 10, their work was largely excluded from mainstream sociological thinking and had little impact on its development. Chapter 10 can be viewed as a first effort to help rectify this omission and exclusion.

C H A P T E R 2

A Historical Sketch of Sociological Theory: The Later Years

Chapter Outline

It is difficult to give a precise date for the founding of sociology in the United States. A course in social problems was taught at Oberlin as early as 1858, Comte's term *sociology* was used by George Fitzhugh in 1854, and William Graham Sumner taught social science courses at Yale beginning in 1873. During the 1880s, courses specifically bearing the title "Sociology" began to appear. The first department with *sociology* in its title was founded at the University of Kansas in 1889. In 1892, Albion Small moved to the University of Chicago and set up the new department of sociology. The Chicago department became the first important center of American sociology in general and of sociological theory in particular (F. Matthews, 1977).

Early American Sociological Theory

Politics

Schwendinger and Schwendinger (1974) argue that the early American sociologists are best described as political liberals and not, as was true of most early European theorists, as conservatives. The liberalism characteristic of early American sociology had basically two elements. First, it operated with a belief in the freedom and welfare of the individual. In this belief, it was influenced far more by Spencer's orientation than by

Comte's more collective position. Second, many sociologists associated with this orientation adopted an evolutionary view of social progress (Fine, 1979). However, they were split over how best to bring about this progress. Some argued that steps should be taken by the government to aid social reform, whereas others pushed a laissez-faire doctrine, arguing that the various components of society should be left to solve their own problems.

Liberalism, taken to its extreme, comes very close to conservatism. The belief in social progress—in reform or a laissez-faire doctrine—and the belief in the importance of the individual both lead to positions supportive of the system as a whole. The overriding belief is that the social system works or can be reformed to work. There is little criticism of the system as a whole; in the American case this means, in particular, that there is little questioning of capitalism. Instead of imminent class struggle, the early sociologists saw a future of class harmony and class cooperation. Ultimately this meant that early American sociological theory helped rationalize exploitation, domestic and international imperialism, and social inequality (Schwendinger and Schwendinger, 1974). In the end, the political liberalism of the early sociologists had enormously conservative implications.

Social Change and Intellectual Currents

In their analyses of the founding of American sociological theory, Roscoe Hinkle (1980) and Ellsworth Fuhrman (1980) outline several basic contexts from which that body of theory emerged. Of utmost importance are the social changes that occurred in American society after the Civil War (Bramson, 1961). In Chapter 1, we discussed an array of factors involved in the development of European sociological theory; several of these factors (such as industrialization and urbanization) were also intimately involved in the development of theory in America. In Fuhrman's view, the early American sociologists saw the positive possibilities of industrialization, but they also were well aware of its dangers. Although these early sociologists were attracted to the ideas generated by the labor movement and socialist groups about dealing with the dangers of industrialization, they were not in favor of radically overhauling society.

Arthur Vidich and Stanford Lyman (1985) make a strong case for the influence of Christianity, especially Protestantism, on the founding of American sociology. American sociologists retained the Protestant interest in saving the world and merely substituted one language (science) for another (religion). "From 1854, when the first works in sociology appeared in the United States, until the outbreak of World War I, sociology was a moral and intellectual response to the problems of American life and thought, institutions, and creeds" (Vidich and Lyman, 1985:1). Sociologists sought to define, study, and help solve these social problems. While the clergyman worked within religion to help improve it and people's lot within it, the sociologist did the same thing within society. Given their religious roots and the religious parallels, the vast majority of sociologists did not challenge the basic legitimacy of society.

Another major factor in the founding of American sociology discussed by both Hinkle and Fuhrman is the simultaneous emergence in America, in the late 1800s, of academic professions (including sociology) and the modern university system. In

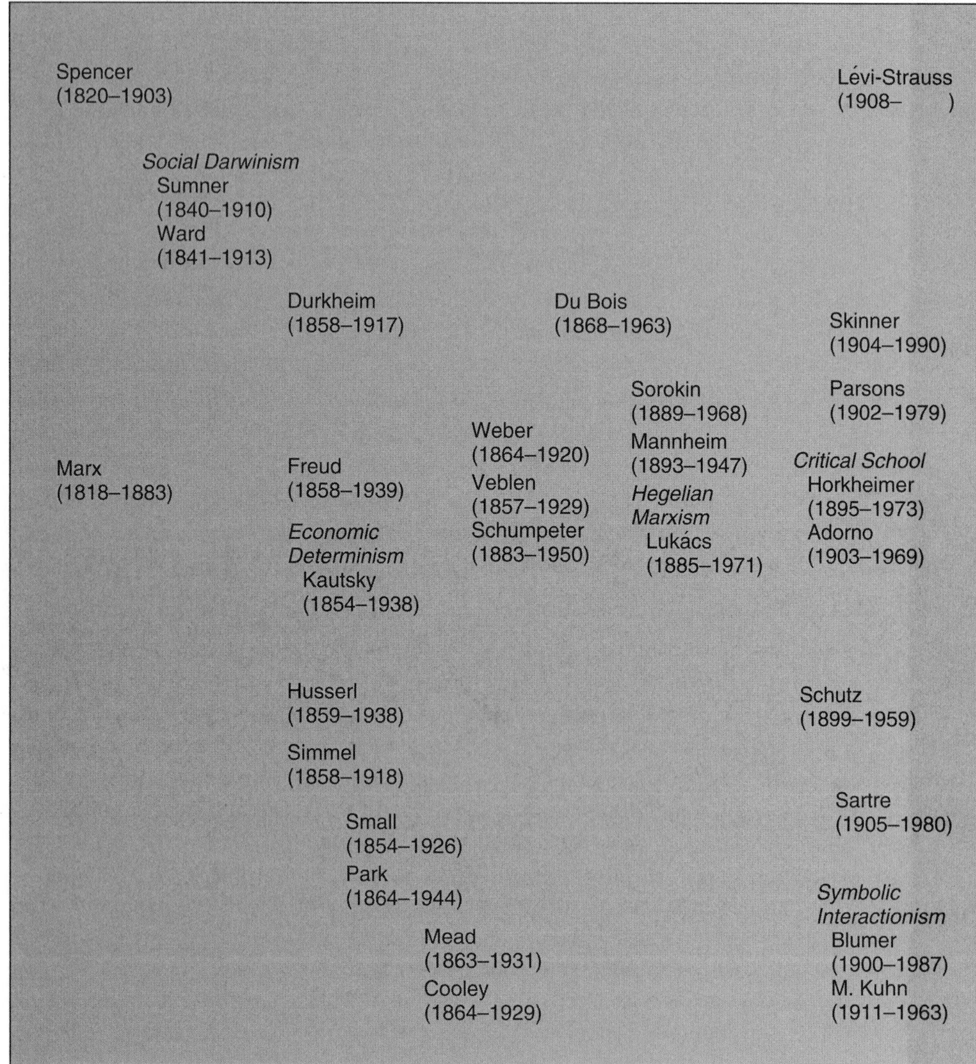

FIGURE 2.1 ***Sociological Theory: The Later Years***

Europe, in contrast, the university system was already well established *before* the emergence of sociology. Although sociology had a difficult time becoming established in Europe, it had easier going in the more fluid setting of the new American university system.

Another characteristic of early American sociology (as well as other social science disciplines) was its turn away from a historical perspective and in the direction of a positivistic, or "scientistic," orientation. As Dorothy Ross puts it, "The desire to achieve universalistic abstraction and quantitative methods turned American social scientists away from interpretive models available in history and cultural anthropology, and from the generalizing and interpretive model offered by Max Weber" (1991:473). Instead of

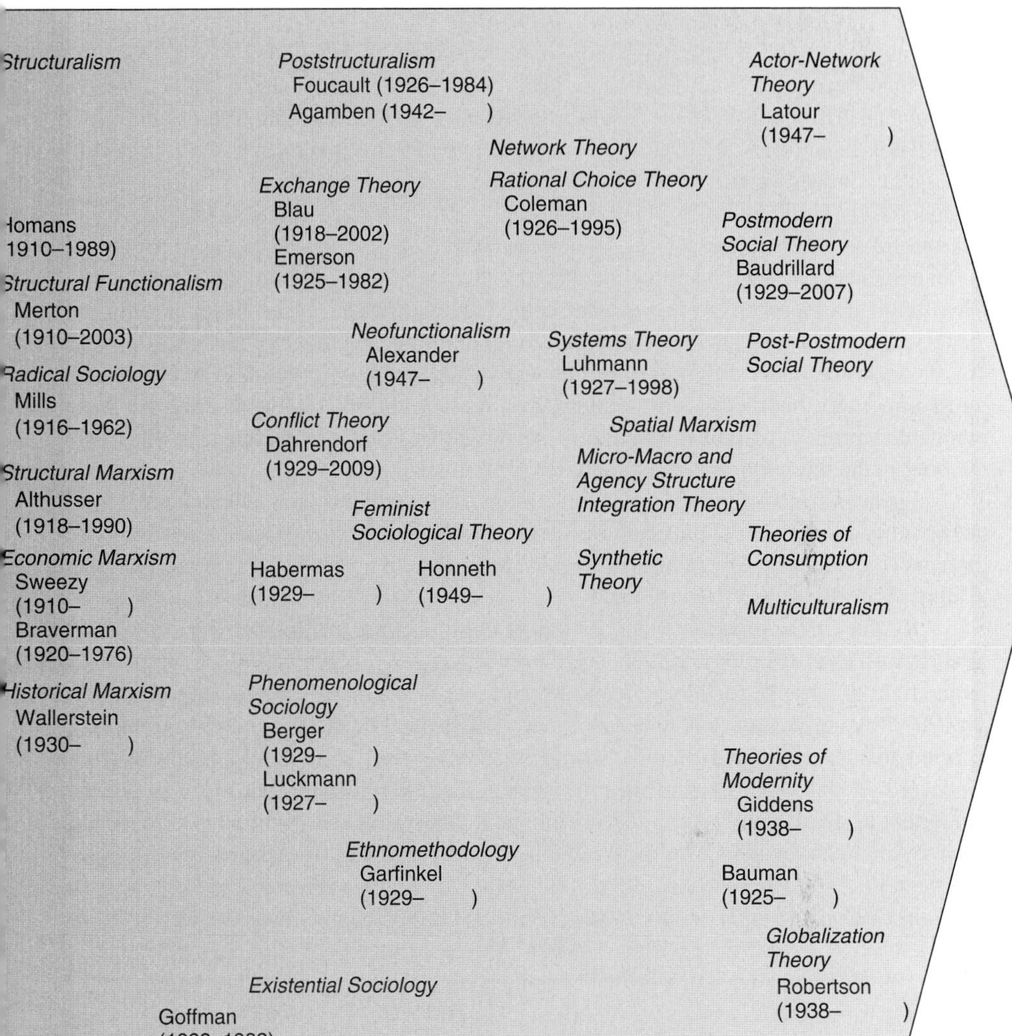

interpreting long-term historical changes, sociology had turned in the direction of scientifically studying short-term processes.

Still another factor was the impact of established European theory on American sociological theory (see Figure 2.1). European theorists largely created sociological theory, and the Americans were able to rely on this groundwork. The Europeans most important to the Americans were Spencer and Comte. Simmel was of some importance in the early years, but the influence of Durkheim, Weber, and Marx was not to have a dramatic effect for a number of years. The history of Herbert Spencer's ideas provides an interesting and informative illustration of the impact of early European theory on American sociology.

Herbert Spencer's Influence on Sociology

Why were Spencer's ideas so much more influential in the early years of American sociology than those of Comte, Durkheim, Marx, and Weber? Hofstadter (1959) offered several explanations. To take the easiest first, Spencer wrote in English, whereas the others did not. In addition, Spencer wrote in nontechnical terms, making his work broadly accessible. Indeed, some have argued that the lack of technicality is traceable to Spencer's *not* being a very sophisticated scholar. But there are other, more important reasons for Spencer's broad appeal. He offered a scientific orientation that was attractive to an audience that was becoming enamored of science and its technological products. He offered a comprehensive theory that seemed to deal with the entire sweep of human history. The breadth of his ideas, as well as the voluminous work he produced, allowed his theory to be many different things to many different people. Finally, and perhaps most important, his theory was soothing and reassuring to a society undergoing the wrenching process of industrialization—society was, according to Spencer, steadily moving in the direction of greater and greater progress.

Spencer's most famous American disciple was William Graham Sumner, who accepted and expanded upon many of Spencer's Social Darwinist ideas. Spencer also influenced other early American sociologists, among them Lester Ward, Charles Horton Cooley, E. A. Ross, and Robert Park.

By the 1930s, however, Spencer was in eclipse in the intellectual world in general, as well as in sociology. His Social Darwinist, laissez-faire ideas seemed ridiculous in the light of massive social problems, a world war, and a major economic depression. In 1937, Talcott Parsons announced Spencer's intellectual death for sociology when he echoed historian Crane Brinton's words of a few years earlier, "Who now reads Spencer?" Today Spencer is of little more than historical interest, but his ideas *were* important in shaping early American sociological theory. Let us look briefly at the work of two American theorists who were influenced, at least in part, by Spencer's work.

William Graham Sumner (1840–1910) William Graham Sumner was the person who taught the first course in the United States that could be called sociology (Delaney, 2005b). Sumner contended that he had begun teaching sociology "years before any such attempt was made at any other university in the world" (Curtis, 1981:63).

Sumner was the major exponent of Social Darwinism in the United States, although he appeared to change his view late in life (N. Smith, 1979). The following exchange between Sumner and one of his students illustrates his "liberal" views on the need for individual freedom and his position against government interference:

> "Professor, don't you believe in any government aid to industries?"
>
> "No! It's root, hog, or die."
>
> "Yes, but hasn't the hog got a right to root?"
>
> "There are no rights. The world owes nobody a living."
>
> "You believe then, Professor, in only one system, the contract-competitive system?"
>
> "That's the only sound economic system. All others are fallacies."
>
> "Well, suppose some professor of political economy came along and took your job away from you. Wouldn't you be sore?"

"Any other professor is welcome to try. If he gets my job, it is my fault. My business is to teach the subject so well that no one can take the job away from me."
(Phelps, cited in Hofstadter, 1959:54)

Sumner basically adopted a survival-of-the-fittest approach to the social world. Like Spencer, he saw people struggling against their environment, and the fittest were those who would be successful. Thus Sumner was a supporter of human aggressiveness and competitiveness. Those who succeeded deserved it, and those who did not succeed deserved to fail. Again like Spencer, Sumner was opposed to efforts, especially government efforts, to aid those who had failed. In his view such intervention operated against the natural selection that, among people as among lower animals, allowed the fit to survive and the unfit to perish. As Sumner put it, "If we do not like the survival of the fittest, we have only one possible alternative, and that is survival of the unfittest" (Curtis, 1981:84). This theoretical system fit in well with the development of capitalism because it provided theoretical legitimacy for the existence of great differences in wealth and power.

Sumner is of little more than historical interest for two main reasons. First, his orientation and Social Darwinism in general have come to be regarded as little more than a crude legitimation of competitive capitalism and the status quo. Second, he failed to build a solid enough base at Yale to build a school of sociology with many disciples. That kind of success was to occur some years later at the University of Chicago (Heyl and Heyl, 1976). In spite of success in his time, "Sumner is remembered by few today" (Curtis, 1981:146).

Lester F. Ward (1841–1913) Lester Ward had an unusual career in that he spent most of it as a paleontologist working for the federal government. During that time, Ward read Spencer and Comte and developed a strong interest in sociology. He published a number of works in the late 1800s and early 1900s in which he expounded his sociological theory. As a result of the fame that this work achieved, in 1906 Ward was elected the first president of the American Sociological Society. It was only then that he took his first academic position, at Brown University, a position that he held until his death (Hill, 2007).

Ward, like Sumner, accepted the idea that people had evolved from lower forms to their present status. He believed that early society was characterized by its simplicity and its moral poverty, whereas modern society was more complex, happier, and offered greater freedom. One task of sociology, *pure sociology,* was to study the basic laws of social change and social structure. But Ward was not content simply to have sociology study social life. He believed that sociology should have a practical side; there should also be an *applied sociology.* This applied sociology involved the conscious use of scientific knowledge to attain a better society. Thus, Ward was not an extreme Social Darwinist; he believed in the need for and importance of social reform.

Although of historical importance, Sumner and Ward have not been of long-term significance to sociological theory. However, now we turn briefly to a theorist of the time, Thorstein Veblen, who has been of long-term significance and whose influence today in sociology is increasing. Then we will look at a group of theorists, especially Mead, and a school, the Chicago school, that came to dominate sociology in America. The Chicago school was unusual in the history of sociology in that it was one of the few (the Durkheimian school in Paris was another) "collective intellectual enterprises of an integrated kind" in the history of sociology (Bulmer, 1984:1). The tradition begun at the University of Chicago is of continuing importance to sociology and its theoretical (and empirical) status.

Thorstein Veblen (1857–1929)

Veblen, who was not a sociologist but mainly held positions in economics departments, and even in economics was a marginal figure, nonetheless produced a body of social theory that is of enduring significance to those in a number of disciplines, including sociology (Powers, 2005). The central problem for Veblen was the clash between business and industry. By *business,* Veblen meant the owners, leaders, and "captains" of industry who focused on the profits of their own companies, but to keep prices and profits high, often engaged in efforts to limit production. In so doing, they obstructed the operation of the industrial system and adversely affected society as a whole (through higher rates of unemployment, for example), which is best served by the unimpeded operation of industry. Thus, business leaders were the source of many problems within society, which, Veblen felt, should be led by people (e.g., engineers) who understood the industrial system and its operation and were interested in the general welfare.

Most of Veblen's importance today is traceable to his book *The Theory of the Leisure Class* (1899/1994; Varul, 2007). Veblen is critical of the leisure class (which is closely tied to business) for its role in fostering wasteful consumption. To impress the rest of society, the leisure class engaged in both *conspicuous leisure* (the nonproductive use of time) and *conspicuous consumption* (spending more money on goods than they are worth). Those in all other social classes are influenced by this example and seek, directly and indirectly, to emulate the leisure class. The result is a society characterized by the waste of time and money. What is of utmost importance about this work is that unlike most other sociological works of the time (as well as most of Veblen's other works), *The Theory of the Leisure Class* focuses on consumption rather than production. Thus, it anticipated the current shift in social theory away from a focus on production and toward a focus on consumption (Ritzer, 2005; Ritzer, Goodman, and Weidenhoft, 2001; Slater, 1997; also a new journal—*Journal of Consumer Culture*—began publication in 2001).

Joseph Schumpeter (1883–1950)

Schumpeter, like Veblen, was an economist not a sociologist, but his work has come to be important to sociologists, especially those who study economic sociology (Swedberg, 1993). Schumpeter's work was motivated by the failure of economics to develop a dynamic theory of the economy. He attempted to deal with this problem by offering such a theory of the economy in general, and of capitalism in particular. At the core of the latter was his thinking on the idea of "creative destruction," that the creation of what was new in capitalism (and that which is new and innovative is essential to capitalism) went hand-in-hand with the destruction of the old (Schumpeter, 1942/1947/1950).

Schumpeter's thinking was related to, and influenced by, the work of Marx and Weber. Schumpeter had a sophisticated sense of Marx's theory and used it in various ways, including thinking about socialism as the stage after capitalism. He also had a strong theory of rationalization, especially the conflict between charismatic entrepreneurs and large, rationalized, industrial organizations. He saw the latter as winning out over the former and its rationalization set the stage for the emergence of the even more rationalized socialism.

The Chicago School[1]

The department of sociology at the University of Chicago was founded in 1892 by Albion Small (Williams, 2007). Small's intellectual work is of less contemporary significance than is the key role he played in the institutionalization of sociology in the United States (Faris, 1970; Matthews, 1977). He was instrumental in creating a department at Chicago that was to become the center of the discipline in the United States for many years. Small collaborated on the first sociology textbook in 1894. In 1895 he founded the *American Journal of Sociology,* a journal that, to this day, is a dominant force in the discipline. In 1905, Small cofounded the American Sociological Society, *the* major professional association of American sociologists to this date (Rhoades, 1981). The embarrassment caused by the initials of the American Sociological Society (ASS) led to the name being changed in 1959 to the American Sociological Association (ASA).

Early Chicago Sociology

The early Chicago department had several distinctive characteristics. For one thing, it had a strong connection with religion. Some members were ministers themselves, and others were sons of ministers. Small, for example, believed that "the ultimate goal of sociology must be essentially Christian" (Matthews, 1977:95). This opinion led to a view that sociology must be interested in social reform, and this view was combined with a belief that sociology should be scientific.[2] Scientific sociology with an objective of social amelioration was to be practiced in the burgeoning city of Chicago, which was beset by the positive *and* negative effects of urbanization and industrialization.

W. I. Thomas (1863–1947) In 1895, W. I. Thomas became a fellow at the Chicago department, where he wrote his dissertation in 1896. Thomas's lasting significance was in his emphasis on the need to do scientific research on sociological issues (Lodge, 1986). Although he championed this position for many years, its major statement came in 1918 with the publication of *The Polish Peasant in Europe and America,* which Thomas coauthored with Florian Znaniecki (Halas, 2005; Stebbins, 2007a, b; Wiley, 2007). Martin Bulmer sees it as a landmark study because it moved sociology away from "abstract theory and library research and toward the study of the empirical world utilizing a theoretical framework" (1984:45). Norbert Wiley sees *The Polish Peasant* as crucial to the founding of sociology in the sense of "clarifying the unique intellectual space into which this discipline alone could see and explore" (1986:20). The book was the product of eight years of research in both Europe and the United States and was primarily a study of social disorganization among Polish migrants. The data were of

[1]See Bulmer (1985) for a discussion of what defines a school and why we can speak of the "Chicago school." Tiryakian (1979, 1986) also deals with schools in general, and the Chicago school in particular, and emphasizes the role played by charismatic leaders as well as methodological innovations. For a discussion of this school within the broader context of developments in American sociological theory, see Hinkle (1994).

[2]As we will see, however, the Chicago school's conception of science was to become too "soft," at least in the eyes of the positivists who later came to dominate sociology.

ROBERT PARK

A Biographical Sketch

Robert Park did not follow the typical career route of an academic sociologist—college, graduate school, professorship. Instead, he had a varied career before he became a sociologist late in life. Despite his late start, Park had a profound effect on sociology in general and on theory in particular. Park's varied experiences gave him an unusual orientation to life, and this view helped shape the Chicago school, symbolic interactionism, and, ultimately, a good portion of sociology.

Park was born in Harveyville, Pennsylvania, on February 14, 1864 (Matthews, 1977). As a student at the University of Michigan, he was exposed to a number of great thinkers, such as John Dewey. Although he was excited by ideas, Park felt a strong need to work in the real world. As Park said, "I made up my mind to go in for experience for its own sake, to gather into my soul . . . 'all the joys and sorrows of the world'" (1927/1973:253). Upon graduation, he began a career as a journalist, which gave him this real-world opportunity. He particularly liked to explore ("hunting down gambling houses and opium dens" [Park, 1927/1973:254]). He wrote about city life in vivid detail. He would go into the field, observe and analyze, and then write up his observations. In fact, he was already doing essentially the kind of research ("scientific reporting") that came to be one of the hallmarks of Chicago sociology—that is, urban ethnology using participant observation techniques (Lindner, 1996).

Although the accurate description of social life remained one of his passions, Park grew dissatisfied with newspaper work because it did not fulfill his familial or, more important, his intellectual needs. Furthermore, it did not seem to contribute to the improvement of the world, and Park had a deep interest in social reform. In 1898, at age thirty-four, Park left newspaper work and enrolled in the philosophy

little lasting importance. However, the methodology was significant. It involved a variety of data sources, including autobiographical material, paid writings, family letters, newspaper files, public documents, and institutional letters.

Although *The Polish Peasant* was primarily a macrosociological study of social institutions, over the course of his career, Thomas gravitated toward a microscopic, social-psychological orientation. He is best known for the following social-psychological statement (made in a book coauthored by Dorothy Thomas): "If men define situations as real, they are real in their consequences" (Thomas and Thomas, 1928:572). The emphasis was on the importance of what people think and how this affects what they do. This microscopic, social-psychological focus stood in contrast to the macroscopic, social-structural and social-cultural perspectives of such European scholars as Marx, Weber, and Durkheim. It was to become one of the defining characteristics of Chicago's theoretical product—symbolic interactionism (Rock, 1979:5).

department at Harvard. He remained there for a year but then decided to move to Germany, which at that time, was the heart of the world's intellectual life. In Berlin he encountered Georg Simmel, whose work was to have a profound influence on Park's sociology. In fact, Simmel's lectures were the *only* formal sociological training that Park received. As Park said, "I got most of my knowledge about society and human nature from my own observations" (1927/1973:257). In 1904, Park completed his doctoral dissertation at the University of Heidelberg. Characteristically, he was dissatisfied with his dissertation: "All I had to show was that little book and I was ashamed of it" (Matthews, 1977:57). He refused a summer teaching job at the University of Chicago and turned away from academe as he had earlier turned away from newspaper work.

His need to contribute to social betterment led him to become secretary and chief publicity officer for the Congo Reform Association, which was set up to help alleviate the brutality and exploitation then taking place in the Belgian Congo. During this period, he met Booker T. Washington and was attracted to the cause of improving the lot of black Americans. He became Washington's secretary and played a key role in the activities of the Tuskegee Institute. In 1912 he met W. I. Thomas, the Chicago sociologist, who was lecturing at Tuskegee. Thomas invited him to give a course on "the Negro in America" to a small group of graduate students at Chicago, and Park did so in 1914. The course was successful, and he gave it again the next year to an audience twice as large. At this time he joined the American Sociological Society, and only a decade later, he became its president. Park gradually worked his way into a full-time appointment at Chicago, although he did not get a full professorship until 1923, when he was fifty-nine years old. Over the approximately two decades that he was affiliated with the University of Chicago, he played a key role in shaping the intellectual orientation of the sociology department.

Park remained peripatetic even after his retirement from Chicago in the early 1930s. He taught courses and oversaw research at Fisk University until he was nearly 80 years old. He traveled extensively. He died on February 7, 1944, one week before his eightieth birthday.

Robert Park (1864–1944) Another figure of significance at Chicago was Robert Park (Shils, 1996). Park had come to Chicago as a part-time instructor in 1914 and quickly worked his way into a central role in the department. Park's importance in the development of sociology lay in several areas. First, he became the dominant figure in the Chicago department, which, in turn, dominated sociology into the 1930s. Second, Park had studied in Europe and was instrumental in bringing Continental thinkers to the attention of Chicago sociologists. Park had taken courses with Simmel, and Simmel's ideas, particularly his focus on action and interaction, were instrumental in the development of the Chicago school's theoretical orientation (Rock, 1979:36–48). Third, prior to becoming a sociologist, Park had been a reporter, and that experience gave him a sense of the importance of urban problems and the need to go out into the field to collect data through personal observation (Lindner, 1996; Strauss, 1996). Out of this emerged the Chicago school's substantive interest in urban ecology (Gaziano, 1996; Maines, Bridger and Ulmer, 1996; Perry, Abbott, and Hutter, 1997). Fourth, Park played a key role in guiding graduate students and helping develop "a cumulative program of graduate research" (Bulmer, 1984:13). Finally, in 1921, Park and Ernest W. Burgess published the first truly important sociology textbook, *An Introduction to the Science of Sociology.* It was to be an influential book for many years and was particularly notable for its commitments to science, research, and the study of a wide range of social phenomena.

Beginning in the late 1920s and early 1930s, Park began to spend less time in Chicago. Finally, his lifelong interest in race relations (he had been secretary to Booker T. Washington before becoming a sociologist) led him to take a position at Fisk University (a black university) in 1934. Although the decline of the Chicago department was not caused solely or even chiefly by Park's departure, its status began to wane in the 1930s. But before we discuss the decline of Chicago sociology and the rise of other departments and theories, we need to return to the early days of the school and the two figures whose work was of the most lasting theoretical significance—Charles Horton Cooley and, most important, George Herbert Mead.[3]

Charles Horton Cooley (1864–1929) The association of Cooley with the Chicago school is interesting in that he spent his career at the University of Michigan. But Cooley's theoretical perspective was in line with the theory of symbolic interactionism that was to become Chicago's most important product (Jacobs, 2006; Sandstrom and Kleinman, 2005; Schubert, 2005, 2007).

Cooley received his Ph.D. from the University of Michigan in 1894. He had developed a strong interest in sociology, but there was as yet no department of sociology at Michigan. As a result, the questions for his Ph.D. examination came from Columbia University, where sociology had been taught since 1889 under the leadership of Franklin Giddings. Cooley began his teaching career at Michigan in 1892 before completion of his doctorate.

Although Cooley theorized about large-scale phenomena such as social classes, social structures, and social institutions, he is remembered today mainly for his insights into the social-psychological aspects of social life (Schubert, 2005, 2007). His work in this area is in line with that of George Herbert Mead, although Mead was to have a deeper and more lasting effect on sociology than Cooley had. Cooley had an interest in consciousness, but he refused (as did Mead) to separate consciousness from the social context. This is best exemplified by a concept of his that survives to this day—the *looking-glass self.* By this concept, Cooley understood that people possess consciousness and that it is shaped in continuing social interaction.

A second basic concept that illustrates Cooley's social-psychological interests, and is also of continuing interest and importance, is that of the primary group. *Primary groups* are intimate, face-to-face groups that play a key role in linking the individual to the larger society. Especially crucial are the primary groups of the young—mainly the family and the peer group. Within these groups, the individual grows into a social being. It is basically within the primary group that the looking-glass self emerges and that the ego-centered child learns to take others into account and, thereby, to become a contributing member of society.

---

[3]There were many other significant figures associated with the Chicago school, including Everett Hughes (Chapoulie, 1996; Strauss, 1996).

Both Cooley (Winterer, 1994) and Mead rejected a *behavioristic* view of human beings, the view that people blindly and unconsciously respond to external stimuli. They believed that people had consciousness, a self, and that it was the responsibility of the sociologist to study this aspect of social reality. Cooley urged sociologists to try to put themselves in the place of the individuals they were studying, to use the method of *sympathetic introspection,* to analyze consciousness. By analyzing what they as individuals might do in various circumstances, sociologists could understand the meanings and motives that are at the base of social behavior. The method of sympathetic introspection seemed to many to be very unscientific. In this area, among others, Mead's work represents an advance over Cooley's. Nevertheless, there is a great deal of similarity in the interests of the two men, not the least of which is their shared view that sociology should focus on such social-psychological phenomena as consciousness, action, and interaction.

George Herbert Mead (1863–1931) The most important thinker associated with the Chicago school and symbolic interactionism was not a sociologist but a philosopher, George Herbert Mead.[4] Mead started teaching philosophy at the University of Chicago in 1894, and he taught there until his death in 1931 (Chriss, 2005b; G. Cook, 1993). He is something of a paradox, given his central importance in the history of sociological theory, both because he taught philosophy, not sociology, and because he published comparatively little during his lifetime. The paradox is, in part, resolved by two facts. First, Mead taught courses in social psychology in the philosophy department, and they were taken by many graduate students in sociology. His ideas had a profound effect on a number of them. These students combined Mead's ideas with those they were getting in the sociology department from people such as Park and Thomas. Although at the time there was no theory known as symbolic interactionism, it was created by students out of these various inputs. Thus Mead had a deep, personal impact on the people who were later to develop symbolic interactionism. Second, these students put together their notes on Mead's courses and published a posthumous volume under his name. The work, *Mind, Self and Society* (Mead, 1934/1962), moved his ideas from the realm of oral to that of written tradition. Widely read to this day, this volume forms the main intellectual pillar of symbolic interactionism.

We deal with Mead's ideas in Chapter 15, but it is necessary at this point to underscore a few points to situate him historically. Mead's ideas need to be seen in the context of psychological behaviorism. Mead was quite impressed with this orientation and accepted many of its tenets. He adopted its focus on the individual and his or her behavior. He regarded as sensible the behaviorists' concern with the rewards and costs involved in the behaviors of the individuals. What troubled Mead was that behaviorism did not seem to go far enough. That is, it excluded consciousness from serious consideration, arguing that it was not amenable to scientific study. Mead vehemently disagreed and sought to extend the principles of behaviorism to an analysis of the mind. In so doing, Mead enunciated a focus similar to that of Cooley. But whereas Cooley's position seemed unscientific, Mead promised a more scientific conception of consciousness by extending the highly scientific principles and methods of psychological behaviorism.

---

[4]For a dissenting view, see Lewis and Smith (1980).

Mead offered American sociology a social-psychological theory that stood in stark contrast to the primarily societal theories offered by most of the major European theorists (Shalin, 2000). The most important exception was Simmel. Thus symbolic interactionism was developed, in large part, out of Simmel's (Low, 2008) interest in action and interaction and Mead's interest in consciousness. However, such a focus led to a weakness in both Mead's work and in symbolic interactionism in general at the societal and cultural levels.

The Waning of Chicago Sociology

Chicago sociology reached its peak in the 1920s, but by the 1930s, with the death of Mead and the departure of Park, the department had begun to lose its position of central importance in American sociology (Cortese, 1995). Fred Matthews (1977; see also Bulmer, 1984) pinpoints several reasons for the decline of Chicago sociology, two of which seem of utmost importance.

First, the discipline had grown increasingly preoccupied with being scientific—that is, using sophisticated methods and employing statistical analysis. However, the Chicago school was viewed as emphasizing descriptive, ethnographic studies (Prus, 1996), often focusing on their subjects' personal orientations (in Thomas's terms, their "definitions of the situation"). Park progressively came to despise statistics (he called it "parlor magic") because it seemed to prohibit the analysis of subjectivity, of the idiosyncratic, and of the peculiar. The fact that important work in quantitative methods was done at Chicago (Bulmer, 1984:151–189) tended to be ignored in the face of its overwhelming association with qualitative methods.

Second, more and more individuals outside Chicago grew increasingly resentful of Chicago's dominance of both the American Sociological Society and the *American Journal of Sociology.* The Eastern Sociological Society was founded in 1930, and eastern sociologists became more vocal about the dominance of the Midwest in general and Chicago in particular (Wiley, 1979:63). By 1935, the revolt against Chicago had led to a non-Chicago secretary of the association and the establishment of a new official journal, the *American Sociological Review* (Lengermann, 1979). According to Wiley, "the Chicago school had fallen like a mighty oak" (1979:63). This signaled the growth of other power centers, most notably Harvard and the Ivy League in general. Symbolic interactionism was largely an indeterminate, oral tradition and as such eventually lost ground to more explicit and codified theoretical systems like the structural functionalism associated with the Ivy League (Rock, 1979:12).

Women in Early Sociology

Simultaneously with the developments at the University of Chicago described in the previous section, even sometimes in concert with them, and at the same time that Durkheim, Weber, and Simmel were creating a European sociology, and sometimes in concert with them as well, a group of women who formed a broad and surprisingly connected network of social reformers were also developing pioneering sociological theories. These women included Jane Addams (1860–1935), Charlotte Perkins Gilman (1860–1935), Anna Julia Cooper (1858–1964), Ida Wells-Barnett (1862–1931),

Marianne Weber (1870–1954), and Beatrice Potter Webb (1858–1943). With the possible exception of Cooper, they can all be connected through their relationship to Jane Addams. That they are not today known or recognized in conventional histories of the discipline as sociologists or sociological theorists is a chilling testimony to the power of gender politics within the discipline of sociology and to sociology's essentially unreflective and uncritical interpretation of its own practices. Although the sociological theory of each of these women is a product of individual theoretical effort, when they are read collectively, they represent a coherent and complementary statement of early feminist sociological theory.

The chief hallmarks of their theories, hallmarks which may in part account for their being passed over in the development of professional sociology, include (1) an emphasis on women's experience and women's lives and works being equal in importance to men's; (2) an awareness that they spoke from a situated and embodied standpoint and therefore, for the most part, not with the tone of imperious objectivity that male sociological theory would come to associate with authoritative theory making (Lemert, 2000); (3) the idea that the purpose of sociology and sociological theory is social reform—that is, the end is to improve people's lives through knowledge; and (4) the claim that the chief problem for amelioration in their time was inequality. What distinguishes these early women most from each other is the nature of and the remedy for the inequality on which they focused—gender, race, or class, or the intersection of these factors. But all these women translated their views into social and political activism that helped shape and change the North Atlantic societies in which they lived, and this activism was as much a part of their sense of practicing sociology as creating theory was. They believed in social science research as part of both their theoretical and activist enactments of sociology and were highly creative innovators of social science method.

As the developing discipline of sociology marginalized these women as sociologists and sociological theorists, it often incorporated their research methods into its own practices, while using their activism as an excuse to define these women as "not sociologists." Thus they are remembered as social activists and social workers rather than sociologists. Their heritage is a sociological theory that is a call to action as well as to thought.

W.E.B. Du Bois and Race Theory[5]

Although W.E.B. Du Bois (1868–1963) taught in a sociology department (Atlanta University) for a considerable amount of time, he usually is not thought of as a sociologist, let alone as a theorist. He is far better known as a public intellectual and for his founding and leadership roles in various civil rights organizations, including the National Association for the Advancement of Colored People (NAACP). However, there is powerful sociology in many of his writings, and there are a number of abstract ideas that can be seen as theory, even though Du Bois (like Marx) was loath to distinguish between theory and practice. That is, he was uninterested in theory in itself, but rather developed abstract ideas in the service of advancing the cause of civil rights, primarily for African Americans.

[5]We will discuss a more specific and contemporary version of race theory—critical theories of race and racism—at the close of this chapter.

Within sociology, Du Bois's reputation has been based to a large degree on his empirical study, *The Philadelphia Negro* (1899/1996). This study of the seventh ward in Philadelphia was conducted single-handedly by Du Bois, and although he employed a multitude of methods, it is best known as a pioneering ethnography. Over his long career, Du Bois wrote an unbelievable number of books, articles, and editorials, but few would be immediately obvious as "theory." However, there is theory in his work, especially in his several unique autobiographical efforts (the best-known of which is *The Souls of Black Folk* [Du Bois, 1903/1996]) that allowed him to develop interesting theoretical ideas in the context of reflections on his own life. Overarching all was his interest in the "race idea," which he considered the "the central thought of all history" (Du Bois, 1897/1995:21), and the "color line," which he saw as drawn across not only the United States but also much of the world. One of his best-known theoretical ideas is the *veil,* which creates a clear separation, or barrier, between African Americans and whites. The imagery is *not* of a wall, but rather of a thin, porous material through which each race can see the other, but which nonetheless serves to separate them. Another key theoretical idea is *double-consciousness,* a sense of "two-ness" or a feeling on the part of African Americans of seeing and measuring themselves through others' eyes. There is not a full-fledged theory of society in Du Bois's work, but there is a series of theoretical ideas about race and race relations in the United States and the world. With the rise of multicultural (and feminist) theories in recent years, Du Bois's focus on race and his view of the world from the African-American perspective have attracted a large number of new admirers and, more important, thinkers who are building on his pioneering ideas, perspectives, and commitments.

Sociological Theory to Mid-Century

The Rise of Harvard, the Ivy League, and Structural Functionalism

We can trace the rise of sociology at Harvard from the arrival of Pitirim Sorokin in 1930 (Avino, 2006; Jeffries, 2005; Johnston, 1995). When Sorokin arrived at Harvard, there was no sociology department, but by the end of his first year, one had been organized, and he had been appointed its head. Although Sorokin was a sociological theorist and continued to publish into the 1960s, his work is surprisingly little cited today. Although some disagree (e.g., Tiryakian, 2007), the dominant view is that his theorizing has not stood the test of time very well. Sorokin's long-term significance may well have been the creation of the Harvard sociology department and the hiring of Talcott Parsons (who had been an instructor of economics at Harvard) for the position of instructor in sociology. Parsons became *the* dominant figure in American sociology for introducing European theorists to an American audience, for his own sociological theories, and for his many students who themselves became major sociological theorists.

Talcott Parsons (1902–1979)

Although he published some early essays, Parsons's major contribution in the early years was his influence on graduate students, many of whom became notable sociological theorists themselves. The most famous was Robert Merton, who received his Ph.D. in 1936 and soon became a major theorist and the heart of Parsonsian-style theorizing at Columbia University. In the same year (1936), Kingsley Davis received his Ph.D., and he, along with Wilbert Moore (who received his Harvard degree in 1940), wrote one of the central works in structural-functional theory, the theory that was to become the major product of Parsons and the Parsonsians. But Parsons's influence was not restricted to the 1930s. Remarkably, he produced graduate students of great influence well into the 1960s.

The pivotal year for Parsons and for American sociological theory was 1937, the year in which he published *The Structure of Social Action.* This book was of significance to sociological theory in America for four main reasons. First, it served to introduce grand European theorizing to a large American audience. The bulk of the book was devoted to Durkheim, Weber, and Pareto. His interpretations of these theorists shaped their images in American sociology for many years.

Second, Parsons devoted almost no attention to Marx or to Simmel (Levine, 1991a), although he emphasized the work of Durkheim, Weber, and even Pareto. As a result, Marxian theory continued to be largely excluded from legitimate sociology.

Third, *The Structure of Social Action* made the case for sociological theorizing as a legitimate and significant sociological activity. The theorizing that has taken place in the United States since then owes a deep debt to Parsons's work (Lidz, 2000).

Finally, Parsons argued for specific sociological theories that were to have a profound influence on sociology. At first, Parsons was thought of, and thought of himself, as an action theorist (Joas, 1996). He seemed to focus on actors and their thoughts and actions. But by the close of his 1937 work and increasingly in his later work, Parsons sounded more like a structural-functional theorist focusing on large-scale social and cultural systems. Although Parsons argued that there was no contradiction between these theories, he became best known as a structural functionalist, and he was the primary exponent of this theory, which gained dominance within sociology and maintained that position until the 1960s. Parsons's theoretical strength, and that of structural functionalism, lay in delineating the relationships among large-scale social structures and institutions.

Parsons's major statements on his structural-functional theory came in the early 1950s in several works, most notably *The Social System* (1951) (Barber, 1994). In that work and others, Parsons tended to concentrate on the structures of society and their relationship to each other. These structures were seen as mutually supportive and tending toward a dynamic equilibrium. The emphasis was on how order was maintained among the various elements of society (Wrong, 1994). Change was seen as an orderly process, and Parsons (1966, 1971) ultimately came to adopt a neoevolutionary view of social change. Parsons was concerned not only with the social system per se but also with its relationship to the other *action systems,* especially the cultural and personality systems. But his basic view on intersystemic relations was essentially the same as his view of intrasystemic relations; that is, that they were defined by cohesion, consensus, and order. In other words, the various *social structures* performed a variety of positive *functions* for each other.

It is clear, then, why Parsons came to be defined primarily as a *structural functionalist.* As his fame grew, so did the strength of structural-functional theory in the

United States. His work lay at the core of this theory, but his students and disciples also concentrated on extending both the theory and its dominance in the United States.

Although Parsons played a number of important and positive roles in the history of sociological theory in the United States, his work also had negative consequences (Holton, 2001). First, he offered interpretations of European theorists that seemed to reflect his own theoretical orientation more than theirs. Many American sociologists were initially exposed to erroneous interpretations of the European masters. Second, as already pointed out, early in his career Parsons largely ignored Marx, which resulted in Marx's ideas being on the periphery of sociology for many years. Third, his own theory, as it developed over the years, had a number of serious weaknesses. However, Parsons's preeminence in American sociology served for many years to mute or overwhelm the critics. Not until much later did the weaknesses of Parsons's theory and structural functionalism in general, receive a full airing.

But returning to the early 1930s and other developments at Harvard, we can gain a good deal of insight into the development of the Harvard department by looking at it through an account of its other major figure, George Homans.

George Homans (1910–1989)

A wealthy Bostonian, George Homans received his bachelor's degree from Harvard in 1932 (Homans, 1962, 1984; see also Bell, 1992). As a result of the Great Depression, he was unemployed but certainly not penniless. In the fall of 1932, L. J. Henderson, a physiologist, was offering a course in the theories of Vilfredo Pareto, and Homans was invited to attend; he accepted. (Parsons also attended the Pareto seminars.) Homans's description of why he was drawn to and taken with Pareto says much about why American sociological theory was so highly conservative, so anti-Marxist:

> I took to Pareto because he made clear to me what I was already prepared to believe. . . . Someone has said that much modern sociology is an effort to answer the arguments of the revolutionaries. As a Republican Bostonian who had not rejected his comparatively wealthy family, I felt during the thirties that I was under personal attack, above all from the Marxists. I was ready to believe Pareto because he provided me with a defense.
>
> (Homans, 1962:4)

Homans's exposure to Pareto led to a book, *An Introduction to Pareto* (coauthored with Charles Curtis), published in 1934. The publication of this book made Homans a sociologist even though Pareto's work was virtually the only sociology he had read up to that point.

In 1934, Homans was named a junior fellow at Harvard, a program started to avoid the problems associated with the Ph.D. program. In fact, Homans never did earn a Ph.D., even though he became one of the major sociological figures of his day. Homans was a junior fellow until 1939, and in those years, he absorbed more and more sociology. In 1939, Homans was affiliated with the sociology department, but the connection was broken by the war.

By the time Homans had returned from the war, the Department of Social Relations had been founded by Parsons at Harvard, and Homans joined it. Although Homans respected some aspects of Parsons's work, he was highly critical of Parsons's style of theorizing. A long-running exchange began between the two men that later manifested itself publicly in the pages of many books and journals. Basically, Homans argued that Parsons's theory was not a theory at all but rather a vast system of intellectual categories into which most aspects of the social world fit. Further, Homans believed that theory should be built from the ground up on the basis of careful observations of the social world. Parsons's theory, however, started on the general theoretical level and worked its way down to the empirical level.

In his own work, Homans amassed a large number of empirical observations over the years, but it was only in the 1950s that he hit upon a satisfactory theoretical approach with which to analyze those data. That theory was psychological behaviorism, as it was best expressed in the ideas of his colleague at Harvard, the psychologist B. F. Skinner. On the basis of this perspective, Homans developed his exchange theory. We will pick up the story of this theoretical development later in this chapter. The crucial point here is that Harvard and its major theoretical product, structural functionalism, became preeminent in sociology in the late 1930s, replacing the Chicago school and symbolic interactionism.

The Chicago School in Decline

We left the Chicago department in the mid-1930s on the wane with the death of Mead, the departure of Park, the revolt of eastern sociologists, and the founding of the *American Sociological Review*. But the Chicago school did not disappear. Into the early 1950s it continued to be an important force in sociology.

The central figure in the Chicago department in this era was Herbert Blumer (1900–1987) (Maines, 2005; *Symbolic Interaction,* 1988). He was a major exponent of the theoretical approach developed at Chicago out of the work of Mead, Cooley, Simmel, Park, Thomas, and others. In fact, it was Blumer who coined the phrase *symbolic interactionism* in 1937. Blumer played a key role in keeping this tradition alive through his teaching at Chicago. He wrote a number of essays that were instrumental in keeping symbolic interactionism vital into the 1950s. Despite this flurry of activity, the Chicago school was in decline, especially given the movement of Blumer in 1952 from Chicago to the University of California at Berkeley. Whatever the state of the Chicago school, the Chicago tradition has remained alive to this day with major exponents dispersed throughout the country and the world (Sandstrom, Martin, and Fine, 2001).

Developments in Marxian Theory

From the early 1900s to the 1930s, Marxian theory continued to develop largely independently of mainstream sociological theory. The exception to this, at least partially, was the emergence of the critical, or Frankfurt, school out of the earlier Hegelian Marxism.

The idea of a school for the development of Marxian theory was the product of Felix J. Weil. The Institute of Social Research was officially founded in Frankfurt, Germany, on February 3, 1923 (Jay, 1973; Wheatland, 2009; Wiggershaus, 1994). Over the years, a number of the most famous thinkers in Marxian theory were associated with the critical school—Max Horkheimer (Schulz, 2007a), Theodor Adorno (Schulz, 2007b),

Erich Fromm (McLaughlin, 2007), Herbert Marcuse (Dandaneau, 2007a), and, more recently, Jurgen Habermas.

The Institute functioned in Germany until 1934, but by then things were growing increasingly uncomfortable under the Nazi regime. The Nazis had little use for the Marxian ideas that dominated the Institute, and their hostility was heightened because many of those associated with it were Jewish. In 1934 Horkheimer, as head of the Institute, came to New York to discuss its status with the president of Columbia University. Much to Horkheimer's surprise, he was invited to affiliate the Institute with the university, and he was even offered a building on campus. And so *a* center of Marxian theory moved to *the* center of the capitalist world. The Institute stayed there until the end of the war, but after the war, pressure mounted to return it to Germany. In 1949, Horkheimer did return to Germany, and he brought the Institute with him. Although the Institute itself moved to Germany, many of the figures associated with it took independent career directions.

It is important to underscore a few of the most significant aspects of critical theory (Calhoun and Karaganis, 2001). In its early years, those associated with the Institute tended to be fairly traditional Marxists, devoting a good portion of their attention to the economic domain. But around 1930, a major change took place as this group of thinkers began to shift its attention from the economy to the cultural system, especially the "culture industry" (Lash and Lury, 2007), which it came to see as the major force in modern capitalist society. This was consistent with, but an extension of, the position taken earlier by Hegelian Marxists such as Georg Lukács. To help them understand the cultural domain, the critical theorists were attracted to the work of Max Weber. The effort to combine Marx and Weber and thereby create "Weberian Marxism"[6] (Dahms, 1997; Lowy, 1996) gave the critical school some of its distinctive orientations and served in later years to make it more legitimate to sociologists who began to grow interested in Marxian theory.

A second major step taken by at least some members of the critical school was to employ the rigorous social-scientific techniques developed by American sociologists to research issues of interest to Marxists. This, like the adoption of Weberian theory, made the critical school more acceptable to mainstream sociologists.

Third, critical theorists made an effort to integrate individually oriented Freudian theory with the societal- and cultural-level insights of Marx and Weber. This seemed to many sociologists to represent a more inclusive theory than that offered by either Marx or Weber alone. If nothing else, the effort to combine such disparate theories proved stimulating to sociologists and many other intellectuals.

The critical school has done much useful work since the 1920s, and a significant amount of it is of relevance to sociologists. However, the critical school had to await the late 1960s before it was "discovered" by large numbers of American theorists.

Karl Mannheim and the Sociology of Knowledge

At this point, the work of Karl Mannheim (1893–1947) should be mentioned briefly (Kettler and Meja, 1995; Ruef, 2007). Born in Hungary, Mannheim was forced to move first to Germany and later to England. Influenced by the ideologies of Marx, Weber,

[6]This label fits some critical theorists better than others, and it also applies to a wide range of other thinkers (Agger, 1998).

Simmel, and the neo-Marxist Georg Lukács, Mannheim is best known for his work on systems of knowledge (for example, conservatism). In fact, he is almost single-handedly responsible for the creation of the contemporary field known as the sociology of knowledge. Also of significance is his thinking on rationality, which tends to pick up themes developed in Weber's work on this topic but deals with them in a far more concise and a much clearer manner (Ritzer, 1998).

From a base in England starting in the 1930s, Karl Mannheim was busy creating a set of theoretical ideas that provided the foundation for an area of sociology—the sociology of knowledge—that continues to be important to this day (McCarthy, 1996, 2007; Stehr, 2001). Mannheim, of course, built on the work of many predecessors, most notably Karl Marx, although Mannheim was far from being a Marxist. Basically, the sociology of knowledge involves the systematic study of knowledge, ideas, or intellectual phenomena in general. To Mannheim, knowledge is determined by social existence. For example, Mannheim seeks to relate the ideas of a group to that group's position in the social structure. Marx did this by relating ideas to social classes, but Mannheim extends this perspective by linking ideas to a variety of different positions within society (for example, differences between generations).

In addition to playing a major role in creating the sociology of knowledge, Mannheim is perhaps best known for his distinction between two idea systems—*ideology* and *utopia* (B. Turner, 1995). An ideology is an idea system that seeks to conceal and conserve the present by interpreting it from the point of view of the past. A utopia, in contrast, is a system of ideas that seeks to transcend the present by focusing on the future. Conflict between ideologies and utopias is an ever-present reality in society (Mannheim, 1931/1936).

Sociological Theory from Mid-Century

Structural Functionalism: Peak and Decline

The 1940s and 1950s were paradoxically the years of greatest dominance and the beginnings of the decline of structural functionalism. In those years, Parsons produced his major statements that clearly reflected his shift from action theory to structural functionalism. Parsons's students had fanned out across the country and occupied dominant positions in many of the major sociology departments (for example, Columbia and Cornell). These students were producing works of their own that were widely recognized contributions to structural-functional theory.

However, just as it was gaining theoretical hegemony, structural functionalism came under attack, and the attacks mounted until they reached a climax in the 1960s and 1970s. There was an attack by C. Wright Mills on Parsons in 1959, and other major criticisms were mounted by David Lockwood (1956), Alvin Gouldner (1959/1967, 1970; Chriss, 2005a), and Irving Horowitz (1962/1967). In the 1950s, these attacks were seen as little more than "guerrilla raids," but as sociology moved into the 1960s, the dominance of structural functionalism was clearly in jeopardy.

George Huaco (1986) linked the rise and decline of structural functionalism to the position of American society in the world order. As America rose to world dominance after 1945, structural functionalism achieved hegemony within sociology. Structural functionalism supported America's dominant position in the world in two ways. First, the structural-functional view that "every pattern has consequences which contribute to the preservation and survival of the larger system" was "nothing less than a celebration of the United States and its world hegemony" (Huaco, 1986:52). Second, the structural-functional emphasis on equilibrium (the best social change is no change) meshed well with the interests of the United States, then "the wealthiest and most powerful empire in the world." The decline of U.S. world dominance in the 1970s coincided with structural functionalism's loss of its preeminent position in sociological theory.

Radical Sociology in America: C. Wright Mills

As we have seen, although Marxian theory was largely ignored or reviled by mainstream American sociologists, there were exceptions, the most notable of which is C. Wright Mills (1916–1962). Mills is noteworthy for his almost single-handed effort to keep a Marxian tradition alive in sociological theory. Modern Marxian sociologists have far outstripped Mills in theoretical sophistication, but they owe him a deep debt nonetheless for the personal and professional activities that helped set the stage for their own work (Alt, 1985–86). Mills was not a Marxist, and he did not read Marx until the mid-1950s. Even then he was restricted to the few available English translations because he could not read German. Because Mills had published most of his major works by then, his work was not informed by a very sophisticated Marxian theory.

Mills published two major works that reflected his radical politics as well as his weaknesses in Marxian theory. The first was *White Collar* (1951), an acid critique of the status of a growing occupational category, white-collar workers. The second was *The Power Elite* (1956), a book that sought to show how America was dominated by a small group of businessmen, politicians, and military leaders (Zweigenhaft and Domhoff, 2006). Sandwiched in between was his most theoretically sophisticated work, *Character and Social Structure* (Gerth and Mills, 1953), coauthored with Hans Gerth (N. Gerth, 1993).

Mills's radicalism put him on the periphery of American sociology. He was the object of much criticism, and he, in turn, became a severe critic of sociology. The critical attitude culminated in *The Sociological Imagination* (1959). Of particular note is Mills's severe criticism of Talcott Parsons and his practice of grand theory.

Mills died in 1962, an outcast in sociology. However, before the decade was out, both radical sociology (Levine, 2005) and Marxian theory would begin to make important inroads into the discipline.

The Development of Conflict Theory

Another precursor to a true union of Marxism and sociological theory was the development of a conflict-theory alternative to structural functionalism. As we have just seen, structural functionalism had no sooner gained leadership in sociological theory than it came under increasing attack. The attack was multifaceted: structural functionalism was accused of such things as being politically conservative, unable to deal with social change because of its focus on static structures, and incapable of adequately analyzing social conflict.

C. Wright Mills

A Biographical Sketch

C. Wright Mills was born on August 28, 1916, in Waco, Texas (Dandaneau, 2007b; Domhoff, 2005 Mills and Mills, 2000; Hayden, 2006;). He came from a conventional middle-class background: his father was an insurance broker, and his mother was a housewife. He attended the University of Texas and by 1939 had obtained both a bachelor's degree and a master's degree. He was quite an unusual student who, by the time he left Texas, already had published articles in the two major sociology journals. Mills did his doctoral work at, and received a Ph.D. from, the University of Wisconsin (Scimecca, 1977). He took his first job at the University of Maryland but spent the bulk of his career, from 1945 until his death, at Columbia University.

Mills was a man in a hurry (Horowitz, 1983). By the time he died at 45 from his fourth heart attack, Mills had made a number of important contributions to sociology.

One of the most striking things about C. Wright Mills was his combativeness; he seemed to be constantly at war (Form, 2007). He had a tumultuous personal life, characterized by many affairs, three marriages, and a child from each marriage. He had an equally tumultuous professional life. He seemed to have fought with and against everyone and everything. As a graduate student at Wisconsin, he took on a number of his professors. Later, in one of his early essays, he engaged in a thinly disguised critique of the ex-chairman of the Wisconsin department. He called the senior theorist at Wisconsin, Howard Becker, a "real fool" (Horowitz, 1983). He eventually came into conflict with his coauthor, Hans Gerth, who called Mills "an excellent operator, whippersnapper, promising young man on the make, and Texas cowboy á la ride and shoot" (Horowitz, 1983:72). As a professor at Columbia, Mills was isolated and estranged from his colleagues. Said one of his Columbia colleagues:

> There was no estrangement between Wright and me. We began estranged. Indeed, at the memorial services or meeting that was organized at Columbia University at his death, I seemed to be the only person who could not say: 'I used to be his friend, but we became somewhat distant.' It was rather the reverse.
>
> (cited in Horowitz, 1983:83)

Mills was an outsider, and he knew it: "I am an outlander, not only regionally, but down deep and for good" (Horowitz, 1983:84). In *The Sociological Imagination* (1959), Mills challenged not only the dominant theorist of his day, Talcott Parsons, but also the dominant methodologist, Paul Lazarsfeld, who also happened to be a colleague at Columbia.

Mills, of course, was at odds not only with people; he was also at odds with American society and challenged it on a variety of fronts. But perhaps most telling is the fact that when Mills visited the Soviet Union and was honored as a major critic of American society, he took the occasion to attack censorship in the Soviet Union with a toast to an early Soviet leader who had been purged and murdered by the Stalinists: "To the day when the complete works of Leon Trotsky are published in the Soviet Union!" (Tilman, 1984:8).

C. Wright Mills died in Nyack, New York, on March 20, 1962.

One of the results of this criticism was an effort on the part of a number of sociologists to overcome the problems of structural functionalism by integrating a concern for structure with an interest in conflict. This work constituted the development of *conflict theory* as an alternative to structural-functional theory. Unfortunately, it often seemed little more than a mirror image of structural functionalism with little intellectual integrity of its own.

The first effort of note was Lewis Coser's (1956) book on the functions of social conflict (Delaney, 2005a; Jaworski, 1991). This work clearly tried to deal with social conflict from within the framework of a structural-functional view of the world. Although it is useful to look at the functions of conflict, there is much more to the study of conflict than an analysis of its positive functions.

The biggest problem with most of conflict theory was that it lacked what it needed most—a sound basis in Marxian theory. After all, Marxian theory was well developed outside of sociology and should have provided a base on which to develop a sophisticated sociological theory of conflict. The one exception here is the work of Ralf Dahrendorf (1929–2009).

Dahrendorf was a European scholar who was well versed in Marxian theory. He sought to embed his conflict theory in the Marxian tradition. However, in the end, his conflict theory looked more like a mirror image of structural functionalism than like a Marxian theory of conflict. Dahrendorf's major work, *Class and Class Conflict in Industrial Society* (1959), was the most influential piece in conflict theory, but that was largely because it sounded so much like structural functionalism that it was palatable to mainstream sociologists. That is, Dahrendorf operated at the same level of analysis as the structural functionalists (structures and institutions) and looked at many of the same issues. In other words, structural functionalism and conflict theory are part of the same paradigm. Dahrendorf recognized that although aspects of the social system could fit together rather neatly, there also could be considerable conflict and tension among them.

In the end, conflict theory should be seen as little more than a transitional development in the history of sociological theory. It failed because it did not go far enough in the direction of Marxian theory. It was still too early in the 1950s and 1960s for American sociology to accept a full-fledged Marxian approach. But conflict theory was helpful in setting the stage for the beginning of that acceptance by the late 1960s.

The Birth of Exchange Theory

Another important theoretical development in the 1950s was the rise of exchange theory (Molm, 2001). The major figure in this development is George Homans, a sociologist whom we left earlier, just as he was being drawn to B. F. Skinner's psychological behaviorism. Skinner's behaviorism is a major source of Homans's, and sociology's, exchange theory.

At first, Homans did not see how Skinner's propositions, developed to help explain the behavior of pigeons, might be useful for understanding human social behavior. But as Homans looked further at data from sociological studies of small groups and anthropological studies of primitive societies, he began to see that Skinner's behaviorism was applicable and that it provided a theoretical alternative to Parsonsian-style structural functionalism. This realization led in 1961 to Homans's book, *Social Behavior: Its Elementary Forms.* This work represented the birth of exchange theory as an important perspective in sociology.

Homans's basic view was that the heart of sociology lies in the study of individual behavior and interaction. He was little interested in consciousness or in the various kinds of large-scale structures and institutions that were of concern to most sociologists. Rather his main interest was in the reinforcement patterns, the history of rewards and costs, that lead people to do what they do. Basically, Homans argued that people continue to do what they have found to be rewarding in the past. Conversely, they cease doing what has proved to be costly in the past. To understand behavior, we need to understand an individual's history of rewards and costs. Thus, the focus of sociology should not be on consciousness or on social structures and institutions but rather on patterns of reinforcement.

As its name suggests, exchange theory is concerned not only with individual behavior but also with interaction between people involving an exchange of rewards and costs. The premise is that interactions are likely to continue when there is an exchange of rewards. Conversely, interactions that are costly to one or both parties are much less likely to continue.

Another major statement in exchange theory is Peter Blau's *Exchange and Power in Social Life,* published in 1964. Blau basically adopted Homans's perspective, but there was an important difference. Whereas Homans was content to deal mainly with elementary forms of social behavior, Blau wanted to integrate this with exchange at the structural and cultural levels, beginning with exchanges among actors, but quickly moving on to the larger structures that emerge out of this exchange. He ended by dealing with exchanges among large-scale structures.

Although he was eclipsed for many years by Homans and Blau, Richard Emerson (1981) has emerged as a central figure in exchange theory (Cook and Whitmeyer, 2000). He is noted particularly for his effort to develop a more integrated micro-macro approach to exchange theory. Exchange theory has now developed into a significant strand of sociological theory, and it continues to attract new adherents and to take new directions (Cook, O'Brien, and Kollock, 1990; Szmatka and Mazur, 1996).

Dramaturgical Analysis: The Work of Erving Goffman

Erving Goffman (1922–1982) is often thought of as the last major thinker associated with the original Chicago school (Scheff, 2006; Smith, 2006; Travers, 1992; Tseelon, 1992); Fine and Manning (2000) see him as arguably the most influential twentieth-century American sociologist. Between the 1950s and the 1970s, Goffman published a series of books and essays that gave birth to dramaturgical analysis as a variant of symbolic interactionism. Although Goffman shifted his attention in his later years, he remained best known for his *dramaturgical theory* (Manning, 2005a, 2007; Alieva, 2008).

Goffman's best-known statement of dramaturgical theory, *Presentation of Self in Everyday Life,* was published in 1959. To put it simply, Goffman saw much in common between theatrical performances and the kinds of "acts" we all put on in our day-to-day actions and interactions. Interaction is seen as very fragile, maintained by social performances. Poor performances or disruptions are seen as great threats to social interaction just as they are to theatrical performances.

Goffman went quite far in his analogy between the stage and social interaction. In all social interaction there is a *front region,* which is the parallel of the stage front in a theatrical performance. Actors both on the stage and in social life are seen as being interested in appearances, wearing costumes, and using props. Furthermore, in both there is a *back region,* a place to which the actors can retire to prepare themselves for their performance. Backstage or offstage, in theater terms, the actors can shed their roles and be themselves.

Dramaturgical analysis is clearly consistent with its symbolic-interactionist roots. It has a focus on actors, action, and interaction. Working in the same arena as traditional symbolic interactionism, Goffman found a brilliant metaphor in the theater to shed new light on small-scale social processes (Manning, 1991, 1992).

The Development of Sociologies of Everyday Life

The 1960s and 1970s witnessed a boom (Ritzer, 1975a, 1975b) in several theoretical perspectives that can be lumped together under the heading of sociologies of everyday life (J. Douglas, 1980; Fontana, 2005; Schutte, 2007; Weigert, 1981).

Phenomenological Sociology and the Work of Alfred Schutz (1899–1959)

The philosophy of phenomenology (Srubar, 2005), with its focus on consciousness, has a long history, but the effort to develop a sociological variant of phenomenology (Ferguson, 2001) can be traced to the publication of Alfred Schutz's *The Phenomenology of the Social World* in Germany in 1932 (Hall, 2007; Prendergast, 2005; Rogers, 2000). Schutz was focally concerned with the way in which people grasp the consciousness of others while they live within their own stream of consciousness. Schutz also used intersubjectivity in a larger sense to mean a concern with the social world, especially the social nature of knowledge.

Much of Schutz's work focuses on an aspect of the social world called the *life-world,* or the world of everyday life. This is an intersubjective world in which people both create social reality and are constrained by the preexisting social and cultural structures created by their predecessors. Although much of the life-world is shared, there are also private (biographically articulated) aspects of that world. Within the life-world, Schutz differentiated between intimate face-to-face relationships ("we-relations") and distant and impersonal relationships ("they-relations"). While face-to-face relations are of great importance in the life-world, it is far easier for the sociologist to study more impersonal relations scientifically. Although Schutz turned away from consciousness to the intersubjective life-world, he did offer insights into consciousness, especially in his thoughts on meaning and people's motives.

Overall, Schutz was concerned with the dialectical relationship between the way people construct social reality and the obdurate social and cultural reality that they inherit from those who preceded them in the social world.

Ethnomethodology

Although there are important differences between them, ethnomethodology and phenomenology are often seen as closely aligned (Langsdorf, 1995). One of the major reasons for this association is that the creator of this theoretical perspective, Harold Garfinkel, was a student of Alfred Schutz at the New School. Interestingly, Garfinkel previously had studied under Talcott Parsons, and it was the fusion of Parsonsian and Schutzian ideas that helped give ethnomethodology its distinctive orientation.

Basically, *ethnomethodology* is the study of "the body of common-sense knowledge and the range of procedures and considerations [the methods] by means of which the ordinary members of society make sense of, find their way about in, and act on the circumstances in which they find themselves" (Heritage, 1984:4). Writers in this tradition are heavily tilted in the direction of the study of everyday life (Sharrock, 2001). Whereas phenomenological sociologists tend to focus on what people think, ethnomethodologists are more concerned with what people actually do. Thus, ethnomethodologists devote a lot of attention to the detailed study of conversations. Such mundane concerns stand in stark contrast to the interest of many mainstream sociologists in such abstractions as bureaucracies, capitalism, the division of labor, and the social system. Ethnomethodologists might be interested in the way a sense of these structures is created in everyday life; they are not interested in such structures as phenomena in themselves.

In the last few pages, we have dealt with several micro theories—exchange theory, phenomenological sociology, and ethnomethodology. Although the last two theories share a sense of a thoughtful and creative actor, such a view is not held by exchange theorists. Nevertheless, all three theories have a primarily micro orientation to actors and their actions and behavior. In the 1970s, such theories grew in strength in sociology and threatened to replace more macro-oriented theories (such as structural functionalism, conflict theory, neo-Marxian theories) as the dominant theories in sociology (Knorr-Cetina, 1981; Ritzer, 1985).

The Rise and Fall (?) of Marxian Sociology

In the late 1960s, Marxian theory finally began to make significant inroads into American sociological theory (Cerullo, 1994). An increasing number of sociologists turned to Marx's original work, as well as to that of many Marxists, for insights that would be useful in the development of a Marxian sociology. At first this simply meant that American theorists were finally reading Marx seriously, but later there emerged many significant pieces of Marxian scholarship by American sociologists.

American theorists were particularly attracted to the work of the critical school, especially because of its fusion of Marxian and Weberian theory (Calhoun and Karaganis, 2001). Many of the works have been translated into English, and a number of scholars have written books about the critical school (for example, Jay, 1973; Kellner, 1993).

Along with an increase in interest came institutional support for such an orientation. Several journals devoted considerable attention to Marxian sociological theory, including *Theory and Society, Telos,* and *Marxist Studies.* A section on Marxist sociology was created in the American Sociological Association in 1977. Not only did the first generation of critical theorists become well known in America, but second-generation thinkers, especially Jurgen Habermas, and even third-generation theorists such as Axel Honneth, received wide recognition.

Of considerable importance was the development of significant pieces of American sociology practiced from a Marxian point of view. One very significant strand is a group of sociologists practicing historical sociology from a Marxian perspective (for example, Skocpol, 1979; Wallerstein, 1974, 1980, 1989). Another is a group analyzing the economic realm from a sociological perspective (e.g., Baran and Sweezy, 1966; Braverman, 1974; Burawoy, 1979). Still others are doing fairly traditional empirical sociology, but work that is informed by a strong sense of Marxian theory (e.g., Kohn, 1976). A relatively recent and promising development is spatial Marxism. A number of important social thinkers (Harvey, 2000; Lefebvre, 1974/1991; Soja, 1989) have been examining social geography from a Marxian perspective.

However, with the disintegration of the Soviet Union and the fall of Marxist regimes around the world, Marxian theory fell on hard times in the 1990s. Some people remain unreconstructed Marxists; others have been forced to develop modified versions of Marxian theory (see the discussion below of the post-Marxists; there is also a journal entitled *Rethinking Marxism*). Still others have come to the conclusion that Marxian theory must be abandoned. Representative of the latter position is Ronald Aronson's book *After Marxism* (1995). The very first line of the book tells the story: "Marxism is over, and we are on our own" (Aronson, 1995:1). This from an avowed Marxist! Although Aronson recognizes that some will continue to work with Marxian theory, he cautions that they must recognize it is no longer part of the larger Marxian project of social transformation. That is, Marxian theory is no longer related, as Marx intended, to a program aimed at changing the basis of society; it is theory without practice. One-time Marxists are on their own in the sense that they can no longer rely on the Marxian project, but rather must grapple with modern society with their "own powers and energies" (Aronson, 1995:4).

Aronson is among the more extreme critics of Marxism from within the Marxian camp. Others recognize the difficulties, but seek in various ways to adapt some variety of Marxian theory to contemporary realities (Brugger, 1995; Kellner, 1995). Nevertheless, larger social changes have posed a grave challenge for Marxian theorists, who are desperately seeking to adapt to these changes in a variety of ways. Whatever else can be said, the "glory days" of Marxian social theory appear to be over. Marxian social theorists of various types will survive, but they are not likely to approach the status and power of their predecessors in the recent history of sociology.

While neo-Marxian theory will never achieve the status it once had, it is undergoing a mini-renaissance (e.g., Hardt and Negri, 2000) in light of globalization, perceptions that the rich nations are growing richer and the poor are growing poorer (Stiglitz, 2002), and the resulting worldwide protests against these disparities and other abuses. There are many who believe that globalization has served to open the entire world, perhaps for the first time, to unbridled capitalism and the excesses that Marxists believe inevitably accompany it (Ritzer, 2004b). If that is the case, and if the excesses continue and even accelerate, we will see a resurgence of interest in Marxian theory, this time applied to a truly global capitalist economy.

The Challenge of Feminist Theory

Beginning in the late 1970s, precisely at the moment when Marxian sociology gained significant acceptance from American sociologists, a new theoretical outsider issued a challenge to established sociological theories—and even to Marxian sociology itself. This latest brand of radical social thought is contemporary feminist theory (Rogers, 2001).

In Western societies, one can trace the record of critical feminist writings back almost 500 years, and there has been an organized political movement by and for women for more than 150 years. In America in 1920, the movement finally won the right for women to vote, fifty-five years after that right had been constitutionally extended to all men. Exhausted and to a degree satiated by victory, the American women's movement over the next thirty years weakened in both size and vigor, only to spring back to life, fully reawakened, in the 1960s. Three factors helped create this new wave of feminist activism: (1) the general climate of critical thinking that characterized the period; (2) the anger of women activists who flocked to the antiwar, civil rights, and student movements only to encounter the sexist attitudes of the liberal and radical men in those movements (Densimore, 1973; Evans, 1980; Morgan, 1970; Shreve, 1989); and (3) women's experience of prejudice and discrimination as they moved in ever larger numbers into wage work and higher education (Bookman and Morgen, 1988; Garland, 1988). For these reasons, particularly the last one, the women's movement continued into the twenty-first century, even though the activism of many other 1960s movements has faded. Moreover, during these years, activism by and for women became an international phenomenon, drawing in women from many societies. Feminist writing has now entered its "third wave" in the writings of women who will spend most of their adult lives in the twenty-first century (C. Bailey, 1997; Orr, 1997). The most significant recent change in the women's movement has been the emergence among activist women of both a feminist and an anti-feminist movement (Fraser, 1989).

A major feature of this international women's movement has been an explosively growing new literature on women that makes visible all aspects of women's previously unconsidered lives and experiences. This literature, which is popularly referred to as *women's studies,* is the work of an international and interdisciplinary community of writers, located both within and outside universities and writing for both the general public and specialized academic audiences. Feminist scholars have launched a probing, multifaceted critique that makes visible the complexity of the system that subordinates women.

Feminist theory is the theoretical strand running through this literature: sometimes implicit in writings on such substantive issues as work or rape or popular culture; sometimes centrally and explicitly presented, as in the analyses of motherhood; and increasingly the sole, systematic project of a piece of writing. Of this recent spate of wholly theoretical writing, certain statements have been particularly salient to sociology because they are directed to sociologists by people well versed in sociological theory. Journals such as *Signs, Feminist Studies, Sociological Inquiry,* and *Gender & Society* bring feminist theory to the attention of sociologists; however, there is hardly a sociological journal that could not be called pro-feminist.

Feminist theory looks at the world from the vantage points of women, with an eye to discovering the significant but unacknowledged ways in which the activities of women—subordinated by gender and variously affected by other stratificational practices such as class, race, age, enforced heterosexuality, and geosocial inequality—help create our world. This viewpoint dramatically reworks our understanding of social life. From this base, feminist theorists have begun to challenge sociological theory, especially its classical statements and early research.

Feminist writings now assume a critical mass in sociology. They offer an exciting paradigm for the study of social life. And those whose experiences and perceptions make them a receptive audience for this theory—women in general and both women and men affected by feminism in particular—may now constitute a numerical majority in the sociological community. For all these reasons, implications of feminist theory are moving increasingly into the mainstream of the discipline; engaging all its subspecialties; influencing many of its long-established theories, both macro and micro; and interacting with the new poststructuralist and postmodernist developments described next.

Structuralism and Poststructuralism

One development that we have said little about up to this point is the increase in interest in *structuralism* (Lemert, 1990). We can get a preliminary feeling for structuralism by delineating the basic differences that exist among those who support a structuralist perspective. There are those who focus on what they call the "deep structures of the mind." It is their view that these unconscious structures lead people to think and act as they do. The work of the psychoanalyst Sigmund Freud might be seen as an example of this orientation. Then there are structuralists who focus on the invisible larger structures of society and see them as determinants of the actions of people as well as of society in general. Marx is sometimes thought of as someone who practiced such a brand of structuralism, with his focus on the unseen economic structure of capitalist society. Still another group sees structures as the models they construct of the social world. Finally, a number of structuralists are concerned with the dialectical relationship between individuals and social structures. They see a link between the structures of the mind and the structures of society. The anthropologist Claude Lévi-Strauss is most often associated with this view.

As structuralism grew within sociology, outside sociology a movement called *poststructuralism* was developing beyond the early premises of structuralism (Lemert, 1990; McCormick, 2007). The major representative of poststructuralism is Michel Foucault (Dean, 2001; J. Miller, 1993; another is Giorgio Agamben). In his early work, Foucault focused on structures, but he later moved beyond structures to focus on power and the linkage between knowledge and power. More generally, poststructuralists accept the importance of structure but go beyond it to encompass a wide range of other concerns.

Poststructuralism is important not only in itself, but also because it is often seen as a precursor to postmodern social theory (to be discussed later in this chapter). In fact, it is difficult, if not impossible, to draw a clear line between poststructuralism and postmodern social theory. Thus Foucault, a poststructuralist, is often seen as a postmodernist, whereas Jean Baudrillard (1972/1981), who is usually labeled a postmodernist, certainly did work that is poststructuralist in character.

Late Twentieth-Century Developments in Sociological Theory

While many of the developments discussed in the preceding pages continued to be important in the late twentieth century, in this section we will deal with three broad movements—micro-macro integration, agency-structure integration, and theoretical syntheses—that were of utmost importance in that era . . . and to this day.

Micro-Macro Integration

A good deal of recent work in American sociological theory has been concerned with the linkage between micro and macro theories and levels of analysis (Barnes, 2001; Berk, 2006; Ryan, 2005). In fact, Ritzer (1990) argued that micro-macro linkage emerged as the central problem in American sociological theory in the 1980s, and it continued to be of focal concern in the 1990s. The contribution of European sociologist Norbert Elias (1939/1994) is an important precursor to contemporary American work on the micro-macro linkage and aids our understanding of the relationship between micro-level manners and the macro-level state (Kilminster and Mennell, 2000; van Krieken, 2001).

There are a number of examples of efforts to link micro-macro levels of analysis and/or theories. Ritzer (1979, 1981) sought to develop a sociological paradigm that integrates micro and macro levels in both their objective and their subjective forms. Thus, there are four major levels of social analysis that must be dealt with in an integrated manner: macro subjectivity, macro objectivity, micro subjectivity, and micro objectivity. Jeffrey Alexander (1982–83) created a "multidimensional sociology" that deals, at least in part, with a model of levels of analysis that closely resembles Ritzer's model. James Coleman (1986) concentrated on the micro-to-macro problem, while Allen Liska (1990) extended Coleman's approach to deal with the macro-to-micro problem as well. Coleman (1990) extended his micro-to-macro model and has developed a much more elaborate theory of the micro-macro relationship based on a rational choice approach derived from economics (see the following section on agency-structure integration).

Agency-Structure Integration

Paralleling the growth in interest in the United States in micro-macro integration has been a concern in Europe for agency-structure integration (Ryan, 2005; Sztompka, 1994). Just as Ritzer saw the micro-macro issue as the central problem in American theory, Margaret Archer (1988) saw the agency-structure topic as the basic concern in European social theory. Although there are many similarities between the micro-macro and agency-structure literatures (Ritzer and Gindoff, 1992, 1994), there are also substantial differences. For example, while agents are usually micro-level actors, collectivities such as labor unions can also be agents. And while structures are usually macro-level phenomena, we also find structures at the micro level. Thus, we must be careful in equating these two bodies of work and must take much care when trying to interrelate them.

There are several major efforts in contemporary European social theory that can be included under the heading of agency-structure integration. The first is Anthony Giddens's (1984) structuration theory (Stones, 2005). Giddens's approach sees agency and structure as a "duality." That is, they cannot be separated from one another: agency is implicated in structure and structure is involved in agency. Giddens refuses to see structure as simply constraining (as, for example, does Durkheim), but instead sees structure as both constraining *and* enabling. Margaret Archer (1982) rejects the idea that agency and structure can be viewed as a duality, but rather sees them as a dualism. That is, agency and structure can and should be separated. In distinguishing them, we become better able to analyze their relationship to one another. Archer (1988) is also noted for extending the agency-structure literature to a concern for the relationship between culture and agency and for developing a more general agency-structure theory (Archer, 1995).

While both Giddens and Archer are British, another major contemporary figure involved in the agency-structure literature is Pierre Bourdieu from France (Bourdieu, 1977; Bourdieu and Wacquant, 1992; Swartz, 1997). In Bourdieu's work, the agency-structure issue translates into a concern for the relationship between habitus and field (Eisenberg, 2007). *Habitus* is an internalized mental, or cognitive, structure through which people deal with the social world. The habitus both produces, and is produced by, the society. The *field* is a network of relations among objective positions. The structure of the field serves to constrain agents, whether they are individuals or collectivities. Overall, Bourdieu is concerned with the relationship between habitus and field. The field conditions the habitus, and the habitus constitutes the field. Thus, there is a dialectical relationship between habitus and field.

The final major theorist of the agency-structure linkage is the German social thinker Jurgen Habermas. We have already mentioned Habermas as a significant contemporary contributor to critical theory. Habermas (1987a) has also dealt with the agency-structure issue under the heading of "the colonization of the life-world." The life-world is a micro world where people interact and communicate. The system has its roots in the life-world, but it ultimately comes to develop its own structural characteristics. As these structures grow in independence and power, they come to exert more and more control over the life-world. In the modern world, the system has come to "colonize" the life-world—that is, to exert control over it.

The theorists discussed in this section are not only the leading theorists on the agency-structure issue, they are arguably (especially Bourdieu, Giddens, and Habermas) the leading theorists in the world today. After a long period of dominance by American theorists (Mead, Parsons, Merton, Homans, and others), the center of social theory seems to be returning to its birthplace—Europe. Furthermore, Nedelmann and Sztompka have argued that with the end of the Cold War and the fall of communism, we were about to "witness another Golden Era of European Sociology" (1993:1). This seems to be supported by the fact that today the works that catch the attention of large numbers of the world's theorists are European.

Theoretical Syntheses

The movements toward micro-macro and agency-structure integration began in the 1980s, and both continued to be strong in the 1990s. They set the stage for the broader movement toward theoretical syntheses, which began at about the beginning of the 1990s. Lewis (1991) has suggested that sociology's problem (assuming it has a problem) may be the result of excessive fragmentation, and that the movement toward greater integration may enhance the status of the discipline. What is involved here is a wide-ranging effort to synthesize two or more theories (for example, structural functionalism and symbolic interactionism). Such efforts have occurred throughout the history of sociological theory (Holmwood and Stewart, 1994). However, there are two distinctive aspects of the recent synthetic work in sociological theory. First, it is very widespread and not restricted to isolated attempts at synthesis. Second, the goal is generally a relatively narrow synthesis of theoretical ideas, and not the development of a grand synthetic theory that encompasses all of sociological theory. These synthetic works are occurring within and among many of the theories discussed in this chapter.

Then there are efforts to bring perspectives from outside sociology into sociological theory. There have been works oriented to bring biological ideas into sociology in an effort to create sociobiology (Crippen, 1994; Maryanski and Turner, 1992). Rational choice theory is based in economics, but it has made inroads into a number of fields including sociology (Coleman, 1990; Heckathorn, 2005). Systems theory has its roots in the hard sciences, but in the late twentieth century, Niklas Luhmann (1984/1995) made a powerful effort to develop a system theory that could be applied to the social world.

Theories of Modernity and Postmodernity

Over the last several decades social theorists[7] have become increasingly preoccupied with whether society (as well as theories about it) has undergone a dramatic transformation. On one side is a group of theorists (for example, Jurgen Habermas, Zygmunt Bauman, and Anthony Giddens) who believe that we continue to live in a society that still can best be described as modern and about which we can theorize in much the same way that social thinkers have long contemplated society. On the other side is a group of thinkers (for example, Jean Baudrillard, Jean-François Lyotard, and Fredric Jameson) who contend that society has changed so dramatically that we now live in a qualitatively different, postmodern society. Furthermore, they argue that this new society needs to be thought about in new and different ways.

The Defenders of Modernity

All the great classical sociological theorists (Marx, Weber, Durkheim, and Simmel) were concerned, in one way or another, with the modern world and its advantages and disadvantages (Sica, 2005). Of course, the last of these (Weber) died in 1920, and the world has changed dramatically since then. Although all contemporary theorists recognize these dramatic changes, there are some who believe that there is more continuity than discontinuity between the world today and the world that existed around the last *fin de siecle*.

Mestrovic (1998:2) has labeled Anthony Giddens "the high priest of modernity." Giddens (1990, 1991, 1992) uses terms such as "radical," "high," or "late" modernity to describe society today and to indicate that while it is not the same society as the one described by the classical theorists, it is continuous with that society. Giddens sees modernity today as a "juggernaut" that is, at least to some degree, out of control.

---

[7]The term "social" rather than "sociological" theorist is used here to reflect the fact that many contributors to the recent literature are not sociologists, although they are theorizing about the social world.

Ulrich Beck (1992; Ekberg, 2007; Jensen and Blok, 2008; Then, 2007) contends that whereas the classical stage of modernity was associated with industrial society, the emerging new modernity is best described as a "risk society." Whereas the central dilemma in classical modernity was wealth and how it ought to be distributed, the central problem in new modernity is the prevention, minimization, and channeling of risk (from, for example, a nuclear accident). Jurgen Habermas (1981, 1987b) sees modernity as an "unfinished project." That is, the central issue in the modern world continues, as it was in Weber's day, to be rationality. The utopian goal is still the maximization of the rationality of both the "system" and the "life-world." Ritzer (2008) also sees rationality as the key process in the world today. However, he picks up on Weber's focus on the problem of increasing formal rationality and the danger of an "iron cage" of rationality. While Weber focused on the bureaucracy, today Ritzer sees the paradigm of this process as the fast-food restaurant, and he describes the increase in formal rationality as the McDonaldization of society. Zygmunt Bauman (2000, 2003, 2005, 2006, 2007) has produced a series of basically modern analyses of what he calls the "liquid" world.

The Proponents of Postmodernity

Postmodernism was hot (Crook, 2001; Kellner, 1989; Ritzer, 1997; Ritzer and Goodman, 2001). Indeed it was so hot and discussed so endlessly in many fields in the late twentieth century, including sociology, that it seems already in the process of burning out (Lemert, 1994b). We need to differentiate, at least initially, between postmodernity and postmodern social theory (Best and Kellner, 1991). *Postmodernity* is a historical epoch that is supposed to have succeeded the modern era, or modernity. *Postmodern social theory* is a way of thinking about postmodernity; the world is so different that it requires entirely new ways of thinking. Postmodernists would tend to reject the theoretical perspectives outlined in the previous section, as well as the ways in which the thinkers involved created their theories.

There are probably as many portrayals of postmodernity as there are postmodern social theorists. To simplify things, we will summarize some of the key elements of a depiction offered by one of the most prominent postmodernists, Fredric Jameson (1984, 1991). First, postmodernity is a depthless, superficial world; it is a world of simulation (for example, a jungle cruise at Disneyland rather than the real thing). Second, it is a world that is lacking in affect and emotion. Third, there is a loss of a sense of one's place in history; it is hard to distinguish past, present, and future. Fourth, instead of the explosive, expanding, productive technologies of modernity (for example, automobile assembly lines), postmodern society is dominated by implosive, flattening, reproductive technologies (television, for example). In these and other ways, postmodern society is very different from modern society.

Such a different world requires a different way of thinking. Rosenau (1992; Ritzer, 1997) defines the postmodern mode of thought in terms of the things that it opposes, largely characteristics of the modern way of thinking. First, postmodernists reject the kind of grand narratives that characterize much of classical sociological theory. Instead, postmodernists prefer more limited explanations, or even no explanations at all. Second, there is a rejection of the tendency to put boundaries between disciplines—to engage in something called sociological (or social) theory that is distinct from, say, philosophical thinking or even novelistic storytelling. Third, postmodernists are often more interested in shocking or startling the reader than they are in engaging in careful, reasoned academic discourse. Finally, instead of looking for the core of society (say, rationality or capitalistic exploitation), postmodernists are more inclined to focus on more peripheral aspects of society.

While postmodern theory seems to have reached its peak, it continues to exert a powerful impact on theory. On the one hand, new contributions to the theory continue to appear (see, for example, Powell and Owen, forthcoming). On the other, it is very difficult to theorize these days without taking into account postmodern theory, especially its critiques of modern theorizing and its analyses of the contemporary world.

Theories to Watch in the Early Twenty-First Century

Multicultural Social Theory, Queer Theory, and Critical Theories of Race and Racism

A recent development, closely tied to postmodernism—especially its emphasis on the periphery and its tendency to level the intellectual playing field—is the rise of multicultural social theory (Lemert, 2001; Rogers, 1996a). This rise of multicultural theory was foreshadowed by the emergence of feminist sociological theory in the 1970s. The feminists complained that sociological theory had been largely closed to women's voices, and in the ensuing years many minority groups echoed the feminists' complaints. In fact, minority women (for example, African Americans and Latinas) began to complain that feminist theory was restricted to white, middle-class females and had to be more receptive to many other voices. Today, feminist theory has become far more diverse, as has sociological theory.

Multicultural theory has taken a series of diverse forms. Examples include Afrocentric theory (Asante, 1996), Appalachian studies (Banks, Billings, and Tice, 1996), Native American theory (Buffalohead, 1996), and even theories of masculinity (Connell, 1996; Kimmel, 1996). Among the things that characterize multicultural theory are the following:

- A rejection of universalistic theories that tend to support those in power; multicultural theories seek to empower those who lack clout.
- Multicultural theory seeks to be inclusive, to offer theory on the behalf of many disempowered groups.
- Multicultural theorists are not value-free; they often theorize on behalf of those without power and work in the social world to change social structure, culture, and the prospects for individuals.
- Multicultural theorists seek to disrupt not only the social world but also the intellectual world; they seek to make it far more open and diverse.
- There is no effort to draw a clear line between theory and other types of narratives.

- There is ordinarily a critical edge to multicultural theory; it is both self-critical and critical of other theories and, most important, of the social world.
- Multicultural theorists recognize that their work is limited by the particular historical, social, and cultural context in which they happen to live (Rogers, 1996b:11–16).

Two of the most important of today's multicultural theories are queer theory and critical theories of race and racism (CTRR).

Queer theory grew out of a series of key publications, academic conferences, political organizations, and published texts largely during the early 1990s. Theoretically, it has its roots in a number of fields including feminist studies, literary criticism, and, most notably, social constructionism and poststructuralism. Queer theory also has political sources, notably in the larger project of queer politics and of groups such as ACT UP and Queer Nation. Academically, queer theory has strong early roots in the works of Michel Foucault, Judith Butler, Eve Kosofsky Sedgwick, and Teresa de Lauretis.

Queer theory involves a range of intellectual ideas rooted in the contention that identities are not fixed and stable and do not determine who we are. Rather, identities are seen as historically and socially constructed processes that are both fluid and contested. Further, these identities need not be gay or lesbian. In fact, queer theory does not seek to explain homosexual or heterosexual identities by themselves, but rather the homosexual/heterosexual divide as a figure of knowledge and power that orders desires, behaviors, social institutions, and social relations. Thus, although queer theory does take sexuality as one of its central concerns, it is a much broader intellectual project than gay and lesbian, or even sexuality, studies. Queer theory is therefore both more than and less than a theory of queers.

Sociologists and other social scientists have been making significant contributions to theories of racism at least since Du Bois's work early in the twentieth century. Such theorizing received an important impetus in recent years from the development of "critical race theory" largely in the field of law (Delgado and Stefancic, 2001). That theory was a result of the growing recognition that the momentum of the civil rights movement of the 1960s had been lost and what was needed was not only a revival of social activism, but also new ways of theorizing race. Among the ideas of critical race theory are that racism is endemic to American life and therefore difficult to deal with; there is little incentive to whites to deal with it; race is a social construction and therefore subject to manipulation, and this leads to skepticism about the law that can be similarly manipulated; different minority groups have been racialized at different times; racial identity is not unidimensional or fixed; the experiences and communities of origin of racial minorities are of great importance, and they serve to give racial minorities a unique expertise; and critical race theory is oriented to the elimination of racial oppression.

Critical theories of race and racism (CTRR) are rooted much more in the social sciences, including sociology, than the critical race theory. Thus, CTRR deals with such cutting-edge issues in theory as the relationship between race and racism and agency-structure, political economy, and globalization (including as race and racism relates to nation-states, nationalism, colonialism, neocolonialism, decolonization, imperialism, and empire). CTRR has a much broader, even global, focus than critical race theory. CTRR is also open to a much wider array of classical and contemporary theories as they apply to race and they adopt a much broader macro-structural and macro-cultural approach, especially one that focuses on power. A general conclusion to be derived from CTRR is that "race matters" and that it continues to matter not only in the legal system, but throughout the structures and institutions of society (West, 1994). For example, Bonilla-Silva (2003) is critical of the view that racism today is of little more than historical interest. Rather, he sees color-blindness as a smokescreen that allows white Americans to continue to perpetuate racial discrimination. Also in tune with CTRR is Bonilla-Silva's proposal for a variety of practical steps to deal with this new form of racism. Another distinctive characteristic of CTRR is its effort to show that race also matters globally (Winant, 2001).

Overall, there is as yet no "theory," critical or otherwise, of race and racism. However, there is a historical body of theory to draw on, many theoretical ideas and perspectives of great relevance, as well as a series of ideas developed already from within CTRR (e.g., intersectionality). It is this heritage, as well as ongoing work, that will provide the base for the continuing development of CTRR.

Postmodern and Post-Postmodern Social Theories

While no longer as hot as it once was, it is safe to assume that postmodern social theories will continue to influence sociology and many other fields. At the same time, there is already well established, primarily in France (the center of theoretical movements such as postmodernism), a body of work that can best be thought of as post-postmodernism. For example, postmodern social theory is associated with a critique of a liberal, humanistic perspective and a shift away from a concern with the human subject. However, Ferry and Renaut (1985/1990) seek to rescue humanism and subjectivity and Lilla (1994:20) offers a defense of human rights. Manent (1994/1998) self-consciously analyzes modernity and the human subject. Lipovetsky (1987/1994) attacks the tendency of postmodern social theorists to be hypercritical of the contemporary world by defending the importance of fashion. He argues, for example, that fashion enhances rather than detracts from individuality.

Theories of Consumption

Coming of age during the Industrial Revolution, and animated by its problems and prospects, sociological theory has long had a "productivist bias." That is, theories have tended to focus on industry, industrial organizations, work, and workers. This is most obvious in Marxian and neo-Marxian theory, but it is found in many other theories, such as Durkheim's thinking on the division of labor, Weber's work on the rise of capitalism in the West and the failure to develop it in other parts of the world, Simmel's analysis of the tragedy of culture produced by the proliferation of human products, the interest of the Chicago school in work, and the concern in conflict theory with relations between employers and employees, leaders and followers, and so on. Much less attention has been devoted to consumption and the consumer. There are exceptions such as Thorstein Veblen's (1899/1994) famous work on "conspicuous consumption" and Simmel's thinking on money and fashion, but for the most part, social theorists have had far less to say about consumption than about production.

Postmodern social theory has tended to define postmodern society as a consumer society, with the result that consumption plays a central role in that theory (Venkatesh, 2007). Most notable is Jean Baudrillard's (1970/1998) *The Consumer Society.* Lipovetsky's post-postmodern work on fashion is reflective of the growing interest in and out of postmodern social theory in consumption. Since consumption is likely to continue to grow in importance, especially in the West, and production is likely to decline, it is safe to assume that we will see a dramatic increase in theoretical (and empirical) work on consumption (Ritzer, Goodman, and Wiedenhoft, 2001; for an overview of extant theories of consumption, see Slater, 1997, 2005). To take one example, we are witnessing something of an outpouring of theoretically based work on the settings in which we consume, such as *Consuming Places* (Urry, 1995), *Enchanting a Disenchanted World: Revolutionizing the Means of Consumption* (Ritzer, 2005), and *Shelf Life: Supermarkets and the Changing Cultures of Consumption* (Humphery, 1998). We are likely to see much more work on such settings, as well as on consumers, consumer goods, and the process of consumption. A very new direction in this domain is work on *Prosumers*, those who simultaneously produce *and* consume, especially on the Internet and Web 2.0 (e.g., blogs, Facebook). (Ritzer, 2009).

Theories of Globalization

While there have been other important developments in theory in the early twentieth century (see below), it seems clear that *the* most important developments are in theories of globalization (Ritzer, 2010; Robinson, 2007). Theorizing globalization is nothing new. In fact, it could be argued that although they lacked the term, classic theorists such as Marx and Weber devoted much attention to theorizing globalization. Similarly, many theories (e.g., modernization, dependency, and world-system theory) and theorists (e.g., Alex Inkeles, Andre Gunder Frank, and Immanuel Wallerstein) were theorizing about globalization in different terms and under other theoretical rubrics. Precursors to theorizing about globalization go back to the 1980s (and even before, see Nettl and Robertson, 1968), began to gain momentum in the 1990s (Albrow, 1996; Albrow and King, 1990; Appadurai, 1996; Bauman, 1998; Garcia Canclini, 1995; Meyer et al., 1997; Robertson, 1992), but such theorizing has really taken off in the twenty-first century (Beck, 2000, 2005; Giddens, 2000; Hardt and Negri, 2000, 2004; Ritzer, 2007; Rosenau, 2003).

There are a wide variety of theories of globalization, but they can be categorized broadly under three main headings—economic, political, and cultural theories. Economic theories are undoubtedly the best known. They can be broadly divided into theories that celebrate the neoliberal global economic market (e.g., Friedman, 2000, 2005; see Antonio, 2007, for a critique of Friedman's celebration of the neoliberal market), and those, often from a Marxian perspective (Hardt and Negri, 2000, 2004; Robinson, 2004), that are critical of it.

In political theory, one position is represented by the liberal approach (derived from the classical work of John Locke, Adam Smith, and others) (MacPherson,

1962), especially in the form of neoliberal thinking (Campbell and Pederson, 2001) (often called the "Washington Consensus" [Williamson, 1990, 1997]), which favors political systems that support and defend the free market. On the other side are thinkers more on the left (e.g., Hardt and Negri, 2000; Harvey, 2005) who are critical of this view.

A central issue in political theory is the continued viability of the nation-state. On the one side are those who see the nation-state as dead or dying in an era of globalization. On the other side on this issue are the defenders of the continued importance of the nation-state, at least one of whom (Rosenberg, 2005) has gone so far as to argue that globalization theory has already come and gone as a result of the continued existence, even reassertion, of the nation-state (e.g., France and the Netherlands vetoing the EU constitution in 2005).

While economic and political issues are of great importance, it is the cultural issues and cultural theories that have attracted the most attention in sociology. We can divide cultural theories into three broad approaches (Pieterse, 2004). The first is *cultural differentialism* in which the argument is made that there are deep and largely impervious differences among cultures that are unaffected, or affected only superficially, by globalization (Huntington, 1996). Second, the proponents of *cultural convergence* argue that while important differences remain among cultures, there is also convergence, increasing homogeneity, across cultures (Boli and Lechner, 2005; DiMaggio and Powell, 1983; Ritzer, 2008, 2004b). Third, there is *cultural hybridization* in which it is contended that the global and the local interpenetrate to create unique indigenous realities that can be seen as "glocalization" (Robertson, 1992, 2001), "hybridization" (Canclini, 1995), and "creolization" (Hannerz, 1987). Much of the sociological thinking on globalization has been concerned with the issue, implied earlier, of the degree to which globalization is leading to homogenization or to heterogenization.

It seems clear that the various theories of globalization, as well as later variants of it, will continue to dominate new developments in sociological theory in the coming years. However, other developments are worth watching.

Actor-Network Theory

Actor-network theory receives more attention in this edition because it is growing increasingly important and expanding its influence into a variety of specific domains in sociology (e.g., in the study of consumption; see Warde, 2005). On the one hand it is part of the broad and increasing interest in networks of various kinds (e.g., Castells, 1996; Mizruchi, 2005). But on the other it has a variety of unique orientations (Latour, 2007) not the least of which is its notion of the *actant,* which involves a number of obvious inclusions such as human agents, but also includes a wide variety of nonhuman actors such as the Internet, ATMs, mobile phones, iPods, and the like. This is in line with the move in the social world toward, and increasingly scholarly interest in, the *posthuman* (Franklin, 2007) and the *postsocial* (Knorr-Cetina, 2001, 2007; Mayall, 2007). That is, we are increasingly involved in networks that encompass both human and nonhuman components; in their relationships with the latter, humans are clearly in a posthuman and postsocial world.

Practice Theory

Another emerging theory is *practice theory.* Actually, the work of some of the major contributors to this theory (such as Garfinkel, Bourdieu, Giddens, and Foucault) has been dealt with previously, but practice theory now shows signs of cohering into a distinctive theory that unites these and many other inputs. The focus is on practice, or human conduct, especially the impact of taken-for-granted assumptions on it. These assumptions are "pretheoretical" in the sense that actors do not fully understand the nature of these assumptions and the degree of their impact on their practice (Biernacki, 2007). Practice is a routinized way of acting in which taken-for-granted assumptions affect how we act, especially how we manage our bodies, handle objects, treat subjects, describe things, and understand the world.

Take bodies, for example. In most other theories, the body is seen as being controlled by rational choices, larger structures, or normative systems, but to practice theory, practices are, at least in part, bodily performances that have been routinized. Practices come about as a result of training the body in a given way. Thus, for example, taking tennis lessons results in the ability of the body to hit a backhand or an overhead smash. This idea also extends to training the body so that talking, reading, and writing are made possible.

This brings us to the close of the chapter reviewing developments in contemporary theory, but this certainly is not meant to imply that we have reached the end of theory development. Some of the theories discussed in this chapter will increase in importance (CTRR) while others (neofunctionalism) will experience a decline. One thing seems sure—the landscape of social theory is likely to be dotted with more theories, none of which is likely to gain hegemony in the field. Postmodernists have criticized the idea of "totalizations," or overarching theoretical frameworks. It seems unlikely that social theory will come to be dominated by a single totalization. Rather, we are likely to see a field with a proliferating number of perspectives that have some supporters and that help us understand part of the social world. Sociological theory will not be a simple world to understand and use, but it will be an exciting world that offers a plethora of old and new ideas.

Summary

This chapter picks up where Chapter 1 left off and deals with the history of sociological theory since the beginning of the twentieth century. We begin with the early history of American sociological theory, which was characterized by its liberalism, by its interest in Social Darwinism, and consequently by the influence of Herbert Spencer. In this context, the work of the two early sociological theorists, Sumner and Ward, is discussed. However, they did not leave a lasting imprint on American sociological theory. In contrast, the Chicago school, as embodied in the work of people such as Small, Park, Thomas, Cooley, and especially Mead, did leave a strong mark on sociological theory, especially on symbolic interactionism.

While the Chicago school was still predominant, a different form of sociological theory began to develop at Harvard. Pitirim Sorokin played a key role in the founding of sociology at Harvard, but it was Talcott Parsons who was to lead Harvard to a position of preeminence in American theory, replacing Chicago's symbolic interactionism. Parsons was important not only for legitimizing "grand theory" in the United States and for introducing European theorists to an American audience, but also for his role in the development of action theory and, more important, structural functionalism. In the 1940s and 1950s, structural functionalism was furthered by the disintegration of the Chicago school that began in the 1930s and was largely complete by the 1950s.

The major development in Marxian theory in the early years of the twentieth century was the creation of the Frankfurt, or critical, school. This Hegelianized form of Marxism also showed the influence of sociologists like Weber and of the psychoanalyst Sigmund Freud. Marxism did not gain a widespread following among sociologists in the early part of the century.

Structural functionalism's dominance within American theory in mid-century was rather short-lived. Although traceable to a much earlier date, phenomenological sociology, especially the work of Alfred Schutz, began to attract significant attention in the 1960s. Marxian theory was still largely excluded from American theory, but C. Wright Mills kept a radical tradition alive in America in the 1940s and 1950s. Mills also was one of the leaders of the attacks on structural functionalism, attacks that mounted in intensity in the 1950s and 1960s. In light of some of these attacks, a conflict-theory alternative to structural functionalism emerged in that period. Although influenced by Marxian theory, conflict theory suffered from an inadequate integration of Marxism. Still another alternative born in the 1950s was exchange theory, which continues to attract a small but steady number of followers. Although symbolic interactionism lost some of its steam, the work of Erving Goffman on dramaturgical analysis in this period gained a following.

Important developments took place in other sociologies of everyday life (symbolic interactionism can be included under this heading) in the 1960s and 1970s, including some increase in interest in phenomenological sociology and, more important, an outburst of work in ethnomethodology. During this period Marxian theories of various types came into their own in sociology, although those theories were seriously compromised by the fall of the Soviet Union and other communist regimes in the late 1980s and early 1990s. Also of note during this period was the growing importance of structuralism and then poststructuralism, especially in the work of Michel Foucault. Of overwhelming significance was the explosion of interest in feminist theory, an outpouring of work that continues apace as we move well beyond the year 2000.

In addition to those just mentioned, three other notable developments occurred in the 1980s and continued into the 1990s. First was the rise in interest in the United States in the micro-macro link. Second was the parallel increase in attention in Europe to the relationship between agency and structure. Third was the growth, especially in the 1990s, of a wide range of synthetic efforts. Finally, there was considerable interest in a series of theories of modernity and postmodernity in the latter part of the twentieth and early twenty-first centuries.

The chapter concludes with a discussion of some theories to watch as we move through the first decade of the new century. Multicultural theories, especially those associated with race (CTRR) and queer theory, are likely to flourish. Postmodern theories will not go away, but more attention may well be devoted to post-postmodern theories: theories that use postmodern ideas and that go beyond them. We can also expect increasing interest in consumption and in theorizing about it. This relates to postmodern theory (consumer society is closely associated with postmodern society), reflects changes in society from an emphasis on production to consumption, as well as a reaction against the productivist bias that has dominated sociological theory since its inception. Perhaps the most dramatic growth is taking place, and is likely to continue to take place, in theories of globalization. Other theories to watch are actor-network and practice theory.

PART II

Classical Sociological Theory

CHAPTER 3

Alexis de Tocqueville

Chapter Outline

Comparative Study

American Politics

The Sociology in Tocqueville's Work

The Key Sociological Problem(s)

Freedom, Democracy, and Socialism

While Alexis de Tocqueville became a famous scholar and public figure after the publication of the first volume of *Democracy in America* in 1835 (the second volume was published in 1840), he has rarely been treated as one of the founders of sociology and sociological theory (Eberts and Witton, 1970). Indeed, until this edition of *Classical Sociological Theory* not only was there not a chapter devoted to him and his theories, there was not one mention of, or citation to, his scholarship or to the enormous body of work that has sprung up around it and that continues to appear in great abundance to this day. It is this enduring interest in Tocqueville's work, as well as the dedication to it by a small number of sociologists,[1] that has led to this chapter.

Another, and more important, reason for this chapter is that it is clear that there *is* a social theory, in particular a sociological theory, to be found in Tocqueville's work (Meyer, 2003). (It is worth pointing out that most sociologists have either ignored this point, or have actively denied it as, for example, in Seidman's (1983:306) case where he argues that Tocqueville posed a key problem in the history of social theory [the different outcomes of liberalism in Europe] "without, however, a concomitant theoretical reckoning"). Up to now, it has been mainly political scientists and political theorists who have recognized the importance of his social theory (although there have been

[1]Indeed, it was at the urging of one of them—Edward Tiryakian—that I decided to include this chapter.

exceptions in sociology; see, for example, Calhoun, 1989; Pope, 1986). This was due, in part, to the fact that Tocqueville described his work as a "new political science," and that became the predominant view of his work. The long first volume of his classic, *Democracy in America* (1835–40/1969), was clearly a "scientific" analysis of the political structure of the United States and how it compared to other states, especially that of his native France. However, it has long been acknowledged that there is also a political *sociology* in his work, and from that it is but a short leap to conclude that there is a broader sociology and sociological theory to be found there, as well. His work is uneven in this regard. The second volume of *Democracy in America,* as Lerner (1994:40; italics added) makes clear, and which is abundantly obvious to any reader, is very different in many ways from the first,[2] including being far more sociological and presenting "a *new social theory* of political man." This chapter will downplay Tocqueville's contributions to an understanding of politics and governments, especially the unique characteristics of the early American government, and focus more on his broader sociology and sociological theory.

However, there is no explicit "theory," especially "grand theory" of the type being produced at the time by Auguste Comte (see Chapter 4), in Tocqueville's work. In fact, he distrusted such theorizing. For example, in his posthumously published recollections, he says:

> I detest these absolute systems, which represent all of the events of history as depending upon great first causes linked by the chain of fatality, and which, as it were, suppress men from the history of the human race. They seem narrow, to my mind, under their pretense of broadness, and false beneath their air of mathematical exactness . . . many important historical facts can only be explained by accidental circumstances, and . . . many others remain totally inexplicable . . . chance . . . plays a great part in all that happens on the world's stage.
>
> (Tocqueville, 1893/1959:64)

Yet, immediately after the preceding statement, Tocqueville (1893/1959:64) goes on to discuss the antecedent factors that shape chance—"the nature of institutions, the cast of mind and the state of morals"—and these constitute a very sociological orientation and offer the base for a larger social theory. In fact, there are at least the rudiments of such a theory in Tocqueville's work.

However, Tocqueville always had more specific and concrete goals in mind in his work such as explaining the reasons for American democracy and the French Revolution. Thus, in order to get at his theory one must look beyond and below the specifics of his work. There is a sophisticated theory there in which Tocqueville, among other things, reconciles macro and micro perspectives on the social and cultural world. Furthermore, Tocqueville avoids the extremes of thinking of culture as an epiphenomenon (as was true of early Marxists) or as an external and coercive (à la Emile Durkheim [see Chapter 7]—all-controlling—force. Tocqueville was also an empiricist, and he generally sought to embed, if not derive, his theory from the data he collected through

---

[2]Although, there are varying views on the precise nature of those differences and where in Volume Two the differences begin.

interviews and observations (the base of *Democracy*), as well as through the analysis of historical records, documents, and archives (the base of his other famous work, *The Old Regime and the French Revolution* [Tocqueville, 1856/1983]).

Tocqueville was a contemporary of Auguste Comte's in France, as well as overlapping significantly with the lives and at least early work of Karl Marx (Chapter 6) in Germany and Herbert Spencer (Chapter 5) in England (among others). However, as far as we know he was not influenced by any of them, and his work appeared not to affect their thinking. While Tocqueville was famous by the 1830s, the others were then either quite young or laboring in obscurity.

Tocqueville does not usually get the credit accorded to these other pioneering social theorists, but there are those who have recognized his importance (Aron, 1965, 1979/2005; Poggi, 1972). In *The Sociological Tradition,* Robert Nisbet (1966:5), a leading sociologist of the day, gives Tocqueville pride of place over those most often seen as the greatest founding social theorists when he says that the "foundations of contemporary sociological thought were being laid by such men as Tocqueville, Marx, Weber, and Durkheim." In the Preface he says: "The towering roles of Tocqueville and Marx will not be missed in the chapters that follow. . . . The sociological tradition may indeed be seen as a kind of magnetic field with Tocqueville and Marx as the two poles of attraction. In the long run the influence of Tocqueville on the sociological tradition has been the greater" (Nisbet, 1966:viii). Throughout that book Tocqueville receives as much attention as, and often more than, that accorded not only to Marx, but the other luminaries mentioned above. Unfortunately, the focus of Nisbet's book is sociology's "unit ideas" with the result that the reader gets, at best, a partial and fragmentary sense from it of Tocqueville's theory and theoretical contributions.

Beyond his association with political science, another factor in the comparative invisibility of Tocqueville in histories of sociological theory is the fact that his views were seen as comparatively conservative (indeed some were appropriated by the "new Right" and even Ronald Reagan; see Goldberg, 2001; Skocpol, 1997) and, as a result, were not seen as acceptable by many sociologists with more liberal or even radical leanings. Tocqueville was an aristocrat, and while, as we will see, he praised (sometimes) democracy, especially American democracy, he was a critic of equality because, as we will see, it went hand-in-hand with governmental centralization and therefore posed a profound threat to the freedom he so cherished. To take this position: to be *for* inequality is a cardinal sin to most sociologists who are almost always highly critical of the negative consequences of social inequality. To take another example of Tocqueville's conservatism, Boyd (2001) contended that in his later letters Tocqueville favored French colonialism in Algeria, argued that some peoples were better suited to self-government than others, and seemed to feel that there was some justification for the civilized to dominate and subjugate those who were barbarous.

Of course, other theorists (Comte, Spencer, Durkheim, Vilfredo Pareto, and so on) also tended to be viewed as conservative (Pareto was even linked with the Italian fascists), but that did not stop them from being of considerable influence in the field, as well as from being the subject of great attention from students in the field. Furthermore, each of them took at least some positions that were offensive to later social thinkers, but it was Tocqueville who came to be ignored by most later social theorists.

Alexis de Tocqueville

A Biographical Sketch

Alexis de Tocqueville was born on July 29, 1805, in Paris. He came from a prominent aristocratic family, although they were not wealthy. The family had suffered during the French Revolution, and although his parents had been arrested, they managed to avoid the guillotine. Tocqueville was well educated, became a lawyer and judge (although not very successful at either), but more importantly became well—and widely—read, especially in the Enlightenment philosophy (Rousseau and Montesquieu) that played such a central role in much classical social theory.

The turning point in Tocqueville's life began on April 2, 1831, when he and a friend (Gustave de Beaumont) journeyed to America ostensibly to study the American penitentiary system. He saw America as a laboratory in which he could study, in their nascent state, such key phenomena to him as democracy, equality, and freedom (Offe, 2005). He traveled widely throughout much of the then-developed (and some undeveloped) parts of the United States (and a bit of Canada), getting as far west as Green Bay (Wisconsin), Memphis (Tennessee), and New Orleans (Louisiana), traveling through large parts of the Northeastern, Middle Atlantic, and Southern states, as well as some Midwestern states east of the Mississippi River. He talked to all sorts of people along the way, asked systematic questions, took copious notes, and allowed his interest to evolve on the basis of what he found along the way. Tocqueville (and Beaumont) returned to France on February 20, 1832, having spent less than a year studying the vast physical and social landscape of the United States as it existed then.

It took Tocqueville some time to get started on the first volume of *Democracy in America,* but he began in earnest in late 1833, and the book was published by 1835. It was a great success and made him famous. The irony here is that one of the classic works on democracy in general, and American democracy in particular, was written by a French aristocrat. He launched a political career while putting the finishing touches on Volume Two of *Democracy,* which appeared in 1840. This book was more sociological (Aron, 1965) than the first, which was clearly about politics, particularly the American political system and how it compared to others, especially

Somewhat astoundingly, in his important recent work entitled *French Social Theory,* Mike Gane (2003) does not once, in spite of the purview of the book, mention Tocqueville. Furthermore, Gane (2003:viii) is focusing on what he calls "the great innovative period of French social thought from 1800–1880," and this is precisely the period in which Tocqueville produced his great works; is concerned with the French Revolution (as was Tocqueville who, as we have seen, wrote a major work on it); and gives central importance to other conservative French thinkers, especially Comte and Durkheim.

the French system (in general, he was very favorably disposed to the American system, although he had reservations about democracy more generally). It was perhaps because of this shift in orientation, as well as the book's more abstract nature, that it was not well received.

Tocqueville continued in politics, and while an aristocrat, was comparatively liberal in many of his views. Of this, he said:

> People ascribe to me alternatively aristocratic and democratic prejudices. If I had been born in another period, or in another country, I might have had either one or the other. But my birth, as it happened, made it easy for me to guard against both. I came into the world at the end of a long revolution, which, after destroying ancient institutions, created none that could last. When I entered life, aristocracy was dead and democracy was yet unborn. My instinct, therefore, could not lead me blindly either to the one or the other.
>
> (Tocqueville, cited in Nisbet, 1976:61)

It is because of this ambivalence that Nisbet (1976–77:65) argues that unlike the development of Marxism flowing from Marx's intellectual certainty, "at no time has there been, or is there likely to be, anything called Tocquevilleism."

Tocqueville lived through the Revolution of 1848 and the abdication of the king. However, he opposed the military coup staged by Louis Napoleon, spent a few days in jail, and saw, as a result, the end of his political career (he had become minister of foreign affairs but was fired by Louis Napoleon). He never accepted the dictatorship of Napoleon III and grew increasingly critical of the political direction taken by France. As a way of critiquing the France of his day, Tocqueville decided to write about the French Revolution of 1789 (although he believed it continued through the first half of the nineteenth century and to his day) in his other well-known book, *The Old Regime and the Revolution,* which was published in 1856. While the book focused on French despotism, it continued the concerns of *Democracy in America* with the relationship among freedom, equality, and democracy. Unlike the second volume of *Democracy in America,* the *Old Regime* was well received and quite successful. It made Tocqueville the "grand old man" of the liberal movement of the day in France.

Tocqueville died at the age of 53 on April 16, 1859 (Mancini, 1994; Zunz and Kahan, 2002). One can gain a great deal of insight into the man and his thinking through *The Recollections of Alexis de Tocqueville* (Tocqueville, 1893/1959), his posthumously published memoirs of the Revolution of 1848 and his role in it.

A leading contemporary French theorist, Alain Touraine (1995), offers a characteristic critique of Tocqueville's theory. Focusing on the second volume of *Democracy in America,* Touraine argues that here Tocqueville contends that increasing equality leads to the danger of the concentration of power. This critique of increasing equality led, in Touraine's (1995:70; italics added) view, to the fact that Tocqueville's argument appealed "mainly to *aristocrats* and all those who remained attached to social and cultural *traditions.*" In fact, Tocqueville (1835–40/1969:230) did retain a favorable view of aristocracy as, for example, when he contended that the aristocrat "does not easily yield to the intoxication of thoughtless passion. An aristocratic body is a firm and enlightened man who never dies." Tocqueville's elite leanings are also clear when he argues that lawyers are the "only counterbalance to democracy" and its excesses in the United States.

Touraine goes on to say: "Although it was very influential in Great Britain and the United States, Tocqueville's work was for a long time marginal to social thought in France. . . . Tocqueville completely rejected the revolutionary idea which dominated French thought and asserted that a unitary and voluntarist movement was leading modern society towards freedom and equality" (Touraine, 1995:71). In the end, Touraine also rejects Toqueville because he associates his work, somewhat unfairly as we will see, with a philosophical approach to politics that focused on ideas and saw people determined by their nature. However, the intellectual world—with its emphasis on political economy rather than philosophy and its focus on action rather than ideas—had left Tocqueville behind.

While largely ignored as a theorist in sociology, Tocqueville has played a role in the field, especially in work that has dealt with the issue of community, particularly its loss. For example, citations to Tocqueville are common in the all-time best-selling sociology book, David Riesman's (1950) *The Lonely Crowd.*[3] Indeed, quotations from Tocqueville's work are used as headers for a number of chapters in that book. Tocqueville is described as "brilliant" by Nisbet (1953:180) in his own community study, *Community and Power.* Tocqueville is the towering intellectual influence in another of the best-selling books in the history of sociology, Robert N. Bellah et al.'s *Habits of the Heart: Individualism and Commitment in American Life* (1985). Indeed, the phrase "habits of the heart" is borrowed from Tocqueville (we will encounter his use of this phrase later in this chapter). The book is concerned with ideas and issues that are dear to him, such as individualism and the threats it poses to community. In fact, the authors of *Habits of the Heart* describe *Democracy in America* as "the most comprehensive and penetrating analysis of the relationship between character and society in America that has *ever been written*" (Bellah et al., 1985:vii). Finally, the more recent and also best-selling *Bowling Alone: The Collapse and Revival of American Community* by political scientist Robert Putnam is clearly in the Tocquevillian tradition and makes use of his ideas at various points in the book. It is worth noting that while he may not be seen as a major figure in sociology, Tocqueville's ideas have strongly influenced a number of very significant books in sociology (even Putnam's book is widely cited by sociologists and used in sociology courses).

Outside of sociology, there is a strong and abiding interest in Tocqueville. For example, there is popular interest in books and articles written by people who have endeavored to replicate, at least in part and in ways, his journey through, and insights into, America (Cohen, 2001). There are societies and newsletters that bear his name, and, of course, there continues to be an outpouring of scholarly books and articles that deal with his work.

---

[3]In fact, Riesman was president of the Tocqueville Society.

What follows will be a selective overview of Tocqueville's contributions to social theory. We will devote little time to what he says about the American government and much more to his thinking on the relationship between and among politics and the social world. It is certainly the case that issues like democracy, freedom, and equality are of enduring importance, but the specifics of what he said about them and their interrelationships are no more important than how he thought about and studied them. For example, as we will see in the following section, Tocqueville was always comparing things in various ways; his work was an early exemplar of what came to be known as the historical/comparative method.

Yet, it is also the case that informing Tocqueville's work is a concern for the *big* kinds of issues and questions that serve to make a theorist part of the canon. Perhaps the biggest issue of concern to him was the growth of centralization, especially centralized (and paternalistic) government. Associated with increasing equality, this centralization brings about a loss of freedom as the central government exerts both hard and soft controls over people. Thus, Tocqueville offers a modern grand narrative (and is a product of the intellectual base of modernity, the Enlightenment, especially the philosophy of Montesquieu) of a historical trend in the direction of increasing equality, increasing centralization, and declining freedom. Thus, he also shares with the other great theorists a passion about an issue that informs his life work. While for Marx it was capitalism, for Durkheim it was anomie, for Weber it was rationalization, and for Georg Simmel (Chapter 9) it was the tragedy of culture, for Tocqueville it was centralization.

Interestingly, Tocqueville had more in common intellectually with the great German theorists than he did with his fellow French social thinker, Emile Durkheim. Like Marx, Weber, and Simmel, Tocqueville was most concerned about the growth of large-scale social and cultural structures and their negative impact on both the social world and the individual. In contrast, Durkheim was concerned about the decline of such phenomena (e.g., the collective conscience) and the negative impact of that on both society and the individual. While, as we will see, it is appropriate to think of Tocqueville as a conservative in many ways, in comparison to Durkheim he aligns better with the more liberal and even radical theorists. The latter see a structural problem and want to replace or modify the structure, while the conservative Durkheim wants to strengthen, rather than weaken or reform, larger structures (e.g., occupational associations). Tocqueville certainly does not want to strengthen centralized government, but rather wants to reform it, make it at least less centralized and therefore less of a threat to freedom.

Comparative Study

Tocqueville's comparative methodology is most obvious in the first volume of *Democracy in America* where he is constantly comparing governmental forms found in the United States to those found mainly in Europe, especially his home country of France.[4] While he wrote much about the United States, his ultimate focus and concern

[4]Tocqueville's study of the American political system is animated by the lessons that could be derived from it that would be of utility in improving the French political system in general and democracy in particular.

was France and what was to happen there. In most cases these involve fairly casual kinds of comparisons; Tocqueville did not engage in the kinds of rigorous and systematic comparative studies that are now *de rigueur* in sociology. Nevertheless, his relentless use of this method yielded great insight into the nature of American government, its strengths and weaknesses, as well as those of the other nations he addressed.

Another kind of comparative analysis is involved in his propensity to compare *democracy* with *aristocracy*. Tocqueville, of course, was himself an aristocrat (see biographical sketch) and the France of his day still had strong aristocratic elements, as did the other European countries. He often compared them to the United States (with its lack of an aristocracy) and its democratic system. He turns again and again to a comparison of democracy and aristocracy, especially in the second volume of *Democracy in America*. What makes this analysis compelling is that the social variables he is analyzing change slightly from section to section, but in most cases he returns to contrast systematically each of those variables in an aristocratic and then in a democratic setting.

In his analysis of democracy as it was practiced in the United States, Tocqueville argues that it is easy to see the problems associated with it, especially in comparison to aristocracy, but one must dig much deeper to get at the advantages of democracy over aristocracy. In terms of disadvantages, an "aristocracy is infinitely more skillful in the science of legislation than democracy can ever be" (Tocqueville, 1835–40/1969:232). Thus, the laws produced by an aristocracy are likely to be stronger, more complete, more timely, and less transitory than those produced by a democracy. However, in spite of these disadvantages, Tocqueville concludes that "democracy's aim in its legislation is more beneficial to humanity than that of aristocracy in its lawmaking . . . that democratic government, for all its faults, is yet best suited of all to make society prosper" (Tocqueville, 1835–40/1969:232). Among the advantages of democracy are:

1. Legislative mistakes are "retrievable."
2. The "governed are more enlightened and alert."
3. They are "constantly occupied . . . with their affairs and jealous of their rights."
4. This prevents "their representatives from deviating from a general line indicated by their interests."
5. Leaders have more interests in common with the masses, and even when they do not they can do less harm because they generally hold their positions for shorter periods of time than those in aristocracies.

He concludes that the "real advantage of democracy is . . . to serve the well-being of the greatest number" (Tocqueville, 1835–40/1969:233). Even though the democratic leaders in America are "often inferior both in capacity and in morality to those whom an aristocracy might bring to power . . . they will never systematically follow a tendency hostile to the majority; they will never turn the government into something exclusive and dangerous" (Tocqueville, 1835–40/1969:233).

The following is a good summary of the relative strengths and weaknesses of the two systems (as well as a use of the idea of "unanticipated" consequences—see italicized phrases next—that Tocqueville employed many times and later would become a staple in sociological theory, although without acknowledging Tocqueville's contributions to it; we will also return to this idea in our discussion of his ideas on social change):

> There is therefore at the bottom of democratic institutions some hidden tendency which often makes men promote the general prosperity, in spite of their vices and their mistakes, whereas in aristocratic institutions there is sometimes a secret bias which, in spite of talents and virtues, leads men to contribute to afflictions of their fellows. In this way it may come about that under aristocratic governments public men do evil *without intending it,* and in democracies they bring about good results *of which they have never thought.*
>
> (Tocqueville, 1835–40/1969:234–235; italics added)

It seems clear that in his comparison of aristocracy and democracy (and elsewhere) Tocqueville is using what Max Weber later called *ideal types* as a methodological basis for his analysis (Nisbet, 1976). While Tocqueville is not as self-conscious as Weber is about this methodology, he is using it nonetheless. He clearly understands that these two political forms can have a wide range of empirical manifestations, and at least in the case of aristocracy he moves back and forth among the ways it manifests itself in various European societies. Yet, Tocqueville offers little in the way of empirical detail about any of these specific aristocracies, and he is most interested in generalizing, oftentimes in a very gross fashion. It is this profusion of great generalizations, generalizations that sometimes read like the grossest of stereotypes, that most dates Tocqueville's work in *Democracy* and differentiates it, say, from Weber's. Weber, after all, embedded his generalizations in comparative/historical research. While Tocqueville did pathbreaking research during his nearly year-long trip to and through America, he did no comparable research on democracy (and aristocracy) in the European societies about which he generalized. Thus, the unevenness of his data leads one to question the results of his comparative analyses, especially what he has to say about European societies. His conclusions about the United States are more credible, but even here he is prone to generalizations, sometimes highly outrageous generalizations.

However, Tocqueville's (1856/1983) historical-comparative research in *The Old Regime and the French Revolution* is much more defensible and closer in quality to that of Weber. In this work he does original archival research in France in order to compare the state of the nation both before and after the French Revolution. While this work did not have the impact that *Democracy* did, it is the stronger work, at least methodologically. That is, his methods allowed him to compare France before and after the revolution, while in *Democracy* his focus on data from his American journey made his comparative views on European political systems questionable since the latter were based on far more casual and less well-documented data.

Tocqueville was also unconstrained by the notion that his work ought to be value-free, or at least as value-free as possible (although he claimed to be impartial [Tocqueville, 1835–40/1969:418]). Thus, while his work is normally quite reasoned, his analysis is liberally studded with strong value judgments. Take, for example, the following from Volume Two of *Democracy in America* in which Tocqueville assails materialism (we will encounter this topic again later in this chapter) in general, and American materialism in particular, by saying that there are many things about it that "*offend me* about the materialists. I think their doctrines *pernicious,* and their pride revolts me. . . . In all nations materialism is a *dangerous malady* of the human spirit, but one must be particularly on guard against it among a democratic people" (Tocqueville, 1835–40/1969:544).

By the way, Tocqueville's often very pointed and acerbic views on this and many other issues (and people) are on display in the posthumously published *The Recollections of Alexis de Tocqueville* (1893/1959). However there are also important theoretical insights in that volume, some of which are to be found throughout this chapter.

American Politics

The first volume of *Democracy* is justly famous for its analysis of politics; it is seen as a landmark in the development of the field of political science. It is, as was pointed out earlier, a comparative study of the American political system (which is described as democratic, although the terms *democracy* and *American government* are not coterminous) and the political systems in other European countries, especially Tocqueville's France. When he compares the specifics of these political systems, he almost always comes down on the side of, and celebrates, the American political system. (This is interesting since he often equates "democracy" with "equality," and he is, as we have seen and will see further, critical of equality, at least in terms of its long-term negative implications for freedom.) However, he is aware of the problems of the American democratic system and makes it clear that he does *not* think "that American institutions are the only ones, or the best, that a democratic nation might adopt" (Tocqueville, 1835–40/1969:231).

He basically sees America as a paradigm case of increasing democratization and as a model from which other nations, especially France, can learn. America is not perfect, but it has moved furthest in this direction. Furthermore, he is clear that France could create a system that is democratic but that is structured differently from the U.S. system. He looks at the U.S. political system for lessons, both positive and negative, for such a system. This constitutes a unique opportunity for a researcher who is able to examine a society (the United States) from its beginnings and in its infancy. Thus, there are similarities between Tocqueville's approach and that of Durkheim (1912/1965) in his study of Australian aborigines. That is, in looking at societies in their "infancy," one is able to see things that would likely be hidden in more developed societies.

Tocqueville's analysis of the American political system is not only quite dated, but it is liberally studded with contentions that, given the benefit of the hindsight of history, are clearly outrageous.[5] However, it is also full of insights into that system and what it has to offer to other societies. What the United States has to offer is clear in comparison to European societies. The vast majority of these comparisons favor America. Indeed, to Tocqueville the United States is the society that is "the most enlightened and the freest" (Tocqueville, 1835–40/1969:291). In spite of his positive view of the American democratic system, Tocqueville is not blind to its weaknesses (e.g., slavery)

[5]For example, "higher education is hardly available to anybody" (55), "the President is an inferior and dependent power . . . , a docile instrument in the hands of the majority" (124; 138), the United States "has no great wars to fear" (169), there is "no religious hatred . . . no class hatred . . . no public distress" (177), "the federal government of the United States is tending to get daily weaker" (394).

The Sociology in Tocqueville's Work

According to Tocqueville (1835–40/1969:277) the "main object" of the first volume of *Democracy in America* was to explain the reasons why the United States was, and continued to be, a "democratic republic." He sees three main reasons or causes, but it is the third, or sociological, cause that is the most important to him (and us). First, there are the *circumstances,* the *accidents of fate,*[6] of the United States as, for example, its geography. Second, there are the *laws* of the United States. Third, there are American *habits and mores.*

Mores

It is the latter, especially mores, that Tocqueville sees as key to American democracy (Maletz, 2005). As he puts it, "I should say that the contributions of physical causes is less than that of the laws, and that of laws less than mores" (Tocqueville, 1835–40/1969:308). More generally, he concludes that the "importance of mores is a universal truth. . . . I find it occupies the central position in my thoughts; all my ideas come back to it in the end" (Tocqueville, 1835–40/1969:308). He is drawing on a long tradition of work on the idea of mores, although he is broadening the concept and giving it unique meaning. He is most reliant on the work of Montesquieu, especially *The Spirit of the Laws,* in which the concept of mores plays a prominent role (Maletz, 2005). Here is the way Tocqueville (1835–40/1969:287) defines *mores* (from the Latin *moeurs*), including using the now famous idea (see earlier) of "habits of the heart":

> I mean it to apply not only to "*moeurs,*" in the strict sense which might be called habits of the heart, but also to the different *notions* possessed by men, the various *opinions* current among them, and the sum of *ideas* that shape *mental habits.*
>
> So I use the word to cover *the whole moral and intellectual state of a people . . .* [italics added]

He goes on to say that his goal is not to describe American mores in general, but only those that relate to its political institutions.

In contemporary terms, Tocqueville can be seen as attempting to understand American political institutions through an examination of American *culture* ("the whole moral and intellectual state"). It is that culture that explains the peculiar development of American democracy and *not* factors like its geography or its laws. This leads, of course, to the issue of exactly what those American mores are and what role they play in American democracy.

Although the idea of mores is introduced in the first volume of *Democracy,* that volume is clearly in the domain of political science. However, the second volume involves a great deal of sociological analysis. The focus shifts from politics to "civil

---

[6]As we saw earlier, the emphasis on chance and accidents is related to Tocqueville's unwillingness to offer grand, all-encompassing theories.

society" (Tocqueville, 1935–40, 1969:417; see the following), and there is much more concern for the social problems associated with democracy. This is clear in the headings for the three parts that make up the second volume.

Part II (the first part in Volume Two; Part I was Volume One) is entitled "The Influence of Democracy on the Sentiments of the Americans." Here his main task can be seen as involving an analysis of the causal relationship between social structure (in this case the political structure of democracy) and the attitudes, beliefs, behaviors, norms, and values—the "sentiments"—of individual Americans. This is clearest in the chapters where Tocqueville deals with the relationship between democracy and Americans' "more ardent and enduring love for equality than liberty" (a cardinal sin to Tocqueville), their "individualism" (another problem, at least mostly, for Tocqueville; see the following), their use of "associations in civil life," their "taste for physical comfort," the display by some of "enthusiastic forms of spirituality," their restlessness, their "excessive love of prosperity" and the harm it can do, and their preference for "industrial callings." All of the latter can be seen as the mores—"the moral and intellectual states"—alluded to earlier.

Part III turns to a focus on the causal relationship between democracy and "mores properly so called." On the one hand, Tocqueville here deals with the relationship between democracy and a set of additional mores such as the ease and simplicity of relationships between Americans, the ease or difficulty with which they are offended, manners, pride, honor, ambition, and so on. In addition, he does what would now be called *institutional* analysis where he discusses the relationship between the political institution (democracy) and various other institutions such as the economy and work, the family, gender relations, and the military. This institutional focus and analysis is also apparent in his work on the French Revolution where he argues that "Its principal and permanent cause was not that it was encouraged by various monarchs, but, rather, the slow, persistent action of our institutions" (Tocqueville, 1856/1983). This kind of institutional analysis is not only highly sociological but also in tune with very contemporary work in sociology that focuses on institutions (the "new" institutionalism; e.g., Powell and DiMaggio, 1991).

In Part IV Tocqueville reverses the causal relationship and examines the "Influence of Democratic Ideas and Feelings on Political Society." That is, the concern is with how feelings and thoughts (also part of what Tocqueville includes under the heading of mores) lead to structural changes in the democratic system. Here Tocqueville is concerned with how these feelings tend to lead to the concentration of political power and how this can lead to a kind of despotism.

Overall, Tocqueville is looking at causal relationships among macro structures (especially democracy), institutions, other large-scale cultural phenomena like mores, norms, and values, and more micro-level objective (behavior) and subjective phenomena (sentiments, feelings, beliefs, and so on). It could be argued that Tocqueville refuses to distinguish between large-scale cultural phenomena and small-scale objective and subjective phenomena. To some, this constitutes a great advantage in his work, but to others it involves a conflation of various "levels" of analysis that would be better clearly distinguished from one another. At the minimum a wide variety of phenomena are included under the heading of mores that would be better carefully distinguished from one another. Nevertheless, Volume Two clearly adopts a very contemporary approach to sociology and to the causal analysis of sociological variables.[7]

Social Class

Perhaps unsurprisingly given his aristocratic background and the threats to it, Tocqueville has a very strong and modern sociological sense of the social class system. For example, he argued that prior to the French Revolution the nobles treated the lower classes well, or at least better than they came to be treated after the revolution. But his deep sense of social classes and the differences in the ways in which they are treated is clear in the following on the way the old regime in France treated different classes:

> The government of the old regime, which in its dealings with the *upper classes* was so lenient and so slow to take offense, was quick to act and often harsh to a degree where members of the *lower orders, peasants* especially, were concerned. Of all the many records I have examined, not one mentions the arrest of *bourgeois* under instructions from the Intendant [a government official]. *Peasants,* on the other hand, were constantly arrested in connection with levies of forced labor or the militia; for begging, for misdemeanors, and countless other minor offense. One *class* of the population could count on impartial tribunals, protracted hearings, and all the safeguards of publicity; the others were tried summarily by the provost, and there was no appeal.
>
> (Tocqueville, 1856/1983:133)

Beyond exemplifying sociological analysis, Volume Two is notable for several sociological ideas that continue to be of great importance to sociology in general, and sociological theory in particular, although their ties to Tocqueville's work are not always acknowledged. Let us look at four of them—individualism, civil associations, materialism, and social change.

Individualism

Tocqueville is often credited with the "invention" of this term. In fact, he claims to have "coined" the term for his "own requirements" (Tocqueville, 1856/1983:96). It has now not only entered wide-scale general use, but also has become an increasing concern in sociology and sociological theory. For example, it is one of the key ideas (often referred to as "individualization") in the work of the important contemporary German social theorists, Ulrich Beck and Elizabeth Beck-Gersheim (Beck and Beck-Gersheim, 2002).

Tocqueville recognizes that individualism is a new idea and that it needs to be contrasted to the older concept of egoism. (Here is another anticipation of later social theory, this time Durkheim's thinking, especially as it relates to suicide, on egoism and the lack of social constraints [linked to individualism] involved in anomie.) He defines

---

[7]It is worth noting that Tocqueville, as a child of the Enlightenment, is here, and throughout his work, doing a very "modern" form of sociological analysis. In many ways he was way ahead of his time, but this also led him to adopt a variety of modern approaches that now, in light of the postmodern critique (Ritzer, 1997), seem highly problematic. Among them are his tendencies to have essentialistic views of peoples, a desire to get to the heart of the matter or to get below surface appearances, and to argue often that there are "invariable rules of social behavior" (Tocqueville, 1835–40/1969:59).

egoism as "a passionate and exaggerated love of self which leads a man to think of all things in terms of himself and to prefer himself to all" (Tocqueville, 1835–40/1969:506). In contrast, *individualism* is "a calm and considered feeling which disposes each citizen to isolate himself from the mass of his fellows and withdraw into the circle of family and friends; with this little society formed to his taste, he gladly leaves the greater society to look after itself" (Tocqueville, 1835–40/1969:506). Let us expand upon and highlight the key differences between these two concepts in Tocqueville's conceptualization.

First, egoism "springs from a blind instinct; individualism is based on misguided judgment rather than depraved feeling" (Tocqueville, 1835–40/1969:506). Individualism is misguided primarily because people are no longer involved with other people (except intimates) and things (especially communities) outside themselves. The latter are left to run themselves; people more or less wash their hands of them and of involvement in them.

Second, egoism relates much more to feelings, while individualism is more closely tied to actions taken and not taken. In that sense, individualism is of far greater sociological consequence than egoism because it involves actions that can have quite material effects on the social world.

Third, egoism is "a vice as old as the world," while "[i]ndividualism is of democratic origin and threatens to grow as conditions get more equal" (Tocqueville, 1835–40/1969:507). Thus, egoism is a more or less stable and universal phenomenon (it is an essentialistic idea), while individualism only came into existence (or at least Tocqueville so argues) in Tocqueville's day, and he saw it as being apt to grow as democracy and equality increased. In other words, egoism seems to be associated with "human nature," while individualism is a more genuinely sociological phenomenon that develops and changes with changing social conditions.

The biggest change, of course, that concerns Tocqueville is from aristocracy to democracy. In the aristocratic age, people "are almost always closely involved with something outside themselves" and "they are often inclined to forget about themselves" (Tocqueville, 1835–40/1969:507). While this is not usually conscious or carefully thought out, "men do often make sacrifices for the sake of certain other men" (Tocqueville, 1835–40/1969:507). In the democratic age, in contrast, "the duties of each to all are much clearer but devoted service to any individual much rarer" (Tocqueville, 1835–40/1969:507).

Clearly, at least in this case (and in others, as we will see), Tocqueville favors aristocracy over democracy and feels that the individualism associated with the latter was having an adverse effect on people and society. Help that would be given to others, as well as to the larger society, is lost with the result that both are worse off than before. People themselves are worse off, too, as the individual "is forever thrown back on himself alone, and there is danger that he may be shut up in the solitude of his own heart" (Tocqueville, 1835–40/1969:508).

Civil Associations

Tocqueville's (1835–40/1969:513) discussion of the importance of "associations in civil life which have no political object" anticipates the enormous concern today in sociology, and elsewhere, in the importance of what is now called "civil society" (Lichterman, 2006; for a critique of this, see Skocpol, 1997). He is interested in, and is highly laudatory toward, the American propensity to form all sorts of civil associations—"religious, moral, serious, futile, very general and very limited, immensely large and very minute" (Tocqueville, 1835–40/1969:513)—and their positive impact on society. The great advantage of these civil associations is that people are able to interact with one another, and it is out of such interaction that "[f]eelings and ideas are renewed, the heart enlarged, and the understanding developed" (Tocqueville, 1835–40/1969:515). Democratic societies tend to eliminate such interactions with the result that they need to be recreated through the creation and development of civil associations.

This is related to Tocqueville's ever-present tendency to compare aristocratic and democratic societies. The basic argument is that there is no need for people in aristocratic societies to form such civil associations since they are already held together quite firmly. However, the situation in democratic societies is very different as is the need for such associations: "among democratic societies all the citizens are independent and weak. They can do hardly anything for themselves, and none of them is in a position to force his fellows to help him. They would all therefore find themselves helpless if they did not learn to help each other voluntarily" (Tocqueville, 1835–40/1969:514). In other words, the structure and nature of democratic societies are conducive to the formation of civil associations.

Materialism

As we saw previously, Tocqueville is highly critical of materialism and was quite willing to express his values on this issue. He sees materialism as a universal problem leading, for example, to "servitude" (Tocqueville, 1856/1983:118), but it is particularly acute in democratic societies. "Democracy favors the taste for physical pleasures. This taste, if it becomes excessive, soon disposes men to believe that nothing but matter exists. Materialism, in its turn, spurs them on to such delights with mad impetuosity. Such is the vicious circle into which democratic nations are driven" (Tocqueville, 1835–40/1969:544). While materialism is also found in aristocratic societies, Tocqueville associates aristocracies more with idealism, especially religion. In fact, he sees religion as a "precious heritage from aristocratic times" and one that must be nurtured in democratic societies in order to ward off the excesses of materialism (Tocqueville, 1835–40/1969:544).

Interestingly, Tocqueville recognizes a variety of economic problems such as materialism, but unlike Marx and many others, he traces them to democracy and not to the capitalist economic system. (To be fair, there was, as yet, no concept of capitalism[8] [Nisbet, 1976:65] and not much of that economic system was in place, especially in America, at the point that Tocqueville undertook his journey there.) For example, he sees "the recurrence of . . . industrial crises . . . [as] an endemic disease among all democratic nations in our day . . . it is not due to accident but to the essential temperament

[8]The concept does not appear as such in Marx's work: it was first used by Pierre Proudhon in 1861 and took off after Werner Sombart used it in 1902 to describe the alternative economic system to socialism (Robbins, 2005:39).

[essentialism again!] of these people" (Tocqueville, 1835–40/1969:554). While he lacks the terminology (he later developed some of that terminology with a sense that the "political struggle will be restricted to those who *have* and those who *have not*; property will form the great field of battle" [Tocqueville, 1893/1959:11; italics added]), Tocqueville describes the emergence of a two-class system in the industrial system he associates with democracy. He sees the division of labor (clearly influenced by Adam Smith) progressively weakening the worker and strengthening the master. The former grows progressively narrow in work and vision, while the latter

> daily embraces a vast field in his vision, and his mind expands as fast as the other's contracts. Soon the [worker] will need no more than bodily strength without intelligence, while to succeed the [master] needs science and almost genius. The [master] becomes more and more like the administrator of a huge empire, and the [worker] more like brute. . . . One is in a state of constant, narrow, and necessary dependence on the other and seems to have been born to obey, as the other was to command."
>
> (Tocqueville, 1835–40/1969:556)

Much of this could clearly have been written by Marx.

However, Tocqueville is restricted in his vision of this problem by his ties to an earlier time period. Thus, he interprets this as the rise of a new "aristocracy." However, unlike the aristocracy of his romantic memory and image, this new one is a "monstrosity" (Tocqueville, 1835–40/1969:557). Here is the way he contrasts the two aristocratic systems:

> The territorial aristocracy of past ages was obliged by law, or thought itself obliged by custom, to come to the help of its servants and relieve their distress. But the industrial aristocracy of our day, when it has impoverished and brutalized the men it uses, abandons them in time of crisis to public charity to feed them.
>
> (Tocqueville, 1835–40/1969:557–558)

Nevertheless, Tocqueville proceeds to make a very prophetic prediction based on this analysis about what came to be known as capitalism: "the friends of democracy should keep their eyes anxiously fixed in that direction. For if ever again permanent inequality of conditions and aristocracy make their way into the world, it will have been by that door that they entered" (Tocqueville, 1835–40/1969:558). Thus, while Tocqueville may have romanticized some aspects of the aristocracy of the past, he was fully aware of the dangers it, especially in its new industrial form, posed for democracy.

Another contrast between Marx and Tocqueville lies in their views on equality/inequality and economic problems. To Marx, economic problems are the result of inequality in capitalism, but while Tocqueville recognizes such inequality, he also argues that it is equality, not inequality, that leads to such problems. The basic logic here is in order to create distinctions in a largely equal world, people are driven to frenzied economic activities and an overemphasis on material goals.

Social Change

The issue of social change, especially revolution, occupies a central position in Tocqueville's work. While the American Revolution certainly involved major social changes, Tocqueville is less sure about the French Revolution (or rather revolutions, since he saw that as a continuing process from 1789 on). He certainly recognized that dramatic changes took place in France (including its increasing "savagery" [Tocqueville, 1856/1983:192]) and ultimately many other countries, but he is at pains to argue that in several very important respects it displayed continuity with the past rather than change. This is especially the case in terms of Tocqueville's obsession with centralization.

He argues that the old, prerevolutionary order was characterized by centralization, and rather than overthrowing it, the revolution took it as its "starting-off point and one of its guiding principles" (Tocqueville, 1856/1983:60). The revolution did *not* overthrow this form of administration. Rather new forms of centralization proliferated *both* before and after the revolution: "this part of the old regime was to be taken over en bloc and integrated into the constitution of modern France" (Tocqueville, 1856/1983:60). Thus, counterintuitively, "the reason why the principle of centralization of power did not perish in the Revolution is that this very centralization was at once the Revolution's starting point and one of its guiding principles" (Tocqueville, 1856/1983:60). The centralization that had characterized the old order was revived by the revolution and, in fact, has "been endorsed by all successive governments" (Tocqueville, 1856/1983:60). And an important reason for this was the destruction of the aristocracy that had previously helped to counter centralization by forming at least a semi-autonomous power base and to moderate the tendency toward centralization. This all leads Tocqueville (1856/1983:65) to a generalization: "History, indeed, is like a picture gallery in which there are the originals and many copies."

Tocqueville also argues that the revolution was not as advantageous as is usually supposed to parties assumed to have benefited from it. He acknowledges that during the old regime the lower classes, especially the peasants, were treated poorly and were bad off. He also recognizes that they were better off after the revolution in that they were free and became, to a modest degree, landowners. However, in another way they were worse off: "the way they were prevented from bettering themselves mentally and materially . . . strikes us today as so inhuman . . . they were left in a state of ignorance and often destitution worse than that of the serfs, their forefathers" (Tocqueville, 1856/1983:133).

Represented here is a kind of view of history associated today with the French social theorist Michel Foucault, in which basic assumptions about the course of history are questioned and ultimately turned completely on their heads. For example, to Foucault (1980a) rather than the Victorian era leading to a suppression of sexuality, it bloomed. Of greater relevance to this discussion, instead of being treated better over time, prisoners (Foucault, 1979) and the mentally ill (Foucault, 1965) actually were, in many ways, more oppressed and repressed. Similarly, Tocqueville (1856/1983:121) argues that the material estrangement of the peasant in the old regime was replaced by a more "prevalent" and "pernicious" kind of spiritual estrangement after the revolution.

More generally, there is a pervasive sense of what later came to be known as "unanticipated consequences" (see earlier) in Tocqueville's work on social change. In addition to the above, he contends that increasingly wealth leads not to more settled conditions but to greater unrest (Tocqueville, 1856/1983:175, 176); increasingly wealth also does not necessarily resolve economic problems, but leads to new ones and perhaps even to revolution (Tocqueville, 1856/1983:179); increased enlightenment and improved conditions can stimulate, rather than retard, revolution (Tocqueville, 1856/1983:186); and, reminiscent of Marx, the elites and the king in the old regime are seen as spawning their own gravediggers. His most general statement on unanticipated consequences is to be found in his memoirs: "the destinies of this world proceed as the result, but often as the contrary result, of the intentions that produce them, similarly to the kite which flies by the antagonistic action of the wind and the cord" (Tocqueville, 1893/1959:26).

The Key Sociological Problem(s)

The key political issue to Tocqueville was the strength (and weakness) of democracy in general, and American democracy in particular, over aristocracy, especially as it existed in Europe, most often France and England.[9] While this issue is not devoid of sociology, it is much more an issue in political science than in sociology. However, in Volume Two of *Democracy in America* Tocqueville is much more of a sociologist, and clear sociological problems emerge in the course of it.

Stagnation

For starters, he fears that a democratic society will lead to a lack of boldness, ambition, pride, a "paltriness of aim," too much humility (632). Later,

> If the citizens continue to shut themselves up more and more narrowly in the little circle of petty domestic interests and keep themselves constantly busy therein, there is a danger that they may in the end become practically out of reach of those great and powerful public emotions which do indeed perturb peoples but which also make them grow and refresh them. Seeing property change hands so quickly, and love of property become so anxious and eager, I cannot help fearing that men may reach a point where they look on every new theory as a danger, every innovation as a toilsome trouble, every social advance as a first step towards a revolution, and that they may absolutely refuse to move at all for fear of being carried off their feet. The prospect really does frighten me that they finally become so engrossed in a cowardly love of immediate pleasures that their interest in their own future and in that of their descendants may vanish, and that they will prefer tamely to follow the course of their destiny rather than make a sudden energetic effort necessary to set things right.
>
> People suppose that the new societies are going to change shape daily, but my fear is that they will end up by being too unalterably fixed with the same institutions, prejudices, and mores, so that mankind will stop progressing and will dig itself in. I fear that the mind may keep folding itself up in a narrower compass forever without producing new ideas, that men will wear themselves out in trivial, lonely, futile activity, and that for all its constant agitation humanity will make no advance.
>
> (Tocqueville, 1835–40/1969:645)

---

[9]Tocqueville was ambivalent about both aristocracy and democracy! (Nisbet, 1976).

Equality

If stagnation is an important problem in democracy, what does Tocqueville see as its causes? A key cause to him is *equality.* While he has positive things to say about equality (it leads to compassion and gentleness [Tocqueville, 1835–40/1969:565]), he is, in the main, critical of it, and it is this that, as pointed out earlier, sets him apart from the vast majority of sociologists and social theorists who are arch critics of *in*equality and in general favor equality. Here we encounter, once again, the reason why Tocqueville is so little dealt with, and so out of favor, in sociology today.

Of equality, Tocqueville (1835–40/1969:527; italics added) says that nothing can prevent

> increasing equality from turning men's minds to look for the useful or disposing each citizen to get wrapped up in himself. . . . One must therefore expect that private interest will more than ever become the chief if not the only driving force behind all behavior. . . . If citizens, attaining equality were to remain ignorant and coarse, it would be difficult to foresee any limit to the *stupid excesses* into which their selfishness might lead them.

Whatever negative things one may say about aristocracies, and Tocqueville did not shrink from saying them, there was in his view less self-interested behavior, more other-oriented behavior, in such societies.

While the end of aristocracy in the name of equality means the end of "troublesome privileges," it leads to another problem: "When men are more or less equal and are following the same path, it is very difficult for any of them to walk faster and get out beyond the uniform crowd surrounding and hemming them in" (Tocqueville, 1835–40/1969:537). Here we get closer to the crux of the problem in the democratic world as far as Tocqueville was concerned: it brought with a loss of creativity, the emergence of mediocrity. For all its faults, aristocratic regimes permitted inequality and therefore fostered creativity and excellence, albeit for the few who were part of the aristocracy.

Despotism

A related problem is that equality leads to *despotism* and to a further weakening of the individual: "everything in Europe seems to tend toward the indefinite extension of the prerogatives of the central power and to make the status of the individual weaker, more subordinate and more precarious" (Tocqueville, 1835–40/1969:679). This is a counter-intuitive argument since we tend to associate despotism with aristocratic regimes. However, Tocqueville argues that the trend for centuries had been for aristocracies to surrender power. In any case, the very nature of the exercise of power is more limited in aristocracies: "The social power in aristocracies was usually limited to directing and supervising the citizens in all matters immediately and patently connected with national interests. In *all other respects* they were left to *freely choose* for themselves." (Tocqueville, 1835–40/1969:681.) In contrast, the democratic nations of his day seem to have held "themselves responsible for the behavior and fate of their subjects as individuals, and have undertaken to guide and instruct them in all they do, and will, if necessary, make them happy against their will" (Tocqueville, 1835–40/1969:681). (The latter is reminiscent of the views of the critical theorists and the ways in which the "culture industry" operates to control and stupefy people [Jay, 1973].)

Another factor in the increasing risk of despotism is the growing individualism discussed earlier. That is, as people grow more individualistic, become more removed from the broader social and political world, the field is left clear for the emergence and victory of a despot.

Centralization

Related to despotism is a parallel concern, and fear, in Tocqueville's work for growing *centralization,*[10] especially bureaucratic centralization in the state. He sees this as "the instinctive desire of every government" (Tocqueville, 1856/1983:58). There is a mutual attraction between centralization and equality. As Nisbet (1976:73) puts it, to Tocqueville: "All centralizing minds . . . are fond of equality, and all egalitarian minds are attracted to centralization." He sees centralization as being accompanied by a loss of freedom as people surrender far more, and far more readily, to bureaucratic "clerks" than they ever did before to the kings of aristocratic societies: "The citizens are perpetually falling under the control of the public administration. They are led insensibly, and perhaps against their will, daily to give up fresh portions of the individual independence to the government and those same men who from time to time have upset a throne and trampled kings beneath their feet bend without resistance to the slightest wishes of some clerk." (Tocqueville, 1835–40/1969:688).[11] Here we have intimations of not only the critical school, but also Weber's fears about bureaucracy and even of Foucault's work.

Centralization is not only a key issue in the second volume of *Democracy,* but it occupies a similar place in *The Old Regime and the French Revolution.* There he argues that in the years leading up to the revolution France underwent a process of increasing governmental administration.[12] He saw this kind of centralized government as a very "modern" institution (Tocqueville, 1856/1983:57). Furthermore, this type of a modern form of government spread to other countries.

Thus, Tocqueville is expressing his deep fears about centralized control (and the closely linked democracy and equality) and especially the loss of freedom and liberty involved in the historical movement from aristocracy to democracy. In his recollections, Tocqueville (1893/1959:189–190) says: "In France there is only one thing we can't set up: that is a free government; and only one institution we can't destroy: that is, centralization." And, he has little hope for the future: "For my part, I own that I have no confidence in the spirit of liberty which seems to animate my contemporaries. I see plainly

---

[10]This is also a concern in Volume One where he distinguishes between governmental and administrative centralization, and argues the United States has no administrative centralization and a high degree of governmental centralization. He feels that the latter is necessary for a nation to live and prosper. Administrative centralization "only serves to enervate peoples that submit to it, because it constantly tends to diminish civic spirit" (Tocqueville, 1835–40/1969:88) Later, centralization is seen as excelling at "preventing, not doing" (Tocqueville, 1835–40/1969:91). More importantly, centralization is linked to despotism, and the lack of administrative centralization acts as an impediment to despotism in the United States.

[11]He also saw centralization as making the French Revolution more likely. In an earlier and less centralized France, movements toward revolution had been successfully resisted (Tocqueville, 1856/1983:204).

[12]He also focused on other forms of centralization such as the growing centrality of Paris vis-à-vis the rest of France. This also made the revolution easier since its success in Paris meant that the whole society would follow suit: "he who reigns in Paris governs France" (Tocqueville, 1893/1959:75).

enough that the nations of this age are turbulent, but it is not clear to me that they are freedom-loving. And I fear that at the end of all these agitations which rock thrones, *sovereigns may be more powerful than ever before*" (Tocqueville, 1835–40/1969:689; italics added). In his later memoirs he is even clearer on this in arguing that centralization (and democratization) leads to a desire to hold public office and earn public money and that this is "the secret malady that has undermined all former governments, and which will undermine all governments to come" (Tocqueville, 1893/1959:32).

These new, more centralized administrations are more powerful in various ways. For one thing, they act "with greater speed, power, and independence" than had previous forms such as kingships (Tocqueville, 1835–40/1969:683). For another, anticipating Foucault's (1980) work, they are seen by Tocqueville (1835–40/1969:682) as "more inquisitive and minute." That is, they intrude, and intrude more deeply, into peoples' lives. Those who hold positions in government gain "pleasure" from "interfering with every one and holding everything in their hands" (Tocqueville, 1893/1959:190). Also similar to Foucault, "they would degrade men rather than torment them" (Tocqueville, 1835–40/1969:691). It is a kind of "soft power" resembling more the power of parents over their children. It serves to keep citizens in a kind of perpetual childhood and "likes to see the citizens enjoy themselves, provided that they think of nothing but enjoyment" (Tocqueville, 1835–40/1969:692). Along these lines, "It does not break men's will, but softens, bends, and guides it; it seldom enjoins, but often inhibits, action; it does not destroy anything, but prevents much from being born; it is not at all tyrannical, but it hinders, restrains, enervates, stifles, and stultifies so much that in the end each nation is no more than a flock of timid and hardworking animals with the government as its shepherd" (Tocqueville, 1835–40/1969:692). Again, reminiscent of Foucault, this governmental control operates in a kind of "capillary" fashion in that it "extends its embrace to include the whole of society. It covers the whole of social life with a network of petty, complicated rules that are both minute and uniform" (Tocqueville, 1835–40/1969:692).

Freedom, Democracy, and Socialism

If Tocqueville is critical of equality and centralization, it is because he is *for* freedom. It, or at least the desire for it, seems to be universal as far as he is concerned. However, it confronts powerful enemies, especially centralization. As a result, freedom was *more* endangered *after* the revolution than before because there was less centralization under the rule of the king than in postrevolutionary France. Centralization under the king did not have the same power it came to have in modern governments. The latter had less control over subordinates, at least in part because public offices were sold to them and thus deprived the old regime "of all the right of appointing or dismissing its officials at will" (Tocqueville, 1856/1983:109). Furthermore, the old regime had fewer inducements to coerce, and fewer means of coercion, over subordinates. As a result, orders were often carried out halfheartedly. The result of all of this was that it was easier for people to defend their freedom in the old regime than in modernity. The French Revolution itself had mixed effects on freedom (Tocqueville, 1856/1983:167), but overall it led to increased centralization and therefore to a reduction in the chances for freedom. Nevertheless, Tocqueville was not arguing for a return to the old regime since while there "was more freedom in that period [of the old regime] than there is today . . . it was a curiously ill-adjusted, intermittent freedom always restricted by class distinctions and tied up with immunities and privileges" (Tocqueville, 1856/1983:119). Whatever its weaknesses, there seemed to be more freedom in the old than the new regime, and the latter is able to mobilize far greater resources to limit, if not threaten, freedom.

If Tocqueville is critical of democracy for this trend toward centralization, and its adverse effects, he is even more critical of socialism, at least as it was articulated in the works on it in his day. To him, "socialism and centralization thrive in the same souls" (Tocqueville, 1856/1983:164). Socialistic ideas tended to support state centralization. It was not only socialism's association with centralization that Tocqueville found alarming,[13] but also ideas like "community of property, the right to be provided with work, absolute *equality,* State control of all of the activities of individuals, despotic legislation, and the total submerging of each citizen's personality in the group mind" (Tocqueville, 1856/1983:164; italics added). This can be seen as a prophetic set of criticisms, at least as socialism came to be practiced in the Soviet bloc countries.

Overall, Tocqueville is critical of *both* democracy and socialism for many of the same reasons, although he clearly sees the prospect of socialism as much more distasteful than democracy. Both tended to foster equality, centralization, and worst of all, the loss of freedom.

What is the solution to these problems associated with the flow of history from aristocracy to democracy (and possibly socialism)? While there is no going back to an older form of aristocracy, Tocqueville sees hope in a new form:

> I am firmly convinced that one cannot found an aristocracy anew in this world, but I think that associations of plain citizens can compose very rich, influential and powerful bodies, in other words, aristocratic bodies. . . . By this means many of the greatest political advantages of an aristocracy could be obtained without its injustices and dangers . . . by defending its private interests against the encroachments of power, it saves the common liberties.
>
> (Tocqueville, 1835–40/1969:697)

However by his work on the French Revolution, Tocqueville seems to have grown less optimistic about the future and more nostalgic for the era of dominance of the nobles and other elites of the earlier French society such as the Catholic clergy and judicial officials. It was the relative independence of these elites that fostered greater freedom not only for themselves, but for much of the rest of society. Their independence also created something of an inhibition, and counterbalance, to centralization. Thus, the centralization of prerevolutionary France was far less of a problem, and far less powerful, than it was to become after the revolution, and less centralization was equated by Tocqueville with greater freedom. It is this kind of thing that led him to write of the "dumb conformity" of his day and longingly of the "good sense of the past" (Tocqueville, 1856/1983:115, 116). He also compares (unfavorably) the "servile mind" of the times to their ancestors' greater freedom and "nobility of mind" (Tocqueville, 1856/1983:119).

---

[13] In other places he ridicules socialistic ideas and finds them "ridiculous" (Tocqueville, 1893/1959:78, 237).

It is for reasons like these that Tocqueville (1856/1983:77) writes of the "catastrophic downfall of the monarchy." Thus, to him the French Revolution was a disaster (even though he was well aware of past problems and that the revolution did away with at least some of them). And he had a low regard for the governments dominated by the middle class that followed (Tocqueville, 1893/1959:3). He saw the revolution as being less due to the impact of the prior American Revolution, than to French ideas—especially such Enlightenment ideas as "natural law" and "rights of man"—and their "naivete" (Tocqueville, 1856/1983:147). With the destruction of the established government (and religion), people were thrown into a state of confusion (something that greatly concerns Tocqueville): "They knew neither what to hold on to, nor where to stop. Revolutionaries of a hitherto unknown breed came on the scene; men who carried audacity to the point of sheer insanity . . . acted with an unprecedented ruthlessness" (Tocqueville, 1856/1983:157). Furthermore, Enlightenment ideas led to views on the way the nation should be governed that were not merely hard to reconcile with free institutions but practically ruled them out. They had come to regard the ideal social system as one whose aristocracy consisted exclusively of government officials and in which an all-powerful bureaucracy not only took charge of affairs of State but controlled men's private lives" (Tocqueville, 1856/1983:167). Tocqueville (1856/1983:169) waxes poetic about the freedom that has been lost: "that lofty aspiration . . . defies analysis . . . it is something one must *feel* and logic has no part in it. It is a privilege of noble minds which God has fitted to receive it, and it inspires them with a generous fervor . . . the sacred flame."

Once again, we see here clearly why Tocqueville's ideas have not stood the test of time well. Few today could accept the idea of an aristocracy in any form. More generally, this reflects his criticisms of equality and his defense of inequality. Making a case for aristocracy and being against equality and for inequality are not the kinds of positions that are going to win favor in sociological and social theory in the twenty-first century. Yet, we must not let our judgments on such issues obscure the fact that Tocqueville was a significant social theorist with much to offer to sociological theory.

Summary

Alexis de Tocqueville was a great social theorist, but he has not yet gotten his full due, especially in sociology where he has tended to be seen as a political scientist and therefore of minimal relevance to the field. Among the reasons that he has not received the credit and recognition due him are that Tocqueville was avowedly an aristocrat, conservative by contemporary standards, and a critic of one of sociology's "sacred cows"—equality. Furthermore, the latter led him in the unpopular direction of *favoring* inequality. Also making it difficult to see the important theory in Tocqueville's work is his deep hostility to abstract grand theory.

However, there clearly is an important theory in Tocqueville's work that revolves mainly around the interrelationship of equality, centralization, and freedom. Overall, he sees greater equality favoring increasing centralization, especially in the government. Such centralization is a problem in itself, but most importantly because it tends to threaten that which is most important to Tocqueville—freedom. He envisions the growth of an increasingly centralized government that intrudes ever more, and ever more deeply, into the lives of its citizens. It is this that lies at the heart of his critique of democracy and more importantly of socialism.

Beyond such a grand theory, Tocqueville also had a series of important insights into theoretical issues that are at the heart of sociology today. His emphasis on mores can be seen as anticipating the cultural turn in recent social theory. His inclusion under the heading of mores of both micro (ideas, mental habits) and macro (the large culture) elements can be seen as in line with current interest in micro-macro and agency-structure integration (although it can also be seen as muddying that which needs to be distinguished). Tocqueville, like Marx, saw materialism as an important problem, although Tocqueville linked it to democracy rather than capitalism (which was not in existence in Tocqueville's time and for which there was as yet no term). Also like Marx, Tocqueville had a strong sense of social class, of the emergence of a two-class system, and of the problems associated with such a system. Presaging the current interest in the topic, Tocqueville coined the term *individualism,* contrasted it to egoism, and saw the problems associated with it, primarily the decline in community interest and involvement, that interest so many today (e.g., Putnam). This is closely tied to his interest in civil associations as a counter to this trend, and this, too, is prescient given the current attention in sociology to civil society. Finally, Tocqueville has a broad theory of social change that is notable for its counterintuitive insights and for its emphasis on unanticipated consequences. It is not just that there is a lot more theory in Tocqueville's work than most have realized; there is simply a great deal of powerful theorizing to be found there.

C H A P T E R 4

Auguste Comte

Chapter Outline

Alfred North Whitehead said: "A science which hesitates to forget its founders is lost" (1917/1974:115). Practitioners in an advanced science such as physics *have* forgotten the field's founders, or at least they have relegated them to works on the history of the field. A student in physics does not ordinarily read about the work of Isaac Newton but rather about the contemporary state of knowledge on the issues that Newton and other classic physicists first addressed. The state of knowledge in contemporary physics has far outstripped that of Newton; hence, there is no need for a student to learn about his ideas. Newton's still useful ideas have long since been integrated into the knowledge base of physics. According to Whitehead, physics is *not* lost; it has (largely) forgotten Isaac Newton and the other important figures in the early history of the field.

Why then are students in sociology being asked to read about the work of an early nineteenth-century thinker like Auguste Comte (1798–1857)? The fact is that in spite of a variety of weaknesses, a number of Comte's ideas (for example, positivism) continue to be important in contemporary sociology. More importantly, many more of his ideas were important in their time and had a significant impact on the development of sociology and sociological theory. Although sociological theory has progressed far beyond many of Comte's ideas, sociology is not yet (and some say it will never be) in the position of physics, able to forget the work of its founders.

Comte's Profound Ambitions

Positivism: The Search for Invariant Laws

Comte is remembered to this day in sociology for his championing of *positivism* (Halfpenny, 1982, 2001; Scharff, 1995; J. Turner, 1985a, 1990). Although this term has a multitude of meanings, it is usually used to mean the search for invariant laws of both the natural and the social world. In Comte's version of positivism, these laws can be derived from doing research on the social world and/or from theorizing about that world. Research is needed to uncover these laws, but in Comte's view the facts derived from research are of secondary importance to sound speculation. Thus Comte's positivism involves empirical research, but that research is subordinated to theory.

Comte's thinking is premised on the idea that there is a real world (for example, biological, sociological) out there and that it is the task of the scientist to discover and report on it. Because of this view, Comte is what we would now call a *realist.* Here is the way Comte put the issue: "Positive philosophers . . . approach the questions with the simple aim of ascertaining the true state of things, and reproducing it with all possible accuracy in their theories" (1830–42/1855:385). Later, Comte argued that positivist philosophy (or any philosophy) "can only be valid insofar as it is an exact and complete representation of the relations naturally existing" (1851/1957:8–9). (This is sometimes called the "copy theory" of truth.)

There are two basic ways of getting at the real world that exists out there—doing research and theorizing. As we saw previously, while Comte recognized the importance of research, he emphasized the need for theory and speculation. In emphasizing theory and speculation, Comte was at variance with what has now come to be thought of as positivism, especially pure empiricism through sensory observations and the belief in quantification. As Pickering puts it, "Comte would not recognize the mutilated version of positivism that exists today" (1993:697).

Although many contemporary sociologists think of themselves as positivists, positivism has come under severe attack in recent years. Considerable work in the philosophy of science has cast doubt on whether positivism fits the natural sciences, and this tends to raise even greater doubts about the possibility of positivistic sociology. Some sociologists (interpretationists) never accepted a positivist approach, and others who did have either totally abandoned it or adopted a modified positivist perspective (for example, Collins, 1989a). Positivism has not disappeared from sociology, but it seems clear that sociology now finds itself in a postpositivist age (Shweder and Fiske, 1986).

Comte's interest in positivism is intimately related to his interest in sociology. Comte "discovered" sociology in 1839. Consistent with his commitment to positivism, he defined *sociology* as a positivistic science. In fact, in defining *sociology,* Comte related it to one of the most positivistic sciences, physics: "Sociology . . . is the term I may be allowed to invent to designate social physics" (1830–42/1855:444).

Comte (1830–42/1855) developed a hierarchy of the positivistic sciences—mathematics, astronomy, physics, biology (physiology), chemistry, and at the pinnacle (at least in his early work)—sociology.[1] (It is interesting to note that Comte leaves no place for psychology, which would seem to be reduced to a series of biological instincts.) This hierarchy descends from the sciences that are the most general, abstract, and remote from people to those that are the most complex, concrete, and interesting to people

---

[1]In his later work, Comte added a seventh science that ranked above sociology—morals. We will have more to say about this later.

(Heilbron, 1990). Sociology builds upon the knowledge and procedures of the sciences that stand beneath it, but in Comte's view, sociology is "the most difficult and important subject of all" (1851/1968:31). Given his high estimation of sociology, it is easy to see why Comte has long been esteemed by sociologists. And given the fact that as a positivist, Comte viewed theorizing as the ultimate activity, it is clear why he has had such high status among theorists.

Comte explicitly identified three basic methods for sociology—three basic ways of doing social research in order to gain empirical knowledge of the real social world. The first is *observation,* but Comte is quick to reject isolated, atheoretical observations of the social world. Without theory, we would not know what to look for in the social world and we would not understand the significance of what we find. Observations should be directed by some theory, and when made, they should be connected to some law. The second of Comte's methods is the *experiment,* but this method is better suited to the other sciences than it is to sociology. It is obviously virtually impossible to interfere with, and to attempt to control, social phenomena. The one possible exception would be a natural experiment in which the consequences of something that happens in one setting (for example, a tornado) are observed and compared to the conditions in settings in which such an event did not occur. Finally, there is *comparison,* which Comte divides into three subtypes. First, we can compare humans to lower animal societies. Second, we can compare societies in different parts of the world. Third, we can compare the different stages of societies over time. Comte found this last subtype particularly important; in fact, he labeled it the "chief scientific device" of sociology (1830–42/1855:481). It is so important that we separate it from the other comparative methods and accord it independent status as Comte's fourth major methodology—*historical research.* In fact, John Stuart Mill sees this as one of Comte's most important contributions in placing the "necessity of historical studies as the foundation of sociological speculation" (1961:86). In his own work, Comte used the historical method almost exclusively, although, as we will see, there are very real questions about how well he actually used this methodology.

Although Comte wrote about research, he most often engaged in speculation or theorizing in order to get at the invariant laws of the social world. He did not derive these laws inductively from observations of the social world; rather, he deduced them from his general theory of human nature. (A critic might ask questions like: How did Comte derive his theory of human nature? Where did he get it from? How can we ascertain whether or not it is true?) In this way Comte (1891/1973:302–304) created a number of general positivistic laws, laws which he applied to the social world.

Law of the Three Stages

Comte's most famous law is the *Law of the Three Stages.* Comte identified three basic stages and proceeded to argue that the human mind, people through the maturation process, all branches of knowledge, and the history of the world (and even, as we will see later, his own mental illness) *all* pass successively through these three stages. Each stage involves the search by human beings for an explanation of the things around them.

1. **The Theological Stage** Comte saw the theological stage as the first stage and the necessary point of departure for the other two stages. In this stage, the human mind is searching for the essential nature of things, particularly their origin (where do they come from?) and their purpose (why do they exist?). What this comes down to is the search for absolute knowledge. It is assumed that all phenomena are created, regulated, and given their purposes by supernatural forces or beings (gods). Although Comte includes *fetishism* (the worship of an object such as a tree) and *polytheism* (the worship of many gods) in the theological stage, the ultimate development in this stage is *monotheism,* or the worship of a single divinity that explains everything.
2. **The Metaphysical Stage** To Comte, this stage is the least important of the three stages. It is a transitional stage between the preceding theological stage and the ensuing positivistic stage. It exists because Comte believes that an immediate jump from the theological to the positivistic stage is too abrupt for people to handle. In the metaphysical stage, abstract forces replace supernatural beings as the explanation for the original causes and purposes of things in the world. For example, mysterious forces such as "nature" are invoked to explain why things are the way they are ("it was an act of nature"). Mill gives as an example of a metaphysical perspective Aristotle's contention that the "rise of water in a pump is attributed to nature's horror of a vacuum" (1961:11). Or to take a more social example, we could say that an event occurred because it was the "will of the people." Although numerous entities can be seen as causes in the metaphysical stage, its ultimate point is reached when one great entity (for example, nature) is seen as the cause of everything.
3. **The Positivist Stage** This, of course, is the final and most important stage in Comte's system. At this point people give up their vain search for original causes or purposes. All we can know are phenomena and the relations among them, not their essential nature or their ultimate causes. People drop such nonscientific ideas as supernatural beings and mysterious forces. Instead, they look for the invariable natural laws that govern *all* phenomena. Examinations of single phenomena are oriented toward linking them to some general fact. The search for these laws involves both doing empirical research and theorizing. Comte differentiated between concrete and abstract laws. Concrete laws must come inductively from empirical research, whereas abstract laws must be derived deductively from theory. Comte was much more interested in creating abstract laws than in creating concrete ones. Although positivism can be characterized by many laws, he sees it ultimately gravitating toward a smaller and smaller number of general abstract laws.

Although Comte recognized an inevitable succession through these three stages, he also acknowledged that at any given point in time all three might be operant. What he envisioned in the future of the world was a time when the positivistic stage would be complete and we would see the elimination of theological or metaphysical thinking.

Comte applied the Law of the Three Stages in a number of arenas. He saw people going through the three stages and viewed the child as a theologian, the adolescent as a metaphysician, and the adult as a positivist.[2] He also saw all the sciences in his hierarchy going through each of these stages. (Because it was a new science in Comte's time, sociology had not yet gone through the positivistic stage. Comte devoted much of his life to the development of positivistic sociology.) And he saw the history of the world in these terms. The early history of the world was the theological stage; the world next went through the metaphysical stage; and during Comte's lifetime the world was entering the last, or positivistic, stage. He believed that in the positivistic stage, people would come to better understand the invariant laws that dominate them and would be able to adapt to these laws "with fewer difficulties and with greater speed" (Comte, 1852/1968:383). These laws would also guide people in making choices that could expedite the emergence, but not alter the course, of inevitable social developments.

Positivism: The Search for Order and Progress

Although Comte used the term *positivism* in the sense of a science committed to the search for invariant laws, he also used it in another way—as the opposite of the negativism that, in his view, dominated the social world of his day. More specifically, that negativity was the moral and political disorder and chaos that occurred in France, and throughout Western Europe, in the wake of the French Revolution of 1789 (Levy-Bruhl, 1903/1973). Among the symptoms of this malaise were intellectual anarchy, political corruption, and incompetence of political leaders. Comte's positive philosophy was designed to counter the negative philosophy and its symptoms that he found all around him.

But although Comte placed great blame on the French Revolution, he found the major source of the disorder to be intellectual anarchy. "The great political and moral crisis that societies are now undergoing is shown by a rigid analysis to arise out of intellectual anarchy" (Comte, 1830–42/1855:36). Comte traced that intellectual anarchy to the coexistence during his lifetime of all three "incompatible" philosophies—theological, metaphysical, and positivistic. Not only did all three exist at one time, but none of them at that point was very strong. Theology and metaphysics were in decay, in a "state of imbecility," and positivism as it relates to the social world (sociology) was as yet unformed. The conflict among, and weaknesses of, these three intellectual schemes allowed a wide variety of "subversive schemes" to grow progressively more dangerous. The answer to this intellectual chaos clearly lay in the emergence of any one of them as preeminent, and given Comte's law, the one that was destined to emerge supreme was positivism. Positivism had already become preeminent within the sciences (except sociology) and had brought order to each, where previously there was chaos. All that was needed was for positivism to bring social phenomena within its domain. Furthermore, Comte saw this as the way to end the revolutionary crisis that was tormenting France and the rest of Western Europe.

Comte also put this issue in terms of two of his great concerns—order and progress. From his point of view, theology offered a system of order, but without progress; it was a stagnant system. Metaphysics offered progress without order; he

[2]Comte came to associate the history of the world with these life stages—infancy (theological), adolescence (metaphysical), and maturity (positivist).

Auguste Comte

A Biographical Sketch

Auguste Comte was born in Montpelier, France, on January 19, 1798 (Pickering, 1993:7; Wernick, 2005). His parents were middle class and his father eventually rose to the position of official local agent for the tax collector. Although a precocious student, Comte never received a college-level degree. He and his whole class were dismissed from the Ecole Polytechnique for their rebelliousness and their political ideas. This expulsion had an adverse effect on Comte's academic career. In 1817 he became secretary (and "adopted son" [Manuel, 1962:251]) to Claude Henri Saint-Simon, a philosopher forty years Comte's senior. They worked closely together for several years and Comte acknowledged his great debt to Saint-Simon: "I certainly owe a great deal intellectually to Saint-Simon . . . he contributed powerfully to launching me in the philosophic direction that I clearly created for myself today and which I will follow without hesitation all my life" (Durkheim, 1928/1962:144). But in 1824 they had a falling out because Comte believed that Saint-Simon wanted to omit Comte's name from one of his contributions. Comte later wrote of his relationship with Saint-Simon as "catastrophic" (Pickering, 1993:238) and described him as a "depraved juggler" (Durkheim, 1928/1962:144). In 1852, Comte said of Saint-Simon, "I owed nothing to this personage" (Pickering, 1993:240).

Heilbron (1995) describes Comte as short (perhaps 5 feet, 2 inches), a bit cross-eyed, and very insecure in social situations, especially involving women. He was also alienated from society as a whole. These facts may help account for the fact that Comte married Caroline Massin (the marriage lasted from 1825 to 1842). She was an illegitimate child who Comte later called a "prostitute," although that label has been questioned recently (Pickering, 1997:37). Comte's personal insecurities stood in contrast to his great security about his own intellectual capacities, and it appears as if this self-esteem was well founded:

> Comte's prodigious memory is famous. Endowed with a photographic memory he could recite backwards the words of any page he had read but once. His powers of concentration were such that he could sketch out an entire book without putting

associated it with the anarchy of his day, in which things were changing in a dizzying and disorderly way. Because of the coexistence of theology and metaphysics (as well as positivism), Comte's time was marked by *dis*order and a *lack* of progress. Positivism was the only system that offered both order *and* progress. On the one hand, positivism would bring order through the restraint of intellectual and social disorder. On the other hand, it would bring progress through an increase in knowledge and through perfection of the relationship among the parts of the social system so that society would move nearer, although never fully attain, its determinate end (the gradual expansion of human pen to paper. His lectures were all delivered without notes. When he sat down to write out his books he wrote everything from memory.

(Schweber, 1991:134)

In 1826, Comte concocted a scheme by which he would present a series of seventy-two public lectures (to be held in his apartment) on his philosophy. The course drew a distinguished audience, but it was halted after three lectures when Comte suffered a nervous breakdown. He continued to suffer from mental problems, and once in 1827 he tried (unsuccessfully) to commit suicide by throwing himself into the Seine River.

Although he could not get a regular position at the Ecole Polytechnique, Comte did get a minor position as a teaching assistant there in 1832. In 1837, Comte was given the additional post of admissions examiner, and this, for the first time, gave him an adequate income (he had often been economically dependent on his family until this time). During this period, Comte worked on the six-volume work for which he is best known, *Cours de Philosophie Positive,* which was finally published in its entirety in 1842 (the first volume had been published in 1830). In that work Comte outlined his view that sociology was the ultimate science. He also attacked the Ecole Polytechnique, and the result was that in 1844 his assistantship there was not renewed. By 1851 he had completed the four-volume *Systeme de Politique Positive,* which had a more practical intent, offering a grand plan for the reorganization of society.

Heilbron argues that a major break took place in Comte's life in 1838 and it was then that he lost hope that anyone would take his work on science in general, and sociology in particular, seriously. It was also at that point that he embarked on his life of "cerebral hygiene"; that is, Comte began to avoid reading the work of other people, with the result that he became hopelessly out of touch with recent intellectual developments. It was after 1838 that he began developing his bizarre ideas about reforming society that found expression in *Systeme de Politique Positive.* Comte came to fancy himself as the high priest of a new religion of humanity; he believed in a world that eventually would be led by sociologist-priests. (Comte had been strongly influenced by his Catholic background.) Interestingly, in spite of such outrageous ideas, Comte eventually developed a considerable following in France, as well as in a number of other countries.

Auguste Comte died on September 5, 1857.

powers). Thus, positivism is the only stage in the history of humankind that offers us both order *and* progress.

Comte saw order and progress in dialectical terms, and in this sense he offered a perspective close to that of Marx (see Chapter 6). This means that Comte refused to see order and progress as separate entities but viewed them as mutually defining and interpenetrating. "Progress may be regarded simply as the development of Order; for the order of nature necessarily contains within itself the germ of all positive progress. . . . Progress then is in its essence identical with Order, and may be looked upon as Order made manifest" (Comte, 1851/1957:116).

It is interesting and important to underscore the fact that in Comte's view the crisis of his time was a *crisis of ideas* and that this crisis could be resolved only by the emergence of a preeminent idea (positivism). In fact, Comte often described positivism as a "spirit." In this sense, Comte is an idealist: "Ideas govern the world" (1830–42/1855:36). On this issue, rather than being in accord with Marx, he stands in stark contrast to Marx (a materialist). Marx saw the capitalist crisis as stemming from the material conflict between capitalists and the proletariat, and he believed that its solution lay in a material revolution in which the economic system of capitalism would be overthrown and replaced by a communist system. Marx scoffed at the idea that he was dealing with a crisis of ideas that could be solved in the ideational realm. Marx was distancing himself from the idealism of Hegel; Comte, in contrast, had adopted a viewpoint that resembled, at least in a few respects, Hegelian idealism.

Comte's Sociology

We turn now more directly to Comte's sociology, or his thoughts about the social world. Here we begin with another of Comte's lasting contributions—his distinction between *social statics* and *social dynamics.* Although we do not use those terms today, the basic distinction remains important in the differentiation between social structure and social change. (By the way, Comte believed that all sciences, not just sociology, are divided into statics and dynamics.)

Social Statics

Comte defines the sociological study of social statics as "the investigation of the laws of action and reaction of the different parts of the social system" (1830–42/1855:457). Contrary to what one might think, the laws of the ways in which parts of the social system interact (social statics) are *not* derived from empirical study. Rather, they are "deduced from the laws of human nature" (Comte, 1852/1968:344–345). Here, again, we see Comte's preference for theory over empirical research.

In his social statics, Comte was anticipating many of the ideas of later structural functionalists (see Chapter 16, on Parsons). Deriving his thoughts from biology (Levine, 1995b), Comte developed a perspective on the parts (or *structures*) of society, the way in which they *function,* and their (functional) relationship to the larger social system. Comte also saw the parts and the whole of the social system in a state of harmony. The idea of harmony was later transformed by structural functionalists into the concept of equilibrium. Methodologically, Comte recommended that because we know about the whole, we start with it and then proceed to the parts. (Later structural functionalists also came to grant priority to the whole [the "social system"] over the parts [the "subsystems"].) For these and many other reasons, Comte is often seen as a forerunner of structural functionalism.

Comte argues that "in Social Statics we must neglect all questions of time, and conceive the organism of society in its fullness. . . . Our ideal" (1852/1968:249). In other words, to use a concept developed by Weber (see Chapter 7), *social statics* describes an "ideal-typical" society. The system of social statics conceived by Comte never really existed; it was an idealized model of the social world at a given point in time. In order to construct such a model, the sociologist must, at least for the purposes of analysis, hold time still.

At a manifest level, Comte is doing a *macro*sociology of social statics (and dynamics) because he is looking at the interrelationship among the parts and the whole of the social system. Indeed, Comte explicitly defined *sociology* as the macro-level study of "collective existence" (1891/1973:172).

The Individual in Comte's Theory

However, Comte's isolated thoughts on micro-level individuals are important not only for understanding his social statics but also for comprehending many other aspects of his work. For example, the individual is a major source of energy in his social system. It is the preponderance of affect or emotion in individuals that gives energy and direction to people's intellectual activities. It is the products of those intellectual activities that lead to changes in the larger social system.

More important for understanding his social statics, as well as his overall view of the world, is the fact that Comte sees the individual as imperfect, dominated by "lower" forms of egoism rather than "higher," more social forms of altruism. In fact, Comte sees this dominance of egoism as rooted in the brain, which is viewed as having both egoistic and altruistic regions. Egoism is seen as having higher energy, thereby helping to ensure the "natural feebleness" of altruism (Comte, 1852/1968:139). Putting egoism and altruism in slightly different terms, Comte argues: "Self-love . . . when left to itself is far stronger than Social Sympathy" (1851/1957:24–25). To Comte (1852/1968:122), the chief problem of human life is the need for altruism to dominate egoism. He sees all the social sciences as being concerned with this problem and with the development of various solutions to it.

Thus, left to themselves, people will, in Comte's view, act in a selfish manner. If we are to hope to be able to create a "better" world, the selfish motives of individuals must be controlled so that the altruistic impulses will emerge. Because egoism cannot be controlled from within the individual, the controls must come from outside the individual, from society. "The higher impulses within us are brought under the influence of a powerful stimulus from without. By its means they are enabled to control our discordant impulses" (Comte, 1851/1957:25–26). Thus Comte, like Durkheim (see Chapter 7), his successor within French sociology, saw people as a problem (egoism was a central concern to both) that could be handled only through external control over people's negative impulses. In terms almost identical to those later used by Durkheim, Comte argues that "true liberty is nothing else than a rational submission to the . . . laws of nature" (1830–42/1855:435). Without such external controls,

> our intellectual faculties, after wasting themselves in wild extravagancies, would sink rapidly into incurable sloth; our nobler feelings would be unable to prevent the ascendancy of the lower instincts; and our active powers would abandon themselves to purposeless agitation. . . . Our propensities are so heterogeneous and so deficient in elevation, that there would be no fixity or consistency in our conduct . . . without them [external restrictions] all its [reason's] deliberations would be confused and purposeless.
>
> (Comte, 1851/1957:29–30)

Thus Comte concludes: "This need of conforming our Acts and our Thoughts to a Necessity without us, far from hampering the real development of our nature, forms the first general condition of progress towards perfection in man" (1852/1968:26).

Not only does Comte have a highly negative view of people and their innate propensity to egoism, but he also has a very limited view of the creative capacities of individuals. "We are powerless to create: all that we can do in bettering our condition is to modify an order in which we can produce no radical change" (Comte, 1851/1957:30). Thus, Comte's actors are not only egoistic but also weak and powerless. In a very real sense, people do not create the social world; rather, the social world creates people, at least those animated by the nobler altruistic motives.

Comte addresses this issue in another way, in terms of the relationship between what he calls the "subjective" and "objective" principles. The subjective principle involves "the subordination of the intellect to the heart," whereas the objective principle entails "the immutable Necessity of the external world . . . actually existing without us"[3] (Comte, 1851/1957:26–27). Given the preceding discussion, it should be clear why Comte argues that the subjective principle must be subordinated to the objective principle. The "heart" (especially its egoism), which dominates the intellect, must be subordinated to external societal constraints so that another aspect of the "heart," altruism, can emerge triumphant.

Comte had other, more specific things to say about the individual. For example, he distinguished among four basic categories of instincts—nutrition, sex, destruction and construction, and pride and vanity (Comte, 1854/1968:249–252). Clearly, all but the constructive instinct are in need of external control. Although Comte does attribute other, more positive instincts to people (attachment to others, veneration of predecessors), it is the instincts in need of external control that define to a great degree his thoughts on the larger society. Larger social structures such as the family and society are needed to restrain individual egoism and to help bring forth individual altruism.

Collective Phenomena

In spite of his clear ideas on the individual, Comte's sociology overtly begins at a more macro level, with the family, which Comte labels the "fundamental institution." The family, *not* the individual, is the building block of Comte's sociology, as he explains: "As every system must be composed of elements of the same nature with itself, the scientific spirit forbids us to regard society as composed of individuals. The true social unit is certainly the family" (1830–42/1855:502). Comte clearly believes that individuals constitute a different "level" of analysis than families (and society), which are, after all, "nothing but our smallest society" (1852/1968:161). These "smaller societies" form the natural building blocks of the larger society. Methodologically, Comte argues that "a system can only be formed out of units similar to itself and differing only in magnitude" (1852/1968:153). Individuals constitute different (microscopic) units, and (macroscopic) society cannot be formed out of them. Families are similar, albeit smaller,

[3]It is the kind of viewpoint that leads us, once again, to think of Comte as a social realist; there is a real world out there.

macroscopic units, and therefore they *can* be the basis of the larger society. In fact, Comte traces a progression whereby out of families tribes emerge, and from tribes come nations. The family is the "true germ of the various characteristics of the social organism" (Comte, 1830–42/1855:502). The family not only is the building block of society but also serves to integrate the individual and society, because it is through the family that people learn to be social; the family is the "school" of society. Thus, it is the family that must play a crucial role in the control of egoistic impulses and the emergence of individual altruism. Furthermore, if we are ever to improve society significantly, a change in the family will be the fundamental basis of any such alteration. Because the family is such a pivotal institution, a change in it will have profound effects both on individuals and the larger society.

Although the family is the most basic and most pivotal institution, the most important institution to Comte is religion, "the universal basis of all society" (1852/1968:7). Doing a kind of structural-functional analysis, Comte identifies two major functions of religion. First, it serves to regulate individual life, once again primarily by subduing egoism and elevating altruism. Second, it has the more macroscopic function of fostering social relationships among people, thereby providing the basis for the emergence of large-scale social structures.

Another important social institution to Comte is language. Language is profoundly social; it is what allows people to interact with one another. Thus, language helps promote unity among people. It connects people not only with their contemporaries but also with their predecessors (we can read their ideas) and their successors (they can read our ideas). Language is also crucial to religion in that it permits the formation, transmission, and application of religious ideas.

Another element of society that serves to hold people together is the division of labor[4] (a view very much like that of Durkheim; see Chapter 7). Social solidarity is enhanced in a system in which individuals are dependent upon others. Society should have a division of labor so that people can occupy the positions for which they qualify on the basis of their abilities and training. Conversely, society should not force people into positions for which they are either underqualified or overqualified (Durkheim calls this the "forced division of labor"). Although Comte argues for the need for a division of labor, he is very concerned here, as he is elsewhere, about the dangers of excessive specialization in work in general and in intellectual work in particular. He worries about the tendency in society toward overspecialization and argues that the government should intervene to emphasize the good of the whole.

The government, in Comte's view, is based on force. Force can hold society together; however, if the use of force gets out of hand, the government will be more of a destructive than an integrative factor in society. To prevent this from occurring, the government needs to be regulated by a "broader and higher society. . . . This is the mission of true Religion" (Comte, 1852/1968:249). Comte clearly did not have a high regard for government, and he felt that religion was needed "to repress or to remedy the evils to which all governments are prone" (1852/1968:252).

---

[4]Or what Comte calls the "division of employments."

Social Dynamics

Comte does have other things to say about social statics, but he devoted more attention to social dynamics. He felt that less was known about social statics than about social dynamics. Furthermore, the topic of social dynamics was, in his opinion, more interesting and of far greater importance than social statics. However, one may question these contentions. How is it that Comte knew more about the history of the world than he did about the nature of his own society? Why is the past (and future) more interesting than the present? In response to these questions, and contrary to Comte, it can be clearly argued that we always know more about the present than the past (or certainly the future) and that the here and now is far more interesting and far more important than the past (or future). Nevertheless, it is on the basis of his beliefs on these issues that Comte abbreviates his discussion of social statics and moves on to the study of social dynamics.

The goal of Comte's social dynamics is to study the laws of succession of social phenomena. Society is always changing, but the change is ordered and subject to social laws. There is an evolutionary process in which society is progressing in a steady fashion to its final harmonious destiny under the laws of positivism: "We are always becoming more intelligent, more active, and more loving" (Comte, 1853/1968:60). Alternatively, Comte labels *social dynamics* the "theory of the Natural Progress of Human Society" (1830–42/1855:515). Overall, Comte sees us evolving toward our "noblest dispositions," toward the dominance of altruism over egoism. Comte also offers a somewhat more specific view of this future state toward which we are evolving:

> The individual life, ruled by personal instincts; the domestic, by sympathetic instincts; and the social, by the special development of intellectual influences, prepare for the states of human existence which are to follow: and that which ensues is, first, personal morality, which subjects the preservation of the individual to a wise discipline; next, domestic morality, which subordinates selfishness to sympathy; and lastly, social morality, which directs all individual tendencies by enlightened reason, always having the general economy in view, so as to bring into concurrence all the faculties of human nature, according to their appropriate laws.
>
> (Comte, 1830–42/1855:515)

In his view, society invariably follows this law of progressive development; only its speed from one time period or one society to another may vary.

Because invariant laws are controlling this process of change, there is relatively little that people can do to affect the overall direction of the process. Nevertheless, people can make a difference by acting "upon the intensity and secondary operation of phenomena, but without affecting their nature or their filiation" (Comte, 1830–42/1855:470). People can modify (for example, speed up) only what is in accord with existing tendencies; that is, people are able to bring about only things that would have happened in any event. It is the fact that people can affect the development of society, if only marginally, that led Comte to his ideas on changing society and his thoughts on the relationship between theory and practice. We will have much more to say about this issue later in this chapter. However, it should be pointed out here that the idea that people can have only a minimal impact did not prevent Comte from developing grandiose plans for the future, positivistic society.

Comte's theory of the evolution of society is based on his theory of the evolution of the mind through the three stages described previously. He contends that he himself has "tested" this law by means of all the major methods—observation, experiment, comparison, historical research—and found it "as fully demonstrated as any other law admitted into any other department of natural philosophy" (Comte, 1830–42/1855:522).

Having derived this social law theoretically (from the laws of human nature), he turns to a "study" of the history of the world to see whether the "data" support his abstract theory. However, Comte's use of the words *study* and *data* is misleading because his methods did not incorporate the criteria that we usually associate with a research study and the data derived from it. For one thing, if Comte's findings contradicted the basic laws of human nature, he would conclude that the research was wrong rather than question the theory (Mill, 1961:85). Comte did no systematic study of the history of the world (how could one systematically study such a vast body of material?), and he did not produce data about that history (he merely provided a series of broad generalizations about vast periods of history). In other words, Comte did not do a research study in the positivistic sense of the term. In fact, Comte acknowledges this by saying that all he is offering is an abstract history; science is not yet ready for a concrete history of the world.

As he had in other areas of his work, Comte offered a dialectical sense of the history of the world. What this meant, in particular, was that he saw the roots of each succeeding stage in history in its prior stage or stages. In addition, each stage prepared the ground for the next stage or stages. In other words, each stage in history is dialectically related to past and future stages. A similar viewpoint is offered by Marx (see Chapter 6), who sees capitalism as being dialectically related to previous economic systems (for example, feudalism) as well as to the future communist society. Although on this point, and on several others, Comte's ideas resemble those of Marx, the reader should bear in mind that the differences between the two thinkers far exceed their similarities. This difference will be clearest when we discuss Comte's conservative views about the future of the world, which are diametrically opposed to Marx's radical communist society.

Never humble, Comte *began* his analysis of social dynamics by asserting, "My principle of social development . . . affords a *perfect* interpretation of the past of human society—at least in its principal phases" (1830–42/1855:541; italics added). Similarly, at the close of the historical discussion briefly outlined next, Comte concluded, "The laws originally deduced from an abstract examination of human nature have been demonstrated to be real laws, *explaining the entire course of the destinies of the human race*" (1853/1968:535; italics added).

History

Comte limited his study to Western Europe (and the "white race") because it had evolved the most and because it was, in his view, the "elite" of humanity. We need not go into great detail here about his historical theory because it is of little lasting significance. Furthermore, because it is more central to Comte's underlying theory, we will focus on the changing nature of ideas rather than on more material transformations (for example, Comte sees society as evolving from the warfare characteristic of the theological stage to industry, which was to dominate the positivist stage). Comte begins with the theological stage, which he traces to antiquity. He divides the theological stage into three succeeding periods—fetishistic, polytheistic, and monotheistic. In the early fetishistic stage, people personify external objects (for example, a tree), give them lives like their own, and then deify those objects. Much later, polytheism in Egypt, Greece, and Rome developed. Finally, Comte analyzes the rise of monotheism, especially Roman Catholicism, in the Middle Ages. Although all of these are part of the theological stage, Comte is careful to show that they also possess the germs of the positivism that was to emerge at a much later point in history.

Comte sees the fourteenth century as a crucial turning point, as theology began a long period of enfeeblement and decline. More specifically, Catholicism was undermined and eventually replaced by Protestantism, which Comte sees as nothing more than a growing protest against the old social order's intellectual basis (theology). This, for Comte, represents the beginning of the negativity that he sought to counteract with his positivism, a negativity that did not begin to be systematized into a doctrine until the mid-seventeenth century. Protestantism laid the groundwork for this negativity by encouraging unlimited free inquiry. This change in ideas, the development of a negative philosophy, led to a corresponding negativity in the social world and to the social crisis that obsessed Comte. This negative doctrine was developed by French thinkers such as Voltaire (1649–1778) and Jean-Jacques Rousseau (1712–1778), whom Comte did not see as systematic thinkers; as a result, he believed they were incapable of producing coherent speculations. Nevertheless, these incoherent theories gained a following among the masses because they appeared at a time when theology was greatly weakened and positivism was not yet ready to take its place. Most generally, this entire period was the transitional period, the metaphysical stage, between theology and positivism.

Comte himself was writing during what he believed to be the close of the metaphysical stage: "We find ourselves therefore living at a period of confusion, without any general view of the past, or sound appreciation of the future, to enlighten us for the crisis prepared by the whole progress yet achieved" (Comte, 1830–42/1855:738–739). Negativity had far outstripped positivity, and there was, as yet, no available intellectual means to reorganize society. Everywhere Comte turned there was crisis—art was "adrift," science was suffering from overspecialization, and philosophy had fallen into "nothingness." Overall, Comte describes the situation as "the philosophical anarchy of our time" (1830–42/1855:738). This philosophical anarchy prepared the way for social revolution, especially the French Revolution, which while negative in many senses, was salutary in that it paved the way for the positivistic reorganization of society. As a social event it demonstrated "the powerlessness of critical principles to do anything but destroy" (Comte, 1830–42/1855:739).

Not only was France the site of the major political revolution, but it was to take the lead in the reorganization of Western Europe. It had the most advanced negative ideas and developments, *and* it had gone furthest in positive directions. In terms of the latter, its industrial activity was most "elevated," its art was most advanced, it was "foremost" in science, and it was closer to the new, positive philosophy (and, of course, his eminence, Auguste Comte, lived there). Although Comte saw signs during this period of the development of positivism, he recognized that in the short run, metaphysics (and the metaphysical stage) had won out. He described the effort in France to develop a constitutional government as being based on metaphysical principles, and he felt that at a philosophical level Rousseau's "retrograde" philosophy had won out. He felt that Rousseau sought to emulate older societies, in which people were freer and more natural, rather than provide a basis for modern society. This negative development held sway for half a century in France, but Comte also saw within it positive developments in industry, art, science, and philosophy.

Comte saw this period as dominated by a focus on the individual and the metaphysical notion of individual rights. Concern for the individual led only to disorder; in its place, Comte, as we have seen, urged a focus on collective phenomena like the family and society. In addition, a focus on individual rights furthered the tendency toward disorder and chaos; Comte sought a society based on what he viewed as the positive idea of *duties* rather than on individual rights. The idea of duties was seen as a positive notion both because it was more scientific (for example, more "precise") and because it had a "calming" influence on people's egoism as well as on the rampant negativity of the day. Instead of focusing on their individual rights, people were urged to concentrate on their duties to the larger society. This emphasis on duties would enable society to control individual egoism and to better bring out the altruism innate in people. These new duties were to help form the basis of a new spiritual authority that would help regenerate society and morality. This new spiritual authority was, of course, positivism.

Theory and Practice

The discussion of the previous section, in broad outline, is Comte's theory of social dynamics. Yet Comte (like Marx) wanted to do more than theorize. He wanted his theoretical ideas to lead to practical social changes; he explicitly and self-consciously sought the "connection between theory and practice" (Comte, 1851/1968:46). To this end, Comte sees two objectives for positivism. The first, covered in the preceding sections, is to generalize scientific conceptions—in other words, to advance the science of humanity. The second, covered in this section, is to systematize the art and practice of life (Comte, 1851/1957:3). Thus, positivism is *both* a scientific philosophy and a political practice; the two "can never be dissevered" (Comte, 1851/1968:1).

Who Will Support Positivism?

One of the first political questions addressed by Comte is: Which social groups are likely to support the new doctrine of positivism? It was assumed by Comte that many philosophers would be ardent supporters of this new set of ideas, but philosophers are limited in terms of their ability to implement their ideas. What of the groups of people who are more actively engaged in the social world?

Comte begins by excluding the upper classes because they are in the thrall of metaphysical theories, are too self-seeking, occupy positions too overly specialized to understand the total situation, are too aristocratic, are absorbed in fighting over remnants of the old system, and are blinded by their educational experiences. Comte also did not expect too much help from the middle classes because they are too busily involved in trying to move into the upper classes.

Comte did expect help from three groups: in addition to the philosophers, who would supply the intellect, the working class would bring the needed action, and women would provide the required feeling. The philosophers, especially those attracted to positivistic ideas, would be involved, but "it is among women, therefore, and among the working classes that the heartiest supporters of the new doctrine will be found" (Comte, 1851/1957:4). Both groups are generally excluded from government positions and thus will be more likely to see the need for political change. Furthermore, discrimination against them in the educational system is less likely to blind them to the need for such change. Comte also sees both women and the working class as possessing "strong social instincts" and "the largest stock of good sense and good feeling" (1851/1957:142).

The Working Class

In Comte's view, the members of the working class are better able to think during the workday because their jobs are not as fully absorbing as those of people in the higher social classes. Presumably this means that the working class has more time and energy to reflect on the benefits of positivism than do the upper classes. The working class is superior not only intellectually, at least in the preceding sense, but also morally. "The life of the workman . . . is far more favourable to the development of the nobler instincts" (1851/1957:144–145). More specifically, Comte attributes a long series of traits to members of the working class, including more affectionate ties at home; the "highest and most genuine types of friendship"; "sincere and simple respect for superiors"; experience with life's miseries, which stimulates them to nobler sympathies; and a greater likelihood of engaging in "prompt and unostentatious self-sacrifice at the call of a great public necessity" (Comte, 1851/1957:145–146).

Comte sees the spread of communism among the working classes in his day as evidence that the trend toward social revolution is focusing in on moral issues. But Comte reinterprets communism as a moral rather than an economic movement so that it fits into his scheme. To Comte, communism was "a simple assertion of the paramount importance of Social Feeling" (1851/1957:169). Clearly, this is a very different meaning of the term *communism* than the one used by Marx (see Chapter 6) and by most other thinkers who have employed the term.

Comte sees positivism as the "only doctrine which can preserve Western Europe from some serious attempt to bring Communism into practical operation" (1851/1957:170). Comte offers a number of contrasts between positivism and communism. First, positivism focuses on moral responses rather than on political responses and economic issues. (Here Comte clearly recognizes that communism, at least as it was being practiced in his time, was an economic and political, rather than a moral, system). Second, communism seeks to suppress individuality, whereas positivism seeks both individuality and cooperation among independent individuals. Third, communism seeks the elimination of the leaders of industry, whereas positivism sees them as essential. (Thus, while the leaders of industry cannot play a role in the positivist revolution, they do play, as we will see later, a central role, along with bankers, in Comte's vision of the revamped positivist society.) Fourth, communism seeks to eliminate inheritance, whereas positivism sees inheritance as important because it provides for historical continuity from generation to generation. In spite of his rejection of communism, Comte sees it as important as another, largely negative, force providing the groundwork for the emergence of positivism.

Women

Comte's interest in the working class as a revolutionary force is not unusual, but his attraction to women as such a group is. His major position was that women brought to politics the needed subordination of intellect to social feeling. And Comte came to believe that feeling was preeminent, far more important than intellect or action: feeling is "the predominating principle, the motive power of our being, the only basis on which the various parts of our natures can be brought into unity" (1851/1957:227). Women are "the best representatives of the fundamental principle on which Positivism rests, the victory of social over selfish affections" (Comte, 1851/1957:232). Nevertheless, in spite of his admiration for women, he clearly sees men as superior practically and intellectually. On the intellectual issue Comte contends, "Women's minds no doubt are less capable than ours of generalizing very widely, or of carrying on long processes of deduction . . . less capable than men of abstract intellectual exertion" (1851/1957:250). Because of their intellectual and practical superiority, it is men who are to take command in the actual implementation of positivism.

On the one hand, Comte clearly admired the moral and affectual aspects of women, and as a result, he was willing to accord them a key revolutionary role. On the other hand, he felt that men excelled in intellect and action, and he tended to demean the intellectual and active capacities of women. In terms of implementing their role in the positivist revolution, women were supposed to alter the educational process within the family and to form "salons" to disseminate positivistic ideas. In spite of his veneration of women, Comte did not believe in equality: "Equality in the position of the two sexes is contrary to their nature" (1851/1957:275). He defended this view on the basis of the fact that positivism has *discovered* the following "axiom": "Man should provide for Woman" (Comte, 1851/1957:276). More practically, positivism would institute a new doctrine: "Worship of Woman, publicly and privately" (Comte, 1851/1957:283).

Thoughts, Feelings, and Actions

Comte's focus on women, and his emphasis on their capacity for feeling, represented a general change in perspective from his earlier positions. As we have seen, Comte emphasized order in social statics and progress in social dynamics. To order and progress he now added the importance of feeling (love), which he associated with women. As a result he came to proclaim the "positivist motto, *Love, Order, Progress*" (Comte, 1851/1957:7). Positivism was no longer important just intellectually but morally as well. Similarly, Comte added the emotional element to his previous commitment to thought and action by arguing that positive philosophy represented a comprehensive perspective encompassing "Thoughts, Feelings, and Actions" (1851/1957:8).

Comte went further than simply according feeling equal status with thought and action; he gave feeling the preeminent place in his system. Feeling was to direct the intellect as well as practical activity. In particular, Comte argued that "individual happiness and public welfare are far more dependent upon the heart than upon the intellect"

(1851/1957:15). It is this kind of viewpoint that led the champion of positivist intellectual life to the anti-intellectualism that is one of the problems we will discuss later in this chapter.

The emphasis on feeling and love led Comte in his later work to add the science of morality (the study of sentiment) to his list of sciences. "Morals is the most *eminent* of the Sciences" (Comte, 1853/1968:41). Morality was a science, which in his system exceeded even sociology. "The field of Morals is at once more *special,* more *complex,* and more *noble* than that of Sociology" (Comte, 1853/1968:40). Not only was morality the most important science, but it was also crucial in giving direction to political changes. In Comte's terms, morality is "the ultimate object of all Philosophy, and the starting point of all Polity" (1851/1957:101). In other words, morality lies at the center of the relationship between theory and practice. Comte sees a natural morality in the world, and it is the task of the positivist to discover its laws. It is these underlying laws of morality that guide our intellectual thoughts and our political actions. Comte concludes, "It is henceforth a fundamental doctrine of Positivism, a doctrine of as great political as philosophical importance, that the Heart preponderates over the Intellect" (1851/1957:18).

Having added morality to the list of his major concerns, Comte returns to his Law of the Three Stages to look at each stage from the point of view of thoughts, feelings, and actions. He sees the theological stage as being dominated by feeling and imagination, with only slight restraint from reason. Theology operated on a purely subjective level, with the result that it was out of touch with the objectivity of practice in the real world. "Theology asserted all phenomena to be under the dominion of Wills more or less arbitrary," but in the real world people were, of course, led by "invariable laws" (Comte, 1851/1957:10). The transitional metaphysical stage continued to be dominated by feeling, was muddled in its thoughts, and was even less able to deal with the practical world. However, positivism finally offered the unity and harmony of thought, feeling, and action. The ideas of positivism are derived from the practical world and are certainly a monumental intellectual achievement. And positivism also came to comprehend the moral sphere. Only when positivism incorporates morality "can the claims of theology be finally set aside" (Comte, 1851/1957:13). Among other things, morality (feeling) is important for giving direction to thought and action. For example, without the direction of morality, positivism is prone to be too specialized and to deal with "useless or insolvable questions" (Comte, 1851/1957:21). Under the guidance of morality, positivism comes to focus on the broadest, most important, most pressing, and most solvable problems of the day.

With morality added to positivism, it is but a short step for Comte to declare positivism a religion: "Thus Positivism becomes, in the true sense of the word, a Religion; the only religion which is real and complete; destined therefore to replace all imperfect and provisional systems resting on the primitive basis of Theology" (1851/1957:365). And this means that Comte and his principal followers become priests of humanity, with far greater influence than any other previous priesthood. In fact, Comte, with customary humility, declared himself the "founder of the Religion of Humanity" (1853/1968:x). The object of worship in the new religion of positivism is not a god or gods but humanity, or what Comte later referred to as the "Great Being," that is, "the whole constituted by the beings [including animals], past, future, and present, which co-operate willingly in perfecting the order of the world" (1854/1968:27). The Great Being lies at the base of the positivist religion: "The Positive Religion inspires all the servants of the Great Being with a sacred zeal to represent that Being as fully as possible" (Comte, 1852/1968:65).

Comte: A Critical Assessment

From the previous discussion of a few of Comte's ideas about the future, the reader might conclude that Comte ought to be dismissed out of hand. In fact, it might even be asked again why a chapter on Comte is included in this book. Thus, we will begin this concluding section with an overview of Comte's most important contributions to sociology. Later we will turn to the far more numerous weaknesses in Comte's work—weaknesses that lead us to conclude that it is safe for the science of sociology to forget much of Comte's work and get on with its own development, which has forged far ahead of Comte's ideas.

Positive Contributions

First, of course, Comte was the first thinker to use the term *sociology;* he can be seen as the "founder" of sociology. Although it is certainly the case that thinkers throughout the course of human history have dealt with sociological issues, Comte was the first to make such a focus explicit and to give it a name.

Second, Comte defined *sociology* as a positivistic science. Although this is, as we will see later, a mixed blessing, the fact is that the majority of contemporary sociologists continue to see sociology as a positivistic science. They believe that there are invariant laws of the social world and that it is their task to discover those laws. Many search for such laws empirically, whereas others (for example, J. Turner, 1985a) follow Comte's model and go about the search for such laws theoretically. Much of contemporary empirical sociology, and a significant segment of sociological theory, continues to accept Comte's positivistic model of sociology.

Third, Comte articulated three major methods for sociology—observation, experiment, and comparison (the historical comparative method is sufficiently important to be distinguished as a fourth methodology)—which continue to be widely used in sociology. Although Comte's work is badly dated in most respects, it is surprisingly contemporary in terms of its methodological pronouncements. For example, there has been a substantial resurgence of interest in historical studies in contemporary sociology (see, for example, Mann, 1986; Wallerstein, 1989).

Fourth, Comte differentiated in sociology between social statics and social dynamics. This continues to be an important differentiation in sociology, but the concepts are now called *social structure* and *social change.* Sociologists continue to focus on society as it is presently constituted as well as on its changing nature.

Fifth, although again a mixed blessing, Comte defined *sociology* in macroscopic terms as the study of collective phenomena. This was to take clearer form in the work of Durkheim, who defined *sociology* as the study of social facts (see Chapter 7). More specifically, many of Comte's ideas played a key role in the development of a major contemporary sociological theory—structural functionalism (see Chapter 2).

Sixth, Comte stated clearly his basic ideas about the domination of human nature, if left on its own, by egoism. Because he is clear about such basic views, the reader gets a sound understanding of where Comte's thoughts on the larger structures of society come from. Basically, those larger structures are needed to control individual egoism and to permit the emergence of individual altruism.

Seventh, Comte offered a dialectical view of macro structures. He saw contemporary macro structures as being the product of past structures and as possessing the seeds of future structures. This view gave his work a strong sense of historical continuity. His dynamic, dialectical view of social structure is superior to positions taken by many later, even contemporary, theorists of social structure who have tended to adopt static, ahistorical perspectives.

Eighth, Comte was not content with simply developing abstract theory, but he was interested in integrating theory and practice. Although this ambition was marred by some of his ludicrous ideas for the future society, the integration of theory and practice remains a cherished objective among contemporary sociologists. In fact, there is a growing interest in what is now called *applied* sociology, and the American Sociological Association has a section on sociological practice.

Basic Weaknesses in Comte's Theory

We can begin the discussion of Comte's specific weaknesses with a quotation from one of his severest critics, Isaiah Berlin:

> His grotesque pedantry, the unreadable dullness of his writing, his vanity, his eccentricity, his solemnity, the pathos of his private life, his insane dogmatism, his authoritarianism, his philosophical fallacies . . . [his] obstinate craving for unity and symmetry at the expense of experience . . . with his fanatically tidy world of human beings joyfully engaged in fulfilling their functions, each within his own rigorously defined province, in the rationally ordered, totally unalterable hierarchy of the perfect society.
>
> (Berlin, 1954:4–5, 22)

One is hard-pressed to think of a more damning critique of any social theorist, yet much of it is warranted. The issue here is: Where and how did Comte go wrong in his social theorizing?

First, Comte's theory was overly influenced by the trials and tribulations of his own life. For one thing, very much ignored in his lifetime, Comte became increasingly grandiose in his theoretical and practical ambitions. For another, his largely unfulfilled relationships with women, especially his beloved Clotilde, led him to a series of outrageous ideas about women and their role in society. This problem was amplified by a sexism that led him to accord feelings to women, while men were given intellectual capacities and political and economic power. Then we must add the fact that Comte was deeply troubled psychologically; one often feels, especially in regard to the later works, that one is reading the rantings of a lunatic.

Second, Comte seemed to fall increasingly out of touch with the real world. After *Positive Philosophy,* his theories were characterized by a spinning out of the internal logic of his own ideas. One reason is that despite his claims, Comte actually did no real empirical research. His idea of doing empirical research was to offer gross generalities about the historical stages and the evolution of the world. Comte's looseness about data analysis is reflected in the following statement: "Verification of this theory may be found *more or less distinctly* in every period of history" (1851/1957:240; italics added). Had Comte been a better data analyst, and had he been more generally in touch with the historical and contemporary worlds, his theories might not have become so outrageous.

Third, Comte also grew progressively out of touch with the intellectual work of his time. Indeed, he is famous for practicing cerebral hygiene rather early in his life. He systematically avoided reading newspapers, periodicals, and books (except for a few favorite poems) and thereby sought to keep the ideas of others from interfering with his own theorizing. In effect, Comte was increasingly anti-intellectual. This ultimately became manifest in his substantive work, in which he urged such things as the abolition of the university and the withdrawal of economic support for science and scientific societies. It is also manifest in his positivist reading list of 100 books. Presumably, this limited list meant that all other books did not need to be read and could be safely burned. Comte's anti-intellectualism is also found in other aspects of his substantive work. For example, in making the case that strong affect helps lead to important scientific findings, Comte downgrades the importance of rigorous scientific work: "Doubtless, the method of pure science leads up to it also; but only by a long and toilsome process, which exhausts the power of thought, and leaves little energy for following out the new results to which this great principle gives rise" (1851/1957:243). The clear lesson of Comte's errors is that a theorist must remain in touch with *both* the empirical and the intellectual worlds.

Fourth, he failed as a positivist, both in his empirical and in his theoretical work. As to his empirical work, we have seen that he did woefully little of it and that the work he did was really little more than a series of gross generalizations about the course of world history. There was certainly little or no induction from data derived from the real world. Regarding his theoretical work, it is hard even to think of many of his bizarre generalizations about the social world as sociological laws. Even if we take Comte's word that these were, in fact, laws, it remains the case that few, if any, social thinkers have confirmed the existence of these invariant laws. Although Comte argued that his laws should be reflections of what actually transpired in the social world, the fact is that he most often seemed to impose his vision on the world.

Fifth, although Comte is credited with creating sociology, there is very little actual sociology in his work. His sketchy overviews of vast sweeps of history hardly qualify as historical sociology. His admittedly weak statements on a few elements of social statics contributed little or nothing to our understanding of social structure. Thus, little, if any, of Comte's substantive sociology survives to this day. John Stuart Mill was quite right when he argued, "Comte has not, in our opinion, created sociology . . . he has, for the first time, made the creation possible" (1961:123–124). Comte's lasting legacy is that he created some domains—sociology, positivist sociology, social statics, social dynamics—which his successors have filled in with some genuine substantive sociology.

Sixth, it can be argued that Comte really made no original contributions.[5] Mill clearly minimizes Comte's contribution in this domain: "The philosophy called

---

[5]Heilbron (1990:155) disagrees, arguing that Comte's original contribution lies in his *"historical and differential theory of science."* (This theory is discussed early in this chapter.)

Positive is not a recent invention of M. Comte, but a simple adherence to the traditions of all the great scientific minds whose discoveries have made the human race what it is" (1961:8–9; see also Heilbron, 1990). Mill also argues that Comte was well aware of his lack of originality: "M. Comte claims no originality for his conception of human knowledge" (1961:6). Comte readily acknowledged his debt to such renowned positivists as Bacon, Descartes, and Galileo. A similar point could be made about Comte's contribution to sociology. Comte clearly recognized important forerunners in sociology, such as Charles de Montesquieu (1689–1755) and Giovanni Vico (1668–1774). He may have invented the term *sociology,* but he certainly did not create the practice of sociology.

Seventh, whatever sociology Comte did have to offer was distorted by a primitive organicism (Levine, 1995b), in which he saw strong similarities between the workings of the human and the social body. For example, Comte argues that composite groups such as social classes and cities are "the counterpart of animal tissues and organs in the organisation of the Great Being" (1852/1968:153). Later, he contends that the family is the social counterpart of cells in an organism. Furthermore, Comte sees an analogy between social disorder and disease in organisms. Just as medicine deals with physical diseases, it "is left for Positivism to put an end to this long disease [social anarchy]" (Comte, 1852/1968:375). This kind of organicism has long been eliminated from sociology.

Eighth, Comte tended to develop theoretical ways of thinking and theoretical tools that he then imposed on whatever issue he happened to be analyzing. For example, Comte seemed to be fond of things that came in threes, and many of his theoretical ideas had three components. In terms of theoretical tools, he was not content to apply his Law of the Three Stages to social history; he also applied it to the history of sciences, the history of the mind, and the development of individuals from infancy through adulthood. A particularly bizarre example of this tendency to apply the Law of the Three Stages to anything and everything is Comte's application of it to his own mental illness:

> I will confine myself to recording here the valuable phenomena I was able to observe in the case of my own cerebral malady in 1826. . . . The complete course . . . enabled me to verify twice over my then recently discovered Law of the Three Stages; for while I passed through those stages, first *inversely,* then *directly,* the order of their succession never varied.
>
> During the three months in which the medical treatment aggravated my malady, I descended gradually from positivism to fetishism, halting first at monotheism, and then longer at polytheism. In the following five months . . . I reascended slowly from fetishism to polytheism, and from that to monotheism, whence I speedily returned to my previous positivism . . . thus furnishing me with a decisive confirmation of my fundamental Law of the Three Stages.
>
> (Comte, 1853/1968:62–63)

Ninth, Comte's "outrageous," "colossal" self-conceit (Mill, 1961) led him to make a series of ridiculous blunders. On the one hand, his never powerful theoretical system grew progressively weak as he increasingly subordinated the intellect to feeling. One manifestation of this is his unrealistic and highly romanticized view of the working class and women as agents of the positivist revolution. This decline in intellect is also manifest in his practice of cerebral hygiene as well as in his limiting of the number of positive books. On the other hand, and more important, his oversized ego led him to suggest a series of social changes, many of which, as we have seen, are ludicrous.

Tenth, Comte seemed to sacrifice much of what he stood for in his later turn toward positivist religion. In the framing of this religion, Comte seemed to be most influenced by the structure of Catholicism. In fact, T. H. Huxley called Comte's system "Catholicism minus Christianity" (cited in Standley, 1981:103). Comte acknowledged his debt to Catholicism when he argued that positivism is "more coherent, as well as more progressive, than the noble but premature attempt of medieval Catholicism" (1851/1957:3). His positivist religion mirrored Catholicism with its priests, vicars, and even its pontiff. Clearly, positivist religion has had no lasting impact, and it certainly served to subvert Comte's scientific pretensions.

Summary

This is not an unbiased presentation of Comte's ideas. It is clear that contemporary sociology has moved far beyond Comtian theory, and this chapter underscores that point. Although there are a number of useful derivatives from Comte's theory, the main point is that there are innumerable weaknesses in that theory. This chapter is concerned with the limited number of positive derivatives from Comte's theories and, more important, the negative lessons that can be of utility to the modern sociologist.

On the positive side, Comte offers us a positivist perspective, and many contemporary sociologists continue to accept the idea of the search for invariant social laws. Comte has also given us the term *sociology,* and his focus within that field on social statics and social dynamics remains a viable distinction. His basic methods of social research—observation, experimentation, comparison, and historical research—remain major methods of social research. Within his work on social statics, he made a number of contributions (a focus on structures, functions, equilibrium) that were important in the development of the contemporary theory of structural functionalism. Also within social statics, it is to Comte's credit that he laid out a detailed view of human nature on which he then erected his macrosociological theory. At the macro level, Comte offers a dialectical sense of structural relations, and his social realism anticipates that of Durkheim and many other later theorists. His work on social dynamics was relevant to later evolutionary theorists. Finally, Comte was not content simply to speculate, but he was interested in linking theory and practice.

Although these are important accomplishments, there are far more things to be critical of in Comte's work. He allowed his theoretical work to be distorted by his personal experiences. He lost touch with both the social and intellectual worlds. His empirical and theoretical work was lacking, given his own positivistic standard. There is really little substantive sociology in his work, and that which he offers is distorted by a primitive organicism. There is little in his work that was new at the time. Comte tended to impose his theoretical schemes on anything and everything, no matter how good the fit. His oversized ego led him to a number of outrageous theoretical blunders as well as many ludicrous suggestions for reforming the social world.

C H A P T E R 5

Herbert Spencer

Chapter Outline

Spencer and Comte
General Theoretical Principles
Sociology
The Evolution of Society
Ethics and Politics

In the theoretical ideas of Herbert Spencer (1820–1903) we see a considerable advance over those of Auguste Comte. Not only was Spencer's work important in the development of sociological theory, but many of his theoretical ideas stand up well from the vantage point of contemporary sociological theory. In spite of this, Jonathan Turner (1985b; see also, Francis, 2007), who is strongly in sympathy with many of Spencer's ideas, points out that modern sociological theorists have been disinclined to take Spencer seriously, relegating him, like Comte, to the "dustbin" of history. (Actually, in superheated terms, Turner argues that contemporary social theorists have been inclined to "spit on the grave of Spencer" [1985b:71].) This negativity is, to a large extent, traceable to Spencer's highly conservative libertarian (*not* liberal) politics and to his belief in a sociological version of survival of the fittest. Although we do not fully share Turner's enthusiasm for Spencer, there is much of merit in Spencer's work. It will be demonstrated that a number of Spencer's theoretical ideas continue to be important and relevant to sociological theory. However, there are also serious problems with Spencer's theory that lead to the conclusion that while it represents an advance over Comtian theory, it is not quite up to the standard of the other major early theorists—Marx, Durkheim, Weber, and Simmel—to be discussed in the ensuing four chapters.

Spencer and Comte

A useful starting point for this discussion is the relationship between Spencer's ideas and those of Auguste Comte. Although the lives of Spencer and Comte overlapped, the two men were separated by the English Channel (Spencer was British, and Comte was French) and there was a substantial difference in their ages (Comte was 22 years old when Spencer was born, and Spencer lived for forty-six years after Comte's death and into the twentieth century). Thus, Comte had completed most of his work before Spencer published his first book, *Social Statics,* in 1850. However, almost as soon as Spencer had published *Social Statics,* comparisons began to be made between his theories and those of Comte. A number of seeming similarities exist between the work of the two men, but Spencer most often felt the need to distinguish his theories from those of Comte.

Spencer commented on Comte's work in various places and even felt compelled to write an essay titled "Reasons for Dissenting from the Philosophy of M. Comte" (1864/1883/1968). Spencer began with great, if only obligatory, praise for Comte's work: "In working out this conception [of positivism] he has shown remarkable breadth of view, great originality, immense fertility of thought, unusual powers of generalization" (1864/1883/1968:118). In spite of such an encomium, Spencer was concerned mainly with positioning himself as one of Comte's "antagonists" and with distinguishing his own ideas from those of Comte because their work was "so utterly different in nature" (Spencer, 1904a:414).

Spencer did acknowledge his terminological debt to Comte by admitting, "I also adopt his word, Sociology" (1864/1883/1968:130). Both derived the terms *structure* and *function* largely from biology, and they tended to use them in similar ways. In utilizing these terms and the perspective they imply, both Spencer and Comte played key historic roles in the development of structural functionalism. However, regarding another set of terms, *social statics* and *social dynamics,* there are important differences between the two men. Although Spencer uses these terms, he denies that they are drawn from or resemble Comte's identical terms. In his autobiography, Spencer contends that when *Social Statics* (1850/1954) was published, he "knew nothing more of Auguste Comte, than that he was a French philosopher" (1904a:414). For Comte, these terms refer to all types of societies, whereas Spencer relates them specifically to his future ideal society. Spencer defines *social statics* as dealing with "the equilibrium of a perfect society" and *social dynamics* as relating to "the forces by which society is advanced toward perfection" (1850/1954:367). Thus, for Spencer the terms *social statics* and *social dynamics* are normative, and for Comte they are descriptive.

Spencer classifies himself, like Comte, as a positivist interested in the discovery of the invariant laws of the social world, but he hastens to add that positivism was not invented by Comte. Although Spencer sees himself as a positivist, he does not accept Comte's version of positivism, especially Comte's sense of a positivist religion. Spencer, like Comte, deals with a wide range of sciences, but unlike Comte, he argues that "the sciences cannot be rightly placed in any linear order whatever" (1883:185). Rather, Spencer views the sciences as being interconnected and interdependent. Another major distinction made by Spencer is between Comte's subjectivity (his concern with ideas) and Spencer's objectivity (his concern with things):

> What is Comte's professed aim? To give a coherent account of the progress of *human conceptions.* What is my aim? To give a coherent account of the progress of the *external world.* Comte proposes to describe the necessary, and the actual, filiation of *ideas.* I propose to describe the necessary, and actual, filiation of *things.* Comte professes to interpret the genesis of *our knowledge of nature.* My aim is to interpret,

Herbert Spencer

A Biographical Sketch

Herbert Spencer was born in Derby, England, on April 27, 1820. He was not schooled in the arts and humanities, but rather in technical and utilitarian matters. In 1837 he began work as a civil engineer for a railway, an occupation he held until 1846. During this period, Spencer continued to study on his own and began to publish scientific and political works (Haines, 2005).

In 1848 Spencer was appointed an editor of *The Economist,* and his intellectual ideas began to solidify. By 1850, he had completed his first major work, *Social Statics.* During the writing of this work, Spencer first began to experience insomnia, and over the years his mental and physical problems mounted. He was to suffer a series of nervous breakdowns throughout the rest of his life.

In 1853 Spencer received an inheritance that allowed him to quit his job and live for the rest of his life as a gentleman scholar. He never earned a university degree or held an academic position. As he grew more isolated, and physical and mental illness mounted, Spencer's productivity as a scholar increased. Eventually, Spencer began to achieve not only fame within England but also an international reputation. As Richard Hofstadter put it: "In the three decades after the Civil War it was impossible to be active in any field of intellectual work without mastering Spencer" (1959:33). Among his supporters was the important industrialist Andrew Carnegie, who wrote the following to Spencer during the latter's fatal illness of 1903:

> Dear Master Teacher . . . you come to me every day in thought, and the everlasting "why" intrudes—Why lies he? Why must he go? . . . The world jogs on unconscious of its greatest mind. . . . But it will wake some day to its teachings and decree Spencer's place is with the greatest.
>
> (Carnegie, cited in Peel, 1971:2)

> as far as it is possible, the genesis of the *phenomena which constitute nature.* The one end is *subjective,* the other is *objective.*
>
> (Spencer, 1904b:570)

Thus, although both Spencer and Comte were concerned with the evolution of the world, Comte was mainly interested in the evolution of ideas, whereas Spencer focused on structural (and functional) evolution.

Finally, there are powerful political differences between Spencer and Comte. As we saw in the previous chapter, Comte wanted to construct a society, even a world, dominated by a positivistic religion of humanity and led by the high priests of positivism. Spencer countered Comte's faith that "the 'Religion of Humanity' will be

But that was not to be Spencer's fate.

One of Spencer's most interesting characteristics, one that was ultimately to be the cause of his intellectual undoing, was his unwillingness to read the work of other people. In this, he resembled another early giant of sociology, Auguste Comte, who practiced "cerebral hygiene." Of the need to read the works of others, Spencer said: "All my life I have been a thinker and not a reader, being able to say with Hobbes that 'if I had read as much as other men I would have known as little'" (Wiltshire, 1978:67). A friend asked Spencer's opinion of a book, and "his reply was that on looking into the book he saw that its fundamental assumption was erroneous, and therefore did not care to read it" (Wiltshire, 1978:67). One author wrote of Spencer's "incomprehensible way of absorbing knowledge through the powers of his skin . . . he never seemed to read books" (Wiltshire, 1978:67).

If he didn't read the work of other scholars, where, then, did Spencer's ideas and insights come from? According to Spencer, they emerged involuntarily and intuitively from his mind. He said that his ideas emerged "little by little, in unobtrusive ways, without conscious intention or appreciable effort" (Wiltshire, 1978:66). Such intuition was deemed by Spencer to be far more effective than careful study and thought: "A solution reached in the way described is more likely to be true than one reached in the pursuance of a determined effort [which] causes perversion of thought" (Wiltshire, 1978:66).

Spencer suffered because of his unwillingness to read seriously the works of other people. In fact, if he read other work, it was often only to find confirmation for his own independently created ideas. He ignored those ideas that did not agree with his. Thus, his contemporary, Charles Darwin, said of Spencer: "If he had trained himself to observe more, even at the expense of . . . some loss of thinking power, he would have been a wonderful man" (Wiltshire, 1978:70). Spencer's disregard for the rules of scholarship led him to a series of outrageous ideas and unsubstantiated assertions about the evolution of the world. For these reasons, sociologists in the twentieth century came to reject Spencer's work and to substitute for it careful scholarship and empirical research.

Spencer died on December 8, 1903.

the religion of the future is a belief countenanced neither by induction nor by deduction" (1873/1961:283). In addition, Spencer had little regard for centralized control, which he felt would do far more harm than good. Thus, Spencer's ideal is a society in which the government is reduced to a minimum and individuals are allowed maximum freedom. We will return to Spencer's political ideas later in the chapter, but suffice it to say that they are radically different from Comte's politics. Spencer was led to muse on how "profoundly opposed" were Comte's and his "avowed or implied ideals of human life and human progress" (1904a:414).

Comte believed that individuals could be taught morality, largely through the positivist religion, but Spencer ridiculed the idea that morality could be taught in any fashion and by any means. Spencer believed that moral ideas emerge from individual action. In arriving at this conclusion, Spencer used here, as he did in many other places in his work, a survival-of-the-fittest perspective. In this specific case, the requirements of an orderly life will force people to act on the basis of their higher moral sentiments and repress their lower sentiments; in other words, people will be rewarded for moral behavior and penalized for immoral behavior. To put it another way, moral actions are likely to survive, whereas immoral actions are not. Spencer concludes that this "natural selection" of moral actions "alone is national education" (1873/1961:340).

In sum, although Spencer and Comte shared concerns with sociology, structures and functions, social statics and social dynamics, positivism, the relationships among the sciences, the evolution of the world, the future ideal society, and morality, there are profound differences in their views on most of these topics as well as in their overall theories. Given this relationship—or, more accurately, this lack of a strong relationship—we turn to a discussion of Spencer's sociological theory.

General Theoretical Principles

Spencer's thoughts on the social world are based on a series of general theoretical principles. He begins by arguing that in the early history of humankind religion and science were unified in their efforts to analyze and understand the world (Spencer, 1902/1958). Gradually, the two begin to separate, with religion coming to focus on the unknowable and science on that which can be known. However, this differentiation is far from complete, even in the modern era, so religion and science continue to overlap and to conflict. In fact, Spencer sees his own work as involving elements of science (intelligence) and religion (morals).

Spencer's main concern was with the knowable world and was therefore much more scientific than it was religious. (This is another contrast to Comte, whose later work became far more religious than scientific.) Science could never know the ultimate nature of things, but it could strive for the highest possible degree of knowledge. Before we can get to Spencer's thoughts on science, we first need to deal with his philosophy, which Spencer sees as transcending the sciences in the search for the complete unification of knowledge, for "truths which unify concrete phenomena belonging to all divisions of Nature" (1902/1958:277). In this section we will discuss Spencer's "general philosophy," in which he deals with "universal truths" for all the world, and later we will analyze his "special philosophies" and the narrower, but still universal, truths of specific areas, especially those relating to the *social* world. In emphasizing the overarching character of philosophy, Spencer rejects the positivistic idea that the goal of science is the reduction of an array of complex laws to a simple law and accepts, instead, the goal of knowledge integrated from a range of specific scientific fields.

Spencer articulates a series of general truths about the world, including the facts that matter is indestructible, that there is continuity of motion and persistence of force, that the relations among forces persist, and that matter and motion are continually redistributed. By a process of *deduction* from these general laws, Spencer articulates a series of ideas that constitute his general *evolutionary theory.*

Evolutionary Theory

Spencer believes that all inorganic, organic, and superorganic (societal) phenomena undergo evolution and devolution, or dissolution. That is, phenomena undergo a process of evolution whereby matter becomes integrated and motion tends to dissipate. Phenomena also undergo a process of devolution in which motion increases and matter moves toward disintegration. Having deduced these general principles of evolution and dissolution from his overarching principles, Spencer then turns to specific areas in order to show that his theory of evolution (and devolution) holds inductively, that is, that "all orders *do* exhibit a progressive integration of Matter and concomitant loss of Motion" (1902/1958:308).

The combination of induction and deduction leads Spencer to his "final" evolutionary formula:

> Evolution is an integration of matter and concomitant dissipation of motion; during which the matter passes from an indefinite, incoherent homogeneity to a definite, coherent, heterogeneity; and during which the retained motion undergoes a parallel transformation.
>
> (Spencer, 1902/1958:394)

Let us decompose this general perspective and examine each of the major elements of Spencer's evolutionary theory.

First, evolution involves progressive change from a less coherent to a more coherent form; in other words, it involves increasing *integration.* Second, accompanying increasing integration is the movement from homogeneity to more and more heterogeneity; in other words, evolution involves increasing *differentiation.* Third, there is a movement from confusion to order, from indeterminacy to determined order, "an increase in the distinctness with which these parts are marked off from one another" (Spencer, 1902/1958:361); in other words, evolution involves movement from the *indefinite to the definite.*

Thus, the three key elements of evolution are increasing integration, heterogeneity, and definiteness. More specifically, Spencer is concerned with these elements and his general theory of evolution as they apply to both *structures* and *functions.* At the most general level, Spencer associates structures with "matter" and sees them growing more integrated, heterogeneous, and definite. Functions are linked to "retained motion," and they, too, are seen as growing increasingly integrated, heterogeneous, and definite. We will have occasion to deal with Spencer's more concrete thoughts on the evolution of functions and structures in his work on society.

Having outlined his general theory of evolution, Spencer turns to the issue of the reasons for the occurrence of evolution. First, Spencer argues that homogeneous phenomena are inherently unstable: "the absolutely homogeneous must lose its equilibrium; and the relatively homogeneous must lapse into the relatively less homogeneous" (1902/1958:426). One reason for this instability is that the different parts of a homogeneous system are constantly subjected to different forces, which tend to differentiate them from one another. Changes in one part of the once homogeneous system will inevitably result in changes in other parts, leading, in turn, to greater multiformity. A second factor in sequence, but not in importance, is the multiplication of effects.

In Spencer's view, the multiplication of effects proceeds in a geometric manner. In other words, a small change in a once homogeneous system has increasingly ramifying effects. Thus, over time, the once homogeneous system grows increasingly heterogeneous. Third, Spencer discusses the effects of segregation on evolution. A sector becomes segregated from the others because of a likeness among its components, which are different from the components of other sectors. This segregation serves to maintain differences among the sectors, and this, in turn, furthers the multiplication of effects when one sector is exposed to and incorporates the distinguishing characteristics of other sectors.

Given that evolution is an inevitable process, the issue becomes: Where is evolution headed? While en route to their end state, phenomena move through a series of transitional states that can be described as "moving equilibria," and the end state of the process is a new equilibrium. It could be argued that we are moving to "a state of quiescence," and it could then be asked: "Are we not manifestly progressing toward omnipresent death" through the dissipation of moving forces (Spencer, 1902/1958:508)? Spencer responds negatively to this question, arguing that we are moving toward universal life through new stages in the evolutionary process. He does, however, posit an end state of the evolutionary process: "Evolution can end only in the establishment of the greatest perfection and the most complete happiness" (Spencer, 1902/1958:511). Spencer obviously has great faith in the evolutionary process, and its ultimate state of perfection gives him a standard by which he can assess all other steps in the evolutionary process.

In spite of his faith in evolution, Spencer recognizes, in a dialectical fashion, that the process of dissolution complements the evolutionary process and periodically leads to its undoing. The dissolution process is likely to occur when evolution has ended and the evolved phenomenon has begun to decay.

Evolution constitutes the focus of Spencer's work in a variety of realms, but our concern is with the evolution of human societies in terms of their growth and with the evolution of structures and functions. Following Spencer's approach, we will look at the evolution of society in general. Spencer's rationale for devoting so much attention to the evolution of society (and its institutions) is his view that a fully adequate understanding of human social relations requires an understanding of their evolution (as well as their cycles and dissolution).

Sociology

Defining the Science of Sociology

Given Spencer's focus on evolution, he defines "the study of Sociology as the study of Evolution in its most complex form" (1873/1961:350). To put it another way, sociology is "the natural history of societies" or, more specifically, "an order among those structural and functional changes which societies pass through" (Spencer, 1873/1961:63–64). However, Spencer does not restrict sociology to historical societies but also accepts the study of the ways in which *contemporary* organizations and institutions "are severally related to other phenomena of their respective times—the political institutions, the class-distinctions, the family arrangements, the modes of distribution and degrees of intercourse between localities, the amounts of knowledge, the religious beliefs, the morals, the sentiments, the customs, the ideas" (1873/1961:120). But while Spencer sanctions the need for contemporaneous research, he feels that the true meaning of his work is found only when it is placed in a historical, evolutionary context. However, whether sociological research focuses on historical or contemporary issues, it is clear that Spencer's sociology concentrates largely on macro-level social phenomena (social aggregates)—societies, social structures, social institutions—as well as the functions of each.[1]

Spencer (1873/1961:115) shares with Comte the view that sociology should deal with social questions in the same scientific manner in which we address issues in the natural sciences. Furthermore, Spencer, like Comte, sees sociology, especially in its evolutionary concerns, as the most complex of sciences.

Although Spencer sees sociology as a (complex) science, he recognizes that it is not an exact science, but he rhetorically wonders, how many sciences are exact sciences? To be a science, in Spencer's view, a field of study need only consist of generalizations (laws) and interpretations based on those generalizations. Sociology seeks laws of social phenomena in the same way that the natural sciences seek the laws of natural phenomena. "Either society has laws or it has not. If it has not, there can be no order, no certainty, no system in its phenomena. If it has, then are they like the other laws of the universe—sure, inflexible, ever active, and having no exceptions?" (Spencer, 1850/1954:40). Although sociology and other sciences seek to make predictions about the future on the basis of laws, in most cases all sciences must be satisfied with only the most general predictions.

Legitimizing Sociology

In endeavoring to lay the groundwork for his kind of scientific sociology, Spencer confronted the problem that many other early sociologists faced—the need to legitimize the field. For example, he felt compelled to argue that laypeople lack the capacity to grasp the complex issues of concern to sociologists: one needs to be a trained sociologist in order to comprehend them. Because in their everyday lives they deal with the same issues that are of concern to sociologists, laypeople in Spencer's day, and to this day as well, are convinced, erroneously, that they can do as good a job of social analysis as trained sociologists can. Spencer also confronted the misplaced confidence of laypeople in their views and their hostility to sociologists by arguing that the incapacity of the layperson "is accompanied by extreme confidence of judgment on sociological questions, and a ridicule of those who, after long discipline, begin to perceive what there is to be understood, and how difficult is the right understanding of it" (1873/1961:115). As a result of these lay attitudes, Spencer saw many barriers to sociology's receiving the recognition it deserves. These include the fact that few laypeople will be able to grasp the complexity of sociology's subject matter, an unconsciousness on the part of laypeople

---

[1]In his work, though, Spencer does offer some insightful micro accounts, especially of rituals in his discussion of ceremonies (see pages 133–134).

that there are any such complex phenomena, the misplaced confidence of laypeople, and the fact that the minds of most laypeople are not adaptable and flexible enough to accept the new perspective offered by sociology.

Spencer felt that sociologists, in contrast to laypeople, require disciplined habits of thought and that those habits are to be derived from a careful study of other sciences. This need to study other sciences is buttressed by an argument similar to one made by Comte, that is, that the science of sociology encompasses the phenomena of concern in all other sciences. Spencer gave particular importance to the need for sociologists to be familiar with the fields of biology and psychology.

Sociology and Biology

Spencer saw three basic linkages between biology and sociology. First, he believed that all social actions are determined by the actions of individuals and that those actions conform to the basic laws of life in general. Thus, to understand social actions, the sociologist must know the basic laws of life, and it is biology that helps us comprehend those laws. Second, there are powerful analogies between sociology and biology. That is, society as a whole, like the living body, is characterized by, among other things, growth, structure, and function. Thus, an understanding of the biology of the living organism, which after all is far easier to study than the social organism, offers many keys to understanding society. Spencer concludes, "There can be no rational apprehension of the truths of Sociology until there has been reached a rational apprehension of the truths of Biology" (1873/1961:305). Third, a kind of natural progression and linkage exist between the two fields because humans are the "terminal" problem for biology and the starting point for sociology.

A more specific similarity between biology and sociology is the operation of the survival-of-the-fittest process in both living and social organisms. Spencer felt that survival of the fittest occurs in both the biological and the social realms and that the lessons of biology from the natural world are that there should be no interference with this process in the social world.

Sociology and Psychology

Spencer also devoted considerable attention to psychology as another major base for sociology. He adopted the general position that "psychological truths underlie sociological truths" (Spencer, 1873/1961:348). As he saw it, psychology is the study of intelligence, feeling, and action. He believed that one of the great lessons of psychology is that feeling, *not* intelligence, is linked to action. This belief led Spencer to emphasize sentiments and to downgrade the importance of intelligence and cognition in his sociological analyses (see the preceding chapter, on Comte, for a similar view). Although people throughout history have been dominated by sentiments and desires, this was especially true in primitive societies. Primitive people were inherently impulsive, and because they were "not much habituated to associated life," they were "habituated to that uncontrolled following of immediate desires" (Spencer, 1908a:64). In contrast, people in the modern world, although still dominated by feelings, emotions, and desires, are better able to control them because they are more habituated to collective life. Thus, Spencer is led to argue that primitive people are characterized by greater selfishness and that there is more altruism in the modern world. This general orientation leads Spencer to focus substantively on collective phenomena, and politically this emphasis on the importance of feelings is one of the factors causing him to oppose conscious and intelligent change of society.

Although Spencer embeds his sociology in a set of assumptions about the psychological characteristics of individuals, he does *not* accept the idea that these characteristics are fixed. Rather, psychological characteristics change with the changes in society as well as with those in the larger environment.

From his study of psychology, and more generally from his basic philosophical orientation, Spencer comes to the "methodological individualist" conclusion that the units of society are individuals and that individuals are the source of social phenomena. Everything in society is derived from the motives of individuals, the combined similar motives of many individuals, or the conflict between those with one set of motives and others with another set. However, Spencer bases his sociology on such psychological principles, but he does not spend much time analyzing the ways in which these psychological phenomena lead to the development of society and its various institutions. Rather, Spencer assumes that individuals are the units, and the base, of society and institutions, and then he proceeds to the macro level to study the evolution of society and its institutions. This lack of concern (with a few exceptions; see the discussion of ceremonial institutions later in this chapter) for how macro-level phenomena (society and institutions) emerge from micro-level units (individuals and their motives) is a serious weakness in Spencer's sociological theory.

Sociological Methods

Within the context of Spencer's definition of sociology as a science, he addressed a range of methodological problems.

Difficulties Facing Sociology

Spencer attempts to show "how greatly the advance of Sociology is hindered by the nature of its subject-matter" (1873/1961:66). He believes that sociology confronts several difficulties that differentiate it from natural sciences. To begin with, there are objective difficulties that involve the intrinsic nature of the facts that sociologists must analyze. For example, social phenomena are not directly perceptible. Unlike natural phenomena, they cannot be studied and measured with such instruments as clocks, thermometers, scales, and microscopes. (Of course, modern sociology has demonstrated that at least some social phenomena *can* be studied and measured with instruments [for example, audiotapes and videotapes].) Another methodological difficulty for sociologists, in Spencer's view, is that they, unlike psychologists, cannot utilize introspection as a method; social facts cannot be studied through introspection, but psychological facts can. (Again, at least some modern sociologists [for example, phenomenologists] do use introspection as a method.)

The facts of concern to sociologists not only are different from those found in the natural sciences and psychology but also are far more complex and difficult to study. Sociologists inevitably deal with an enormous range of highly dispersed details. It is often difficult to gain a sense of what is happening, because things occur over a wide geographic area and over long periods of time. Thus, for example, Spencer contends that the increasing division of labor is very difficult to study and was under way for quite some time before its development was recognized.

Another objective difficulty facing sociology is the untrustworthiness of its data, derived from *both* past and present societies. For one thing, the data are often distorted by the subjective states of the witnesses to the events under study, but sociologists must rely on the reports of such witnesses for their data. For another, the sociological observer is often misled by superficial and trivial facts and fails to see what is truly important. Spencer offers a number of cautions to sociologists: "In every case we have to beware of the many modes in which evidence may be vitiated—have to estimate its worth when it has been discounted in various ways; and have to take care that our conclusions do not depend on any particular class of facts gathered from any particular place or time" (1873/1961:102). Spencer recognizes that the objective difficulties are formidable, but he still believes that sociology can deal scientifically with general classes of facts, although not with specific facts.

Sociologists must also confront the reality that they are the human observers of humanly created phenomena. As human beings, sociologists use modes of observation and reasoning in their daily lives, and such habits may not be useful in, or may even be impediments to, sociological study. Sociologists must be wary of assessing others on the basis of their own standards. They are likely to experience difficulties in their own society, and those difficulties are greatly magnified when sociologists examine other societies.

Biases Sociologists also have a very different relationship to the facts they observe than do natural scientists. Sociologists' emotions may affect their judgments of social phenomena or lead them to make judgments without sufficient evidence. Spencer argues that "minds thus swayed by disproportionate hates and admirations, cannot frame those balanced conclusions respecting social phenomena which alone constitute Social Science" (1873/1961:144). In this context, Spencer deals with a number of specific emotional biases such as those stemming from social class, politics, and religion.

Spencer's Approach

In seeking to exclude these and other biases from sociological research, Spencer is articulating a "value-free" position for the discipline (see Chapter 8, on Weber, for a more complex view of this issue). He argues, for example, that

> in pursuing our sociological inquiries . . . we must, as much as possible, exclude whatever emotions the facts are calculated to excite . . . trustworthy interpretations of social arrangements imply an almost passionless consciousness. Though feeling cannot and ought not to be excluded from the mind when otherwise contemplating them, yet it ought to be excluded when contemplating them as natural phenomena to be understood in their causes and effects.
>
> (Spencer, 1908b:230, 232)

In his own work, Spencer employed what has come to be called the *comparative-historical* method. That is, he engaged mainly in the comparative study of the different stages of societies over time as well as of various kinds of contemporary societies. His goal in this research was always to seek out, inductively, support (or, presumably, lack of support) for the theories derived deductively from his most general orientation. He was also interested in developing empirical generalizations based on his comparative, especially evolutionary, studies.

We must not close this section without mentioning the fifteen volumes of data on various societies (for example, ancient Mexicans, ancient Romans) commissioned by Spencer but put together by others in accord with a category system developed by Spencer (J. Turner, 1985b:95–104). Although these volumes have been little read or used by sociologists, and although they are almost impossible to find today, they reflect Spencer's commitment to empirical research of the comparative-historical variety in order to create a base whereby he and others could inductively support, or fail to support, theories derived deductively.

The Evolution of Society

Spencer employs his evolutionary theory in his massive three-volume work, *The Principles of Sociology* (1908a, 1908b, 1908c). (Much of this work had been published in serial form in magazines in the late 1800s.) In his more specific focus on the evolution of society and its major institutions, Spencer employs the three general dimensions outlined earlier—increasing *integration* (increasing size and coalescence of masses of people), *heterogeneity,* and *definiteness* (clearly demarcated social institutions). In addition, he employs a fourth dimension, the *increasing coherence* of social groups (modern civilized nations hold together far longer than early wandering groups of people). Thus, he offers the following statement as his general formula of social evolution: "There is progress toward greater size, coherence, multiformity and definiteness" (Spencer, 1908a:597).

Before we go any further, it is important to make clear that in spite of appearances, Spencer does *not* adopt an inevitable, unilinear view of social evolution. That is, evolution does not have to occur, and it does *not* always move in a single direction. Societies are constantly changing in light of changes in their environs, but these changes are not necessarily evolutionary. "Only now and then does the environing change initiate in the organism a new complication, and so produce a somewhat higher structure" (Spencer, 1908a:95–96). It is possible at any given moment for there to be no change, dissolution, *or* evolution. Not only is evolution not inevitable, but when it does occur, it does not take the form of a simple unilinear pattern; the stages do not necessarily occur in serial order (Haines, 1997).

Before getting to the actual evolution of society, we need a definition of *society.* Spencer discusses the issue of *nominalism* (society is nothing more than its component parts) versus *realism* (society is a distinct and separable entity) and comes down on the side of realism because of the "permanence of the relations among component parts which constitutes the individuality of a whole" (1908a:447). "Thus we consistently regard society as an entity, because, though formed of discrete units, a certain concreteness in the aggregate of them is implied by the general persistence of the arrangements among them throughout the area occupied" (Spencer, 1908a:448). Thus, Spencer considers society a "thing," but it is unlike any other thing except for parallel principles in the way the component parts are arranged.

It should be pointed out here that there is an uncomfortable fit between Spencer's social realism and his previously discussed methodological individualism. Methodological individualism generally leads to, and is more comfortable with, a nominalist position on society. Conversely, methodological individualism generally rules out a realist orientation to society. Spencer holds to both without telling us much about how he is able to adopt two such discordant perspectives or how they are linked to one another. In other words, how do individuals create a "real" society? Spencer begins with assumptions about individuals, imposes the existence of society, and then ends (as we will see later) with a series of concerns about the negative impact of society on individuals.

Spencer sees societies as being like organic bodies (but unlike inorganic bodies) in that they are characterized by permanent relations among the component parts (Levine, 1995b). Spencer's *organicism* led him to see a number of parallelisms between society and organic entities. Among other similarities, both entities increase in size and are subject to structural and functional differentiation. Furthermore, both are characterized by an increasing division of labor, the development of interrelated differentiations that make still other differentiations possible. The component parts of both society and an organism are interconnected and in need of each other. In addition, if the whole of society or an organism dies, parts can live on; conversely, the whole can live on even if parts die (for example, society continues even after individuals die).

One issue here is whether Spencer believed that society is an organism or that there are simply important analogies between the two. Although at times Spencer discussed society as an organism, his avowed position was that there are merely important parallels between the two and that one could improve one's understanding of society by better understanding the parallelisms.

In a more concrete sense, Spencer (1908b) sees society as a gathering of people forming a group in which there is cooperation to seek common ends. Cooperation in society implies some form of organization. In Spencer's view, there are two basic types of cooperation. The first is the division of labor, which is a spontaneously and unconsciously developed system that directly serves the interests of individuals and indirectly serves the interests of society. Here we have a situation in which individuals consciously pursue their private ends, and the unconsciously evolving organization is *not* coercive. The second cooperative system is the one for defense and government, that is, the political organization, which is a consciously and purposefully created system that directly serves the interests of society and indirectly those of the individual. The political system involves the conscious pursuit of public ends, and this consciously evolving organization is coercive in regard to individuals.

The first element in Spencer's work on the evolution of society is society's growth in size. In his view, societies, similar to living organisms, "begin as germs" (Spencer, 1908a:463). "Superorganic" (social) phenomena, like organisms, grow through both the multiplication of individuals and the union ("compounding") of groups (for example, tribes), both of which may go on simultaneously.

The increase in the size of society is accompanied by an increase in *structure*. Spencer defines a *structure* as "an organization" (1908c:3). Greater size requires more differentiation, a greater unlikeness of parts. In fact, Spencer argues that "to reach great size [society] must acquire great complexity" (1908a:471). More generally, he contends that "all social structures result from specializations of a relatively homogeneous mass" (Spencer, 1908c:181). The first differentiation is the emergence of one or more people claiming and/or exercising authority. This is followed soon after by the division between the *regulative* and the *sustaining* structures of society. We will have more to say about these structures later, but at this early stage the regulative structure is associated with military activities, whereas economic activities that maintain the group are linked to the sustaining structures. At first, this differentiation is closely linked to the division of labor among the sexes, with men handling the regulative structure (the military) and women the sustaining structures. As society evolves, each of these structures undergoes further differentiation; for example, the regulative agency acquires a system of kings, local rulers, petty chiefs, and so on. Then there are differentiations of social classes as the military, the priestly, and the slave classes emerge. Further differentiations occur *within* each social class; in the priestly class, for example, sorcerers, priests, diviners, and exorcists develop. Overall, society moves toward increasing structural differentiation and complexity.

The increasing differentiation of structures is accompanied by increasingly differentiated functions. A *function* is "the need subserved" by a structure (Spencer, 1908c:3). Spencer argues that "changes of structures cannot occur without changes of functions" (1908a:485). More generally, he contends that one cannot truly understand structures without a clear conception of their functions, or the needs served by the structures. In a relatively undifferentiated state, the various parts of society can perform each other's functions. Thus, in a primitive society the male warriors could raise food and the females could fight if it became necessary. However, as society grows increasingly complex structurally, it is more and more difficult for highly specialized parts to perform each other's functions. Evolution brings functional progress along with structural progress: "With advance of organization, every part, more limited in its office, performs its office [that is, function] better; the means of exchanging benefits becomes greater; each aids all, and all aid each with increasing efficiency; and the total activity we call life, individual or national, augments" (Spencer, 1908a:489).

Having argued that societies evolve both structurally and functionally, Spencer returns to the sustaining and regulative systems mentioned previously and adds a third, the *distributing* system. In the discussion of these three systems, Spencer makes great use of analogies between social systems and organisms. In both social systems and organisms the sustaining system is concerned with the *internal* matters needed to keep them alive. In the living body the sustaining system takes the form of the alimentary organs, whereas in the social system it adopts the form of the various elements of the industrial system. *External* matters for both social systems and organisms are handled by the regulative system. The regulative system takes the form of the neuromuscular system in organisms and the government-military apparatus in social systems. Both are concerned with warfare with other systems and conflicts with the environment. Finally, the distributive system links the sustaining and regulative organs and systems. Here Spencer sees an analogy between blood vessels (in organisms) and roads (in social systems), "channels which carry, in the one case blood-corpuscles and serum, and in the other case men and commodities" (1908a:510). In addition to describing each of these structures and the functions they perform, Spencer also demonstrates how each is undergoing a process of evolution.

Simple and Compounded Societies

On the basis of what he claims are inductions from the evolution of past and present societies, Spencer develops two systems for classifying societies. The first, or primary, method is based on the increasing number of members of the aggregate as well as the degree to which that aggregate is *compounded,* or added to, by combining with other aggregates through such means as conquest or peaceful merger. Although, as we saw earlier, Spencer has argued in general against a simple unilinear theory of evolution, the latter is just what he seems to offer here: "The stages of compounding and recompounding *have to be passed through in succession.* No tribe becomes a nation by simple growth; and no great society is formed by the direct union of the smallest societies" (1908a:555; italics added).

Spencer identifies four types of societies on the basis of their degree of compounding. First, there are *simple* societies, which constitute single working entities that are not connected with any other entities. These are relatively homogeneous and uncivilized societies that have not gone through a compounding process. Second, we find *compound* societies, in which there is some increase in heterogeneity. For example, here we may find the emergence of a supreme chief who rules over the chiefs of several simple groups. Obviously, because there are now several groups, some compounding has occurred either by conquest or by peaceful means. We also find in compound societies, as a result of increasing heterogeneity, an increase in the division of economic labor and in organization. Third, there are *doubly-compound* societies, formed on the basis of the recompounding of compound groups. Here we find still more heterogeneity and further advances in civilization. Thus, in the political realm we find even more developed and stable governments. Spencer describes many other advances in these societies, such as the development of an ecclesiastical hierarchy, a more complex division of economic labor, law emerging from custom, more towns and roads, and more advanced knowledge and arts. Finally, there are the *trebly-compound* societies, or the great nations of the world, which are even more advanced in the areas just mentioned, as well as in many others. Included in this category are both older societies, like the Roman Empire, and modern nations.

Militant and Industrial Societies

Spencer offers a secondary system of classifying societies, although this one became better known than his primary system of classifying societies by their degree of compounding. This is his famous distinction between *militant* and *industrial* societies and the character of societies as they oscillate between the two. Militant societies tend to be dominated by the regulative system, whereas industrial societies are characterized by their more highly developed sustaining systems. These are ideal types, as Spencer recognizes: "During social evolution there has habitually been a mingling of the two"

(1908b:568). Spencer sees a long-term evolutionary trend from militant to industrial societies, although here he is more careful to be clear that this trend is *not* unilinear. Spencer also briefly mentions the possibility of a future, "higher" type of society characterized by intellectual and esthetic concerns (Perrin, 1976), but he has little to say of a substantive nature about the possibility of this third type of society.

Spencer goes into much more detail about militant societies than about industrial societies, and what he says about them is much clearer, because militant societies had long been in existence, whereas industrial societies were still emerging in his day.

Militant societies are characterized by highly structured organizations for offensive and defensive warfare. In effect, the army and the nation are one: "The army is the nation mobilized while the nation is the quiescent army, and which, therefore, acquires a structure common to army and nation" (Spencer, 1908a:557). The militant society is dominated by its regulative system, with centralized and despotic government control, unlimited political control over personal conduct, and a rigidly controlled, disciplined, and regimented population. The cooperation that exists in society is a result of compulsion. The individual exists for the good of the collectivity: "Under the militant type the individual is owned by the state. While preservation of the society is the primary end, preservation of each member is a secondary end" (Spencer, 1908b:572). There is a rigid status hierarchy, and individual positions are fixed as to rank, occupation, and locality. Industry, such as it is, exists largely to fill the needs of the government-military.

Although he is critical of warfare, and he hopes for a future society in which warfare is reduced or eliminated, Spencer believes that war is useful in militant societies in producing social aggregation (by, for example, military conquest). It is also useful in laying the groundwork for industrial society: "Without war large aggregates of men cannot be formed, and . . . without large aggregates of men there cannot be a developed industrial state" (Spencer, 1873/1961:176). This attitude toward warfare is also linked to Spencer's views on survival of the fittest: "We must recognize the truth that the struggles for existence between societies have been instrumental to their evolution" (1908b:241). However, with the development of industrial society, war becomes more dysfunctional than functional, as it serves to block industrial growth, consumes needed people and materials, draws off intellectual resources, and fosters antisocial attitudes and behaviors in a society that values harmony.

As is his normal pattern, Spencer arrives at the characteristics of the militant society deductively and then demonstrates that they are supported by induction from actual militant societies. However, he is forced to deviate from his usual pattern in the case of industrial societies because their characteristics are not fully emergent and continue to be hidden by the militant characteristics of society. Therefore, in his depiction of industrial societies, Spencer is forced to rely even more heavily on the deductive method, although he does find some support in data derived from societies with industrial characteristics.

The industrial society is dominated by the sustaining system, and its industrial system is more developed and diverse. The regulative control that continues to exist tends to be negative (people shall *not* do certain things) rather than positive (people must do certain things). There is no need for despotic control, and the government tends to be democratic, with representatives of the people exercising power. The control that remains tends to be much more decentralized. There is voluntary cooperation among people, and the collectivity exists to serve the welfare of the people. Individuality is protected and permitted to flourish. The military system is subordinated to the needs of the industrial system. Control is exercised by contracts voluntarily entered into by individuals. Harmony, rather than conflict and warfare, characterizes industrial societies. Although militant societies are forced to be economically autonomous because of the hostility from and toward their neighbors, industrial societies are much more interdependent economically. Whereas militant societies tend to be rather inflexible, industrial societies are much more changeable and adaptable.

Of course, these societies are ideal types that vary greatly from one setting to another. Spencer made clear the ideal-typical character of his depiction of a militant society: "Having contemplated the society *ideally* organized for war, we shall be prepared to recognize in real societies the characteristics which war has brought about" (1908b:569; italics added). Spencer details a number of factors that contribute to variation within each of these types, including racial composition, the nature of the immediately preceding society, the habitat, and surrounding societies. Spencer also discusses "hybrid societies," which are only partially militant or industrial, although he contends that hybrid societies are likely to be more like militant societies than industrial societies. In fact, he describes the society in which he lived as such a transitional hybrid—semi-militant and semi-industrial (Spencer, 1908c:551). Finally, although there is a general evolutionary trend toward industrial societies, Spencer recognizes that regression to more militant societies is possible. For example, an international conflict can cause an industrial society to grow more militant, engaging in more aggressive external acts and developing a more repressive internal government. Although Spencer sees a continual threat of rebarbarization, he hopes for some sort of federation of the nations of the world that would forbid wars among member nations. Thus, in his militant-industrial categorization system, Spencer does *not* offer a unilinear view of the evolution of society.

Ethics and Politics

In his earliest book, *Social Statics* (1850/1954), and in much later books, especially his two-volume *The Principles of Ethics* (1897/1978), Spencer articulated a rather consistent ethical and political position that informs, and is informed by, his substantive work. He subtitled *Social Statics* "The conditions essential to human happiness specified, and the first of them developed," and he described *The Principles of Ethics* as a set of "rules of right conduct on a scientific basis" (Spencer, 1897/1978:xiv). We will briefly examine in this section Spencer's ethical and political ideas. A key issue is whether these ideas greatly enhanced or fatally injured his sociology.

Spencer's moral and political ideas are derived, to a large extent, from his methodological individualism. As we have seen throughout this chapter, Spencer focused on macro-level phenomena, but he did so with the view that the base of these phenomena was individual "units." This specific view of the social world is deduced, like many others, from his general principles: "As a multitude is but an assemblage of units, and as the characteristics of a multitude result from the properties of its units, so social phenomena are consequences of the natures of individual men" (Spencer,

1902/1958:8). Or, more strongly, "The properties of the units determine the properties of the aggregate" (Spencer, 1873/1961:41).[2] The characteristics of people in an associated state are derived from the inherent properties of individuals: "No phenomenon can be presented by a corporate body but what there is a preexisting capacity in its individual members for producing" (Spencer, 1850/1954:17). Just as macro-level phenomena are derived from individuals, so too is the moral law of society: "The right ruling of humanity in its state of *multitude* is to be found in humanity in its state of *unitude*" (Spencer, 1850/1954:18). Spencer believes that individuals are endowed with a moral sense that dictates their actions and ultimately the structure and functioning of society.

Although individuals are the proximate cause of social morality, the more distant cause is God. The things that people come to view as moral are in line with divine rule. Spencer castigates those who "doubt the foresight and efficiency of the Divine arrangements" (1850/1954:47). He further argues that "human happiness is the divine will" (Spencer, 1850/1954:67). Thus, society is seen as evolving toward an increasing state of perfection and happiness.

Another factor in this evolution to a perfect moral state is that evil, in Spencer's view, progressively disappears. To explain this disappearance, Spencer once again employs the survival-of-the-fittest argument.[3] As he sees it, evil is a result of nonadaptation to external conditions, or "unfitness to the conditions of existence" (Spencer, 1850/1954:59). However, such nonadaptation is constantly diminishing and must ultimately disappear. More generally, Spencer argues that "all excess and all deficiency must disappear; that is, all unfitness must disappear; that is, all imperfection must disappear" (1850/1954:59). As a result of the survival-of-the-fittest argument applied to evil, Spencer concludes that "the ultimate development of the ideal man is logically certain" (1850/1954:59).

Turning the argument around, Spencer contends that human happiness comes from the satisfaction of desires and that gratification can come only from an exercise of human faculties. Thus, people must be free to exercise their faculties; that is, they must have liberty. Spencer invokes God on the side of this viewpoint as well: "God intends he [the human] should have that liberty. Therefore he has a right to that liberty" (1850/1954:69). He also embeds this argument in his methodological individualism by contending that people are endowed with "an *instinct of personal rights*" (Spencer, 1850/1954:86). Furthermore, this liberty must not be the right of just a few; because everyone has these faculties, all individuals have the right to exercise them freely.

However, there are limits on personal liberty, most important in the fact that an individual, in exercising his or her liberty, cannot be allowed to infringe on the liberty of others. However, because individuals are not endowed with the capacity to prevent their

---

[2]Although we see here (and have seen elsewhere) that individual units lie at the base of aggregates, Spencer also recognizes a dialectic in which changes in the aggregate in turn alter the units. Spencer specifies a number of superorganic products that serve to modify the individual, including material "appliances" (for example, the steam engine), language, knowledge, science, customs and laws, esthetic products (literature), and so on.

[3]By the way, Spencer (1897/1978) later makes it clear that his ideas on evolution are *not* indebted to Charles Darwin, whose book *On the Origin of the Species* appeared in 1859, almost a decade *after* Spencer had published *Social Statics*. However, in the preface to the fourth edition of *First Principles* (1902/1958), Spencer did admit to altering some of his ideas as a result of Darwin's influence.

actions from infringing on the rights of others, society is needed to perform this function. This leads to Spencer's libertarian political position that there is a role for the state but it is a highly limited one. In his view, the state must protect the liberty of individuals, but "it ought to do nothing more than protect" (Spencer, 1850/1954:264–265). Because he does see this limited role for the state, Spencer rejects the label "laissez-faire theorist" that some affixed to him.

Of course, such a libertarian position fits well with Spencer's views on evolution and survival of the fittest. Other than protecting individual liberty, the state is to get out of the way and allow the "law" and dynamics of evolution to work themselves out. Here is one of the ways in which Spencer describes that law:

> The well-being of existing humanity and the unfolding of it into this ultimate perfection are both secured by that same beneficent, though severe, discipline to which animate creation at large is subject: a discipline which is pitiless in the working out of good: a felicity-pursuing law which never swerves for the avoidance of partial and temporary suffering. The poverty of the incapable, the distresses that come upon the imprudent, the starvation of the idle, and those shoulderings aside of the weak by the strong, which leaves so many "in shallows and in miseries," are the decrees of a large, far-seeing benevolence.
>
> (Spencer, 1850/1954:288–289)

Thus, Spencer does not look upon such "harsh realities" as hunger and disease as evil; rather, they "are seen to be full of the highest benificence—the same benificence which brings to early graves the children of diseased parents and singles out the low-spirited, the intemperate, and the debilitated as the victims of an epidemic" (Spencer, 1850/1954:289). Similarly, and more harshly, "Society is constantly excreting its unhealthy, imbecile slow, vacillating, faithless members" (Spencer, 1850/1954:289). To put it more directly, those who are not healthy, not smart, not steadfast, and not believers in the divine should, and will, for the benefit of the larger society, die, as long as the natural process of evolution is left to operate in accord with its basic laws. Spencer does not totally deny that some of the disadvantaged may need care, but they should be taken care of through what he called, "positive private benificence" (Offer, 1999).

Thus, we return to Spencer's libertarian politics. The state, as well as private philanthropists, is enjoined from preventing misery because to do so would cause greater misery for future generations. That is, if the unfit are allowed to survive, they will produce only similarly unfit offspring and that will only increase the magnitude of the problem for societies of the future. Those individuals, both in and out of the government, who think of themselves as doing good are in fact doing great harm to society. Interference by the state (and other agencies) serves only to encourage the multiplication of the unfit, to discourage the multiplication of the fit, and to stop the "purifying" process of natural evolution. Those who interfere "bequeath to posterity a continually increasing curse" (Spencer, 1850/1954:290).

Specifically, Spencer opposes state-administered charity (or any charity, for that matter) and state-run education. He even opposes government involvement in sanitation matters, such as garbage removal. Throughout his work, Spencer often returns to the theme of the evils of state intervention. In the end, the government is to refrain from intervention not only because such interference hampers the natural process of evolution but also because it curtails individual rights: "For a government to take from a citizen more property than is needful for the efficient defense of that citizen's rights is to infringe his rights" (Spencer, 1850/1954:333). What Spencer seeks is a "society organized upon the same [evolutionary] system as an individual being" (1850/1954:403).

In his autobiography, Spencer railed against the distortion of his libertarian position ("genuine liberalism") by the "modern perversion of it which, while giving them nominal liberties in the shape of votes . . . is busily decreasing their liberties, both by the multiplication of restraints and commands, and by taking away larger parts of their incomes to be spent not as they individually like, but as public officials like" (1904a:487–488). Elsewhere, Spencer described the contrast in this way: "Liberalism habitually stood for individual freedom *versus* State-coercion" (1892/1965:5).

In response to the critics of his position, Spencer (1873/1961) expressed shock at being seen as an enemy of the poor and other unfortunate members of society. He depicts himself as more humane than that. He argues that he is not for inaction but rather for the use of "fit means" to deal with the problems of the unfortunate. Of course, one wonders about the credibility of such a position in light of views such as his concern that "the diligent and provident labourer had to pay that the good-for-nothings might not suffer" (Spencer, 1892/1965:113). Obviously, Spencer had little regard for those on the public dole and wished that those who worked hard should not have to pay for the poor, with the result, presumably, that the poor would be permitted to suffer and ultimately die.

Obviously, if Spencer is opposed to state intervention, he would certainly be opposed to any radical (for example, socialist, communist) alteration of society. He believes that sociology, with its focus on the long history of unintentional evolutionary changes, will help disabuse us of the notion that "social evils admit of radical cures" (Spencer, 1873/1961:19). Societies arise by slow evolution, not by human manufacture and certainly not by human demolition and remanufacture. Spencer's fears about the controls exercised by the capitalist state were nothing in comparison to his fears about socialistic control, which he equated with slavery and tyranny. As a result of this view, Spencer associates socialism with militant societies and argues that it will "cease to be normal as fast as the society becomes predominantly industrial in its type" (1908c:577).

Spencer differentiates his own ideal society from that of socialists and communists by arguing that he is not in favor of giving people equal shares of things but rather of giving "each an opportunity of acquiring the objects he desires" (Spencer, 1850/1954:118). Spencer sees socialism as standing in opposition to the selfishness that he feels is an inherent part of human nature. It is unrealistic to expect that selfish people will voluntarily surrender their excess productivity to others; selfish people cannot produce an unselfish system. Relatedly, as we saw earlier in this chapter, Spencer views people as being endowed with an "instinct for personal rights," and one of those rights, which he sees as an element of human nature, is a desire for property. Therefore, socialism stands in opposition to this element of human nature and, as a result, cannot survive.

Spencer's opposition to socialism and communism is also related to his opposition to any abrupt or revolutionary change. This follows from his oft-stated view that evolution is, and must be, a gradual process. Not only does abrupt change violate evolution, but it also would lead to a radically altered society that would be out of harmony with human nature, which changes glacially.

The moral and political views previously outlined, as well as many others, led many sociologists, as Jonathan Turner (1985b) argues, to dismiss Spencer's theoretical perspective. That is, contemporary, often liberal or radical, sociological theorists tend to reject the kind of conservative morality and politics preached by Spencer. Their rejection of his morality and politics led to a rejection of his sociological theory. We agree with Turner that this is not a good reason to reject a theory. That is, one should not reject a theory merely because one opposes the morals or politics of its creator. However, there is another reason to question Spencer's theory, and that is on the basis of the feeling that his scientific sociology is shaped and distorted by his moral and political views. From our perspective, there is a very suspicious fit between Spencer's "scientific" sociology and his moral and political views. In fact, it could be argued that Spencer's claim to being scientific is vitiated by the fact that his work is biased by his moral and political proclivities. (Of course, similar things could be said about Marx, Weber, Simmel, and many other classical theorists.) Spencer cautioned sociologists about being biased in their work, but it seems clear that Spencer's sociological theory is weakened by his own biases. Thus it is not Spencer's specific morality or politics that leads us to question his work but rather the fact that they biased and distorted his theory.

However, we should not lose sight of the fact that there is much more of merit in Spencer's sociological theory than he is usually given credit for today. His meritorious ideas have been analyzed and underscored throughout this chapter.

Summary

Herbert Spencer has a more powerful theory, and his work has more contemporary significance, than that of the other significant figure in the "prehistory" of sociological theory, Auguste Comte. Their theories have some similarities (for example, positivism) but far more differences (for example, Comte's faith in a positivist religion and Spencer's opposition to any centralized system of control).

Spencer offers a series of general principles from which he deduces an evolutionary theory: increasing integration, heterogeneity, and definiteness of both structures and functions. Indeed, sociology, for Spencer, is the study of the evolution of societies. Although Spencer sought to legitimize sociology as a science, he also felt that sociology is linked to, and should draw upon, other sciences such as biology (especially the idea of survival of the fittest) and psychology (especially the importance of sentiments). In part from his concern with psychology, Spencer developed his methodological-individualist approach to the study of society.

Spencer addresses a number of the methodological difficulties confronting sociology as a science. He is especially concerned with various biases the sociologist must overcome—educational, patriotic, class, political, and theological. In seeking to exclude these biases, Spencer articulates a "value-free" position for sociology. In much of his substantive work, Spencer employs the comparative-historical method.

The evolution of society occupies a central place in Spencer's sociology. In his analysis of societal evolution, Spencer employs the three general aspects of evolution mentioned previously—increasing integration (increasing size and coalescence of masses of people), heterogeneity, and definiteness (here, clearly demarcated institutions)—as well as a fourth aspect—the increasing coherence of social groups. In his evolutionary social theory, Spencer traces, among other things, the movement from simple to compounded societies and from militant to industrial societies.

Spencer also articulates a series of ethical and political ideals. Consistent with his methodological individualism, Spencer argues that people must be free to exercise their abilities; they must have liberty. The only role for the state is the protection of individual liberty. Such a laissez-faire political perspective fits well with Spencer's ideas on evolution and survival of the fittest. Given his perspective on the gradual evolution of society, Spencer also rejects the idea of any radical solution (for example, communism) to society's problems.

C H A P T E R **6**

Karl Marx

Chapter Outline

The Dialectic
Dialectical Method
Human Potential
Alienation
The Structures of Capitalist Society
Materialist Conception of History
Cultural Aspects of Capitalist Society
Marx's Economics: A Case Study
Communism
Criticisms

Marx began his most famous work, *The Manifesto of the Communist Party* (Marx and Engels, 1848/1948), with the following line: "There is a spectre haunting Europe, the spectre of communism." It might be said that the same ghost is haunting our understanding of Marx. It is difficult to separate the ideas of Marx from the political movements that they inspired. Nevertheless, as Tom Rockmore (2002:96) tells us, we must try "to free Marx from Marxism."

For many, Marx has become more of an icon than a thinker deserving of serious study. The symbolism of his name tends to muddle our understanding of his ideas. Marx is the only theorist we will study who has had political movements and social systems named after him. He is probably the only theorist your friends and family have strong opinions about. He is often criticized, as well as praised, by people who have never actually read his work. Even among his followers, Marx's ideas frequently are reduced to slogans such as "the opium of the people" and "the dictatorship of proletariat," but the role of these slogans in Marx's encompassing theory often is ignored.

There are many reasons for this lack of understanding of Marx's social theory, the main one being that he never really completed his social theory. He planned, early in his career, to publish separate works on economics, law, morals, politics, etc., and then "in a special work, to present them once again as a connected whole, to show the relationship between the parts. . . ." (Marx, 1964:280). He never did this final work and never even completed his separate work on economics. Instead, much of his time was taken up by study, journalism, political activity, and a series of minor intellectual and political arguments with friends and adversaries.

In addition, although Marx could write clear and inspiring prose, especially in his political tracts, he often preferred a vocabulary that relied on complex philosophical traditions, and he would make these terms even more difficult to understand by implicitly redefining them for his own use. Vilfredo Pareto made the classic critique of Marx by comparing his words to a fable about bats. When someone said they were birds, the bats would cry, "No, we are mice." When someone said they were mice, they protested that they were birds. Whatever interpretation one makes of Marx, others can offer alternative interpretations. For example, some stress Marx's early work on human potential and tend to discount his political economy (see, for example, Ollman, 1976; Wallimann, 1981; Wartenberg, 1982). Others stress Marx's later work on the economic structures of society and see that work as distinct from his early, largely philosophical work on human nature (see Althusser, 1969; Gandy, 1979; McMurty, 1978).[1] A recent interpreter of Marx made the following comment, which applies equally to this chapter: "Virtually every paragraph in this chapter could be accompanied by three concise paragraphs describing why other readers of Marx, erudite and influential, think that this paragraph is wrong, in emphasis or substance" (Miller, 1991:105). And, of course, the differing interpretations have political consequences, making any disagreement extremely contentious.[2]

Despite these problems, Marx's theories have produced one of sociology's most productive and significant research programs. When Marx died in 1883, the eleven mourners at his funeral seemed to belie what Engels said in his eulogy: "His name and work will endure through the ages." Nevertheless, Engels seems to have been right. His ideas have been so influential that even one of his critics admitted that, in a sense, "we are all Marxists now" (Singer, 1980:1). As Hannah Arendt (2002:274) wrote, if Marx seems to be forgotten, it is not "because Marx's thought and the methods he introduced have been abandoned, but rather because they have become so axiomatic that their origin is no longer remembered."

It is for these reasons that a return to Marx has proven so productive to those working in sociology. Thinking about Marx helps us to clarify what sociology and, indeed, our society have taken for granted. Rediscoveries and reinterpretation of Marx have often renewed sociology and opened up a fresh perspective on such issues as alienation, globalization, and, most recently, the environment (Foster, 2000).

Despite differing interpretations, there is general agreement that Marx's main interest was in the historical basis of inequality, especially the unique form that it takes under capitalism. However, Marx's approach is different from many of the theories that we will examine. For Marx, a theory about how society works would be partial, because what he mainly sought was a theory about how to change society. Marx's theory, then, is an analysis of inequality under capitalism and how to change it.

---

[1]Our approach is based on the premise that there is no discontinuity or contradiction between Marx's early work on human potential and his later work on the structures of capitalist society. We believe that his early ideas continue, at least implicitly, in his later work even though these ideas were certainly modified by his study of the economic structures of capitalism.

[2]In Josef Stalin's Soviet Union, there was no problem about the "correct" interpretation of Marx, since Stalin provided the interpretation and brutally eliminated all those, such as Leon Trotsky, who disagreed.

As capitalism has come to dominate the globe and the most significant communist alternatives have disappeared, some might argue that Marx's theories have lost their relevance. However, once we realize that Marx provides us with an analysis of capitalism, we can see that his theories are more relevant now than ever (McLennan, 2001:43). Marx provides a diagnosis of capitalism that is able to reveal its tendencies to crises, point out its perennial inequalities, and, if nothing else, demand that capitalism live up to its own promises. The example of Marx makes an important point about theory. Even when its particular predictions are disproved—even when the proletariat revolution that Marx believed to be imminent did not come about—theories still hold a value as an alternative to our current society. Theories may not tell us what will happen, but they can argue for what should happen and help us develop a plan for carrying out the change that the theory envisions and/or resisting the change that the theory predicts.

The Dialectic

Vladimir Lenin (1972:180) said that no one can fully understand Marx's work without a prior understanding of the German philosopher G.W.F. Hegel. We can only hope that this is not true, since Hegel was one of the most purposefully difficult philosophers ever to have written. Nevertheless, we must understand some of Hegel in order to appreciate the central Marxian conception of the dialectic.

The idea of a dialectical philosophy had been around for centuries (Gadamer, 1989). Its basic idea is the centrality of contradiction. While most philosophies, and indeed common sense, treat contradictions as mistakes, a dialectical philosophy believes that contradictions exist in reality and that the most appropriate way to understand reality is to study the development of those contradictions. Hegel used the idea of contradiction to understand historical change. According to Hegel, historical change has been driven by the contradictory understandings that are the essence of reality, our attempts to resolve the contradictions, and the new contradictions that develop.

Marx also accepted the centrality of contradictions to historical change. We see this in such well-known formulations as the "contradictions of capitalism" and "class contradictions." However, unlike Hegel, Marx did not believe that these contradictions could be worked out in our understanding, that is, in our minds. Instead, for Marx these are real existing contradictions (Wilde, 1991:277). For Marx, such contradictions are not resolved by the philosopher sitting in an armchair, but by a life-and-death struggle that changes the social world. This was a crucial transformation because it allowed Marx to move the dialectic out of the realm of philosophy and into the realm of a study of social relations grounded in the material world. It is this focus that makes Marx's work so relevant to sociology, even though the dialectical approach is very different from the mode of thinking used by most sociologists. The dialectic leads to an interest in the conflicts and contradictions among various levels of social reality, rather than to the more traditional sociological interest in the ways these various levels mesh neatly into a cohesive whole.

For example, one of the contradictions within capitalism is the relationship between the workers and the capitalists who own the factories and other means of production with which the work is done. The capitalist must exploit the workers in order to make a profit from the workers' labor. The workers, in contradiction to the capitalists, want to keep at least some of the profit for themselves. Marx believed that this contradiction was at the heart of capitalism, and that it would grow worse as capitalists drove more and more people to become workers by forcing small firms out of business and as competition between the capitalists forced them to further exploit the workers to make a profit. As capitalism expands, the number of workers exploited, as well as the degree of exploitation, increases. This contradiction cannot be resolved through philosophy, but only through social change. The tendency for the level of exploitation to escalate leads to more and more resistance on the part of the workers. Resistance begets more exploitation and oppression, and the likely result is a confrontation between the two classes (Boswell and Dixon, 1993).

Dialectical Method

Marx's focus on real existing contradictions led to a particular method for studying social phenomena that has also come to be called dialectical (Ball, 1991; Friedrichs, 1972; Ollman, 1976; Schneider, 1971; Starosta, 2008).

Fact and Value

In dialectical analysis, social values are not separable from social facts. Many sociologists believe that their values can and must be separated from their study of facts about the social world. The dialectical thinker believes that it is not only impossible to keep values out of the study of the social world but also undesirable, because it produces a dispassionate, inhuman sociology that has little to offer to people in search of answers to the problems they confront. Facts and values are inevitably intertwined, with the result that the study of social phenomena is value-laden. Thus, to Marx it was impossible and, even if possible, undesirable to be dispassionate in his analysis of capitalist society. But Marx's emotional involvement in what he was studying did not mean that his observations were inaccurate. It could even be argued that Marx's passionate views on these issues gave him unparalleled insight into the nature of capitalist society. A less passionate student might have delved less deeply into the dynamics of the system. In fact, research into the work of scientists indicates that the idea of a dispassionate scientist is largely a myth and that the very best scientists are the ones who are most passionate about, and committed to, their ideas (Mitroff, 1974).

Reciprocal Relations

The dialectical method of analysis does not see a simple, one-way, cause-and-effect relationship among the various parts of the social world. For the dialectical thinker, social influences never simply flow in one direction as they often do for cause-and-effect thinkers. To the dialectician, one factor may have an effect on another, but it is just as likely that the latter will have a simultaneous effect on the former. For example, the increasing exploitation of the workers by the capitalist may cause the workers to

Karl Marx

A Biographical Sketch

Karl Marx was born in Trier, Prussia, on May 5, 1818 (Beilharz, 2005b). His father, a lawyer, provided the family with a fairly typical middle-class existence. Both parents were from rabbinical families, but for business reasons the father had converted to Lutheranism when Karl was very young. In 1841 Marx received his doctorate in philosophy from the University of Berlin, a school heavily influenced by Hegel and the Young Hegelians, supportive, yet critical, of their master. Marx's doctorate was a dry philosophical treatise, but it did anticipate many of his later ideas. After graduation he became a writer for a liberal-radical newspaper and within ten months had become its editor-in-chief. However, because of its political positions, the paper was closed shortly thereafter by the government. The early essays published in this period began to reflect a number of the positions that would guide Marx throughout his life. They were liberally sprinkled with democratic principles, humanism, and youthful idealism. He rejected the abstractness of Hegelian philosophy, the naive dreaming of utopian communists, and those activists who were urging what he considered to be premature political action. In rejecting these activists, Marx laid the groundwork for his own life's work:

> Practical attempts, even by the masses, can be answered with a cannon as soon as they become dangerous, but ideas that have overcome our intellect and conquered our conviction, ideas to which reason has riveted our conscience, are chains from which one cannot break loose without breaking one's heart; they are demons that one can only overcome by submitting to them.
>
> (Marx, 1842/1977:20)

Marx married in 1843 and soon thereafter was forced to leave Germany for the more liberal atmosphere of Paris. There he continued to grapple with the ideas of Hegel and his supporters, but he also encountered two new sets of ideas—French socialism and English political economy. It was the unique way in which he combined Hegelianism, socialism, and political economy that shaped his intellectual orientation. Also of great importance at this point was his meeting the man who was to become his lifelong friend, benefactor, and collaborator—Friedrich Engels (Carver, 1983). The son of a textile manufacturer, Engels had become a socialist critical of the conditions facing the working class. Much of Marx's compassion for the misery of the working class came from his exposure to Engels and his ideas. In 1844 Engels and Marx had a lengthy conversation in a famous café in Paris and laid the groundwork for a lifelong association. Of that conversation Engels said, "Our complete agreement in all theoretical fields became obvious . . . and our joint work dates from that time" (McLellan, 1973:131). In the following year, Engels published a notable work, *The Condition of the Working Class in England.* During this period

Marx wrote a number of abstruse works (many unpublished in his lifetime), including *The Holy Family* and *The German Ideology* (both coauthored with Engels), but he also produced *The Economic and Philosophic Manuscripts of 1844,* which better foreshadowed his increasing preoccupation with the economic domain.

While Marx and Engels shared a theoretical orientation, there were many differences between the two men. Marx tended to be theoretical, a disorderly intellectual, and very oriented to his family. Engels was a practical thinker, a neat and tidy businessman, and a person who did not believe in the institution of the family. In spite of their differences, Marx and Engels forged a close union in which they collaborated on books and articles and worked together in radical organizations, and Engels even helped support Marx throughout the rest of his life so that Marx could devote himself to his intellectual and political endeavors.

In spite of the close association of the names of Marx and Engels, Engels made it clear that he was the junior partner:

> Marx could very well have done without me. What Marx accomplished I would not have achieved. Marx stood higher, saw farther, and took a wider and quicker view than the rest of us. Marx was a genius.
>
> (Engels, cited in McLellan, 1973:131–132)

In fact, many believe that Engels failed to understand many of the subtleties of Marx's work (C. Smith, 1997). After Marx's death, Engels became the leading spokesperson for Marxian theory and in various ways distorted and oversimplified it, although he remained faithful to the political perspective he had forged with Marx.

Because some of his writings had upset the Prussian government, the French government (at the request of the Prussians) expelled Marx in 1845, and he moved to Brussels. His radicalism was growing, and he had become an active member of the international revolutionary movement. He also associated with the Communist League and was asked to write a document (with Engels) expounding its aims and beliefs. The result was the *Communist Manifesto* of 1848, a work that was characterized by ringing political slogans (for example, "Working men of all countries, unite!").

In 1849 Marx moved to London, and, in light of the failure of the political revolutions of 1848, he began to withdraw from active revolutionary activity and to move into more serious and detailed research on the workings of the capitalist system. In 1852, he began his famous studies in the British Museum of the working conditions in capitalism. These studies ultimately resulted in the three volumes of *Capital,* the first of which was published in 1867; the other two were published posthumously. He lived in poverty during these years, barely managing to survive on a small income from his writings and the support of Engels. In 1864 Marx became reinvolved in political activity by joining the International, an international movement of workers. He soon gained preeminence within the movement and devoted a number of years to it. He began to gain fame both as a leader of the International and as the author of *Capital.* But the disintegration of the International by 1876, the failure of various revolutionary movements, and personal illness took their toll on Marx. His wife died in 1881, a daughter in 1882, and Marx himself on March 14, 1883.

become increasingly dissatisfied and more militant, but the increasing militancy of the proletariat may well cause the capitalists to react by becoming even more exploitative in order to crush the resistance of the workers. This kind of thinking does not mean that the dialectician never considers causal relationships in the social world. It does mean that when dialectical thinkers talk about causality, they are always attuned to reciprocal relationships among social factors as well as to the dialectical totality of social life in which they are embedded.

Past, Present, Future

Dialecticians are interested not only in the relationships of social phenomena in the contemporary world but also in the relationship of those contemporary realities to both past (Bauman, 1976:81) and future social phenomena. This has two distinct implications for a dialectical sociology. First, it means that dialectical sociologists are concerned with studying the historical roots of the contemporary world as Marx (1857–58/1964) did in his study of the sources of modern capitalism. In fact, dialectical thinkers are very critical of modern sociology for its failure to do much historical research. A good example of Marx's thinking in this regard is found in the following famous quotation from *The Eighteenth Brumaire of Louis Bonaparte*:

> Men make their own history, but they do not make it just as they please; they do not make it under circumstances chosen by themselves, but under circumstances directly encountered from the past. The tradition of all the dead generations weighs like a nightmare on the brain of the living.
>
> (Marx, 1852/1963:15)

Second, many dialectical thinkers are attuned to current social trends in order to understand the possible future directions of society. This interest in future possibilities is one of the main reasons dialectical sociology is inherently political. It is interested in encouraging practical activities that would bring new possibilities into existence. However, dialecticians believe that the nature of this future world can be discerned only through a careful study of the contemporary world. It is their view that the sources of the future exist in the present.

No Inevitabilities

The dialectical view of the relationship between the present and the future need not imply that the future is determined by the present. Terence Ball (1991) describes Marx as a "political possibilist" rather than a "historical inevitabilist." Because social phenomena are constantly acting and reacting, the social world defies a simple, deterministic model. The future may be based on some contemporary model, but not inevitably.[3] Marx's historical studies had shown him that people make choices, but that these choices are limited. For instance, Marx believed that society was engaged in a class struggle and that people could choose to participate either in "the revolutionary reconstitution of society at large,

---

[3]Marx did, however, occasionally discuss the inevitability of socialism.

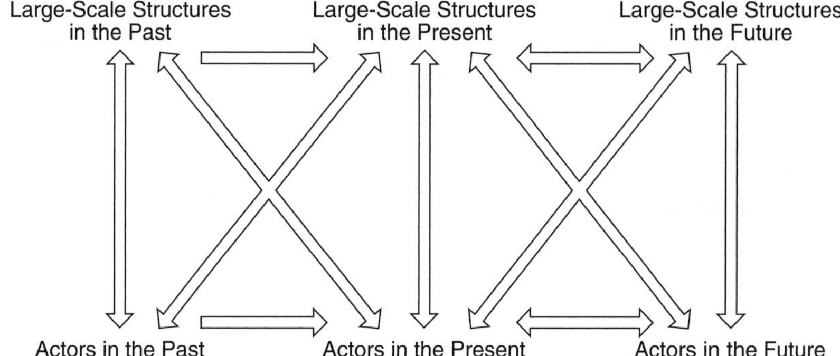

FIGURE 6.1 ***Schematic Representation of a Sociologically Relevant Dialectic***

or in the common ruin of the contending classes" (Marx and Engels, 1848/1948). Marx hoped and believed that the future was to be found in communism, but he did not believe that the workers could simply wait passively for it to arrive. Communism would come only through their choices and struggles.

This disinclination to think deterministically is what makes the best-known model of the dialectic—thesis, antithesis, synthesis—inadequate for sociological use. This simple model implies that a social phenomenon will inevitably spawn an opposing form and that the clash between the two will inevitably lead to a new, synthetic social form. But in the real world, there are no inevitabilities. Furthermore, social phenomena are not easily divided into the simple thesis, antithesis, and synthesis categories adopted by some Marxists. The dialectician is interested in the study of real relationships rather than grand abstractions. It is this disinclination to deal in grand abstractions that led Marx away from Hegel and would lead him today to reject such a great oversimplification of the dialectic as thesis, antithesis, synthesis.

Actors and Structures

Dialectical thinkers are also interested in the dynamic relationship between actors and social structures. Marx was certainly attuned to the ongoing interplay among the major levels of social analysis. The heart of Marx's thought lies in the relationship between people and the large-scale structures they create (Lefebvre, 1968:8). On the one hand, these large-scale structures help people fulfill themselves; on the other, they represent a grave threat to humanity. But the dialectical method is even more complex than this, because, as we have already seen, the dialectician considers past, present, and future circumstances, and this applies to both actors and structures. Figure 6.1 is a simplified schematic representation of this enormously complex and sophisticated perspective.

Human Potential

A good portion of this chapter will be devoted to a discussion of Marx's macrosociology, in particular his analysis of the macrostructures of capitalism. But before we can analyze these topics, we need to begin with Marx's thoughts on the more microsociological aspects of social reality. Marx built his critical analysis of the contradictions of capitalist society on his premises about human potential (or nature), its relation to labor, and its potential for alienation under capitalism. He believed that there was a real contradiction between our human potential and the way that we must work in capitalist society.

Marx (1964:64) wrote in an early work that human beings are an "ensemble of social relations." He indicates by this that our human potential is intertwined with our specific social relations and our institutional context. Therefore, human nature is not a static thing, but varies historically and socially. To understand human potential, we need to understand social history, because human nature is shaped by the same dialectical contradictions that Marx believed shapes the history of society.

For Marx, a conception of human potential that does not take social and historical factors into account is wrong, but to take them into account is not the same as being without a conception of human nature. It simply complicates this conception. For Marx, there is a human potential in general, but what is more important is the way that it is "modified in each historical epoch" (Marx, 1842/1977:609). When speaking of our general human potential, Marx often used the term *species being*. By this he meant the potentials and powers that are uniquely human and that distinguish us from other species.

Some Marxists, such as Louis Althusser (1969:229), have contended that the mature Marx did not believe in human nature. There are certainly reasons to downplay human nature for someone interested in changing society. Ideas about human nature—such as our "natural" greed, our "natural" tendency to violence, our "natural" gender differences—have often been used to argue against any social change. Such conceptions of human nature are innately conservative. If our problems are due to human nature, we had better learn to just adapt instead of trying to change things.

Nevertheless, there is much evidence that Marx did have a notion of human nature (Geras, 1983). Indeed, it makes little sense to say there is no human nature. Even if we are like a blank chalkboard, the chalkboard must be made out of something, and must have a nature such that chalk marks can show up on it. Some conception of human nature is part of any sociological theory. Our concept of human nature dictates how society can be sustained and how it can be changed, but most importantly for Marx's theory, it suggests how society *should* be changed. The real question is not whether we have a human nature, but what kind of nature it is—unchanging or open to historical processes (the use of the idea of human potential here indicates that we think it is open).

> Unless we confront the idea, however dangerous, of our human nature and species being and get some understanding of them, we cannot know what it is we might be alienated from or what emancipation might mean. Nor can we determine which of our "slumbering powers" must be awakened to achieve emancipatory goals. A working definition of human nature, however tentative and insecure, is a necessary step in the search for real as opposed to fantastic alternatives. A conversation about our "species being" is desperately called for.
>
> (Harvey, 2000:207)

Labor

For Marx, our species being and our human potential are intimately related to labor:

> Labour is, in the first place, a process in which both man and Nature participate, and in which man of his own accord starts, regulates, and controls the material reactions between himself and Nature. . . . By thus acting on the external world and changing it, he at the same time changes his own nature. He develops his slumbering powers and compels them to act in obedience to his sway. . . . We presuppose labour in a form that stamps it as exclusively human. A spider conducts operations that resemble those of a weaver and a bee puts to shame many an architect in the construction of her cells. But what distinguishes the worst architect from the best of bees is this, that the architect raises his structure in imagination before he erects it in reality. At the end of every labour process we get a result that existed in the imagination of the labourer at its commencement. He not only effects a change of form in the material on which he works, but he also realizes a purpose.
>
> (Marx, 1867/1967:177–178)

We see in the above quotation many important parts of Marx's view of the relation between labor and human nature. First, what distinguishes us from other animals—our species being—is that our labor creates something in reality that previously existed only in our imagination. Our production reflects our purpose. Marx calls this process where we create external objects out of our internal thoughts *objectification.* Second, this labor is material. It works with material nature in order to satisfy our material needs. Finally, Marx believed that this labor does not just transform nature, it also transforms us, including our needs, our consciousness, and our human nature. Labor is thus at the same time (1) the objectification of our purpose, (2) the establishment of an essential relation between human need and the material objects of our need, and (3) the transformation of our human nature.

Marx's use of the term *labor* is not restricted to economic activities but encompasses all productive actions where we transform material nature in accordance with our purpose. Whatever is created through this free purposive activity is both an expression of our human nature and a transformation of it. As we will see next, the process of labor has been changed under capitalism, making it difficult for us to understand Marx's conception, but we get close to Marx's concept when we think of the creative activity of the artist. The art work is a representation of the thought of the artist. In Marx's terms, the art work is an objectivation of the artist. However, it is also true that the process of creating the art changes the artist. Through the process of producing the art, the artist's ideas of it change or the artist may become aware of a new vision that needs objectivation. In addition, the completed artwork can take on a new meaning for the artist and transform the artist's conceptions of that particular piece or of art in general.

Labor, even artistic labor, is in response to a need, and the transformation that labor entails also transforms our needs. The satisfaction of our needs can lead to the creation of new needs (Marx and Engels, 1845–46/1970:43). For example, the production of cars to satisfy our need for long-distance transportation led to a new need for highways. Even more significantly, although few people thought they needed cars when cars were invented, now most people feel that they need one. A similar change has occurred with the computer. Whereas two generations ago few thought they needed a personal computer, now many people need one, as well as all of the software and peripherals that go with it.

We labor in response to our needs, but the labor itself transforms our needs, which can lead to new forms of productive activity. According to Marx, it is this transformation of our needs through labor that is the engine of human history.

> Not only do the objective conditions change in the act of production . . . but the producers change, too, in that they bring out new qualities in themselves, develop themselves in production, transform themselves, develop new powers and ideas, new modes of intercourse, new needs and new language.
>
> (Marx, 1857–58/1974:494)

Labor, for Marx, is the development of our truly human powers and potentials. By transforming material reality to fit our purpose, we also transform ourselves. Furthermore, labor is a social activity. Work involves others, directly in joint productions, or because others provide us with the necessary tools or raw materials for our work, or because they enjoy the fruits of our labor. Labor does not just transform the individual human, it transforms society. Indeed, for Marx, the emergence of a human as an individual depends on a society. Marx wrote, "Man is in the most literal sense of the word a *zoon politikon*, not only a social animal, but an animal which can develop into an individual only in society" (1857–58/1964:84). In addition, Marx tells us that this transformation includes even our consciousness: "Consciousness is, therefore, from the very beginning a social product, and remains so as long as men exist at all" (Marx and Engels, 1845–46/1970:51). Consequently, the transformation of the individual through labor and the transformation of society are not separable.

Alienation

Although Marx believed that there is an inherent relation between labor and human nature, he thought that this relation is perverted by capitalism. He calls this perverted relation *alienation* (Beilharz, 2005a; D. Cooper, 1991; Meisenhelder, 1991). Our discussion of Marx's concept of human nature and of alienation is derived mainly from Marx's early work. Even though he shied away from such a heavily philosophical term later in his work on the nature of capitalist society, alienation remained one of his main concerns (Barbalet, 1983:95).

Marx analyzed the peculiar form that our relation to our own labor has taken under capitalism. We no longer see our labor as an expression of our purpose. There is no objectivation. Instead, we labor in accordance with the purpose of the capitalist who has hired us and pays us. Rather than being an end in itself—an expression of human capabilities—labor in capitalism is reduced to a means to an end—earning money (Marx, 1932/1964:173). Because our labor is not our own, it no longer transforms us. Instead we are alienated from our labor and therefore alienated from our true human nature.

Although it is the individual who feels alienated in capitalist society, Marx's basic analytic concern was with the structures of capitalism that cause this alienation (Israel, 1971). Marx uses the concept of alienation to reveal the devastating effect of capitalist production on human beings and on society. Of crucial significance here is the two-class system in which the capitalists employ the workers (and thereby own their labor time) and own the means of production (tools and raw materials) as well as the ultimate products. In order to survive, workers are forced to sell their labor time to capitalists. This is the sociological basis of alienation.

> First, the fact that labor is external to the worker, i.e., it does not belong to his essential being; that in his work, therefore, he does not affirm himself but denies himself, does not feel content but unhappy, does not develop freely his physical and mental energy but mortifies his body and ruins his mind. The worker therefore only feels himself outside his work, and in his work feels outside himself. He is at home when he is not working, and when he is working he is not at home. His labor therefore is not voluntary, but coerced; it is forced labor. It is therefore not the satisfaction of a need; it is merely a means to satisfy needs external to it.
>
> (Marx, 1964:72)

As a result, people feel freely active only in their animal functions—eating, drinking, procreating—while in the essentially human process of labor, they no longer feel themselves to be anything but an animal. What is animal becomes human, and what is human becomes animal. Certainly eating, drinking, procreating, etc., are also genuinely human functions, but separated from the sphere of all other human activity and turned into sole and ultimate ends, they are animal functions.

Alienation can be seen as having four basic components. First, the workers in capitalist society are alienated from their *productive activity.* Workers do not produce objects according to their own ideas or to directly satisfy their own needs. Instead, they work for capitalists, who pay them a subsistence wage in return for the right to use the workers in any way they see fit. Because productive activity belongs to the capitalists, and because they decide what is to be done with it, we can say that workers are alienated from that activity. Furthermore, many workers perform highly specialized tasks and as a result have little sense of their role in the total production process. For example, automobile assembly-line workers who tighten a few bolts on an engine may have little feel for how their labor contributes to the production of the entire car. They do not objectivate their ideas, and they are not transformed by the labor in any meaningful way. Instead of being a process that is satisfying in and of itself, productive activity in capitalism is reduced, Marx argued, to an often boring and stultifying means to the fulfillment of the only end that really matters in capitalism—earning enough money to survive.

Second, the workers are alienated not only from productive activities but also from the object of those activities—the *product.* The product of their labor does not belong to the workers. Instead, the product belongs to the capitalists, who may use it in any way they wish, because the product is the capitalists' private property. Marx (1932/1964:117) tells us, "Private property is thus the product, the result, the necessary consequence of alienated labour." The capitalist will use his or her ownership in order to sell the product for a profit.

If workers wish to own the product of their own labor, they must buy it like anyone else. No matter how desperate the workers' need, they cannot use the products of their own labor to satisfy their need. Even workers in a bakery can starve if they don't have the money to buy the bread that they have made. Because of this peculiar relation, things that we buy—that are made by others—seem to us to be more an expression of ourselves than the things we make at our jobs. People's personalities are judged more by the cars that they drive, the clothes that they wear, the gadgets that they use—none of which they have made—than by what they actually produce in their daily work, which appears to be an arbitrary and accidental means for making money in order to buy things.

Third, the workers in capitalism are *alienated from their fellow workers.* Marx's assumption was that people basically need and want to work cooperatively in order to appropriate from nature what they require to survive. But in capitalism this cooperation is disrupted, and people, often strangers, are forced to work side by side for the capitalist. Even if the workers on the assembly line are close friends, the nature of the technology makes for a great deal of isolation. Here is the way one worker describes his social situation on the assembly line:

> You can work next to a guy for months without even knowing his name. One thing, you're too busy to talk. Can't hear. . . . You have to holler in his ear. They got these little guys coming around in white shirts and if they see you runnin' your mouth, they say, "This guy needs more work." Man, he's got no time to talk.
>
> (Terkel, 1974:165)

Of course, much the same is true in the newest version of the assembly line, the office cubicle. But this social situation is worse than simple isolation; the workers are often forced into outright competition, and sometimes conflict, with one another. In order to extract maximum productivity and to prevent the development of cooperative relationships, the capitalist pits one worker against another to see who can produce more, work more quickly, or please the boss more. The ones who succeed are given a few extra rewards; those who fail are discarded. In either case, considerable hostility is generated among the workers toward their peers. This is useful to the capitalists because it tends to deflect hostility that otherwise would be aimed at them. The isolation and the interpersonal hostility tend to make workers in capitalism alienated from their fellow workers.

Finally, and most generally, workers in capitalist society are alienated from their own *human potential.* Instead of work being the transformation and fulfillment of our human nature, work is where we feel least human, least ourselves. Individuals perform less and less like human beings as they are reduced in their work to machines. Even our smiles and greetings are programmed and scripted. Consciousness is numbed and, ultimately, destroyed as relations with other humans and with nature are progressively controlled. The result is a mass of people who are unable to express their essential human qualities, a mass of alienated workers.

Alienation is an example of the sort of contradiction that Marx's dialectical approach focused on. There is a real contradiction between our human nature that is defined and transformed by labor and the actual social conditions of our labor under capitalism. What Marx wanted to stress is that this contradiction cannot be resolved merely in thought. We are not any less alienated because we identify with our employer or with the things that our wages can purchase. Indeed, these things are a symptom of our alienation, which can be resolved only through real social change.

The Structures of Capitalist Society

Europe in Marx's time was undergoing increasing industrialization. People were being forced to leave agricultural and artisan trades and work in factories where the conditions were often literally inhuman. By the 1840s, when Marx was entering his most productive period, Europe was experiencing a widespread sense of social crisis (Seigel, 1978:106). This led to a series of revolts across Europe in 1848 (soon after the publication of Marx and Engel's *Communist Manifesto*). The effects of industrialization and its political connotations were especially evident in the group of mostly rural states collectively referred to as Germany. At the beginning of the nineteenth century, cheap manufactured goods from England and France began to destroy the less efficient manufacturers in Germany. In response, the German states imposed capitalism on the still mainly feudal society. The resulting poverty, dislocation, and alienation were particularly evident because of the imposed rapidity of the change. It was also clearly a political as well as an economic process.

Marx's analysis of alienation was a response to the economic, social, and political changes that he saw going on around him. He did not want to understand alienation as a philosophical problem. He wanted to understand what changes are needed to create a society in which human potential can be adequately expressed. In relation to this, Marx developed an important insight: The capitalist economic system is the primary cause of alienation. Marx's work on human nature and its alienation led him both to a critique of capitalist society and to a political program oriented to overcoming the structures of capitalism so that people could express their essential humanity (Mészáros, 1970).

Capitalism is an economic system in which a great number of workers who own little produce commodities for the profit of a small number of capitalists who own all of the following: the commodities, the means of producing the commodities, and even the labor time of the workers because they have purchased it through wages (Wolf, 2005b). But one of Marx's central insights is that capitalism is much more than just an economic system. Most significantly, capitalism is also a system of power. The secret of capitalism is that political powers have been transformed into economic relations (Wood, 1995). Capitalists are able to coerce the workers through their power to dismiss workers or close plants. Because of this, capitalists seldom need to use brute force. Capitalism, then, is not simply an economic system; it is at the same time a political system, a mode of exercising power, and a process for exploiting the workers.

Under capitalism, the economy appears to us as a natural force. People are laid off, wages are reduced, factories are closed all because of the "economy." We do not see these as social or political decisions. The links between human suffering and the economic structures are treated as irrelevant or trivial. For example, you might read in the newspaper that the Federal Reserve Board of the United States has raised interest rates. A reason often given for this is that the economy is "overheated," which is to say that there is the possibility of inflation. Raising interest rates does indeed "cool-off" the economy; that is, it puts people out of work so that workers are afraid to demand higher wages that might get passed on as higher prices. Thus, inflation is averted. Even though this is presented as an economic decision, notice its political dimensions. Inflation makes money worth less; therefore, it primarily hurts people who have accumulated money. If people live from paycheck to paycheck, they are not hurt by inflation because their income and their cost of living both go up. Consequently, capitalists are more hurt by inflation because the money they have accumulated goes down in value. However, the people who are hurt by rising interest rates are disproportionably the poor, because they are the first to lose their jobs in a slowing economy. In raising interest rates, then, the Federal Reserve Board adopts a policy that helps capitalists and hurts workers. Nevertheless, this decision usually is presented as a purely economic one. Marx would see this as a political decision that favors the capitalists at the expense of the workers.

Marx's aim is to make the social and political aspects of the economy clearer by revealing "the economic law of motion of modern society" (quoted in Ollman 1976:168). Furthermore, Marx intends to reveal the internal contradictions that he hopes will inevitably transform capitalism.

Commodities

The basis of all of Marx's work on social structures, and the place in which that work is most clearly tied to his views on human potential, is his analysis of commodities, or products of labor intended primarily for exchange. As Georg Lukács (1922/1968:83) put it, "The problem of commodities is . . . the central, structural problem of capitalist society." By starting with the commodity, Marx is able to reveal the nature of capitalism.

Marx's view of the commodity was rooted in his materialist orientation, with its focus on the productive activities of actors. As we saw earlier, it was Marx's view that in their interactions with nature and with other actors, people produce the objects that they need in order to survive. These objects are produced for use by oneself or by others in the immediate environment. This is what Marx called the commodity's *use value.* However, in capitalism this process takes on a new and dangerous form. Instead of producing for themselves or their immediate associates, the actors produce for someone else (the capitalist). The products have *exchange value;* that is, instead of being used immediately, they are exchanged in the market for money or for other objects.

Use value is connected to the intimate relation between human needs and the actual objects that can satisfy those needs. It is difficult to compare different use values. Bread has the use value of satisfying hunger; shoes have the use value of protecting our feet. It is difficult to say that one has more use value than the other. They are *qualitatively* different. Furthermore, use value is tied to the physical properties of a commodity. Shoes cannot satisfy our hunger and bread cannot protect our feet because they are physically different kinds of objects. However, in the process of exchange, commodities are compared to one another. One pair of shoes can be exchanged for six loaves of bread. Or if we use money, as is common, the shoes are worth six times as much money as a loaf of bread. Exchange values are *quantitatively* different. One can say that a pair of shoes has more exchange value than a loaf of bread. Furthermore, exchange value is separate from the physical property of the commodity. Only things that can be eaten can have the use value of satisfying hunger, but any type of thing can have the exchange value of a dollar.

Fetishism of Commodities

Commodities are the product of human labor, but they can become separated from the needs and purposes of their creator. Because exchange value floats free from the actual commodity and seems to exist in its own quantitative realm separate from any human use, we are led to believe that these objects and the market for them have an independent existence. In fully developed capitalism, this belief turns into reality as the objects and their market do become real, independent phenomena. The commodity becomes an independent, almost mystical external reality (Marx, 1867/1967:35). Marx called this the *fetishism of commodities* (Dant, 1996; Sherlock, 1997). Marx did not mean that commodities take on sexual meanings, since he wrote before Freud gave the term *fetish* this twist. Marx was referring to the ways in which the members of some religions, such as the Zunis, carve figures and then worship them. This is what Marx meant by fetish, a thing that we have made ourselves, but that we now worship as if it were a god.

In capitalism, the products that we make, their values, and the economy that is made up of our exchanges all seem to take on a life of their own. They are separate from any human needs or decisions. Most important, even our own labor—the thing that makes us truly human—becomes a commodity that is bought and sold on the market. Our labor acquires an exchange value that is separate from us. It is turned into an abstract thing and used by the capitalist to make objects that come to dominate us. Hence, the commodity is the source of the alienation discussed earlier. Even the labor of self-employed commodity producers is alienated, because they must produce for the market instead of according to their own purpose and need.

Thus, the economy takes on a function that Marx believed only actors could perform: the production of value. For Marx, the true value of a thing comes from the fact that labor produces it and that someone needs it. Its value represents human social relations, but in capitalism Marx tells us, "A definite social relation between men . . . assumes, in their eyes, the fantastic form of a relation between things" (1867/1967:72). Granting reality to commodities and the market, the individual in capitalism progressively loses control over them.

> A commodity is therefore a mysterious thing, simply because in it the social character of men's labor appears to them as an objective character stamped upon the product of that labor: because the relations of the producers to the sum total of their own labor is presented to them as a social relation, existing not between themselves, but between the products of their labor.
>
> (Marx, 1867/1967:72)

Think, for example, of the cup of coffee that you might have bought before sitting down to read this text. In that simple transaction, you entered into a relationship with hundreds of others: the waitperson, the owner of the coffee shop, the people working at the roaster, the importer, the truck driver, the dockworkers, all the people on the ship that brought the beans, the coffee plantation owner, the pickers, etc. In addition, you supported a particular trading relation between countries, a particular form of government in the grower's country that has been historically shaped by the coffee trade, a particular relation between the plantation owner and the worker, and many other social relations. You did all this by exchanging money for a cup of coffee. In the relation between these objects lies hidden all these social relations between people.

Marx's discussion of commodities and their fetishism takes us from the level of the individual actor to the level of large-scale social structures. The fetishism of commodities imparts to the economy an independent objective reality that is external to, and coercive of, the actor. Looked at in this way, the fetishism of commodities is translated into the concept of *reification* (Lukács, 1922/1968; Sherlock, 1997). Reification can be thought of as "thingification," or the process of coming to believe that humanly created social forms are natural, universal, and absolute things, and as a result, those social forms do acquire those characteristics. The concept of reification implies that people believe that social structures are beyond their control and unchangeable. Reification occurs when this belief comes to be a self-fulfilling prophecy. Then the structures actually do acquire the character people endowed them with. People become mesmerized by the seeming objectivity and authority of the economy. People lose their jobs, make career choices, or move across the country because of the economy. But according to Marx, the economy is not an objective, natural thing. It is a form of domination, and decisions about interest rates and layoffs are political decisions that tend to benefit one group over another.

By using this concept, we can see that people reify the whole range of social relationships and social structures. Just as people reify commodities and other economic phenomena (for example, the division of labor [Rattansi, 1982; Walliman, 1981]), they also reify religious (Barbalet, 1983:147), political, and organizational structures. Marx made a similar point in reference to the state: "And out of this very contradiction between the individual and . . . the community the latter takes an independent form as the State, divorced from the real interests of individual and community" (cited in Bender, 1970:176). Capitalism is made up of particular types of social relations that tend to take forms that appear to be and eventually are independent of the actual people involved. As Moishe Postone (1993) tells us, "The result is a new, increasingly abstract form of social domination—one that subjects people to impersonal structural imperatives and constraints that cannot be adequately grasped in terms of concrete domination (e.g., personal or group domination)."

Capital, Capitalists, and Proletariat

Marx found the heart of capitalist society within the commodity. A society dominated by objects whose main value is exchange produces certain categories of people. The two main types that concerned Marx were the proletariat and the capitalist. Let us start with the proletariat.

Proletariat are workers who sell their labor and who do not own their own means of production. They do not own their own tools or their factories, but Marx (1867/1967:714–15) further believed that members of the proletariat would even lose their own skills as they increasingly just serviced the machines that had the workers' skills built into them. Because members of the proletariat produce only for exchange, they are also consumers. Since they do not have the means to produce for their own needs, they must instead use their wages to buy what they need. Consequently, the proletariat is completely dependent on its wages in order to live. This makes the proletariat dependent on those who pay the wages.

Those who pay the wages are the capitalists. Briefly, the capitalists are those who own the means of production. However, before we can fully understand a capitalist, we must first understand what is *capital* (Wolf, 2005a). To begin with, capital is money that produces more money. In other words, capital is money that is invested rather than being used to satisfy human needs or desires. We can make this clearer by looking at what Marx considered to be "the starting-point of capital" (1867/1967:146), the *circulation of commodities.* Marx discussed two types of circulation of commodities. One of these types of circulation—Money→Commodities→(a larger sum of) Money (M_1-C-M_2)—is characteristic of capital; the other—Commodities→Money→Commodities (C_1-M-C_2)—is not.

In noncapitalist circulation of commodities, the circuit C_1-M-C_2 predominates. An example of C_1-M-C_2 would be the fisherman who sells his catch (C_1) and then uses the money (M) to buy bread (C_2). In other words, the primary goal of exchange in noncapitalist circulation is a commodity that one can use and enjoy.

Conversely, the capitalist circulation of commodities (M_1-C-M_2) has the goal of producing more money. Commodities are purchased in order to make a profit, not necessarily to use. In the capitalist circuit, referred to by Marx as "buying in order to sell" (1867/1967:147), the individual actor buys a commodity with money and in turn exchanges it for presumably more money. Here a store owner would buy (M_1) the fish (C) in order to sell them for more money (M_2). To further increase profits, the store owner might buy the boat and fishing equipment and pay the fisherman a wage. The end of this circuit is not the consumption of the use value, as it is in the simple circulation of commodities. The end is more money. The particular properties of the commodity used to make money are irrelevant. The commodity can be fish or it can be labor. Also, the real needs and desires of human beings are irrelevant; all that matters is what will produce more money.

Capital, then, is money that produces more money, but Marx tells us it is more than that: It is also a particular social relation. In other words, money becomes capital only because of a social relation between, on the one hand, the proletariat who do the work and must purchase the product and, on the other hand, those who have invested the money. The capacity of capital to make a profit appears "as a power endowed by Nature—a productive power that is immanent in Capital" (1867/1967:333), but it is, according to Marx, a relation of power. Capital cannot increase except by exploiting those who actually do the work. The workers are exploited by a system, and the irony is that it is a system that is produced through the workers' own labor. The capitalist system is the social structure that emerges on the basis of that exploitive relationship. Capitalists are those who live off the profit of their capital, and we can see now that they are the beneficiaries of the proletariat's exploitation. Within the idea of capital is already contained a social relation between those who own the means of production and those whose wage labor is exploited.

Exploitation

For Marx, exploitation and domination are more than an accidentally unequal distribution of wealth and power. *Exploitation* is a necessary part of the capitalist economy. Of course, all societies have exploitation, but what is peculiar in capitalism is that the exploitation is accomplished by the impersonal and "objective" economic system. It seems to be less a matter of power and more a matter of economists' charts and figures. Furthermore, the coercion is rarely naked force and is instead the worker's own needs, which can now be satisfied only through wage labor. Dripping irony, Marx describes the freedom of this wage labor:

> For the conversion of his money into capital . . . the owner of money must meet in the market with the free labourer, free in the double sense, that as a free man he can dispose of his labour-power as his own commodity, and that on the other hand he has no other commodity for sale, is short of everything necessary for the realization of his labour-power.
>
> (Marx, 1867/1967:169)

Workers appear to be "free laborers," entering into free contracts with capitalists. But Marx believed that the workers must take the terms the capitalists offer them, because the workers can no longer produce for their own needs. This is especially true because capitalism usually creates what Marx referred to as a *reserve army* of the unemployed. If the worker does not want to do the job at the wage that the capitalist offers, someone else in the reserve army of the unemployed will. This, for example, is what Barbara Ehrenreich discovered is the purpose of many of the want ads for low-paying jobs:

> Only later will I realize that the want ads are not a reliable measure of the actual jobs available at any particular time. They are . . . the employers' insurance policy against the relentless turnover of the low-wage workforce. Most of the big hotels run ads almost continually if only to build a supply of applicants to replace the current workers as they drift away or are fired. . . .
>
> (Ehrenreich, 2001:15)

The capitalists pay the workers less than the value the workers produce and keep the rest for themselves. This leads us to Marx's central concept of *surplus value*. This is defined as the difference between the value of the product when it is sold and the value of the elements consumed in the formation of that product (including the worker's labor). The capitalists can use this profit for private consumption, but that would not lead to the expansion of capitalism. Rather, capitalists expand their enterprise by converting it into a base for the creation of still more surplus value.

It should be stressed that this is not simply an economic concept. Surplus value, like capital, is a particular social relation and a form of domination, because labor is the real source of surplus value. "The rate of surplus-value is therefore an exact expression for the degree of exploitation of labor-power by capital, or of the laborer by the capitalist" (Marx, 1867/1967:218). This points to one of Marx's more colorful metaphors: "Capital is dead labor, that, vampire-like, only lives by sucking living labor, and lives the more, the more labor it sucks" (1867/1967:233).

Marx (1857–58/1974:414) makes one other important point about capital: "Capital exists and can only exist as many capitals." What he means by this is that capitalism is always driven by incessant competition. Capitalists may seem to be in control, but even they are driven by the constant competition between capitals. The capitalist is driven to make more profit in order to accumulate and invest more capital. The capitalist who does not do this will be outcompeted by the others who will. "As such, he shares with the miser an absolute drive towards self-enrichment. But what appears in the miser as the mania of an individual is in the capitalist the effect of a social mechanism in which he is merely a cog" (Marx, 1867/1967:739).

The desire for more profit and more surplus value for expansion pushes capitalism toward what Marx called the *general law of capitalist accumulation.* The capitalists seek to exploit workers as much as possible: "The constant tendency of capital is to force the cost of labor back towards . . . zero" (Marx, 1867/1967:600). Marx basically argued that the structure and the ethos of capitalism push the capitalists in the direction of the accumulation of more and more capital. In order to do this, given Marx's view that labor is the source of value, the capitalists are led to intensify the exploitation of the proletariat. This is what drives class conflict.

Class Conflict

Marx often used the term *class* in his writings, but he never systematically defined what he meant (So and Suwarsono, 1990:35). He usually is taken to have meant a group of people in similar situations with respect to their control of the means of production. This, however, is not a complete description of the way that Marx used the term. *Class,* for Marx, was always defined in terms of its potential for conflict. Individuals form a class insofar as they are in a common conflict with others over the surplus value. In capitalism there is an inherent conflict of interest between those who hire wage laborers and those whose labor is turned into surplus value. It is this inherent conflict that produces classes (Ollman, 1976).

Because class is defined by the potential for conflict, it is a theoretical and historically variant concept. A theory about where potential conflict exists in a society is required before identifying a class.[4] Richard Miller (1991:99) tells us that "there is no rule that could, in principle, be used to sort out people in a society into classes without studying the actual interactions among economic processes on the one hand and between political and cultural processes on the other."

For Marx, a class truly exists only when people become aware of their conflicting relation to other classes. Without this awareness, they only constitute what Marx called a class *in itself.* When they become aware of the conflict, they become a true class, a class *for itself.*

In capitalism, Marx's analysis discovered two primary classes: bourgeoisie and proletariat.[5] The *bourgeoisie* is the particular name for the capitalists in the modern economy. They own the means of production and employ wage labor. The conflict between bourgeoisie and proletariat is another example of a real material contradiction. This contradiction grows out of the previously mentioned contradiction between labor and capitalism. None of these contradictions can be resolved except by changing the

---

[4]Marx did acknowledge that class conflict often is affected by other forms of stratification, such as ethnic, racial, gender, and religious; however, he did not accept that these could be primary.

[5]Although his theoretical work looked mainly at these two classes, his historical studies examined a number of different class formations. Most significant are the petty bourgeois—small shopkeepers employing at most a few workers—and the lumpenproletariat—the proletariat who readily sell out to the capitalists. For Marx, these other classes can be understood only in terms of the primary relationship between bourgeoisie and proletariat.

capitalist structure. In fact, until that change occurs, the contradiction will only become worse. Society will be increasingly polarized into these two great opposing classes. Competition with megastores and franchise chains will shut down many small, independent businesses; mechanization will replace skilled artisans; and even some capitalists will be squeezed out through attempts to establish monopolies, for example, by means of mergers. All these displaced people will be forced down into the ranks of the proletariat. Marx called this inevitable increase in the proletariat *proletarianization.*

In addition, because capitalists have already reduced the workers to laboring machines performing a series of simple operations, mechanization becomes increasingly easy. As mechanization proceeds, more and more people are put out of work and fall from the proletariat to the industrial reserve army. In the end, Marx foresaw a situation in which society would be characterized by a tiny number of exploitative capitalists and a huge mass of proletariat and members of the industrial reserve army. By reducing so many people to this condition, capitalism creates the masses that will lead to its own overthrow. The increased centralization of factory work, as well as the shared suffering, increases the possibility of an organized resistance to capitalism. Furthermore, the international linking of factories and markets encourages workers to be aware of more than their own local interests. This is likely to lead to revolution.

The capitalists, of course, seek to forestall this revolution. For example, they sponsor colonial adventures with the objective of shifting at least some of the burden of exploitation from the home front to the colonies. However, in Marx's view (1867/1967:10), these efforts are ultimately doomed to failure, since the capitalist is as much controlled by the laws of the capitalist economy as are the workers. The capitalists are under competitive pressure from one another, forcing each to try to reduce labor costs and intensify exploitation—even though this intensified exploitation will increase the likelihood of revolution and therefore contribute to the capitalists' demise. Even good-hearted capitalists will be forced to further exploit their workers in order to compete: "The law of capitalist accumulation, metamorphosed by economists into pretended law of nature, in reality merely states that the very nature of accumulation excludes every diminution in the degree of exploitation" (Marx, 1867/1967:582).

Although no Marxist, Robert Reich, the former secretary of labor, echoes Marx's analysis that it is not the evil of individual capitalists but the capitalist system that explains the increasing layoffs in America and the movement of manufacturing to take advantage of cheaper overseas labor:

> It's tempting to conclude from all this that enterprises are becoming colder-hearted, and executives more ruthless—and to blame it on an ethic of unbridled greed that seems to have taken hold in recent years and appears to be increasing. But this conclusion would be inaccurate. The underlying cause isn't a change in the American character. It is to be found in the increasing ease by which buyers and investors can get better deals, and the competitive pressure this imposes on all enterprises.
>
> (Reich, 2000:71)

Whether they want to or not, capitalists must move their factories where labor is cheaper; they must exploit the workers. If one capitalist does not, he or she will not be able to compete with those who do. Marx usually did not blame individual members of the bourgeoisie for their actions; he saw these actions as largely determined by the logic of the capitalist system. This is consistent with his view that actors in capitalism generally are devoid of creative independence.[6] However, the developmental process inherent in capitalism provides the conditions necessary for the ultimate reemergence of such creative action and, with it, the overthrow of the capitalist system. The logic of the capitalist system is forcing the capitalists to produce a more exploited proletariat, and these are the very people who will bring an end to capitalism through their revolt. "What the bourgeoisie, therefore, produces, is, above all, its own gravediggers" (Marx and Engels, 1848/1948).

It is not only the ultimate proletariat revolution that Marx sees as caused by the underlying contradictions of capitalism, but also many of the various personal and social crises that beset modern society. On the personal side, we have already discussed some of the facets of the alienation that Marx believed was at the root of the feeling of meaninglessness in so many people's lives. At the economic level, Marx predicted a series of booms and depressions as capitalists overproduced or laid off workers in their attempts to increase their profits. At the political level, Marx predicted the increasing inability of a civil society to discuss and solve social problems. Instead we would see the growth of a state whose only purposes are the protection of the capitalists' private property and an occasional brutal intervention when economic coercion by the capitalist fails.

Capitalism as a Good Thing

Despite his focus on the inevitable crises of capitalism and his portrayal of it as a system of domination and exploitation, Marx saw capitalism as primarily a good thing. Certainly, Marx did not want to return to the traditional values of precapitalism. Past generations were just as exploited; the only difference is that the old exploitation was not veiled behind an economic system. Notwithstanding its exploitation, the birth of capitalism opened up new possibilities for the freedom of the workers. The capitalist system provides the possibility for freedom from the traditions that have bound all previous societies. Even if the worker is not yet truly free, the promise is there. Similarly, as the most powerful economic system ever developed, capitalism holds the promise of freedom from hunger and other forms of material deprivation. It was from the viewpoint of these promises that Marx criticized capitalism.

In addition, Marx believed that capitalism is the root cause of the defining characteristics of the modern age. Modernity's constant change and propensity to challenge all accepted traditions are driven by the inherent competition of capitalism, which pushes the capitalists to continuously revolutionize the means of production and transform society.

> Constant revolutionizing of production, uninterrupted disturbance of all social conditions, everlasting uncertainty and agitation distinguish the bourgeois epoch from all earlier ones. All fixed, fast-frozen relations, with their train of ancient and venerable prejudices and opinions, are swept away, all new-formed ones become antiquated before they can ossify. All that is solid melts into air, all that is holy is

---

[6]Marx might be seen as an exception to his own theory. He does acknowledge that it is possible for some individuals among the bourgeoisie to lay aside their class characteristics and adopt a communist consciousness (Marx and Engels, 1845–46/1970:69).

> profaned, and man is at last compelled to face with sober senses, his real conditions of life, and his relations with his kind.
>
> (Marx and Engels, 1848/1948:11)

Capitalism has been a truly revolutionary force. It has created a global society; it has introduced unrelenting technological change; it has overthrown the traditional world, but now, Marx believed, it must be overthrown. Capitalism's role is finished, and it is time for the new stage of communism to begin. This was the perspective from which Marx criticized capitalism, from its potential future.

Materialist Conception of History

Marx was able to criticize capitalism from the perspective of its future because of his belief that history would follow a predictable course. This was based on his materialist conception of history (often simply shortened to the term *historical materialism* [Vandenberghe, 2005]). The general claim of Marx's historical materialism is that the way in which people provide for their material needs determines or, in general, conditions the relations that people have with each other, their social institutions, and even their prevalent ideas.[7]

Because of the importance of the way in which people provide for their material needs, this, along with the resultant economic relations, are often referred to as the *base* while the noneconomic relations, other social institutions, and prevalent ideas are referred to as the *superstructure.*

It should be noted that Marx's view of history does not envision a straightforward trend where the superstructure simply comes into line with the base. Human history is set into motion by the attempt to satisfy needs, but as we noted earlier, these needs are themselves historically changing. Consequently, advances in the satisfaction of needs tend to produce more needs so that human needs are both the motivating foundation and the result of the economic base.

The following quote is one of Marx's best summaries of his materialist conception of history:

> In the social production which men carry on they enter into definite relations that are indispensable and independent of their will. These relations of production correspond to a definite stage of development of their material forces of production. The totality of these relations of production constitutes the economic structure of society, which is the real foundation on top of which arises a legal and political superstructure to which correspond definite forms of social consciousness. At a certain stage of their development, the material forces of production in society come in conflict with the existing relations of production or—what is but a legal expression of the same thing—with the property relations within which they had been at work before. From forms of development of the forces of production these relations turn into their fetters. Then

[7]Antonio (2000:119–20) distinguishes between a hard and a soft material determinism. "Although hard determinist passages exist in Marx's texts, he suggested much more often a complex, historically contingent materialism, which ought not to be reduced to 'technological determinism' (i.e., social change arises from technical change) or to 'reflection theory' (i.e., ideas are mere emanations of material reality)."

> occurs a period of social revolution. With the change of the economic foundation the entire immense superstructure is more or less rapidly transformed.
>
> (Marx, 1859/1970:20–21)

The place to start in the preceding quote is with the material *forces of production.* These are the actual tools, machinery, factories, and so forth, used to satisfy human needs. The *relations of production* refer to the kinds of associations that people have with each other in satisfying their needs. Marx's theory holds that a society will tend to adopt the system of social relations that best facilitates the employment and development of its productive powers. Therefore, the relations of production correspond to the state of the material forces of production. For example, certain stages of low technology correspond to social relations characterized by a few large landowners and a large number of serfs who work the land in return for a share of the produce. The higher technology of capitalism corresponds to a few capitalists who are able to invest in the expensive machinery and factories and a large number of wage workers. As Marx succinctly, if somewhat simplistically, puts it, "the hand-mill gives you society with the feudal lord; the steam-mill society with the capitalist" (Marx, 1847/1963:95). Marx adds that these relations between people also can be expressed as property relations: the capitalist owns the means of production, and the wage laborer does not.

Capitalist economies have unique relations between people, and they carry certain expectations, obligations, and duties. For example, wage laborers must show a certain deference to the capitalist if they want to keep their jobs. For Marx, what was important about these relations of production was their propensity to class conflict, but it is also possible to see the effect of the relations of production in family and personal relations. The socialization necessary to produce the "good" male worker also produces a certain type of husband. Similarly, early capitalism's requirement that the man leave the home to work all day led to a definition of the mother as the primary caretaker of the children. Hence, changes in the forces of production led to deep changes in the family structure. These changes too can be seen as relations of production.

Marx is never quite clear about where the relations of production leave off and the superstructure starts. However, he clearly felt that there are some relations and forms of "social consciousness" that play only a supporting role in the material means of production. Marx predicted that although these are not directly involved, they tend to take a form that will support the relations of production.

Marx's view of history was a dynamic one, and he therefore believed that the forces of production will change to become better at providing for material needs. For example, this is what happened with the advent of capitalism, when technological changes made factories possible. However, before capitalism could actually occur there had to be changes in society, changes in the relations of production. Factories, capitalists, and wage laborers were not compatible with feudal relations. The feudal lords, who tied their wealth solely to the ownership of land and who felt a moral obligation to provide for their serfs, had to be replaced by capitalists who tied their wealth to capital and who felt no moral obligation to the wage laborer. Similarly, the serf's feeling of personal loyalty to the lord had to be replaced by proletariats who will sell their labor to whomever will pay. The old relations of production were in conflict with the new forces of production.

A revolution is often required in order to change relations of production. We see that the main source of the revolution is the material contradiction between the forces of production and the relations of production. However, this revolution takes the form of another contradiction, that between the exploiters and the exploited. According to Marx, the contradiction between the exploiters and the exploited has always existed. It leads to a revolutionary change when the exploited line up on the side of a change in the relations of production that favors the changes occurring in the forces of production. This means that Marx did not believe that all workers' revolts could be effective, only those that were on the side of a change in the forces of production. And this revolution, according to Marx, will cause the supporting relations, institutions, and prevalent ideas to change so that they sanction the new relations of production.

Cultural Aspects of Capitalist Society

In addition to his focus on the material structures of capitalism, Marx also theorized about its culture aspects.

Ideology

Not only do the existing relations of production tend to prevent the necessary changes for the development of the forces of production, but similarly, the supporting relations, institutions, and, in particular, prevalent ideas also tend to prevent these changes. When prevalent ideas perform this function, Marx gave them a special name: *ideologies.*

As with many terms, Marx is not always precise about his use of the word ideology. He seems to use it to indicate two related sorts of ideas. First, ideology refers to those ideas that naturally emerge out of everyday life in capitalism, but which, because of the nature of capitalism, reflect reality in an inverted manner (Larrain, 1979). For this he used the metaphor of a *camera obscura,* which employs an optical quirk to show a real image reflected upside down. This is the type of ideology represented by the fetishism of commodities or by money. Even though we know that money is nothing but a piece of paper that has value only because of underlying social relations, we must, in our daily lives, treat money as though it had its own value. Instead of seeing that we give money its value, it often seems that money gives us value.

This type of ideology is vulnerable to disruption because it is based on underlying material contradictions. Human value is not really dependent on money, and we often meet people who are living proof of that contradiction. In fact, it is at this level that we usually become aware of the material contradictions that Marx believed will drive capitalism to the next phase. We become aware, for example, that the economy is not an objective, independent system, but a political sphere. We become aware that our labor is not just another commodity, and that its sale through wages produces alienation. Or if we don't become aware of the underlying truth, we at least become aware of the disruption because of a blatantly political move in the economic system or our own feeling of alienation. It is in addressing these disruptions that the second use of ideology is relevant.

When disruptions occur and the underlying material contradictions are revealed, or are in danger of being revealed, a second type of ideology will emerge. Here Marx uses the term *ideology* to refer to those systems of ruling ideas that attempt once again to hide the contradictions that are at the heart of the capitalist system. In most cases, they do this in one of three ways: (1) they present a system of ideas—a religion, a philosophy, a literature, a legal system—that makes the contradictions appear to be coherent; (2) they explain away those experiences that reveal the contradictions, usually as personal problems or individual idiosyncrasies; or (3) they present the capitalist contradiction as really being a contradiction in human nature and therefore one that cannot be fixed by social change.

In general, those of the ruling class create this second type of ideology. For example, Marx refers to bourgeois economists who present the commodity form as natural and universal. Or he criticizes bourgeois philosophers, such as Hegel, for pretending that the material contradictions can be resolved by changing how we think. However, even the proletariat can create this type of ideology. People who have given up the hope of actually changing society need such ideologies. But no matter who creates it, these ideologies always benefit the ruling class by hiding the contradictions that would lead to social change.

Freedom, Equality, and Ideology

For an example of ideology, we will look at Marx's ideas about the bourgeois conception of equality and freedom. According to Marx, our particular ideas of equality and freedom emerge out of capitalism. Although we take our belief in freedom and equality to be an obvious thing, any historical study will demonstrate that it is not. Most societies would have considered the idea that all people are essentially equal as absurd. For most cultures throughout history, slavery seemed quite natural. Now, under capitalism, we believe quite the opposite: inequality is absurd, and slavery is unnatural.

Marx thought that this change in our ideas could be traced to the everyday practices of capitalism. The act of exchange that is the basis of capitalism presupposes the equality of the people in the exchange, just as it presupposes the equality of the commodities in the exchange. For the commodities, the particular qualitative differences of their use values are hidden by their exchange value. In other words, apples and oranges are made equal by reducing them to their monetary value. The same thing happens to the differences between the people involved in the exchange. Most exchanges in advanced capitalism involve people who never meet and don't know each other. We don't care who grew the apples and oranges we buy. This anonymity and indifference constitutes a kind of equality.

Furthermore, freedom is assumed in this exchange, since any of the partners to the exchange are presumed to be free to exchange or not as they see fit. The very idea of capitalist exchange means that commodities are not taken by force, but freely traded. This is also true of the exchange of labor time for wages. It is assumed that the worker or the employer is free to enter into the exchange and free to terminate it. Marx (1857–58/1974:245) concludes that "equality and freedom are not only respected in exchange which is based on exchange values, but the exchange of exchange values is the real productive basis of all equality and freedom." Nevertheless, Marx believed that capitalist practices result in an inverted view of freedom. It seems that we are free, but in fact, it is capital that is free and we who are enslaved.

For Marx, freedom means the ability to have control over your own labor and its products. Although individuals may seem free under capitalism, they are not. Under previous social forms, people were directly dominated by others and so were aware of their unfreedom. Under capitalism, people are dominated by capitalist relations that seem to be objective and natural, and therefore are not perceived as a form of domination. Marx (1857–58/1974:652) decries "the insipidity of the view that free competition is the ultimate development of human freedom. . . . This kind of individual freedom is therefore at the same time the most complete suspension of all individual freedom, and the most complete subjugation of individuality under social conditions which assume the form of objective powers. . . ."

Because the capitalist owns the means of production, the exchange of wages for labor time cannot be free. The proletariat must work in order to live, but the capitalist has the choice to hire others from the reserve army of labor, or to mechanize, or to let the factory sit idle until the workers become desperate enough to "freely" accept the capitalist's wages. The worker is neither free nor equal to the capitalist.

Hence, we see that the first level of the ideology of freedom and equality emerges from the practices of exchange in capitalism, but that our ideas are inverted and do not represent real freedom and equality. It is capital that is freely and equally exchanged; it is capital that is accepted without prejudice; it is capital that is able to do as it wishes; not us. As we noted earlier, this first type of ideology is easily disrupted, and our awareness of this disruption drives capitalism to the next phase. Despite the ideology of equality and freedom, few workers feel equal to their employers; few feel free in their jobs. This is why the second type of ideology is necessary. These disruptions somehow must be explained away or made to look inevitable.

This is especially true with the ideology of equality and freedom, since these ideas are among the most threatening to capitalism. They are another example of how capitalism creates its own gravediggers. Older forms of unfreedom and inequality were clearly tied to people, and there was hope, therefore, of becoming free and equal by changing the hearts of the people who oppressed us. When we become aware of the source of unfreedom and inequality under capitalism, we begin to realize that capitalism itself must be changed. Ideologies therefore must be created to protect the capitalist system, and one way in which they do this is by portraying inequality as equality and unfreedom as freedom.

Marx believed that the capitalist system is inherently unequal. The capitalists automatically benefit more from the capitalist system, while the workers are automatically disadvantaged. Under capitalism, those who own the means of production, those with capital, make money from their money. Under capitalism, capital begets more capital—that is, investments give a return—and as we saw earlier, Marx believed that this was derived from the exploitation of the workers. Not only are the workers automatically exploited, they also bear the burden of unemployment due to technological changes, geographical shifts, and other economic dislocations, all of which benefit the capitalist. The rule of capitalism is reflected in the common saying that the rich get richer while the poor get poorer. Constantly increasing inequality is built into the capitalist system.

Any attempt toward a more equal society must take into account this automatic propensity of the capitalist system to increased inequality. Nevertheless, attempts to make the capitalist system more equal often are portrayed as forms of inequality. From the Marxist viewpoint these would be the second form of ideology. For example, ideologues promote a "flat tax" which taxes the rich and the poor at the same rate. They argue that because the rate is the same for rich and poor, it is equal. They ignore the fact that a graduated tax rate may be just compensation for the built-in inequality of capitalism. They create an ideology by portraying the obvious inequalities of the capitalist system as inevitable or as being due to the laziness of the poor. In this way, inequality is portrayed as equality, and the freedom of the rich to keep the fruits of exploitation trumps the freedom of the workers.

We see in this example not only the two types of ideology, but also another instance of how Marx thought that capitalism is a good thing. The ideas of freedom and equality emerge from capitalism itself, and it is these ideas that drive us toward the dissolution of capitalism, toward communism.

Religion

Marx also sees religion as an ideology. He famously refers to religion as the opiate of the people, but it is worthwhile to look at the entire quote:

> Religious distress is at the same time the expression of real distress and also the protest against real distress. Religion is the sigh of the oppressed creature, the heart of a heartless world, just as it is the spirit of spiritless conditions. It is the opium of the people.
>
> (Marx, 1843/1970)

Marx believed that religion, like all ideology, reflects a truth, but that it is inverted. Because people cannot see that their distress and oppression are produced by the capitalist system, they are given a religious form. Marx clearly says that he is not against religion per se, but against a system that requires the illusions of religion.

This religious form is vulnerable to disruption, and therefore always is liable to become the basis of a revolutionary movement. We do indeed see that religious movements have often been in the forefront of opposition to capitalism (see, for example, liberation theology). Nevertheless, Marx felt that religion is especially amenable to becoming the second form of ideology by portraying the injustice of capitalism as a test for the faithful and pushing any revolutionary change off into the afterlife. In this way, the cry of the oppressed is used to further oppression.

Marx's Economics: A Case Study

This chapter is devoted to an analysis of Marx's sociology, but of course it is his economics for which he is far better known. Although we have touched on a number of aspects of Marx's economics, we have not dealt with it in a coherent fashion. In this closing section, we will look at Marx's economics, not as economics per se, but rather as an exemplification of his sociological theory. There is much more to Marxian economics, but this is the most relevant way to deal with it in a book devoted to sociological theory.

A starting point for Marxian economics is in the concepts, previously touched on, of use value and exchange value. People have always created use values; that is, they have always produced things that directly satisfy their wants. A *use value* is defined qualitatively; that is, something either is or is not useful. An *exchange value*, however, is defined quantitatively, not qualitatively. It is defined by the amount of labor needed to appropriate useful qualities. Whereas use values are produced to satisfy one's own needs, exchange values are produced to be exchanged for values of another use. Whereas the production of use values is a natural human expression, the existence of exchange values sets in motion a process by which humanity is distorted. The entire edifice of capitalism, including commodities, the market, money, and so forth, is erected on the basis of exchange values.

To Marx, the basic source of any value was the amount of socially necessary labor-time needed to produce an article under the normal conditions of production and with the average degree of skill and intensity of the time. This is the well-known *labor theory of value*. Although it is clear that labor lies at the base of use value, this fact grows progressively less clear as we move to exchange values, commodities, the market, and capitalism. To put it another way, "The determination of the magnitude of value by labor-time is therefore a secret, hidden under the apparent fluctuations in relative values of commodities" (Marx, 1867/1967:75). Labor, as the source of all value, is a secret in capitalism that allows the capitalists to exploit the workers.

According to Peter Worsley, Marx "put at the heart of his sociology—as no other sociology does—the theme of exploitation" (Worsley, 1982). The capitalists pay the workers *less* than the value the workers produce and keep the rest for themselves. The workers are not aware of this exploitation, and often, neither are the capitalists. The capitalists believe that this extra value is derived from their own cleverness, their capital investment, their manipulation of the market, and so on. Marx stated that "so long as trade is good, the capitalist is too much absorbed in money grubbing to take notice of this gratuitous gift of labor" (1867/1967:207). In sum, Marx said:

> The capitalist does not know that the normal price of labor also includes a definite quantity of unpaid labor, and that this very unpaid labor is the normal source of his gain. The category, surplus labor-time, does not exist at all for him, since it is included in the normal working-day, which he thinks he has paid for in the day's wages.
>
> (Marx, 1867/1967:550)

This leads us to Marx's central concept of *surplus value*. This is defined as the difference between the value of the product when it is sold and the value of the elements consumed in the formation of that product. Although means of production (raw materials and tools, the value of which comes from the labor involved in extracting or producing them) are consumed in the production process, it is labor that is the real source of surplus value. "The rate of surplus-value is therefore an exact expression for the degree of exploitation of labor-power by capital, or of the laborer by the capitalist" (Marx, 1867/1967:218). This points to one of Marx's more colorful metaphors: "Capital is dead labor, that, vampire-like, only lives by sucking living labor, and lives the more, the more labor it sucks" (1867/1967:233).

The surplus derived from this process is used by the capitalists to pay for such things as rent to landowners and interest to banks. But the most important derivation from it is profit. The capitalists can use this profit for private consumption, but that would not lead to the expansion of capitalism. Rather they expand their enterprise by converting it into a base for the creation of still more surplus value.

The desire for more profit and more surplus value for expansion pushes capitalism toward what Marx called the *general law of capitalist accumulation.* The capitalists seek to exploit workers as much as possible: "The constant tendency of capital is to force the cost of labor back towards . . . zero" (Marx, 1867/1967:600). Marx basically argued that the structure and the ethos of capitalism push the capitalists in the direction of the accumulation of more and more capital. In order to do this, given Marx's view that labor is the source of value, the capitalists are led to intensify the exploitation of the proletariat. Ultimately, however, increased exploitation yields fewer and fewer gains; an upper limit of exploitation is reached. In addition, as this limit is approached, the government is forced by pressure from the working class to place restrictions on the actions of capitalists (for example, laws limiting the length of the workday). As a result of these restrictions, the capitalists must look for other devices, and a major one is the substitution of machines for people. This substitution is made relatively easy, because the capitalists already have reduced the workers to laboring machines performing a series of simple operations. This shift to capital-intensive production is, paradoxically, a cause of the declining rate of profit since it is labor (not machines) which is the ultimate source of profit.

As mechanization proceeds, more and more people are put out of work and fall from the proletariat to the "industrial reserve army." At the same time, heightening competition and the burgeoning costs of technology lead to a progressive decline in the number of capitalists. In the end, Marx foresaw a situation in which society would be characterized by a tiny number of exploitative capitalists and a huge mass of proletarians and members of the industrial reserve army. In these extreme circumstances, capitalism would be most vulnerable to revolution. As Marx put it, the expropriation of the masses by the capitalists would be replaced by "the expropriation of a few usurpers by the mass of people" (1867/1967:764). The capitalists, of course, seek to forestall their demise. For example, they sponsor colonial adventures with the objective of shifting at least some of the burden of exploitation from the home front to the colonies. However, in Marx's view these efforts are ultimately doomed to failure, and the capitalists will face rebellion at home and abroad.

The key point about the general law of capitalist accumulation is the degree to which actors, both capitalist and proletarian, are impelled by the structure and ethos of capitalism to do what they do. Marx usually did not blame individual capitalists for their actions; he saw these actions as largely determined by the logic of the capitalist system. This is consistent with his view that actors in capitalism generally are devoid of creative independence. However, the developmental process inherent in capitalism provides the conditions necessary for the ultimate reemergence of such creative action and, with it, the overthrow of the capitalist system.

Communism

Marx often wrote as though changes in the mode of production were inevitable, as in the earlier quote where the hand-mill gives you feudalism and the steam-mill gives you capitalism. Unless one wishes to find reasons for rejecting Marx's theories, it is probably best to interpret Marx's historical materialism as motivated by a desire to identify some predictable trends and to use these trends to discover the points where political action could be most effective. This is certainly the way that Marx used his theories in his concrete political and economic studies, such as *Class Struggles in France* (1850) and *The Eighteenth Brumaire of Louis Bonaparte* (1963). The truth of historical materialism, then, does not depend on the inevitability of its historical predictions, but upon whether a focus on the way that we satisfy our material needs is the best way to reveal the opportunities for effective political intervention.

If the goal of Marx's materialist view of history was to predict those points where political action could be most effective, then it is his view of what changes will lead to the next stage that is most important. Marx thought that capitalism had developed its productive powers so that it was ready to enter a new mode of production, which he called communism. Most of his analysis dwelt on those conflicts in the present that will lead to this new economic form.

Despite the importance to Marx of the future communist society, he spent surprisingly little time depicting what this world would be like. He refused to write "recipes for the kitchens of the future" (Marx, cited in T. Ball, 1991:139). The era in which Marx wrote was filled with talk of revolutions and new forms of society—of communism, socialism, anarchy, and many more now forgotten. Charismatic political leaders appeared upon the historical stage and stirred audiences with their speeches. Marx, however, was intellectually opposed to painting utopic visions of the future. To Marx, the most important task was the critical analysis of contemporary capitalist society. He believed that such criticism would help bring down capitalism and create the conditions for the rise of a new socialist world. There would be time to construct communist society once capitalism was overcome. In general, however, Marx believed that communism would involve making decisions about what is to be produced away from the reified economy that runs in the interests of the few capitalists and putting in its place some sort of social decision making that would allow the needs of the many to be taken into account.

Criticisms

There are several problems in Marx's theory that need to be discussed. The first is the problem of actually existing communism. The failure of communist societies and their turn to a more capitalistically oriented economy force us to address what this means for the role of Marxian theory within sociology (Antonio, 2000; Aronson, 1995; Hudelson, 1993; Manuel, 1992). Marx's ideas seem to have already been tried and to have failed. At one time, almost one-third of the world's population lived under states inspired by the ideas of Marx. Now, many of these formerly Marxist states have become capitalist, and even those that still claim to be Marxist are nothing but a highly bureaucratized form of capitalism.

Against this criticism, it could be argued that these states never truly followed Marxist precepts, and that it is unfair for the critics to blame Marx for every misuse of his theory. However, those making the criticism claim that Marx himself insisted that

Marxist theory should not be split from its actually existing practice. As Alvin Gouldner (1970:3) writes, "Having set out to change the world, rather than produce one more interpretation of it, Marxist theory must ultimately be weighed on the scales of history." If Marxism never works out in practice, then, for Marx, the theory would be useless at best and ideological at worst. Furthermore, it seems clear that Marx's lack of a theory regarding the problems of state bureaucracy has contributed to the failures of actually existing communism. Had he developed a complete theory of state bureaucracy, it is conceivable that Marx might have preferred the evils of capitalism.

The second problem is often referred to as the *missing emancipatory subject*. This is the idea that Marx's theory places the proletariat at the heart of the social change leading to communism, but, in fact, members of the proletariat have rarely assumed this leading position and often are among the groups that are most opposed to communism. This is compounded by the fact that intellectuals—for example, academic sociologists—have leapt into the gap left by the proletariat and substituted intellectual activity for class struggle. In addition, the intellectuals' disappointment at the proletariat's conservativism is transformed into a theory that emphasizes the role of ideology much more strongly than Marx did and that tends to see the "heroes" of the future revolution as manipulated dupes.

The third problem is the missing dimension of gender. One of the main points of Marx's theory is that labor becomes a commodity under capitalism, yet it is a historical fact that this has happened less to women than to men. To a large degree, men's paid labor still depends on the unpaid labor of women. This is especially true when it comes to the all-important rearing of the next generation of workers. Sayer (1991) points out that not only does this leave a hole in his analysis, it affects his primary argument that capitalism is defined by its growing dependence on wage labor, since the growth of wage labor has been dependent on the unpaid labor of women. Patriarchy may be an essential foundation for the emergence of capitalism that Marx simply ignores.

The fourth problem is that Marx saw the economy as driven almost solely by production and ignored the role of consumption. The focus on production led him to predict that concerns for efficiency and cost cutting would lead to proletarianization, increasing alienation, and deepening class conflict. It could be argued that the central role of consumption in the modern economy encourages some creativity and entrepreneurship and that this provides at least some wage labor jobs that are not alienating. People who create new video games or direct movies or perform popular music are less alienated from their work, even though they are firmly entrenched in a capitalist system. Although there are only a few such jobs, this gives a concrete hope to the alienated masses who can anticipate that they, or at least their children, might someday work in interesting and creative jobs.

Finally, some might point to Marx's uncritical acceptance of Western conceptions of progress as a problem. Marx believed that the engine of history is humanity's always improving exploitation of nature for its material needs. In addition, Marx thought that the essence of human nature is our ability to shape nature to our purposes. It may be that these assumptions are a root cause of many of our current and future ecological crises.

Summary

Marx presents a complex and still relevant analysis of the historical basis of inequality in capitalism and how to change it. Marx's theories are open to many interpretations, but we have tried to present one that makes his theories consistent with his actual historical studies.

The chapter begins with a discussion of the dialectical approach that Marx derived from Hegel and that shapes all of Marx's work. The important point here is that Marx believed that society is structured around contradictions that can be resolved only through actual social change. One of the primary contradictions that Marx looked at was that between human potential (nature) and the conditions for labor in capitalism. For Marx, human potential is intimately tied to labor, which both expresses and transforms our nature. Under capitalism, our labor is sold as a commodity, and this leads to alienation from our productive activity, the objects that we make, our fellow workers, and even ourselves.

Next the chapter presents Marx's analysis of capitalist society. We begin with the central concept of commodities and then look at the contradiction between their use value and their exchange value. In capitalism, the exchange value of commodities tends to predominate over their actual usefulness in satisfying human needs; therefore, the commodities begin to appear to be separate from human labor and human need and eventually appear to have power over humans. Marx called this the fetishism of commodities. This fetishism is a form of reification, and it affects more than just commodities; in particular, it affects the economic system, which begins to seem like an objective, nonpolitical force that determines our lives. Because of this reification we don't see that the very idea of capital contains a contradictory social relation between those who profit from their investments and those whose actual labor provides the surplus value that constitutes the profit. In other words, the ability of capital to provide a profit really rests on the exploitation of the proletariat. This underlying contradiction leads to class conflict between the proletariat and bourgeoisie that eventually will result in revolution because proletarianization will swell the ranks of the proletariat. We conclude this section by stressing that despite his criticisms, Marx believed that capitalism has been good and that his criticisms of it are from the perspective of its potential future.

Marx felt that he was able to take the view from capitalism's potential future because of his materialist conception of history. By focusing on the forces of production, Marx was able to predict historical trends that allowed him to identify where political action could be effective. Political action and even revolution are necessary because relations of production and ideology hold back the necessary development of the forces of production. In Marx's view these changes eventually will lead to a communist society.

We also offer a discussion of some of the most important non-material (cultural) aspects of Marx's theory-especially ideology and religion-as well as some of his famous ideas on economics, especially the labor theory of value.

We conclude the chapter by presenting some criticisms of Marx's theories. Despite their significance, we believe that these and other criticisms have contributed to the strength of the Marxist approach, even where this has meant abandoning some of Marx's most strongly held positions.

CHAPTER 7

Emile Durkheim

Chapter Outline

Social Facts

The Division of Labor in Society

Suicide

Elementary Forms of Religious Life

Moral Education and Social Reform

Criticisms

There are two main themes in the work of Emile Durkheim. The first is the priority of the social over the individual, and the second is the idea that society can be studied scientifically. Because both of these themes continue to be controversial, Durkheim is still relevant today.

We live in a society that tends to see everything as attributable to individuals, even clearly social problems such as racism, pollution, and economic recessions. Durkheim approaches things from the opposite perspective, stressing the social dimension of all human phenomena. However, even some who recognize the importance of society tend to see it as an amorphous entity that can be intuitively understood, but never scientifically studied. Here again, Durkheim provides the opposing approach. For Durkheim, society is made up of "social facts" that exceed our intuitive understanding and must be investigated through observations and measurements. These ideas are so central to sociology that Durkheim is often seen as the "father" of sociology (Gouldner, 1958; Tiryakian, 2009). To found sociology as a discipline was indeed one of Durkheim's primary goals.

Durkheim (1900/1973b:3) believed that sociology, as an idea, was born in France in the nineteenth century. He wanted to turn this idea into a discipline, a well-defined field of study. He recognized the roots of sociology in the ancient philosophers—such as Plato and Aristotle—and more proximate sources in French philosophers such as Montesquieu and Condorcet. However, in Durkheim's (1900/1973b:6) view, previous philosophers did not go far enough, because they did not try to create an entirely new discipline.

Although the term *sociology* had been coined some years earlier by Auguste Comte, there was no field of sociology per se in late nineteenth-century universities. There were no schools, departments, or even professors of sociology. There were a few thinkers who were dealing with ideas that were in one way or another sociological, but there was as yet no disciplinary "home" for sociology. Indeed, there was strong opposition from existing disciplines to the founding of such a field. The most significant opposition came from psychology and philosophy, two fields that claimed already to cover the domain sought by sociology. The dilemma for Durkheim, given his aspirations for sociology, was how to create for it a separate and identifiable niche.

To separate it from philosophy, Durkheim argued that sociology should be oriented toward empirical research. This seems simple enough, but the situation was complicated by Durkheim's belief that sociology was also threatened by a philosophical school within sociology itself. In his view, the two other major figures of the epoch who thought of themselves as sociologists, Comte and Herbert Spencer, were far more interested in philosophizing, in abstract theorizing, than they were in studying the social world empirically. If the field continued in the direction set by Comte and Spencer, Durkheim felt, it would become nothing more than a branch of philosophy. As a result, he found it necessary to attack both Comte and Spencer (Durkheim, 1895/1982:19–20) for relying on preconceived ideas of social phenomena instead of actually studying the real world. Thus Comte was said to be guilty of assuming theoretically that the social world was evolving in the direction of an increasingly perfect society, rather than engaging in the hard, rigorous, and basic work of actually studying the changing nature of various societies. Similarly, Spencer was accused of assuming harmony in society rather than studying whether harmony actually existed.

Social Facts

In order to help sociology move away from philosophy and to give it a clear and separate identity, Durkheim (1895/1982) proposed that the distinctive subject matter of sociology should be the study of social facts (see Gane, 1988; Gilbert, 1994; Nielson, 2005; and the special edition of *Sociological Perspectives* [1995]). Briefly, *social facts* are the social structures and cultural norms and values that are external to, and coercive of, actors. Students, for example, are constrained by such social structures as the university bureaucracy as well as the norms and values of American society, which place great importance on a college education. Similar social facts constrain people in all areas of social life.

Crucial in separating sociology from philosophy is the idea that social facts are to be treated as "things" (S. Jones, 1996) and studied empirically. This means that social facts must be studied by acquiring data from outside of our own minds through observation and experimentation. This empirical study of social facts as things sets Durkheimian sociology apart from more philosophical approaches.[1]

> A social fact is every way of acting, fixed or not, capable of exercising on the individual an external constraint; or again, every way of acting which is general throughout a given society, while at the same time existing in its own right independent of its individual manifestations.
>
> (Durkheim, 1895/1982:13)

[1]For a critique of Durkheim's attempt to separate sociology from philosophy, see Boudon (1995).

Note that Durkheim gave two ways of defining a social fact so that sociology is distinguished from psychology. First, it is experienced as an external constraint rather than an internal drive; second, it is general throughout the society and is not attached to any particular individual.

Durkheim argued that social facts cannot be reduced to individuals, but must be studied as their own reality. Durkheim referred to social facts with the Latin term *sui generis,* which means "unique." He used this term to claim that social facts have their own unique character that is not reducible to individual consciousness. To allow that social facts could be explained by reference to individuals would be to reduce sociology to psychology. Instead, social facts can be explained only by other social facts. We will study some examples of this type of explanation later, where Durkheim explains the division of labor and even the rate of suicide with other social facts rather than individual intentions. To summarize, social facts can be empirically studied, are external to the individual, are coercive of the individual, and are explained by other social facts.

Durkheim himself gave several examples of social facts, including legal rules, moral obligations, and social conventions. He also refers to language as a social fact, and it provides an easily understood example. First, language is a "thing" that must be studied empirically. One cannot simply philosophize about the logical rules of language. Certainly, all languages have some logical rules regarding grammar, pronunciation, spelling, and so forth; however, all languages also have important exceptions to these logical rules (Quine, 1972). What follows the rules and what are exceptions must be discovered empirically by studying actual language use, especially since language use changes over time in ways that are not completely predictable.

Second, language is external to the individual. Although individuals use a language, language is not defined or created by the individual. The fact that individuals adapt language to their own use indicates that language is first external to the individual and in need of adaptation for individual use. Indeed, some philosophers (Kripke, 1982; Wittgenstein, 1953) have argued that there cannot be such a thing as a private language. A collection of words with only private meanings would not qualify as a language since it could not perform the basic function of a language: communication. Language is, by definition, social and therefore external to any particular individual.

Third, language is coercive of the individual. The language that we use makes some things extremely difficult to say. For example, people in lifelong relationships with same-sex partners have a very difficult time referring to each other. Should they call each other partners—leading people into thinking they are in business together—significant others, lovers, spouses, special friends? Each seems to have its disadvantages. Language is part of the system of social facts that makes life with a same-sex partner difficult even if every individual should be personally accepting of same-sex relationships.

Finally, changes in language can be explained only by other social facts and never by one individual's intentions. Even in those rare instances where a change in language can be traced to an individual, the actual explanation for the change is the social facts that have made society open to this change. For example, the most changeable part of language is slang, which almost always originates in a marginal social group. We may assume that an individual first originates a slang term, but which individual is irrelevant. It is the fact of the marginal social group that truly explains the history and function of the slang.

EMILE DURKHEIM

A Biographical Sketch

Emile Durkheim was born on April 15, 1858, in Epinal, France. He was descended from a long line of rabbis and himself studied to be a rabbi, but by the time he was in his teens, he had largely disavowed his heritage (Strenski, 1997:4). From that time on, his lifelong interest in religion was more academic than theological (Mestrovic, 1988). He was dissatisfied not only with his religious training but also with his general education and its emphasis on literary and esthetic matters. He longed for schooling in scientific methods and in the moral principles needed to guide social life. He rejected a traditional academic career in philosophy and sought instead to acquire the scientific training needed to contribute to the moral guidance of society. Although he was interested in scientific sociology, there was no field of sociology at that time, so between 1882 and 1887 he taught philosophy in a number of provincial schools in the Paris area.

His appetite for science was whetted further by a trip to Germany, where he was exposed to the scientific psychology being pioneered by Wilhelm Wundt (Durkheim, 1887/1993). In the years immediately after his visit to Germany, Durkheim published a good deal, basing his work, in part, on his experiences there (R. Jones, 1994). These publications helped him gain a position in the department of philosophy at the University of Bordeaux in 1887 (Pearce, 2005). There Durkheim offered the first course in social science in a French university. This was a particularly impressive accomplishment, because only a decade earlier, a furor had erupted in a French university after the mention of Auguste Comte in a student dissertation. Durkheim's main responsibility, however, was teaching courses in education to schoolteachers, and his most important course was in the area of moral education. His goal was to communicate a moral system to the educators, who he hoped would then pass the system on to young people in an effort to help reverse the moral degeneration he saw around him in French society.

The years that followed were characterized by a series of personal successes for Durkheim. In 1893 he published his French doctoral thesis, *The Division of Labor in Society*, as well as his Latin thesis on Montesquieu (Durkheim, 1892/1997; W. Miller, 1993). His major methodological statement, *The Rules of Sociological Method,* appeared in 1895, followed (in 1897) by his empirical application of those methods in the study *Suicide* (Hamlin and Brym, 2006). By 1896 he had become a full professor at Bordeaux. In 1902 he was summoned to the famous French university the Sorbonne, and in 1906 he was named professor of the science of education, a title that was changed in 1913 to professor of the science of education and sociology. The other of his most famous works, *The Elementary Forms of Religious Life,* was published in 1912.

Durkheim is most often thought of today as a political conservative, and his influence within sociology certainly has been a conservative one. But in his time, he was considered a liberal, and this was exemplified by the active public role he played in the defense of Alfred Dreyfus, the Jewish army captain whose court-martial for treason was felt by many to be anti-Semitic (Farrell, 1997).

Durkheim was deeply offended by the Dreyfus affair, particularly its anti-Semitism (Goldberg, 2008). But Durkheim did not attribute this anti-Semitism to racism among the French people. Characteristically, he saw it as a symptom of the moral sickness confronting French society as a whole (Birnbaum and Todd, 1995). He said:

> When society undergoes suffering, it feels the need to find someone whom it can hold responsible for its sickness, on whom it can avenge its misfortunes: and those against whom public opinion already discriminates are naturally designated for this role. These are the pariahs who serve as expiatory victims. What confirms me in this interpretation is the way in which the result of Dreyfus's trial was greeted in 1894. There was a surge of joy in the boulevards. People celebrated as a triumph what should have been a cause for public mourning. At least they knew whom to blame for the economic troubles and moral distress in which they lived. The trouble came from the Jews. The charge had been officially proved. By this very fact alone, things already seemed to be getting better and people felt consoled.
>
> (Lukes, 1972:345)

Thus, Durkheim's interest in the Dreyfus affair stemmed from his deep and lifelong interest in morality and the moral crisis confronting modern society.

To Durkheim, the answer to the Dreyfus affair and crises like it lay in ending the moral disorder in society. Because that could not be done quickly or easily, Durkheim suggested more specific actions such as severe repression of those who incite hatred of others and government efforts to show the public how it is being misled. He urged people to "have the courage to proclaim aloud what they think, and to unite together in order to achieve victory in the struggle against public madness" (Lukes, 1972:347).

Durkheim's (1928/1962) interest in socialism is also taken as evidence against the idea that he was a conservative, but his kind of socialism was very different from the kind that interested Marx and his followers. In fact, Durkheim labeled Marxism as a set of "disputable and out-of-date hypotheses" (Lukes, 1972:323). To Durkheim, socialism represented a movement aimed at the moral regeneration of society through scientific morality, and he was not interested in short-term political methods or the economic aspects of socialism. He did not see the proletariat as the salvation of society, and he was greatly opposed to agitation or violence. Socialism for Durkheim was very different from what we usually think of as socialism; it simply represented a system in which the moral principles discovered by scientific sociology were to be applied.

Durkheim, as we will see throughout this book, had a profound influence on the development of sociology, but his influence was not restricted to it (Halls, 1996). Much of his impact on other fields came through the journal *L'année sociologique,* which he founded in 1898. An intellectual circle arose around the journal with Durkheim at its center. Through it, he and his ideas influenced such fields as anthropology, history (especially the "Annales school" [Nielsen, 2005]), linguistics, and—somewhat ironically, considering his early attacks on the field—psychology.

Durkheim died on November 15, 1917, a celebrated figure in French intellectual circles, but it was not until over twenty years later, with the publication of Talcott Parsons's *The Structure of Social Action* (1937), that his work became a significant influence on American sociology.

Some sociologists feel that Durkheim took an "extremist" position (Karady, 1983:79–80) in limiting sociology to the study of social facts. This position has limited at least some branches of sociology to the present day. Furthermore, Durkheim seemed to artificially sever sociology from neighboring fields. As Lemert (1994a:91) puts it, "Because he defined sociology so exclusively in relation to its own facts, Durkheim cut it off from the other sciences of man." Nevertheless, whatever its subsequent drawbacks, Durkheim's idea of social facts both established sociology as an independent field of study and provided one of the most convincing arguments for studying society as it is before we decide what it should be.

Material and Nonmaterial Social Facts

Durkheim differentiated between two broad types of social facts—material and nonmaterial. *Material social facts,* such as styles of architecture, forms of technology, and legal codes, are the easier to understand of the two because they are directly observable. Clearly, such things as laws are external to individuals and coercive over them. More importantly, these material social facts often express a far larger and more powerful realm of moral forces that are at least equally external to individuals and coercive over them. These are nonmaterial social facts.

The bulk of Durkheim's studies, and the heart of his sociology, lies in the study of nonmaterial social facts. Durkheim said: "Not all social consciousness achieves . . . externalization and materialization" (1897/1951:315). What sociologists now call norms and values, or more generally culture (Alexander, 1988a), are good examples of what Durkheim meant by *nonmaterial social facts.* But this idea creates a problem: How can nonmaterial social facts like norms and values be external to the actor? Where could they be found except in the minds of actors? And if they are in the minds of actors, are they not internal rather than external?

Durkheim recognized that nonmaterial social facts are, to a certain extent, found in the minds of individuals. However, it was his belief that when people begin to interact in complex ways, their interactions will "obey laws all their own" (Durkheim, 1912/1965:471). Individuals are still necessary as a kind of substrate for the nonmaterial social facts, but the particular form and content will be determined by the complex interactions and not by the individuals. Hence, Durkheim could write in the same work first that "Social things are actualized only through men; they are the product of human activity" (1895/1982:17) and second that "Society is not a mere sum of individuals" (1895/1982:103). Despite the fact that society is made up only of human beings and contains no immaterial "spiritual" substance, it can be understood only through studying the interactions rather than the individuals. The interactions, even when nonmaterial, have their own levels of reality. This has been called "relational realism" (Alpert, 1939).

Durkheim saw social facts along a continuum of materiality (Lukes, 1972:9–10). The sociologist usually begins a study by focusing on material social facts, which are empirically accessible, in order to understand nonmaterial social facts, which are the real focus of his work. The most material are such things as population size and density, channels of communication, and housing arrangements (Andrews, 1993). Durkheim called these facts *morphological,* and they figure most importantly in his first book, *The*

Division of Labor in Society. At another level are structural components (a bureaucracy, for example), which are a mixture of morphological components (the density of people in a building and their lines of communication) and nonmaterial social facts (such as the bureaucratic norms).

Types of Nonmaterial Social Facts

Since nonmaterial social facts are so important to Durkheim, we will present a brief discussion of four different types—morality, collective conscience, collective representations, and social currents—before examining how Durkheim used these types in his studies.

Morality

Durkheim was a sociologist of morality in the broadest sense of the word (Hall, 1987; Mestrovic, 1988; Varga, 2006). Studying him reminds us that a concern with morality was at the foundation of sociology as a discipline. Durkheim's view of morality had two aspects. First, Durkheim was convinced that morality is a social fact, in other words, that morality can be empirically studied, is external to the individual, is coercive of the individual, and is explained by other social facts. This means that morality is not something that one can philosophize about, but something that one has to study as an empirical phenomenon. This is particularly true because morality is intimately related to the social structure. To understand the morality of any particular institution, you have to *first study* how the institution is constituted, how it came to assume its present form, what its place is in the overall structure of society, how the various institutional obligations are related to the social good, and so forth.

Second, Durkheim was a sociologist of morality because his studies were driven by his concern about the moral "health" of modern society. Much of Durkheim's sociology can be seen as a by-product of his concern with moral issues. Indeed, one of Durkheim's associates wrote in a review of his life's work that "one will fail to understand his works if one does not take account of the fact that morality was their center and object" (Davy, trans. in Hall, 1987:5).

This second point needs more explanation if we are to understand Durkheim's perspective. It was not that Durkheim thought that society had become, or was in danger of becoming, immoral. That was simply impossible because morality was, for Durkheim (1925/1961:59), identified with society. Therefore, society could not be immoral, but it could certainly lose its moral force if the collective interest of society became nothing but the sum of self-interests. Only to the extent that morality was a social fact could it impose an obligation on individuals that superseded their self-interest. Consequently, Durkheim believed that society needs a strong common morality. What the morality should be was of less interest to him.

Durkheim's great concern with morality was related to his curious definition of freedom. In Durkheim's view, people were in danger of a "pathological" loosening of moral bonds. These moral bonds were important to Durkheim, for without them the individual would be enslaved by ever-expanding and insatiable passions. People would be impelled by their passions into a mad search for gratification, but each new gratification would lead only to more and more needs. According to Durkheim, the one thing that every human will always want is "more." And, of course, that is the one thing we ultimately cannot have. If society does not limit us, we will become slaves to the pursuit of more. Consequently, Durkheim held the seemingly paradoxical view that the individual needs morality and external control in order to be free. This view of the insatiable desire at the core of every human is central to his sociology.

Collective Conscience

Durkheim attempted to deal with his interest in common morality in various ways and with different concepts. In his early efforts to deal with this issue, Durkheim developed the idea of the *collective conscience.* In French, the word *conscience* means both "consciousness" and "moral conscience." Durkheim characterized the collective conscience in the following way:

> The totality of beliefs and sentiments common to average citizens of the same society forms a determinate system which has its own life; one may call it the collective or common conscience. . . . It is, thus, an entirely different thing from particular consciences, although it can be realized only through them.
>
> (Durkheim, 1893/1964:79–80)

Several points are worth underscoring in this definition. First, it is clear that Durkheim thought of the collective conscience as occurring throughout a given society when he wrote of the "totality" of people's beliefs and sentiments. Second, Durkheim clearly conceived of the collective conscience as being independent and capable of determining other social facts. It is not just a reflection of a material base as Marx sometimes suggested. Finally, although he held such views of the collective conscience, Durkheim also wrote of its being "realized" through individual consciousness.

Collective conscience refers to the general structure of shared understandings, norms, and beliefs. It is therefore an all-embracing and amorphous concept. As we will see later, Durkheim employed this concept to argue that "primitive" societies had a stronger collective conscience—that is, more shared understandings, norms, and beliefs—than modern societies.

Collective Representations

Because collective conscience is such a broad and amorphous idea, it is impossible to study directly, but must be approached through related material social facts. (Later, for example, we will look at Durkheim's use of the legal system to say something about the collective conscience.) Durkheim's dissatisfaction with this limitation led him to use the collective conscience less in his later work in favor of the much more specific concept of *collective representations* (Nemedi, 1995; Schmaus, 1994). The French word *représentation* literally means "idea." Durkheim used the term to refer to both a collective concept and a social "force." Examples of collective representations are religious symbols, myths, and popular legends. All of these are ways in which society reflects on itself (Durkheim, 1895/1982:40). They represent collective beliefs, norms, and values, and they motivate us to conform to these collective claims.

Collective representations also cannot be reduced to individuals, because they emerge out of social interactions, but they can be studied more directly because they are more liable to be connected to material symbols such as flags, icons, and pictures or connected to practices such as rituals. Therefore, the sociologist can begin to study how certain collective representations fit well together, or have an affinity, and others do not. As an example, we can look at a recent sociological study that shows how representations of Abraham Lincoln have changed in response to other social facts.

> Between the turn of the century and 1945, Lincoln, like other heroic presidents, was idealized. Prints showed him holding Theodore Roosevelt's hand and pointing him in the right direction, or hovering in ethereal splendor behind Woodrow Wilson as he contemplated matters of war and peace, or placing his reassuring hand on Franklin Roosevelt's shoulder. Cartoons showed admirers looking up to his statue or portrait. Neoclassical statues depicted him larger than life; state portraits enveloped him in the majesty of presidential power; "grand style" history painting showed him altering the fate of the nation. By the 1960s, however, traditional pictures had disappeared and been replaced by a new kind of representation on billboards, posters, cartoons, and magazine covers. Here Lincoln is shown wearing a party hat and blowing a whistle to mark a bank's anniversary; there he is playing a saxophone to announce a rock concert; elsewhere he is depicted arm in arm with a seductive Marilyn Monroe, or sitting upon his Lincoln Memorial chair of state grasping a can of beer, or wearing sunglasses and looking "cool," or exchanging Valentine cards with George Washington to signify that Valentine's Day had displaced their own traditional birthday celebrations. Post-1960s commemorative iconography articulates the diminishing of Lincoln's dignity.
>
> (Schwartz, 1998:73)

Abraham Lincoln functions in American society as a collective representation in that his various representations allow a people to think about themselves as Americans—as either American patriots or American consumers. His image is also a force that motivates us to perform a patriotic duty or to buy a greeting card. A study of this representation allows us to better understand changes in American society.

Social Currents

Most of the examples of social facts that Durkheim refers to are associated with social organizations. However, he made it clear that there are social facts "which do not present themselves in this already crystallized form" (1895/1982:52). Durkheim called these *social currents.* He gave as examples "the great waves of enthusiasm, indignation, and pity" that are produced in public gatherings (Durkheim, 1895/1982:52–53). Although social currents are less concrete than other social facts, they are nevertheless social facts because they cannot be reduced to the individual. We are swept along by such social currents, and this has a coercive power over us even if we become aware of it only when we struggle against the common feelings.

It is possible for these nonmaterial and ephemeral social facts to affect even the strongest institutions. Ramet (1991), for example, reports that the social currents that are potentially created among a crowd at a rock concert were looked at as a threat by Eastern European communist governments and, indeed, contributed to their downfall. Rock concerts were places for the emergence and dissemination of "cultural standards, fashions, and behavioral syndromes independent of party control" (Ramet, 1991:216). In particular, members of the audience were apt to see an expression of their alienation in the concert. Their own feelings were thereby affirmed, strengthened, and given new social and political meanings. In other words, political leaders were afraid of rock concerts because of the potential for the depressing individual feelings of alienation to be transformed into the motivating social fact of alienation. This provides another example of how social facts are related to but different from individual feelings and intentions.

A Group Mind?

Given the emphasis on norms, values, and culture in contemporary sociology, we have little difficulty accepting Durkheim's interest in nonmaterial social facts. However, the concept of social currents does cause us a few problems. Particularly troublesome is the idea of a set of independent social currents "coursing" through the social world as if they were somehow suspended in a social void. This problem has led many to criticize Durkheim for having a group-mind orientation (Pope, 1976:192–194). (Such an idea was prevalent in the United States in the late 1800s and early 1900s, especially in the work of Franklin A. Giddings [Chriss, 2006].) Those who accuse Durkheim of having such a perspective argue that he accorded nonmaterial social facts an autonomous existence, separate from actors. But cultural phenomena cannot float by themselves in a social void, and Durkheim was well aware of this.

> But how are we to conceive of this social consciousness? Is it a simple and transcendent being, soaring above society? . . . It is certain that experience shows us nothing of the sort. The collective mind [*l'esprit collectif*] is only a composite of individual minds. But the latter are not mechanically juxtaposed and closed off from one another. They are in perpetual interaction through the exchange of symbols; they interpenetrate one another. They group themselves according to their natural affinities; they coordinate and systematize themselves. In this way is formed an entirely new psychological being, one without equal in the world. The consciousness with which it is endowed is infinitely more intense and more vast than those which resonate within it. For it is "a consciousness of consciousnesses" [*une conscience de consciences*]. Within it, we find condensed at once all the vitality of the present and of the past.
>
> (Durkheim, 1885/1978:103)

Social currents can be viewed as sets of meanings that are shared by the members of a collectivity. As such, they cannot be explained in terms of the mind of any given individual. Individuals certainly contribute to social currents, but by becoming social something new develops through their interactions. They can only be explained intersubjectively, that is, in terms of the *interactions* between individuals. They exist at the level of interactions, not at the level of individuals. These collective "moods," or social currents, vary from one collectivity to another, with the result that there is variation in the rate of certain behaviors, including, as we will see later, something as seemingly individualistic as suicide.

In fact, there are very strong similarities between Durkheim's theory of social facts and current theories about the relation between the brain and the mind (Sawyer, 2002). Both theories use the idea that complex, constantly changing systems will begin to display new properties that "cannot be predicted from a full and complete description of the component units of the system" (Sawyer, 2002:228). Even though modern philosophy assumes that the mind is nothing but brain functions, the argument is that the complexity of the interconnections in the brain creates a new level of reality, the mind, that is not explainable in terms of individual neurons. This was precisely Durkheim's argument: that the complexity and intensity of interactions between individuals cause a new level of reality to emerge that cannot be explained in terms of the individuals. Hence, it could be argued that Durkheim had a very modern conception of nonmaterial social facts that encompasses norms, values, culture, and a variety of shared social-psychological phenomena (Emirbayer, 1996).

The Division of Labor in Society

The Division of Labor in Society (Durkheim, 1893/1964; Gibbs, 2003) has been called sociology's first classic (Tiryakian, 1994). In this work, Durkheim traced the development of the modern relation between individuals and society. In particular, Durkheim wanted to use his new science of sociology to examine what many at the time had come to see as the modern crisis of morality. The preface to the first edition begins, "This book is above all an attempt to treat the facts of moral life according to the methods of the positive sciences."

In France in Durkheim's day, there was a widespread feeling of moral crisis. The French Revolution had ushered in a focus on the rights of the individual that often expressed itself as an attack on traditional authority and religious beliefs. This trend continued even after the fall of the revolutionary government. By the mid-nineteenth century, many people felt that social order was threatened because people thought only about themselves and not about society. In the less than 100 years between the French Revolution and Durkheim's maturity, France went through three monarchies, two empires, and three republics. These regimes produced fourteen constitutions. The feeling of moral crisis was brought to a head by Prussia's crushing defeat of France in 1870, which included the annexation of Durkheim's birthplace by Prussia. This was followed by the short-lived and violent revolution known as the Paris Commune.[2] Both the defeat and the subsequent revolt were blamed on the problem of rampant individualism.

August Comte argued that much of this could be traced to the increasing division of labor. In simpler societies, people do basically the same thing, such as farming, and they share common experiences and consequently have common values. In modern society, everyone has a different job. When different people are assigned various specialized tasks, they no longer share common experiences. This undermines the shared moral beliefs that are necessary for a society. Consequently, people will not sacrifice in times of social need. Comte proposed that sociology create a new pseudo-religion that would reinstate social cohesion. To a large degree, *The Division of Labor in Society* can be seen as a refutation of Comte's analysis (Gouldner, 1962). Durkheim argues that the division of labor does not represent the disappearance of social morality so much as a new kind of social morality.

---

[2]Before its bloody repression, Marx saw the Paris Commune as the harbinger of the proletariat revolution.

The thesis of *The Division of Labor in Society* is that modern society is not held together by the similarities between people who do basically similar things. Instead, it is the division of labor itself that pulls people together by forcing them to be dependent on each other. It may seem that the division of labor is an economic necessity that corrodes the feeling of solidarity, but Durkheim (1893/1964:17) argued that "the economic services that it can render are insignificant compared with the moral effect that it produces and its true function is to create between two or more people a feeling of solidarity."

Mechanical and Organic Solidarity

The change in the division of labor has had enormous implications for the structure of society. Durkheim was most interested in the changed way in which social solidarity is produced, in other words, the changed way in which society is held together and how its members see themselves as part of a whole. To capture this difference, Durkheim referred to two types of solidarity—mechanical and organic. A society characterized by mechanical solidarity is unified because all people are generalists. The bond among people is that they are all engaged in similar activities and have similar responsibilities. In contrast, a society characterized by organic solidarity is held together by the differences among people, by the fact that all have different tasks and responsibilities.[3]

Because people in modern society perform a relatively narrow range of tasks, they need many other people in order to survive. The primitive family headed by father–hunter and mother–food gatherer is practically self-sufficient, but the modern family needs the grocer, baker, butcher, auto mechanic, teacher, police officer, and so forth. These people, in turn, need the kinds of services that others provide in order to live in the modern world. Modern society, in Durkheim's view, is thus held together by the specialization of people and their need for the services of many others. This specialization includes not only that of individuals but also of groups, structures, and institutions.

Durkheim argued that primitive societies have a stronger collective conscience, that is, more shared understandings, norms, and beliefs. The increasing division of labor has caused a diminution of the collective conscience. The collective conscience is of much less significance in a society with organic solidarity than it is in a society with mechanical solidarity. People in modern society are more likely to be held together by the division of labor and the resulting need for the functions performed by others than they are by a shared and powerful collective conscience. Nevertheless, even organic societies have a collective consciousness, albeit in a weaker form that allows for more individual differences.

Anthony Giddens (1972) points out that the collective conscience in the two types of society can be differentiated on four dimensions—volume, intensity, rigidity, and content. Volume refers to the number of people enveloped by the collective conscience; intensity, to how deeply the individuals feel about it; rigidity, to how clearly it is defined; and content, to the form that the collective conscience takes in the two types of society (see Table 7.1).

---

[3]For a comparison with Spencer's evolutionary theory, see Perrin (1995).

TABLE 7.1

The Four Dimensions of the Collective Conscience

Solidarity	Volume	Intensity	Rigidity	Content
Mechanical	Entire society	High	High	Religious
Organic	Particular groups	Low	Low	Moral individualism

In a society characterized by mechanical solidarity, the collective conscience covers virtually the entire society and all its members; it is believed in with great intensity; it is extremely rigid; and its content is highly religious in character. In a society with organic solidarity, the collective conscience is limited to particular groups; it is adhered to with much less intensity; it is not very rigid; and its content is the elevation of the importance of the individual to a moral precept.

Dynamic Density

The division of labor was a material social fact to Durkheim because it is a pattern of interactions in the social world. As we indicated earlier, social facts must be explained by other social facts. Durkheim believed that the cause of the transition from mechanical to organic solidarity was dynamic density. This concept refers to the number of people in a society and the amount of interaction that occurs among them. More people means an increase in the competition for scarce resources, and more interaction means a more intense struggle for survival among the basically similar components of society.

The problems associated with dynamic density usually are resolved through differentiation and, ultimately, the emergence of new forms of social organization. The rise of the division of labor allows people to complement, rather than conflict with, one another. Furthermore, the increased division of labor makes for greater efficiency, with the result that resources increase, making the competition over them more peaceful.

This points to one final difference between mechanical and organic solidarity. In societies with organic solidarity, less competition and more differentiation allow people to cooperate more and to all be supported by the same resource base. Therefore, difference allows for even closer bonds between people than does similarity. Thus, a society characterized by organic solidarity leads to both more solidarity and more individuality than does one characterized by mechanical solidarity (Rueschemeyer, 1994). Individuality, then, is not the opposite of close social bonds, but a requirement for it (Muller, 1994).

Repressive and Restitutive Law

The division of labor and dynamic density are material social facts, but Durkheim's main interest was in the forms of solidarity, which are nonmaterial social facts. Durkheim felt that it was difficult to study nonmaterial social facts directly, especially something as pervasive as a collective conscience. In order to study nonmaterial social facts scientifically, the sociologist should examine material social facts that reflect the nature of, and changes in, nonmaterial social facts. In *The Division of Labor in Society,* Durkheim chose to study the differences between law in societies with mechanical solidarity and law in societies with organic solidarity (Cotterrell, 1999).

Durkheim argued that a society with mechanical solidarity is characterized by *repressive law.* Because people are very similar in this type of society, and because they tend to believe very strongly in a common morality, any offense against their shared value system is likely to be of significance to most individuals. Since everyone feels the offense and believes deeply in the common morality, a wrongdoer is likely to be punished severely for any action that offends the collective moral system. Theft might lead to the cutting off of the offender's hands; blaspheming might result in the removal of one's tongue. Even minor offenses against the moral system are likely to be met with severe punishment.

In contrast, a society with organic solidarity is characterized by *restitutive law,* where offenders must make restitution for their crimes. In such societies, offenses are more likely to be seen as committed against a particular individual or segment of society than against the moral system itself. Because there is a weak common morality, most people do not react emotionally to a breach of the law. Instead of being severely punished for every offense against the collective morality, offenders in an organic society are likely to be asked to make restitution to those who have been harmed by their actions. Although some repressive law continues to exist in a society with organic solidarity (for example, the death penalty), restitutive law predominates, especially for minor offenses.

In summary, Durkheim argues in *The Division of Labor* that the form of moral solidarity has changed in modern society, not disappeared. We have a new form of solidarity that allows for more interdependence and closer, less competitive relations and that produces a new form of law based on restitution. However, this book was far from a celebration of modern society. Durkheim argued that this new form of solidarity is prone to certain kinds of social pathologies.

Normal and Pathological

Perhaps the most controversial of Durkheim's claims was that the sociologist is able to distinguish between healthy and pathological societies. After using this idea in *The Division of Labor in Society,* Durkheim wrote another book, *The Rules of Sociological Method,* in which, among other things, he attempted to refine and defend this idea. He claimed that a healthy society can be recognized because the sociologist will find similar conditions in other societies in similar stages. If a society departs from what is normally found, it is probably pathological.

This idea was attacked at the time, and there are few sociologists today who subscribe to it. Even Durkheim, when he wrote the "Preface to the Second Edition" of *The Rules,* no longer attempted to defend it: "It seems pointless for us to revert to the other controversies that this book has given rise to, for they do not touch upon anything essential. The general orientation of the method does not depend upon the procedures preferred to classify social types or distinguish the normal from the pathological" (1895/1982:45).

Nevertheless, there is one interesting idea that Durkheim derived from this argument: the idea that crime (Smith, 2008) is normal rather than pathological. He argued that since crime is found in every society, it must be normal and provide a useful function. Crime, he claimed, helps societies define and delineate their collective conscience: "Imagine a community of saints in an exemplary and perfect monastery. In it crime as such will be unknown, but faults that appear venial to the ordinary person will arouse the same scandal as does normal crime in ordinary consciences. If therefore that community has the power to judge and punish, it will term such acts criminal and deal with them as such" (1895/1982:100).

In *The Division of Labo*r, he used the idea of pathology to criticize some of the "abnormal" forms that the division of labor takes in modern society. He identified three abnormal forms: (1) the anomic division of labor, (2) the forced division of labor, and (3) the poorly coordinated division of labor. Durkheim maintained that the moral crises of modernity that Comte and others had identified with the division of labor was really caused by these abnormal forms.

The *anomic division of labor* refers to the lack of regulation in a society that celebrates isolated individuality and refrains from telling people what they should do. Durkheim further develops this concept of *anomie* in his work on suicide discussed later. In both works, he uses the term to refer to those social conditions where humans lack sufficient moral restraint (Bar-Haim, 1997; Hilbert, 1986). For Durkheim, modern society is always prone to anomie, but it comes to the fore in times of social and economic crises.

Without the strong common morality of mechanical solidarity, people might not have a clear concept of what is and what is not proper and acceptable behavior. Even though the division of labor is a source of cohesion in modern society, it cannot entirely make up for the weakening of the common morality. Individuals can become isolated and be cut adrift in their highly specialized activities. They can more easily cease to feel a common bond with those who work and live around them. This gives rise to anomie. Organic solidarity is prone to this particular "pathology," but it is important to remember that Durkheim saw this as an abnormal situation. The modern division of labor has the capacity to promote increased moral interactions rather than reduce people to isolated and meaningless tasks and positions.

While Durkheim believed that people needed rules and regulation to tell them what to do, his second abnormal form pointed to a kind of rule that could lead to conflict and isolation and therefore increase anomie. He called this the *forced division of labor*. This second pathology refers to the fact that outdated norms and expectations can force individuals, groups, and classes into positions for which they are ill suited. Traditions, economic power, or status can determine who performs what jobs regardless of talent and qualification. It is here that Durkheim comes closest to a Marxist position.

> If one class in society is obliged, in order to live, to take any price for its services, while another class can pass over this situation, because of the resources already at its disposal, resources that, however, are not necessarily the result of some social superiority, the latter group has an unjust advantage over the former with respect to the law.
>
> (Durkheim, 1895/1982:319)

Finally, the third form of abnormal division of labor is where the specialized functions performed by different people are *poorly coordinated.* Again Durkheim makes the point that organic solidarity flows from the interdependence of people. If people's specializations do not result in increased interdependence but simply in isolation, the division of labor will not result in social solidarity.

Justice

For the division of labor to function as a moral and socially solidifying force in modern society, anomie, the forced division of labor, and the improper coordination of specialization must be addressed. Modern societies are no longer held together by shared experiences and common beliefs. Instead, they are held together through their very differences, so long as those differences are allowed to develop in a way that promotes interdependence. Key to this for Durkheim is social justice.

> The task of the most advanced societies is, then, a work of justice. . . . Just as the idea of lower societies was to create or maintain as intense a common life as possible, in which the individual was absorbed, so our ideal is to make social relations always more equitable, so as to assure the free development of all our socially useful forces.
>
> (Durkheim, 1893/1964:387)

Morality, social solidarity, justice—these were big themes for a first book in a fledgling field. Durkheim was to return to these ideas again in his work, but never again would he look at them in terms of society as a whole. He predicted in his second book, *The Rules of Sociological Method* (1895/1982:184), that sociology itself would succumb to the division of labor and break down into a collection of specialties. Whether this has led to an increased interdependence and an organic solidarity in sociology is still an open question.

Suicide

It has been suggested that Durkheim's study of suicide is the paradigmatic example of how a sociologist should connect theory and research (Merton, 1968). Indeed, Durkheim makes it clear in the "Preface" that he intended this study not only to contribute to the understanding of a particular social problem, but also to serve as an example of his new sociological method. (For a series of appraisals of *Suicide* nearly 100 years after its publication, see Lester, 1994.)

Durkheim chose to study suicide because it is a relatively concrete and specific phenomenon for which there were comparatively good data available. However, Durkheim's most important reason for studying suicide was to prove the power of the new science of sociology. Suicide is generally considered to be one of the most private and personal acts. Durkheim believed that if he could show that sociology had a role to play in explaining such a seemingly individualistic act as suicide, it would be relatively easy to extend sociology's domain to phenomena that are much more readily seen as open to sociological analysis.

As a sociologist, Durkheim was not concerned with studying why any specific individual committed suicide (for a critique of this, see Berk, 2006). That was to be left to the psychologists. Instead, Durkheim was interested in explaining differences in *suicide rates;* that is, he was interested in why one group had a higher rate of suicide than did another. Psychological or biological factors may explain why a particular individual in a group commits suicide, but Durkheim assumed that only social facts could explain why one group had a higher rate of suicide than did another. (For a critique of this approach and an argument for the need to include cultural and psychological factors in the study of suicide, see Hamlin and Brym, 2006.)

Durkheim proposed two related ways of evaluating suicide rates. One way is to compare different societies or other types of collectivities. Another way is to look at the changes in the suicide rate in the same collectivity over time. In either case, cross-culturally or historically, the logic of the argument is essentially the same. If there is variation in suicide rates from one group to another or from one time period to another, Durkheim believed that the difference would be the consequence of variations in sociological factors, in particular, social currents. Durkheim acknowledged that individuals may have reasons for committing suicide, but these reasons are not the real cause: "They may be said to indicate the individual's weak points, where the outside current bearing the impulse to self-destruction most easily finds introduction. But they are no part of this current itself, and consequently cannot help us to understand it" (1897/1951:151).

Durkheim began *Suicide* by testing and rejecting a series of alternative ideas about the causes of suicide. Among these are individual psychopathology, alcoholism, race, heredity, and climate. Not all of Durkheim's arguments are convincing (see, for example, Skog, 1991 for an examination of Durkheim's argument against alcoholism). However, what is important is his method of empirically dismissing what he considered extraneous factors so that he could get to what he thought of as the most important causal variables.

In addition, Durkheim examined and rejected the imitation theory associated with one of his contemporaries, the French social psychologist Gabriel Tarde (1843–1904). The theory of imitation argues that people commit suicide (and engage in a wide range of other actions) because they are imitating the actions of others. This social-psychological approach was the most important competitor to Durkheim's focus on social facts. As a result, Durkheim took great pains to discredit it. For example, Durkheim reasoned that if imitation were truly important, we should find that nations that border on a country with a high suicide rate would themselves have high rates, but an examination of the data showed that no such relationship existed. Durkheim admitted that some individual suicides may be the result of imitation, but it is such a minor factor that it has no significant effect on the overall suicide rate.

Durkheim concluded that the critical factors in differences in suicide rates were to be found in differences at the level of social facts. Different groups have different collective sentiments[4] that produce different social currents. It is these social currents that affect individual decisions about suicide. In other words, changes in the collective sentiments lead to changes in social currents, which, in turn, lead to changes in suicide rates.

---

[4]Durkheim is moving away from using the term *collective conscience* in this work, but he has not fully developed the idea of collective representations. We see no substantial difference between his use of collective sentiments in *Suicide* and his use of collective conscience in *The Division of Labor*.

TABLE 7.2

The Four Types of Suicide

Integration	Low	Egoistic suicide
	High	Altruistic suicide
Regulation	Low	Anomic suicide
	High	Fatalistic suicide

The Four Types of Suicide

Durkheim's theory of suicide can be seen more clearly if we examine the relation between the types of suicide and his two underlying social facts—integration and regulation (Pope, 1976). *Integration* refers to the strength of the attachment that we have to society. *Regulation* refers to the degree of external constraint on people. For Durkheim, the two social currents are continuous variables, and suicide rates go up when either of these currents are too low or too high. We therefore have four types of suicide, as shown in Table 7.2. If integration is high, Durkheim calls that type of suicide altruistic. Low integration results in an increase in egoistic suicides. Fatalistic suicide is associated with high regulation, and anomic suicide with low regulation.

Egoistic Suicide

High rates of *egoistic suicide* (Berk, 2006) are likely to be found in those societies or groups in which the individual is not well integrated into the larger social unit. This lack of integration leads to a feeling that the individual is not part of society, but this also means that society is not part of the individual. Durkheim believed that the best parts of a human being—our morality, values, and sense of purpose—come from society. An integrated society provides us with these things, as well as a general feeling of moral support to get us through the daily small indignities and trivial disappointments. Without this, we are liable to commit suicide at the smallest frustration.

The lack of social integration produces distinctive social currents, and these currents cause differences in suicide rates. For example, Durkheim talked of societal disintegration leading to "currents of depression and disillusionment" (1897/1951:214). Politics is dominated by a sense of futility, morality is seen as an individual choice, and popular philosophies stress the meaninglessness of life. In contrast, strongly integrated groups discourage suicide. The protective, enveloping social currents produced by integrated societies prevent the widespread occurrence of egoistic suicide by, among other things, providing people with a sense of the broader meaning of their lives. Here is the way Durkheim puts it regarding religious groups:

> Religion protects man against the desire for self-destruction. . . . What constitutes religion is the existence of a certain number of beliefs and practices common to all the faithful, traditional and thus obligatory. The more numerous and strong these

> collective states of mind are, the stronger the integration of the religious community, also the greater its preservative value.
>
> (Durkheim, 1897/1951:170)

However, Durkheim demonstrated that not all religions provide the same degree of protection from suicide. Protestant religions with their emphasis on individual faith over church community and their lack of communal rituals tend to provide less protection. His principal point is that it is not the particular beliefs of the religion that are important, but the degree of integration.

Durkheim's statistics also showed that suicide rates go up for those who are unmarried and therefore less integrated into a family, whereas the rates go down in times of national political crises such as wars and revolutions, when social causes and revolutionary or nationalist fervor give people's life a greater meaning. He argues that the only thing that all of these have in common is the increased feeling of integration.

Interestingly, Durkheim affirms the importance of social forces even in the case of egoistic suicide, where the individual might be thought to be free of social constraints. Actors are never free of the force of the collectivity: "However individualized a man may be, there is always something collective remaining—the very depression and melancholy resulting from this same exaggerated individualism. He effects communion through sadness when he no longer has anything else with which to achieve it" (Durkheim, 1897/1951:214). The case of egoistic suicide indicates that in even the most individualistic, most private of acts, social facts are the key determinant.

Altruistic Suicide

The second type of suicide discussed by Durkheim is altruistic suicide. Whereas egoistic suicide is more likely to occur when social integration is too weak, *altruistic suicide* is more likely to occur when "social integration is too strong" (Durkheim, 1897/1951:217). The individual is literally forced into committing suicide.

One notorious example of altruistic suicide was the mass suicide of the followers of the Reverend Jim Jones in Jonestown, Guyana, in 1978. They knowingly took a poisoned drink and in some cases had their children drink it as well. They clearly were committing suicide because they were so tightly integrated into the society of Jones's fanatical followers. Durkheim notes that this is also the explanation for those who seek to be martyrs (Durkheim, 1897/1951:225), as in the terrorist attack of September 11, 2001. More generally, those who commit altruistic suicide do so because they feel that it is their duty to do so. Durkheim argued that this is particularly likely in the military, where the degree of integration is so strong that the individual will feel that he has disgraced the entire group by the most trivial of failures.

Whereas higher rates of egoistic suicide stem from "incurable weariness and sad depression," the increased likelihood of altruistic suicide "springs from hope, for it depends on the belief in beautiful perspectives beyond this life" (Durkheim, 1897/1951:225). When integration is low, people will commit suicide because they have no greater good to sustain them. When integration is high, they commit suicide in the name of that greater good.

Anomic Suicide

The third major form of suicide discussed by Durkheim is *anomic suicide,* which is more likely to occur when the regulative powers of society are disrupted. Such disruptions are likely to leave individuals dissatisfied because there is little control over their passions, which are free to run wild in an insatiable race for gratification. Rates of anomic suicide are likely to rise whether the nature of the disruption is positive (for example, an economic boom) or negative (an economic depression). Either type of disruption renders the collectivity temporarily incapable of exercising its authority over individuals. Such changes put people in new situations in which the old norms no longer apply but new ones have yet to develop. Periods of disruption unleash currents of anomie—moods of rootlessness and normlessness—and these currents lead to an increase in rates of anomic suicide. This is relatively easy to envisage in the case of an economic depression. The closing of a factory because of a depression may lead to the loss of a job, with the result that the individual is cut adrift from the regulative effect that both the company and the job may have had. Being cut off from these structures or others (for example, family, religion, and state) can leave an individual highly vulnerable to the effects of currents of anomie.

Somewhat more difficult to imagine is the effect of an economic boom. In this case, Durkheim argued that sudden success leads individuals away from the traditional structures in which they are embedded. They may lead individuals to quit their jobs, move to a new community, perhaps even find a new spouse. All these changes disrupt the regulative effect of extant structures and leave the individual in boom periods vulnerable to anomic social currents. In such a condition, people's activity is released from regulation and even their dreams are no longer restrained. People in an economic boom seem to have limitless prospects, and "reality seems valueless by comparison with the dreams of fevered imaginations" (Durkheim, 1897/1951:256).

The increases in rates of anomic suicide during periods of deregulation of social life are consistent with Durkheim's views on the pernicious effect of individual passions when freed of external constraint. People thus freed will become slaves to their passions and as a result, in Durkheim's view, commit a wide range of destructive acts, including killing themselves.

Fatalistic Suicide

There is a little-mentioned fourth type of suicide—fatalistic—that Durkheim discussed only in a footnote in *Suicide* (Acevedo, 2005; Besnard, 1993). Whereas anomic suicide is more likely to occur in situations in which regulation is too weak, *fatalistic suicide* is more likely to occur when regulation is excessive. Durkheim (1897/1951:276) described those who are more likely to commit fatalistic suicide as "persons with futures pitilessly blocked and passions violently choked by oppressive discipline." The classic example is the slave who takes his own life because of the hopelessness associated with the oppressive regulation of his every action. Too much regulation—oppression—unleashes currents of melancholy that, in turn, cause a rise in the rate of fatalistic suicide.

Durkheim argued that social currents cause changes in the rates of suicides. Individual suicides are affected by these underlying currents of egoism, altruism, anomie, and fatalism. This proved, for Durkheim, that these currents are more than just the sum of individuals, but are *sui generis* forces, because they dominate the decisions of individuals. Without this assumption, the stability of the suicide rate for any particular society could not be explained.

Suicide Rates and Social Reform

Durkheim concludes his study of suicide with an examination of what reforms could be undertaken to prevent it. Most attempts to prevent suicide have failed because it has been seen as an individual problem. For Durkheim, attempts to directly convince individuals not to commit suicide are futile, since its real causes are in society.

Of course, the first question to be asked is whether suicide should be prevented or whether it counts among those social phenomena that Durkheim would call normal because of its widespread prevalence. This is an especially important question for Durkheim because his theory says that suicides result from social currents that, in a less exaggerated form, are good for society. We would not want to stop all economic booms because they lead to anomic suicides, nor would we stop valuing individuality because it leads to egoistic suicide. Similarly, altruistic suicide results from our virtuous tendency to sacrifice ourselves for the community. The pursuit of progress, the belief in the individual, and the spirit of sacrifice all have their place in society, and cannot exist without generating some suicides.

Durkheim admits that some suicide is normal, but he argues that modern society has seen a pathological increase in both egoistic and anomic suicides. Here his position can be traced back to *The Division of Labor,* where he argued that the anomie of modern culture is due to the abnormal way in which labor is divided so that it leads to isolation rather than interdependence. What is needed, then, is a way to preserve the benefits of modernity without unduly increasing suicides—a way of balancing these social currents. In our society, Durkheim believes, these currents are out of balance. In particular, social regulation and integration are too low, leading to an abnormal rate of anomic and egoistic suicides.

Many of the existing institutions for connecting the individual and society have failed, and Durkheim sees little hope of their success. The modern state is too distant from the individual to influence his or her life with enough force and continuity. The church cannot exert its integrating effect without at the same time repressing freedom of thought. Even the family, possibly the most integrative institution in modern society, will fail in this task since it is subject to the same corrosive conditions that are increasing suicide.

Instead, what Durkheim suggests is the need of a different institution based on occupational groups. We will discuss these occupational associations more later, but what is important here is that Durkheim proposes a social solution to a social problem.

Elementary Forms of Religious Life

Early and Late Durkheimian Theory

Before we go on to Durkheim's last great sociological work, *The Elementary Forms of Religious Life,* we should say some things about the way in which his ideas were received into American sociology. As we said, Durkheim is seen as the "father" of modern sociology, but, unlike biological paternity, the parentage of disciplines is not susceptible to DNA tests and therefore must be seen as a social construction. To a large degree, Durkheim was awarded his status of "father" by one of America's greatest theorists, Talcott Parsons (1937), and this has influenced subsequent views of Durkheim.

Parsons presented Durkheim as undergoing a theoretical change between *Suicide* and *The Elementary Forms.* He believed that the early Durkheim was primarily a positivist who tried to apply the methods of the natural sciences to the study of society, while the later Durkheim was an idealist who traced social changes to changes in collective ideas. Even though Parsons (1975) later admitted that this division was "overdone," it has made its way into many sociologists' understanding of Durkheim. For the most part, sociologists tend to find an early or a late Durkheim they agree with and emphasize that aspect of his work.

There is some truth to this periodization of Durkheim, but it seems to be more a matter of his focus than any great theoretical shift. Durkheim always believed that social forces were akin to natural forces and always believed that collective ideas shaped social practices as well as vice versa. However, there is no doubt that after *Suicide,* the question of religion became of overriding importance in Durkheim's sociological theory. It would be wrong to see this as a form of idealism. In fact, we see in the text that Durkheim was actually worried that he would be seen as too materialistic since he assumed that religious beliefs are dependent upon such concrete social practices as rituals.

In addition, Durkheim, in his later period, more directly addressed how individuals internalize social structures. Durkheim's often overly zealous arguments for sociology and against psychology have led many to argue that he had little to offer on how social facts affected the consciousnesses of human actors (Lukes, 1972:228). This was particularly true in his early work, where he dealt with the link between social facts and individual consciousness in only a vague and cursory way. Nevertheless, Durkheim's ultimate goal was to explain how individual humans are shaped by social facts. We see his clear announcement of that intent in regard to *The Elementary Forms of Religious Life.* "In general, we hold that sociology has not completely achieved its task so long as it has not penetrated into the mind . . . of the individual in order to relate the institutions it seeks to explain to their psychological conditions. . . . Man is for us less a point of departure than a point of arrival" (Durkheim, cited in Lukes, 1972:498–499). As we will see in what follows, he proposed a theory of ritual and effervescence that addressed the link between social facts and human consciousness, as did his work on moral education.

Theory of Religion—The Sacred and the Profane

Raymond Aron (1965:45) said of *The Elementary Forms of Religious Life* that it was Durkheim's most important, most profound, and most original work. Collins and Makowsky (1998:107) call it "perhaps the greatest single book of the twentieth century." In this book, Durkheim put forward both a sociology of religion and a theory of knowledge. His sociology of religion consisted of an attempt to identify the enduring essence of religion through an analysis of its most primitive forms. His theory of knowledge attempted to connect the fundamental categories of human thought to their social origins. It was Durkheim's great genius to propose a sociological connection between these two disparate puzzles. Put briefly, he found the enduring essence of religion in the setting apart of the *sacred* from all that is profane (Edwards, 2007). This sacred is created through rituals that transform the moral power of society into religious symbols that bind individuals to the group. Durkheim's most daring argument is that this moral bond becomes a cognitive bond because the categories for understanding, such as classification, time, space, and causation, are also derived from religious rituals.

Let us start with Durkheim's theory of religion. Society (through individuals) creates religion by defining certain phenomena as sacred and others as profane. Those aspects of social reality that are defined as sacred—that is, that are set apart from the everyday—form the essence of religion. The rest are defined as *profane*—the commonplace, the utilitarian, the mundane aspects of life. On the one hand, the sacred brings out an attitude of reverence, awe, and obligation. On the other hand, it is the attitude accorded to these phenomena that transforms them from profane to sacred. The question for Durkheim was, What is the source of this reverence, awe, and obligation?

Here he proposed to both retain the essential truth of religion while revealing its sociological reality.[5] Durkheim refused to believe that all religion is nothing but an illusion. Such a pervasive social phenomenon must have some truth. However, that truth need not be precisely that which is believed by the participants. Indeed, as a strict agnostic, Durkheim could not believe that anything supernatural was the source of these religious feelings. There really is a superior moral power that inspires believers, but it is society and not God. Durkheim argued that religion symbolically embodies society itself. Religion is the system of symbols by means of which society becomes conscious of itself. This was the only way that he could explain why every society has had religious beliefs but each has had different beliefs.

Society is a power that is greater than we are. It transcends us, demands our sacrifices, suppresses our selfish tendencies, and fills us with energy. Society, according to Durkheim, exercises these powers through representations. In God, he sees "only society transfigured and symbolically expressed" (Durkheim, 1906/1974:52). Thus, society is the source of the sacred.

Beliefs, Rituals, and Church

The differentiation between the sacred and the profane and the elevation of some aspects of social life to the sacred level are necessary but not sufficient conditions for the development of religion. Three other conditions are needed. First, there must be the development of a set of religious beliefs. These *beliefs* are "the representations which express the nature of sacred things and the relations which they sustain, either with each other or with profane things" (Durkheim, 1912/1965:56). Second, a set of religious *rituals* is necessary. These are "the rules of conduct which prescribe how a man should comport himself in the presence of these sacred objects" (Durkheim, 1912/1965:56). Finally, a religion requires a *church,* or a single overarching moral community. The

[5]Other sociologies of religion, for example, by Marx, Weber, and Simmel, saw religions as false explanations of natural phenomena (B. Turner, 1991).

interrelationships among the sacred, beliefs, rituals, and church led Durkheim to the following definition of a religion: "A religion is a unified system of beliefs and practices which unite into one single moral community called a Church, all those who adhere to them" (1912/1965:62).

Rituals and the church are important to Durkheim's theory of religion because they connect the representations of the social to individual practices. Durkheim often assumes that social currents are simply absorbed by individuals through some sort of contagion, but here he spells out how such a process might work. Individuals learn about the sacred and its associated beliefs through participating in rituals and in the community of the church. As we will see later, this is also how individuals learn the categories of understanding (Rawls, 1996). Furthermore, rituals and the church keep social representations from dissipating and losing their force by dramatically reenacting the collective memory of the group. Finally, they reconnect individuals to the social, a source of greater energy that inspires them when they return to their mundane pursuits.

Why Primitive?

Although the research reported in *The Elementary Forms* was not Durkheim's own, he felt it necessary, given his commitment to empirical science, to embed his thinking on religion in published data. The major sources of his data were studies of a clan-based Australian tribe, the Arunta, who, for Durkheim, represented primitive culture. Although today we are very skeptical of the idea that some cultures are more primitive than others, Durkheim wanted to study religion within a "primitive" culture for several reasons. First, he believed that it is much easier to gain insight into the essential nature of religion in a primitive culture because the ideological systems of primitive religions are less well developed than are those of modern religions, with the result that there is less obfuscation. Religious forms in primitive society could be "shown in all their nudity," and it would require "only the slightest effort to lay them open" (Durkheim, 1912/1965:18). In addition, whereas religion in modern society takes diverse forms, in primitive society there is "intellectual and moral conformity" (Durkheim, 1912/1965:18). This makes it easier to relate the common beliefs to the common social structures.

Durkheim studied primitive religion only in order to shed light on religion in modern society. Religion in a nonmodern society is an all-encompassing collective conscience. But as society grows more specialized, religion comes to occupy an increasingly narrow domain. It becomes simply one of a number of collective representations. Although it expresses some collective sentiments, other institutions (for example, law and science) come to express other aspects of the collective morality. Durkheim recognized that religion per se comes to occupy an ever narrower domain, but he also contended that most, if not all, of the various collective representations of modern society have their origin in the all-encompassing religion of primitive society.

Totemism

Because Durkheim believed that society is the source of religion, he was particularly interested in totemism among the Australian Arunta. *Totemism* is a religious system in which certain things, particularly animals and plants, come to be regarded as sacred and as emblems of the clan. Durkheim viewed totemism as the simplest, most primitive form of religion and believed it to be associated with a similarly simple form of social organization, the clan.

Durkheim argued that the totem is nothing but the representation of the clan itself. Individuals who experience the heightened energy of social force in a gathering of the clan seek some explanation for this state. Durkheim believed that the gathering itself was the real cause, but even today, people are reluctant to attribute this power to social forces. Instead, the clan member mistakenly attributes the energy he or she feels to the symbols of the clan. The totems are the material representations of the nonmaterial force that is at their base, and that nonmaterial force is none other than society. Totemism, and more generally religion, is derived from the collective morality and becomes itself an impersonal force. It is not simply a series of mythical animals, plants, personalities, spirits, or gods.

As a study of primitive religion, the specifics of Durkheim's interpretation have been questioned (Hiatt, 1996). However, even if totemism is not the most primitive religion, it was certainly the best vehicle to develop Durkheim's new theory linking together religion, knowledge, and society.

Although a society may have a large number of totems, Durkheim did not view these totems as representing a series of separate, fragmentary beliefs about specific animals or plants. Instead, he saw them as an interrelated set of ideas that give the society a more or less complete representation of the world. In totemism, three classes of things are connected: the totemic symbol, the animal or plant, and the members of the clan. As such, totemism provides a way to classify natural objects that reflects the social organization of the tribe. Hence, Durkheim was able to argue that the ability to classify nature into cognitive categories is derived from religious and ultimately social experiences. Later, society may develop better ways to classify nature and its symbols, for example, into scientific genera and species, but the basic idea of classification comes from social experiences. He expanded on this idea that the social world grounds our mental categories in his earlier essay with his nephew Marcel Mauss:

> Society was not simply a model which classificatory thought followed; it was its own divisions which served as divisions for the system of classification. The first logical categories were social categories; the first classes of things were classes of men. . . . It was because men were grouped, and thought of themselves in the form of groups, that in their ideas they grouped other things, and in the beginning the two modes of grouping were merged to the point of being indistinct.
>
> (Durkheim and Mauss, 1903/1963:82–83)

Sociology of Knowledge

Whereas the early Durkheim was concerned with differentiating sociology from philosophy, he now wanted to show that sociology could answer the most intractable philosophical questions. Philosophy had proposed two general models for how humans are able to develop concepts from their sense impressions. One, called *empiricism,* contends that our concepts are just generalizations from our sense impressions. The problem with this philosophy is that we seem to need some initial concepts such as space, time, and categories even to begin to group sense impressions together so that we can generalize from them. Consequently, another school of philosophy, *apriorism,* contends that we must be born with some initial categories of understanding. For Durkheim, this was really no explanation at all. How is it that we are born with these particular categories? How are they transmitted to each new generation? These are questions that Durkheim felt the philosophers could not answer. Instead, philosophers usually imply some sort of transcendental source. In other words, their philosophy has a religious character, and we already know what Durkheim thinks is the ultimate source of religion.

Durkheim contended that human knowledge is not a product of experience alone, nor are we just born with certain mental categories that are applied to experience. Instead our categories are social creations. They are collective representations. Marx had already proposed a sociology of knowledge, but his was purely in the negative sense. Ideology was the distortion of our knowledge by social forces. In that sense, it was a theory of false knowledge. Durkheim offers a much more powerful sociology of knowledge that explains our "true" knowledge in terms of social forces.

Categories of Understanding

The Elementary Forms presents an argument for the social origin of six fundamental categories that some philosophers had identified as essential to human understanding: time, space, classification, force, causality, and totality. *Time* comes from the rhythms of social life. The category of *space* develops from the division of space occupied by society. We've already discussed how in totemism, *classification* is tied to the human group. *Force* is derived from experiences with social forces. Imitative rituals are the origin of the concept of *causality.* Finally, society itself is the representation of *totality* (Nielsen, 1999). These descriptions are necessarily brief, but the important point is that the fundamental categories that allow us to transform our sense impressions into abstract concepts are derived from social experiences, in particular experiences of religious rituals. In these rituals, the bodily involvement of participants in the ritual's sounds and movements creates feelings that give rise to the categories of understanding (Rawls, 2001).

Even if our abstract concepts are based on social experiences, this does not mean that our thoughts are determined by society. Remember that social facts acquire laws of development and association of their own, and they are not reducible to their source. Although social facts emerge out of other social facts, their subsequent development is autonomous. Consequently, even though these concepts have a religious source, they can develop into nonreligious systems. In fact, this is exactly what Durkheim sees as having happened with science. Rather than being opposed to religion, science has developed out of religion.

Despite their autonomous development, some categories are universal and necessary. This is the case because these categories develop in order to facilitate social interaction. Without them, all contact between individual minds would be impossible, and social life would cease. This explains why they are universal to humanity, because everywhere human beings have lived in societies. This also explains why they are necessary.

> Hence society cannot leave the categories up to the free choice of individuals without abandoning itself. To live, it requires not only a minimum moral consensus but also a minimum logical consensus that it cannot do without either. Thus, in order to prevent

> dissidence, society weighs on its members with all its authority. Does a mind seek to free itself from these norms of all thought? Society no longer considers this a human mind in the full sense, and treats it accordingly.
>
> (Durkheim, 1912/1965:16)

Collective Effervescence

Nevertheless, there are times when even the most fundamental moral and cognitive categories can change or be created anew. Durkheim calls this *collective effervescence* (Ono, 1996; Tiryakian, 1995). The notion of collective effervescence is not well spelled out in any of Durkheim's works. He seemed to have in mind, in a general sense, the great moments in history when a collectivity is able to achieve a new and heightened level of collective exaltation that in turn can lead to great changes in the structure of society. The Reformation and the Renaissance would be examples of historical periods when collective effervescence had a marked effect on the structure of society. As described later, effervescence is possible even in a classroom. It was during such a period of collective effervescence that the clan members created totemism. Collective effervescences are the decisive formative moments in social development. They are social facts at their birth.

To summarize Durkheim's theory of religion, society is the source of religion, the concept of God, and ultimately everything that is sacred (as opposed to profane). In a very real sense, then, we can argue that the sacred, God, and society are one and the same. Durkheim believed that this is fairly clear-cut in primitive society and that it remains true today, even though the relationship is greatly obscured by the complexities of modern society. To summarize Durkheim's sociology of knowledge, he claimed that concepts and even our most fundamental categories are collective representations that society produces, at least initially, through religious rituals. Religion is what connects society and the individual, since it is through sacred rituals that social categories become the basis for individual concepts.

Moral Education and Social Reform

Durkheim did not consider himself to be political and indeed avoided most partisan politics as not compatible with scientific objectivity. Nevertheless, as we've seen, most of his writings dealt with social issues, and, unlike some who see themselves as objective scientists today, he was not shy about suggesting specific social reforms, in particular regarding education and occupational associations. Gane (2001:79) writes that Durkheim "believed the role of social science was to provide guidance for specific kinds of social intervention."

Durkheim saw problems in modern society as temporary aberrations and not as inherent difficulties (Fenton, 1984:45). Therefore, he believed in social reform. In taking this position, he stood in opposition to both the conservatives and the radicals of his day. Conservatives saw no hope in modern society and sought instead the restoration of the monarchy or of the political power of the Roman Catholic Church. Radicals like the socialists of Durkheim's time agreed that the world could not be reformed, but they hoped that a revolution would bring into existence socialism or communism.

Both Durkheim's programs for reform and his reformist approach were due to his belief that society is the source of any morality. His reform programs were dictated by the fact that society needs to be able to produce moral direction for the individual. To the extent that society is losing that capacity, it must be reformed. His reformist approach was dictated by the fact that the source for any reform has to be the actually existing society. It does no good to formulate reform programs from the viewpoint of an abstract morality. The program must be generated by that society's social forces and not from some philosopher's, or even sociologist's, ethical system. "Ideals cannot be legislated into existence; they must be understood, loved and striven for by the body whose duty it is to realize them" (Durkheim, 1938/1977:38).

Morality

Durkheim offered courses and gave public lectures on moral education and the sociology of morals. And he intended, had he lived long enough, to culminate his oeuvre with a comprehensive presentation of his science of morals. The connection that Durkheim saw between sociology and morality has not until recently been appreciated by most sociologists:

> It is not a coincidence, it seems to me, that the new emphasis on Durkheim should be in the areas of morality, philosophy, and intellectual milieu; it is indicative of a growing reflective need of sociology for ontological problems, those which relate professional concerns to the socio-historical situation of the profession. Whereas only a decade or so ago many sociologists might have been embarrassed if not vexed to discuss "ethics" and "morality," the increasing amorality and immorality of the public and private sectors of our society may be tacitly leading or forcing us back to fundamental inquiries, such as the moral basis of modern society, ideal and actual. This was a central theoretical and existential concern of Durkheim.
>
> (Tiryakian, 1974:769)

As we have said, Durkheim was centrally concerned with morality, but it is not easy to classify his theory of morality according to the typical categories. On the one hand, he was a moral relativist who believed that ethical rules do and should change in response to other social facts. On the other hand, he was a traditionalist because he did not believe that one could simply create a new morality. Any new morality could only grow out of our collective moral traditions. He insisted that one must "see in morality itself a fact the nature of which one must investigate attentively, I would even say respectfully, before daring to modify" (Durkheim cited in Bellah, 1973:xv). Durkheim's sociological theory of morality cuts across most of the positions concerning morality today and offers the possibility of a fresh perspective on contemporary debates over such issues as traditional families and the moral content of popular culture.

Morality, for Durkheim, has three components. First, morality involves discipline, that is, a sense of authority that resists idiosyncratic impulses. Second, morality involves attachment to society since society is the source of our morality. Third, it involves autonomy, a sense of individual responsibility for our actions.

Discipline

Durkheim usually discussed *discipline* in terms of constraint upon one's egoistic impulses. Such constraint is necessary because individual interests and group interests are not the same and may, at least in the short term, be in conflict. Discipline confronts one with one's moral duty, which, for Durkheim, is one's duty to society. As discussed earlier, this social discipline also makes the individual happier, since it limits his or her limitless desires and therefore provides the only chance of happiness for a being who otherwise would always want more.

Attachment

But Durkheim did not see morality as simply a matter of constraint. His second element in morality is *attachment* to social groups—the warm, voluntary, positive aspect of group commitment—not out of external duty but out of willing attachment.

> It is society that we consider the most important part of ourselves. From this point of view, one can readily see how it can become the thing to which we are bound. In fact, we could not disengage ourselves from society without cutting ourselves off from ourselves. Between it and us there is the strongest and most intimate connection, since it is a part of our own being, since in a sense it constitutes what is best in us. . . . Consequently, . . . when we hold to ourselves, we hold to something other than ourselves. . . . Thus, just as morality limits and constrains us, in response to the requirements of our nature, so in requiring our commitment and subordination to the group does it compel us to realize ourselves.
>
> (Durkheim, 1925/1961:71–72)

These two elements of morality—discipline and attachment—complement and support each other because they are both simply different aspects of society. The former is society seen as making demands on us, and the latter is society seen as part of us.

Autonomy

The third element of morality is *autonomy.* Here Durkheim follows Kant's philosophical definition and sees it as a rationally grounded impulse of the will, with the sociological twist that the rational grounding is ultimately social.

Durkheim's focus on society as the source of morality has led many to assume that his ideal actor is one who is almost wholly controlled from without—a total conformist. However, Durkheim did not subscribe to such an extreme view of the actor: "Conformity must not be pushed to the point where it completely subjugates the intellect. Thus it does not follow from a belief in the need for discipline that it must be blind and slavish" (cited in Giddens, 1972:113).

Autonomy only comes to full force in modernity with the decline of the myths and symbols that previous moral systems used to demand discipline and encourage attachment. Durkheim believed that now that these myths have passed away, only scientific understanding can provide the foundation for moral autonomy. In particular, modern morality should be based on the relation between individuals and society as revealed by Durkheim's new science of sociology. The only way for this sociological understanding to become a true morality is through education.

Moral Education

Durkheim's most consistent attempts to reform society in order to enable a modern morality were directed at education (Dill, 2007). Education was defined by Durkheim as the process by which the individual acquires the physical, intellectual, and, most important to Durkheim, moral tools needed to function in society (Durkheim, 1922/1956:71). As Lukes (1972:359) reports, Durkheim had always believed "that the relation of the science of sociology to education was that of theory to practice." In 1902, he was given the powerful position of head of the Sorbonne's education department. "It is scarcely an exaggeration to say that every young mind in Paris, in the decade prior to World War I, came directly or indirectly under his influence" (Gerstein, 1983:239).

Before Durkheim began to reform education there had been two approaches. One saw education as an extension of the Church, and the other saw education as the unfolding of the natural individual. In contrast, Durkheim argued that education should help children develop a moral attitude toward society. He believed that the schools were practically the only existing institution that could provide a social foundation for modern morality.

For Durkheim, the classroom is a small society, and he concluded that its collective effervescence could be made powerful enough to inculcate a moral attitude. The classroom could provide the rich collective milieu necessary for reproducing collective representations (Durkheim, 1925/1961:229). This would allow education to present and reproduce all three elements of morality.

First, it would provide individuals with the discipline they need to restrain the passions that threaten to engulf them. Second, education could develop in the students a sense of devotion to society and to its moral system. Most important is education's role in the development of autonomy, in which discipline is "freely desired," and the attachment to society is by virtue of "enlightened assent" (Durkheim, 1925/1961:120).

> For to teach morality is neither to preach nor to indoctrinate; it is to explain. If we refuse the child all explanation of this sort, if we do not try to help him understand the reasons for the rules he should abide by, we would be condemning him to an incomplete and inferior morality.
>
> (Durkheim, 1925/1961:120–121)

Occupational Associations

As we discussed earlier, the primary problem that Durkheim saw in modern society was the lack of integration and regulation. Even though the cult of the individual provided a collective representation, Durkheim believed that there was a lack of social organizations that people could feel part of and that could tell people what they should and should not do. The modern state is too distant to influence most individuals. The church tends to integrate people by repressing freedom of thought. And the family is too particular and does not integrate individuals into society as a whole. As we've seen, the schools provided an excellent milieu for children. For adults, Durkheim proposed another institution: the *occupational association.*

Genuine moral commitments require a concrete group that is tied to the basic organizing principle of modern society, the division of labor. Durkheim proposed the development of occupational associations. All the workers, managers, and owners involved in a particular industry should join together in an association that would be both professional and social. Durkheim did not believe that there was a basic conflict of interest among the owners, managers, and workers within an industry. In this, of course, he took a position diametrically opposed to that of Marx, who saw an essential conflict of interest between the owners and the workers. Durkheim believed that any such conflict occurred only because the various people involved lacked a common morality that was traceable to the lack of an integrative structure. He suggested that the structure that was needed to provide this integrative morality was the occupational association, which would encompass "all the agents of the same industry united and organized into a single group" (Durkheim, 1893/1964:5). Such an organization was deemed to be superior to such organizations as labor unions and employer associations, which in Durkheim's view served only to intensify the differences between owners, managers, and workers. Involved in a common organization, people in these categories would recognize their common interests as well as their common need for an integrative moral system. That moral system, with its derived rules and laws, would serve to counteract the tendency toward atomization in modern society as well as help stop the decline in the significance of collective morality.

Criticisms

As mentioned earlier, Durkheim's reception into American sociology was strongly influenced by Talcott Parsons, who presented him as both a functionalist and a positivist. Although we don't feel that these labels fairly characterize Durkheim's position, a number of criticisms have been directed at his ideas on the basis of these characterizations. Since the sociology student is bound to come across these criticisms, we feel we should briefly address them here.

Functionalism and Positivism

Durkheim's focus on macro-level social facts was one of the reasons why his work played a central role in the development of structural functionalism, which has a similar, macro-level orientation (see Chapter 16 on Parsons). However, whether Durkheim was himself a functionalist is open to debate and depends upon how one defines functionalism. Functionalism can be defined in two different ways: a weak sense and a strong sense. When Kingsley Davis (1959) said that all sociologists are functionalists, he referred to the weak sense: that functionalism is an approach that attempts "to relate the parts of society to the whole, and to relate one part to another." A stronger definition of functionalism is given by Turner and Maryanski (1988), who define it as an approach that is based on seeing society as analogous to a biological organism and attempts to explain particular social structures in terms of the needs of society as a whole.

In this second sense, Durkheim was only an occasional and, one might say, accidental functionalist. Durkheim was not absolutely opposed to drawing analogies between biological organisms and social structures (Lehmann, 1993a:15), but he did not believe that sociologists can infer sociological laws by analogy with biology. Durkheim (1898/1974:1) called such inferences "worthless."

Durkheim urged that we distinguish functions from the historical causes of social facts. The historical study is primary because social needs cannot simply call structures into existence. Certainly, Durkheim's initial hypothesis was always that enduring social facts probably perform some sort of function, but he recognized that some social facts are historical accidents. Furthermore, we see in Durkheim no attempt to predefine the needs of society. Instead, the needs of a particular society can be established only by studying that society. Consequently, any functionalist approach must be preceded by a historical study.

Despite this theoretical injunction, it must be admitted that Durkheim did sometimes slip into functional analysis (Turner and Maryanski, 1988:111–112). Consequently, there are many places where one can fairly criticize Durkheim for assuming that societies as a whole have needs and that social structures automatically emerge to respond to these needs.

Durkheim also is often criticized for being a positivist, and indeed, he used the term to describe himself. However, as Robert Hall notes, the meaning of the term has changed:

> The term "positive" was needed to distinguish the new approach from those of the philosophers who had taken to calling their ethical theories "scientific" and who used this term to indicate the dialectical reasoning they employed. In an age in which one could still speak of the "science" of metaphysics, the term "positive" simply indicated an empirical approach.
>
> (Hall, 1987:137)

Today, positivism refers to the belief that social phenomena should be studied with the same methods as the natural sciences, and it is likely that Durkheim would accept this. However, it has also come to mean a focus on invariant laws (Turner, 1993), and we find little of that in Durkheim. Social facts were, for Durkheim, autonomous from their substrate, but also autonomous in their relation to other social facts. Each social fact required historical investigation, and none could be predicted on the basis of invariant laws.

Other Criticisms

There are some other problems with Durkheim's theory that need to be discussed. The first has to do with the crucial idea of a social fact. It is not at all clear that social facts can be approached in the objective manner that Durkheim recommends. Even such seemingly objective evidence for these social facts as a suicide rate can be seen as an accumulation of interpretations. In other words, whether a particular death is a suicide depends upon ascertaining the intention of a dead person (Douglas, 1967). This may be especially difficult in such cases as drug overdoses. In addition, the interpretation may be biased in a systemic manner so that, for example, deaths among those of high status may be less likely to be interpreted as suicides, even if the body is found clutching the fatal gun. Social facts and the evidence for them should always be approached as interpretations, and even the sociologist's own use of the social fact should be seen as such.

There are also some problems with Durkheim's view of the individual. Despite having made a number of crucial assumptions about human nature, Durkheim denied that he had done so. He argued that he did not begin by postulating a certain conception of human nature in order to deduce a sociology from it. Instead, he said that it was from sociology that he sought an increasing understanding of human nature. However, Durkheim may have been less than honest with his readers, and perhaps even with himself.

One of Durkheim's assumptions about human nature—one that we have already encountered—may be viewed as the basis of his entire sociology. That assumption is that people are impelled by their passions into a mad search for gratification that always leads to a need for more. If these passions are unrestrained, they multiply to the point where the individual is enslaved by them and they become a threat to the individual as well as to society. It can be argued that Durkheim's entire theoretical edifice, especially his emphasis on collective morality, was erected on this basic assumption about people's passions. However, Durkheim provides no evidence for this assumption, and indeed, his own theories would suggest that such an insatiable subject may be a creation of social structures rather than the other way around.

In addition, Durkheim failed to give consciousness an active role in the social process. He treated the actor and the actor's mental processes as secondary factors or, more commonly, as dependent variables to be explained by the independent and decisive variables—social facts. Individuals are, in general, controlled by social forces in his theories; they do not actively control those forces. Autonomy, for Durkheim, meant nothing more than freely accepting those social forces. However, even if we accept that consciousness and some mental processes are types of social facts, there is no reason to suppose that they cannot develop the same autonomy that Durkheim recognized in other social facts. Just as science has developed its own autonomous rules, making its religious roots almost unrecognizable, couldn't consciousness do the same?

The final set of criticisms that we will discuss have to do with the centrality of morality in Durkheim's sociology. All sociologists are driven by moral concerns, but for Durkheim, morality was more than just the driving force behind sociology, it was also its ultimate goal. Durkheim believed that the sociological study of morality would produce a science of morality. As Everett White (1961:xx) wrote, "To say that the moral is an inevitable aspect of the social—is a far cry from asserting, as Durkheim does, that there can be a science of morality."

Furthermore, even without the fantasy of a science of morality, a sociology that attempts to determine what *should be done* from what *now exists* is inherently conservative. This conservatism is the most frequently cited criticism of Durkheim (Pearce, 1989). This is often attributed to his functionalism and positivism, but it is more correctly traced to the connection that he sees between morality and sociology. Whatever value there is in the scientific study of morality, it cannot relieve us of making moral choices. Indeed, it is likely that such study will make moral choice more difficult even as it makes us more flexible and responsive to changing social situations.

We should note, however, that Durkheim is not alone in having failed to work out the proper relation between morality and sociology. This problem disturbs modern sociology at least as much as it does Durkheim's theories. In an increasingly pluralistic culture, it is clear that we cannot just accept our moral traditions. For one thing, it is impossible to say whose moral traditions we should accept. It is equally clear, thanks in part to Durkheim's insight, that we cannot just create a new morality that is separate from our moral traditions. A new morality must emerge, and it must emerge from our moral traditions, but what role sociology can and should play in this is a question that appears to be both unanswerable and unavoidable.

Summary

The two main themes in Durkheim's sociology were the priority of the social over the individual and the idea that society can be studied scientifically. These themes led to his concept of social facts. Social facts can be empirically studied, are external to the individual, are coercive of the individual, and are explained by other social facts. Durkheim differentiated between two basic types of social facts—material and nonmaterial. The most important focus for Durkheim was on nonmaterial social facts. He dealt with a number of them, including morality, collective conscience, collective representations, and social currents.

Durkheim's first major work was *The Division of Labor in Society,* in which he argued that the collective conscience of societies with mechanical solidarity had been replaced by a new organic solidarity based on mutual interdependence in a society organized by a division of labor. He investigated the difference between mechanical and organic solidarity through an analysis of their different legal systems. He argued that mechanical solidarity is associated with repressive laws while organic solidarity is associated with legal systems based on restitution.

Durkheim's next book, a study of suicide, is a good illustration of the significance of nonmaterial social facts in his work. In his basic causal model, changes in nonmaterial social facts ultimately cause differences in suicide rates. Durkheim differentiated among four types of suicide—egoistic, altruistic, anomic, and fatalistic—and showed how each is affected by different changes in social currents. The study of suicide was taken by Durkheim and his supporters as evidence that sociology has a legitimate place in the social sciences. After all, it was argued, if sociology could explain so individualistic an act as suicide, it certainly could be used to explain other, less individual aspects of social life.

In his last major work, *The Elementary Forms of Religious Life,* Durkheim focused on another aspect of culture: religion. In his analysis of primitive religion, Durkheim sought to show the roots of religion in the social structure of society. It is society that defines certain things as sacred and others as profane. Durkheim demonstrated the social sources of religion in his analysis of primitive totemism and its roots in the social structure of the clan. Durkheim concluded that religion and society are one and the same, two manifestations of the same general process. He also presented a sociology of knowledge in this work. He claimed that concepts and even our most fundamental mental categories are collective representations that society produces, at least initially, through religious rituals.

Although Durkheim was against any radical change, his central concern with morality led him to propose two reforms in society that he hoped would lead to a stronger collective morality. For children, he successfully implemented a new program for moral education in France that focused on teaching children discipline, attachment to society, and autonomy. For adults, he proposed occupational associations to restore collective morality and to cope with some of the curable pathologies of the modern division of labor.

We conclude the chapter by presenting some criticisms of Durkheim's theories. We find serious problems with his basic idea of the social fact, with his assumptions about human nature, and with his sociology of morality.

CHAPTER 8

Max Weber

Chapter Outline

Methodology

Substantive Sociology

Criticisms

Max Weber (1864–1920) is probably the best known and most influential figure in sociological theory (Burger, 1993; R. Collins, 1985; Kalberg, 2000; Sica, 2001; Whimster, 2001, 2005a).[1] Weber's work is so varied and subject to so many interpretations that it has influenced a wide array of sociological theories. It certainly had an influence on structural functionalism, especially through the work of Talcott Parsons. It has also come to be seen as important to the conflict tradition (R. Collins, 1975, 1990) and to critical theory, which was shaped almost as much by Weber's ideas as it was by Marx's orientation, as well as to Jurgen Habermas, the major inheritor of the critical-theory tradition (Outhwaite, 1994). Symbolic interactionists have been affected by Weber's ideas on *verstehen,* as well as by others of Weber's ideas. Alfred Schutz was powerfully affected by Weber's work on meanings and motives, and he, in turn, played a crucial role in the development of ethnomethodology (see Chapter 2). Recently, rational choice theorists have acknowledged their debt to Weber (Norkus, 2000). Weber was and is a widely influential theorist.

We begin this chapter with a discussion of Weber's (1903–17/1949) ideas on the methodology of the social sciences, which remain remarkably relevant and fruitful even today (Ringer, 1997:171). A clear understanding of these ideas is necessary in dealing with Weber's substantive and theoretical ideas. Weber was opposed to pure abstract theorizing. Instead, his theoretical ideas are embedded in his empirical, usually historical, research. Weber's methodology shaped his research, and the combination of the two lies at the base of his theoretical orientation.

[1]For a time, his position was threatened by the increase in interest in the work of Karl Marx, who was already much better known to those in other fields and to the general public. But with the demise of world communism, Weber's position of preeminence seems secure once again.

Methodology

History and Sociology

Weber tended to deemphasize methodological issues. As Lassman and Velody put it, "Clearly Weber has no concern with methodology in the sense of rulebooks for correct practice. . . . His methodological essays are more in the nature of philosophical reflections upon the nature and significance of claims to historical and social knowledge" (1989:192). A discussion of even these general matters was viewed by Weber as "mainly a precondition of fruitful intellectual work" (1903–17/1949:115; see also Marianne Weber, 1975:309). Weber focused on substantive work: "Only by laying bare and solving *substantive problems* can sciences be established and their methods developed. On the other hand, purely epistemological and methodological reflections have never played the crucial role in such developments" (1903–17/1949:116).

Even though Weber was a student of, and took his first academic job in, law, his early career was dominated by an interest in history. As Weber moved more in the direction of the relatively new field of sociology, he sought to clarify its relationship to the established field of history. Although Weber felt that each field needed the other, his view was that the task of sociology was to provide a needed "service" to history (Roth, 1976:307). In Weber's words, sociology performed only a "preliminary, quite modest task" (cited in R. Frank, 1976:21). Weber explained the difference between sociology and history: "Sociology seeks to formulate type concepts and generalized uniformities of empirical processes. This distinguishes it from history, which is oriented to the causal analysis and explanation of individual actions, structures, and personalities possessing cultural significance" (1921/1968:19). Despite this seemingly clear-cut differentiation, in his own work Weber was able to combine the two. His sociology was oriented to the development of clear concepts so that he could perform a causal analysis of historical phenomena. Weber defined his ideal procedure as "the sure imputation of individual concrete events occurring in historical reality *to concrete, historically* given causes through the study of precise empirical data which have been selected from specific points of view" (1903–17/1949:69). We can think of Weber as a historical sociologist.

In fact, his doctoral dissertations were historical studies of the Middle Ages and of Rome. In his later years, however, he identified more and more with sociology. It has been argued that it was in 1909, the year Weber started writing his massive *Economy and Society,* that he began to devote himself fully to sociology (R. Frank, 1976:13).

Weber's thinking on sociology was profoundly shaped by a series of intellectual debates (*Methodenstreit*) raging in Germany during his time. The most important of these debates was over the issue of the relationship between history and science. At the poles in this debate were those (the positivists [Halfpenny, 2005]) who thought that history was composed of general (*nomothetic*) laws and those (the subjectivists) who reduced history to idiosyncratic (*idiographic*) actions and events. (The positivists thought that history could be like a natural science; the subjectivists saw the two as radically different.) For example, a nomothetic thinker would generalize about social revolutions, whereas an idiographic analyst would focus on the specific events leading up to the American Revolution. Weber rejected both extremes and in the process developed a distinctive way of dealing with historical sociology. In Weber's view, history is composed of unique empirical events; there can be no generalizations at the empirical level. Sociologists must, therefore, separate the empirical world from the conceptual universe that they construct. The concepts never completely capture the empirical world, but they can be used as heuristic tools for gaining a better understanding of reality. With these concepts, sociologists can develop generalizations, but these generalizations are not history and must not be confused with empirical reality.

Although Weber was clearly in favor of generalizing, he also rejected historians who sought to reduce history to a simple set of laws: "For the knowledge of historical phenomena in their concreteness, the most general laws, because they are devoid of content, are also the least valuable" (1903–17/1949:80). For example, Weber rejected one historian (Wilhelm Roscher) who took as his task the search for the laws of the historical evolution of a people and who believed that all peoples went through a typical sequence of stages (1903–06/1975). As Weber put it, "The reduction of empirical reality . . . to 'laws' is meaningless" (1903–17/1949:80). In other terms: "A systematic science of culture . . . would be senseless in itself" (Weber, 1903–17/1949:84). This view is reflected in various specific historical studies. For example, in his study of ancient civilizations, Weber admitted that although in some respects earlier times were precursors of things to come, "the long and continuous history of Mediterranean-European civilization does not show either closed cycles or linear progress. Sometimes phenomena of ancient civilizations have disappeared entirely and then come to light again in an entirely new context" (1896–1906/1976:366).

In rejecting these opposing views of German historical scholarship, Weber fashioned his own perspective, which constituted a fusion of the two orientations. Weber felt that history (that is, historical sociology) was appropriately concerned with both individuality *and* generality. The unification was accomplished through the development and utilization of general concepts (what we later will call "ideal types") in the study of particular individuals, events, or societies. These general concepts are to be used "to identify and define the individuality of each development, the characteristics which made the one conclude in a manner so different from that of the other. Thus done, one can then determine the causes which led to the differences" (Weber, 1896–1906/1976:385). In doing this kind of causal analysis, Weber rejected, at least at a conscious level, the idea of searching for a single causal agent throughout history.[2] He instead used his conceptual arsenal to rank the various factors involved in a given historical case in terms of their causal significance (Roth, 1971).

Weber's views on historical sociology were shaped in part by the availability of, and his commitment to the study of, empirical historical data. His was the first generation of scholars to have available reliable data on historical phenomena from many parts of the world (MacRae, 1974). Weber was more inclined to immerse himself in these historical data than he was to dream up abstract generalizations about the basic thrust of

[2]Ironically, Weber did seem (as we will see later in this chapter) to argue in his substantive work that there was such a causal agent in society—rationalization.

MAX WEBER

A Biographical Sketch

Max Weber was born in Erfurt, Germany, on April 21, 1864, into a decidedly middle-class family.

Important differences between his parents had a profound effect upon both his intellectual orientation and his psychological development. His father was a bureaucrat who rose to a relatively important political position. He was clearly a part of the political establishment and as a result eschewed any activity or idealism that would require personal sacrifice or threaten his position within the system. In addition, the senior Weber was a man who enjoyed earthly pleasures, and in this and many other ways he stood in sharp contrast to his wife. Max Weber's mother was a devout Calvinist, a woman who sought to lead an ascetic life largely devoid of the pleasures craved by her husband. Her concerns were more otherworldly; she was disturbed by the imperfections that were signs that she was not destined for salvation. These deep differences between the parents led to marital tension, and both the differences and the tension had an immense impact on Weber.

Because it was impossible to emulate both parents, Weber was presented with a clear choice as a child (Marianne Weber, 1975:62). He first seemed to opt for his father's orientation to life, but later he drew closer to his mother's approach. Whatever the choice, the tension produced by the need to choose between such polar opposites negatively affected Max Weber's psyche.

At age 18, Max Weber left home for a short time to attend the University of Heidelberg. Weber had already demonstrated intellectual precocity, but on a social level he entered Heidelberg shy and underdeveloped. However, that quickly changed after he gravitated toward his father's way of life and joined his father's old dueling fraternity. There he developed socially, at least in part because of the huge quantities of beer he consumed with his peers. In addition, he proudly displayed the dueling scars that were the trademark of such fraternities. Weber not only manifested his identity with his father's way of life in these ways but also chose, at least for the time being, his father's career—the law.

After three terms, Weber left Heidelberg for military service, and in 1884 he returned to Berlin and to his parents' home to take courses at the University of Berlin. He remained there for most of the next eight years as he completed his studies, earned his Ph.D., became a lawyer (see Turner and Factor, 1994, for a discussion of the impact of legal thinking on Weber's theorizing), and started teaching at the University of Berlin. In the process, his interests shifted more toward his lifelong concerns—economics, history, and sociology. During his eight years in Berlin, Weber was financially dependent on his father, a circumstance he progressively grew to dislike. At the same time, he moved closer to his mother's values, and his antipathy to his father increased. He adopted an ascetic life and plunged deeply into his work. For example, during one semester as a student, his work habits were described as follows: "He continues the rigid work discipline, regulates his life by the clock, divides the daily routine into exact sections for the various subjects, saves in his way, by feeding himself evenings in his room with a pound of raw chopped beef and four fried eggs" (Mitzman, 1969/1971:48; Marianne Weber, 1975:105). Thus, Weber, following his mother, had become ascetic and diligent, a compulsive worker—in contemporary terms a "workaholic."

This compulsion for work led in 1896 to a position as professor of economics at Heidelberg. But in 1897, when Weber's academic career was blossoming, his father died following a violent argument between them. Shortly thereafter Weber began to manifest symptoms that were to culminate in a nervous breakdown. Often unable to sleep or to work, Weber spent the next six or seven years in near-total collapse. After a long hiatus, some of his powers began to return in 1903, but it was not until 1904, when he delivered (in the United States) his first lecture in six and a half years, that Weber was able to begin to return to active academic life. In 1904 and 1905, he published one of his best-known works, *The Protestant Ethic and the Spirit of Capitalism*. In this work, Weber announced the ascendance of his mother's religion on an academic level. Weber devoted much of his time to the study of religion, though he was not personally religious.

Although he continued to be plagued by psychological problems, after 1904 Weber was able to function, indeed to produce some of his most important work. In these years, Weber published his studies of the world's religions in world-historical perspective (for example, China, India, and ancient Judaism). At the time of his death (June 14, 1920), he was working on his most important work, *Economy and Society*. Although this book was published, and subsequently translated into many languages, it was unfinished.

In addition to producing voluminous writings in this period, Weber undertook a number of other activities. He helped found the German Sociological Society in 1910. His home became a center for a wide range of intellectuals, including sociologists such as Georg Simmel, Robert Michels, and his brother Alfred Weber, as well as the philosopher and literary critic Georg Lukács (Scaff, 1989:186–222). In addition, Max Weber was active politically and wrote essays on the issues of the day.

There was a tension in Weber's life and, more important, in his work between the bureaucratic mind, as represented by his father, and his mother's religiosity. This unresolved tension permeates Weber's work as it permeated his personal life.

history. Although this led him to some important insights, it also created serious problems in understanding his work; he often got so involved in historical detail that he lost sight of the basic reasons for the historical study. In addition, the sweep of his historical studies encompassed so many epochs and so many societies that he could do little more than make rough generalizations (Roth, 1971). Despite these problems, Weber's commitment to the scientific study of empirical phenomena made him attractive to the developing discipline of sociology in the United States.

In sum, Weber believed that history is composed of an inexhaustible array of specific phenomena. To study these phenomena, it was necessary to develop a variety of concepts designed to be useful for research on the real world. As a general rule, although Weber (as we will see) did not adhere to it strictly and neither do most sociologists and historians, the task of sociology was to develop these concepts, which history was to use in causal analyses of specific historical phenomena. In this way, Weber sought to combine the specific and the general in an effort to develop a science that did justice to the complex nature of social life.

Verstehen

Weber felt that sociologists had an advantage over natural scientists. That advantage resided in the sociologist's ability to *understand* social phenomena, whereas the natural scientist could not gain a similar understanding of the behavior of an atom or a chemical compound. The German word for understanding is *verstehen* (Soeffner, 2005). Weber's special use of the term *verstehen* in his historical research is one of his best-known, and most controversial, contributions to the methodology of contemporary sociology. As we clarify what Weber meant by *verstehen,* we will also underscore some of the problems involved in his conceptualization of it. The controversy surrounding the concept of *verstehen,* as well as some of the problems involved in interpreting what Weber meant, grows out of a general problem with Weber's methodological thoughts. As Thomas Burger argued, Weber was neither very sophisticated nor very consistent in his methodological pronouncements (1976; see also Hekman, 1983:26). He tended to be careless and imprecise because he felt that he was simply repeating ideas that were well known in his day among German historians. Furthermore, as pointed out earlier, Weber did not think too highly of methodological reflections.

Weber's thoughts on *verstehen* were relatively common among German historians of his day and were derived from a field known as *hermeneutics* (Brown, 2005; Martin, 2000; Pressler and Dasilva, 1996). Hermeneutics was a special approach to the understanding and interpretation of published writings. Its goal was to understand the thinking of the author as well as the basic structure of the text. Weber and others (for example, Wilhelm Dilthey) sought to extend this idea from the understanding of texts to the understanding of social life:

> Once we have realized that the historical method is nothing more or less than the classical method of interpretation applied to overt action instead of to texts, a method aiming at identifying a human design, a "meaning" behind observable events, we shall have no difficulty in accepting that it can be just as well applied to human interaction

as to individual actors. From this point of view all history is interaction, which has to be interpreted in terms of the rival plans of various actors.

(Lachman, 1971:20)

In other words, Weber sought to use the tools of hermeneutics to understand actors, interaction, and indeed all of human history.[3]

One common misconception about *verstehen* is that it is simply the use of "intuition" by the researcher. Thus, many critics see it as a "soft," irrational, subjective research methodology. However, Weber categorically rejected the idea that *verstehen* involved simply intuition, sympathetic participation, or empathy (1903–17/1949). To him, *verstehen* involved doing systematic and rigorous research rather than simply getting a "feeling" for a text or social phenomenon. In other words, for Weber (1921/1968) *verstehen* was a rational procedure of study.

The key question in interpreting Weber's concept of *verstehen* is whether he thought that it was most appropriately applied to the subjective states of individual actors or to the subjective aspects of large-scale units of analysis (for example, culture). As we will see, Weber's focus on the cultural and social-structural contexts of action leads us to the view that *verstehen* is a tool for macro-level analysis.

Causality

Another aspect of Weber's methodology was his commitment to the study of causality (Ringer, 1997:75). Weber was inclined to see the study of the causes of social phenomena as being within the domain of history, not sociology. Yet to the degree that history and sociology cannot be clearly separated—and they certainly are not clearly separated in Weber's substantive work—the issue of causality is relevant to sociology. Causality is also important because it is, as we will see, another place in which Weber sought to combine nomothetic and idiographic approaches.

By *causality* Weber (1921/1968) simply meant the probability that an event will be followed or accompanied by another event. It was not, in his view, enough to look for historical constants, repetitions, analogies, and parallels, as many historians are content to do. Instead, the researcher has to look at the reasons for, as well as the meanings of, historical changes (Roth, 1971). Although Weber can be seen as having a one-way causal model—in contrast to Marx's dialectical mode of reasoning—in his substantive sociology he was always attuned to the interrelationships among the economy, society, polity, organization, social stratification, religion, and so forth (Roth, 1968). Thus, Weber operates with a multicausal approach in which "*hosts* of interactive influences are very often effective causal factors" (Kalberg, 1994:13).

Weber was quite clear on the issue of multiple causality in his study of the relationship between Protestantism and the spirit of capitalism. Although he is sometimes interpreted differently, Weber (1904–05/1958) simply argued that the Protestant ethic was *one* of the causal factors in the rise of the modern spirit of capitalism. He labeled as

---

[3]Hermeneutics has become a major intellectual concern in recent years, especially in the work of Martin Heidegger, Hans-Georg Gadamer, and Jurgen Habermas (Bleicher, 1980). For a strong argument in favor of using hermeneutics today, see Sica (1986), and for an appreciation of Weber's hermeneutics, see Oliver (1983).

"foolish" the idea that Protestantism was the sole cause. Similarly foolish, in Weber's view, was the idea that capitalism could have arisen "only" as a result of the Protestant Reformation; other factors could have led to the same result. Here is the way Weber made his point:

> We shall as far as possible clarify the manner and the general *direction* in which . . . the religious movements have influenced the development of material culture. Only when this has been determined with reasonable accuracy can the attempt be made to estimate to what extent the historical development of modern culture can be attributed to those *religious forces and to what extent to others.*
>
> (Weber, 1904–05/1958:91–92; italics added)

In *The Protestant Ethic and the Spirit of Capitalism,* as well as in most of the rest of his historical work, Weber was interested in the question of causality, but he did not operate with a simple one-way model; he was always attuned to the interrelationships among a number of social factors.

The critical thing to remember about Weber's thinking on causality is his belief that because we can have a special understanding of social life (*verstehen*), the causal knowledge of the social sciences is different from the causal knowledge of the natural sciences. As Weber put it: "'Meaningfully' interpretable human conduct ('action') is identifiable by reference to 'valuations' and meanings. For this reason, our criteria for *causal* explanation have a unique kind of satisfaction in the 'historical' explanation of such an 'entity'" (1903–06/1975:185). Thus the causal knowledge of the social scientist is different from the causal knowledge of the natural scientist.

Weber's thoughts on causality were intimately related to his efforts to come to grips with the conflict between nomothetic and idiographic knowledge. Those who subscribe to a nomothetic point of view would argue that there is a necessary relationship among social phenomena, whereas the supporters of an idiographic perspective would be inclined to see only random relationships among these entities. As usual, Weber took a middle position, epitomized in his concept of "adequate causality." The notion of *adequate causality* adopts the view that the best we can do in sociology is make probabilistic statements about the relationship between social phenomena; that is, if x occurs, then it is *probable* that y will occur. The goal is to "estimate the *degree* to which a certain effect is 'favored' by certain 'conditions'" (Weber, 1903–17/1949:183).

Ideal Types

The ideal type is one of Weber's best-known contributions to contemporary sociology (Drysdale, 1996; Hekman, 1983; Lindbekk, 1992; McKinney, 1966; Zijderveld, 2005). As we have seen, Weber believed it was the responsibility of sociologists to develop conceptual tools, which could be used later by historians and sociologists. The most important such conceptual tool was the ideal type:

> An ideal type is formed by the one-sided *accentuation* of one or more points of view and by the synthesis of a great many diffuse, discrete, more or less present and occasionally absent *concrete individual* phenomena, which are arranged according to those one-sidedly emphasized viewpoints into a unified *analytical* construct. . . .

> In its conceptual purity, this mental construct . . . cannot be found empirically anywhere in reality.
>
> (Weber, 1903–17/1949:90)

In spite of this definition, Weber was not totally consistent in the way he used the ideal type. To grasp what the concept means initially, we will have to overlook some of the inconsistencies. At its most basic level, an *ideal type* is a concept constructed by a social scientist, on the basis of his or her interests and theoretical orientation, to capture the essential features of some social phenomenon.

The most important thing about ideal types is that they are heuristic devices; they are to be useful and helpful in doing empirical research and in understanding a specific aspect of the social world (or a "historical individual"). As Lachman said, an ideal type is "essentially a measuring rod" (1971:26), or in Kalberg's terms, a "yardstick" (1994:87). Here is the way Weber put it: "Its function is the comparison with empirical reality in order to establish its divergences or similarities, to describe them with the *most unambiguously intelligible concepts,* and to understand and explain them causally" (1903–17/1949:43). Ideal types are heuristic devices to be used in the study of slices of historical reality. For example, social scientists would construct an ideal-typical bureaucracy on the basis of their immersion in historical data. This ideal type can then be compared to actual bureaucracies. The researcher looks for divergences in the real case from the exaggerated ideal type. Next, the social scientist must look for the causes of the deviations. Some typical reasons for these divergences are:

- Actions of bureaucrats that are motivated by *misinformation.*
- *Strategic errors,* primarily by the bureaucratic leaders.
- *Logical fallacies* undergirding the actions of leaders and followers.
- Decisions made in the bureaucracy on the basis of *emotion.*
- Any *irrationality* in the action of bureaucratic leaders and followers.

To take another example, an ideal-typical military battle delineates the principal components of such a battle—opposing armies, opposing strategies, materiel at the disposal of each, disputed land ("no-man's-land"), supply and support forces, command centers, and leadership qualities. Actual battles may not have all these elements, and that is one thing a researcher wants to know. The basic point is that the elements of any particular military battle may be compared with the elements identified in the ideal type.

The elements of an ideal type (such as the components of the ideal-typical military battle) are not to be thrown together arbitrarily; they are combined on the basis of their compatibility. As Hekman puts it, "Ideal types are not the product of the whim or fancy of a social scientist, but are logically constructed concepts" (1983:32). (However, they can and should reflect the interests of the social scientist.)

In Weber's view, the ideal type was to be derived inductively from the real world of social history. Weber did not believe that it was enough to offer a carefully defined set of concepts, especially if they were deductively derived from an abstract theory. The concepts had to be empirically adequate (Roth, 1971). Thus, in order to produce ideal types, researchers had first to immerse themselves in historical reality and then derive the types from that reality.

In line with Weber's efforts to find a middle ground between nomothetic and idiographic knowledge, he argued that ideal types should be neither too general nor too specific. For example, in the case of religion he would reject ideal types of the history of religion in general, but he would also be critical of ideal types of very specific phenomena, such as an individual's religious experience. Rather, ideal types are developed of intermediate phenomena such as Calvinism, Pietism, Methodism, and Baptism (Weber, 1904–05/1958).

Although ideal types are to be derived from the real world, they are not to be mirror images of that world. Rather, they are to be one-sided exaggerations (based on the researcher's interests) of the essence of what goes on in the real world. In Weber's view, the more exaggerated the ideal type, the more useful it will be for historical research.

The use of the word *ideal* or *utopia* should not be construed to mean that the concept being described is in any sense the best of all possible worlds. As used by Weber, the term meant that the form described in the concept was rarely, if ever, found in the real world. In fact, Weber argued that the ideal type need not be positive or correct; it can just as easily be negative or even morally repugnant (1903–17/1949).

Ideal types should make sense in themselves, the meaning of their components should be compatible, and they should aid us in making sense of the real world. Although we have come to think of ideal types as describing static entities, Weber believed that they could describe either static or dynamic entities. Thus we can have an ideal type of a structure, such as a bureaucracy, or of a social development, such as bureaucratization.

Ideal types also are not developed once and for all. Because society is constantly changing, and the interests of social scientists are as well, it is necessary to develop new typologies to fit the changing reality. This is in line with Weber's view that there can be no timeless concepts in the social sciences (Roth, 1968).

Although we have presented a relatively unambiguous image of the ideal type, there are contradictions in the way Weber defined the concept. In addition, in his own substantive work, Weber used the ideal type in ways that differed from the ways he said it was to be used. As Burger noted, "The ideal types presented in *Economy and Society* are a mixture of definitions, classification, and specific hypotheses seemingly too divergent to be reconcilable with Weber's statements" (1976:118). Although she disagrees with Burger on Weber's inconsistency in defining ideal types, Hekman (1983:38–59) also recognizes that Weber offers several varieties of ideal types:

- *Historical ideal types.* These relate to phenomena found in some particular historical epoch (for example, the modern capitalistic marketplace).
- *General sociological ideal types.* These relate to phenomena that cut across a number of historical periods and societies (for example, bureaucracy).
- *Action ideal types.* These are pure types of action based on the motivations of the actor (for example, affectual action).
- *Structural ideal types.* These are forms taken by the causes and consequences of social action (for example, traditional domination).

Clearly Weber developed an array of varieties of ideal types, and some of the richness in his work stems from their diversity, although common to them all is their mode of construction.

Kalberg (1994) argues that while the heuristic use of ideal types in empirical research is important, it should not be forgotten that they also play a key *theoretical* role in Weber's work. Although Weber rejects the idea of theoretical laws, he does use ideal types in various ways to create theoretical models. Thus, ideal types constitute the theoretical building blocks for the construction of a variety of theoretical models (for example, the routinization of charisma and the rationalization of society—both of which are discussed later in this chapter), and these models are then used to analyze specific historical developments.

Values

Modern sociological thinking in America on the role of values in the social sciences has been shaped to a large degree by an interpretation, often simplistic and erroneous, of Weber's notion of *value-free* sociology (Hennis, 1994; McFalls, 2007). A common perception of Weber's view is that social scientists should *not* let their personal values influence their scientific research in any way. As we will see, Weber's work on values is far more complicated and should not be reduced to the simplistic notion that values should be kept out of sociology (Tribe, 1989:3).

Values and Teaching

Weber (1903–17/1949) was most clear about the need for teachers to control their personal values in the classroom. From his point of view, academicians have a perfect right to express their personal values freely in speeches, in the press, and so forth, but the academic lecture hall is different. Weber was opposed to those teachers who preached "their evaluations on ultimate questions 'in the name of science' in governmentally privileged lecture halls in which they are neither controlled, checked by discussion, nor subject to contradiction . . . the lecture hall should be held separate from the arena of public discussion" (1903–17/1949:4). The most important difference between a public speech and an academic lecture lies in the nature of the audience. A crowd watching a public speaker has chosen to be there and can leave at any time. But students, if they want to succeed, have little choice but to listen attentively to their professor's value-laden positions. There is little ambiguity in this aspect of Weber's position on value-freedom. The academician is to express "facts," not personal values, in the classroom. Although teachers may be tempted to insert values because they make a course more interesting, teachers should be wary of employing values, because such values will "weaken the students' taste for sober empirical analysis" (Weber, 1903–17/1949:9). The only question is whether it is realistic to think that professors could eliminate most values from their presentations. Weber could adopt this position because he believed it possible to separate fact and value. However, Marx would disagree, because in his view fact and value are intertwined, dialectically interrelated.

Values and Research

Weber's position on the place of values in social research is far more ambiguous. Weber did believe in the ability to separate fact from value, and this view could be extended to the research world: "Investigator and teacher should keep unconditionally separate the establishment of empirical facts . . . and *his* own personal evaluations, i.e., his evaluation of these facts as satisfactory or unsatisfactory" (1903–17/1949:11). He often differentiated between existential knowledge of what is and normative knowledge of what ought to be (Weber, 1903–17/1949). For example, on the founding of the German Sociological Society, he said: "The Association rejects, in principle and definitely, all propaganda for action-oriented ideas from its midst." Instead, the association was pointed in the direction of the study of "what is, why something is the way it is, for what historical and social reasons" (Roth, 1968:5).

However, several facts point in a different direction and show that despite the evidence we have described, Weber did not operate with the simplistic view that values should be totally eliminated from social research. While, as we will see, Weber perceived a role for values in a specific aspect of the research process, he thought that they should be kept out of the actual collection of research data. By this Weber meant that we should employ the regular procedures of scientific investigation, such as accurate observation and systematic comparison.

Values are to be restricted to the time before social research begins. They should shape the selection of what we choose to study. Weber's (1903–17/1949:21) ideas on the role of values prior to social research are captured in his concept of *value-relevance.* As with many of Weber's methodological concepts, value-relevance is derived from the work of the German historicist Heinrich Rickert, for whom it involved "a selection of those parts of empirical reality which for human beings embody one or several of those general cultural values which are held by people in the society in which the scientific observers live" (Burger, 1976:36). In historical research, this would mean that the choice of objects to study would be made on the basis of what is considered important in the particular society in which the researchers live. That is, they choose what to study of the past on the basis of the contemporary value system. In his specific case, Weber wrote of value-relevance from the "standpoint of the interests of the modern European" (1903–17/1949:30). For example, bureaucracy was a very important part of the German society of Weber's time, and he chose, as a result, to study that phenomenon (or the lack of it) in various historical settings.

Thus, to Weber, value judgments are not to be withdrawn completely from scientific discourse. Although Weber was opposed to confusing fact and value, he did not believe that values should be excised from the social sciences: "An *attitude of moral indifference* has no connection with *scientific* 'objectivity'" (1903–17/1949:60). He was prepared to admit that values have a certain place, though he warned researchers to be careful about the role of values: "It should be constantly made clear . . . exactly at which point the scientific investigator becomes silent and the evaluating and acting person begins to speak" (Weber, 1903–17/1949:60). When expressing value positions, sociological researchers must always keep themselves and their audiences aware of those positions.

There is a gap between what Weber said and what he actually did. Weber was not afraid to express a value judgment, even in the midst of the analysis of historical data. For example, he said that the Roman state suffered from a convulsive sickness of its social body. It can be argued that in Weber's actual work values not only were a basic device for selecting subjects to study but also were involved in the acquisition of meaningful knowledge of the social world. Gary Abraham (1992) has made the point that Weber's work, especially his views on Judaism as a world religion, was distorted by his values. In his sociology of religion (discussed later in this chapter), Weber termed the Jews "pariah people." Weber traced this position of outsider more to the desire of Jews to segregate themselves than to their exclusion by the rest of society. Thus Weber, accepting the general view of the day, argued that Jews would need to surrender Judaism in order to be assimilated into German society. Abraham argues that this sort of bias affected not only Weber's ideas on Judaism, but his work in general. This casts further doubt on Weber as a "value-free" sociologist, as well as on the conventional view of Weber as a liberal thinker. As Abraham says, "Max Weber was probably as close to tolerant liberalism as majority Germany could offer at the time" (1992:22). Weber was more of a nationalist supporting the assimilation of minority groups than he was a classical liberal favoring pluralism, and those values had a profound effect on his work (Roth, 2000).

Most American sociologists regard Weber as an exponent of value-free sociology. The truth is that most American sociologists themselves subscribe to the idea of value-freedom, and they find it useful to invoke Weber's name in support of their position. As we have seen, however, Weber's work is studded with values.

One other aspect of Weber's work on values worth noting is his ideas on the role of the social sciences in helping people make choices among various ultimate value positions. Basically, Weber's view is that there is *no* way of scientifically choosing among alternative value positions. Thus, social scientists cannot presume to make such choices for people. "The social sciences, which are strictly empirical sciences, are the least fitted to presume to save the individual the difficulty of making a choice" (Weber, 1903–17/1949:19). The social scientist can derive certain factual conclusions from social research, but this research cannot tell people what they "ought" to do. Empirical research can help people choose an adequate means to an end, but it cannot help them choose that end as opposed to other ends. Weber says, "It can never be the task of an empirical science to provide binding norms and ideals from which directions for immediate practical activity can be derived" (1903–17/1949:52).

Substantive Sociology

We turn now to Weber's substantive sociology. We will begin, as did Weber in his monumental *Economy and Society,* at the levels of action and interaction, but we will soon encounter the basic paradox in Weber's work: despite his seeming commitment to a sociology of small-scale processes, his work is primarily at the large-scale levels of the social world. (Many Weberians would disagree with this portrayal of paradox in Weber's work. Kalberg [1994], for example, argues that Weber offers a more fully integrated micro-macro, or agency-structure, theory.)

What is Sociology?

In articulating his view on sociology, Weber often took a stance against the large-scale evolutionary sociology, the organicism, that was preeminent in the field at the time. For example, Weber said: "I became one [a sociologist] in order to put an end to collectivist notions. In other words, sociology, too, can only be practiced by proceeding from the action of one or more, few or many, individuals, that means, by employing a strictly 'individualist' method" (Roth, 1976:306). Despite his stated adherence to an "individualist" method, Weber was forced to admit that it is impossible to eliminate totally collective ideas from sociology.[4] But even when he admitted the significance of collective concepts, Weber ultimately reduced them to patterns and regularities of individual action: "For the subjective interpretation of action in sociological work these collectivities must be treated as *solely* the resultants and modes of organization of the particular acts of individual persons, since these alone can be treated as agents in a course of subjectively understandable action" (1921/1968:13).

At the individual level, Weber was deeply concerned with meaning, and the way in which it was formed. There seems little doubt that Weber believed in, and intended to undertake, a microsociology. But is that, in fact, what he did? Guenther Roth, one of Weber's foremost interpreters, provides us with an unequivocal answer in his description of the overall thrust of *Economy and Society:* "the first strictly *empirical comparison of social structure* and normative order in *world-historical* depth" (1968:xxvii). Mary Fulbrook directly addresses the discontinuity in Weber's work:

> Weber's overt emphasis on the importance of [individual] meanings and motives in causal explanation of social action does not correspond adequately with the true mode of explanation involved in his comparative-historical studies of the world religions. Rather, the ultimate level of causal explanation in Weber's substantive writings is that of the social-structural conditions under which certain forms of meaning and motivation can achieve historical efficacy.
>
> (Fulbrook, 1978:71)

Lars Udehn (1981) has cast light on this problem in interpreting Weber's work by distinguishing between Weber's methodology and his substantive concerns and recognizing that there is a conflict or tension between them. In Udehn's view, Weber uses an "individualist and subjectivist methodology" (1981:131). In terms of the latter, Weber is interested in what individuals do and why they do it (their subjective motives). In the former, Weber is interested in reducing collectivities to the actions of individuals. However, in most of his substantive sociology (as we will see), Weber focuses on large-scale structure (such as bureaucracy or capitalism) and is not focally concerned with what individuals do or why they do it.[5] Such structures are not reduced by Weber to the actions of individuals, and the actions of those in them are determined by the structures, not by their motives. There is little doubt that there is an enormous contradiction in Weber's work, and it will concern us through much of this chapter.

With this as background, we are now ready for Weber's definition of *sociology:* "Sociology . . . is a *science* concerning itself with the *interpretive understanding* of

---

[4]In fact, Weber's ideal types *are* collective concepts.

[5]Udehn argues that one exception is Weber's analysis of the behavior of leaders.

social action and thereby with a *causal* explanation of its course and consequences" (1921/1968:4). Among the themes discussed earlier that are mentioned or implied in this definition are:

Sociology should be a science.
Sociology should be concerned with causality. (Here, apparently, Weber was combining sociology and history.)
Sociology should utilize interpretive understanding *(verstehen).*

We are now ready for what Weber meant by social action.

Social Action

Weber's entire sociology, if we accept his words at face value, was based on his conception of social action (S. Turner, 1983). He differentiated between action and purely reactive behavior. The concept of behavior is reserved, then as now, for automatic behavior that involves no thought processes. A stimulus is presented and behavior occurs, with little intervening between stimulus and response. Such behavior was not of interest in Weber's sociology. He was concerned with action that clearly involved the intervention of thought processes (and the resulting meaningful action) between the occurrence of a stimulus and the ultimate response. To put it slightly differently, action was said to occur when individuals attached subjective meanings to their action. To Weber, the task of sociological analysis involved "the interpretation of action in terms of its subjective meaning" (1921/1968:8). A good, and more specific, example of Weber's thinking on action is found in his discussion of *economic action,* which he defined as "a *conscious, primary* orientation to economic consideration . . . for what matters is not the objective necessity of making economic provision, but the belief that it is necessary" (1921/1968:64).

In embedding his analysis in mental processes and the resulting meaningful action, Weber (1921/1968) was careful to point out that it is erroneous to regard psychology as the foundation of the sociological interpretation of action. Weber seemed to be making essentially the same point made by Durkheim in discussing at least some nonmaterial social facts. That is, sociologists are interested in mental processes, but this is not the same as psychologists' interest in the mind, personality, and so forth.

Although Weber implied that he had a great concern with mental processes, he actually spent little time on them. Hans Gerth and C. Wright Mills called attention to Weber's lack of concern with mental processes: "Weber sees in the concept of personality a much abused notion referring to a profoundly irrational center of creativity, a center before which analytical inquiry comes to a halt" (1958:55). Schutz (1932/1967) was quite correct when he pointed out that although Weber's work on mental processes is suggestive, it is hardly the basis for a systematic microsociology. But it was the suggestiveness of Weber's work that made him relevant to those who developed theories of individuals and their behavior—symbolic interactionism, phenomenology, and so forth.

In his action theory, Weber's clear intent was to focus on individuals and patterns and regularities of action and not on the collectivity. "Action in the sense of subjectively understandable orientation of behavior exists only as the behavior of one or more *individual* human beings" (Weber, 1921/1968:13). Weber was prepared to admit that for some purposes we may have to treat collectivities as individuals, "but for the subjective interpretation of action in sociological work these collectivities must be treated as *solely* the resultants and modes of organization of the particular acts of individual persons, since these alone can be treated as agents in a course of subjectively understandable action" (1921/1968:13). It would seem that Weber could hardly be more explicit: the sociology of action is ultimately concerned with individuals, *not* collectivities.

Weber utilized his ideal-type methodology to clarify the meaning of *action* by identifying four basic types of action. Not only is this typology significant for understanding what Weber meant by action, but it is also, in part, the basis for Weber's concern with larger social structures and institutions. Of greatest importance is Weber's differentiation between the two basic types of rational action. The first is *means–ends rationality,* or action that is "determined by expectations as to the behavior of objects in the environment and of other human beings; these expectations are used as 'conditions' or 'means' for the attainment of the actor's own rationally pursued and calculated ends" (Weber, 1921/1968:24). The second is *value rationality,* or action that is "determined by a conscious belief in the value for its own sake of some ethical, aesthetic, religious, or other form of behavior, independently of its prospects for success" (Weber, 1921/1968:24–25). *Affectual* action (which was of little concern to Weber) is determined by the emotional state of the actor. *Traditional* action (which was of far greater concern to Weber) is determined by the actor's habitual and customary ways of behaving.

It should be noted that although Weber differentiated four ideal-typical forms of action, he was well aware that any given action usually involves a combination of all four ideal types of action. In addition, Weber argued that sociologists have a much better chance of understanding action of the more rational variety than they do of understanding action dominated by affect or tradition.

We turn now to Weber's thoughts on social stratification, or his famous ideas on class, status, and party (or power). His analysis of stratification is one area in which Weber does operate, at least at first, as an action theorist.

Class, Status, and Party

One important aspect of this analysis is that Weber refused to reduce stratification to economic factors (or class, in Weber's terms) but saw it as multidimensional. Thus, society is stratified on the bases of economics, status, and power. One resulting implication is that people can rank high on one or two of these dimensions of stratification and low on the other (or others), permitting a far more sophisticated analysis of social stratification than is possible when stratification is simply reduced (as it was by some Marxists) to variations in one's economic situation.

Starting with class, Weber adhered to his action orientation by arguing that a class is not a community. Rather, a class is a group of people whose shared situation is a possible, and sometimes frequent, basis for action by the group (Smith, 2007). Weber contends that a "class situation" exists when three conditions are met:

> (1) A number of people have in common a specific causal component of their life chances, insofar as (2) this component is represented exclusively by economic

> interests in the possession of goods and opportunities for income, and (3) is represented under the conditions of the commodity or labor markets. This is "class situation."
>
> (Weber, 1921/1968:927)

The concept of "class" refers to any group of people found in the same class situation. Thus, a class is *not* a community but merely a group of people in the same economic, or market, situation.

In contrast to class, status does normally refer to communities; status groups are ordinarily communities, albeit rather amorphous ones. "Status situation" is defined by Weber as "every typical component of the life of men that is determined by a specific, positive or negative, social estimation of *honor*" (1921/1968:932). As a general rule, status is associated with a style of life. (Status relates to consumption of goods produced, while class relates to economic production.) Those at the top of the status hierarchy have a different lifestyle than do those at the bottom. In this case, lifestyle, or status, is related to class situation. But class and status are not necessarily linked to one another: "Money and an entrepreneurial position are not in themselves status qualifications, although they may lead to them; and the lack of property is not in itself a status disqualification, although this may be a reason for it" (Weber, 1921/1968:306). There is a complex set of relationships between class and status, and it is made even more complicated when we add the dimension of party.

While classes exist in the economic order and status groups in the social order, parties can be found in the political order. To Weber, parties "are always *structures* struggling for domination" (cited in Gerth and Mills, 1958:195; italics added). Thus, parties are the most organized elements of Weber's stratification system. Weber thinks of parties very broadly as including not only those that exist in the state but also those that may exist in a social club. Parties usually, but not always, represent class and/or status groups. Whatever they represent, parties are oriented to the attainment of power.

While Weber remained close to his action approach in his ideas on social stratification, these ideas already indicate a movement in the direction of macro-level communities and structures. In most of his other work, Weber focused on such large-scale units of analysis. Not that Weber lost sight of the action; the actor simply moved from being the focus of his concern to being largely a dependent variable determined by a variety of large-scale forces. For example, as we will see, Weber believed that individual Calvinists are impelled to act in various ways by the norms, values, and beliefs of their religion, but his focus was not on the individual but on the collective forces that impel the actor.

Structures of Authority

Weber's sociological interest in the structures of authority was motivated, at least in part, by his political interests (Eliaeson, 2000). Weber was no political radical; in fact, he was often called the "bourgeois Marx" to reflect the similarities in the intellectual interests of Marx and Weber as well as their very different political orientations. Although Weber was almost as critical of modern capitalism as Marx was, he did not advocate revolution. He wanted to change society gradually, not overthrow it. He had little faith in the ability of the masses to create a "better" society. But Weber also saw little hope in the middle classes, which he felt were dominated by shortsighted, petty bureaucrats. Weber was critical of authoritarian political leaders like Bismarck. Nevertheless, for Weber the hope—if indeed he had any hope—lay with the great political leaders rather than with the masses or the bureaucrats. Along with his faith in political leaders went his unswerving nationalism. He placed the nation above all else: "The vital interests of the nation stand, of course, above democracy and parliamentarianism" (Weber, 1921/1968:1383). Weber preferred democracy as a political form not because he believed in the masses but because it offered maximum dynamism and the best milieu to generate political leaders (Mommsen, 1974). Weber noted that authority structures exist in every social institution, and his political views were related to his analysis of these structures in all settings. Of course, they were most relevant to his views on the polity.

Weber began his analysis of authority structures in a way that was consistent with his assumptions about the nature of action. He defined *domination* as the "probability that certain specific commands (or all commands) will be obeyed by a given group of persons" (Weber, 1921/1968:212). Domination can have a variety of bases, legitimate as well as illegitimate, but what mainly interested Weber were the legitimate forms of domination, or what he called *authority* (Leggewie, 2005). What concerned Weber, and what played a central role in much of his sociology, were the three bases on which authority is made legitimate to followers—rational, traditional, and charismatic. In defining these three bases, Weber remained fairly close to his ideas on individual action, but he rapidly moved to the large-scale structures of authority. Authority legitimized on *rational* grounds rests "on a belief in the legality of enacted rules and the right of those elevated to authority under such rules to issue commands" (Weber, 1921/1968:215). Authority legitimized on *traditional* grounds is based on "an established belief in the sanctity of immemorial traditions and the legitimacy of those exercising authority under them" (Weber, 1921/1968:215). Finally, authority legitimized by *charisma*[6] rests on the devotion of followers to the exceptional sanctity, exemplary character, heroism, or special powers (for example, the ability to work miracles) of leaders, as well as on the normative order sanctioned by them. All these modes of legitimizing authority clearly imply individual actors, thought processes (beliefs), and actions. But from this point, Weber, in his thinking about authority, did move quite far from an individual action base, as we will see when we discuss the authority structures erected on the basis of these types of legitimacy.

Legal Authority

Legal authority can take a variety of structural forms, but the one that interested Weber most was the *bureaucracy,* which he considered "the purest type of exercise of legal authority" (1921/1968:220).

Ideal-Typical Bureaucracy Weber depicted bureaucracies in ideal-typical terms:

> From a purely technical point of view, a bureaucracy is capable of attaining the highest degree of efficiency, and is in this sense formally the most rational known means of exercising authority over human beings. It is superior to any other form in

[6]The term *charisma* is used in Weber's work in a variety of other ways and contexts as well; see Miyahara (1983).

> precision, in stability, in the stringency of its discipline, and in its reliability. It thus makes possible a particularly high degree of calculability of results for the heads of the organization and for those acting in relation to it. It is finally superior both in intensive efficiency and in the scope of its operations and is formally capable of application to all kinds of administrative tasks.
>
> (Weber, 1921/1968:223)

Despite his discussion of the positive characteristics of bureaucracies, here and elsewhere in his work, there is a fundamental ambivalence in his attitude toward them. Although he detailed their advantages, he was well aware of their problems. Weber expressed various reservations about bureaucratic organizations. For example, he was cognizant of the "red tape" that often makes dealing with bureaucracies so trying and so difficult. His major fear, however, was that the rationalization that dominates all aspects of bureaucratic life was a threat to individual liberty. As Weber put it:

> No machinery in the world functions so precisely as this apparatus of men and, moreover, so cheaply. . . . Rational calculation . . . reduces every worker to a cog in this bureaucratic machine and, seeing himself in this light, he will merely ask how to transform himself into a somewhat bigger cog. . . . The passion for bureaucratization drives us to despair.
>
> (Weber, 1921/1968:liii)

Weber was appalled by the effects of bureaucratization and, more generally, of the rationalization of the world of which bureaucratization is but one component, but he saw no way out. He described bureaucracies as "escape proof," "practically unshatterable," and among the hardest institutions to destroy once they are established. Along the same lines, he felt that individual bureaucrats could not "squirm out" of the bureaucracy once they were "harnessed" in it (for a less ominous view of bureaucratization, see Klagge, 1997). Weber concluded that "the future belongs to bureaucratization" (1921/1968:1401), and time has borne out his prediction.

Weber would say that his depiction of the advantages of bureaucracy is part of his ideal-typical image of the way it operates. The ideal-typical bureaucracy is a purposeful exaggeration of the rational characteristics of bureaucracies. Such an exaggerated model is useful for heuristic purposes and for studies of organizations in the real world, but it is not to be mistaken for a realistic depiction of the way bureaucracies actually operate.

Weber distinguished the ideal-typical bureaucracy from the ideal-typical bureaucrat. He conceived of bureaucracies as structures and of bureaucrats as positions within those structures. He did *not,* as his action orientation might lead us to expect, offer a social psychology of organizations or of the individuals who inhabit those bureaucracies (as modern symbolic interactionists might).

The ideal-typical bureaucracy is a type of organization. Its basic units are offices organized in a hierarchical manner with rules, functions, written documents, and means of compulsion. All these are, to varying degrees, large-scale structures that represent the thrust of Weber's thinking. He could, after all, have constructed an ideal-typical bureaucracy that focused on the thoughts and actions of individuals within the bureaucracy. There is a whole school of thought in the study of organizations that focuses precisely on this level rather than on the structures of bureaucracies (see, for example, Blankenship, 1977).

The following are the major characteristics of the ideal-typical bureaucracy:

1. It consists of a continuous organization of official functions (offices) bound by rules.
2. Each office has a specified sphere of competence. The office carries with it a set of obligations to perform various functions, the authority to carry out these functions, and the means of compulsion required to do the job.
3. The offices are organized into a hierarchical system.
4. The offices may carry with them technical qualifications that require that the participants obtain suitable training.
5. The staff that fills these offices does not own the means of production associated with them;[7] staff members are provided with the use of those things that they need to do the job.
6. The incumbent is not allowed to appropriate the position; it always remains part of the organization.
7. Administrative acts, decisions, and rules are formulated and recorded in writing.

Any Alternatives? A bureaucracy is one of the rational structures that is playing an ever-increasing role in modern society, but one may wonder whether there is any alternative to the bureaucratic structure. Weber's clear and unequivocal answer was that there is no possible alternative: "The needs of mass administration make it today completely indispensable. The choice is only between bureaucracy and dilettantism in the field of administration" (1921/1968:223).

Although we might admit that bureaucracy is an intrinsic part of modern capitalism, we might ask whether a socialist society might be different. Is it possible to create a socialist society without bureaucracies and bureaucrats? Once again, Weber was unequivocal: "When those subject to bureaucratic control seek to escape the influence of existing bureaucratic apparatus, this is normally possible only by creating an organization of their own which is equally subject to the process of bureaucratization" (1921/1968:224). In fact, Weber believed that in the case of socialism we would see an increase, not a decrease, in bureaucratization. If socialism were to achieve a level of efficiency comparable to capitalism, "it would mean a tremendous increase in the importance of professional bureaucrats" (Weber, 1921/1968:224). In capitalism, at least the owners are not bureaucrats and therefore would be able to restrain the bureaucrats, but in socialism, even the top-level leaders would be bureaucrats. Weber thus believed that even with its problems "capitalism presented the best chances for the preservation of individual freedom and creative leadership in a bureaucratic world" (Mommsen, 1974:xv). We are once again at a key theme in Weber's work: his view that there is really no hope for a better world. Socialists can, in Weber's view, only make things worse by expanding the degree of bureaucratization in society. Weber noted: "Not summer's bloom lies ahead of us, but rather a polar night of icy darkness and hardness, no matter which group may triumph externally now" (cited in Gerth and Mills, 1958:128).

---

[7]Here and elsewhere in his work Weber adopts a Marxian interest in the means of production. This is paralleled by his concern with alienation, not only in the economic sector but throughout social life (science, politics, and so forth).

Any Hope? A ray of hope in Weber's work—and it is a small one—is that professionals who stand outside the bureaucratic system can control it to some degree. In this category, Weber included professional politicians, scientists, intellectuals (Sadri, 1992), and even capitalists, as well as the supreme heads of the bureaucracies. For example, Weber said that politicians "must be the countervailing force against bureaucratic domination" (1921/1968:1417). His famous essay "Politics as a Vocation" is basically a plea for the development of political leaders with a calling to oppose the rule of bureaucracies and of bureaucrats. But in the end these appear to be rather feeble hopes. In fact, a good case can be made that these professionals are simply another aspect of the rationalization process and that their development serves only to accelerate that process (Nass, 1986; Ritzer, 1975c; Ritzer and Walczak, 1988).

In Weber's "'Churches' and 'Sects' in North America: An Ecclesiastical Socio-Political Sketch" (1906/1985), Colin Loader and Jeffrey Alexander (1985) see a forerunner of Weber's thoughts on the hope provided by an ethic of responsibility in the face of the expansion of bureaucratization. American sects such as the Quakers practice an ethic of responsibility by combining rationality and larger values. Rogers Brubaker defines the *ethic of responsibility* as "the passionate commitment to ultimate values with the dispassionate analysis of alternative means of pursuing them" (1984:108). He contrasts this to the *ethic of conviction,* in which a rational choice of means is foregone and the actor orients "his action to the realization of some absolute value or unconditional demand" (1984:106; for a somewhat different view, see Gane, 1997). The ethic of conviction often involves a withdrawal from the rational world, whereas the ethic of responsibility involves a struggle within that world for greater humanness. The ethic of responsibility provides at least a modicum of hope in the face of the onslaught of rationalization and bureaucratization.

Traditional Authority

Whereas legal authority stems from the legitimacy of a rational-legal system, traditional authority is based on a claim by the leaders, and a belief on the part of the followers, that there is virtue in the sanctity of age-old rules and powers. The leader in such a system is not a superior but a personal master. The administrative staff, if any, consists not of officials but mainly of personal retainers. In Weber's words, "Personal loyalty, not the official's impersonal duty, determines the relations of the administrative staff to the master" (1921/1968:227). Although the bureaucratic staff owes its allegiance and obedience to enacted rules and to the leader, who acts in their name, the staff of the traditional leader obeys because the leader carries the weight of tradition—he or she has been chosen for that position in the traditional manner.

Weber was interested in the staff of the traditional leader and how it measured up to the ideal-typical bureaucratic staff. He concluded that it was lacking on a number of counts. The traditional staff lacks offices with clearly defined spheres of competence that are subject to impersonal rules. It also does not have a rational ordering of relations of superiority and inferiority; it lacks a clear hierarchy. There is no regular system of appointment and promotion on the basis of free contracts. Technical training is not a regular requirement for obtaining a position or an appointment. Appointments do not carry with them fixed salaries paid in money.

Weber also used his ideal-type methodology to analyze historically the different forms of traditional authority. He differentiated between two very early forms of traditional authority. A *gerontocracy* involves rule by elders, whereas *primary patriarchalism* involves leaders who inherit their positions. Both of these forms have a supreme chief but lack an administrative staff. A more modern form is *patrimonialism,* which is traditional domination with an administration and a military force that are purely personal instruments of the master (Eisenberg, 1998). Still more modern is *feudalism,* which limits the discretion of the master through the development of more routinized, even contractual, relationships between leader and subordinate. This restraint, in turn, leads to more stabilized power positions than exist in patrimonialism. All four of these forms may be seen as structural variations of traditional authority, and all of them differ significantly from rational-legal authority.

Weber saw structures of traditional authority, in any form, as barriers to the development of rationality. This is our first encounter with an overriding theme in Weber's work—factors that facilitate or impede the development of (formal) rationality (see the next section). Over and over we find Weber concerned, as he was here, with the structural factors conducive to rationality in the Western world and the structural and cultural impediments to the development of a similar rationality throughout the rest of the world. In this specific case, Weber argued that the structures and practices of traditional authority constitute a barrier to the rise of rational economic structures—in particular, capitalism—as well as to various other components of a rational society. Even patrimonialism—a more modern form of traditionalism—while permitting the development of certain forms of "primitive" capitalism, does not allow for the rise of the highly rational type of capitalism characteristic of the modern West.

Charismatic Authority

Charisma is a concept that has come to be used very broadly (Adair-Tateff, 2005; Oakes, 1997; Turner, 2003; Werbner and Basu, 1998). The news media and the general public are quick to point to a politician, a movie star, or a rock musician as a charismatic individual. By this they most often mean that the person in question is endowed with extraordinary qualities. The concept of charisma plays an important role in the work of Max Weber, but his conception of it was very different from that held by most laypeople today. Although Weber did not deny that a charismatic leader may have outstanding characteristics, his sense of charisma was more dependent on the group of disciples and the way that they *define* the charismatic leader. To put Weber's position bluntly, if the disciples define a leader as charismatic, then he or she is likely to be a charismatic leader irrespective of whether he or she actually possesses any outstanding traits. A charismatic leader, then, can be someone who is quite ordinary. What is crucial is the process by which such a leader is set apart from ordinary people and treated as if endowed with supernatural, superhuman, or at least exceptional powers or qualities that are not accessible to the ordinary person (Miyahara, 1983).

Charisma and Revolution To Weber, charisma was a revolutionary force, one of the most important revolutionary forces in the social world. Whereas traditional authority clearly is inherently conservative, the rise of a charismatic leader may well pose a threat to that system (as well as to a rational-legal system) and lead to a dramatic change in that system. What distinguishes charisma as a revolutionary force is that it leads to changes in the minds of actors; it causes a "subjective or internal reorientation." Such changes may lead to "a radical alteration of the central attitudes and direction of action with a completely new orientation of all attitudes toward different problems of the world" (Weber, 1921/1968:245). Although Weber was here addressing changes in the thoughts and actions of individuals, such changes are clearly reduced to the status of dependent variables. Weber focused on changes in the structure of authority, that is, the rise of charismatic authority. When such a new authority structure emerges, it is likely to change people's thoughts and actions dramatically.

The other major revolutionary force in Weber's theoretical system, and the one with which he was much more concerned, is (formal) rationality. Whereas charisma is an internal revolutionary force that changes the minds of actors, Weber saw (formal) rationality as an external revolutionary force changing the structures of society first and then ultimately the thoughts and actions of individuals. We will have more to say about rationality as a revolutionary force later, but this closes our discussion of charisma as a revolutionary factor, because Weber had very little to say about it. Weber was interested in the revolutionary character of charisma as well as its structure and the necessity that its basic character be transformed and routinized in order for it to survive as a system of authority.

Charismatic Organizations and the Routinization of Charisma In his analysis of charisma, Weber began, as he did with traditional authority, with the ideal-typical bureaucracy. He sought to determine to what degree the structure of charismatic authority, with its disciples and staff, differs from the bureaucratic system. Compared to that of the ideal-typical bureaucracy, the staff of the charismatic leader is lacking on virtually all counts. The staff members are not technically trained but are chosen instead for their possession of charismatic qualities or, at least, of qualities similar to those possessed by the charismatic leader. The offices they occupy form no clear hierarchy. Their work does not constitute a career, and there are no promotions, clear appointments, or dismissals. The charismatic leader is free to intervene whenever he or she feels that the staff cannot handle a situation. The organization has no formal rules, no established administrative organs, and no precedents to guide new judgments. In these and other ways, Weber found the staff of the charismatic leader to be "greatly inferior" to the staff in a bureaucratic form of organization.

Weber's interest in the organization behind the charismatic leader and the staff that inhabits it led him to the question of what happens to charismatic authority when the leader dies. After all, a charismatic system is inherently fragile; it would seem to be able to survive only as long as the charismatic leader lives. But is it possible for such an organization to live after the leader dies? The answer to this question is of the greatest consequence to the staff members of the charismatic leader, for they are likely to live on after the leader dies. They are also likely to have a vested interest in the continued existence of the organization: if the organization ceases to exist, they are out of work. Thus, the challenge for the staff is to create a situation in which charisma in some adulterated form persists even after the leader's death. It is a difficult struggle because, for Weber, charisma is by its nature unstable; it exists in its pure form only as long as the charismatic leader lives.

In order to cope with the departure of the charismatic leader, the staff (as well as the followers) may adopt a variety of strategies to create a more lasting organization. The staff may search out a new charismatic leader, but even if the search is successful, the new leader is unlikely to have the same aura as his or her predecessor. A set of rules also may be developed that allows the group to identify future charismatic leaders. But such rules rapidly become tradition, and what was charismatic leadership is on the way toward becoming traditional authority. In any case, the nature of leadership is radically changed as the purely personal character of charisma is eliminated. Still another technique is to allow the charismatic leader to designate his or her successor and thereby to transfer charisma symbolically to the next in line. Again it is questionable whether this is ever very successful or whether it can be successful in the long run. Another strategy is having the staff designate a successor and having its choice accepted by the larger community. The staff could also create ritual tests, with the new charismatic leader being the one who successfully undergoes the tests. However, all these efforts are doomed to failure. In the long run, charisma cannot be routinized and still be charisma; it must be transformed into either traditional or rational-legal authority (or into some sort of institutionalized charisma like the Catholic Church).

Indeed, we find a basic theory of history in Weber's work. If successful, charisma almost immediately moves in the direction of routinization. But once routinized, charisma is en route to becoming either traditional or rational-legal authority. Once it achieves one of those states, the stage is set for the cycle to begin all over again. However, despite a general adherence to a cyclical theory, Weber believed that a basic change has occurred in the modern world and that we are more and more likely to see charisma routinized in the direction of rational-legal authority. Furthermore, he saw rational systems of authority as stronger and as increasingly impervious to charismatic movements. The modern, rationalized world may well mean the death of charisma as a significant revolutionary force (Seligman, 1993). Weber contended that rationality—not charisma—is the most irresistible and important revolutionary force in the modern world.

Types of Authority and the "Real World"

In this section, we have discussed the three types of authority as ideal types, but Weber was well aware that in the real world, any specific form of authority involves a combination of all three. Thus, we can think of Franklin D. Roosevelt as a president of the United States who ruled on all three bases. He was elected president in accordance with a series of rational-legal principles. By the time he was elected president for the fourth time, a good part of this rule had traditional elements. Finally, many disciples and followers regarded him as a charismatic leader (McCann, 1997).

Although we have presented the three forms of authority as parallel structures, in the real world there is constant tension and, sometimes, conflict among them. The charismatic leader is a constant threat to the other forms of authority. Once in power, the charismatic leader must address the threat posed to him or her by the other two forms. Even if charismatic authority is successfully routinized, there then arises the problem of maintaining its dynamism and its original revolutionary qualities. Then there is the conflict produced by the constant development of rational-legal authority and the threat it poses to the continued existence of the other forms. If Weber was right, however, we might face a future in which the tension among the three forms of authority is eliminated, a world of the uncontested hegemony of the rational-legal system. This is the "iron cage" of a totally rationalized society that worried Weber so much. In such a society, the only hope lies with isolated charismatic individuals who manage somehow to avoid the coercive power of society. But a small number of isolated individuals hardly represent a significant hope in the face of an increasingly powerful bureaucratic machine.

Rationalization

There has been a growing realization in recent years that rationalization lies at the heart of Weber's substantive sociology (Brubaker, 1984; R. Collins, 1980; Eisen, 1978; Kalberg, 1980, 1990; Levine, 1981a; Ritzer, 2005; Scaff, 1989, 2005; Schluchter, 1981; Sica, 1988). As Kalberg put it, "It *is* the case that Weber's interest in a broad and overarching theme—the 'specific and peculiar "rationalism" of Western culture' and its unique origins and development—stands at the center of his sociology" (1994:18). However, it is difficult to extract a clear definition of *rationalization* from Weber's work.[8] In fact, he operated with a number of different definitions of the term, and he often failed to specify which definition he was using in a particular discussion (Brubaker, 1984:1). As we saw earlier, Weber did define *rationality;* indeed, he differentiated between two types—means–ends and value rationality. However, these concepts refer to types of *action.* They are the basis of, but not coterminous with, Weber's larger-scale sense of rationalization. Weber is interested in far more than fragmented action orientations; his main concern is with regularities and patterns of action within civilizations, institutions, organizations, strata, classes, and groups. Donald Levine (1981a) argues that Weber is interested in "objectified" rationality, that is, action that is in accord with some process of external systematization. Stephen Kalberg (1980) performs a useful service by identifying four basic types of ("objective") rationality in Weber's work. (Levine offers a very similar differentiation.) These types of rationality were "the basic heuristic tools [Weber] employed to scrutinize the historical fates of rationalization as sociocultural processes" (Kalberg, 1980:1172; for an application, see Takayama, 1998).

Types of Rationality

The first type is *practical rationality,* which is defined by Kalberg as "every way of life that views and judges worldly activity in relation to the individual's purely pragmatic and egoistic interests" (1980:1151). People who practice practical rationality accept given realities and merely calculate the most expedient ways of dealing with the difficulties that they present. This type of rationality arose with the severing of the bonds of primitive magic, and it exists trans-civilizationally and trans-historically; that is, it is not

[8]It might be argued that there is no single definition because the various forms of rationality are so different from one another that they preclude such a definition. We would like to thank Jere Cohen for this point.

restricted to the modern Occident. This type of rationality stands in opposition to anything that threatens to transcend everyday routine. It leads people to distrust all impractical values, either religious or secular-utopian, as well as the theoretical rationality of the intellectuals, the type of rationality to which we now turn.

Theoretical rationality involves a cognitive effort to master reality through increasingly abstract concepts rather than through action. It involves such abstract cognitive processes as logical deduction, induction, attribution of causality, and the like. This type of rationality was accomplished early in history by sorcerers and ritualistic priests and later by philosophers, judges, and scientists. Unlike practical rationality, theoretical rationality leads the actor to transcend daily realities in a quest to understand the world as a meaningful cosmos. Like practical rationality, it is trans-civilizational and trans-historical. The effect of intellectual rationality on action is limited. In that it involves cognitive processes, it need not affect action taken, and it has the potential to introduce new patterns of action only indirectly.

Substantive rationality (like practical rationality but *not* theoretical rationality) directly orders action into patterns through clusters of values. Substantive rationality involves a choice of means to ends within the context of a system of values. One value system is no more (substantively) rational than another. Thus, this type of rationality also exists trans-civilizationally and trans-historically, wherever consistent value postulates exist.

Finally, and most important from the author's point of view, is *formal rationality,* which involves means–ends calculation (Cockerham, Abel, and Luschen, 1993). But whereas in practical rationality this calculation occurs in reference to pragmatic self-interests, in formal rationality it occurs with reference to "universally applied rules, laws, and regulations." As Brubaker puts it, "Common to the rationality of industrial capitalism, formalistic law and bureaucratic administration is its objectified, institutionalized, supra-individual form; in each sphere, rationality is embodied in the social structure and confronts individuals as something external to them" (1984:9). Weber makes this quite clear in the specific case of bureaucratic rationalization:

> Bureaucratic rationalization . . . revolutionizes with *technical means,* in principle, as does every economic reorganization, "from without": It *first* changes the material and social orders, and *through* them the people, by changing the conditions of adaptation, and perhaps the opportunities for adaptation, through a rational determination of means and ends.
>
> (Weber, 1921/1968:1116)

Although all the other types of rationality are trans-civilizational and epoch-transcending, formal rationality arose *only* in the West with the coming of industrialization. The universally applied rules, laws, and regulations that characterize formal rationality in the West are found particularly in the economic, legal, and scientific institutions, as well as in the bureaucratic form of domination. Thus, we have already encountered formal rationality in our discussion of rational-legal authority and the bureaucracy.

An Overarching Theory?

Although Weber had a complex, multifaceted sense of rationalization, he used it most powerfully and meaningfully in his image of the modern Western world, especially in the capitalistic economy (R. Collins, 1980; Weber, 1927/1981) and bureaucratic organizations (I. Cohen, 1981:xxxi; Weber, 1921/1968:956–1005), as an iron cage (Mitzman, 1969/1971; Tiryakian, 1981) of formally rational structures. Weber described capitalism and bureaucracies as "two great rationalizing forces" (1921/1968:698).[9] In fact, Weber saw capitalism and bureaucracies as being derived from the same basic sources (especially innerworldly asceticism), involving similarly rational and methodical action, and reinforcing one another and in the process furthering the rationalization of the Occident.[10] In Weber's (1921/1968:227, 994) view, the only real rival to the bureaucrat in technical expertise and factual knowledge was the capitalist.

However, if we take Weber at his word, it is difficult to argue that he had an overarching theory of rationalization. He rejected the idea of "general evolutionary sequence" (Weber, 1927/1981:34). He was critical of thinkers like Hegel and Marx, who he felt offered general, teleological theories of society. In his own work, he tended to shy away from studies of, or proclamations about, whole societies. Instead, he tended to focus, in turn, on social structures and institutions such as bureaucracy, stratification, law, the city, religion, the polity, and the economy. Lacking a sense of the whole, he was unlikely to make global generalizations, especially about future directions. Furthermore, the rationalization process that Weber described in one social structure or institution was usually quite different from the rationalization of another structure or institution. As Weber put it, the process of rationalization assumes "unusually varied forms" (1922–23/1958:293; see also Weber, 1921/1958: 30; 1904–05/1958:78), and "the history of rationalism shows a development which by no means follows parallel lines in the various departments of life" (1904–05/1958:77; see also Brubaker, 1984:9; Kalberg, 1980:1147). Weber also looked at many things other than rationalization in his various comparative-historical studies (Kalberg, 1994).

This being said, it is clear that Weber does have a deep concern for the overarching effect of the formal rationalization of the economy and bureaucracies on the Western world (Brubaker, 1984). For example, in *Economy and Society,* Weber says:

> This whole process of rationalization in the factory as elsewhere, and especially in the bureaucratic state machine, parallels the centralization of the material implements of organization in the hands of the master. Thus, discipline inexorably takes over ever larger areas as the satisfaction of political and economic needs is increasingly rationalized. This universal phenomenon more and more restricts the importance of charisma and of individually differentiated conduct.
>
> (Weber, 1921/1968:1156)

Formal rationalization will be our main, but certainly not only, concern in this section.

---

[9]In the 1920 introduction to *The Protestant Ethic and the Spirit of Capitalism,* Weber focused on "a specially trained organization of officials" (bureaucracy) in his discussion of rationalization, but he also mentioned capitalism in the same context as "the most fateful force in our modern life."

[10]Of course, these are not completely distinct because large capitalistic enterprises are one of the places in which we find bureaucracies (Weber, 1922–23/1958:299). However, Weber also sees the possibility that bureaucracies can stand in opposition to, can impede, capitalism.

Formal and Substantive Rationality

Various efforts have been made to delineate the basic characteristics of formal rationality. In our view, formal rationality may be defined in terms of six basic characteristics (Ritzer, 1983, 2004a). First, formally rational structures and institutions emphasize *calculability,* or those things that can be counted or quantified. Second, there is a focus on *efficiency,* on finding the best means to a given end. Third, there is great concern with ensuring *predictability,* or that things operate in the same way from one time or place to another. Fourth, a formally rational system progressively reduces human technology and ultimately *replaces human technology with nonhuman technology.* Nonhuman technologies (such as computerized systems) are viewed as more calculable, more efficient, and more predictable than human technologies. Fifth, formally rational systems seek to gain *control* over an array of uncertainties, especially the uncertainties posed by human beings who work in, or are served by, them. Finally, rational systems tend to have a series of *irrational consequences* for the people involved with them and for the systems themselves, as well as for the larger society (Sica, 1988). One of the irrationalities of rationality, from Weber's point of view, is that the world tends to become less enchanted, less magical, and ultimately less meaningful to people (MacKinnon, 2001; Ritzer, 2005; M. Schneider, 1993).[11]

Formal rationality stands in contrast to all the other types of rationality but is especially in conflict with substantive rationality (Brubaker, 1984:4). Kalberg argues that Weber believed that the conflict between these two types of rationality played "a particularly fateful role in the unfolding of rationalization processes in the West" (1980:1157).

In addition to differentiating among the four types of rationality, Kalberg deals with their capacity to introduce methodical ways of life. Practical rationality lacks this ability because it involves reactions to situations rather than efforts to order them. Theoretical rationality is cognitive and therefore has a highly limited ability to suppress practical rationality and seems to be more of an end product than a producer. To Weber, substantive rationality is the *only* type with the "potential to introduce methodical ways of life" (Kalberg, 1980:1165). Thus, in the West, a particular substantive rationality with an emphasis on a methodical way of life—Calvinism—subjugated practical rationality and led to the development of formal rationality.

Weber's fear was that substantive rationality was becoming less significant than the other types of rationality, especially formal rationality, in the West. Thus practitioners of formal rationality, like the bureaucrat and the capitalist, were coming to dominate the West, and the type that "embodied Western civilization's highest ideals: the autonomous and free individual whose actions were given continuity by their reference to ultimate values" (Kalberg, 1980:1176) was fading away (for an alternative view on this, see Titunik, 1997).

---

[11]However, M. Schneider argues that Weber overstated the case and that in spite of rationalization, parts of the world continue to be enchanted: "Enchantment, we suggest, is part of our normal condition, and far from having fled with the rise of science [one of Weber's rationalized systems], it continues to exist (though often unrecognized) wherever our capacity to explain the world's behavior is slim, that is, where neither science nor practical knowledge seem of much utility" (1993:x). Ritzer (2005) argues that disenchanted realms will try to find ways to, at least, temporarily be re-enchanted. This is particularly true of consumer-driven economic systems that depend on enchanted consumers.

Rationalization in Various Social Settings

Although we have emphasized the differences among Weber's four types of rationalization, there are a number of commonalities among them. Thus, as we move from setting to setting, we, like Weber, focus sometimes on rationalization in general and at other times on the specific types of rationalization.

Economy Engerman (2000:258) argues that, although this is rarely cited, "Weber laid out much of the methodological underpinning to what is conventionally called neoclassical economics." This includes the ideal type, methodological individualism, and, most important, rationality and rationalization. The most systematic presentation of Weber's thoughts on the rationalization of the economic institution is to be found in his *General Economic History.* Weber's concern is with the development of the rational capitalistic economy in the Occident, which is a specific example of a rational economy defined as a "functional organization oriented to money-prices which originate in the interest-struggles of men in the *market*" (Weber, 1915/1958:331). Although there is a general evolutionary trend, Weber, as always, is careful to point out that there are various sources of capitalism, alternative routes to it, and a range of results emanating from it (Swedberg, 1998). In fact, in the course of rejecting the socialistic theory of evolutionary change, Weber rejects the whole idea of a "general evolutionary sequence" (1927/1981:34).

Weber begins by depicting various irrational and traditional forms, such as the household, clan, village, and manorial economies. For example, the lord of the manor in feudalism was described by Weber as being traditionalistic, "too lacking in initiative to build up a business enterprise in a large scale into which the peasants would have fitted as a labor force" (1927/1981:72). However, by the twelfth and thirteenth centuries in the Occident, feudalism began to break down as the peasants and the land were freed from control by the lord and a money economy was introduced. With this breakdown, the manorial system "showed a strong tendency to develop in a capitalistic direction" (Weber, 1927/1981:79).

At the same time, in the Middle Ages, cities were beginning to develop. Weber focuses on the largely urban development of industry involved in the transformation of raw materials. Especially important to Weber is the development of such industrial production beyond the immediate needs of the house community. Notable here is the rise of free craftsmen in the cities. They developed in the Middle Ages in the Occident because, for one thing, this society had developed consumptive needs greater than those of any other. In general, there were larger markets and more purchasers, and the peasantry had greater purchasing power. On the other side, forces operated against the major alternative to craftsmen—slaves. Slavery was found to be too unprofitable and too unstable, and it was made increasingly more unstable by the growth of the towns that offered freedom to the slaves.

In the Occident, along with free craftsmen came the development of the *guild,* defined by Weber as "an organization of craft workers specialized in accordance with the type of occupation . . . [with] internal regulation of work and monopolization against outsiders" (1927/1981:136). Freedom of association was also characteristic of the guilds. But although rational in many senses, guilds also had traditional, anticapitalistic aspects. For example, one master was not supposed to have more capital than another, and this requirement was a barrier to the development of large capitalistic organizations.

As the Middle Ages came to a close, the guilds began to disintegrate. This disintegration was crucial because the traditional guilds stood in the way of technological advance. With the dissolution of the guild system came the rise of the domestic system of production, especially the "putting out" system in the textile industry. In such a system, production was decentralized, with much of it taking place within the homes of the workers. Although domestic systems were found throughout the world, it was only in the Occident that the owners controlled the means of production (for example, tools, raw materials) and provided them to the workers in exchange for the right to dispose of the product. Whereas a fully developed domestic system developed in the West, it was impeded in other parts of the world by such barriers as the clan system (China), the caste system (India), traditionalism, and the lack of free workers.

Next, Weber details the development of the workshop (a central work setting without advanced machinery) and then the emergence of the factory in the fourteenth through sixteenth centuries. In Weber's view, the factory did not arise out of craft work or the domestic system, but alongside them. Similarly, the factory was not called into existence by advances in machinery; the two developments were correlated with each other. The factory was characterized by free labor that performed specialized and coordinated activities, ownership of the means of production by the entrepreneur, the fixed capital of the entrepreneur, and the system of accounting that is indispensable to such capitalization. Such a factory was, in Weber's view, a capitalistic organization. In addition to the development of the factory, Weber details the rise of other components of a modern capitalistic economy, such as advanced machinery, transportation systems, money, banking, interest, bookkeeping systems, and so on.

What most clearly defines modern rational capitalistic enterprises for Weber is their calculability, which is best represented in their reliance on modern bookkeeping. Isolated calculable enterprises existed in the past in the Occident as well as in other societies. However, an entire society is considered capitalistic only when the everyday requirements of the population are supplied by capitalistic methods and enterprises. Such a society is found only in the Occident, and there only since the mid-nineteenth century.

The development of a capitalistic system hinged on a variety of developments within the economy as well as within the larger society. Within the economy, some of the prerequisites included a free market with large and steady demand, a money economy, inexpensive and rational technologies, a free labor force, a disciplined labor force, rational capital-accounting techniques, and the commercialization of economic life involving the use of shares, stocks, and the like. Many of the economic prerequisites were found only in the Occident. Outside the economy, Weber identified a variety of needed developments, such as a modern state with "professional administration, specialized officialdom, and law based on the concept of citizenship" (1927/1981:313), rational law "made by jurists and rationally interpreted and applied" (1927/1981:313), cities, and modern science and technology. To these Weber adds a factor that will concern us in the next section: "a rational ethic for the conduct of life . . . a religious basis for the ordering of life which consistently followed out must lead to explicit rationalism" (1927/1981:313–314). Like the economic prerequisites, these noneconomic presuppositions occurred together only in the Occident. The basic point is that a rational economy is dependent upon a variety of noneconomic forces throughout the rest of society in order to develop.

Religion Although we will focus on the rationalization of religion in this section, Weber spent much time analyzing the degree to which early, more primitive religions—and religions in much of the world—acted as impediments to the rise of rationality. Weber noted that "the sacred is the uniquely unalterable" (1921/1968:406). Despite this view, religion in the West did prove to be alterable; it was amenable to rationalization, and it did play a key role in the rationalization of other sectors of society (Kalberg, 1990).

Early religion was composed of a bewildering array of gods, but with rationalization, a clear and coherent set of gods (a pantheon) emerged. Early religions had household gods, kin-group gods, local political gods, and occupational and vocational gods. We get the clear feeling that Weber did believe that a cultural force of (theoretical) rationality impelled the emergence of this set of gods: "*Reason* favored the primacy of universal gods; and every consistent crystallization of a pantheon followed systematic *rational* principles" (1921/1968:417). A pantheon of gods was not the only aspect of the rationalization of religion discussed by Weber. He also considered the delimitation of the jurisdiction of gods, monotheism, and the anthropomorphization of gods as part of this development. Although the pressure for rationalization exists in many of the world's religions, in areas outside the Western world, the barriers to rationalization more than counterbalance the pressures for rationalization.

Although Weber had a cultural conception of rationalization, he did not view it simply as a force "out there" that impels people to act. He did not have a group-mind concept. In religion, rationalization is tied to concrete groups of people, in particular to priests. Specifically, the professionally trained priesthood is the carrier[12] and the expediter of rationalization. In this, priests stand in contrast to magicians, who support a more irrational religious system. The greater rationality of the priesthood is traceable to several factors. Members go through a systematic training program, whereas the training of magicians is unsystematic. Also, priests are fairly highly specialized, whereas magicians tend to be unspecialized. Finally, priests possess a systematic set of religious concepts, and this, too, sets them apart from magicians. We can say that priests are both the products and the expediters of the process of rationalization.

The priesthood is not the only group that plays a key role in rationalization. Prophets and a laity are also important in the process. Prophets can be distinguished from priests by their personal calling, their emotional preaching, their proclamation of a doctrine, and the fact that they tend to be unpopular and often work alone. The key role of the prophet is the mobilization of the laity, because there would be no religion without a group of followers. Unlike priests, prophets do not tend to the needs of a congregation. Weber differentiated between two types of prophets: ethical and exemplary. *Ethical prophets* (Mohammad, Jesus Christ, and the Old Testament prophets) believe that they have received a commission directly from God and demand obedience from

[12]For a general discussion of the role of carriers in Weber's work, see Kalberg (1994:58–62).

followers as an ethical duty. *Exemplary prophets* (Buddha is a model) demonstrate to others by personal example the way to religious salvation. In either case, successful prophets are able to attract large numbers of followers, and it is this mass, along with the priests, that forms the heart of religion. Prophets are likely at first to attract a personal following, but it is necessary that that group be transformed into a permanent congregation. Once such a laity has been formed, major strides have been made in the direction of the rationalization of religion.

Prophets play a key initial role, but once a congregation is formed, they are no longer needed. In fact, because they are largely irrational, they represent a barrier to that rationalization of religion. A conflict develops between priests and prophets, but it is a conflict that must be won in the long run by the more rational priesthood. In their conflict, the priests are aided by the rationalization proceeding in the rest of society. As the secular world becomes more and more literate and bureaucratized, the task of educating the masses falls increasingly to the priests, whose literacy gives them a tremendous advantage over the prophets. In addition, while the prophets tend to do the preaching, the priests take over the task of day-to-day pastoral care. Although preaching is important during extraordinary times, pastoral care, or the daily religious cultivation of the laity, is an important instrument in the growing power of the priesthood. It was the church in the Western world that combined a rationalized pastoral character with an ethical religion to form a peculiarly influential and rational form of religion. This rationalized religion proved particularly well suited to winning converts among the urban middle class, and it was there that it played a key role in the rationalization of economic life as well as all other sectors of life.

Law As with his analysis of religion, Weber began his treatment of law with the primitive, which he saw as highly irrational. Primitive law was a rather undifferentiated system of norms. For example, no distinction was made between a civil wrong (a tort) and a crime. Thus, cases involving differences over a piece of land and homicide were likely to be handled, and offenders punished, in much the same way. In addition, primitive law tended to lack any official machinery. Vengeance dominated reactions to a crime, and law was generally free from procedural formality or rules. Leaders, especially, were virtually unrestrained in what they could do to followers. From this early irrational period, Weber traced a direct line of development to a formalized legal procedure. And as was usual in Weber's thinking, it is only in the West that a rational, systematic theory of law is held to have developed.

Weber traced several stages in the development of a more rational legal system (Shamir, 1993). An early stage involves charismatic legal revelation through law prophets. Then there is the empirical creation and founding of law by honorary legal officials. Later there is the imposition of law by secular or theocratic powers. Finally, in the most modern case, we have the systematic elaboration of law and professionalized administration of justice by persons who have received their legal training formally and systematically.

In law, as in religion, Weber placed great weight on the process of professionalization: the legal profession is crucial to the rationalization of Western law. There are certainly other factors (for example, the influence of Roman law), but the legal profession was central to his thinking: "Formally elaborated law constituting a complex of maxims consciously applied in decisions has never come into existence without the decisive cooperation of trained specialists" (Weber, 1921/1968:775). Although Weber was aware that there was a series of external pressures—especially from the rationalizing economy—impelling law toward rationalization, his view was that the most important force was the internal factor of the professionalization of the legal profession (1921/1968:776).

Weber differentiated between two types of legal training but saw only one as contributing to the development of rational law. The first is *craft training,* in which apprentices learn from masters, primarily during the actual practice of law. This kind of training produces a formalistic type of law dominated by precedents. The goal is not the creation of a comprehensive, rational system of law but, instead, the production of practically useful precedents for dealing with recurring situations. Because these precedents are tied to specific issues in the real world, a general, rational, and systematic body of law cannot emerge.

In contrast, *academic legal training* laid the groundwork for the rational law of the West. In this system, law is taught in special schools where the emphasis is placed on legal theory and science—in other words, where legal phenomena are given rational and systematic treatment. The legal concepts produced have the character of abstract norms. Interpretation of these laws occurs in a rigorously formal and logical manner. They are general, in contrast to the specific, precedent-bound laws produced in the case of craft training.

Academic legal training leads to the development of a rational legal system with a number of characteristics, including the following:

- Every concrete legal decision involves the application of abstract legal propositions to concrete situations.
- It must be possible in every concrete case to derive the decision logically from abstract legal propositions.
- Law must tend to be a gapless system of legal propositions or at least be treated as one.
- The gapless legal system should be applicable to all social actions.

Weber seemed to adopt the view that history has seen law evolve from a cultural system of norms to a more structured system of formal laws. In general, actors are increasingly constrained by a more and more rational legal system. Although this is true, Weber was too good a sociologist to lose sight completely of the independent significance of the actor. For one thing, Weber (1921/1968:754–755) saw actors as crucial in the emergence of, and change in, law. However, the most important aspect of Weber's work in this area—for the purposes of this discussion—is the degree to which law is regarded as part of the general process of rationalization throughout the West.

Polity The rationalization of the political system is intimately linked to the rationalization of law and, ultimately, to the rationalization of all elements of the social system. For example, Weber argued that the more rational the political structure becomes, the more likely it is to eliminate systematically the irrational elements within the law. A rational polity cannot function with an irrational legal system, and vice versa. Weber did not believe that political leaders follow a conscious policy of rationalizing the law; rather, they are impelled in that direction by the demands of their own increasingly rational means of administration. Once again, Weber took the position that actors are being impelled by structural (the state) and cultural (rationalization) forces.

Weber defined the *polity* as "a community whose social action is aimed at subordinating to orderly domination by the participants a territory and the conduct of the persons within it, through readiness to resort to physical force, including normally force of arms" (1921/1968:901). This type of polity has existed neither everywhere nor always. It does not exist as a separate entity where the task of armed defense against enemies is assigned to the household, the neighborhood association, an economic group, and so forth. Although Weber clearly viewed the polity as a social structure, he was more careful to link his thinking here to his individual action orientations. In his view, modern political associations rest on the prestige bestowed upon them by their members.

As was his usual strategy, Weber went back to the primitive case in order to trace the development of the polity. He made it clear that violent social action is primordial. However, the monopolization and rational ordering of legitimate violence did not exist in early societies but evolved over the centuries. Not only is rational control over violence lacking in primitive society, but other basic functions of the modern state either are totally absent or are not ordered in a rational manner. Included here would be functions like legislation, police, justice, administration, and the military. The development of the polity in the West involves the progressive differentiation and elaboration of these functions. But the most important step is their subordination under a single, dominant, rationally ordered state.

The City Weber was also interested in the rise of the city in the West. The city provided an alternative to the feudal order and a setting in which modern capitalism and, more generally, rationality could develop. He defined a *city* as having the following characteristics:

- It is a relatively closed settlement.
- It is relatively large.
- It possesses a marketplace.
- It has partial political autonomy.

Although many cities in many societies had these characteristics, Western cities developed a peculiarly rational character with, among other things, a rationally organized marketplace and political structure.

Weber looked at various other societies in order to determine why they did not develop the rational form of the city. He concluded that barriers like the traditional community in China and the caste system in India impeded the rise of such a city. But in the West, a number of rationalizing forces coalesced to create the modern city. For example, the development of a city requires a relatively rational economy. But of course the converse is also true: the development of a rational economy requires the modern city.

Art Forms To give the reader a sense of the breadth of Weber's thinking, we need to say a few words about his work on the rationalization of various art forms. For example, Weber (1921/1958) viewed music in the West as having developed in a peculiarly rational direction. Musical creativity is reduced to routine procedures based on comprehensive principles. Music in the Western world has undergone a "transformation of the process of musical production into a calculable affair operating with known means, effective instruments, and understandable rules" (Weber, 1921/1958:li). Although the process of rationalization engenders tension in all the institutions in which it occurs, that tension is nowhere more noticeable than in music. After all, music is supposed to be an arena of expressive flexibility, but it is being progressively reduced to a rational, and ultimately mathematical, system.

Weber (1904–05/1958) sees a similar development in other art forms. For example, in painting, Weber emphasizes "the rational utilization of lines and spatial perspective—which the Renaissance created for us" (1904–05/1958:15). In architecture, "the rational use of the Gothic vault as a means of distributing pressure and of roofing spaces of all forms, and above all as the constructive principle of great monumental buildings and the foundation of a *style* extending to sculpture and painting, such as that created by our Middle Ages, does not occur elsewhere [in the world]" (Weber, 1904–05/1958:15).

We have now spent a number of pages examining Weber's ideas on rationalization in various aspects of social life. Although nowhere does he explicitly say so, we believe that Weber adopted the view that changes in the cultural level of rationality are leading to changes in the structures as well as in the individual thoughts and actions of the modern world. The rationalization process is not left to float alone above concrete phenomena but is embedded in various social structures and in the thoughts and actions of individuals. To put it slightly differently, the key point is that the cultural system of rationality occupies a position of causal priority in Weber's work. We can illustrate this in still another way by looking at Weber's work on the relationship between religion and economics—more specifically, the relationship between religion and the development, or lack of development, of a capitalist economy.

Religion and the Rise of Capitalism

Weber spent much of his life studying religion—this in spite of, or perhaps because of, his being areligious, or, as he once described himself, "religiously unmusical" (Gerth and Mills, 1958:25). One of his overriding concerns was the relationship among a variety of the world's religions and the development only in the West of a capitalist economic system (Schlucter, 1996). It is clear that the vast bulk of this work is done at the social-structural and cultural levels; the thoughts and actions of Calvinists, Buddhists, Confucians, Jews, Muslims (B. Turner, 1974; Nafassi, 1998), and others are held to be affected by changes in social structures and social institutions. Weber was interested primarily in the systems of ideas of the world's religions, in the "spirit" of capitalism, and in rationalization as a modern system of norms and values. He was also very interested in the structures of the world's religions, the various structural components of the societies in which they exist that serve to facilitate or impede rationalization, and the structural aspects of capitalism and the rest of the modern world.

Weber's work on religion and capitalism involved an enormous body of cross-cultural historical research; here, as elsewhere, he did comparative-historical sociology (Kalberg, 1997). Freund summarized the complicated interrelationships involved in this research:

1. Economic forces influenced Protestantism.
2. Economic forces influenced religions other than Protestantism (for example, Hinduism, Confucianism, and Taoism).
3. Religious idea systems influenced individual thoughts and actions—in particular, economic thoughts and actions.
4. Religious idea systems have been influential throughout the world.
5. Religious idea systems (particularly Protestantism) have had the unique effect in the West of helping to rationalize the economic sector and virtually every other institution.

(Freund, 1968:213)

To this we can add:

6. Religious idea systems in the non-Western world have created overwhelming structural barriers to rationalization.

By according the religious factor great importance, Weber appeared to be simultaneously building on and criticizing his image of Marx's work. Weber, like Marx, operated with a complicated model of the interrelationship of primarily large-scale systems: "Weber's sociology is related to Marx's thought in the common attempt to grasp the interrelations of institutional orders making up a social structure: In Weber's work, military and religious, political and juridical institutional systems are functionally related to the economic order in a variety of ways" (Gerth and Mills, 1958:49). In fact, Weber's affinities with Marx are even greater than is often recognized. Although Weber, especially early in his career, gave primacy to religious ideas, he later came to see that material forces, not idea systems, are of greater importance (Kalberg, 1985:61). As Weber said, "Not ideas, but material and ideal interests, directly govern men's conduct. Yet very frequently the 'world images' that have been created by 'ideas' have, like switchmen, determined the tracks along which action has been pushed by the dynamic of interest" (cited in Gerth and Mills, 1958:280).

Paths to Salvation

In analyzing the relationship between the world's religions and the economy, Weber (1921/1963) developed a typology of the paths of salvation. *Asceticism* is the first broad type of religiosity, and it combines an orientation toward action with the commitment of believers to denying themselves the pleasures of the world. Ascetic religions are divided into two subtypes. *Otherworldly asceticism* involves a set of norms and values that command the followers not to work within the secular world and to fight against its temptations (Kalberg, 2001). Of greater interest to Weber, because it encompasses Calvinism, was *innerworldly asceticism.* Such a religion does not reject the world; instead, it actively urges its members to work within the world so that they can find salvation, or at least signs of it. The distinctive goal here is the strict, methodical control of the members' patterns of life, thought, and action. Members are urged to reject everything unethical, esthetic, or dependent on their emotional reactions to the secular world. Innerworldly ascetics are motivated to systematize their own conduct.

Whereas both types of asceticism involve some type of action and self-denial, *mysticism* involves contemplation, emotion, and inaction. Weber subdivided mysticism in the same way as asceticism. *World-rejecting mysticism* involves total flight from the world. *Innerworldly mysticism* leads to contemplative efforts to understand the meaning of the world, but these efforts are doomed to failure, because the world is viewed as being beyond individual comprehension. In any case, both types of mysticism and world-rejecting asceticism can be seen as idea systems that inhibit the development of capitalism and rationality. In contrast, innerworldly asceticism is the system of norms and values that contributed to the development of these phenomena in the West.

The Protestant Ethic and the Spirit of Capitalism In Max Weber's best-known work, *The Protestant Ethic and the Spirit of Capitalism* (1904–05/1958), he traced the impact of ascetic Protestantism—primarily Calvinism—on the rise of the spirit of capitalism (Breiner, 2005; H. Jones, 1997). This work is but a small part of a larger body of scholarship that traces the relationship between religion and modern capitalism throughout much of the world.

Weber, especially later in his work, made it clear that his most general interest was in the rise of the distinctive rationality of the West. Capitalism, with its rational organization of free labor, its open market, and its rational bookkeeping system, is only one component of that developing system. He directly linked it to the parallel development of rationalized science, law, politics, art, architecture, literature, universities, and the polity.

Weber did not directly link the idea system of the Protestant ethic to the structures of the capitalist system; instead, he was content to link the Protestant ethic to another system of ideas, the "spirit of capitalism." In other words, two systems of ideas are directly linked in this work. Although links of the capitalist economic system to the material world are certainly implied and indicated, they were not Weber's primary concern. Thus, *The Protestant Ethic* is not about the rise of modern capitalism but is about the origin of a peculiar spirit that eventually made modern rational capitalism (some form of capitalism had existed since early times) expand and come to dominate the economy.

Weber began by examining and rejecting alternative explanations of why capitalism arose in the West in the sixteenth and seventeenth centuries (for an alternative view on this, see R. Collins, 1997a). To those who contended that capitalism arose because the material conditions were right at that time, Weber retorted that material conditions were also ripe at other times and capitalism did not arise. Weber also rejected the psychological theory that the development of capitalism was due simply to the acquisitive instinct. In his view, such an instinct always has existed, yet it did not produce capitalism in other situations.

Evidence for Weber's views on the significance of Protestantism was found in an examination of countries with mixed religious systems. In looking at these countries, he discovered that the leaders of the economic system—business leaders, owners of capital, high-grade skilled labor, and more advanced technically and commercially trained personnel—were all overwhelmingly Protestant. This suggested that Protestantism was a significant cause in the choice of these occupations and, conversely, that other religions (for example, Roman Catholicism) failed to produce idea systems that impelled individuals into these vocations.

In Weber's view, the spirit of capitalism is not defined simply by economic greed; it is in many ways the exact opposite. It is a moral and ethical system, an ethos, that among other things stresses economic success. In fact, it was the turning of profit making into an ethos that was critical in the West. In other societies, the pursuit of profit was seen as an individual act motivated at least in part by greed. Thus, it was viewed by many as morally suspect. However, Protestantism succeeded in turning the pursuit of profit into a moral crusade. It was the backing of the moral system that led to the unprecedented expansion of profit seeking and, ultimately, to the capitalist system. On a theoretical level, by stressing that he was dealing with the relationship between one ethos (Protestantism) and another (the spirit of capitalism), Weber was able to keep his analysis primarily at the level of systems of ideas.

The spirit of capitalism can be seen as a normative system that involves a number of interrelated ideas. For example, its goal is to instill an "attitude which seeks profit rationally and systematically" (Weber, 1904–05/1958:64). In addition, it preaches an avoidance of life's pleasures: "Seest thou a man diligent in business? He shall stand before kings" (Weber, 1904–05/1958:53). Also included in the spirit of capitalism are ideas such as "time is money," "be industrious," "be frugal," "be punctual," "be fair," and "earning money is a legitimate end in itself." Above all, there is the idea that it is people's duty to increase their wealth ceaselessly. This takes the spirit of capitalism out of the realm of individual ambition and into the category of an ethical imperative. Although Weber admitted that a type of capitalism (for example, adventurer capitalism) existed in China, India, Babylon, and the classical world and during the Middle Ages, it was different from Western capitalism, primarily because it lacked "this particular ethos" (1904–05/1958:52).

Weber was interested not simply in describing this ethical system but also in explaining its derivations. He thought that Protestantism, particularly Calvinism, was crucial to the rise of the spirit of capitalism. Calvinism is no longer necessary to the continuation of that economic system. In fact, in many senses modern capitalism, given its secularity, stands in opposition to Calvinism and to religion in general. Capitalism today has become a real entity that combines norms, values, market, money, and laws. It has become, in Durkheim's terms, a social fact that is external to, and coercive of, the individual. As Weber put it:

> Capitalism is today an immense cosmos into which the individual is born, and which presents itself to him, at least as an individual, as an unalterable order of things in which he must live. It forces the individual, in so far as he is involved in the system of market relationships, to conform to capitalist rules of action.
>
> (Weber, 1904–05/1958:54)

Another crucial point here is that Calvinists did not consciously seek to create a capitalist system. In Weber's view, capitalism was an *unanticipated consequence*

(Cherkaoui, 2007) of the Protestant ethic. The concept of unanticipated consequences has broad significance in Weber's work, for he believed that what individuals and groups intend by their actions often leads to a set of consequences that are at variance with their intentions. Although Weber did not explain this point, it seems that it is related to his theoretical view that people create social structures but that those structures soon take on a life of their own, over which the creators have little or no control. Because people lack control over them, structures are free to develop in a variety of totally unanticipated directions. Weber's line of thinking led Arthur Mitzman (1969/1971) to argue that Weber created a sociology of reification. Reified social structures are free to move in unanticipated directions, as both Marx and Weber showed in their analyses of capitalism.

Calvinism and the Spirit of Capitalism Calvinism was the version of Protestantism that interested Weber most. One feature of Calvinism was the idea that only a small number of people are chosen for salvation. In addition, Calvinism entailed the idea of predestination; people were predestined to be either among the saved or among the damned. There was nothing that the individual or the religion as a whole could do to affect that fate. Yet the idea of predestination left people uncertain about whether they were among the saved. To reduce this uncertainty, the Calvinists developed the idea that *signs* could be used as indicators of whether a person was saved. People were urged to work hard, because if they were diligent, they would uncover the signs of salvation, which were to be found in economic success. In sum, the Calvinist was urged to engage in intense, worldly activity and to become a "man of vocation."

However, isolated actions were not enough. Calvinism, as an ethic, required self-control and a systematized style of life that involved an integrated round of activities, particularly business activities. This stood in contrast to the Christian ideal of the Middle Ages, in which individuals simply engaged in isolated acts as the occasion arose in order to atone for particular sins and to increase their chances of salvation. "The God of Calvinism demanded of his believers not single good works, but a life of good works combined into a unified system" (Weber, 1904–05/1958:117). Calvinism produced an ethical system and ultimately a group of people who were nascent capitalists. Calvinism "has the highest ethical appreciation of the sober, middle-class, self-made man" (Weber, 1904–05/1958:163). Weber neatly summarized his own position on Calvinism and its relationship to capitalism as follows:

> The religious valuation of restless, continuous, systematic work in a worldly calling, as the highest means of asceticism, and at the same time the surest and most evident proof of rebirth and genuine faith, must have been the most powerful conceivable lever for the expansion of . . . the spirit of capitalism.
>
> (Weber, 1904–05/1958:172)

In addition to its general link to the spirit of capitalism, Calvinism had some more specific links. First, as already mentioned, capitalists could ruthlessly pursue their economic interests and feel that such pursuit was not merely self-interest but was, in fact, their ethical duty. This not only permitted unprecedented mercilessness in business but also silenced potential critics, who could not simply reduce these actions to self-interest. Second, Calvinism provided the rising capitalist "with sober, conscientious and unusually industrious workmen who clung to their work as to a life purpose willed by god" (Weber, 1904–05/1958:117). With such a work force, the nascent capitalist could raise the level of exploitation to unprecedented heights. Third, Calvinism legitimized an unequal stratification system by giving the capitalist the "comforting assurances that the unequal distribution of the goods of this world was a special dispensation of Divine Providence" (Weber, 1904–05/1958:117).

Weber also had reservations about the capitalist system, as he did about all aspects of the rationalized world. For example, he pointed out that capitalism tends to produce "specialists without spirit, sensualists without heart; this nullity imagines that it has attained a level of civilization never before achieved" (Weber, 1904–05/1958:182).

Although in *The Protestant Ethic* Weber focused on the effect of Calvinism on the spirit of capitalism, he was well aware that social and economic conditions have a reciprocal impact on religion. He chose not to deal with such relationships in this book, but he made it clear that his goal was not to substitute a one-sided spiritualist interpretation for the one-sided materialist explanation that he attributed to Marxists. (The same is true of much of the rest of his work, including his essays on the Russian Revolution; see Wells and Baehr, 1995:22.) As Kalberg (1996) has pointed out, *The Protestant Ethic* raises a wide number of issues that go to the heart of contemporary sociological theory.

If Calvinism was one of the causal factors in the rise of capitalism in the West, then the question arises: Why didn't capitalism arise in other societies? In his effort to answer this question, Weber dealt with spiritual and material barriers to the rise of capitalism. Let us look briefly at Weber's analysis of those barriers in two societies—China and India.

Religion and Capitalism in China

One crucial assumption that allowed Weber to make legitimate the comparison between the West and China is that both had the prerequisites for the development of capitalism. In China, there was a tradition of intense acquisitiveness and unscrupulous competition. There was great industry and an enormous capacity for work in the populace. Powerful guilds existed. The population was expanding. And there was a steady growth in precious metals. With these and other material prerequisites, why didn't capitalism arise in China? As has been pointed out before, Weber's general answer was that social, structural, and religious barriers in China prevented the development of capitalism. This is not to say that capitalism was entirely absent in China (Love, 2000). There were moneylenders and purveyors who sought high rates of profit. But a market, as well as various other components of a rational capitalistic system, was absent. In Weber's view, the rudimentary capitalism of China "pointed in a direction opposite to the development of rational economic corporate enterprises" (1916/1964:86).

Structural Barriers Weber listed several structural barriers to the rise of capitalism in China. First, there was the structure of the typical Chinese community. It was held together by rigid kinship bonds in the form of sibs. The sibs were ruled by elders, who made them bastions of traditionalism. The sibs were self-contained entities, and there was little dealing with other sibs. This encouraged small, encapsulated land holdings and a household-based, rather than a market, economy. The extensive partitioning of the land prevented major technological developments, because economies of scale were impossible. Agricultural production remained in the hands of peasants, industrial production in the hands of small-scale artisans. Modern cities, which were to become the centers of Western capitalism, were inhibited in their development because the people retained their allegiance to the sibs. Because of the sibs' autonomy, the central government was never able to govern these units effectively or to mold them into a unified whole.

The structure of the Chinese state was a second barrier to the rise of capitalism. The state was largely patrimonial and governed by tradition, prerogative, and favoritism. In Weber's view, a rational and calculable system of administration and law enforcement, which was necessary for industrial development, did not exist. There were very few formal laws covering commerce, there was no central court, and legal formalism was rejected. This irrational type of administrative structure was a barrier to the rise of capitalism, as Weber made clear: "Capital investment in industry is far too sensitive to such irrational rule and too dependent upon the possibility of calculating the steady and rational operation of the state machinery to emerge within an administration of this type" (1916/1964:103). In addition to its general structure, a number of more specific components of the state acted against the development of capitalism. For example, the officials of the bureaucratic administration had vested material interests that made them oppose capitalism. Officials often bought offices primarily to make a profit, and this kind of orientation did not necessarily make for a high degree of efficiency.

A third structural barrier to the rise of capitalism was the nature of the Chinese language. In Weber's view, it militated against rationality by making systematic thought difficult. It remained largely in the realm of the "pictorial" and the "descriptive." Logical thinking was also inhibited because intellectual thought remained largely in the form of parables, and this hardly was the basis for the development of a cumulative body of knowledge.

Although there were other structural barriers to the rise of capitalism (for example, a country without wars or overseas trade), a key factor was the lack of the required "mentality," the lack of the needed idea system. Weber looked at the two dominant systems of religious ideas in China—Confucianism and Taoism—and the characteristics of both that militated against the development of a spirit of capitalism.

Confucianism A central characteristic of Confucian thinking was its emphasis on a literary education as a prerequisite for office and for social status. To acquire a position in the ruling strata, a person had to be a member of the literati. Movement up the hierarchy was based on a system of ideas that tested literary knowledge, not the technical knowledge needed to conduct the office in question. What was valued and tested was whether the individual's mind was steeped in culture and whether it was characterized by ways of thought suitable to a cultured man. In Weber's terms, Confucianism encouraged "a highly bookish literary education." The literati produced by this system came to see the actual work of administration as beneath them, mere tasks to be delegated to subordinates. Instead, the literati aspired to clever puns, euphemisms, and allusions to classical quotations—a purely literary kind of intellectuality. With this kind of orientation, it is easy to see why the literati were unconcerned with the state of the economy or with economic activities. The world view of the Confucians ultimately grew to be the policy of the state. As a result, the Chinese state came to be only minimally involved in rationally influencing the economy and the rest of society. The Confucians maintained their influence by having the constitution decree that only they could serve as officials, and competitors to Confucians (for example, the bourgeoisie, prophets, and priests) were blocked from serving in the government. In fact, if the emperor dared to deviate from this rule, he was thought to be toying with disaster and his potential downfall.

Many other components of Confucianism militated against capitalism. It was basically an ethic of adjustment to the world and to its order and its conventions. Rather than viewing material success and wealth as a sign of salvation as the Calvinist did, the Confucian simply was led to accept things as they were. In fact, there was no idea of salvation in Confucianism, and this lack of tension between religion and the world also acted to inhibit the rise of capitalism. The snobbish Confucian was urged to reject thrift, because it was something that commoners practiced. In contrast to the Puritan work ethic, it was not regarded as proper for a Confucian gentleman to work, although wealth was prized. Active engagement in a profitable enterprise was regarded as morally dubious and unbecoming to a Confucian's station. The acceptable goal for such a gentleman was a good position, not high profits. The ethic emphasized the abilities of a gentleman rather than the highly specialized skills that could have proved useful to a developing capitalist system. In sum, Weber contended that Confucianism became a relentless canonization of tradition.

Taoism Weber perceived Taoism as a mystical Chinese religion in which the supreme good was deemed to be a psychic state, a state of mind, and not a state of grace to be obtained by conduct in the real world. As a result, Taoists did not operate in a rational way to affect the external world. Taoism was essentially traditional, and one of its basic tenets was "Do not introduce innovations" (Weber, 1916/1964:203). Such an idea system was unlikely to produce any major changes, let alone one as far-reaching as capitalism.

One trait common to Taoism and Confucianism is that neither produced enough tension, or conflict, among the members to motivate them to much innovative action in this world:

> Neither in its official state cult nor in its Taoist aspect could Chinese religiosity produce sufficiently strong motives for a religiously oriented life for the individual such as the Puritan method represents. Both forms of religion lacked even the traces of the Satanic force or evil against which [the] pious Chinese might have struggled for his salvation.
>
> (Weber, 1916/1964:206)

As was true of Confucianism, there was no inherent force in Taoism to impel actors to change the world or, more specifically, to build a capitalist system.

Religion and Capitalism in India

For our purposes, a very brief discussion of Weber's (1916–17/1958) thinking on the relationship between religion and capitalism in India will suffice. The argument, though not its details, parallels the Chinese case. For example, Weber discussed the structural barriers of the caste system (Gellner, 1982:534). Among other things, the caste system erected overwhelming barriers to social mobility, and it tended to regulate even the most minute aspects of people's lives. The idea system of the Brahmans had a number of components. For example, Brahmans were expected to avoid vulgar occupations and to observe elegance in manners and proprieties in conduct. Indifference to the world's mundane affairs was the crowning idea of Brahman religiosity. The Brahmans also emphasized a highly literary kind of education. Although there certainly were important differences between Brahmans and Confucians, the ethos of each presented overwhelming barriers to the rise of capitalism.

The Hindu religion posed similar ideational barriers. Its key idea was reincarnation. To the Hindu, a person is born into the caste that he or she deserves by virtue of behavior in a past life. Through faithful adherence to the ritual of caste, the Hindu gains merit for the next life. Hinduism, unlike Calvinism, was traditional in the sense that salvation was to be achieved by faithfully following the rules; innovation, particularly in the economic sphere, could not lead to a higher caste in the next life. Activity in this world was not important, because the world was seen as a transient abode and an impediment to the spiritual quest. In these and other ways, the idea system associated with Hinduism failed to produce the kind of people who could create a capitalist economic system and, more generally, a rationally ordered society.

Criticisms

There have been numerous criticisms of Weber. We will deal with four of the most important. The first criticism has to do with Weber's *verstehen* method. Weber was caught between two problem in regards to *verstehen*. On the one hand, it could not simply mean a subjective intuition because this would not be scientific. On the other hand, the sociologist could not just proclaim the "objective" meaning of the social phenomenon. Weber declared that his method fell between these two choices, but he never fully explained how (Herva, 1988). The deficiencies in his methodology are not always clear when we are reading Weber's insightful analysis based on his own interpretations, but it becomes perfectly clear when we try to apply his method to our own research or, even more so, when we attempt to teach *verstehen* to others. Clearly, the method involves systemic and rigorous research, but the magic of turning that research into Weber's illuminating insights eludes us. This has led some (Abel, 1948) to relegate *verstehen* to a heuristic operation of discovery that precedes the real scientific work of sociology. Others have suggested that *verstehen* needs to be seen as itself a social process and that our understanding of others always proceeds out of a dialogue (Shields, 1996).

The second criticism is that Weber lacks a fully theorized macrosociology. We have already spent some time discussing the contradiction between Weber's individualistic method and his focus on large-scale social structures and world-historical norms. In Weber's method, class is reduced to a collection of people in the same economic situation. Political structure is reduced to the acceptance of domination because of subjectively perceived legitimacy in terms of rationality, charisma, or traditions. Weber certainly recognizes that class and political structures have effects on people—not to mention such macrophenomena as religion and rationalization—but he has no way to theorize these effects except as a collection of uinintended consequences. He has no theory of how these work as systems behind the back of individuals and, in some cases, even to determine the intention of actors (Turner, 1981).

The third criticism of Weber is that he lacks a critical theory. In other words, others have said that Weber's theory cannot be used to point out opportunities for constructive change. We can demonstrate this criticism through examining Weber's theory of rationalization.

Weber used the term *rationalization* in a number of ways, but of these, Weber was primarily concerned with two types. One concerns the development of bureaucracy and its legal form of authority (see pp. 241–244). The other refers to the subjective changes in attitude that he called formal rationality (see pp. 249–251). In the confluence of bureaucracy and formal rationality we see what Weber described as unintended consequences. The creation of bureaucracy and the adaptation of formal rationality ends up undermining the very purposes that the rationalization was meant to serve. This is what we have called the irrational consequences of rationality. Weber's famous iron cage is one of these irrational consequences. Bureaucracy and formal rationality were initially developed because of their efficiency, predictability, calculability, and control in achieving a given goal (for example, to help the poor). But as rationalization proceeds, the original goal tends to be forgotten and the organization increasingly devotes itself to efficiency, predictability, calculability, and control for their own sakes. For example, welfare bureaucracies measure their success by their efficiency in "dealing" with clients, even their efficiency in getting them off welfare, regardless of whether doing so actually serves the original goal of helping the poor to better their situations.

In some of his most quoted passages, Weber implies that this process is inevitable, as for example in his metaphor of the iron cage. However, as argued earlier, it would be wrong to see this as a general evolutionary sequence of inevitable rationalization. Johannes Weiss (1987) maintains that rationalization is only inevitable to the extent that we want it to be so. It is simply that our world is so complex that it is difficult to conceive of accomplishing any significant task without the efficiency, calculability, predictability, and control of rationalization—even if it inevitably ends in its own peculiar irrationality. We may dream of a world without bureaucracies, but, "the real question is whether—with due regard to the obligations of intellectual honesty—we seriously strive to attain it or ever could" (Weiss, 1987:162).

Many people prefer to ignore their own complicity and to see rationalization as something that is imposed on them. Indeed, one of the most cited criticisms of Weber is that he did not provide a strategy for opposing this rationalization (Marcuse, 1971). Since both of the authors work in bureaucracies (universities), deal with them everyday, and will complain when they are not efficient or predictable enough, we are not in a position to make such a strong criticism of Weber. Nevertheless, part of the reason for our complicity is the lack of fully developed alternatives to an increasingly bureaucratized world. Consequently, it is quite fair to criticize Weber for not offering such an alternative, and it is right for those who follow Weber to work at providing a theory of an alternative.

The final criticism is of the unremitting pessimism of Weber's sociology. We can see from Weber's sociological method that he firmly believed in the centrality of individual meaning; however, his substantive work on rationalization and domination indicated that we are trapped in an increasingly meaningless and disenchanted world. It could be said that anyone who still feels optimistic about our culture after reading the closing pages of *The Protestant Ethic* simply hasn't understood them. This alone is not a criticism of Weber. It is shortsighted to criticize someone who points out your cage, if in fact you are in one. Nevertheless, not only did Weber not attempt to provide us with alternatives, he seems to have missed the fact that some of the unintended consequences may be beneficial.

Summary

Max Weber has had a more powerful positive impact on a wide range of sociological theories than any other sociological theorist. This influence is traceable to the sophistication, complexity, and sometimes even confusion of Weberian theory. Despite its problems, Weber's work represents a remarkable fusion of historical research and sociological theorizing.

We open this chapter with a discussion of the theoretical roots and methodological orientations of Weberian theory. We see that Weber, over the course of his career, moved progressively toward a fusion of history and sociology, that is, toward the development of a historical sociology. One of his most critical methodological concepts is *verstehen.* Although this is often interpreted as a tool to be used to analyze individual consciousness, in Weber's hands it was more often a scientific tool to analyze structural and institutional constraints on actors. We also discuss other aspects of Weber's methodology, including his propensity to think in terms of causality and to employ ideal types. In addition, we examine his analysis of the relationship between values and sociology.

The heart of Weberian sociology lies in substantive sociology, not in methodological statements. Although Weber based his theories on his thoughts about social action and social relationships, his main interest was the large-scale structures and institutions of society. We deal especially with his analysis of the three structures of authority—legal, traditional, and charismatic. In the context of legal authority, we deal with his famous ideal-typical bureaucracy and show how he used that tool to analyze traditional and charismatic authority. Of particular interest is Weber's work on charisma. Not only did he have a clear sense of it as a structure of authority, he was also interested in the processes by which such a structure is produced.

Although his work on social structures—such as authority—is important, it is at the cultural level, in his work on the rationalization of the world, that Weber's most important insights lie. Weber articulated the idea that the world is becoming increasingly dominated by norms and values of rationalization. In this context, we discuss Weber's work on the economy, religion, law, the polity, the city, and art forms. Weber argued that rationalization was sweeping across all these institutions in the West, whereas there were major barriers to this process in the rest of the world.

Weber's thoughts on rationalization and various other issues are illustrated in his work on the relationship between religion and capitalism. At one level, this is a series of studies of the relationship between ideas (religious ideas) and the development of the spirit of capitalism and, ultimately, capitalism itself. At another level, it is a study of how the West developed a distinctively rational religious system (Calvinism) that played a key role in the rise of a rational economic system (capitalism). Weber also studied other societies, in which he found religious systems (for example, Confucianism, Taoism, and Hinduism) that inhibit the growth of a rational economic system. It is this kind of majestic sweep over the history of many sectors of the world that helps give Weberian theory its enduring significance.

CHAPTER 9

Georg Simmel

Chapter Outline

The impact of the ideas of Georg Simmel (1858–1918) on American sociological theory, as well as sociological theory in general, differs markedly from that of the three theorists discussed in the preceding three chapters of this book (see Dahme, 1990; Featherstone, 1991; Helle, 2005; Kaern, Phillips, and Cohen, 1990; for a good overview of the secondary literature on Simmel, see Frisby, 1994; Nedelmann, 2001; Scaff, 2000). Marx, Durkheim, and Weber, despite their later significance, had relatively little influence on American theory in the early twentieth century. Simmel was much better known to the early American sociologists (Jaworski, 1997). Simmel was eclipsed by Marx, Durkheim, and Weber, although he is far more influential today than classical thinkers such as Comte and Spencer. In recent years we have seen an increase in Simmel's impact on sociological theory (Aronowitz, 1994; D. Levine, 1985, 1989, 1997; Scaff, 2000) as a result of the growing influence of one of his most important works, *The Philosophy of Money* (for an analysis of this work, see Poggi, 1993), as well as the linking of his ideas to one of the most important developments in social thought—postmodern social theory (Weinstein and Weinstein, 1993, 1998).

Primary Concerns

Although we will focus on Simmel's contributions to sociological theory, we should point out that he was primarily a philosopher and that many of his publications dealt with philosophical issues (for example, ethics) and other philosophers (for example, Kant).

GEORG SIMMEL

A Biographical Sketch

Georg Simmel was born in the heart of Berlin on March 1, 1858. He studied a wide range of subjects at the University of Berlin. However, his first effort to produce a dissertation was rejected, and one of his professors remarked, "We would do him a great service if we do not encourage him further in this direction" (Frisby, 1984:23). Despite this, Simmel persevered and received his doctorate in philosophy in 1881. He remained at the university in a teaching capacity until 1914, although he occupied a relatively unimportant position as *Privatdozent* from 1885 to 1900. In the latter position, Simmel served as an unpaid lecturer whose livelihood was dependent on student fees. Despite his marginality, Simmel did rather well in this position, largely because he was an excellent lecturer and attracted large numbers of (paying) students (Frisby, 1981:17; Salomon, 1963/1997). His style was so popular that even cultured members of Berlin society were drawn to his lectures, which became public events (Leck, 2000).

Simmel's marginality is paralleled by the fact that he was a somewhat contradictory and therefore bewildering person:

> If we put together the testimonials left by relatives, friends, students, contemporaries, we find a number of sometimes contradictory indications concerning Georg Simmel. He is depicted by some as being tall and slender, by others as being short and as bearing a forlorn expression. His appearance is reported to be unattractive, typically Jewish, but also intensely intellectual and noble. He is reported to be hard-working, but also humorous and overarticulate as a lecturer. Finally we hear that he was intellectually brilliant [Lukács, 1991:145], friendly, well-disposed—but also that *inside* he was irrational, opaque, and wild.
>
> (Schnabel, cited in Poggi, 1993:55)

Simmel wrote innumerable articles ("The Metropolis and Mental Life") and books (*The Philosophy of Money*). He was well known in German academic circles and even had an international following, especially in the United States, where his work was of great significance in the birth of sociology. Finally, in 1900, Simmel received

With the exception of his contribution to the primarily macroscopic conflict theory (Coser, 1956; Simmel, 1908/1955), Georg Simmel is best known as a microsociologist who played a significant role in the development of small-group research (Caplow, 1968), symbolic interactionism, and exchange theory. All of Simmel's contributions in these areas reflect his belief that sociologists should study primarily forms and types of social interaction. Robert Nisbet presents this view of Simmel's contribution to sociology:

official recognition, a purely honorary title at the University of Berlin, which did not give him full academic status. Simmel tried to obtain many academic positions, but he failed in spite of the support of such scholars as Max Weber.

One of the reasons for Simmel's failure was that he was a Jew in a nineteenth-century Germany rife with anti-Semitism (Birnbaum, 2008; Kasler, 1985). Thus, in a report on Simmel written to a minister of education, Simmel was described as "an Israelite through and through, in his external appearance, in his bearing and in his mode of thought" (Frisby, 1981:25). Another reason was the kind of work that he did. Many of his articles appeared in newspapers and magazines; they were written for an audience more general than simply academic sociologists (Rammstedt, 1991). In addition, because he did not hold a regular academic appointment, he was forced to earn his living through public lectures. Simmel's audience, both for his writings and for his lectures, was more the intellectual public than professional sociologists, and this tended to lead to derisive judgments from fellow professionals. For example, one of his contemporaries damned him because "his influence remained . . . upon the general atmosphere and affected, above all, the higher levels of journalism" (Troeltsch, cited in Frisby, 1981:13). Simmel's personal failures can also be linked to the low esteem that German academicians of that day had for sociology.

In 1914 Simmel finally obtained a regular academic appointment at a minor university (Strasbourg), but he once again felt estranged. On the one hand, he regretted leaving his audience of Berlin intellectuals. Thus his wife wrote to Max Weber's wife: "Georg has taken leave of the auditorium very badly. . . . The students were very affectionate and sympathetic. . . . It was a departure at the full height of life" (Frisby, 1981:29). On the other hand, Simmel did not feel a part of the life of his new university. Thus, he wrote to Mrs. Weber: "There is hardly anything to report from us. We live . . . a cloistered, closed-off, indifferent, desolate external existence. Academic activity is = 0, the people . . . alien and inwardly hostile" (Frisby, 1981:32).

World War I started soon after Simmel's appointment at Strasbourg; lecture halls were turned into military hospitals, and students went off to war. Thus, Simmel remained a marginal figure in German academia until his death in 1918. He never did have a normal academic career. Nevertheless, Simmel attracted a large academic following in his day, and his fame as a scholar has, if anything, grown over the years.

> It is the *microsociological* character of Simmel's work that may always give him an edge in timeliness over the other pioneers. He did not disdain the small and the intimate elements of human association, nor did he ever lose sight of the primacy of human beings, of concrete individuals, in his analysis of institutions.
>
> (Nisbet, 1959:480)

David Frisby makes a similar point: "The grounding of sociology in some psychological categories may be one reason why Simmel's sociology has proved attractive not merely to the interactionist but also to social psychology" (1984:57; see also Frisby, 1992:20–41). However, it is often forgotten that Simmel's microsociological work on the forms of interaction is embedded in a broader theory of the relations between individuals and the larger society.

Levels and Areas of Concern

Simmel had a much more complicated and sophisticated theory of social reality than he commonly is given credit for in contemporary American sociology. Tom Bottomore and David Frisby (1978) argue that there are four basic levels of concern in Simmel's work. First are his microscopic assumptions about the psychological components of social life. Second, on a slightly larger scale, is his interest in the sociological components of interpersonal relationships. Third, and most macroscopic, is his work on the structure of, and changes in, the social and cultural "spirit" of his times. Not only did Simmel operate with this image of a three-tiered social reality, he adopted the principle of *emergence* (Sawyer, 2005), the idea that the higher levels emerge out of the lower levels: "Further development replaces the immediacy of interacting forces with the creation of higher supra-individual formations, which appear as independent representatives of these forces and absorb and mediate the relations between individuals" (1907/1978:174). He also said, "If society is to be an autonomous object of an independent science, then it can only be so through the fact that, out of the sum of the individual elements that constitute it, a new entity emerges; otherwise all problems of social science would only be those of individual psychology" (Frisby, 1984:56–57). Overarching these three tiers is a fourth that involves ultimate metaphysical principles of life. These eternal truths affect all of Simmel's work and, as we will see, lead to his image of the future direction of the world.

This concern with multiple levels of social reality is reflected in Simmel's definition of three separable problem "areas" in sociology in "The Problem Areas of Sociology" (1950; originally published in 1917). The first he described as "pure" sociology. In this area, psychological variables are combined with forms of interactions. Although Simmel clearly assumed that actors have creative mental abilities, he gave little explicit attention to this aspect of social reality. His most microscopic work is with the *forms* that interaction takes as well as with the *types* of people who engage in interaction (Korllos, 1994). The forms include subordination, superordination, exchange, conflict, and sociability. In his work on types, he differentiated between positions in the interactional structure, such as "competitor" and "coquette," and orientations to the world, such as "miser," "spendthrift," "stranger," and "adventurer." At the intermediate level is Simmel's "general" sociology, dealing with the social and cultural products of human history. Here Simmel manifested his larger-scale interests in the group, the structure, and history of societies and cultures. Finally, in Simmel's "philosophical" sociology, he dealt with his views on the basic nature, and inevitable fate, of humankind. Throughout this chapter, we will touch on all these levels and sociologies. We will find that although Simmel sometimes separated the different levels and sociologies, he more often integrated them into a broader totality.

Dialectical Thinking

Simmel's way of dealing with the interrelationships among three basic levels of social reality (leaving out his fourth, metaphysical, level) gave his sociology a dialectical character reminiscent of Marx's sociology (Levine, 1991b:109). A dialectical approach, as we saw earlier, is multicausal and multidirectional, integrates fact and value, rejects the idea that there are hard-and-fast dividing lines between social phenomena, focuses on social relations (B. Turner, 1986), looks not only at the present but also at the past and the future, and is deeply concerned with both conflicts and contradictions.

In spite of the similarities between Marx and Simmel in their use of a dialectical approach, there are important differences between them. Of greatest importance is the fact that they focused on very different aspects of the social world and offered very different images of the future of the world. Instead of Marx's revolutionary optimism, Simmel had a view of the future closer to Weber's image of an "iron cage" from which there is no escape (for more on the intellectual relationship between Simmel and Weber, see Scaff, 1989:121–151).

Simmel manifested his commitment to the dialectic in various ways (Featherstone, 1991:7). For one thing, Simmel's sociology was always concerned with relationships (Lichtblau and Ritter, 1991), especially interaction (*association*). More generally, Simmel was a "methodological relationist" (Ritzer and Gindoff, 1992) operating with the "principle that everything interacts in some way with everything else" (Simmel, cited in Frisby, 1992:9). Overall he was ever attuned to dualisms, conflicts, and contradictions in whatever realm of the social world he happened to be working on (Sellerberg, 1994). Donald Levine states that this perspective reflects Simmel's belief that "*the world can best be understood in terms of conflicts and contrasts between opposed categories*" (1971:xxxv). Rather than try to deal with this mode of thinking throughout Simmel's work, let us illustrate it from his work on one of his forms of interaction—*fashion.* Simmel used a similar mode of dialectical thinking in most of his essays on social forms and social types, but this discussion of fashion amply illustrates his method of dealing with these phenomena. We will also deal with the dialectic in Simmel's thoughts on subjective-objective culture and the concepts of "more-life" and "more-than-life."

Fashion

In one of his typically fascinating and dualistic essays, Simmel (1904/1971; Gronow, 1997; Nedelmann, 1990) illustrated the contradictions in fashion in a variety of ways. On the one hand, fashion is a form of social relationship that allows those who wish to conform to the demands of the group to do so. On the other hand, fashion also provides the norm from which those who wish to be individualistic can deviate. Fashion involves a historical process as well: at the initial stage, everyone accepts what is fashionable; inevitably, individuals deviate from this; and finally, in the process of deviation, they may adopt a whole new view of what is in fashion. Fashion is also dialectical in the sense that the success and spread of any given fashion lead to its eventual failure. That is, the distinctiveness of something leads to its being considered fashionable; however, as large numbers of people come to accept it, it ceases to be distinctive and hence it loses its attractiveness. Still another duality involves the role of the leader of a fashion movement. Such a person leads the group, paradoxically, by *following* the fashion better than anyone else, that is, by adopting it more determinedly. Finally, Simmel argued that not only does following what is in fashion involve dualities, so does the effort on the part of some people to be out of fashion. Unfashionable people view those who follow a fashion as being imitators and themselves as mavericks, but Simmel argued that the latter are simply engaging in an inverse form of imitation. Individuals may avoid what is in fashion because they are afraid that they, like their peers, will lose their individuality, but in Simmel's view, such a fear is hardly a sign of great personal strength and independence. In sum, Simmel noted that in fashion "all . . . leading antithetical tendencies . . . are represented in one way or another" (1904/1971:317).

Simmel's dialectical thinking can be seen at a more general level as well. As we will see throughout this chapter, he was most interested in the conflicts and contradictions that exist between the individual and the larger social and cultural structures that individuals construct. These structures ultimately come to have a life of their own, over which the individual can exert little or no control.

Individual (Subjective) Culture and Objective Culture

People are influenced, and in Simmel's view threatened, by social structures and, more important for Simmel, by their cultural products. Simmel distinguished between individual culture and objective culture. *Objective culture* refers to those things that people produce (art, science, philosophy, and so on). *Individual (subjective) culture* is the capacity of the actor to produce, absorb, and control the elements of objective culture. In an ideal sense, individual culture shapes, and is shaped by, objective culture. The problem is that objective culture comes to have a life of its own. As Simmel put it, "They [the elements of culture] acquire fixed identities, a logic and lawfulness of their own; this new rigidity inevitably places them at a distance from the spiritual dynamic which created them and which makes them independent" (1921/1968:11). The existence of these cultural products creates a contradiction with the actors who created them because it is an example of

> the deep estrangement or animosity which exists between organic and creative processes of the soul and its contents and products: the vibrating, restless life of the creative soul; which develops toward the infinite contrasts with its fixed and ideally unchanging product and its uncanny feedback effect, which arrests and indeed rigidifies this liveliness. Frequently it appears as if creative movement of the soul was dying from its own product.
>
> (Simmel, 1921/1968:42)

As K. Peter Etzkorn said, "In Simmel's dialectic, man is always in danger of being slain by those objects of his own creation which have lost their organic human coefficient" (1968:2).

More-Life and More-Than-Life

Another area of Simmel's thinking, his philosophical sociology, is an even more general manifestation of his dialectical thinking. In discussing the emergence of social and cultural structures, Simmel took a position very similar to some of Marx's ideas. Marx used the concept of the fetishism of commodities to illustrate the separation between people and their products. For Marx, this separation reached its apex in capitalism, could be overcome only in the future socialist society, and thus was a specific historical phenomenon. But for Simmel this separation is inherent in the nature of human life. In philosophical terms, there is an inherent and inevitable contradiction between "more-life" and "more-than-life" (Oakes, 1984:6; Weingartner, 1959).

The issue of more-life and more-than-life is central in Simmel's essay "The Transcendent Character of Life" (1918/1971). As the title suggests and as Simmel makes clear, "*Transcendence is immanent in life*" (1918/1971:361). People possess a doubly transcendent capability. First, because of their restless, creative capacities (more-life), people are able to transcend themselves. Second, this transcendent, creative ability makes it possible for people to constantly produce sets of objects that transcend them. The objective existence of these phenomena (more-than-life) comes to stand in irreconcilable opposition to the creative forces (more-life) that produced the objects in the first place. In other words, social life "creates and sets free from itself something that is not life but 'which has its own significance and follows its own law'" (Weingartner, citing Simmel, 1959:53). Life is found in the unity, and the conflict, between the two. As Simmel concludes, "Life finds its essence, its process, in being more-life and more-than-life" (1918/1971:374).

Thus, because of his metaphysical conceptions, Simmel came to an image of the world far closer to Weber's than to Marx's. Simmel, like Weber, saw the world as becoming an iron cage of objective culture from which people have progressively less chance of escape. We will have more to say about a number of these issues in the following sections, which deal with Simmel's thoughts on the major components of social reality.

Individual Consciousness

At the individual level, Simmel focused on forms of association and paid relatively little attention to the issue of individual consciousness (for at least one exception, a discussion of memory, see Jedlowski, 1990), which was rarely dealt with directly in his work. Still, Simmel clearly operated with a sense that human beings possess creative consciousness. As Frisby put it, the bases of social life to Simmel were "conscious individuals or groups of individuals who interact with one another for a variety of motives, purposes, and interests" (1984:61). This interest in creativity is manifest in Simmel's discussion of the diverse forms of interaction, the ability of actors to create social structures, as well as the disastrous effects those structures have on the creativity of individuals.

All of Simmel's discussions of the forms of interaction imply that actors must be consciously oriented to one another. Thus, for example, interaction in a stratified system requires that superordinates and subordinates orient themselves to each other. The interaction would cease and the stratification system would collapse if a process of mutual orientation did not exist. The same is true of all other forms of interaction.

Consciousness plays other roles in Simmel's work. For example, although Simmel believed that social (and cultural) structures come to have a life of their own, he realized that people must conceptualize such structures in order for them to have an effect on the people. Simmel stated that society is not simply "out there" but is also "'my representation'—something dependent on the activity of consciousness" (1908/1959a:339).

Simmel also had a sense of individual conscience and of the fact that the norms and values of society become internalized in individual consciousness. The existence of norms and values both internally and externally

> explains the dual character of the moral command: that on the one hand, it confronts us as an impersonal order to which we simply have to submit, but that, on the other, no external power, but only our most private and internal impulses, imposes it upon us. At any rate, here is one of the cases where the individual, within his own consciousness, repeats the relationships which exist between him, as a total personality, and the group.
>
> (Simmel, 1908/1950a:254)

This very modern conception of internalization is a relatively undeveloped assumption in Simmel's work.

In addition, Simmel had a conception of people's ability to confront themselves mentally, to set themselves apart from their own actions, that is very similar to the views of George Herbert Mead (see Chapter 14) and the symbolic interactionists (Simmel, 1918/1971:364; see also Simmel, 1907/1978:64). The actor can take in external stimuli, assess them, try out different courses of action, and then decide what to do. Because of these mental capacities, the actor is not simply enslaved by external forces. But there is a paradox in Simmel's conception of the actor's mental capacities. The mind can keep people from being enslaved by external stimuli, but it also has the capacity to reify social reality, to create the very objects that come to enslave it. As Simmel said, "Our mind has a remarkable ability to think of contents as being independent of the act of thinking" (1907/1978:65). Thus, although their intelligence enables people to avoid being enslaved by the same external stimuli that constrain lower animals, it also creates the structures and institutions that constrain their thoughts and actions.

Although we can find manifestations of Simmel's concern with consciousness in various places in his work, he did very little more than assume its existence. Raymond Aron clearly makes this point: "He [Simmel] must know the laws of behavior . . . of human reaction. But he does not try to discover or to explain what goes on in the mind itself" (1965:5–6).

Social Interaction ("Association")

Georg Simmel is best known in contemporary sociology for his contributions to our understanding of the patterns, or forms, of social interaction. He expressed his interest in this level of social reality in this way:

> We are dealing here with microscopic-molecular processes within human material, so to speak. These processes are the actual occurrences that are concatenated or hypostatized into those macrocosmic, solid units and systems. That people look at one another and are jealous of one another; that they exchange letters or have dinner together; that apart from all tangible interests they strike one another as pleasant or unpleasant; that gratitude for altruistic acts makes for inseparable union; that one asks another to point out a certain street; that people dress and adorn themselves for each other—these are a few casually chosen illustrations from the whole range of relations that play between one person and another. They may be momentary or permanent,

> conscious or unconscious, ephemeral or of grave consequence, but they incessantly tie men together. At each moment such threads are spun, dropped, taken up again, displaced by others, interwoven with others. These interactions among the atoms of society are accessible only to psychological microscopy.
>
> (Simmel, 1908/1959b:327–328)

Simmel made clear here that one of his primary interests was interaction (association) among conscious actors and that his intent was to look at a wide range of interactions that may seem trivial at some times but crucially important at others. His was not a Durkheimian expression of interest in social facts but a declaration of a smaller-scale focus for sociology.

Because Simmel sometimes took an exaggerated position on the importance of interaction in his sociology, many have lost sight of his insights into the larger-scale aspects of social reality. At times, for example, he equated society with interaction: "Society . . . is only the synthesis or the general term for the totality of these specific interactions. . . . 'Society' is identical with the sum total of these relations" (Simmel, 1907/1978:175). Such statements may be taken as a reaffirmation of his interest in interaction, but as we will see, in his general and philosophical sociologies, Simmel held a much larger-scale conception of society as well as culture.

Interaction: Forms and Types

One of Simmel's dominant concerns was the *form* rather than the *content* of social interaction. This concern stemmed from Simmel's identification with the Kantian tradition in philosophy, in which much is made of the difference between form and content. Simmel's position here, however, was quite simple. From Simmel's point of view, the real world is composed of innumerable events, actions, interactions, and so forth. To cope with this maze of reality (the "contents"), people order it by imposing patterns, or forms, on it. Thus, instead of a bewildering array of specific events, the actor is confronted with a limited number of forms. In Simmel's view, the sociologist's task is to do precisely what the layperson does, that is, impose a limited number of forms on social reality, on interaction in particular, so that it may be better analyzed. This methodology generally involves extracting commonalities that are found in a wide array of specific interactions. For example, the superordination and subordination forms of interaction are found in a wide range of settings, "in the state as well as in a religious community, in a band of conspirators as in an economic association, in art school as in a family" (Simmel, 1908/1959b:317). Donald Levine, one of Simmel's foremost contemporary analysts, describes Simmel's method of doing formal interactional sociology in this way: "His method is to select some bounded, finite phenomenon from the world of flux; to examine the multiplicity of elements which compose it; and to ascertain the cause of their coherence by disclosing its form. Secondarily, he investigates the origins of this form and its structural implications" (1971:xxxi). More specifically, Levine points out that "forms are the patterns exhibited by the associations" of people (1981b:65).[1]

---

[1]In the specific case of interaction, contents are the "*drives, purposes and ideas which lead people to associate* with one another" (Levine, 1981b:65).

Simmel's interest in the forms of social interaction has been subjected to various criticisms. For example, he has been accused of imposing order where there is none and of producing a series of unrelated studies that in the end really impose no better order on the complexities of social reality than does the layperson. Some of these criticisms are valid only if we focus on Simmel's concern with forms of interaction, his formal sociology, and ignore the other types of sociology he practiced.

However, there are a number of ways to defend Simmel's approach to formal sociology. First, it is close to reality, as reflected by the innumerable real-life examples employed by Simmel. Second, it does not impose arbitrary and rigid categories on social reality but tries instead to allow the forms to flow from social reality. Third, Simmel's approach does not employ a general theoretical schema into which all aspects of the social world are forced. He thus avoided the reification of a theoretical schema that plagues a theorist like Talcott Parsons. Finally, formal sociology militates against the poorly conceptualized empiricism that is characteristic of much of sociology. Simmel certainly used empirical "data," but they are subordinated to his effort to impose some order on the bewildering world of social reality.

Social Geometry

In Simmel's formal sociology, one sees most clearly his effort to develop a "geometry" of social relations. Two of the geometric coefficients that interested him are numbers and distance (others are position, valence, self-involvement, and symmetry [Levine, 1981b]).

Numbers Simmel's interest in the impact of numbers of people on the quality of interaction can be seen in his discussion of the difference between a dyad and a triad.

Dyad and Triad. For Simmel (1950) there was a crucial difference between the *dyad* (two-person group) and the *triad* (three-person group). The addition of a third person causes a radical and fundamental change. Increasing the membership beyond three has nowhere near the same impact as does adding a third member. Unlike all other groups, the dyad does not achieve a meaning beyond the two individuals involved. There is no independent group structure in a dyad; there is nothing more to the group than the two separable individuals. Thus, each member of a dyad retains a high level of individuality. The individual is not lowered to the level of the group. This is not the case in a triad. A triad does have the possibility of obtaining a meaning beyond the individuals involved. There is likely to be more to a triad than the individuals involved. It is likely to develop an independent group structure. As a result, there is a greater threat to the individuality of the members. A triad can have a general leveling effect on the members.

With the addition of a third party to the group, a number of new social roles become possible. For example, the third party can take the role of arbitrator or mediator in disputes within the group. Then the third party can use disputes between the other two for his or her own gain or become an object of competition between the other two parties. The third member also can intentionally foster conflict between the other two parties in order to gain superiority (divide and rule). A stratification system and an authority structure then can emerge. The movement from dyad to triad is essential to the development of social structures that can become separate from, and dominant over, individuals. Such a possibility does not exist in a dyad.

The process that is begun in the transition from a dyad to a triad continues as larger and larger groups and, ultimately, societies emerge. In these large social structures, the individual, increasingly separated from the structure of society, grows more and more alone, isolated, and segmented. This results finally in a dialectical relationship between individuals and social structures: "According to Simmel, the socialized individual always remains in a dual relation toward society: he is incorporated within it and yet stands against it. . . . The individual is determined, yet determining; acted upon, yet self-actuating" (Coser, 1965:11). The contradiction here is that "society allows the emergence of individuality and autonomy, but it also impedes it" (Coser, 1965:11).

Group Size. At a more general level, there is Simmel's (1908/1971a) ambivalent attitude toward the impact of group *size.* On the one hand, he took the position that the increase in the size of a group or society increases individual freedom. A small group or society is likely to control the individual completely. However, in a larger society, the individual is likely to be involved in a number of groups, each of which controls only a small portion of his or her total personality. In other words, "*Individuality in being and action generally increases to the degree that the social circle encompassing the individual expands*" (Simmel, 1908/1971a:252). However, Simmel took the view that large societies create a set of problems that ultimately threaten individual freedom. For example, he saw the masses as likely to be dominated by one idea, the simplest idea. The physical proximity of a mass makes people suggestible and more likely to follow simplistic ideas, to engage in mindless, emotional actions.

Perhaps most important, in terms of Simmel's interest in forms of interaction, is that increasing size and differentiation tend to loosen the bonds between individuals and leave in their place much more distant, impersonal, and segmental relationships. Paradoxically, the large group that frees the individual simultaneously threatens that individuality. Also paradoxical is Simmel's belief that one way for individuals to cope with the threat of the mass society is to immerse themselves in small groups such as the family.

Distance Another of Simmel's concerns in social geometry was *distance.* Levine offers a good summation of Simmel's views on the role of distance in social relationships: "*The properties of forms and the meanings of things are a function of the relative distances between individuals and other individuals or things*" (1971:xxxiv). This concern with distance is manifest in various places in Simmel's work. We will discuss it in two different contexts—in Simmel's massive *The Philosophy of Money* and in one of his cleverest essays, "The Stranger."

In *The Philosophy of Money* (1907/1978), Simmel enunciated some general principles about value—and about what makes things valuable—that served as the basis for his analysis of money. Because we deal with this work in detail later in this chapter, we discuss this issue only briefly here. The essential point is that the value of something is determined by its distance from the actor. It is not valuable if it is either too close and too easy to obtain or too distant and too difficult to obtain. Objects that are attainable, but only with great effort, are the most valuable.

Distance also plays a central role in Simmel's "The Stranger" (1908/1971b; Tabboni, 1995; McVeigh and Sikkink, 2005), an essay on a type of actor who is neither too close nor too far. If he (or she) were too close, he would no longer be a stranger, but if he were too far, he would cease to have any contact with the group. The interaction that the stranger engages in with the group members involves a combination of closeness and distance. The peculiar distance of the stranger from the group allows him to have a series of unusual interaction patterns with the members. For example, the stranger can be more objective in his relationships with the group members. Because he is a stranger, other group members feel more comfortable expressing confidences to him. In these and other ways, a pattern of coordination and consistent interaction emerges between the stranger and the other group members. The stranger becomes an organic member of the group. But Simmel not only considered the stranger a social type, he considered strangeness a form of social interaction. A degree of strangeness, involving a combination of nearness and remoteness, enters into all social relationships, even the most intimate. Thus, we can examine a wide range of specific interactions in order to discover the degree of strangeness found in each.

Although geometric dimensions enter a number of Simmel's types and forms, there is much more to them than simply geometry. The types and forms are constructs that Simmel used to gain a greater understanding of a wide range of interaction patterns.

Social Types

We have already encountered one of Simmel's types, the stranger; others include the miser, the spendthrift, the adventurer, and the nobleman. To illustrate his mode of thinking in this area, we will focus on one of his types, the poor.

The Poor As is typical of types in Simmel's work, the *poor* were defined in terms of social relationships, as being aided by other people or at least having the right to that aid. Here Simmel quite clearly did not hold the view that *poverty* is defined by a quantity, or rather a lack of quantity, of money.

Although Simmel focused on the poor in terms of characteristic relationships and interaction patterns, he also used the occasion of his essay "The Poor" (1908/1971c) to develop a wide range of interesting insights into the poor and poverty. It was characteristic of Simmel to offer a profusion of insights in every essay. Indeed, this is one of his great claims to fame. For example, Simmel argued that a reciprocal set of rights and obligations defines the relationship between the needy and the givers. The needy have the right to receive aid, and this right makes receiving aid less painful. Conversely, the giver has the obligation to give to the needy. Simmel also took the functionalist position that aid to the poor by society helps support the system. Society requires aid to the poor "so that the poor will not become active and dangerous enemies of society, so as to make their reduced energies more productive, and so as to prevent the degeneration of their progeny" (Simmel, 1908/1971c:154). Thus, aid to the poor is for the sake of society, not so much for the poor per se. The state plays a key role here, and, as Simmel saw it, the treatment of the poor grows increasingly impersonal as the mechanism for giving aid becomes more bureaucratized.

Simmel also had a relativistic view of poverty; that is, the poor are not simply those who stand at the bottom of society. From his point of view, poverty is found in *all* social strata. This concept foreshadowed the later sociological concept of *relative deprivation.* If people who are members of the upper classes have less than their peers do, they are likely to feel poor in comparison to them. Therefore, government programs aimed at eradicating poverty can never succeed. Even if those at the bottom are elevated, many people throughout the stratification system will still feel poor in comparison to their peers.

Social Forms

As with social types, Simmel looked at a wide range of social forms, including exchange, conflict, prostitution, and sociability. We can illustrate Simmel's (1908/1971d) work on social forms through his discussion of domination, that is, superordination and subordination.

Superordination and Subordination Superordination and subordination have a reciprocal relationship. The leader does not want to determine completely the thoughts and actions of others. Rather, the leader expects the subordinate to react either positively or negatively. Neither this nor any other form of interaction can exist without mutual relationships. Even in the most oppressive form of domination, subordinates have at least some degree of personal freedom.

To most people, superordination involves an effort to eliminate completely the independence of subordinates, but Simmel argued that a social relationship would cease to exist if this were the case.

Simmel asserted that one can be subordinated to an individual, a group, or an objective force. Leadership by a single individual generally leads to a tightly knit group either in support of or in opposition to the leader. Even when opposition arises in such a group, discord can be resolved more easily when the parties stand under the same higher power. Subordination under a plurality can have very uneven effects. On the one hand, the objectivity of rule by a plurality may make for greater unity in the group than does the more arbitrary rule of an individual. On the other hand, hostility is likely to be engendered among subordinates if they do not get the personal attention of a leader.

Simmel found subordination under an objective principle to be most offensive, perhaps because human relationships and social interactions are eliminated. People feel they are determined by an impersonal law that they have no ability to affect. Simmel saw subordination to an individual as freer and more spontaneous: "Subordination under a person has an element of freedom and dignity in comparison with which all obedience to laws has something mechanical and passive" (1908/1971d:115). Even worse is subordination to objects (for example, icons), which Simmel found a "humiliatingly harsh and unconditional kind of subordination" (1908/1971d:115). Because the individual is dominated by a thing, "he himself psychologically sinks to the category of mere thing" (Simmel, 1908/1971d:117).

Social Forms and Simmel's Larger Problematic Guy Oakes (1984) linked Simmel's discussion of forms to his basic problematic, the growing gap between objective and subjective culture. He begins with the position that in "Simmel's view, the discovery of objectivity—the independence of things from the condition of their subjective or psychological genesis—was the greatest achievement in the cultural history of the West" (Oakes, 1984:3). One of the ways in which Simmel addresses this objectivity is in his discussion of forms, but although such formalization and objectification are necessary and desirable, they can come to be quite undesirable:

> On the one hand, forms are necessary conditions for the expression and the realization of the energies and interests of life. On the other hand, these forms become increasingly detached and remote from life. When this happens, a conflict develops between the process of life and the configurations in which it is expressed. Ultimately, this conflict threatens to nullify the relationship between life and form, and thus to destroy the conditions under which the process of life can be realized in autonomous structures.
>
> (Oakes, 1984:4)

Social Structures

Simmel said relatively little directly about the large-scale structures of society. In fact, at times, given his focus on patterns of interaction, he denied the existence of that level of social reality. A good example of this is found in his effort to define *society,* where he rejected the realist position exemplified by Emile Durkheim that society is a real, material entity. Lewis Coser notes, "He did not see society as a thing or an organism" (1965:5). Simmel was also uncomfortable with the nominalist conception that society is nothing more than a collection of isolated individuals. He adopted an intermediate position, conceiving of society as a set of interactions (Spykman, 1925/1966:88). "*Society* is merely the name for a number of individuals connected by 'interaction' " (Simmel, cited in Coser, 1965:5).

Although Simmel enunciated this interactionist position, in much of his work he operated as a realist, as if society were a real material structure. There is, then, a basic contradiction in Simmel's work on the social-structural level. Simmel noted, "Society transcends the individual and lives its own life which follows its own laws. It, too, confronts the individual with a historical, imperative firmness" (1908/1950a:258). Coser catches the essence of this aspect of Simmel's thought: "The larger superindividual structures—the state, the clan, the family, the city, or the trade union—turn out to be but crystallizations of this interaction, even though they may attain autonomy and permanency and confront the individual as if they were alien powers" (1965:5). Rudolph Heberle makes essentially the same point: "One can scarcely escape the impression that Simmel views society as an interplay of structural factors, in which the human beings appear as passive objects rather than as live and willing actors" (1965:117).

The resolution of this paradox lies in the difference between Simmel's formal sociology, in which he tended to adhere to an interactionist view of society, and his historical and philosophical sociologies, in which he was much more inclined to see society as an independent, coercive social structure. In the latter sociologies, he saw society as part of the broader process of the development of objective culture, which worried him. Although objective culture is best seen as part of the cultural realm, Simmel included the growth of large-scale social structures as part of this process. That Simmel related the growth of social structures to the spread of objective culture is clear in this statement: "The increasing objectification of our culture, whose phenomena consist more and more of impersonal elements and less and less absorb the subjective totality of the individual . . . also involves sociological structures" (1908/1950b:318). In addition to clarifying the relationship between society and objective culture, this statement leads to Simmel's thoughts on the cultural level of social reality.

Objective Culture

One of the main focuses of Simmel's historical and philosophical sociology is the cultural level of social reality, or what he called the "objective culture." In Simmel's view, people produce culture, but because of their ability to reify social reality, the cultural world and the social world come to have lives of their own, lives that come increasingly to dominate the actors who created, and daily re-create, them. "The cultural objects become more and more linked to each other in a self-contained world which has increasingly fewer contacts with the [individual] subjective psyche and its desires and sensibilities" (Coser, 1965:22). Although people always retain the capacity to create and re-create culture, the long-term trend of history is for culture to exert a more and more coercive force on the actor.

> The preponderance of objective over [individual] subjective culture that developed during the nineteenth century . . . this discrepancy seems to widen steadily. Every day and from all sides, the wealth of objective culture increases, but the individual mind can enrich the forms and content of its own development only by distancing itself still further from that culture and developing its own at a much slower pace.
>
> (Simmel, 1907/1978:449)

In various places in his work, Simmel identified a number of components of the objective culture, for example, tools, means of transport, products of science, technology, arts, language, the intellectual sphere, conventional wisdom, religious dogma, philosophical systems, legal systems, moral codes, and ideals (for example, the "fatherland"). The objective culture grows and expands in various ways. First, its absolute size grows with increasing modernization. This can be seen most obviously in the case of scientific knowledge, which is expanding exponentially, although this is just as true of most other aspects of the cultural realm. Second, the number of different components of the cultural realm also grows. Finally, and perhaps most important, the various elements of the cultural world become more and more intertwined in an ever more powerful, self-contained world that is increasingly beyond the control of the actors (Oakes, 1984:12). Simmel not only was interested in describing the growth of objective culture but also was greatly disturbed by it: "Simmel was impressed—if not depressed—by the bewildering number and variety of human products which in the contemporary world surround and unceasingly impinge upon the individual" (Weingartner, 1959:33).

What worried Simmel most was the threat to individual culture posed by the growth of objective culture. Simmel's personal sympathies were with a world dominated by individual culture, but he saw the possibility of such a world as more and more unlikely. It is this that Simmel described as the "tragedy of culture." (We will comment on this in detail in the discussion of *The Philosophy of Money*.) Simmel's specific analysis of the growth of objective culture over individual subjective culture is simply one example of a general principle that dominates all of life: "The total value of something increases to the same extent as the value of its individual parts declines" (1907/1978:199).

We can relate Simmel's general argument about objective culture to his more basic analysis of forms of interaction. In one of his best-known essays, "The Metropolis and Mental Life" (1903/1971), Simmel analyzed the forms of interaction that take place in the modern city (Vidler, 1991). He saw the modern metropolis as the "genuine arena" of the growth of objective culture and the decline of individual culture. It is the scene of the predominance of the money economy, and money, as Simmel often made clear, has a profound effect on the nature of human relationships. The widespread use of money leads to an emphasis on calculability and rationality in all spheres of life. Thus genuine human relationships decline, and social relationships tend to be dominated by a blasé and reserved attitude. Whereas the small town was characterized by greater feeling and emotionality, the modern city is characterized by a shallow intellectuality that matches the calculability needed by a money economy. The city is also the center of the division of labor, and as we have seen, specialization plays a central role in the production of an ever-expanding objective culture, with a corresponding decline in individual culture. The city is a "frightful leveler," in which virtually everyone is reduced to emphasizing unfeeling calculability. It is more and more difficult to maintain individuality in the face of the expansion of objective culture (Lohmann and Wilkes, 1996).

It should be pointed out that in his essay on the city (as well as in many other places in his work) Simmel also discussed the liberating effect of this modern development. For example, he emphasized the fact that people are freer in the modern city than in the tight social confines of the small town. We will have more to say about Simmel's thoughts on the liberating impact of modernity at the close of the following section, devoted to Simmel's book *The Philosophy of Money.*

Before we get to that work, it is necessary to indicate that one of the many ironies of Simmel's influence on the development of sociology is that his micro-analytic work is used, but its broader implications are ignored almost totally. Take the example of Simmel's work on exchange relationships. He saw exchange as the "purest and most developed kind" of interaction (Simmel, 1907/1978:82). Although all forms of interaction involve some sacrifice, it occurs most clearly in exchange relationships. Simmel thought of all social exchanges as involving "profit and loss." Such an orientation was crucial to Simmel's microsociological work and specifically to the development of his largely micro-oriented exchange theory. However, his thoughts on exchange are also expressed in his broader work on money. To Simmel, money is the purest form of exchange. In contrast to a barter economy, where the cycle ends when one object has been exchanged for another, an economy based on money allows for an endless series of exchanges. This possibility is crucial for Simmel because it provides the basis for the widespread development of social structures and objective culture. Consequently, money as a form of exchange represented for Simmel one of the root causes of the alienation of people in a modern reified social structure.

In his treatment of the city and exchange, one can see the elegance of Simmel's thinking as he related small-scale sociological forms of exchange to the development of modern society in its totality. Although this link can be found in his specific essays (especially Simmel, 1991), it is clearest in *The Philosophy of Money.*

The Philosophy of Money

The Philosophy of Money (1907/1978) illustrates well the breadth and sophistication of Simmel's thinking (Deflem, 2003). It demonstrates conclusively that Simmel deserves at least as much recognition for his general theory as for his essays on microsociology, many of which can be seen as specific manifestations of his general theory.

Although the title makes it clear that Simmel's focus is money, his interest in that phenomenon is embedded in a set of his broader theoretical and philosophical concerns. For example, as we have already seen, Simmel was interested in the broad issue of value, and money can be seen as simply a specific form of value. At another level, Simmel was interested not in money per se but in its impact on such a wide range of phenomena as the "inner world" of actors and the objective culture as a whole. At still another level, he treated money as a specific phenomenon linked with a variety of other components of life, including "exchange, ownership, greed, extravagance, cynicism, individual freedom, the style of life, culture, the value of the personality, etc." (Siegfried Kracauer, cited in Bottomore and Frisby, 1978:7). Finally, and most generally, Simmel saw money as a specific component of life capable of helping us understand the totality of life. As Tom Bottomore and David Frisby put it, Simmel sought no less than to extract "the totality of the spirit of the age from his analysis of money" (1978:7).

The Philosophy of Money has much in common with the work of Karl Marx. Like Marx, Simmel focused on capitalism and the problems created by a money economy. Despite this common ground, however, the differences are overwhelming. For example, Simmel saw the economic problems of his time as simply a specific manifestation of a more general cultural problem, the alienation of objective from subjective culture (Poggi, 1993). To Marx these problems are specific to capitalism, but to Simmel they are part of a universal tragedy—the increasing powerlessness of the individual in the face of the growth of objective culture. Whereas Marx's analysis is historically specific, Simmel's analysis seeks to extract timeless truths from the flux of human history. As Frisby says, "In his *The Philosophy of Money* . . . [w]hat is missing . . . is a historical sociology of money relationships" (1984:58). This difference in their analyses is related to a crucial political difference between Simmel and Marx. Because Marx saw economic problems as time-bound, the product of capitalist society, he believed that eventually they could be solved. Simmel, however, saw the basic problems as inherent in human life and held out no hope for future improvement. In fact, Simmel believed that socialism, instead of improving the situation, would heighten the kinds of problems discussed in *The Philosophy of Money.* Despite some substantive similarities to Marxian theory, Simmel's thought is far closer to that of Weber and his "iron cage" in terms of his image of both the modern world and its future.

The Philosophy of Money begins with a discussion of the general forms of money and value. Later the discussion moves to the impact of money on the "inner world" of actors and on culture in general. Because the argument is so complex, we can only highlight it here.

Money and Value

One of Simmel's initial concerns in the work, as we discussed briefly earlier, is the relationship between money and value (Kamolnick, 2001). In general, he argued that people create value by making objects, separating themselves from those objects, and then seeking to overcome the "distance, obstacles, difficulties" (Simmel, 1907/1978:66). The greater the difficulty of obtaining an object, the greater its value. However, difficulty of attainment has a "lower and an upper limit" (Simmel, 1907/1978:72). The general principle is that the value of things comes from the ability of people to distance themselves properly from objects. Things that are too close, too easily obtained, are not very valuable. Some exertion is needed for something to be considered valuable. Conversely, things that are too far, too difficult, or nearly impossible to obtain are also not very valuable. Things that defy most, if not all, of our efforts to obtain them cease to be valuable to us. Those things that are most valuable are neither too distant nor too close. Among the factors involved in the distance of an object from an actor are the time it takes to obtain it, its scarcity, the difficulties involved in acquiring it, and the need to give up other things in order to acquire it. People try to place themselves at a proper distance from objects, which must be attainable, but not too easily.

In this general context of value, Simmel discussed money. In the economic realm, money serves both to create distance from objects and to provide the means to overcome it. The money value attached to objects in a modern economy places them at a distance from us; we cannot obtain them without money of our own. The difficulty in obtaining the money and therefore the objects makes them valuable to us. At the same time, once we obtain enough money, we are able to overcome the distance between ourselves and the objects. Money thus performs the interesting function of creating distance between people and objects and then providing the means to overcome that distance.

Money, Reification, and Rationalization

In the process of creating value, money also provides the basis for the development of the market, the modern economy, and ultimately modern (capitalistic) society (Poggi, 1996). Money provides the means by which these entities acquire a life of their own that is external to, and coercive of, the actor. This stands in contrast to earlier societies in which barter or trade could not lead to the reified world that is the distinctive product of a money economy. Money permits this development in various ways. For example, Simmel argued that money allows for "long-range calculations, large-scale enterprises and long-term credits" (1907/1978:125). Later, Simmel said that "money has . . . developed . . . the most objective practices, the most logical, purely mathematical norms, the absolute freedom from everything personal" (1907/1978:128). He saw this process of reification as only part of the more general process by which the mind embodies and symbolizes itself in objects. These embodiments, these symbolic structures, become reified and come to exert a controlling force on actors.

Not only does money help create a reified social world, it also contributes to the increasing rationalization of that social world (Deutschmann, 1996; B. Turner, 1986). This is another of the concerns that Simmel shared with Weber (Levine, 2000). A money economy fosters an emphasis on quantitative rather than qualitative factors. Simmel stated:

> It would be easy to multiply the examples that illustrate the growing preponderance of the category of quantity over that of quality, or more precisely the tendency to dissolve quality into quantity, to remove the elements more and more from quality, to grant them only specific forms of motion and to interpret everything that is specifically, individually, and qualitatively determined as the more or less, the bigger or smaller, the wider or narrower, the more or less frequent of those colourless elements and awarenesses that are only accessible to numerical determination—even though this tendency may never absolutely attain its goal by mortal means. . . .
>
> Thus, one of the major tendencies of life—the reduction of quality to quantity—achieves its highest and uniquely perfect representation in money. Here, too, money is the pinnacle of a cultural historical series of developments which unambiguously determines its direction.
>
> (Simmel, 1907/1978:278–280)

Less obviously, money contributes to rationalization by increasing the importance of intellectuality in the modern world (B. Turner, 1986; Deutschmann, 1996). On the one hand, the development of a money economy presupposes a significant expansion of mental processes. As an example, Simmel pointed to the complicated mental processes that are required by such money transactions as covering bank notes with cash reserves. On the other hand, a money economy contributes to a considerable change in the norms and values of society; it aids in the "fundamental reorientation of culture towards intellectuality" (Simmel, 1907/1978:152). In part because of a money economy, intellect has come to be considered the most valuable of our mental energies.

Simmel saw the significance of the individual declining as money transactions become an increasingly important part of society and as reified structures expand. This is part of his general argument on the decline of individual subjective culture in the face of the expansion of objective culture (the "tragedy of culture"):

> The rapid circulation of money induces habits of spending and acquisition; it makes a specific quantity of money psychologically less significant and valuable, while money in general becomes increasingly important because money matters now affect the individual more vitally than they do in a less agitated style of life. We are confronted here with a very common phenomenon; namely, that the total value of something increases to the same extent as the value of its individual parts declines. For example, the size and significance of a social group often becomes greater the less highly the lives and interests of its individual members are valued; the objective culture, the diversity and liveliness of its content attain their highest point through a division of labour that often condemns the individual representative and participant in this culture to a monotonous specialization, narrowness, and stunted growth. The whole becomes more perfect and harmonious, the less the individual is a harmonious being.
>
> (Simmel, 1907/1978:199)

Jorge Arditi (1996) has put this issue in slightly different terms. Arditi recognizes the theme of increasing rationalization in Simmel's work, but argues that it must be seen in the context of Simmel's thinking on the nonrational. "According to Simmel, the nonrational is a primary, essential element of 'life,' an integral aspect of our humanity. Its gradual eclipse in the expanses of a modern, highly rationalized world implies, then, an unquestionable impoverishment of being" (Arditi, 1996:95). One example of the nonrational is love (others are emotions and faith), and it is nonrational because, among other things, it is impractical, is the opposite of intellectual experience, does not necessarily have real value, is impulsive, nothing social or cultural intervenes between lover and beloved, and it springs "'from the completely *nonrational* depths of life'" (Simmel, in Arditi, 1996:96). With increasing rationalization, we begin to lose the nonrational and with it "we lose . . . the most meaningful of our human attributes: our authenticity" (Arditi, 1996:103). This loss of authenticity, of the nonrational, is a real human tragedy.

In some senses, it may be difficult to see how money can take on the central role that it does in modern society. On the surface, it appears that money is simply a means to a variety of ends or, in Simmel's worlds, "the purest form of the tool" (1907/1978:210). However, money has come to be the most extreme example of a means that has become an end in itself:

> Never has an object that owes its value exclusively to its quality as a means, to its convertibility into more definite values, so thoroughly and unreservedly developed into a psychological value absolute, into a completely engrossing final purpose governing our practical consciousness. This ultimate craving for money must increase to the extent that money takes on the quality of a pure means. For this implies that the range of objects made available to money grows continuously, that things submit more and more defencelessly to the power of money, that money itself becomes more and more lacking in quality yet thereby at the same time becomes powerful in relation to the quality of things.
>
> (Simmel, 1907/1978:232)

Negative Effects

A society in which money becomes an end in itself, indeed the ultimate end, has a number of negative effects on individuals (Beilharz, 1996), two of the most interesting of which are the increase in cynicism and the increase in a blasé attitude. Cynicism is induced when both the highest and the lowest aspects of social life are for sale, reduced to a common denominator—money. Thus we can "buy" beauty or truth or intelligence almost as easily as we can buy cornflakes or underarm deodorant. This leveling of everything to a common denominator leads to the cynical attitude that everything has its price, that anything can be bought or sold in the market. A money economy also induces a blasé attitude, "all things as being of an equally dull and grey hue, as not worth getting excited about" (Simmel, 1907/1978:256). The blasé person has lost completely the ability to make value differentiations among the ultimate objects of purchase. Put slightly differently, money is the absolute enemy of esthetics, reducing everything to formlessness, to purely quantitative phenomena.

Another negative effect of a money economy is the increasingly impersonal relations among people. Instead of dealing with individuals with their own personalities, we are increasingly likely to deal solely with positions—the delivery person, the baker, and so forth—regardless of who occupies those positions. In the modern division of labor characteristic of a money economy, we have the paradoxical situation that while we grow more dependent on other positions for our survival, we know less about the people who occupy those positions. The specific individual who fills a given position becomes progressively insignificant. Personalities tend to disappear behind positions that demand only a small part of them. Because so little is demanded of them, many individuals can fill the same position equally well. People thus become interchangeable parts.

A related issue is the impact of the money economy on individual freedom. A money economy leads to an increase in individual enslavement. The individual in the modern world becomes atomized and isolated. No longer embedded within a group, the individual stands alone in the face of an ever-expanding and increasingly coercive objective culture. The individual in the modern world is thus enslaved by a massive objective culture.

Another impact of the money economy is the reduction of all human values to dollar terms, "the tendency to reduce the value of man to a monetary expression" (Simmel, 1907/1978:356). For example, Simmel offers the case in primitive society of atonement for a murder by a money payment. But his best example is the exchange of sex for money. The expansion of prostitution is traceable in part to the growth of the money economy.

Some of Simmel's most interesting insights lie in his thoughts on the impact of money on people's styles of life. For example, a society dominated by a money economy tends to reduce everything to a string of causal connections that can be comprehended intellectually, not emotionally. Related to this is what Simmel called the "calculating character" of life in the modern world. The specific form of intellectuality that is peculiarly suited to a money economy is a mathematical mode of thinking. This, in turn, is related to the tendency to emphasize quantitative rather than qualitative factors in the social world. Simmel concluded that "the lives of many people are absorbed by such evaluating, weighing, calculating, and reducing of qualitative values to quantitative ones" (1907/1978:444).

The key to Simmel's discussion of money's impact on style of life is in the growth of objective culture at the expense of individual culture. The gap between the two grows larger at an accelerating rate:

> This discrepancy seems to widen steadily. Every day and from all sides, the wealth of objective culture increases, but the individual mind can enrich the forms and contents of its own development only by distancing itself still further from that culture and developing its own at a much slower pace.
>
> (Simmel, 1907/1978:449)

Tragedy of Culture

The major cause of this increasing disparity is the increasing division of labor in modern society (Oakes, 1984:19). Increased specialization leads to an improved ability to create the various components of the cultural world. But at the same time, the highly specialized individual loses a sense of the total culture and loses the ability to control it. As objective culture grows, individual culture atrophies. One of the examples of this is that language in its totality has clearly expanded enormously, yet the linguistic abilities of given individuals seem to be declining. Similarly, with the growth of technology and machinery, the abilities of the individual worker and the skills required have declined dramatically. Finally, although there has been an enormous expansion of the intellectual sphere, fewer and fewer individuals seem to deserve the label "intellectual." Highly specialized individuals are confronted with an increasingly closed and interconnected world of products over which they have little or no control. A mechanical world devoid of spirituality comes to dominate individuals, and their lifestyles are affected in various ways. Acts of production come to be meaningless exercises in which individuals do not see their roles in the overall process or in the production of the final product. Relationships among people are highly specialized and impersonal. Consumption becomes little more than the devouring of one meaningless product after another.

The massive expansion of objective culture has had a dramatic effect upon the rhythm of life. In general, the unevenness that was characteristic of earlier epochs has been leveled and replaced in modern society by a much more consistent pattern of living. Examples of this leveling of modern culture abound.

In times past, food consumption was cyclical and often very uncertain. What foods were consumed and when they were available depended on the harvest. Today, with improved methods of preservation and transportation, we can consume virtually any food at any time. Furthermore, the ability to preserve and store huge quantities of food has helped offset disruptions caused by bad harvests, natural catastrophes, and so forth.

In communication the infrequent and unpredictable mail coach has been replaced by the telegraph, telephone, daily mail service, fax machines, cell phones, and e-mail, which make communication available at all times.

In an earlier time, night and day gave life a natural rhythm. Now, with artificial lighting, the natural rhythm has been altered greatly. Many activities formerly restricted to daylight hours can now be performed at night as well.

Intellectual stimulation, which formerly was restricted to an occasional conversation or a rare book, is now available at all times because of the ready availability of books and magazines. In this realm, as in all the others, the situation has grown even more pronounced since Simmel's time. With radio, television, videotape and DVD players and recorders, and home computers, the availability and possibilities of intellectual stimulation have grown far beyond anything Simmel could have imagined.

There are positive elements to all this, of course. For example, people have much more freedom because they are less restricted by the natural rhythm of life. In spite of the human gains, problems arise because all these developments are at the level of objective culture and are integral parts of the process by which objective culture grows and further impoverishes individual culture.

In the end, money has come to be the symbol of, and a major factor in, the development of a relativistic mode of existence. Money allows us to reduce the most disparate phenomena to numbers of dollars, and this allows them to be compared to each other. In other words, money allows us to relativize *everything*. Our relativistic way of life stands in contrast to earlier methods of living in which people believed in a number of eternal verities. A money economy destroys such eternal truths. The gains to people in terms of increased freedom from absolute ideas are far outweighed by the costs. The alienation endemic to the expanding objective culture of a modern money economy is a far greater threat to people, in Simmel's eyes, than the evils of absolutism. Perhaps Simmel would not wish us to return to an earlier, simpler time, but he certainly would warn us to be wary of the seductive dangers associated with the growth of a money economy and objective culture in the modern world.

While we have focused most of our attention on the negative effects of the modern money economy, such an economy also has its liberating aspects (Beilharz, 1996; Levine, 1981b, 1991b; Poggi, 1993). First, it allows us to deal with many more people in a much-expanded marketplace. Second, our obligations to one another are highly limited (to specific services or products) rather than all-encompassing. Third, the money economy allows people to find gratifications that were unavailable in earlier economic systems. Fourth, people have greater freedom in such an environment to develop their individuality to a fuller extent. Fifth, people are better able to maintain and protect their subjective center, since they are involved only in very limited relationships. Sixth, the separation of the worker from the means of production, as Simmel points out, allows the individual some freedom from those productive forces. Finally, money helps people grow increasingly free of the constraints of their social groups. For example, in a barter economy people are largely controlled by their groups, but in the modern economic world such constraints are loosened, with the result that people are freer to make their own economic deals. However, while Simmel is careful to point out a variety of liberating effects of the money economy, and of modernity in general, in our view the heart of his work lies in his discussion of the problems associated with modernity, especially the "tragedy of culture."

Secrecy: A Case Study in Simmel's Sociology

While *The Philosophy of Money* demonstrates that Simmel has a theoretical scope that rivals that of Marx, Weber, and Durkheim, it remains an atypical example of his work. Thus, in this closing section we return to a more characteristic type of Simmelian scholarship, his work on a specific form of interaction—secrecy. *Secrecy* is defined as the condition in which one person has the intention of hiding something while the other person is seeking to reveal that which is being hidden. In this discussion, we are interested not only in outlining Simmel's many insightful ideas on secrecy but also in bringing together under one heading many of the sociological ideas raised through this chapter.

Simmel begins with the basic fact that people must know some things about other people in order to interact with them. For instance, we must know with whom we are dealing (for example, a friend, a relative, a shopkeeper). We may come to know a great deal about other people, but we can never know them absolutely. That is, we can never know all the thoughts, moods, and so on, of other people. However, we do form some sort of unitary conception of other people out of the bits and pieces that we know about them; we form a fairly coherent mental picture of the people with whom we interact. Simmel sees a dialectical relationship between interaction (being) and the mental picture we have of others (conceiving): "Our relationships thus develop upon the basis of reciprocal knowledge, and this knowledge upon the basis of actual relations. Both are inextricably interwoven" (1906/1950:309).

In all aspects of our lives we acquire not only truth but also ignorance and error. However, it is in the interaction with other people that ignorance and error acquire a distinctive character. This relates to the inner lives of the people with whom we interact.

People, in contrast to any other object of knowledge, have the capacity to *intentionally* reveal the truth about themselves *or* to lie and conceal such information.

The fact is that even if people wanted to reveal all (and they almost always do not), they could not do so because so much information "would drive everybody into the insane asylum" (Simmel, 1906/1950:312). Thus, people must select the things that they report to others. From the point of view of Simmel's concern with quantitative issues, we report only "fragments" of our inner lives to others. Furthermore, we choose which fragments to reveal and which to conceal. Thus, in all interaction, we reveal only a part of ourselves, and which part we opt to show depends on how we select and arrange the fragments we choose to reveal.

This brings us to the *lie,* a form of interaction in which the liar *intentionally* hides the truth from others. In the lie, it is not just that others are left with an erroneous conception but also that the error is traceable to the fact that the liar intended that the others be deceived.

Simmel discusses the lie in terms of social geometry, specifically his ideas on distance. For example, in Simmel's view, we can better accept and come to terms with the lies of those who are distant from us. Thus, we have little difficulty learning that the politicians who habituate Washington, D.C., frequently lie to us. In contrast, "If the persons closest to us lie, life becomes unbearable" (Simmel, 1906/1950:313). The lie of a spouse, lover, or child has a far more devastating impact on us than does the lie of a government official whom we know only through the television screen.

More generally, in terms of distance, all everyday communication combines elements known to both parties with facts known to only one or the other. It is the existence of the latter that leads to "distanceness" in all social relationships. Indeed, Simmel argues that social relationships require both elements that are known to the interactants *and* those that are unknown to one party or the other. In other words, even the most intimate relationships require both nearness and distance, reciprocal knowledge and mutual concealment. Thus, secrecy is an integral part of all social relationships, although a relationship may be destroyed if the secret becomes known to the person from whom it was being kept.

Secrecy is linked to the size of society. In small groups, it is difficult to develop secrets; "Everybody is too close to everybody else and his circumstances, and frequency and intimacy of contact involve too many temptations to revelation" (Simmel, 1906/1950:335). Furthermore, in small groups, secrets are not even needed because everyone is much like everyone else. In large groups, in contrast, secrets can more easily develop and are much more needed because there are important differences among people.

On the issue of size, at the most macroscopic level, we should note that secrecy not only is a form of interaction (which, as we have seen, affects many other forms) but also can come to characterize a group in its entirety. Unlike the secret possessed by a single individual, the secret in a *secret society* is shared by all the members and determines the reciprocal relations among them. As with the individual case, however, the secret of the secret society cannot be hidden forever. In such a society there is a constant tension caused by the fact that the secret can be uncovered, or revealed, and thus the entire basis for the existence of the secret society can be eliminated.

Secrecy and Social Relationships

Simmel examines various forms of social relationships from the point of view of reciprocal knowledge and secrecy. For example, we all are involved in a range of interest groups in which we interact with other people on a very limited basis, and the total personalities of these people are irrelevant to our specific concerns. Thus, in the university the student is concerned with what the professor says and does in the classroom and not in all aspects of the professor's life and personality. Linking this to his ideas on the larger society, Simmel argues that the increasing objectification of culture brings with it more and more limited-interest groups and the kinds of relationships associated with them. Such relationships require less and less of the subjective totality of the individual (individual culture) than do associations in premodern societies.

In the impersonal relationships characteristic of modern objectified society, *confidence,* as a form of interaction, becomes increasingly important. To Simmel "confidence is intermediate between knowledge and ignorance about a man" (1906/1950:318). In premodern societies people are much more likely to know a great deal about the people they deal with. But in the modern world we do not, and cannot, have a great deal of knowledge about most of the people with whom we have associations. Thus, students do not know a great deal about their professors (and vice versa), but they must have the confidence that their professors will show up at the appointed times and talk about what they are supposed to discuss.

Another form of social relationship is *acquaintanceship.* We know our acquaintances, but we do not have intimate knowledge of them: "One knows of the other only what he is toward the outside, either in the purely social-representative sense, or in the sense of that which he shows us" (Simmel, 1906/1950:320). Thus, there is far more secretiveness among acquaintances than there is among intimates.

Under the heading of "acquaintanceship," Simmel discusses another form of association—*discretion.* We are discrete with our acquaintances, staying "away from the knowledge of all the other does not expressly reveal to us. It does not refer to anything particular which we are not permitted to know, but to a quite general reserve in regard to the total personality" (Simmel, 1906/1950:321). In spite of being discrete, we often come to know more about other people than they reveal to us voluntarily. More specifically, we often come to learn things that others would prefer we do not know. Simmel offers a very Freudian example of how we learn such things: "To the man with the psychologically fine ear, people innumerable times betray their most secret thoughts and qualities, not only *although,* but often *because,* they anxiously try to guard them" (1906/1950:323–324). In fact, Simmel argues that human interaction is dependent on both discretion *and* the fact that we often come to know more than we are supposed to know.

Turning to another form of association, *friendship,* Simmel contradicts the assumption that friendship is based on total intimacy, full reciprocal knowledge. This lack of full intimacy is especially true of friendships in modern, differentiated society: "Modern man, possibly, has too much to hide to sustain a friendship in the ancient sense" (Simmel, 1906/1950:326). Thus, we have a series of differentiated friendships based on such things as common intellectual pursuits, religion, and shared experiences.

There is a very limited kind of intimacy in such friendships and thus a good deal of secrecy. However, in spite of these limitations, friendship still involves some intimacy:

> But the relation which is thus restricted and surrounded by discretions, may yet stem from the center of the total personality. It may yet be reached by the sap of the ultimate roots of the personality, even though it feeds only part of the person's periphery. In its idea, it involves the same affective depth and the same readiness for sacrifice, which less differentiated epochs and persons connect only with a common *total* sphere of life, for which reservations and discretion constitute no problem.
>
> (Simmel, 1906/1950:326)

Then there is what is usually thought of as the most intimate, least secret form of association—*marriage*. Simmel argues that there is a temptation in marriage to reveal all to the partner, to have no secrets. However, in his view, this would be a mistake. For one thing, all social relationships require "a certain proportion of truth and error," and thus it would be impossible to remove all error from a social relationship (Simmel, 1906/1950:329). More specifically, complete self-revelation (assuming such a thing is even possible) would make a marriage matter-of-fact and remove all possibility of the unexpected. Finally, most of us have limited internal resources, and every revelation reduces the (secret) treasures that we have to offer to others. Only those few with a great storehouse of personal accomplishments can afford numerous revelations to a marriage partner. All others are left denuded (and uninteresting) by excessive self-revelation.

Other Thoughts on Secrecy

Next, Simmel turns to an analysis of the functions, the positive consequences, of secrecy. Simmel sees the secret as "one of man's greatest achievements . . . the secret produces an immense enlargement of life: numerous contents of life cannot even emerge in the presence of full publicity. The secret offers, so to speak, the possibility of a second world alongside the manifest world" (1906/1950:330). More specifically in terms of its functionality, the secret, especially if it is shared by a number of people, makes for a strong "we feeling" among those who know the secret. High status is also associated with the secret; there is something mysterious about superordinate positions and superior achievements.

Human interaction in general is shaped by secrecy and its logical opposite, *betrayal.* The secret is always accompanied dialectically by the possibility that it can be discovered. Betrayal can come from two sources. Externally, another person can discover our secret, while internally there is always the possibility that we will reveal our secret to others. "The secret puts a barrier between men but, at the same time, it creates the tempting challenge to break through it, by gossip or confession. . . . Out of the counterplay of these two interests, in concealing and revealing, spring nuances and fates of human interaction that permeate it in its entirety" (Simmel, 1906/1950:334).

Simmel links his ideas on the lie to his views on the larger society of the modern world. To Simmel, the modern world is much more dependent on honesty than earlier societies were. For one thing, the modern economy is increasingly a credit economy, and credit is dependent on the fact that people will repay what they promise. For another, in modern science, researchers are dependent on the results of many other studies that they cannot examine in minute detail. Those studies are produced by innumerable other scientists whom the researchers are unlikely to know personally. Thus, the modern scientist is dependent on the honesty of all other scientists. Simmel concludes: "Under modern conditions, the lie, therefore, becomes something much more devastating than it was earlier, something which questions the very foundations of our life" (1906/1950:313).

More generally, Simmel connects secrecy to his thoughts on the social structure of modern society. On the one hand, a highly differentiated society permits and requires a high degree of secrecy. On the other hand, and dialectically, the secret serves to intensify such differentiation.

Simmel associates the secret with the modern money economy; money makes possible a level of secrecy that was unattainable previously. First, money's "compressibility" makes it possible to make others rich by simply slipping them checks without anyone else noticing the act. Second, the abstractness and the qualityless character of money make it possible to hide "transactions, acquisitions, and changes in ownership" that could not be hidden if more tangible objects were exchanged (Simmel, 1906/1950:335). Third, money can be invested in very distant things, thereby making the transaction invisible to those in the immediate environment.

Simmel also sees that in the modern world, public matters, such as those relating to politics, have tended to lose their secrecy and inaccessibility. In contrast, private affairs are much more secret than they are in premodern societies. Here Simmel ties his thoughts on secrecy to those on the modern city by arguing that "modern life has developed, in the midst of metropolitan crowdedness, a technique for making and keeping private matters secret" (Simmel, 1906/1950:337). Overall, "what is public becomes even more public, and what is private becomes even more private" (Simmel, 1906/1950:337).

Thus, Simmel's work on secrecy illustrates many aspects of his theoretical orientation.

Criticisms

We have already discussed some criticisms of Simmel's particular ideas, for example that his emphasis on forms imposes order where none exists and that he seems to contradict himself by viewing social structures, on the one hand, as simply a form of interaction and, on the other hand, as coercive and independent of interactions. In addition, we have described the difference between Marx and Simmel on alienation, which suggests the primary Marxist criticism of Simmel. This criticism is that Simmel does not suggest a way out of the tragedy of culture, because he considers alienation to be inherent to the human condition. For Simmel, the disjuncture between objective and subjective culture is as much a part of our "species being" as labor is to Marx. Therefore, whereas Marx believes that alienation will be swept away with the coming of socialism, Simmel has no such political hope.

Undoubtedly, the most frequently cited criticism of Simmel is the fragmentary nature of his work. Simmel is accused of having no coherent theoretical approach, but instead a set of fragmentary or "impressionistic" (Frisby, 1981) approaches. It certainly is true, as we have argued here, that Simmel focused on forms and types of association, but that is hardly the sort of theoretical unity that we see in the other founders of sociology. Indeed, one of Simmel's most enthusiastic living supporters in American sociology, Donald Levine et al (1976a:814) admits that, "although literate American sociologists today could be expected to produce a coherent statement of the theoretical frameworks and principal themes of Marx, Durkheim, and Weber, few would be able to do the same for Simmel." Further, Levine et al (1976b:1128) admits that it is not the obtuseness of modern interpreters, but "the character of Simmel's work itself: the scatter of topics, the failure to integrate related materials, the paucity of coherent general statements, and the cavalier attitude toward academic tradition." Although Levine attempts to present the core of Simmel's unique approach (as we have here), he must admit that, "in spite of these achievements of Simmelian scholarship, there remains for the reader the undeniable experience of Simmel as an unsystematic writer. Indeed, although many have found his work powerfully stimulating, virtually no one knows how to practice as a full-blown proponent of Simmelian social science" (Levine 1997:200).

Despite the fact that there are few Simmelians, Simmel has often been recognized as an "innovator of ideas and theoretical lead" (Tenbruck, 1959:61). This really is exactly what Simmel intended.

> I know that I shall die without spiritual heirs (and that is good). The estate I leave is like cash distributed among many heirs, each of whom puts his share to use in some trade that is compatible with his nature but which can no longer be recognized as coming from that estate.
>
> (Simmel in Frisby, 1984:150)

Consequently, Simmel has often been regarded as a natural resource of insights to be mined for empirical hypothesis rather than as a coherent framework for theoretical analysis.

Nevertheless, we do not feel that its potential for positivistic hypothesis is a satisfactory answer to the objection that Simmel's work is fragmentary. If these are the terms by which Simmel is measured, he most certainly must be judged a failure whose ideas are only saved because of the work of his more scientific successors. This was, in fact, Durkheim's (1979:328) assessment of Simmel's work. We, however, agree more with Nisbet's (1959:481) assessment that there is, in Simmel's work, "a larger element of irreducible humanism and . . . it will always be possible to derive something of importance from him directly that cannot be absorbed by the impersonal propositions of science."

With all of the classical theorists, it is important for the student to directly encounter their original writings, even if only in translation. The power and humor of Marx's language evaporates when we summarize his theories. The broad strokes of our précis obscure Durkheim's carefully detailed arguments. The optimistic faith in scholarship that lies behind Weber's pessimistic conclusions are missed. But this is most true with Simmel. There simply is no substitute for picking up one of Simmel's essays and being taught to look anew at fashion (1904/1971) or flirting (1984) or the stranger (1908/1971b) or secrecy (1906/1950).

Summary

The work of Georg Simmel has been influential in American sociological theory for many years. The focus of this influence seems to be shifting from microsociology to a general sociological theory. Simmel's microsociology is embedded in a broad dialectical theory that interrelates the cultural and individual levels. We identify four basic levels of concern in Simmel's work: psychological, interactional, structural and institutional, and the ultimate metaphysics of life.

Simmel operated with a dialectical orientation, although it is not as well articulated as that of Karl Marx. We illustrate Simmel's dialectical concerns in various ways. We deal with the way they are manifested in forms of interaction—specifically, fashion. Simmel also was interested in the conflicts between the individual and social structures, but his greatest concern was those conflicts that develop between individual culture and objective culture. He perceived a general process by which objective culture expands and individual culture becomes increasingly impoverished in the face of this development. Simmel saw this conflict, in turn, as part of a broader philosophical conflict between more-life and more-than-life.

The bulk of this chapter is devoted to Simmel's thoughts on each of the four levels of social reality. Although he has many useful assumptions about consciousness, he did comparatively little with them. He had much more to offer on forms of interaction and types of interactants. In this formal sociology, we see Simmel's great interest in social geometry, for example, numbers of people. In this context, we examine Simmel's work on the crucial transition from a dyad to a triad. With the addition of one person, we move from a dyad to a triad and with it the possibility of the development of large-scale structures that can become separate from, and dominant over, individuals. This creates the possibility of conflict and contradiction between the individual and the larger society. In his social geometry, Simmel was also concerned with the issue of distance, as in, for example, his essay on the "stranger," including "strangeness" in social life. Simmel's interest in social types is illustrated in a discussion of the poor, and his thoughts on social forms are illustrated in a discussion of domination, that is, superordination and subordination.

At the macro level, Simmel had comparatively little to say about social structures. In fact, at times he seemed to manifest a disturbing tendency to reduce social structures to little more than interaction patterns. Simmel's real interest at the macro level was objective culture. He was interested in both the expansion of this culture and its destructive effects on individuals (the "tragedy of culture"). This general concern is manifest in a variety of his specific essays, for example, those on the city and exchange.

In *The Philosophy of Money* Simmel's discussion progressed from money to value to the problems of modern society and, ultimately, to the problems of life in general. Of particular concern is Simmel's interest in the tragedy of culture as part of a broader set of apprehensions about culture. Finally, we discussed Simmel's work on secrecy in order to illustrate the full range of his theoretical ideas. The discussion of Simmel's work on money, as well as his ideas on secrecy, demonstrates that he has a far more elegant and sophisticated theoretical orientation than he is usually given credit for by those who are familiar with only his thoughts on micro-level phenomena.

C H A P T E R 10

Early Women Sociologists and Classical Sociological Theory: 1830–1930

Patricia Madoo Lengermann
The George Washington University

Gillian Niebrugge
American University

Chapter Outline

The traditional telling of the history of sociological theory has been shaped by a politics of gender that tends to emphasize male achievement and erase female contributions. (For an account of how this erasure occurred, see Lengermann and Niebrugge, 1998/2007.) As conventionally told, the creation of sociological theory is presented as the work of two generations of men: a "founding" generation who, in the middle third of the nineteenth century, acted as public educators outside any formal university base—particularly, Comte, Spencer, and Marx—and a second "classical" generation, a larger cohort of university-based men—notably, Durkheim, Weber, Simmel, Mead, and Park—who between 1890 and 1930 set out to establish a profession and a discipline. This historical account raises the critical question of mobilized feminism—*"And what about the women?"*

This chapter modifies this conventional history in the following ways. First, we add one woman, Harriet Martineau (1802–1876), to the first mid-nineteenth century generation of sociology's founders, affirming that Martineau is not only a key theorist of this generation but that she is perhaps sociology's original founder. Second, we describe a larger, interconnected community of women on both sides of the Atlantic who, in the period of sociology's emergence 1890–1930, worked with extraordinary energy to create their own models for sociological theory and practice. We review the ideas of just a few of these women—Charlotte Perkins Gilman, Jane Addams, Florence Kelley, Anna Julia Cooper, Ida Wells-Barnett, Marianne Weber, and Beatrice Potter Webb. The women who contributed are so numerous and the records so incomplete that we have had to be very selective in our presentation; important women omitted here include Helen Campbell, Caroline Bartlett Crane, Katharine Bement Davis, Jenny P. d'Héricourt, Crystal Eastman, Isabel Eaton, Lucille Eaves, Emma Goldman, Rosa Luxembourg, Florence Nightingale, Olive Schreiner, Mary Kingsbury Simkhovitch, Anna Garlin Spencer, Jessie Taft, Flora Tristan, Mary van Kleeck, and Fannie Barrier Williams.

The retelling here, part of the only half-completed feminist revolution in sociology (Alway, 1995; Chafetz, 1997; Delamont, 2003; Stacey and Thorne, 1985, 1996; Thistle, 2000), is important because a discipline is significantly defined by the canon of its classic works. That canon changes over time, depending in part on whether the discipline is engaged in the practice of "normal" or "revolutionary" science (Kuhn, 1970). In moments of revolutionary science, the discipline of sociology has frequently reached out to incorporate new or forgotten figures (for example, Parsons's reintroduction of Weber in the 1930s and the collective effort to incorporate Marx in the 1960s). This reclamation is currently under way in the burgeoning of feminist-inspired research of the last two decades (Arni and Mueller, 2004; Broschart, 1991a, b; Collins, 1990; Costin, 1983; Deegan, 1988, 1991, 2002a, 2002b; Deegan and Rynbrandt, 2002; Elshtain, 2002; Fish, 1981, 1985; Fitzpatrick, 1990; Grant, Stalp, and Ward, 2002; Hill, 1989, 2005; Hill and Hoecker-Drysdale, 2001; Hoecker-Drysdale, 1994, 2000; Keith, 1991; Lemert, 1995, 2002; Lemert and Bhan, 1998; Lengermann and Niebrugge-Brantley, 1998, 2001a, 2001b, 2002, 2006; McDonald, 1994, 1998; Reinharz, 1992, 1993; Rosenberg, 1982; Rynbrandt, 1999; Seigfried, 1996, 1999; Sklar, 1995; Thomas and Kukulan, 2004).

In making our selection, we have been guided by Dorothy E. Smith's conception that "a sociology is a systematically developed consciousness of society and of social relations" (1987:2). By "systematically developed consciousness," we mean that the person doing the thinking is doing so with a view to understanding society, and that understanding finds expression in an ability to identify and relate the parts that constitute society and social relations. The parts that seem essential to any social theory are some sense of (1) the fundamental organization of society, (2) the nature of the human being, (3) the relation between ideas and materiality, (4) the purpose and methods appropriate to social-science study, and (5) a definition of the social role of the sociologist. The women whose theories we describe developed such an understanding, and that understanding is essentially feminist. And this fact adds a sixth point to be looked for in their understanding of society and social relations: their articulation of a principle from which to judge the essential fairness of the society in place.

By describing these theories as feminist, we mean that from the vantage point of contemporary feminist sociological theory, we recognize certain themes and concerns central to the theories of these women. These include (1) the theorist's awareness of her gender and her stance in that gender identity as she develops her sociological theory,

Harriet Martineau

A Biographical Sketch

Harriet Martineau was born on June 12, 1802, in Norwich, England. The sixth of eight children in a business family of comfortable means and of the liberal Unitarian faith, Harriet, as a child, was given as good an education as her brothers. An able student, she turned eagerly to scholarship, not only because of its intrinsic appeal, but also as a respite from her childhood shyness and from the deafness that overcame her in early adolescence. She had an extraordinary facility for writing and began publishing in 1820, writing on women's unequal treatment in education and religion for the Unitarian journal *The Repository*.

The failure of the family business left her penniless in 1829. Faced with the choice of earning her—and her mother's—living as a seamstress or as a writer, she chose the latter, settling on a plan for writing in which she would educate the public, in a pleasing and acceptable form, in the principles of the emerging discipline of sociology. Between 1832 and 1834, she wrote didactic novels in the series, *Illustrations of Political Economy*. The series was enormously successful, averaging 10,000 copies a month at its height and outselling even Dickens. The success of this venture won her financial independence, fame, and political influence.

In 1834, Martineau followed this enormously successful venture into public education with more theoretical work: she drafted the first text on sociological research techniques, *How to Observe Morals and Manners* (which was published in 1838). Between 1834 and 1836, she applied and expanded these research strategies in an extensive field study of American society, published in 1836 in three volumes as *Society in America*—though she had wanted it titled "Theory and Practice of Society in America" to better capture the intent of her social-science project. By

(2) an awareness of the situatedness of her analysis and of the situatedness of the vantage points of others, (3) a consistent focus on the lives and work of women, (4) a critical concern with the practices of social inequality, and (5) a commitment to the practice of sociology in pursuit of social amelioration.

Harriet Martineau (1802–1876)

As recent feminist research shows (Annandale, 2009; Boucher, 2006; Broschart, 2005; Deegan, 1991, 2008; Hill, 1989; Hill and Hoecker-Drysdale, 2001; Hoecker-Drysdale, 1994, 2000, 2002, 2005; Lengermann and Niebrugge-Brantley, 1998, 2001b, 2005; Rossi, 1973; Yates, 1985), Harriet Martineau indisputably belongs in that founding generation of sociologists usually represented by Comte, Spencer, and Marx, thinkers who undertook the ambitious task of delineating an intellectual undertaking that would systematically and scientifically study human society.

1837, her reputation as Britain's preeminent social analyst led to a request from her publishers that she "become editor of a proposed new periodical 'to treat of philosophical principles, abstract and applied, of sociology'" (cited in Hoecker-Drysdale, 1994:70–71).[1] Personal uncertainty and family pressure led Martineau to refuse the offer, but she continued her projects of social research and of popularizing sociology. In 1853 she published an extensively edited English translation of Comte's *Positive Philosophy,* a version he so approved that he substituted it, translated back into French, for his original edition. It is only in this relationship to Comte that, until recently, Martineau's name survived in the record of sociology's history. But the claim may indeed be made that she is the first sociologist—sociology's "founding mother."

Martineau would write for the rest of her life for her living, for social reputation, and for political influence. She published more than seventy volumes in many genres, including adult fiction, children's stories, poetry, history, religious tracts, autobiography, literary criticism, and social and political analysis. She also wrote more than 1,500 newspaper columns.

Despite this grueling writing schedule, Martineau was not a recluse. She traveled extensively in Britain, the United States, and the Middle East. She spoke and traveled on behalf of innumerable public causes, including women's rights and the abolition of slavery. A prominent feminist thinker, she led a busy social life and was connected to the significant British intellectuals of her day.

The quality that comes through most strongly as we study her life and writings is her valor in the face of deafness, poor health, financial vulnerability, and the disadvantages of being a woman making her way from modest beginnings on her own in nineteenth-century England. Harriet Martineau was determined to make the best of what life had dealt her, and she did so with enormous discipline, considerable talent, and a capacity for joy in the details of her daily experiences. She died on June 27, 1876, at the home she had earned for herself—The Knoll, Ambleside, in England's Lake District.

The Social Role of the Sociologist

Martineau's first venture into this new science was an attempt to popularize "political economy," an intellectual forerunner both of economics and sociology (a science which is, as both Comte and Spencer later also portray it, about material and moral existence). Between 1832 and 1834 she published twenty-five didactic novels in a series called *Illustrations of Political Economy,* intended to teach the principles of the new science of society to a general middle-class and working-class readership through the medium of stories (often set in some distant or exotic place); Martineau concluded each volume with a summary of the principles of the new science that shaped her plot. The role of

[1]The phrase "to treat of philosophical principles, abstract and applied, of *sociology*" (italics added) is from two letters from Harriet to her brother James, December 12 and 21, 1837 (as cited in Hoecker-Drysdale, 1994:77). Although Comte is conventionally seen as inventing the word "sociology," Martineau's use here shows that the term had general currency in the 1830s and that her usage, together with Comte's, may reflect some emerging consensus about the name for the new field.

sociologist as that of public educator, and defined her Martineau saw audience democratically and inclusively—the educated intelligentsia like herself, the political class of Britain, the ordinary working people of both the middle and working classes, women, children (by means of a popular series of children's stories), her public in America (where since 1837 her popularity had been enormous), feminists and abolitionists on both sides of the Atlantic, even—in what must be a sociological first—the disabled—in this case, those who, like her, were deaf (1830/1836).

Despite this project of making sociology popular, Martineau held that the formulation of sociology, its subject matter and its method, should be developed in a disciplined and systematic way:

> In an attempt to develop any science, whether deductive or inductive, the very first step . . . is to define your subject methodically, to lay down the definition of your terms and instruments, and to ascertain what are the principles upon which the science essentially turns.
>
> (Martineau, cited in Hoecker-Drysdale, 1994:112)

The Organization of Society

Sociology's subject matter, for Martineau, is *social life in society*—its patterns, causes, consequences, and problems. Like Comte and Spencer, she chooses society, understood as roughly equivalent to a nation state or politico-cultural entity, as the object for sociological investigation, and believes that the life of any society is influenced by general social laws, including the principle of progress, the emergence of science as the most advanced product of human intellectual endeavor, and the significance of population dynamics and the natural environment. But for Martineau, the most important law of social life is that "the great ends of human association" aim above all "to the grand one,—the only general one,— . . . human happiness" (1838b:12). This is the principle by which she judges the essential fairness of society. She argues that a system of social arrangements is conducive to human happiness to the extent that it allows individuals to realize their basic human nature as autonomous moral and practical agents. The opposite of autonomy is domination, the enforced "submission of one's will to another" (1838a:411).

Morals and Manners

Sociology's project is, thus, to assess the extent to which a people develop "morals and manners" that produce or subvert this great end of all social life, human happiness. By "morals," Martineau means a society's collective ideas of prescribed and proscribed behavior; by "manners," its patterns of action and association. The principle that the aim of human association is human happiness—for Martineau as much a "law of nature" as any of the others, that is, one to which societies should conform if they are to progress—distinguishes her sociology from that of Comte and Spencer, giving her theory of society a critical tone essentially absent from their theories. She shares that critical posture with Marx, although his theory would focus on class injustice and be militant, whereas hers would be woman-centered and reformist.

Martineau's sociology, unlike that of Comte and Spencer, is interested much less in building a model of an ideal-typical, ahistorical, generalized "social system" or creating an abstract typology of societies in terms of their "stages" of development.

Rather, she chooses to study the fundamental organization of society in the actual patterns of human relationships and activities, in historically developed societies—England, Ireland, the United States, and those of the Middle East. In the truest sense of the term, she is a qualitative, comparative sociologist. In her analysis, the actions and interactions of a society can be classified as relating to various institutional zones—government, economy, law, education, marriage and family, religion, communication, popular culture, and so on. But social activities can also be constructed less formally, as the fluid relational tissue or texture of social life. Thus, Martineau studies hospitality, travel, colloquialisms, attitudes toward money and toward nature, decorum and entertainment, children's comportment, norms of housing, relations around sexuality, and so on. The life of each society in its uniqueness from, as well as its similarities to, other societies is her immediate subject of attention.

Anomaly

Together with this descriptive task, Martineau wishes to analyze each society in terms of its general economic and moral well-being. She sets out to discover the moral principles that the society's members have collectively set up for themselves, their cultural aspirations or "Morals." The well-being of a society is in part to be assessed in terms of the alignment between moral codes and actual behaviors or manners. Martineau calls a misalignment between a society's morals or ideals and its manners or everyday practices an *anomaly.* In *Society in America* (1836–37), she identifies four anomalies that she feels will eventually disrupt U.S. society—that is, four ways the society's practices do not meet its stated ideals of assuring all individuals the rights to life, liberty, and the pursuit of happiness. These anomalies are the institution of slavery, the unequal status of women, the pursuit of wealth, and the fear of public opinion. She tries to ascertain a society's progress or malaise in terms of the degree to which it promotes autonomy or allows domination; she develops three measures of this progress: (1) the condition of the less powerful—women, racial minorities, prisoners, servants, those in need of charity; (2) cultural attitudes toward authority and autonomy; (3) the extent to which all people are provided with the necessities for autonomous moral and practical action. In this last measure, Martineau links ideas and materiality.

Methods

"Things" and Sympathy

This concern with issues of measurement is part of Martineau's deep interest in methods for research and for sound scientific thinking. In *How to Observe Morals and Manners* (1838b), she focuses more sharply on the research work of the social scientist and develops the first methods text in the history of sociology. Again she believes everyone capable of instruction in social scientific procedures of observation, and she takes as her audience the person in everyday life who in the role of "traveler" wants to make informed observations about society. In *How to Observe,* Martineau gives instruction in the appropriate attitude of the sociologist toward the research experience, in problems of sampling, and in the identification of social indicators. She also develops the first guidelines for the practice of interpretive sociology. She argues that the sociologist must try to develop a sympathetic understanding as a strategy for discovering the meanings of an activity for the actors—for "actions and habits do not always carry their moral impress visibly to all eyes" (1838b:17). To overcome problems of sampling, the sociologist must look for "things" that represent the collectivity. In a passage that anticipates Durkheim's much later statement (*Rules of Sociological Method,* 1895/1982), she says that one must begin the "'inquiry into morals and manners with the study of THINGS' . . . facts to be collected from architectural remains, epitaphs, civic registers, national music or any other of the thousand manifestations of the common mind which may be found among every people" (1838b:63). She goes on to elaborate strategies for field work, including a diary of one's views, a journal of one's observations, a notebook for recording events. This concern with disciplined research is sustained after the American investigation in all her other sociological investigations. In the detail of her directives and her application of these directives in social research, Martineau is much more advanced methodologically than Comte or Spencer, and she anticipates the work of the next generation of academically based or trained sociologists, both male and female. If Martineau is the founder of a feminist sociology, then that sociology is to be both theoretical and firmly grounded in empirical research.

Feminism

Martineau's feminist approach to social analysis is evident in *Society in America* (1836–37) in her pervasive interest in and investigation of the conditions of women's lives. She makes the relational facts of marriage in the United States a key index of the moral condition of that society (her conclusions are pessimistic). The enslavement of the African-American population is her second key index, and she does not miss the significance of the interplay of gender and race. For Martineau, the domination of women closely parallels the domination of slaves. Like the slave, the woman is described—even to herself—as being indulged, but "indulgence is given her as a substitute for justice. Her case differs from that of the slave, as the principle, just so far as this; that the indulgence is large and universal, instead of petty and capricious. In both cases, justice is denied on no better plea than the right of the strongest" (1836–37:II:227).

In her writing and research after the study of U.S. society, Martineau continued this woman-centered sociology with investigations of women's education, family, marriage and the law, violence against women, the tyranny of fashion, the inhumanity of the Arab harem, the inhumanity of the British treatment of prostitution, and in study after study, the nature of women's paid work, in terms of its brutally heavy physical demands and wretchedly low wages. Her particular focus was on the wage labor of working-class women—in factories, in agriculture, in domestic service. In these studies, she brings together the double oppressions of class and gender.

Martineau did not restrict the sociology she was developing to women's issues. She expanded her analytic efforts to an enormous number of other topics. She continued her comparative case studies with field research in Ireland and in the Middle East; the latter research was published in the three-volume work *Eastern Life: Present and Past* in 1848. Later, Martineau wrote about the origins and functions of religion; crime and its punishment; the lives of the poor; labor conflicts; colonialism and war; illness, both physical and mental; and health care practices related to illness. Her sociological perspective, though anchored in her gendered life experience and permeated by a woman-centered sensibility, did not produce only a sociology of gender. It is a general sociology with theoretical relevance for all aspects of social life.

To some extent, the most basic connection of Martineau's sociology and her feminism was her understanding of herself as a gendered being in a world in which gender mattered and in which the fact that she was a woman would always frame others' response to her and her work. Her consciousness of this gender framing and, consequently, of a particular duty to women is visible from her very first publications—"Female Writers on Practical Divinity" (1822) and "On Female Education" (1823)—to her great achievements, *Society in America* (1836–37) and *How to Observe Morals and Manners* (1838b). She opens *Society in America* by answering the charge that her being a woman has made her research difficult—"In this I do not agree. I am sure, I have seen much more of domestic life than could possibly have been exhibited to any gentleman traveling through the country. The nursery, the boudoir, the kitchen are all excellent schools in which to learn the morals and manners of a people" (1836–37:I:xiii).

In the end, Harriet Martineau was defeated by the very issue she knew to be inseparable from others' reactions to her work—her gender. Although she worked with modesty, discipline, and prodigious productivity to prove her worth as a human being and a woman, and although she maintained a public reputation as a social scientist, political advocate, and intellectual in her lifetime, at her death the patriarchal currents in both general intellectual life and in sociology would flood in to defeat her. The record of her achievement would be washed away almost without trace in the century in which the field in which she had been so creative and dedicated—sociology—would emerge as a distinct scholarly discipline.

Charlotte Perkins Gilman (1860–1935)

In her analytic writings, Charlotte Perkins Gilman, more than any other female sociologist of the classic period, approximates in tone and intention the work of her male contemporaries in sociology—Durkheim (see Chapter 7), Weber (see Chapter 8), Simmel (see Chapter 9), Mead (see Chapter 15), and Park (see Chapter 2). Gilman's project was to present, in the impersonal, objective voice that we have come to associate with authoritative theorizing, a formal, theoretical analysis of society, understood both as a general or typical phenomenon and in its particular industrialized patternings in turn-of-the-century North Atlantic societies. Theory-building is Gilman's method of doing sociology, and it is as a theorist that she defined her social role as a sociologist (but like Martineau, a theorist speaking to a general audience).

The Organization of Society

The Sexuo-Economic Relation

In a passage that presents us with the central thesis of her feminist sociological theory of society, Gilman writes:

> Since we learned to study the development of human life as we study . . . species through the animal kingdom. . . . [w]e begin to see that . . . our lives are the results of natural causes. . . . the material universe . . . and the effect of our own activity. . . . What

CHARLOTTE PERKINS GILMAN

A Biographical Sketch

Charlotte Perkins Gilman was a woman of extraordinary energy. She was most fulfilled when she was most active, a personal experience that she would generalize to her sociological views about human nature. She published more than 2,000 works in her lifetime—novels, poetry, journalistic accounts, autobiography, and above all, sociological commentary on society, politics, and women's lives. She was an activist and organizer on women's issues, a public speaker in constant demand, the editor and sole author of her own journal, *The Forerunner,* from 1909 to 1916, and a constant traveler who crisscrossed the United States and visited Europe on several occasions.

Born in Hartford, Connecticut, on July 3, 1860, she was related on her father's side to the eminent and established Beecher family (her aunt was Harriet Beecher Stowe, author of *Uncle Tom's Cabin*), but her own life was marked by instability and unconventionality. After her parents divorced in 1869, she was raised in genteel poverty by her mother, moving from one relative's home to another and erratically receiving education. Her first marriage, in 1884, pushed her to the edge of madness, vividly portrayed in *The Yellow Wall-Paper* (1892/1973), and ended in divorce a decade later. Determined to have an independent lifestyle, Gilman helped effect the marriage of her best friend to her former husband and

> we do, as well as what is done to us, makes us what we are. But beyond these forces, we come under the effect of a third set of conditions peculiar to our human status; namely, social conditions. In the organic interchanges which constitute social life, we are affected to a degree beyond what is found even among the most gregarious of animals. Throughout all these environing conditions, . . . economic necessities are most marked in their influence. . . . the individual is . . . inexorably modified by his means of livelihood . . . the daily processes of supplying economic needs. . . .
>
> In view of these facts, attention is now called to certain marked and peculiar economic conditions affecting the human race, and unparalleled in organic life. We are the only animal species in which the female depends on the male for food, the only animal species in which the sex-relation is also an economic relation. With us an entire sex lives in a relation of economic dependence upon the other sex, and the economic relation is combined with the sex-relation.
>
> (Gilman, 1898/1966:1–5)

Gilman thus argues that in the foundational social institutions, the economy and the family, we find a basic stratificational practice that explains most of the ills observable in societies, in individual experience, and in history: that practice is gender inequality. Gilman, who like all the writers of this period lacked the term and concept "gender," uses the term *excessive sex distinction* to name the stratificational practice she identifies turned her daughter over to them while she pursued her public and professional career. In 1900, after several passionate attachments with other women, she married a cousin, Houghton Gilman, who was considerably younger than she and who supported her need for independence and public visibility in what was to be a very satisfactory marriage for them both.

In her own life, Gilman achieved enormous visibility. Her book *Women and Economics* (1898/1966) went through nine editions in her lifetime, was translated into seven languages, and was reviewed by the male establishment and by almost all the women sociologists discussed in this chapter—Addams, Kelley, Taft, Weber, and Webb. All her other sociological books received significant attention. She was an active member of both the sociological and economic scholarly communities, an occasional resident at Hull House, and a cofounder, with Jane Addams, of the Women's Peace Party. Like many feminist writers today, Gilman experimented with the forms in which her views of the individual in society might be presented. But the overwhelming majority of her 2,173 publications (Scharnhorst, 1985) were social commentary and analysis. She published hundreds of articles of this type, not only in her own journal, *The Forerunner,* which she founded in 1909 and both edited and wrote until 1916, but also in mainstream publications like *The Independent* and sociological journals like *The American Journal of Sociology, Annals of the American Academy of Political and Social Science,* and *Publications of the American Sociological Society,* which later became the *American Sociological Review* (Keith, 1991).

Ill with inoperable breast cancer, she died by her own hand on August 17, 1935.

and theorizes. "Sex" in her usage conflates physiological sex traits with sociocultural gender processes and sociocultural emotional patternings of sexuality. "Excessive" sex distinction is the marking of differences between men and women beyond that which arises directly out of biological reproduction. Thus conceptualized, gender stratification is the primary tension in the economies of all known societies, producing in effect, two sex classes—men as a "master class" and women as a class of subordinated and disempowered social beings. Gilman calls this pattern the *sexuo-economic relation.*

Gilman's explication of the consequences of this sexuo-economic arrangement parallels Marx's exploration of the implications of economic class conflict for history and society. For Gilman, as for Marx, the economy is the basic social institution, the area of physical human work that produces individual and social life and moves society progressively forward. It is through work that individuals potentially realize their species-nature as agentic producers. Our personalities are formed by our actual experiences of work. In her best-known work, the novella *The Yellow Wall-Paper,* written in 1892, six years before her first sociological book, *Women and Economics,* Gilman horrifyingly dramatizes this theme as the female first-person narrator descends into madness because of the inactivity enforced on her by her doctor-husband and relatives, that is, by the sexuo-economic arrangements in society. This understanding of human nature is developed in all of Gilman's sociological writings: meaningful work is the essence of human self-realization; restricting or denying the individual access to meaningful work reduces the individual to a condition of nonhumanity. This is the criterion by which she judges the essential fairness or unfairness of the society in place.

The sexuo-economic arrangement presents just this barrier to self-actualizing work, for both women and men, though for women much more than men. This systemic pollution of the human essence leads not merely to individual unhappiness but to an enormous catalogue of social pathologies: class conflict, political corruption, distorted sexuality, greed, poverty, waste and environmental exploitation, inhuman conditions in both wage labor and unpaid household labor, harmful educational practices, child neglect and abuse, ideological excess, war, and above all, a systemic structural condition of human alienation. Working systematically through this comprehensive and critical theory of society and gender is the project of Gilman's feminist sociology.

Gilman developed this thesis six books of sociological theory in; *Women and Economics* (1898/1966) lays out her basic thesis; *Concerning Children* (1900) presents her theory of child development, socialization, education, gender education, and the essential reforms needed in all these areas; *The Home* (1903) is an exploration of the contemporary household and of the organization of domestic work, with radical, concrete suggestions for the reorganization of this institution, and consequently for both family relations and society; *Human Work* (1904) offers an ambitious assessment of both paid and unpaid human labor and of human alienation and class struggle in contemporary society; *The Man-Made World or Our Androcentric Culture* (1911) traces the ramifications of cultural themes of masculinity and femininity on "family, health and beauty, art, literature, games and sports, ethics and religion, education, society and fashion, law and government, crime and punishment, politics and warfare, and industry and economics" (Ceplair, 1991:189); and *His Religion and Hers* (1923) explores religion as an institution from a consciously feminist sociological viewpoint. In combination, these books give us as comprehensive an analysis of society as any offered by Gilman's male contemporaries—an analysis that traces the complex interaction between materiality and ideas in the sexuo-economic relation.

Origins of Gender Stratification

Central to much of Gilman's work is an exploration of the processes that produce gender stratification. Here she uses evolutionary imagery in much the same way as Engels, for example, in *The Origins of the Family, Private Property, and the State* (1884/1970), develops a mythic prehistory for humankind. But stripped of this imagery, Gilman in fact makes a remarkable claim: *man's domination of woman springs from his need for sociability with or recognition by an Other.* This is an argument with much currency in modern feminism (Benjamin, 1988; Chodorow, 1978; Lengermann and Niebrugge, 1995). Gilman writes in *Women and Economics:*

> [T]he human individual [has] the imperative demand for the establishment of a common consciousness between . . . hitherto irreconcilable individuals. The first step in nature towards this end is found in the relation between mother and child . . . [when] we have the overlapping of personality, the mutual need . . . that holds

> together these interacting personalities. . . . Therefore between the mother and child [is] born . . . the common consciousness . . . mutual attraction. . . . As the male . . . steadily encroaches upon the freedom of the female until she is reduced to the state of . . . dependence . . . [h]e fulfils . . . in his own person the thwarted uses of maternity . . . [the] common interest, existing now not only between mother and child, but between father, mother and child.
>
> (Gilman, 1898/1966:124–125)

Out of this primary though distorted need for sociability or recognition arises male domination and female subordination. "So he instituted the custom of enslaving the female" (Gilman, 1898/1966:60), psychologically bonding with her while increasingly appropriating all economic agency in the relationship and thus all relational control. She, thus, becomes increasingly dependent, increasingly disempowered economically, increasingly maimed in terms of personal growth. Gender will be her only instrument of countervailing power, the wiles of femininity, a focus on sexuality, the fact as well as the ploy of her economic helplessness.

Androcentric Culture

Out of this class arrangement arises masculinity and femininity as pervasive cultural themes—the aggressive, assertive man, the yielding, compliant woman. These structures become deeply embedded in the dailiness of habit and go sociologically unscrutinized because they are assumed to be attributes of the individual person. From birth on, socialization and education inculcate these relational, structural, and stratificational modes, and all of culture conspires to reinforce them through life. Thus the sexuo-economic relation is continuously reproduced by androcentric culture.

Public and Private Spheres

The ramifications of this system are not only psychological and cultural; they profoundly penetrate and distort economic and community life. The sexuo-economic arrangement gives rise to the individual family, the individual mating or married couple, the individual household. Unlike economic class relations, dominants and subordinates in the sexuo-economic system are intimately linked in pairs, each pair isolated in its own "little household." Society can be understood as dividing between the public economy of the marketplace and the private economy of the household. The first is the sphere of manly action, and women are marginal to it. The second is the sphere of women's labor, labor dependent on the economic power of the man. The household is an area of untrained, unprofessional demanding labor, wasteful of the woman, wasteful of society's economic resources in its replication of need from house to house—an area often of unregulated consumption. The market is a place where man's gender power becomes an oppressive economic responsibility for the provision of his household. From this pressure arises a social system encouraging individualism, competition, conflict, class divisions, excessive greed, and wealth hand in hand with crippling exploitation and deprivation. In this pathological system, people wander unguided into whatever occupation comes to hand, and there, trapped by the burden of the household, they remain if they can, "square pegs in round holes," hanging on to security, but in their deep unfulfillment doing second-rate work, and thus reproducing the incompetence, waste, inefficiency, and alienation of the contemporary economy (Gilman, 1904:157–226).

Feminism

The solution to this wasteful sexuo-economic arrangement is to break up the arrangement of the sex classes. The first step to achieving this is the economic emancipation of women—one goal of the women's movement of Gilman's own day, as it is in ours. This goal is not a simple one for Gilman. It requires fundamental changes in gender socialization and in education. It requires the physical development of women to their full size and strength, a rethinking and renegotiation of the personal, relational, and sexual expectations between women and men. But most basically, it requires the rational dismantling and reconstruction of the institution of the household, so that women can have freedom to do the work they choose and so that society may thus be enriched by their labor. In this last strategy, we have Gilman's most novel and problematic approach to a revolution in gender relations. In extraordinary detail she sets herself the project of redesigning domestic space and domestic activity. In Gilman's transformed world of the home, each person will have "a room of their own" and space for association with the family of their choice and construction. Child care, food service, laundry, and household cleaning will be handled professionally by enlightened, well-paid workers, in humane work spaces—and by people who find their calling and their dignity in such work. Surrounding them all—those working in the newly designed domestic spaces, those being reared there, and those coming "home" there from work elsewhere—will be cultural, intellectual, recreational, and health facilities for the new communal lifestyle, paid for by the saving from earlier wasteful domestic drudgery and earlier wasteful marketplace drudgery. This scenario was Gilman's utopia, as communism was Marx's utopia. In its closest real-world realization, perhaps, and on a scale much smaller than Gilman envisioned, this was the organizational form of Jane Addams's Hull House, which we will discuss shortly.

Erasure

Although she did everything that one might expect of a significant sociological theorist in a language, English, that means she has always been accessible to American sociologists, Charlotte Perkins Gilman has been systematically written out of American sociology's construction of its past. Gilman was a member of the American Sociological Society from its foundation in 1895 to her death in 1935. She presented before its annual convention in 1908 and 1909. Her writing is replete with the awareness that she is bringing a sociological consciousness to her work. Her tone is recognizably that of the sociological theorist, for whom theory is her intended project. That theory includes the familiar "markers" of classical sociological theory—comparison with other species (Darwin, Spencer, Park, Mead); an assumption of human societal development (Spencer, Durkheim, Weber, Mead, Park); conditioning social facts (Marx, Durkheim) and interactions (Simmel, Mead, Park); the centrality of economic life (Marx, Weber). The arrangement of these arguments is both sufficiently familiar and sufficiently innovative to distinguish Gilman's work as a distinctive body of theory. It is true that social evolutionary vocabulary permeates many of her statements and that these referents have fallen out of favor, but Spencer, Durkheim, Mead, and Park—even, to a degree, Marx—also weave this vocabulary through their presentations. Together with the explications of her theoretical effort, and its embedded sociological referents, we also have the massive production of her writings, their enormous visibility in her own time, and her explicit engagement with and acknowledgment by the professional sociological communities—both male and female—of her day.

Only a complex process of antiwoman and antifeminist bias explains Gilman's disappearance from the record of sociology and sociological theory. As with all the other women discovered in this chapter, Gilman's gender diminished her authority as a sociological spokesperson in an increasingly male-dominated profession. So too did her women-centered concerns—home, children, sexuality, housework, gender identity, femininity, and masculinity. Moreover, her activist and feminist stance, would make her seem too political and valuational to a field moving rapidly toward a value-neutral stance, a field that by the 1930s would make Weber's "Politics as a Vocation" and "Science as a Vocation" guiding documents. Without a large population of women in the profession or a strong feminist movement in society after 1920, Gilman could be first marginalized and then allowed to disappear. Only with the reversal of both these trends has the work of recovery begun (Deutscher, 2004; Ganobscsik-Williams, 1999; Hill, 2005; Hill and Deegan, 2004; Salinas, 2004; Schaefer, 2004; Squier, 2002; Van Staveren, 2003; Wolosky, 2003).

Jane Addams (1860–1935) and the Chicago Women's School

At the same time that men at the University of Chicago were building what was to become "the Chicago school" (see Chapter 2), the group of women we shall call "the Chicago women's school" were also creating a sociology and a sociological theory. The focal energy in this group was Jane Addams (1860–1935). The women worked out of two bases, the University of Chicago and Hull House, the settlement founded by Jane Addams and Ellen Gates Starr in 1889.

Although connected to the men of the University of Chicago (Deegan, 1988), these women formed their real professional and personal networks with each other (Fitzpatrick, 1990; Gordon, 1994; Muncy, 1991; Rosenberg, 1982). It is hard to overstate the significance of this network for the women personally, for U.S. history in the Progressive Era (1880–1916) and beyond, and for a feminist reconstruction of the history of sociology. This network included women who studied or taught at the University of Chicago and/or who lived as residents or did research instituted by Hull House. Besides Addams, this network included: Edith and Grace Abbott, Sophonisba Breckinridge, Florence Kelley, Frances Kellor, Julia Lathrop, Annie Marion MacLean, Virginia Robinson, Anna Garlin Spencer, Jessie Taft, and Marion Talbot, among others. They were part of a larger women's network described by Gordon (1994), "social innovators" (Scott, 1964) who devised an astounding range of policies and associations to protect subordinate groups as the United States confronted the effects of the Industrial Revolution and its own classist, racist, and sexist politics. Further, this network touched the lives and work of other women discussed in this chapter: Charlotte Perkins Gilman was a resident at Hull House from 1895 to 1896; Marianne Weber visited there, as did Beatrice Potter Webb; Ida B. Wells-Barnett and Jane Addams were partners in the struggle for African-American and women's rights. (To close the circle, we note that Edith Abbott [1906] wrote an article on Harriet Martineau in *The Journal of Political Economy,* and Martineau herself had written a lively description of Chicago as a frontier settlement in 1836.)

The Social Role of the Sociologist

The women of Chicago defined the purpose of sociology and their role as sociologists as the reform and improvement of society. The years from 1890 to 1914 were a golden era for the reform movement of "Progressivism." Inspired by the theories of "reform Social Darwinism," the teaching of the "social gospel" and the philosophy of pragmatism, Progressives sought to take control of the chaotic and exploitative conditions of life created by the interconnected events of the Industrial Revolution, the influx of immigrants and the rise of the cities.

Although battling intense sexism in university and professional life (Deegan, 1988; Fitzpatrick, 1990; Rosenberg, 1982), the women used sociological theory, analysis, and research to win numerous victories for the rights of women and for the Progressive movement. The Chicago women helped lead the fight for women's suffrage, factory legislation, child labor laws, protection of working women, aid for dependent mothers and children, better sanitation in the cities, trade unions, arbitration of labor disputes, minimum wages, and minimum-wage boards. Much of what the women fought for became the stuff of New Deal legislation in the 1930s.

Jane Addams and the women of Chicago were both products and creators of this extraordinary period. What they may have created above all was a tremendous energy born of the faith that something could indeed be done.

Jane Addams (1860–1935)

Jane Addams by her life and example helped create the career possibility of "social activist." Her sociology grew directly out of her social activism, but until about twenty years ago, she was remembered only for her social activism. The work of reclaiming Addams as a sociologist and locating her career in the gender politics of sociology has been done in Mary Jo Deegan's landmark study, *Jane Addams and the Men of the Chicago School* (1988) and extended in Elshtain (2001, 2002, 2008), Forte (2003), Gross, 2009; Hewitt, 2008; Knight, 2006, Lengermann and Niebrugge-Brantley (1998, 2001a, 2002, 2006), Moyers (2003), Ross (1998), Seigfried (1996), and Whipps (2004). Here we focus on Addams's sociological theory.

The Basic Thesis

What distinguishes Addams from the other reformist arguments of early sociologists is her proposition that the particular amelioration that is needed in her time is to create a society based in the practice of a "democratic social ethics," that is, to achieve the democratic transformation of all parts of the society through the inculcation of *social ethics.*

Social ethics is Addams's most original concept and the lynchpin of her theory; it is what united the goal of a society that is democratic in all its relations with the practical action necessary to its achievement. Addams spent much of her career elaborating on the meaning of and the strategies necessary for creating social ethics; here, we offer a starting definition that we will expand on as we explore Addams's theory; in its simplest form, Addams defines social ethics as the practice of rules of right relationship that produce and sustain in the individual an orientation to action based on "concern for the welfare of a community" or "identification with the common lot" (1902/1907: 226, 11).

Methods

In order to understand her theory, we must first understand something about the epistemology and method undergirding it. Addams chose her life's work as an activist and social theorist after a series of experiences of "bifurcated consciousness," the awareness of a division between formal textual descriptions of life and one's own lived experience (Dorothy E. Smith, 1987). For Addams, this bifurcation was in the division between the world seen through literature read in college and a series of glimpses of the real life of the poor as she traveled in Europe after graduation. Addams condemns herself for doing what she felt many women of her class were doing, substituting sentiment and book learning for action. Her sociological theory reflects her attempt to turn herself to life and action and in that attempt she adopts a philosophical pragmatist epistemology—truth emerges through living: "While I may receive valuable suggestions from classic literature, when I really want to learn about life, I must depend upon my neighbors, for, as William James insists, the most instructive human documents live along the beaten pathway" (Addams, 1916:xi). As a pragmatist, Addams values her own experience over textual authority.

Because she "privileges" personal experience over theory, Addams has a distinctive method of doing sociology and creating theory. Her analysis is developed not so much through the crafting of theoretical generalizations as through the presentation of paradigmatic case studies from participant observation and key informants at Hull House and in the city of Chicago. She makes fewer generalizations than do most male theorists, she rarely speaks in their tone of detached objectivity, and her illustrations are strikingly concrete and particular. She illustrates a point not with hypothetical, ahistorical figures, but with detailed accounts of the lives of men and women she has known. Addams seeks something more than *verstehen;* she seeks to establish what contemporary feminist theorists call for in research: an authentic, caring relation between the researcher and the subject of the research. This practice she called "the neighborly relation" as it emerged for her out of her living as a neighbor in the Hull House community. In all her research Addams pursues the issue of *vantage point*—the practice of rendering accounts of social reality from the perspectives of the various individuals involved.

The Organization of Society

Addams develops the central tenet of her sociological theory, the need for a social ethic, on the basis of a series of implicit propositions about the fundamental organization of society, human nature, and social change. Addams envisions society as a vast network of

Jane Addams

A Biographical Sketch

Jane Addams, though often trivialized in popular schooling as an ever-beloved "Lady Bountiful," was a deeply thoughtful, ethically committed person, of only modest personal wealth, who genuinely tried to love her neighbors, and who in her lifetime both was on the FBI's list of "most dangerous radicals" (during the 1920s "Red Scare") and won the Nobel Peace Prize (in 1931).

Born in Cedarville, Illinois, on September 6, 1860, into a family involved in both business and politics, she attended Rockford Seminary, where she began some serious spiritual thinking and excelled academically, graduating as valedictorian in 1881.

The years from 1881 to 1888, when she at last settled on the plan that would become Hull House, were difficult ones—marked by her father's death, her own illness, and illness in her family which demanded her attention. Worse though, she found that she did not know what to do with her life; she had leisure but not purpose. In her travels in Europe, she gradually formed the conviction that she should try to imitate the settlement experiment she had seen in London.

In 1889, she and Ellen Gates Starr arranged to rent Hull House on Halsted Street in Chicago's nineteenth ward, an area of impoverished working-class immigrants. Their plan, which Addams recounts in *Twenty Years at Hull-House* (1910/1990), was to try to learn and help by living simply as neighbors among the poor. Addams showed a remarkable ability to do just that. Hull House attracted

individual human beings coming together to realize both material interests and ethical ideals. This network takes form in a variety of diverse and not necessarily analytically parallel structures—family, household, neighborhood, industry, education, war and peace, philanthropy, recreation, art. Her interest is not in establishing the appropriate analytic categories to name these structures—"institutions," "organizations," "processes"—but in seeing how to make them all possess certain common qualities—qualities of social democracy—that she assumes that evolution now demands.

Human Nature and Ethics She understands the human being to be an embodied subjectivity, that is, a mind capable of reason and emotion, in a body that materially experiences the world. The democratic social ideal rests in the recognition of the independent agentic subjectivity of this embodied subject. This capacity of the individual subjectivity to hold to her or his own will or sense of the world has been, Addams other "residents," mainly educated young women who wanted to put their education to use. Collectively they embarked upon a range of social experiments including social clubs, garbage collection, apartments for working women, consumer cooperatives, evening classes, trade unions, industrial reform legislation, investigations of working conditions, debating societies, and interventions in strikes, solutions to unemployment, and platforms for Hull House debates). Hull House became identified in the public mind of Addams's own day not simply with good works but with radical thought and change. This identification was all but sealed when Addams held to her commitment to pacifism during the patriotic fervor of World War I.

Following the pragmatic creed of testing the truth of ideas by experience, Addams drew on her Hull House work to develop a sociological theory based on the conviction that people had now to begin to work collectively and cooperatively—which meant learning to tolerate differences. She traces the need for cooperation and growth in understanding in a series of books and articles, among the most important of which are *Twenty Years at Hull-House* (1910), *Democracy and Social Ethics* (1902/1907), *Newer Ideals of Peace* (1907), *The Long Road of Woman's Memory* (1916), *Peace and Bread in Times of War* (1922), and *The Second Twenty Years at Hull-House* (1930).

Her most noted personal quality—her ability to understand another person's position without necessarily agreeing with it and to communicate that understanding—may also be the quality that most emerges for the feminist reader of her sociology. Her long-time friend Emily Greene Balch remembers Addams's special concern with vantage point: "Significant of her relation to her Halsted Street neighbors is the habit that she had when she made a speech about Hull House of taking one of them with her so that they all knew that when Hull House was described to important people downtown it sounded exactly like Hull House as they knew it" (1941/1972:206). Jane Addams died on May 21, 1935.

argues, too little realized in social thought. She criticizes the "first type of humanitarian who loves the people without really knowing them . . . and expects the people whom he does not know to forswear altogether the right of going their own way, and to be convinced of the beauty and value of his way" (Addams, 1905:425–426). Drawing on her Hull House experience, Addams argues that a democracy cannot be built by people who expect other people to "see the light," that such demands for change are grounded in a lack of respect for the vantage point of the other.

Further, she conceives of human subjectivity as a complex of reason and emotion, especially the emotion of kindness. On the basis of this understanding of human nature, Addams rests her argument that ethical systems are a foundational feature of social life. She sees reason and emotion working together, manifesting themselves in the coexistence in the individual of rational judgment and sympathy. All people, no matter how materially hard-pressed, desire "an outlet for more kindliness," seek "to do a favor for a friend," to find expression for that "kindheartedness [that] lies in ambush to incorporate itself in our larger relations," hoping that "it shall be given some form of governmental expression" (Addams, 1907:2–3). Addams describes this desire as what the French mean in the "phrase *l'imperieuse bonté* by which they designate those impulses towards compassionate conduct which will not be denied" (1907:21). The idea of human beings desiring sociality is well developed in sociology in the theories of Simmel, Mead, W. I. Thomas, and Park. But the extension of this desire into a description of an embodied person who actively seeks to be in right or ethical relation with others is Addams's distinctive contribution.

Social Production and Ethics The human being is located in a society that is always evolving or changing, but this process of change is one that humans must now control through the collective exercise of mind. Change does not necessarily proceed at the same pace in all parts of society; many social problems are the result of a disjunction between the rate and type of change in one part and those of another—a disjunction that Addams and other women of Chicago speak of as "belatedness." Although Addams sees that industrial change is currently forcing adjustments in other areas of social life, she does not accept that the material base always determines the pace and direction of change. Rather, she sees materiality and ideas as mutually interdependent; ethical systems must be aligned with the social relations of production, but will in turn determine the forms of those relations. She explains social tensions much less in terms of class conflict than of people caught in processes of change that they have not yet brought into alignment.

The Social Ethic

Addams finds herself at a moment in history when humans must, by the invention of new means of association, realize the democratic social ethic.

> [W]e are . . . brought to a conception of Democracy not merely as a sentiment which desires the well-being of all men, nor yet as a creed which believes in the essential dignity and equality of all men, but as that which affords a rule of living as well as a test of faith. . . . To attain individual morality in an age demanding social morality, to pride oneself on the results of personal effort when the time demands social adjustment, is utterly to fail to apprehend the situation.
>
> (Addams, 1902/1907:2–3, 6)

A democratic social ethic would be based on the facts, revealed in one's own experience, that (1) no "one set of people are of so much less importance than another, that a valuable side of life pertaining to them should be sacrificed for the other" (Addams, 1902/1907:124); (2) that all people may be active agents, not simply included in the hopes of some elite but themselves actively hoping, planning, participating, thinking; (3) that as active agents all people seek opportunities to enact the imperative to kindliness which has evolved in humanity, and (4) that the personal safety of all members of the democratic social unit is tied to the personal safety of each.

Much of Addams's sociological theory is devoted to analyzing how to transform democracy from a political creed, enacted occasionally in elections, into a social creed informing all human interactions. One problem is that people cling to belated ethics that are misaligned or inappropriate to the organization of material production that Addams sees as characterized above all by "the discovery of the power to combine" (1895:183).

Belated Ethics The belated ethic of individualism shows itself in the insistence of owners on keeping absolute control of production processes, enforcing specialization on the workers and refusing to share organizational control with them. "The division of labor" instituted by the factory owner "robs" the workers of a common and shared interest in their work and leaves only "the mere mechanical fact of interdependence" (Addams, 1902/1907:211). This alienation can be overcome only by an industrial democracy that allows workers to participate in the organization of production.

Within the household and family, the belated ethic of the family claim restricts women's sense of ethical responsibility for the larger society, leading them to feel ethically adequate even when they exploit their domestic help so long as the needs of their family and immediate circle of friends are addressed. Addams's arguments for women's suffrage turn not upon any assertion of natural rights (an assertion she felt assumed a fixed rather than an evolving human nature), but upon her understanding that changes in the organization of society brought new duties and required new ethics. The dominant fact of her age—the growth in size and complexity of human relationships—meant that women could no longer live within the narrow confines of the family claim. Indeed, if they were to take care of their families in this new world, they must assume a social ethic, which meant taking responsibility for the welfare of the whole community to which they were now irrevocably attached.

Situated Vantage Points In establishing the social ethic a second problem is that the practice depends upon an ability to take the vantage point of the other. A recurring theme in the narratives Addams used to present her social theory is the clash of standpoints: the failure of an elite class to understand the real and valuable ethics of the poor, the lack of a general ethic that understands the world of multiple viewpoints, the difference between "organized" charity and neighborly outreach.

> Let us take a neighborhood of poor people, and test their ethical standards by those of the charity visitor. . . . A most striking incongruity, at once apparent, is the difference between the emotional kindness with which relief is given by one poor neighbor, and the guarded care with which relief is given by the charity visitor to the charity recipient. The neighborhood mind is at once confronted not only by the difference of method, but by an absolute clashing of two ethical standards.
>
> (Addams, 1902/1907:20–21)

Learning the Social Ethic Addams offers three strategies for establishing democratic social ethics as the necessary complement to industrialization. One, people can be taught the legitimacy of the social claim through formal education if the educational system is reformed, along lines suggested by Dewey (a frequent Hull House visitor), to "give the child's own social experience a value" (Addams, 1902/1907:180). But the schools often fail to teach this principle of "connectedness" because "the same tendency to division of labor has also produced over-specialization in scholarship, with the sad result that . . . the scholar . . . cannot bring healing and solace because he himself is suffering from the same disease" (Addams, 1902/1907:206).

A second way for people to learn democracy as a way of relating is through constant and varied experiences of social interaction; people learn to work together by working together. People can change old habits and develop new norms and sensibilities through social interaction "not so much by the teaching of moral theorems [but] by the direct expression of social sentiments and by the cultivation of practical habits" (Addams, 1907:8). Hull House, trade unions, labor arbitration, social clubs, debating societies, elections, government committees, and neighborhood organizations are for Addams all avenues for the direct expression of social sentiments and the cultivation of practical habits of social interaction.

A third way Addams sees change occurring is in individuals' "memory"—or reflection shared and retold with others. In *The Long Road of Woman's Memory* (1916), Addams links women's memory, or individual subjectivity, and social change, arguing that memory is used in two different but often complementary ways: for "interpreting and appeasing life for the individual" and as "a selective agency in social reorganization" (Addams, 1916:xi). People often remember events of their lives in ways that lead them to react against conventions or to reinterpret their part in historic changes so as to experience their own connectedness. *The Long Road of Woman's Memory* contains some of Addams's most persuasive case histories. Through these histories, Addams argues that memory may be a kind of consciousness-raising in which people realign themselves with the larger impersonal forces that have shaped their lives and in that realignment prepare the way for social change.

The Chicago Women's School

Addams's core belief—that society needs not individual but collective action realized in democratic association—is clearly visible in the relationships, work, and sociology of the circle we have called "the Chicago women's school": Edith and Grace Abbott, Sophonisba Breckinridge, Florence Kelley, Frances Kellor, Julia Lathrop, Annie Marion MacLean, Virginia Robinson, Anna Garlin Spencer, Jessie Taft, and Marion Talbot, among others. It is possible, as Gordon (1994) has documented, to see these women as clannish and inbred, but it is also possible to see this network of women possessing, as both Gordon (1994:70) and Costin (1983:100) quote, what Supreme Court Justice Felix Frankfurter described as "'a rare degree of disinterestedness and indifference to the share of [their] own ego in the cosmos.'" A recovery of these women as sociologists is as yet only partial (Clark and Foster 2006; Dauder, 2008; Gi-Juarez, 2008; Hallett and Joffers, 2008; Lengermann and Niebrugge-Brantley, 1998/2007; Timming, 2004).

The Organization of Society and Social Role of the Sociologist

Four major propositions frame their sociological theory. First, the fundamental organizational principle of modern society is the interdependence of human beings and of the structures in which they come together. One cannot separately analyze industry, family, neighborhood, education, recreation, municipal government, and so on. Every person and activity potentially relates to every other. Everything that happens potentially affects women's lives, and women must find ways to exercise greater power. Second, people must now act collectively to shape the environment and direct future human development, a proposition that turns on an understanding of the human being as an agentic moral agent. The world is evolving not by the action of some invisible law but through the efforts of men and women. These efforts, heretofore uncoordinated, now require that people become inventive in forms of association and in the formulation of state policies as one means for the enactment of the collective will. Third, the groups most affected by change and the failures to control change are the socially disenfranchised: women, children, the elderly poor, immigrants, African Americans, and working-class and poor people in general. This proposition reflects a basic critical position of "equity," that is, that all people are entitled to a fair share of society's goods. Fourth, the role of the social scientist is to give people the tools for understanding and action by presenting facts about social conditions, plans for associations, and proposals for state policies. Besides conducting research, the Chicago women helped found the Urban League, the National Consumers League, the National Association for the Advancement of Colored People, the National Federation of Women's Clubs, the Association of College Alumnae (later to be the American Association of University Women), and other associations for social amelioration.

Methods

Perhaps because they reinforced each other in this view of society, certainly because they were philosophic pragmatists, their sociological theory came to focus on those epistemological issues typically denoted as methodology. One of their great sociological innovations is the methods they designed for studying and publicizing a problem—indeed, they were inventors of "social problems," in the sense that they took situations that most people took for granted as unavoidable and redefined them as subject to social control, social improvement, and social elimination. In presenting the taken-for-granted as a social problem, these women invented an array of techniques for discovering and reporting their evidence using both primary and secondary quantitative and qualitative data sources—personal and historic documents, statistical tables, maps of demographic traits, interviews, key informants, participant observations, and photographs. Good examples of the use of multiple research strategies are Edith Abbott's *Women in Industry* (1910) and *The Tenements of Chicago* (1936/1970), Sophonisba Breckinridge's *New Homes for Old* (1921/1971), Frances Kellor's *Out of Work* (1905/1915), and *Hull-House Maps and Papers* (1895), compiled under the general direction of Florence Kelley. Probably the first published report of sociological participant observation is Annie Marion MacLean's "Two Weeks in Department Stores," in *The American Journal of Sociology,* May 1899, which illustrates the Chicago women's attention to methodology, their emphasis on empirical data, their commitment to fostering social change, and their interconnectedness as thinkers and researchers. MacLean undertook this research as part of the work of the new Consumers' League of Illinois, "organized by the collegiate alumnae" of Chicago as an early attempt to get consumers to use their power to improve working conditions for women and children. MacLean introduces her purpose:

> The necessity for a thorough investigation of the work of women and children in the large department stores in the city was apparent and the difficulties manifold. With a view to ascertaining some things which could be learned only from the inside, . . . [i]t seemed evident that valuable information could be obtained if someone were willing to endure the hardships of the saleswoman's life, and from personal experience be able to pass judgment upon observed conditions. [This] led me to join the ranks of the retail clerks for two weeks during the rush of the holiday trade.
>
> (MacLean, 1899:721–722)

Collective Action and Social Change

The most daring explorations of collective action may have been done by Florence Kelley (1859–1932), who in 1887 published both the first English translation of Engels's *The Conditions of the Working Class in England in 1844* and a remarkable work of her own, "The Need for Theoretical Preparation for Philanthropic Work." The theoretical preparation Kelley proposes is the application of Marxist theory to philanthropy. In this essay, which she first presented at a meeting of the New York chapter of the Association of Collegiate Alumnae, Kelley argues that all bourgeois philanthropy, no matter how well intended, is really only a palliative, a restitution to the working class, the real creators of wealth, of what has been taken from them. She presents an absolute statement of class conflict, describing a "division of society into two warring classes," producing two different kinds of philanthropy, bourgeois and proletarian.

> Our bourgeois philanthropy, whatever form it may take, is really only the effort to give back to the workers a little bit of that which our whole social system, systematically, robs them of, and so to prop up that system yet a little longer. . . . It is the workers who produce all values; but the lion's share of what they produce falls to the lion—the capitalist class. . . . [F]or the capitalist class as a whole, all philanthropic effort is a work of restitution for self-preservation.
>
> (Kelley, 1887/1986:94)

Settling into work at Hull House, Kelley became Chief Inspector of Factories under the reform Illinois Factory and Workshop Inspection Law of 1893. She fought its gutting by the Illinois Supreme Court until she was replaced by the next governor for a too vigorous enforcement. Her analysis of this and other attempts at reform legislation are offered in *Some Ethical Gains through Legislation* (1905/1969).

Momentarily defeated in terms of state policies, Kelley turned her attention to the possibility of voluntary associations bringing about changes in industrial organization. By the end of 1899, she published in *The American Journal of Sociology* "Aims and Principles of the Consumers' League." Here Kelley attempts to give consciousness to a new social category, "consumers." She will call consumers into being as a conscious social aggregate to redress the balance between capital and labor, which the state seems impotent or unwilling to do.

> [T]hroughout our lives we are choosing, or choice is made for us, as to the disposal of money. . . . As we [make these choices], we help to decide, however unconsciously,

> how our fellow-men shall spend their time in making what we buy. . . . Those of us who enjoy the privilege of voting may help, once or twice in a year. . . . But all of us, all the time, are deciding by our expenditures what industries shall survive at all, and under what conditions. Broadly stated, it is the aim of the National Consumers' League to moralize this decision, to gather and make available information which may enable us all to decide in the light of knowledge, and to appeal to the consciences, so that the decision when made shall be a righteous one.
>
> (Kelley, 1899:289–290)

The essential principles of the sociology of the Chicago women are all in this statement: that social science must act for change; that all citizens, including women still denied suffrage, are nevertheless morally responsible for the welfare of the country; that every action ties a person to other people; that effective personal virtue today must be done through associations because it is only in associations that people can gain the knowledge and the power to make their individual action truly "righteous"—that is, both democratic and effective.

Anna Julia Cooper (1859–1964) and Ida Wells-Barnett (1862–1931)

Anna Julia Cooper and Ida Wells-Barnett were African American women of the same generation as Gilman, Addams, and many of the Chicago women sociologists discussed in the previous section. Their ideas are being incorporated into classical sociological theory by contemporary feminist sociologists (Broschart, 1991b; P. Collins, 1990; Deegan, 1991) and by sociologists and others influenced by feminism (Bailey, 2004; Glass, 2005; Lemert, 1995, 1999; Lemert and Bhan, 1998; May, 2004, Schechter 2001). Though possibly neither Cooper nor Wells-Barnett self-identified herself as a sociologist, both women worked out of an explicitly acknowledged sociological orientation. Wells-Barnett opens her empirical study of lynching, *A Red Record,* with a claim to a sociological perspective:

> The student of American sociology will find the year 1894 marked by a pronounced awakening of the public conscience to a system of anarchy and outlawry which had grown up during [the past] ten years.
>
> (Wells-Barnett, 1894/1969:7)

Cooper, in her best-known book, *A Voice from the South* (1892), discusses Comte and Spencer and presents her most general principle of societal organization as a sociological one:

> This . . . law holds good in sociology as in the world of matter, *that equilibrium, not repression among conflicting forces is the condition of natural harmony, of permanent progress, and of universal freedom.*
>
> (Cooper, 1892/1969:160)

Cooper and Wells-Barnett both consciously drew on their lived experiences as African American women to develop a "systematic consciousness of society and social relations." They lay the foundation for a feminist sociological theory based in the interests of women of color.

Anna Julia Cooper & Ida Wells-Barnett

Biographical Sketches

Anna Julia Hayward Cooper was born a slave in Raleigh, North Carolina, in 1859, to a slave mother and to a master whom, she presumed, was also her father. Freed by the Emancipation Proclamation of 1863, and apparently of extraordinary intellectual ability, she battled racism, sexism, and limited finances all her life in pursuit of an education. By age nine she was working as a "pupil-teacher" at St. Augustine's Normal and Collegiate Institute, an Episcopal freedman's school for African Americans, where she was one of a very few female students. She worked her way, as a student-tutor, through Oberlin College in the 1880s—Oberlin being one of the very few white colleges to admit blacks—earning her bachelor's degree in 1884 and an honorary master's degree in 1887. Supporting herself all her life as a teacher, she taught for forty years in the Washington, D.C., school system, where from 1901 to 1906 she served as principal of the M Street High School (later Dunbar High School), the second black woman principal in the school's history. From that base, she actively fought racism on behalf of her students and herself, lectured widely, and in 1892 published *A Voice from the South by a Black Woman from the South,* the primary statement of her sociological views. Studying at Columbia University and at the Sorbonne, in Paris, during summer breaks and various leaves of absence, she completed the work for her doctoral degree from the Sorbonne in 1925, defending her dissertation and accepting her degree at age 65. Her dissertation, *Slavery and the French Revolutionists 1788–1805,* was written in French (she was a gifted linguist) and has been available in English only since 1988. These two works, which show Cooper to be a significant sociological theorist of race and society both in the United States and globally, form the basis of our discussion here.

Ida Wells-Barnett was born to slave parents in Holly Springs, Mississippi, in 1862. After supporting her orphaned siblings as a teacher from 1878 to 1883, she moved to Memphis in 1883, where she studied at both Fiske and LeMoyne Institute. A lifelong activist on behalf of African American and women's rights, she worked primarily as a journalist, initiating a one-woman campaign against lynching in 1883 with a series of publications that present a detailed empirical study of that horrific practice of racial terrorism. That campaign would build into a national and international protest. Living in Chicago for most of her adult life, Wells-Barnett was well acquainted with Jane Addams, Hull House, and the activist social-science work of that institution (Wells-Barnett, 1970). A prominent figure in the women's-club movement of this period, Wells-Barnett helped found the National Association of Colored Women, the National Afro-American Council, and the National Association for the Advancement of Colored People. Her writings on lynching were compiled in 1969 into a single volume, *On Lynchings* (1894/1969).

Methods

Ida Wells-Barnett was primarily a researcher whose theory of society is implicit in her research. This research is sociological and inventive. It uses statistics, interviews, and secondary accounts to describe the lynching of African Americans that became epidemic in the southern United States during the 1890s (and continued into the 1930s) and to analyze the causes of this development. Wells-Barnett's method is a pioneering adaptation of secondary data analysis that uses the oppressor's own reports as the main source. She builds her analysis on white newspaper reports of lynchings in an effort to protect herself from the charge of distorting her research. She then "deconstructs" those reports to find their underlying themes of domination and oppression.

Cooper, in contrast, is explicitly engaged in theoretical work. She seeks to describe the patterns of social life and to situate herself in that work of theoretical creation. Although her theory of societal organization is more extensively developed than Wells-Barnett's, Cooper also uses the oppressor's own texts—statistics, popular literature, and historical records—as a key database.

The Lens of Race Relations

Groups and Power

In the social theory of both Cooper and Wells-Barnett, power is the fundamental relation of social life. They understood that power can range from manipulation to unqualified physical oppression and that power resources can include coercion, material advantage, ideology, interactional norms, communication—and pure passion, the will to dominate.

Cooper and Wells-Barnett base this theory of power on their understanding of race relations. Cooper writes:

> Black slavery was an institution founded solely on the abuse of power. In all aspects created by a barbarous and shortsighted politics, and maintained by violence. . . . [I]t was done without pretext and without excuse. And only in the name of the right of the strongest.
>
> (Cooper, 1925/1988:131)

And in a more concrete and journalistic style, Wells-Barnett would say of lynching, "The more I studied the situation the more I was convinced that the Southerner had never gotten over his resentment that the Negro was no longer his plaything, his servant, and his source of income" (Wells-Barnett, 1970:10). Race, then, is at the center of both women's social theories; the power relations between whites and blacks in Western history and contemporary American society give them their paradigm of domination and of stratification. In this insistence that domination, inequality, and injustice are structurally pervasive in modern society, Cooper and Wells-Barnett differ from the white women sociologists of their day, all of whom, even the radical feminist Gilman, blur the issue of domination in themes about evolution and progress.

Intersections: Race, Gender, Class

Using race relations as a lens on oppression and stratification, both Cooper and Wells-Barnett explore other social practices of stratification. Cooper analyzes gender inequality between white women and men and between African American women and men (1892/1969:9–149). And she explores the complex interplay of race and gender through her own embodied experience in society. She analyzes a moment when, traveling by train, she arrived at a shabby railway station and looked for a bathroom: "I see two dingy little rooms with 'For Ladies' swinging over one and 'For Colored People' over the other, while wondering under which head I come" (1892/1969:96). More generally, she writes, "The colored woman today occupies . . . a unique position. . . . She is confronted by both a woman question and a race problem, and is as yet an unknown or unacknowledged factor in both" (1892/1969:134).

Wells-Barnett looks at an even more explosive interaction of race and gender, exploring the interplay of those issues around sexuality. She dissolves the rationale for the lynching of black men offered by white society, the myth that the victim has raped a white woman. She provides case studies of the emotional/sexual attraction between white women and black men as a normal part of social relations in the South and of the attraction of white men to black women. The former is so taboo a possibility that when it occurs it is labeled rape and leads to lynching. The latter is so condoned and unreprimanded, no matter how resisted by black women, that it has resulted in "the many shades of the race." Wells-Barnett's Memphis newspaper was burned to the ground and her life threatened for opening up this topic in the 1890s.

Both women further expand the theme of social inequality to class relations. Cooper describes the relation between capitalists and labor (her terms) in modern society, the interpolation of class and race in both urban and rural America, the internal economic and status divisions in the African American population, the interaction of class and race in educated women's circles, shade stratification in the societies of the Caribbean, and status differences among African American women. Wells-Barnett traces social class tensions in the women's club movement of her day and in Great Britain, to which she traveled as part of her antilynching campaign. She also locates some of the problems of lynching in the class/race nexus: "Lynching was an excuse to get rid of Negroes who were acquiring wealth and property and thus 'keep the nigger down'" (Wells-Barnett, 1970:64). Finally, both women understand that domination, inequality, and race conflict are not only issues in the various nation-states of the West, but a process in the "global order" of capitalism. Wells-Barnett discusses the situation of Indians in Britain in the heyday of the British Empire. Cooper's dissertation (1925/1988) focuses on the contradiction between black enslavement as an economic "resource" for eighteenth-century capitalist economies and the democratic aspiration of white, bourgeois revolutionists. Slavery gave the lie to the democratic revolutionary claims of the French (and supposedly the American) Revolution and resulted in the defeat of white lower- and working-class aspirations in those revolutions.

The Organization of Society

From this systematic grasp of domination and inequality, Cooper develops both a theory of social organization and an epistemology for her project of social critique. Society she sees as a system—of institutions such as economy, family, education and religion; of stratificational groupings resulting from class, race, and gender distinctions and from their parallel as well as overlapping dynamics; and of cultural aspirations and themes. She gives serious attention to the cultural themes of masculinity and femininity and to the outcome of those themes for personality and for societal functioning. Order in this system may take two forms. It may result from domination and oppression, the situation in much of the contemporary world, or it may result from "equilibrium," a dynamic and competitive interdependence between all sectors of a society. Her criterion for a critical evaluation of society is whether it is characterized by equilibrium or domination, not that it is free of conflict.

Vantage Point and "the Singing Something"

Epistemologically, Cooper presents us with an argument that resonates with that of contemporary African-American feminism. She will insert herself into sociological analysis by speaking from her distinctive vantage point as a black woman—the claim for which she is best known (Alexander, 1995; Giddings, 1984; Harley, 1978). "The 'other side' has not been represented by one who 'lives there.' And not many can more sensibly . . . tell the weight and the fret of the 'long dull pain' than the open-eyed but still voiceless Black woman. . . ." (Cooper, 1892/1969:i, ii, 31). This claim of vantage point is based in Cooper's understanding of human nature, an understanding she shares with Wells-Barnett, which emphasizes above all the human being as possessed of "that *Singing* Something, which distinguished the first man from the last ape, which in a subtle way tagged him with the picturesque Greek title *anthropos,* the *upward face*" (Cooper, 1925/1998:293), that is, as a being whose species nature contains the possibility of rising in aspiration out of the most degrading and oppressive circumstances.

Marianne Schnitger Weber (1870–1954)

Marianne Weber is known in American sociology solely through her biography of her husband, *Max Weber: A Biography* (1926/1975; see Chapter 8). Her self-portrait there is of the dutiful, uncritical, self-effacing Victorian wife, hovering on the edge of the grand life and figure of Max Weber. Perhaps this depiction amused her, for it hides much of the truth of her life. She was among the first generation of German women formally admitted for university study (Roth, 1990:67). Her studies were in the general area of social science. After Max's nervous breakdown in 1897 and his retreat to a semireclusive life, Marianne became the public figure in the marriage, building her reputation as a feminist scholar and public speaker. She published her first book on the relationship of Fichte and Marx in 1900, her first journal article "Politics and the Woman's Movement" in 1901, and over the next thirty-five years eight books and dozens of articles in sociology and on feminist issues. In 1918, German women won the vote, and in 1919, Marianne became the first female member of parliament for Baden. In 1920, the year of Max's death, she was president of the Federation of German Women's Organizations, Germany's most powerful feminist organization. In 1924 she was granted an honorary doctorate in law by Heidelberg University "in recognition of her legal study and editorial work" (Kippenberg, 2005; Roth, 1990:66).

It is part of the gender politics of sociology that until recently none of Marianne Weber's writings had been translated into English except her biography of Max, and we can glean only a few details of her sociological work from brief English discussions of her, which frequently lack an appropriate framing in feminist sociology (Britton, 1979; Hackett, 1976; Kandal, 1988; Roth, 1990, 2005; Scaff, 1988; J. Thomas, 1985; Tijssen, 1991; Whimster, 2005b; Wobbe, 2004). In 1998, the first essays from her 1919 collection, *Reflections on Women and Women's Issues,* became available in English (see translation by Elizabeth Kirchen in Lengermann and Niebrugge-Brantley, 1998). From these materials, we can see that she wrote as a feminist social theorist who drew on and responded critically to the theories of Simmel, Max Weber, Marx and Engels, and feminist writers such as Charlotte Perkins Gilman, whom we discussed earlier in this chapter.

The Stand Point of Women

Marianne Weber's social theory grounds an understanding of the fundamental organization of society in an understanding of the human being, and both of these are seen through her self-defined role as a feminist sociologist. She sees the human being, in the tradition of German Idealism, as an individual who wants to control his or her own destiny and to become all he or she is created capable of becoming. This gives her the critical lens through which she evaluates society: how well do social structures make such self-fulfillment a possibility for women as well as for men?

These understandings lead Marianne Weber to her central theoretical project, the creation of a sociology from the standpoint of women. She claims that there is a distinctive women's standpoint. She partly defines this standpoint by contrasting women's experiences and understandings with men's—of marriage, public and household life, the importance of housework, power and other relational arrangements, ethics, and war. She develops three major themes around this central concern: the need for an autonomy for women equal to that of men (a debate with Max); the significance of women's work in the production of culture (a debate with Simmel); the situated differences of standpoint among women (a debate partially with Gilman). Marianne Weber uses legal research, historical data, and statistical data as empirical bases for her theoretical arguments.

Gender and Power: Authority is Autonomy

In the work that established her as a leading feminist scholar, *Ehefrau und Mutter in der Rechtsentwicklung* ("Marriage and Motherhood in the Development of Law") (1907), and her 1912 essay presenting a formal conceptualization of some of its major arguments, "Authority and Autonomy in Marriage," Marianne Weber brings a woman-centered perspective to bear on Max Weber's famous typology of power. For women, she argues, in their experiences of masculine domination within marriage, the key distinction is not between legitimate power (authority) and illegitimate power (coercion). Because all societies have framed marriage relations with law, all legal power relations between husband and wife are culturally legitimate. But over the long course of Western history, which she chronicles in detail, men have transformed law and culture in the direction of greater individual autonomy for themselves, greater possibilities for freedom in self-definition. The tension then may be construed not as one between coercion and authority but as one between autonomy and domination, between a free exercise of one's will in action and subordinating one's will to another. While men have changed law and culture to gain such autonomy, they have skillfully contrived to keep the family patriarchal, their "authority" perhaps softened a little but essentially intact; women continue to experience this relationship of male "authority" as one that denies them autonomous action and will. Weber explores legal, normative, and cultural changes that might lead to a transformation of marriage into one of a bond between independent actors, something she regards as a difficult achievement (Marianne Weber 1912a/1919/1998). In her later book, *Women and Love* (1935), she explores conventional and unconventional ways in which women may find the love they typically seek through marriage—the latter include relationships between younger men and older women, between women, and the sublimated ideal of public service. All these are alternatives to the structure of conventional marriage.[2]

Gender and Culture: Objective Culture, Personal Culture, and 'The Middle Ground of Daily Life'

Continuing her exploration of structural conditions for autonomy, Marianne rebuts Georg Simmel's (Chapter 9) sociology of gender in which he idealizes women's distinct and spiritual nature and suggests the existence of two distinctive spheres of culture: the "objective" or male world of public achievement and the "personal" or female world of inner self development (Oakes, 1984; Tijssen, 1991). Weber begins very practically by pointing out that there is much about women's work in the household that is not spiritual but intensely practical, instrumental, and objective. She then moves to suggest that women's work in the home constitutes a third realm of culture production, which she calls "the middle ground of immediate daily life," in which the individual person is constructed and reproduced as a social being capable of sympathetic and intelligent responses to others. She questions Simmel's assumption of distinctively male and female natures, arguing that although one can discern some typical differences between the two genders, individuals within each gender vary too much to support the assumption of separate natures. She concludes that it is more useful to think of a common nature and of typical maleness and femaleness as circles intersecting within the common space. This idea allows one to think of women developing their autonomy more fully, men their capacities for caring, and individuals of each gender moving as freely between public and private culture as they individually choose (Marianne Weber, 1918–19/1998).

Differences Among Women

But she also sees that there are differences among women in standpoint because of social-class stratification. This theme is developed in "Jobs and Marriage" (1905/1919)

---

[2]Our discussion also draws on initial aid in translation by C. Joanna Sheldon of Ithaca, New York, to whom we express our deepest appreciation for her help.

and "The Valuation of Housework" (1912/1919b/1998), in which she grounds her theory of women's standpoint in her sociological understanding of societal organization, social class stratification, and the data of the German census. She contrasts the life experiences of women in agricultural work, paid domestic employment, factory work, and professional employment. She points out that much of women's "professional" work is relatively low status (61 percent of this category are midwives). Only a small fraction (2 percent) of professional women in Germany hold the high-status, self-actualizing jobs that she sees the women's movement depicting as the ideal for women's workplace participation. Yet the standpoint of the spokespersons of this movement is in this tiny privileged group. Weber argues that it is absurd to speak from this standpoint about the reforms needed in all women's home and work lives. She chides her "American sister in struggle" Gilman for succumbing to this totalizing error.

The interaction of capitalism and patriarchy creates barriers to the attempts of women, especially non-elite women, to seek greater liberty and autonomy. Capitalistic work arrangements doom most women to wage-sector work that is typically exhausting, onerous, and grossly underpaid—and an experience of meaninglessness and alienation. Indeed, most working women have not chosen to work outside the home but have been forced by capitalistic and class pressures to seek wages, however small. Working women bear the double burden of wage-work demands and unaltered expectations that they are fully responsible for child care and housework. Under these conditions, working-class women's lives are little improved by wage-sector involvement. Nor does Weber romanticize the home situations of women as an alternative to wage work. She sees that housework for most women is an area of incessant drudgery, that women who stay at home, whatever their class, are oppressed by economic dependency and by patriarchal male authority.

Social Change

Only fundamental reform holds any hope for women's escape from these two sites of oppression. Weber discusses legal reforms such as spousal rights, job training for women as a route to better employment and more meaningful lives, and, most radical of all, various formulae that would provide monetary independence for the housewife.

She sees that capitalism may offer some emancipation for women in its acceleration of individualism and its erosion of ancient relational patterns like patriarchy (J. Thomas, 1985). But her position is that to improve women's situation one should begin by reforming the patriarchal household rather than the capitalistic workplace. A reformed, that is, nonpatriarchal household, is one setting in which women can find vocation and self-actualization. Weber's acute consciousness of women's varied vantage points, however, leads her also to recommend the pursuit of a public career, either paid or voluntary, as another avenue to self-actualization for some women.

The exploration of Marianne Weber's theory is currently under way. What is apparent is that she is a significant contributor to an international effort by women sociologists to create a feminist sociological theory in the classic period of sociology's history.

Beatrice Potter Webb (1858–1943)

Beatrice Potter Webb was an amalgam of contradictions—a woman born to extreme wealth, she was nevertheless "self-made"; a member of the British upper class, she devoted herself as a sociologist and theorist to the problems of "poverty amidst riches" (1926:209); a student and lifelong friend of Herbert Spencer, she became a leading British socialist; a solid empiricist, she is nevertheless moved to her descriptive and analytic studies by what she calls "a consciousness of sin" (1926:167). Webb's father, Richard Potter, was a wealthy industrialist who made his living in railroad speculation; her mother, Laurencina, was a close friend of Spencer, a frequent visitor to the Potter household. Webb grew to maturity just before women began to be admitted to British universities and was largely self-educated through reading, travels with her father, conversation with Spencer, and reflection in her voluminous personal diaries. Two paths were primarily open to her as a member of her class, generation, and gender—a "suitable" marriage or good works; she chose neither. She chose instead to become what she describes as "a female brain worker" (in contrast to a manual worker), a social investigator; the problems she focused on were economic inequality, the causes of poverty, and ways to reform the capitalist economy. The marriage she eventually made, to Sidney Webb, a British Fabian socialist, considered "unsuitable" by her family, was an intellectual and political partnership that produced a policy-oriented body of empirical research foundational to the twentieth-century British welfare state.

In her autobiography, *My Apprenticeship* (1926), Webb explores the motivations that led her to social research: "Why did I select the chronic destitution of whole sections of the people, whether illustrated by overcrowded homes, by demoralized casual labor at the docks, or by the low wages, long hours, and insanitary conditions of the sweated industries, as the first subject for enquiry?" (1926:167). She admits that she was not moved by charity but by an unease affecting much of the class of wealthy British capitalists to which her family belonged as they confronted the fact that four-fifths of the population of Britain had not benefited from the Industrial Revolution and were indeed the worse off for it. Her intellectual curiosity was a response to debates about whether the misery of the many must be a necessary condition for the wealth and advancement of the few and whether the poor are responsible for their poverty or are the victims of larger social forces. This question guides her evaluation of how just contemporary society is.

Method: Natural Experiments

Seeking to understand the causes of poverty, Webb first worked as "a charity visitor," but her interest was not in good works but in understanding. She moved from this charity work to assisting Charles Booth in his seventeen-volume study, *The Life and Labour of the People of London* (1892–1902). Her experiences working with the poor and with Booth led her to the insight that the best way to understand how to reform the capitalist economic system was not to study the desperately poor but to find examples of working-class people successfully organizing to create alternative economic systems. She came to argue that in real social life, "experiments" of this type were taking place all the time in businesses, collectives, and local government. The presence of these social experiments suggests both Webb's understanding of human beings as a species with the potential for collective creativity and her sense of social organization as changing in response to material production. This line of thought culminated in her most important single-authored monograph, *The Co-operative Movement in Great Britain* (1891). In this study, which she did as participant observation research in Lancastershire, Webb outlines how economic equity can be arrived at through democratic decision-making by showing how a British working-class buyers' co-operative functioned, that is, how working people could combine their purchasing power to control the price and quality—and potentially, the conditions of production—of material goods and services.

Social Change: Permeation

This research led Webb to an interest in Fabian Socialism and her acquaintance with Sidney Webb. The Fabian Socialists, a relatively small party, sought to influence the course of reform in Britain by a process of "permeation," that is, by supplying information and platform planks to any political party that would champion any aspect of the reform of inequality. The Webbs as Fabians were guided by three main principles: (1) that Marx is wrong in his prediction of the "withering away of the state"; rather the state must intervene in order to control—or socialize—basic elements of the economy; (2) inequality has advanced to such a point of social crisis that such intervention is inevitable; and (3) therefore, it is possible for socialists to advocate gradual rather than revolutionary reforms because gradualism is inevitable.

Webb's vision of society is, above all, of *the working out of processes between the structures in which people are contained*—structures such as state, class, trade unions, and sweatshops. The key structures she concentrates on are the state and social classes. The key process she believes she is witnessing in her lifetime is the growth of state intervention in the conduct of the economy and the society. She accounts for this growth in intervention by the fact that in her lifetime, conditions of inequality in Great Britain and the world are reaching a point where there is no choice but for state intervention. What Webb sees as the great social change of her day is that "our actions whether legislative or voluntary, individual or collective, are becoming more and more inspired and guided by *descriptions* of our social state" ([1887] 1926:403), that is, that actions increasingly are taken on the basis of information about society. She points to the vast increase in the interventions of government in the conduct of the economy as her prime proof.

The Social Role of the Sociologist

Webb sees that if reforms are to work, it is of critical importance that information be accurate, and she devotes much of her sociology to detailed explanations of how to do both quantitative and qualitative empirical research. She sees the primary role of the sociologist as being to provide the information on which a reformist state can be established and make policy. With Sidney, she writes some eight major books encompassing some 4,000 pages; the direction of this work is what we may term "a critical empiricism," that is, it is quantitative and qualitative research done with a view to social change.

With few exceptions, Webb's sociological significance has not received the attention it deserves (Castillo and Castillo, 2004). One reason for Webb's relative neglect as a sociologist may lie in feminist sociologists' reaction to her antisuffrage stance in the 1880s and 1890s. Although Webb later claimed that she was sorry almost immediately after signing an antisuffrage petition, she did not publicly recant for twenty years; she gave her essential reason for her stance as "I had never myself suffered the disabilities assumed to arise from my sex" (1926:343). Yet this assertion is shown as decidedly untrue in various incidents in *My Apprenticeship*. What is more likely the case is that Webb could not see herself as a *member* of a subordinate class, in this case, women, though she would work all her life to help the subordinated.

Summary

The history of the development of sociological theory in the classic period 1830–1930 is typically a description of the work of male theorists. A complex gender politics in academic life, in sociology, in intellectual productivity, and in historiography explains the absence of women from these histories. As part of the contemporary feminist project of deconstructing this politics and of affirming women's contribution to the world of intellectual achievement, this chapter introduces the ideas of several women to the record, and hopefully the canon, of sociology's theoretical development. Harriet Martineau is restored to her rightful place in sociology's founding generation, and a selection of theorists including Charlotte Perkins Gilman, Jane Addams and her network of women sociologists, Anna Julia Cooper, Ida Wells-Barnett, Marianne Schnitger Weber, and Beatrice Potter Webb are discussed as contributors to sociology's classic period of theoretical development, from 1890 to 1930.

Each of these women had that "systematic consciousness of society and social relations" that is the hallmark of a sociological theorist. And although each woman's theory is distinctively framed by the intellectual and social influences of her biography and by her theoretical and ethical preferences, all these theories are also patterned by some common themes: awareness of the fact that they spoke from the particular vantage point of women, an analysis and ethical concern with society's power arrangements, a commitment to sound research as a necessary means to social amelioration and change. Each woman's theory can thus be understood and evaluated as a distinctive individual contribution to sociology. But taken together, these women can also be rediscovered as the collectivity who introduced a feminist theoretical tradition into the history of the discipline.

CHAPTER 11

W.E.B. Du Bois[1]

Chapter Outline

Not too many years ago, one would have been unlikely to see a chapter on W.E.B. Du Bois in a book devoted to classical sociological theory (Rabaka, 2006; 2007).[2] Du Bois's work tends to lack references to, and is not clearly embedded in, the theoretical traditions that are part of, and that inform, this book. He is best known in sociology for his empirical study, *The Philadelphia Negro* (Du Bois, 1899/1996; Lemert, 2005), a work that is not only highly descriptive, but devoid of what is usually thought of as theory. Furthermore, the bulk of Du Bois's enormous body of work produced over many years takes a variety of other forms, including autobiography, poetry, essays, short stories, political commentary, book reviews, newspaper articles, editorials, and so on. In many of his best-known works, he placed great emphasis on the esthetics of what he wrote—how he said things seemed at times to be at least as important as what he said. Most important, he was an activist and he had a profound effect on the state of blacks and others (for example, women) in society. Nevertheless, he certainly was influential within sociology, and if anything, that influence has increased, but he influenced many other disciplines as well.

Du Bois's ideas meet our definition of sociological theory: they have a wide range of application, especially to issues involving minority groups; they deal with the increasingly important issue of race; they have stood the test of time; indeed, they have greater scholarly impact today than they did during Du Bois's lifetime. He was

[1]Many thanks to Professor Norman R. Yetman, University of Kansas, for his many insightful suggestions and comments on this chapter.

[2]In fact, on getting an award late in life from a Czechoslovakian university, Du Bois (1968:25) himself noted: "No American university (except Negro institutions in understandable self-defense) has ever recognized that I had any claim to scholarship."

a sociologist[3] and his ideas are defined as important within that field (and many others). One reflection of that is the fact that one of the major awards given annually by the American Sociological Association is the Du Bois-Johnson-Frazier Award (Johnson and Frazier were also noted sociologists).

It would have been hard to think of Du Bois as a social theorist from a modern (circa 1950) point of view. However, from the perspective of the early twenty-first century and the emergence of postmodern, feminist, and multicultural theories, Du Bois can more easily be thought of as such a theorist. He offered what today would be called by feminists (and others) a "standpoint" theory, and the standpoint from which he theorized was that of black Americans. Like the thinking of many feminists, and especially multiculturalists, his theorizing often did not take the conventional modern form (heavy, theoretical tomes), but a range of theoretical ideas is embedded in his empirical studies, autobiographical sketches, essays, poems, and the like. As a result of recent developments such as those previously mentioned, our sense of what constitutes theory has expanded greatly. It no longer has to be written in a certain way by people trained to do theory in that way. We can now see that theory can come in various forms and be written in ways that we do not necessarily recognize immediately as theory. To allow theory to move beyond the traditional canon of the "dead white men" dealt with throughout most of this book, we need to have the kind of revised vision of theory offered by the viewpoints that have emerged in the last several decades. That new perspective on theory allows us to see, perhaps for the first time, that while Du Bois (like Marx and others) was many things, he was a sociological theorist.

Science

Although only a small portion of his work could be considered scientific, Du Bois (like Comte, Spencer, Durkheim and other classical theorists) was a strong believer in and advocate of science, especially the social-scientific study of race. As a student at Harvard, Du Bois (1968:148) describes how the influence of some of his professors "turned me back from the lonely but sterile land of philosophic speculation, to the social sciences as the field for gathering and interpreting that body of fact which would apply to my program for the Negro. . . . In other words, I was trying to make my first steps toward sociology as the science of human action. It goes without saying that no such field of study was then recognized at Harvard or came to be recognized for 20 years after." During his days in Germany, he turned even more resolutely in the direction of positivism (although he was well aware of the difficulties associated with it): "I . . . began to grasp the idea of a world of human beings whose actions, like those of the physical world, were subject to law" (Du Bois, 1968:205). Indeed, Du Bois thought of much of his early work (through 1910) as kind of laboratory experiments on the "Negro

---

[3]Not only did he teach in a sociology department at two different points in his career, but he was a member of the American Sociological Society (from 1905), attended its meetings, and published in leading journals such as the *American Journal of Sociology* (Lewis, 1993:372–373).

Problem" in which he "hoped to make the laws of social living clearer, surer, and more definite" (Du Bois, 1968:216).[4]

For its day, *The Philadelphia Negro* (Du Bois, 1899/1996) was an impressive scientific study that relied on a variety of kinds of data to analyze the state of Negro[5] life in Philadelphia's seventh ward. It was, for example, loaded with statistical information on the history and current status of Negroes in Philadelphia, as well as maps, observations, interview data, and so on.

One of the things that was especially notable about the study from a scientific perspective was how "value free" (for more on this, see Chapter 8 on Weber) Du Bois attempted to be in his analysis and conclusions. He tried hard to let the data, and to a lesser degree the people, speak for themselves. His own "voice" is quite muted and dispassionate. Although he is critical of white America for what it was doing to Negroes, he was equally hard on the latter, making it clear that they bore some of the responsibility for their plight.

However, *The Philadelphia Negro,* published early in Du Bois's career, proved to be very different from the vast majority of the work that he did over the succeeding half century and more. For example, although he continued to point an accusatory finger at black Americans, at least for a time, he ultimately came to focus almost all his attention on, and anger at, white America and what it was doing to black Americans. Eventually, he took a broader focus and critically analyzed the world as a whole, focusing on the prejudice and discrimination of whites against the "darker" races—black, brown, yellow, and so on. He wrote about these issues with increasingly great passion and anger—this work was anything but value-free. Nevertheless, he continued to argue for the dispassionate, scientific study of race relations, even though he himself was less and less inclined to do such studies himself.

The direction taken by Du Bois in his own work was a reflection of the path he took in his career. He was an academic sociologist for many years, especially at Atlanta University, and he later became an activist involved in the founding of not only the National Association of Colored People (NAACP), but also its predecessor—the Niagara Movement. Later, he was actively involved in many important movements, meetings, and events, not only in the United States, but throughout the world. He came to edit *Crisis,* the magazine of the NAACP, and in it wrote seemingly endless editorials on the plight of black Americans. He was also in demand as a writer for many newspapers, popular magazines, and political tracts; such writing demanded not science, but its seeming opposite—heated political rhetoric. Nonetheless, Du Bois did not surrender his academic, value-free side, and among other things, Du Bois was one of the founders of a scientific journal for the study of race, *Phylon,* in 1940.

The Philadelphia Negro was clearly intended to be a scientific work, and although Du Bois's values creep in now and then, in the main it is a balanced, dispassionate

---

[4]However, Du Bois (1968:222) was later to surrender, at least in part, his commitment to such scientific work because there was little interest in it and, more importantly, because "one could not be a calm, cool, and detached scientist while Negroes were lynched, murdered and starved." In fact, upon later joining the NAACP, he said: "My career as a scientist was to be swallowed up in my role as a master of propaganda. This was not wholly to my liking" (Du Bois, 1968:253).

[5]I use this now old-fashioned term at times in this chapter because Du Bois does and because it was the most commonly used term during the era in which Du Bois lived. At other times I will use the more contemporary terms—"black" and "African American."

treatment of the "Negro Problem" in Philadelphia. From 1898–1910, Du Bois published the Atlanta University Studies,[6] which were similar in tone and orientation. He often argued for the need for careful, systematic, scientific study of issues that relate to Negroes. However, Lewis (1995:151) points out, although Du Bois "professed a commitment to objective social science, he was temperamentally incapable of neutrality."

Du Bois and the "New" Social Theory

The heated political rhetoric of most of Du Bois's work is one of the things that would have made it hard in the (modern) past to consider him a sociological theorist. Marx, as we have seen, had much the same problem, but his work became part of the canon in the United States by about 1970 (it had been accepted long before in other parts of the world), in part because of a recognition that amid all the rhetoric there was a profound theory. In addition, Marx's work was accorded this status because it had such a powerful effect on the thinking of many classical and contemporary theorists who were themselves unquestionably part of the canon. Although the latter was not true of Du Bois's work—it remained largely sequestered within the study of race relations—the former argument, that amid the rhetoric there is serious theory, became clear to more and more social theorists outside the area of the study of race relations a decade or two after Marx's work was accorded general recognition as an important theory.

Those associated with feminist, multicultural, and postmodern theory developed a critique of the canon and a new vision of social theory. Du Bois's manner of thinking not only fit well within this new type of theory, but was something of an exemplar of it. First, as mentioned previously, Du Bois offered a *standpoint theory* of the kind espoused and created by feminists and multiculturalists. The latter (as well as the postmodernists) were critical of the value-free perspective, the "view from nowhere," the so-called "god's eye" view, espoused by modernists. They argued that such a perspective was impossible—one could never be value-free, be nowhere, adopt a godlike perspective. They were also seen as poses that allowed seemingly scientific social scientists (and others) to adopt ideas that adversely affected minorities, be they women, gays, or blacks, among others. The new social theorists argued for the need to recognize this and to develop theories that self-consciously looked at the social world from the standpoint of such minority groups. In this, they were building on the work of Marx, especially, who looked at the capitalist world from the standpoint of the proletariat.

Du Bois can be seen, especially after *The Philadelphia Negro* and his other early scientific works, to be offering a view of society from the standpoint of black Americans and more generally of the world from the perspective of all minority races. At the minimum, being black gives observers the ability to see things whites cannot see: "We who are dark can see America in a way that white Americans cannot" (Du Bois, 1926/1995a:509).

---

[6]In terms of the history of sociology, Du Bois (1940/1995:216) claims that these studies constituted "the beginning of applied Sociology and Anthropology to group problems."

W.E.B. Du Bois

A Biographical Sketch

William Edward Burghardt Du Bois was born on February 23, 1868, in Great Barrington, Massachusetts (Lewis, 1993). Compared to the vast majority of blacks of his day, Du Bois had a comparatively advantaged upbringing that led to college at Fisk University and later to a Ph.D. from Harvard University, with a stop along the way at the University of Berlin. At Harvard and in Germany, Du Bois came into contact with some of the important thinkers of his day, including philosophers William James and Josiah Royce, as well as the great social theorist, Max Weber.

Du Bois took his first job teaching Greek and Latin at a black college (Wilberforce). He notes that "the institution would have no sociology, even though I offered to teach it on my own time" (Du Bois, 1968:189). Du Bois moved on in the fall of 1896 when he was offered a position as assistant instructor at the University of Pennsylvania to do research on blacks in Philadelphia. That research led to the publication of one of the classic works of early sociology, *The Philadelphia Negro* (1899/1996). When that project was completed, Du Bois moved (he never had a regular faculty position at Pennsylvania and that, like many other things in his lifetime, rankled him) to Atlanta University where he taught sociology from 1897 to 1910 and was responsible for a number of research reports on various aspects of Negro life in America. It was also in this period that he authored the first and most important of his autobiographical memoirs, *The Souls of Black Folk* (1903/1996). This was a highly literary and deeply personal work that also made a series of general theoretical points and contributed greatly to the understanding of black Americans and of race relations. Du Bois published a number of such autobiographical works during the course of his life, including *Darkwater: Voices from within the Veil* (1920/1999), *Dusk of Dawn: An Essay Toward an Autobiography of a Race Concept* (1940/1968) and *The Autobiography of W.E.B. Du Bois: A Soliloquy on Viewing My Life from the Last Decade of Its First Century* (1968). Of *Dusk of Dawn*, Du Bois (1968:2) says, "I have written then what is meant to be not so much my autobiography as the autobiography of a concept of race, elucidated, magnified and doubtless distorted in the thoughts and deeds that were mine." (Du Bois was not lacking in self-esteem and he has often been criticized for his outsized ego.)

While at Atlanta University, Du Bois became more publicly and politically engaged. In 1905 he called for and attended a meeting near Buffalo, New York, that led to the formation of the Niagara Movement, an interracial civil rights organization interested in such things as the "abolition of all caste distinctions based simply on race and color" (Du Bois, 1968:249). This formed the basis of the similarly interracial National Association of Colored People (NAACP), which came into existence in 1910, and Du Bois became its Director of Publications and Research. He founded the NAACP's magazine, *The Crisis,* and in its pages authored many essays on a wide range of issues relating to the state of the Negro in America. Du Bois took this new position because it offered him a platform for the widespread dissemination of his ideas (he was solely responsible for the editorial opinions of *The Crisis*). In addition, his position at Atlanta University had become untenable because of his conflict with the then very popular and powerful Booker T. Washington, who was regarded by most white leaders and politicians as the spokesman for black America. Du Bois came to view Washington as far too conservative and much too willing to subordinate Negroes to whites in general and specifically within the white-dominated economy where they were to be trained for, and satisfied with, manual work.

For the next half century, Du Bois was a tireless writer and activist on behalf of Negro and other racial causes (Lewis, 2000). He attended and participated in meetings throughout the United States and much of the world on Negroes in particular and all "colored" races in general. He took positions on many of the pressing issues of the day, almost always from the vantage point of Negroes and other minorities. For example, he had views on which presidential candidates Negroes should support, whether the United States should enter World Wars I and II, and whether Negroes should support those wars and participate in them.

By the early 1930s, the Depression had begun to wreak havoc on the circulation of *The Crisis* and Du Bois lost control to young dissidents within the NAACP. He returned to Atlanta University, to scholarly work, and among other things authored *Black Reconstruction in America, 1860–1880* (1935/1998). His tenure lasted a little more than a decade, and in 1944 Du Bois (then 76) was forcibly retired by the university. Under pressure, the NAACP invited him back as an ornamental figure, but Du Bois refused to play that role or to act his age, and he was dismissed in 1948. His ideas and his work grew increasingly radical over the ensuing nearly two decades of his life. He joined and participated in various peace organizations and eventually was indicted by a grand jury in 1951 for failing to register as an agent of a foreign power in the peace movement.

Early in his life, Du Bois had hope in America in general and, more specifically, that it could solve its racial problems peacefully within the context of a capitalist society. Over the years he lost faith in capitalists and capitalism and grew more supportive of socialism. Eventually, he grew more radical in his views and drifted toward communism. He was quite impressed with the advances communism brought to the Soviet Union and China. In the end, he joined the Communist Party. Toward the very end of his long life, Du Bois seemed to give up hope in the United States, and he moved to the African nation of Ghana. Du Bois died there—a citizen of Ghana—on August 27, 1963, ironically the day before the March on Washington. He was 95 years of age.

Although wide-scale recognition of Du Bois as an important theorist may be relatively recent, he has long been influential within the black community. For example, on becoming Chairman of the Board of the NAACP, Julian Bond said: "I think for people of my age and generation, this [a picture in his home of a young Bond holding Du Bois's hand] was a normal experience—not to have Du Bois in your home, but to have his name in your home, to know about him in your home. . . . This was table conversation for us" (cited in Lemert, 2000:346).

More specifically, in a famous essay, "The Souls of White Folk," Du Bois argues that his standpoint as a black American gave him special insight into white Americans:

> Of them I am singularly clairvoyant. I see in and through them. I view them from unusual points of vantage. Not as a foreigner do I come, for I am, native, not foreign, bone of their thought and flesh of their language. Mine is not the knowledge of the traveler. . . . Rather I see these souls undressed and from the back and side. I see the working of their entrails. I know their thoughts and they know that I know . . . I see them stripped,—ugly, human.
>
> Du Bois (1920/1999:17)

Late twentieth-century thinkers who adopted the standpoint of black Americans saw Du Bois as a pioneer in this kind of work, and feminists, queer theorists, and others also applauded and resonated with his efforts.

Another perspective that emerged at this point—the rejection of general theories and a greater appreciation of *local* theories—also aided in the renewed appreciation of Du Bois's work. That is, unlike, say, Weber, Durkheim, or Parsons, Du Bois did not endeavor to develop a general theory of society; in the main, his theory focused much more narrowly on race and race relations. The view emerged that a general theory of society was another of modernism's many impossible illusions. Furthermore, such general theories tended to ignore, subordinate, and/or denigrate minorities. What was needed, instead, were narrower, more focused theories of the kind developed by Du Bois. Among others, feminists had long created such theories, and such theorizing expanded enormously in the last few decades of the twentieth century and into the twenty-first century. Furthermore, minority women came to the view that even feminist theory was too general and what was needed was even more local forms of theory, especially those from the standpoints of a wide array of minority women. Some of the most important work of this genre came from black feminists (for example, Collins, 1990; 1998) who clearly were working in a tradition pioneered by Du Bois.

Yet another idea that aided in the emergence of the recognition of Du Bois as an important social theorist was the rejection of the idea of value-free thinking. Not only did feminists, multiculturalists, and postmodernists think that such an idea was still another modern illusion, but they also believed in the importance of thinking that was deeply implicated with the values of theorists and the communities from which they emanated and with which they sympathized. And, of course, there were few better models of this kind of thinking than the work of Du Bois.

However, in spite of these and other proclivities, it is important to remember that Du Bois was in many other ways a modernist; given the era in which he wrote, he had little choice. First, of course, as we have seen, Du Bois believed in science and in the scientific study of the situation confronting black Americans. Second, for most of his life he believed in progress, especially for black Americans, even though that progress was being thwarted, largely by whites. Third, he bought into socialism early in his career and toward the end of his life became a firm believer in communism, both as an ideology and in the way it was practiced in the Soviet Union and in China. There are no better examples of modern thinking, especially of "grand narratives" whose conclusions lead ultimately to a better world, if not nirvana, than socialist and communist theories. For these and other reasons, it would be a mistake to consider Du Bois a postmodernist, or even a forerunner of it. Yet, his value-laden and single-minded focus on race puts him in accord with a range of radical new ideas in social theory that emerged in the late twentieth century.

Studying Race Scientifically: *The Philadelphia Negro*

Although it is not a work in theory ("Of the theory back of the plan of this study of Negroes I neither knew nor cared" [Du Bois, 1968:197]), and it was not typical of the vast bulk of Du Bois's work, it is necessary to discuss, at least briefly, his pioneering study of the seventh ward in Philadelphia. Important in itself, it also helps us to understand the later development of Du Bois's thinking. Elijah Anderson (1999), who did his own study of the same ward in recent years, regards *The Philadelphia Negro* as a "masterpiece": "One of the first works to combine the use of urban ethnography, social history, and descriptive statistics, it has become a classic work in the social science literature" (Anderson, 1996:ix). In its use of multiple methods, and in its many very contemporary sounding conclusions about black Americans and race relations, it is a book that has aged well and stands up in comparison to the widely acknowledged classics of this genre.

Several things stand out about this piece of work. First, Du Bois did it all *on his own fieldwork*; he had *no* research assistant to help him collect the wide array of data amassed in the study. He walked the streets of the seventh ward, observing, mapping, asking questions, and doing more formal interviews.[7] Second, his inquiries focused on topics that a similar study done today would also concern itself with, including the demographic characteristics of Negroes in this area of Philadelphia, the geographic origins of this population, marriage and the family, education (and illiteracy), work, the church, housing and community, and politics and voting. In addition to covering most of what we would today call social structures and social institutions, Du Bois also examined key contemporary social problems such as illiteracy, crime, and racial prejudice and discrimination. Any contemporary study of this type would need to cover these topics, and those that Du Bois did not concern himself with probably did not exist at the time. For example, Anderson (1999) rightly points to the enormous problems associated with drug use in the seventh ward in Philadelphia today, but drug abuse was virtually absent at the close of the nineteenth century in that area (or virtually anywhere else).

The Philadelphia Negro is a largely descriptive study; it is not overtly shaped by any theoretical perspective, nor does it come to any broad theoretical conclusion. Du Bois begins by describing the history of the Negro in Philadelphia that led up to the point of his study—the late nineteenth century. After examining the history from 1638 to the time of his writing, especially the period following the end of the Civil War,[8] Du Bois (1899/1996:43) concludes that developments had been disappointing: "an abnormal

[7]Later, in *The Souls of Black Folk*, Du Bois (1903/1996:155) was critical of the "car-window sociologist" who was content with research that involved "the few leisure hours of a holiday trip." The work involved in *The Philadelphia Negro* (and other early research by Du Bois) was, in contrast, extraordinarily intense and intensive. However, later in his career, Du Bois became content with armchair reflections without even the casual observations of the "car-window sociologist."

[8]This was in many senses a comparative-historical study, involving not only historical comparisons, but also contemporaneous comparisons with various European groups.

and growing amount of crime and poverty can justly be charged to the Negro; he is not a large taxpayer, holds no conspicuous place in the business world or the world of letters, and even as a working man seems to be losing ground."

Du Bois shows a very contemporary sense of important issues in the social sciences, especially time, space, and their intersection. Time is represented through his historical analysis, whereas his spatial orientation is reflected in his detailed analysis of the geography (social ecology) of the seventh ward. One of the things that becomes clear quickly is that seventh ward is *not* uniform; there is great diversity, from subarea to subarea, even block to block. In particular, Du Bois makes it clear that there are important social class distinctions in the area, and the issue of social class is an important element throughout Du Bois's work (see later in this chapter), although it is increasingly subordinated to race, which is, by far, the most important factor in his studies and analyses.

One of the things that strikes today's reader is the multifaceted character of Du Bois's analysis; he sees virtually everything in multifactorial terms. A good example is found in the realm of the occupations held by Negroes and the incomes derived from that work. He accounts for their relatively lowly status on both dimensions in terms of (1) their lack of previous training leading to low work-related efficiency; (2) the competition from others, especially white immigrants, who are seen as "eager," "well-trained," and "ruthless;" (3) industrial changes leading to the replacement of small businesses by increasingly large industries for whose work Negroes were ill-prepared; (4) wide-ranging discrimination against Negroes on the basis of race. Interestingly, the latter reinforces itself because as a result of discrimination, whites rarely come into contact with Negroes on the job, and this lack of contact serves to reinforce the prejudice that lies at the base of discrimination.

Although most of the blame, explicitly and implicitly, is placed on whites and their prejudice and discrimination, Negroes do not escape unscathed. On the one side, Du Bois (1899/1966:121) argues that when Negroes seek to advance economically, "almost unconsciously the whole countenance and aid of the [white] community is thrown against the Negro." On the other side, Du Bois describes the ways in which Negroes contribute to their own economic difficulties. For example, he argues that they tend to go to white physicians and lawyers, thereby having an adverse effect on the small numbers of Negroes who make it into these occupations, as well as on the motivation of others to make the effort.

Crime

One of the most impressive aspects of *The Philadelphia Negro* is its analysis of the high crime rates among Negroes. Du Bois shows a very contemporary caution about earlier statistics showing a higher crime rate for Negroes. For example, he demonstrates the role played by discrimination in these statistics, arguing that Negroes were "arrested for less cause and given longer sentences than whites" (Du Bois, 1899/1996:239). He also makes the point that many of the Negroes arrested were never brought to trial, with the result that their guilt or innocence was never proven.

Du Bois was careful to analyze the social causes of high crime rates among Negroes after the close of the Civil War. Among the factors that he points to is the heritage of slavery and emancipation, the influx of larger numbers of Negroes (and others) into the city, increasing competition for jobs, the increasing complexity of life, and the environment, including "the world of custom and thought in which he (the Negro) must live and work, the physical surrounding of house and home and ward, the moral encouragements and discouragements which he encounters" (Du Bois, 1899/1996:284). Turning to causes within the white community, Du Bois (1899/1996:241) points to the "stinging oppression and ridicule" heaped on blacks and later concludes: "The real foundation of the difference (of the social conditions facing Negroes) is the widespread feeling all over the land . . . that the Negro is something less than an American and ought not to be much more than he is" (Du Bois, 1899/1996:284). He concludes that crime is a "symptom of countless wrong social conditions" (Du Bois, 1899/1996:242).

Although Du Bois (1899/1996:322) finds that whites are in general "quite unconscious of any such powerful and vindictive feeling," Negroes "regard this prejudice as the chief cause of their present unfortunate condition." Here, Du Bois isolates an important difference between the races that continues to this day and, if possible, the differences in perception have increased. Nonetheless, Du Bois refuses to make a simplistic association between prejudice (and discrimination) and crime (as well other problems confronting Negroes). He sees the linkages as both subtler and more dangerous.

Ironically, Du Bois (1899/1996:352) finds that the city of Philadelphia, through its institutions, charities, and sympathy, had supported "the criminal, the lazy and the shiftless," but the city is found to have "no use" for "the educated and industrious young colored man."

Intermarriage

On the issue of intermarriage, Du Bois (1899/1996:358) argues that Negroes (and presumably whites) must see marriage as a "private contract" and that "it does not concern any one but themselves as to whether one of them be white, black or red." However, whatever Du Bois (1899/1996:359) would like, he recognizes that the reality is quite different—"the average white person does not marry a Negro; and the average Negro, despite his theory, himself marries one of his race, and frowns darkly on his fellows unless they do likewise."

Social Inequality: Caste and Class

Although Du Bois certainly privileged race as a factor in this analysis, and he steadfastly retained such a focus throughout his long career, he was also very interested in social class.[9] He differentiated among whites in terms of social class (we will discuss his thoughts on an elite group—"benevolent despots"—below and later we will discuss his analysis and criticisms of the white working class), but in *The Philadelphia Negro* there is much about social class among Negroes. For example, one of his class systems is: Grade 1 (respectable families earning enough income to live well); Grade 2

[9]Although Du Bois usually talks in terms of social classes, at times he uses the stronger term of a "caste" system to describe the situation confronting blacks in America. In this context he discusses the "Jim Crow" laws that established *de facto* (legal) segregation and discrimination on the basis of race.

(respectable working class with steady paying work); Grade 3 (the poor and very poor without enough steady income); Grade 4 (the "lowest class of criminals, prostitutes and loafers; the 'submerged tenth'" [Du Bois, 1899/1996:311]).[10]

Du Bois not only wants to make it clear that there are vast differences within the black community in terms of class (and in terms of spatial distribution, as we saw earlier), that they are not on one piece, but he also wants to give special importance to the highest classes within the Negro community. He argues that "the better classes of the Negroes should recognize their duty toward the masses . . . toward lifting the rabble" (Du Bois, 1899/1996:392–393). Given his elite background and training, Du Bois,[11] at this early stage in his career, accords great importance to the elites of both races. Indeed, he argues for the need for elite whites interested in helping to "recognize the existence of the better class of Negroes [who] must gain their active aid and cooperation by generous and polite conduct" (Du Bois, 1899/1996:396). *The Philadelphia Negro* concludes not with a rallying cry to black Americans, but with talk of the need for whites to be "polite and sympathetic" and "generous" to Negroes while, for their part, the latter are urged to engage in "proper striving." Together, whites and African Americans will be able to "realize what the great founder of the city meant when he named it the City of Brotherly Love" (Du Bois, 1899/1996:397).[12]

Du Bois came to be known for the phrase "The Talented Tenth" to describe the small group at the top that were to be the leaders of the Negro community. He revisited that idea late in his career in light of being criticized for his elitism, and because he began to take Marx's ideas increasingly seriously. The latter's ideas, of course, pointed to a revolution from below emanating from the masses. Although Du Bois did not abandon his views on the importance of leadership, he did modify them. In his later work, it was no longer enough for these leaders to be talented in a general sense, they also had to be experts in economics and its effect on Negroes. The "Talented Tenth" became the "Guiding Hundredth"[13] and they had to be willing to "sacrifice and plan such economic revolution in industry and just distribution of wealth, as would make the rise of our group possible." (Du Bois, 1948/1995:350).

The Benevolent Despot

If there is a hopeful figure in *The Philadelphia Negro* it is the "benevolent despot," often a benevolent capitalist. At this early stage in his work, Du Bois retains some faith in whites, strong and benevolent leaders, *and* in capitalism. Thus, on the issue of economic and work-related problems, Du Bois argues that a benevolent despot might have sought to deal with the lack of training of the Negro and the discrimination practiced against them. However, there was "no benevolent despot, no philanthropist, no far-seeing captain of industry to prevent the Negro from losing even the skill he had learned or to inspire

---

[10]Du Bois (1898/1995) describes a similar class system in a study of African Americans in Farmville, Virginia.

[11]Indeed, Du Bois was often criticized as being an elitist, especially in his early work.

[12]As we will see, Du Bois was to radically revise his thinking and abandon such romantic rhetoric as his thinking evolved and changed.

[13]Of course, in a sense, the smaller number involved in this group (a hundredth rather than a tenth) implied even greater elitism.

him by opportunities to learn more" (Du Bois, 1899/1996:127). However, characteristically Du Bois (1899/1996:130) is quick not to let Negroes off the hook and to simply blame others: "Undoubtedly much blame can rightly be laid at the door of Negroes for submitting rather tamely to their organized opposition." More positively, in terms of health-related problems, Du Bois (1899/1996:163) argues: "The main movement of reform must come from the Negroes themselves, and should start with a crusade for fresh air, cleanliness, healthfully located homes and proper food."

Du Bois did not long hold out much hope for aid from the benevolent despot and, more specifically, from the capitalist. Indeed, in a later analysis of the economy of the post-Civil War South, he points an accusatory finger at northern capitalists "who have come to take charge of the industrial exploitation of the New South . . . there is in these new captains of industry neither love nor hate, neither sympathy nor romance; it is a cold question of dollars and dividends" (Du Bois, 1903/1996:170). And in a still later work, *Black Reconstruction in America, 1860–1880* (Du Bois, 1935/1998), capitalists, especially those from the North, are accorded much of the blame for the failure of Reconstruction after the Civil War.

Appeal to White Self-Interest

An approach taken by Du Bois in this early study, and utilized many times over the course of his career, is to seek to improve the situation for Negroes by appealing to white self-interest. That is, he argues that whites, as well as society as a whole, would benefit from black educational and economic advancement as well as an amelioration of problems within the black community. For example, white employers and the economy as a whole would benefit from better-trained black workers with greater ability to succeed occupationally and in terms of income. The fact that whites are unwilling to recognize this, let alone help blacks, points to the fact that "one of the great postulates in the science of economics—that men will seek their economic advantage—is in this case untrue" (Du Bois, 1899/1996:146).[14] That is, even though it is to whites' collective advantage to have Negroes succeed economically, they are unwilling to help them and may even act to their further detriment. After describing the relatively poor health of Negroes (which he attributes largely to poor social conditions), Du Bois makes the same point—whites and the community in general would benefit from better health among Negroes (a healthier workforce would provide more workers and be less of a drain on the community). More generally, Du Bois (1898/1996:394) concludes: "Such discrimination is morally wrong, politically dangerous, industrially wasteful, and socially silly. It is the duty of whites to stop it, and to do so primarily for their own sakes."

Theoretical Contributions

Although there is no "theory" in a modern sense in Du Bois's work, there certainly are a series of general ideas that continue to be useful in thinking in theoretical terms about race in general, and black Americans in particular. There is no general theory in his

[14]This constitutes a critique of what today is called rational-choice theory.

work because he never set out to create one and because he was involved in many other kinds of work, including *The Philadelphia Negro* (and other empirical works that occupied most of his attention until roughly 1910), later more autobiographical writings (in which, however, theoretical ideas were embedded), political tracts, and political activities of great variety and importance. Nevertheless, it is possible to identify several important theoretical ideas and twists and turns in his work.

Racialism and Race Pride

In an early essay, Du Bois (1897/1995:21) argues that the "race idea" is "the central thought of all history" and this is followed immediately with a definition of race: "a family of human beings, generally of common blood and language, always of common history, traditions and impulses, who are both voluntarily and involuntarily striving together for the accomplishment of certain more or less vividly conceived ideals of life." This leads Du Bois (1897/1995:23) to the view that the goal of American Negroes (and implicitly of all races) is *not* integration, and certainly *not* "absorption by the white Americans," but rather, to serve as the "advance guard" of "Pan-Negroism."[15] In various ways, Du Bois (1923/1995:471–477) sees Negroes as superior to whites, and it is their role to "soften" the hardness of "the "twisted white American environment" (Du Bois, 1933/1995a:73). Here he points to such things as Negro music (the only truly original American music, he argues),[16] fairy tales, and humor.[17] More generally, Du Bois (1915/1995:53) argues that "in its normal condition" the Negro race is "at once the strongest and gentlest of the races of men." Whereas whites are seen as immersed in a "mad money-getting plutocracy" (Du Bois, 1897/1995:25), blacks are seen as being able to ameliorate these excesses by infusing American society with their softer, gentler culture. To accomplish this goal, as well as to defend and further their self-interests, Du Bois urges race organization, solidarity, and unity.

> It is the race-conscious black man cooperating together in his own institutions and movements who will eventually emancipate the colored race, and the great step ahead today is for the American Negro to accomplish his economic emancipation through voluntary determined cooperative effort.
>
> (Du Bois, 1934/1995:558)

Along these lines, he makes it clear that he is not opposed to segregation per se, but segregation accompanied by discrimination. As long as segregated facilities are more or less equal and operate on the basis of the same principles, he has no problem with their segregation on the basis of race. However, he later came to the realization that such "separate but equal" facilities are "rarely possible" (Du Bois, 1944/1995:615).

Race, of course, was at the base of what Du Bois famously called the "Negro Problem," or the frictions between the races in America. He thought in terms of a

---

[15]Yet, at least in his critique of the separatism (back to Africa) of Marcus Garvey, Du Bois (1923/1995:337) sees the "exchange of one race supremacy for another" as futile and spiritually bankrupt.

[16]In fact, *The Souls of Black Folk* (Du Bois, 1903/1996) is organized around, and each chapter begins with, verses from Negro songs.

[17]Du Bois also sees the gift of spirit, or religion, as an important contribution, although he was most often quite critical of black religion.

"color-line" in the United States in general, and in the South in particular. (As early as his college-student years, Du Bois [1968:125] says that he "developed a belligerent attitude toward the color bar.") For example, he described a

> frightful chasm at the color-line across which men pass at their peril. Thus, then and now, there stand in the South two separate worlds; and separate not simply in the higher realms of social intercourse, but also in church and school, on railway and street-car, in hotels and theatres, in streets and city sections, in books and newspapers, in asylums and jails, in hospitals and graveyards.
>
> (Du Bois, 1903/1996:97)

However, later Du Bois came to broaden his perspective and to see the American case as part of a global color line. In fact, he had anticipated that position earlier in one of his most famous statements, and one that seems even more true in the early years of the twenty-first century:

> The problem of the twentieth century is the problem of the colour line, the question is to how far differences of race . . . are going to be made, hereafter, the basis of denying to over half the world the right of sharing to their utmost ability the opportunities and privileges of modern civilization.
>
> (Du Bois, 1900/1995:639)

Thus, Du Bois (1903/1996:15) no longer focused exclusively on the United States, but looked at Negroes in "Asia and Africa and the islands of the sea" and more generally at other races throughout the world. Du Bois came to think more broadly in terms of race rather than focusing exclusively on one race—the Negro. Furthermore, he began to discuss not just the need for Negro organizations (including Negro colleges), but for unified organizations involving all "colored races."[18] However, in spite of this focus on race, Du Bois recognized that there were no "pure" races and that the vast majority of the differences between the races stemmed from differences in their environment, especially their social environment.

Du Bois's more general focus on race led him in a variety of directions, some more defensible than others. For example, as early as 1936, Du Bois (1936/1995b:81) expressed concern over the plight of Jews in Germany as victims of "race hate." On the other hand, for a time, Du Bois seemed to be blind to the abuses committed by the Japanese before and during WWII. For example, he talked of an absence of "racial or color caste" in Manchuria, which was occupied by the Japanese before World War II (Du Bois, 1937/1995:83). Even at the close of that war, while he condemned the attack on Pearl Harbor ("unwise," "ill-considered"), Du Bois (1945/1995:86–87) praised the Japanese people ("fine and progressive"), criticized an American admiral ("he is fighting and hating a colored race"), and fretted over the occupation of Japan by white troops.

---

[18]Du Bois even called for all laborers, white and nonwhite, throughout the world to join together. However, this was an atypical position for Du Bois who ordinarily saw white laborers (and their unions) as the enemy of black (and other nonwhite) workers. This opposition is also seen as a key factor in the failure of Reconstruction (Du Bois, 1935/1998).

The Veil

One of Du Bois's most famous concepts is that of the *Veil.*[19] By this idea, he means that there is a clear separation, a barrier, between Negroes and whites. The imagery is *not* one of a wall, but rather of thin, porous material through which each race can see the other. However, no matter how thin and porous the Veil, no matter how easy it is to see through, it still clearly separates the races. In his "Forethought" to *The Souls of Black Folk,* Du Bois makes it clear that it is his intention to "lift" the Veil, to venture behind or within it, in order to examine, and let his (white) readers glimpse, the "souls" of Negroes in America:

> Leaving, then, the white world, I have stepped within the Veil, raising it that you may view faintly its deeper recesses,—the meaning of its religion, the passion of its human sorrow, and the struggle of its greater souls. . . . And, finally, need I add that I who speak here am bone of the bone and flesh of the flesh of them that live within the Veil?
>
> (Du Bois, 1903/1996:xxiv)

Although the Veil is usually seen as capable of being seen through and of being lifted, there are times when Du Bois sees it as more opaque and impossible to lift, let alone breach. For example, in describing the "older South," he argues that "we build around them walls so high, and hang between them and the light a Veil so thick, that they shall not even think of breaking through" (Du Bois, 1903/1996:90).

Du Bois discusses the Veil in a number of ways:

- as something that shuts blacks out from the rest of the world and within which they live
- as something that blacks are born with
- that falls or lays between blacks and whites (for example, Du Bois [1903/1996:65] describes an incident where he was greeted amiably by a white commissioner, but when it came time for dinner "then fell the awful shadow of the Veil, for they ate first, then I—alone") even though at times it was lifted, at least partially
- as something that affects the way Negroes and whites see each other
- that hangs between Negroes and opportunity
- that through education and truth, it would become possible, as he does, to "dwell above the Veil" (Du Bois, 1903/1996:110)
- that it is also possible to dwell above the Veil in death[20]
- that negatively affects both blacks and whites
- that impoverishes them in different ways, including their "souls"
- as something that he hopes someday might be lifted in order to "set the prisoned free" (Du Bois, 1903/1996:215)

Overall, "worlds within and without the Veil of Color are changing, and changing rapidly, but not at the same rate, not in the same way; and this must produce a peculiar

[19]Du Bois also used the metaphor of a "cave" to illustrate the position of African Americans who could be seen as peering out from it, being ignored by white passersby, and as screaming out in a vacuum (Lewis, 2000:474).

[20]After the death of his infant son, Du Bois (1903/1996:214) saw "the world . . . darkly through the Veil."

wrenching of the soul, a peculiar sense of doubt and bewilderment" (Du Bois, 1903/1996:203).

The following is one of Du Bois's best and most lyrical statements on the Veil:

> And then—the Veil, the Veil of color. It drops as drops the night on southern seas—vast, sudden, unanswering. There is Hate behind it, and Cruelty and Tears. As one peers through its intricate, unfathomable pattern of ancient, old, old design, one sees blood and guilt and misunderstanding. And yet it hangs there, this Veil, between then and now, between Pale and Colored and Black and White—between You and Me. Surely it is but a thought-thing, tenuous, intangible; yet just as surely is it true and terrible and not in our little day may you and I lift it. We may feverishly unravel its edges and even climb slow with giant shears to where its ringed and gilded top nestles close to the throne of Eternity. But as we work and climb we shall see through streaming eyes and hear with aching ears, lynching and murder, cheating and despising, degrading and lying, so flashed and flashed through this vast hanging darkness that the Doer never sees the Deed and the Victim knows not the Victor and Each hate All in wild and bitter ignorance. Listen, O Isles, to those voices from within the Veil, for they portray the most human hurt of the Twentieth Cycle.
>
> (Du Bois, 1920/1999:143–144)

Among the notable things about this statement is Du Bois's recognition that while the Veil is a "thought thing," an idea or rather a series of ideas, it is not easily lifted, cut, or destroyed. It will be a long-term struggle to lift the Veil and that event was not to come anytime soon. That something like the Veil described by Du Bois continues to exist points to the continued importance of this view, indeed all of his thinking on the Veil.

Double Consciousness, or "Twoness"

Closely related to the concept of the Veil, is one of Du Bois's best-known and most influential ideas—*double-consciousness.* By this, he means that a black person has an unusual feeling, a sensation of

> always looking at one's self through the eyes of others, of measuring one's soul by the tape of a world that looks on in amused contempt and pity. One ever feels this twoness,—an American, a Negro; two souls, two thoughts, two unreconciled strivings; two warring ideals in one dark body, whose dogged strength alone keeps it from being torn asunder.
>
> (Du Bois, 1903/1996:5)

To put this another way, African Americans were simultaneously outsiders and insiders, or more specifically, outsiders within. That is, they were (and to some degree still are) both inside and outside of the dominant white society (separated, of course, by the Veil). On the one hand, this position gives them unique and perhaps enhanced insight into society as a whole (see his standpoint theory discussed earlier), and on the other it produces enormous tension that manifests itself in all sorts of pathologies within the black community. As Du Bois (1903/1996:7) puts it, "this seeking to satisfy two unreconciled ideals, has wrought sad havoc with the courage and faith and deeds" of Negro Americans.

Given the existence of this double consciousness, Du Bois (1903/1996:6) argues that the American Negro longs "to attain self-conscious manhood, to merge his double self into a better and truer self. In this merging he wishes neither of the older [Negro, American] selves to be lost. . . . He simply wishes to make it possible for a man to be both a Negro and an American, without being cursed and spit upon by his fellows, without having the doors of Opportunity closed roughly in his face."

Du Bois's thinking on double consciousness resonates with a number of classical and contemporary theoretical ideas. For example, Simmel's "stranger" (see Chapter 9) would likely suffer from double consciousness, and black Americans can be thought of as strangers within white-dominated American society. More contemporaneously, Patricia Hill Collins's (1990; 1998) work on "the outsider within" has strong resemblances to Du Bois's thinking on double consciousness. The point is that although Du Bois was largely ignored by the mainstream within sociology in general, and sociological theory in particular, and he generally ignored it, his ideas do resonate with a number of strands of theory and empirical research within the mainstream.

Economics

Du Bois devoted a great deal of attention to economic factors, and although he discussed many other factors (social, political, and so on), in the end he usually came back to economics as the most basic and most important factor. For example: "The main weakness of the Negro's position is that since emancipation he has never had an adequate economic foundation" (Du Bois, 1935/1998:565). He tied this position into the kind of economic determinism often associated with Marx: "I believe in the dictum of Karl Marx, that the economic foundation of a nation is widely decisive for its politics, its art and its culture" (Du Bois, 1944/1995:610). As Lemert (2000:357) puts it, "Du Bois's most distinctive theoretical conviction [was]: that race never stands alone, apart from economic realities. . . . Race makes little sense apart from class."

However, although Du Bois recognized the ultimate importance of economic factors, he was highly critical of the attention accorded, and the amount of time and energy devoted, to the striving for economic success. At first, he criticized white America for its fetishization of money; for its overarching materialism. Later, he criticized the United States as a whole for this. He thought there were more important, "higher," things in life that had been lost sight of by white Americans. In contrast, Negroes had not yet accorded as much importance to material success (perhaps, at least in part, because they had not been given a real opportunity to achieve it) and Du Bois hoped they never would attach too much importance to material success. This is part of the reason why Du Bois argued so often and so determinedly for the importance of education, especially higher education, in the black community. Education would permit blacks to achieve a range of higher goals and objectives than mere economic success. This is also one of the central reasons why Du Bois was critical of Booker T. Washington, especially the latter's economic focus on success in industry and the trades. Not only did Washington's philosophy relegate Negroes to secondary economic status, but also lost in this focus is the need for leadership, morality, and "self-respecting manhood for black folk" (Du Bois, 1904/1995:330). This is closely linked to Du Bois's view that Washington preached subservience and to Du Bois's (1904/1995:331) refusal, as he puts it, "to kiss the hands that smite us."

Karl Marx, Socialism, and Communism

We have seen that early in his career, DuBois could have been considered in some respects quite conservative, even elitist. After completing the early scientific phase of his career, he became active in the Niagara Movement and in the NAACP in an effort to improve the situation of Negro Americans. However, these were reformist organizations seeking change of, and within, the system. Indeed, Du Bois (1921/1995:555) admits this when in editorializing for the NAACP, he says: "We do not believe in revolution." Earlier, he had said: "By every civilized and peaceful method we must strive for the rights which the world accords to men" (Du Bois, 1903/1996:61). In these initial phases of his career he, like most other American social scientists and public intellectuals of the day, placed great faith in reforms of various types (for example, education) and even allowed himself romantic notions of harmony between blacks and whites: "Only by a union of intelligence and sympathy across the color-line in this critical period of the Republic shall justice and right triumph (Du Bois, 1903/1996:189).

At the turn of the twentieth century, Du Bois (1903/1996:151) was critical of socialism, characterizing it as "cheap and dangerous." However, as widespread reform movements proved ineffective, Du Bois was drawn to socialism and he retained an interest, sympathy, and hope in it for the rest of his life. He joined the Socialist Party in 1911. Although he soon resigned, he continued to consider himself a socialist. Toward the end of his life, Du Bois (1958/1995:147) retained that orientation, although he had come to collapse the distinction between socialism and communism: "I believe in socialism. I seek a world where the ideals of communism will triumph—to each according to his need; from each according to his ability."

Early on, Du Bois was critical of socialist party organizations (as well as the labor movement) for continuing to discriminate against Negroes. More important, even as late as 1933, Du Bois continued to adhere to the view that the "lowest and most fatal degree of its [Negro labor's] suffering comes not from capitalists but from fellow white laborers" (1933/1995b:541). This was a view that goes all the way back to *The Philadelphia Negro,* where Du Bois saw Negro workers suffering from competition from white laborers, primarily immigrants. As a result, at this point Du Bois holds out little hope for a union of black and white workers, Marxian theory, socialism, and communism:

> How now does the philosophy of Karl Marx apply today to colored labor? First of all colored labor has no common ground with white labor. No soviet of technocrats would do more than exploit colored labor in order to raise the status of whites. No revolt of a white proletariat could be started if its object was to make black workers their economic, political and social equals. It is for this reason that American socialism for fifty years has been dumb on the Negro problem, and the communists cannot even get a respectful hearing in America unless they begin by expelling Negroes. . . . There is not at present the slightest indication that a Marxian revolution based on a united class-conscious proletariat is anywhere on the American far horizon.
>
> (Du Bois, 1933/1995b:542–544)

However, by the 1940s, Du Bois had come to the view that the white working class could come to form an alliance with black workers, at least in the South (Du Bois, 1947/1995:545–550). Ultimately, Du Bois (1957/1995:357) came to the conclusion "that without the overthrow of capitalist monopoly the Negro cannot survive in the United States as a self-respecting cultural unit, integrating gradually into the nation, but not on terms which imply self-destruction or loss of his possible gifts to America."

Gradually, in his later years, Du Bois moved fitfully in the direction of communism. This was motivated, in part, by the experiences he had during his travels around the world, especially the Soviet Union. Following an early visit there, he proclaimed: "I am a Bolshevik" (Du Bois, 1926/1995b:582). Although he continued to have reservations about communism as it was practiced in the Soviet Union, he was especially critical of American communism and its leaders ("young jackasses") (Du Bois, 1931/1995:588). Still later, in another of his dramatic shifts, he became something of a worshiper of both the Soviet Union and China. This led to some unfortunate and embarrassing statements, including applauding "democracy" in the Soviet Union, welcoming the Soviet repression of the Hungarian uprising, contending that "Joseph Stalin was a great man" (Du Bois, 1953/1995:796), and arguing that "It was only a matter of time and a comparatively short time when the Soviet Union will lead the world in industry" (Du Bois, 1968:39).

By the 1950s, discouraged by the continuing humiliation of, and discrimination against, African Americans, Du Bois was arguing for some sort of socialist/communist change within the United States. He suggested "drastically curbing the present power of concentrated wealth, by assuming ownership of some natural resources, by administering many of our key industries and by socializing our services for public welfare" (Du Bois, 1951/1995:621). And, he seemed now to accord social class far more importance than he had earlier. In fact, he foresaw a time when "Negroes will be divided into classes even more sharply than now, and the main mass will become a part of the working class of the nation and the world, which will surely go socialist" (Du Bois, 1951/1995:625).

On October 1, 1961, Du Bois, at the age of 93, applied for membership in the Communist Party of the United States. In his letter of application, he said: "Capitalism cannot reform itself; it is doomed to self-destruction. . . . In the end Communism will triumph. I want to help to bring that day" (Du Bois, 1961/1995:632). Here is the way he defined communism:

> I mean by communism, a planned way of life in the production of wealth and work designed for building a state whose object is the highest welfare of its people and not merely the profit of a part. I believe that all men should be employed according to their ability and that wealth and services should be distributed according to need.
>
> (Du Bois, 1968:57)

Early in his career, Du Bois admits to not having read Marx's work (he was certainly not the only social theorist and/or sociologist of the day guilty of this). Of his days at Fisk, Du Bois (1968:126) says, "In class I do not remember ever hearing Karl Marx mentioned nor socialism discussed." At Harvard, he recalls "Karl Marx was mentioned but only incidentally and as one whose doubtful theories had long since been refuted. Socialism as dream of philanthropy or as will-o-wisp hotheads was dismissed as unimportant" (Du Bois, 1968:133).[21] Of his time in Germany, Du Bois (1968:168) said, "The

---

[21]However, Lewis (1993:111) argues that one of Du Bois's papers shows that he "knew far more about Marxist economic theory at Harvard than he subsequently let on."

history of the development of Marxism and of revisionists . . . was too complicated for a student like myself to understand, who had received no real teaching along this line."

However, he began to read Marx seriously during WWI and claims that he later mastered Marx's theory. By the 1930s he was using texts such as *The Communist Manifesto* in his classes at Atlanta University.[22] The influence of Marx in general, and the *Manifesto* in particular, is clear in the following call to Africa and Pan-African Socialism (Kendhammar, 2007):

> You have nothing to lose but your Chains!
> You have a continent to regain!
> You have freedom and human dignity to attain!
>
> (Du Bois, 1968:404)

Although he was influenced by Marxian theory, Du Bois was disinclined to write scholarly metatheoretical treatises, with the result that what one is likely to get is elliptical statements, or brief sketches—even caricatures—of, Marx's theory in his work (Du Bois, 1933/1995b:539–540). This is reflected in Du Bois's rather simplistic definition of communism (see the preceding quote), a definition that reflects his lack of deep engagement with Marx's ideas as well as those of the wide variety of neo-Marxists.

Yet, to be fair to Du Bois, he never sought to do this kind of scholarly work, even though he was certainly exposed to it, and how it was to be done, in his graduate days at Harvard and Berlin. It seems fair to say that in Marxian terms, Du Bois was always drawn to an integration of theory and praxis. In addition, he was writing to be read by a larger audience and not just by other scholars. This is reflected both in his literary and poetic works on the one hand and also in his numerous editorials, magazine articles, and newspaper pieces.

Marxian theory, in a simplified and perhaps distorted[23] form, plays a central role in *Black Reconstruction in America: 1860–1880* (Du Bois, 1935/1998). He begins with the black worker[24] (the slave) who was the "ultimate exploited," the source of surplus value, and the "underlying cause" of "civil war in America" (Du Bois, 1935/1998:15–16). Du Bois turns his attention next to the white worker who, in an argument reminiscent of his findings in Philadelphia's seventh ward, are described as feeling threatened by competition from black workers. Thus, with the end of slavery in 1863, white workers welcomed the caste system that served to protect them from open competition with black workers. Underlying the race issue was the ultimately more important, or at least more general, issue of economics. Northern (and later Southern) capitalists were willing to accept the subordination, even exclusion, of blacks as long as they could use the same methods of control and exploitation on Southern white workers that they were already using on Northern whites. Du Bois (1935/1998:584) saw this capitalist hegemony evolving into a dictatorship of property and capital, of "super-capital" and

---

[22]By this time Du Bois had assembled "one of the most comprehensive private libraries on scientific socialism in the country" (Lewis, 2000:263).

[23]For example, he makes highly questionable use of the idea of a "general strike" in his discussion of actions taken by slaves during the Civil War.

[24]Later in the book, Du Bois substitutes "proletariat" for both black and white "worker."

"great corporations," ultimately forming a kind of "super-government." To Du Bois, it was capitalism that had undermined Reconstruction and it was that economic system that was destroying America and much of the rest of the world in his day.

Summary

There is no question that in addition to being a towering public figure throughout the first half of the twentieth century, W.E.B. Du Bois was also a sociologist and social thinker of great importance. *The Philadelphia Negro* was unquestionably a pioneering urban ethnography, one that remains of interest and use to this day. And *Black Reconstruction in America: 1860–1880,* in spite of its problems associated with an unsophisticated and questionable use of Marxian theory, remains of use to students today interested in the events of that period and how to better understand them.

Although he is not what is conventionally thought of as a social theorist, Du Bois certainly developed a number of theoretical ideas that continue to be useful in terms of thinking about race (and many other issues—for example, gender). Especially notable is his early recognition of, and thinking about, the *race issue* and the *color line.* Ideas on concepts like the *Veil* and *double consciousness* not only continue to be relevant, but are worthy of further thought and exploration by contemporary students of race. Especially interesting is Du Bois's struggle over many years with the theories of socialism, communism, and especially with those of Karl Marx. He not only vacillated, but changed course rather abruptly at many points in his career. It would be interesting to see further explorations, perhaps by researchers with access to the Du Bois archives, of the true extent of his knowledge of and commitment to Marxian theory. This also leads to the need to assess Du Bois's place in Marxian and neo-Marxian theory. Just as he has rarely been included in discussions of the major classical social theorists, he has also not been included in overviews of major Marxian thinkers. Inclusion in those pantheons, and discussions of his place in them, are both now more likely as recognition grows of Du Bois's importance as a sociologist and a social thinker.

C H A P T E R 12

Thorstein Veblen

Chapter Outline

Intellectual Influences

Basic Premises

Substantive Issues

In Thorstein Veblen we encounter a unique figure in the pantheon of classical social theorists. Veblen has always had a small, but significant, following in the social sciences. However, his influence has increased recently because his famous work on "conspicuous consumption" is in line with both the growing importance of consumption (both absolutely and in comparison to production) in American society and much of the rest of the world, as well as the increasing interest in sociology (and other fields) in consumption.[1] Yet, the irony is that Veblen was very much a product of his times (late eighteenth- and early nineteenth-century America) and, as a result, he shares with the other classical theorists of the day a focal interest in issues relating to production. The increasing interest in his work on consumption has led to a reexamination of Veblen's work on production and although it is not without its problems (for example, the repetition of a single theme in a series of books and articles covering a span of many decades), there is much more to Veblen's theorizing than his valuable work on consumption (Rosenberg, 1956).

Intellectual Influences

Thorstein Veblen was influenced by the ideas of a wide range of social thinkers, but he synthesized inputs from those bodies of thought and, in the process, created a perspective that is quite distinctive. Among those who influenced Veblen were Karl Marx, a variety of evolutionary thinkers (Charles Darwin, Herbert Spencer, William Graham Sumner), a number of economists (Adam Smith, Alfred Marshall), and even some "anonymous authors of the Icelandic sagas" (Rosenberg, 1963:2).[2] It would be useful at the beginning of this chapter to introduce the complex relationship between the thinking of Veblen and Marxian theory, as well as the impact of evolutionary and economic theory on Veblen.

[1]It is also seen as a contribution to at least one other contemporary field, leisure studies (Rojek, 1995).

[2]There were other inputs, as well, including philosophy (for example, John Dewey).

Marxian Theory

Although he recognizes many subdivisions within each social class, Veblen, like Marx, operates with essentially a two-class model of social stratification (the business and industrial classes, with the former controlling the latter), but in contrast to Marx, Veblen's model is *not* based on ownership of the means of production, but rather on amount of wealth and whether or not control is exercised over others. The *business class* "own[s] wealth invested in large holdings and . . . thereby control[s] the conditions of life for the rest"; the *industrial class* does "not own wealth in sufficiently large holdings, and [its] conditions of life are therefore controlled by others" (Veblen, 1919/1964:161). Other ways of putting the distinction between the two classes is that there is a division between those "who live on free income [essentially, unearned income; see below] and those who live by work"; "between those who control the conditions of work and the rate and volume of output and to whom the net output of industry goes as free income, on the one hand, and those others who have the work to do and to whom a livelihood is allowed by these persons in control, on the other hand"; "between the kept classes and the underlying community from which their keep is drawn" (Veblen, 1919/1964:162). Later, Veblen (1923:9) puts the issue in an explicitly non-Marxist way: "this . . . cleavage, in material interest and in sentiment, runs not between those who own something and those who own nothing, as has habitually been set out in the formulas of the doctrinaires, but between those who own more than they personally can use and those who have urgent use for more than they own."

Another key difference between Marx and Veblen is that for Marx the creative force is labor, whereas Veblen sees the "industrial arts" (defined by Veblen [1923:63] as "the accumulated knowledge of ways and means"), especially technology, as creative forces (we will have more to say about the industrial arts later in this chapter).[3] For example, Veblen (1923:63) argues, "The state of the industrial arts . . . must in the nature of things always be the prime factor in human industry." One consequence of this is that labor and its emancipation does not occupy the central role in Veblen's work that it does in Marx's. In fact, Veblen has a rather low regard for the working class. It is those who create and maintain the industrial arts—the technologists and engineers—who are central and who would lead a revolution against the business class, were it to occur. Workers, at best, would follow their lead.

One of the basic principles that Veblen does share with Marx is a materialistic orientation. Veblen (1923:205) defines material conditions as "the ways and means of living and of procuring a livelihood." The industrial arts are part of the material conditions, as is the population base. Veblen argues: "in the long run, of course, the pressure of changing material circumstances will have to shape the lines of human conduct, on pain of extinction" (Veblen, 1923:17). Thus, for example, changes in norms, values, and ways of thinking follow changes in the material bases (and are therefore always out of date; see p. 356 for a discussion of Veblen's contribution to our understanding of "cultural lag").

---

[3]However, it is the case that the "instinct of workmanship" (see p. 357) plays a role in Veblen's work that has some resemblance to the role played by "species being" in Marx's work.

In spite of a number of similarities, Veblen (1906/1963) was *not* a Marxist.[4] Veblen criticizes Marx for a number of things, including buying into the doctrine of natural rights (for example, the laborer's right to the entire product of labor); being in the thrall of Hegelian philosophy; adopting the latter's theory of change rather than a Darwinian evolutionary perspective of a cumulative sequence of change without a teleology, or final perfect end (to Veblen [1906/1963:72], "Darwinism has largely supplanted Hegelianism"); operating with other ideas (conscious class struggle) that do not fit well with a Hegelian approach; using outmoded psychological assumptions (hedonistic calculus based on self-interest); using the ideas of the political economists in ways that were not consistent with their intended use; having nothing to say about the future society that is supposed to replace capitalism; and making a series of predictions that have not been borne out by later events. Overall, although Veblen was not a Marxist, at least some of his ideas show the impact of Marxian theory.

Evolutionary Theory

Influenced by Darwin and the Social Darwinists (especially Herbert Spencer and William Graham Sumner), Veblen operated with an evolutionary perspective (Tilman, 2007). He views human society as being dominated by a struggle for existence with the fittest social institutions and habits of thought surviving. He sees progress in human history with not only the fit social institutions and individuals surviving, but the unfit perishing. Furthermore, he sees a process of institutions and habits of thought adapting to changing circumstances. Above all, and most generally, an evolutionary perspective is useful to Veblen in allowing him to emphasize that social institutions change and develop.

The selective adaptation that lies at the core of evolutionary theory is never totally successful. Institutions are received from the past and exist in the present because they have survived the process of selective adaptation. However, they are still derived from the past and as such are never fully in tune with present circumstances; institutions adapted from the past can never catch up with changing social circumstances. Thus, Veblen (1899/1994:191) concludes, "institutions of to-day—the present accepted scheme of life—do not entirely fit the situation of to-day." However, as a result of inherent inertia or conservatism, there is a tendency for social institutions to persist even when they are not fully adapted to changing circumstances. This means that people are, at least to some degree, rendered ill-equipped to handle present-day demands. However, they are likely to become aware of the discontinuity between the demands of their current life and the social institutions that are holdovers from the past. This awareness is one of the things that leads to changes in social institutions designed to bring them more into line with present realities. However, some groups (such as the leisure class to be discussed later) are sheltered from everyday realities, especially everyday economic exigencies, with the result that their way of life is able to remain more attuned to past realities. Such groups, especially if they are of high status and are emulated by other groups, are likely to be conservative forces that retard social

[4]Paul Sweezy (1958:180), among others, disagrees, arguing that "the Veblenian framework is fundamentally Marxian."

progress and the efforts of others to bring social institutions up to date. In spite of such opposition, social institutions do change and develop; they selectively adapt to changing circumstances.

Veblen distinguishes between the evolution of the community and the evolution of the individual. He argues that the difference between them has led to an important discontinuity in evolution. Communities have, in Veblen's view, evolved to the point where they no longer need to compete with one another, but rather need to cooperate in industrial matters. However, individuals have retained the need to compete in order to succeed and further their own interests and careers. Thus, individuals "lag" behind changes at the collective level.

Overall, Veblen operated with a basic, two-stage model of evolution. The earlier stage is termed "savage society" and Veblen tends to have a positive view of it describing it as a good society being characterized by peace and cooperation. In contrast to Hobbes, Veblen saw the primitive, savage state as pointing rather to "peace than to war as the habitual situation" (Veblen, 1922/1964:100). The later stage of predatory "barbarism" is viewed much more negatively as being characterized by a warlike and competitive character. The focus here is on the achievement of the individual rather than the well-being of the collectivity. In the early, savage culture, the industrial arts were employed for the common good. However, in the predatory, barbarian culture, the focus shifts to self-interest and to using the industrial arts to gain advantages at the expense of others. Although the world had moved beyond the early stages of barbarism through handicrafts and the machine age, Veblen believed that the society he analyzed and lived in was only a later stage of barbarism. Thus, even the machine age is characterized by individual competitiveness and is, as we will see, conducive to warlike relations among nations.

A key aspect of this evolutionary process is a shift from free workmanship in savage society, a situation in which workmanship is the basis of industry, to the predatory, barbarian society in which property relations, or pecuniary interests, control industry. The basis for pecuniary control arises when production yields income above and beyond that which is needed by the workers to subsist. In addition, material factors such as raw material and technology tie industry to a particular place with the result that the surveillance, control, and economic exploitation of workers becomes more possible. It becomes profitable to own the material means of industry and along with that comes control over the more immaterial aspects of the industrial arts. Ownership of the means of production often comes about as a result of warfare and, as a result, is clearly part of a predatory, barbarian culture. All of this finds its most perfect expression in the great pecuniary cultures of the Occident.

Although not devoid of utility, Veblen's evolutionary theory now seems like an unfortunate product of his intellectual times, which were dominated by Darwinian theory, Social Darwinism, and Spencerian evolutionism. It leads, to put it mildly, to a questionable and simplistic model of human history. It also gives his work a very dated feel and it leads Veblen into some very unfortunate positions. For example, he adopts a racist view of evolution when he discusses the evolution of "lower ethnic elements" (Veblen, 1899/1994:217), viewing "the negro population of the South" as "low in economic efficiency, or in intelligence, or both" (Veblen, 1899/1994:322).

Economic Theory

If Veblen was identified with any field during his lifetime, it was economics (he was offered the presidency of the American Economic Association, but refused the position). However, Veblen was highly critical of mainstream economics (he was associated with institutional economics [Seckler, 1975], which has been pushed to the margins of the discipline by the kind of economics of which he was so critical). Among other things, he was critical of economic theory for adopting the idea of natural laws that led to the orderly unfolding of human conduct to reach the ordained end of human happiness (Veblen, 1899/1900/1964). Adam Smith, among others, is accused of operating with such a perspective and for making the facts fit with his preconceptions about natural law and the teleology of the theory. Later economists replaced the achievement of such an end with a hedonistic, utilitarian view, which sees conduct as "the pursuit of the greatest gain or least sacrifice" (Veblen, 1899/1900/1964:97). Still later economists (for example, Alfred Marshall) offered a sense of a "consummately [sic] conceived and self-balanced mechanism" (Veblen, 1899/1900/1964:143). All of these are rejected for Veblen's preferred Darwinian evolutionary view of a "cumulatively unfolding process of an institutional adaptation to cumulatively unfolding exigencies" (Veblen, 1899/1900/1964:143).

Veblen (1909/1964) sees more recent marginal utility economics as a variant of, and sharing some of the same problems with, classical economic theory. It is a static, hedonistic, rationalistic, teleological (current events are governed by their future consequences), deductive theory that accepts natural rights, especially that of ownership. Marginal utility theory is seen as solely concerned with distribution and having little to offer on such issues as consumption. More important, it is dominated by an interest in "the method of inference by which an individual is presumed invariably to balance pleasure and pain under given conditions that are presumed to be normal and invariable" (Veblen, 1909/1964:162). Given its teleological and deductive character, it has little to say on cause and effect in general, and more specifically on that which is of greatest importance to Veblen (1909/1964:152), "the causes of change or the unfolding sequence of the phenomena of economic life." Thus, on what, as we will see, is the most important issue in economic life to Veblen, the growth of the industrial arts (as well as the pecuniary interests of business) in the preceding two centuries, marginal utility theory had, in Veblen's view, been silent.

Marginal utility theory is also accused of ignoring larger cultural and institutional issues and concentrating, instead, on making theoretical deductions. The focus is on hedonistic actors making rational choices in order to maximize their pleasure (and minimize their pain), and larger cultural factors are, in the main, ignored by marginal utility theorists. Also ignored are "discriminating forethought," habit, and convention, because marginal utility economists focus solely on rational calculation based on future consequences. Finally, in Veblen's view, marginal utility theory reflects the current business and pecuniary situation, but it mistakes that for the only way in which economic behavior can occur.

Basic Premises

In this section we deal with some of the basic premises of Veblen's theory, including his ideas on human nature, the industrial arts, cultural lag, and cultural borrowing.

Thorstein Veblen

A Biographical Sketch

Thorstein Veblen was born in rural Wisconsin on July 30, 1857. His parents were poor farmers of Norwegian origin (Dorfman, 1966). Thorstein was the sixth of twelve children. He was able to escape the farm and at the age of 17 began studying at Carleton College in Northfield, Minnesota. Early in his schooling he demonstrated both the bitterness and the sense of humor that were to characterize his later work. He met his future first wife, the niece of the president of Carleton College, at the school (they eventually married in 1888). Veblen graduated in 1880 and obtained a teaching position, but the school soon closed and he went East to study philosophy at Johns Hopkins University. However, he failed to obtain a scholarship and moved on to Yale in the hopes of finding economic support for his studies. He managed to get by economically and obtained his Ph.D. from Yale in 1884 (one of his teachers was an early giant of sociology, William Graham Sumner). However, in spite of strong letters of recommendation, he was unable to obtain a university position because, at least in part, of his agnosticism, his lack (at the time) of a professional reputation, and the fact that he was perceived as an immigrant lacking the polish needed to hold a university post. He was idle for the next few years (he attributed this idleness to ill health), but by 1891 he returned to his studies, this time focusing more on the social sciences at Cornell University. With the help of one of his professors of economics (A. Laurence Laughlin), who was moving to the University of Chicago, Veblen was able to become a fellow at that university in 1892. He did much of the editorial work associated with *The Journal of Political Economy,* one of the many new academic journals created during this period at Chicago. Veblen was a marginal figure at Chicago, but he did teach some courses and, more important, used the *Journal of Political Economy* as an outlet for his writings. His work also began to appear in other outlets, including *The American Journal of Sociology,* another of the University of Chicago's new journals.

In 1899 he published his first and what became his best-known book, *The Theory of the Leisure Class,* but his position at Chicago remained tenuous. In fact, when he asked for a customary raise of a few hundred dollars, the university president made it clear that he would not be displeased if Veblen left the university. But the book received a great deal of attention and Veblen was eventually promoted to the position of assistant professor. While some students found his teaching inspiring, most found it abysmal. One of his Chicago students said that he was "an exceedingly queer fish. . . . Very commonly with his cheek in hand, or in some such position, he talked in a low, placid monotone, in itself a most uninteresting delivery and manner of conducting the class" (Dorfman, 1966:248–249). It was not unusual for him to begin a course with a large number of students who had heard of his growing fame, but for the class to dwindle to a few diehards by the end of the semester.

Veblen's days at Chicago were numbered for various reasons, including the fact that his marriage was crumbling and he offended Victorian sentiments with affairs with other women. In 1906, Veblen took an associate professorship at Stanford University.

Unlike the situation at Chicago, he taught mainly undergraduates at Stanford and many of them were put off by his appearance (one said he looked like a "tramp") and his boring teaching style. But what did Veblen in again was his womanizing, which forced him to resign from Stanford in 1909 under circumstances that made it difficult for him to find another academic position. But with the help of a colleague and friend who was the head of the department of economics at the University of Missouri, Veblen was able to obtain a position there in 1911. He also obtained a divorce in that year, and in 1914, he married a divorcee and former student.

Veblen's appointment at Missouri was at a lower rank (lecturer) and it paid less than the position at Stanford. In addition, he hated the then-small town, Columbia, Missouri, that was the home of the university (he reportedly called it a "woodpecker hole of a town" and the state a "rotten stump" [Dorfman, 1966:306]). However, it was during his stay at Missouri that another of his best-known books, *The Instinct of Workmanship and the State of the Industrial Arts* appeared. Veblen's stormy academic career took another turn in 1917 when he moved to Washington, D.C., to work with a group commissioned by President Wilson to analyze possible peace settlements for World War I. After working for the U.S. Food Administration for a short time, Veblen moved to New York City as one of the editors of a magazine, *The Dial*. The magazine shifted its orientation and within a year Veblen lost his editorial position. However, in the interim he had become connected with the New School for Social Research. His pay there was comparatively high (a good portion of it contributed by one of his former students at Chicago) and because he lived frugally, the great critic of American business began investing his money, at first in raisin vineyards in California and later in the stock market.

Veblen returned to California in 1926 and by the next year was living in a town shack in northern California. His economic situation became a disaster as he lost the money he had invested in the raisin industry and his stocks became worthless. He continued to earn $500 to $600 a year from royalties, and his former Chicago student continued to send him $500 a year.

Veblen was, to put it mildly, an unusual man. For example, he could often sit for hours and contribute little or nothing to a conversation going on around him. His friends and admirers made it possible for him to become president of the American Economic Association, but he declined the offer. The following vignette offered by a bookseller gives a bit more sense of this complex man:

> a man used to appear every six or eight weeks quite regularly, an ascetic, mysterious person . . . with a gentle air. He wore his hair long. . . . I used to try to interest him in economics . . . I even once tried to get him to begin with *The Theory of the Leisure Class*. I explained to him what a brilliant port of entry it is to social consciousness. . . . He listened attentively to all I said and melted like a snow drop through the door. One day he ordered a volume of Latin hymns. "I shall have to take your name because we will order this expressly for you," I told him. "We shall not have an audience for such a book as this again in a long time, I am afraid." "My name is Thorstein Veblen," he breathed rather than said.
>
> (cited in Tilman, 1992:9–10)

Thorstein Veblen died on August 3, 1929, just before the Depression that many felt his work anticipated.

Human Nature

Veblen operates with a very strong sense of human nature and of its importance in social life. *Instincts* are at the core of his thinking about human nature (Ayres, 1958), and they are defined as "the innate and persistent propensities of human nature" (Veblen, 1922/1964:2). There are a number of such inherited human instincts. They all relate to the objective ends of human endeavors; in other words, instincts are teleological. In fact, instincts differ from one another on the basis of their ends or purposes. Another component of Veblen's thinking on human nature is "tropismatic action." Tropismatic action is seen as "automatic" behavior involving no conscious thought processes, as mere "physiological reflexes" (F. Hill, 1958:134). In contrast, instinctive action involves intelligence, or "consciousness and adaptation to an end aimed at" (Veblen, 1922/1964:4). With the ends of life defined instinctively, the ways and means to those ends are defined intelligently, socially, and culturally. The latter is especially important to Veblen. Over time, intelligently chosen means become traditional and part of the larger culture; they become habitual. Ultimately, they become institutionalized; they become conventional, consistent, and sanctioned by the larger culture. Thus, although Veblen bases his thinking on instincts, they are inherently intertwined with larger social factors.

There are, in Veblen's view, individual and racial differences in instincts. Here, he accords an advantage to groups such as Europeans (and their colonies), which are composed of racially mixed, or "hybrid," stocks. Because of racial homogeneity, "lower cultures" are at a disadvantage relative to Europeans. In terms of instincts, there is greater evolutionary adaptation on the part of the European "races" than is found in the lower cultures. This is because "the hybrid populations afford a greater scope and range of variation in their human nature than could be had within the limits of any pure-bred race" (Veblen, 1922/1964:23). Although Veblen sees only slight genetic differences between the races, those differences may come to represent decisive differences as they work themselves out over time. Thus, Veblen (1922/1964:24) does accord much importance to race, and "in the last resort any race is at the mercy of its instincts."

Whereas race and attendant instincts are generally stable (although mutations are possible), the associated habitual elements of life, the social institutions, change continually. Although such changes are necessary, it is possible that social institutions will arise that are, as we have already seen, at variance with the demands of various instincts. Institutions that are at such variance are what Veblen often calls "imbecile institutions."

Instinct of Workmanship

The primary human instinct, and one that has a crucial place in Veblen's thinking, is the instinct of workmanship. It involves the efficient use of available means and adequate management of available resources. It is concerned with "practical expedients, ways and means, devices and contrivances of efficiency and economy, proficiency, creative work, and technological mastery of facts . . . a proclivity for taking pains" (Veblen, 1922/1964:33). Although it sounds as if it deals with means, the instinct of workmanship, as well as those things involved in it, is an end in its own right. This instinct is manifest at the micro level in terms of the technical efficiency of the individual worker and at the macro level in the technological proficiency and accomplishments of the community as a whole (the "industrial arts"). Although it is primary, the instinct of workmanship, like all instincts, must work itself out in a give-and-take with all other instincts. The instinct of workmanship is manifest throughout the social world in domains as diverse as the arts, religion, and law. In a way, this instinct relates to all ends because it is concerned with achieving ends in the best possible way.

As important as it is, the instinct of workmanship has certain weaknesses. For example, it does not have the tenacity of other instincts and is likely to yield to them. It is also relatively easy to bend this instinct to institutional developments of one kind or another. In lower cultures, there was little institutional development to adversely affect the instinct of workmanship, but in later cultures a more developed institutional system has a far more negative impact on that instinct. However, the most important obstruction to the instinct of workmanship comes, at least theoretically, from within the instinct itself in the form of *animism.* By this, Veblen means the belief that inanimate objects are invested with souls and the ability to do things. More specifically, within the instinct of workmanship this involves "the sentimental propensity to impute workmanlike qualities and conduct to external facts" (Veblen, 1922/1964:80). One example might be the view that it is the "market" or the organization that accomplishes work rather than workers endowed with the instinct of workmanship. Such mystical views stand in contrast to the matter-of-factness that lies at the heart of the instinct of workmanship.

Parental Bent

The only instinct close to the instinct of workmanship in importance is the "parental bent," and the two have much in common. The parental bent is defined as "an unselfish solicitude for the well-being of the incoming generation—a bias for the highest efficiency and fullest volume of life in the group" (Veblen, 1922/1964:46).

Idle Curiosity

Veblen (1922/1964:85) sees people as endowed with an instinctive curiosity, "an 'idle' curiosity by force of which men, more or less insistently, want to know things, when graver interests do not engage their attention." Although it may be pushed to the background in the short run by more immediate needs such as food, in the long run it has led to our most important achievements in systematic knowledge. This instinct plays a central role in Veblen's discussion of "higher learning" (Kaplan, 1958; see the following).

Veblen does not emphasize the fact that this curiosity is "hard-wired" in people, but rather focuses on how it has developed into ancient habits of thought that have persisted through centuries of existence and use. Especially important are the "habitual canons of knowledge and belief" through which people "construct those canons of conduct which serve as guide and standards in practical life" (Veblen, 1919/1964:6). As important as these habits of thinking are, they are constantly subject to revision as a result of changes in the material environment. This makes it clear, again, that Veblen was ultimately a materialist, believing that what shapes everything else is "the exigencies that beset men in their everyday dealings with the material means of life; inasmuch as these material facts are insistent and uncompromising" (Veblen, 1919/1964:9). The economy is one of the key elements of material existence. As it changes, people's habits of thought (also defined as social institutions) change, but social and cultural change is limited by "changeless native proclivities" (Veblen, 1919/1964:11). In fact, if habits of thought grow too far out of line with human nature, those ways of thinking will be modified so that they are in better alignment with human nature.

Emulation

Veblen relates the instinct of workmanship to yet another of his instincts—emulation: "Men are moved by many impulses and driven by many instinctive dispositions. Among these abiding dispositions are a strong bent to admire and defer to persons of achievement and distinction, as well as a workmanlike disposition to find merit in any work that serves the common good" (Veblen, 1923:115). We will have more to say about this instinct in our later discussion of conspicuous consumption and waste.

The Industrial Arts

The industrial arts, or technological knowledge, is "a common stock, held and carried forward collectively by the community, which is in this relation to be conceived as a going concern" (Veblen, 1922/1964:103). It is a historical product and it is continually changing. However, the new additions are slight in comparison to the total body handed down from the past. He sees the industrial arts as a collective possession, and Veblen offers a very contemporary sounding micro-macro model of its genesis:

> Each successive move in advance, every new wrinkle of novelty, improvement, invention, adaptation, every further detail of workmanlike innovation, is of course made by individuals and comes out of individual experience and initiative, since the generations of mankind live only in individuals. But each move so made is necessarily made by individuals immersed in the community and exposed to the discipline of group life as it runs in the community, since all life is necessarily group life. . . . Any new technological departure necessarily takes its rise in the workmanlike endeavours of given individuals, but it can do so only by force of their familiarity with the body of knowledge which the group already has in hand.
>
> (Veblen, 1922/1964:104)

Just as the industrial arts of the collectivity could not exist without the contributions of individuals, individual workers would be helpless without access to that collective body of knowledge and skill.

The industrial efficiency of individual workers, as well as the community as a whole, is a function of the state of the industrial arts. Efficiency is apt to be high when the arts are well-developed and it is likely to be low when they are underdeveloped.

As in many places in his work, race plays a role here. The state of industrial arts depends on the individual abilities of the worker, but the kind and the degree of the abilities of individuals in this regard vary among the races.

Cultural Lag

As we have already seen several times, Veblen operates with a theory of cultural lag, an idea that is usually more associated with William Fielding Ogburn (1922/1964). This concept is most notable in his discussion of the advances in science and technology in the modern world and the resulting centrality of a matter-of-fact, mechanistic way of thinking. In fact, he sees this way of thinking, and its scientific and practical application, as the "main line of march for civilisation" (Veblen, 1919/1964:12). The "lag" occurs because "the system of law and custom, which governs the relations of men to one another and defines their mutual rights, obligations, advantages and disabilities" has tended to be "somewhat in arrears" (Veblen, 1919/1964:11–12). More specifically, Veblen (1923:206) argues, "The principles (habits of thought) which govern knowledge and belief, law and morals, have accordingly lagged behind, as contrasted with the forward drive in industry and in the resulting workday conditions of living." However, it was in his view only a matter of time until those systems of thought would be brought more into line with the matter-of-fact way of thinking predominant in science and technology.

Among the system of laws and customs, Veblen focuses on the vested right of ownership and the time-honored principles that lie at its base. From his point of view, these vested rights have "become the focus of vexation and misery in the life of civilised peoples" (Veblen, 1919/1964:22). They have done so because they have lagged behind and put limits on the development of the industrial arts with its factories, mechanical equipment, standardized procedures and possession of the "accumulated technological wisdom of the community" (Veblen, 1919/1964:37). The expansion of the industrial arts has been accompanied by a change in ownership, with the personal employer-owner being progressively replaced by impersonal corporate capital. The problem is that those who possess such capital have come to gain control over the industrial arts at the same time that they have grown increasingly distant from, and less knowledgeable about, them. Thus, capital has come to be a barrier to the industrial arts and their further development. To put it another way, ownership and the ideas that lie at its base have tended to lag behind changes in the industrial arts and, given their position, they have had the ability to impede the operation and progress of the industrial arts. In sum, "Twentieth-century technology has outgrown the eighteenth-century system of vested rights" (Veblen 1921:100).

Substantive Issues

A number of substantive issues lie at the core of Veblen's thinking, including his theories of the leisure class, the inherent conflict between business and industry, higher learning, and politics.

Theory of the Leisure Class

Veblen's first and best-known book, *The Theory of the Leisure Class,* was also his most important work. He begins by making an early variant of a distinction that, as we alluded to earlier (although in other terms) and will discuss more extensively later (under the heading "Business versus Industry"), informs his life work. He argues that activities fall into two classes in primitive society. First, there is *industry* (or "drudgery"), the "effort that goes to create a new thing, with a new purpose given it by the fashioning hand of its maker out of passive ('brute') material" (Veblen, 1899/1994:12). Then there is *exploit,* which involves "so far as it results in an outcome useful to the agent . . . the conversion to his own ends of energies previously directed to some other end by another agent" (Veblen, 1899/1994:12–13). An "invidious distinction"[5] (a key phrase in Veblen's work) is made between the two with employment involving exploit coming to be seen as "worthy, honourable, noble," whereas that involving industry (or drudgery) is viewed as "unworthy, debasing, ignoble" (Veblen, 1899/1994:13). It is this distinction that lies at the root of the development of social classes.

Veblen explores the "psychological ground" of this invidious distinction, which he sees as rooted in a concept that, as we have seen, is fundamental to his work—the instinct of workmanship. He describes this aptitude (or propensity) as follows: "man is an agent . . . seeking in every act the accomplishment of some concrete, objective, impersonal end. By force of his being such an agent he is possessed of a taste for effective work, and a distaste for futile effort. He has a sense of the merit of serviceability or efficiency and of the demerit of futility, waste, or incapacity" (Veblen, 1899/1994:13). Invidious comparisons tend to be made between people on the basis of their efficiency in doing work. As a result, people seek to make their efficiency visible to others so that they may gain esteem and be emulated by others. In peaceful barbarian societies this most often takes the form of gaining esteem on the basis of one's industrial efficiency. Later, in more predatory societies, the focus shifts to exploit and to the demonstration of tangible evidence of prowess and aggression, such as booty and trophies. Obtaining these by force comes to be valued with the result that obtaining them by other methods, including industry, comes to be disesteemed. An invidious distinction is made between exploit and industry, and the latter comes to be seen as lacking in dignity and even irksome to perform.

Operating with an evolutionary model that, as we saw earlier, pervades all his work, Veblen argues that with the beginning of ownership there dawns a leisure class. The roots of ownership lie in the seizure of women as trophies, as demonstrations of male prowess. From there ownership extends to the products of industry. Most often, ownership of private property is traced to the need for subsistence, but although this may be true in earlier societies, in more contemporary societies the motive that lies at the base of owning and accumulating things is emulation. That is, private property is the basis of esteem and everyone else in society seeks to emulate, or even outdo, those who have a great deal of it. This is true of manual workers, but it is even more true in the higher reaches of the stratification system.

In an earlier era, wealth was seen as evidence of efficiency, of the instinct of workmanship. However, more recently, the possession of wealth itself has come to be seen as meritorious. The importance of how one acquired the wealth, whether or not one gained it on the basis of efficient industry, tends to fade from view. In fact, at a later stage, greater prestige is awarded to wealth obtained by inheritance than to that obtained by

---

[5]Veblen claims, somewhat disingenuously, that he is not using this term in a negative sense. Rather, he contends that he is using it "in a technical sense as describing a comparison of persons with a view to rating and grading them in respect of relative worth or value—in an aesthetic or moral sense—and so awarding and defining the relative degrees of complacency with which they may legitimately be contemplated by themselves and by others. An invidious comparison is a process of valuation of persons in respect of worth" (Veblen, 1899/1994:34).

dint of a person's own efforts. Self-esteem comes to be based on material possessions and whether one has as many, or (better) more, possessions than do those one considers one's peers. Thus, emulation lies at the base of this desire for material goods. As a result, the desire for wealth can never be satisfied as it might be if it were driven by the need to subsist: "since the struggle is substantially a race for reputability on the basis of invidious comparison, no approach to a definitive attainment is possible" (Veblen, 1899/1994:32). Thus, the instinct of workmanship is transformed into an effort to outdo others in terms of the possession of the symbols of economic achievement.

Conspicuous Leisure

In the working class there persists, at least to some degree, a focus on work and an emulation of those who are good at what they do. However, this is not the case in the leisure, or superior pecuniary, class. Until the early industrial stage of development, the leisure class tends to demonstrate its wealth, and thereby gain esteem, by leading a life of leisure; by ostentatiously *not* working. This Veblen calls *conspicuous leisure.* It is not that the leisure class is necessarily indolent or quiescent, but rather that it consumes time nonproductively because of a sense that productive work is unworthy. Such activity is also evidence of its ability to be able to afford to devote its life to idleness. The leisure class seeks to develop and present "evidence" that it has not been engaged in productive labor and such evidence includes "the knowledge of dead languages and the occult sciences; of correct spelling; of syntax and prosody; of the various forms of domestic music and other household art; of the latest properties of dress, furniture, and equipage; of games, sports, and fancy-bred animals, such as dogs and race-horses" (Veblen, 1899/1994:45). Similar evidence comes from demonstrations of "manners and breeding, polite usage, decorum, and formal and ceremonial observances generally" (Veblen, 1899/1994:45–46). The leisure class is apt to employ servants who, because they produce nothing, also serve to demonstrate that time is being wasted in the care and maintenance of the master and his household and that the master has the ability to pay for such a waste of time. In addition, wives do the consumption for the master, further demonstrating his leisure and his ability to pay for it.

Conspicuous Consumption

As society evolves further, *conspicuous consumption* tends to replace conspicuous leisure among the leisure class. In modern societies the only practicable way of impressing large numbers of transient others is with abundantly obvious indicators of one's ability to waste money, and consumer goods are more obvious than leisure activities. Both conspicuous consumption and conspicuous leisure involve waste.[6] The latter involves the waste of time and the former, the waste of money. The leisure class is expected to consume not only a great deal, but also the best "in food, drink, narcotics, shelter, services, ornaments, apparel, weapons and accoutrements, amusements, amulets, and idols or

[6]In another disingenuous aside, Veblen (1899/1994:97–98) claims that he is not using the term *waste* in a negative sense as illegitimate or to deprecate the ends or motives of the consumer. Rather, *waste* is used "technically" as expenditures that do "not serve human life or human well-being on the whole." However, he quickly adds that from the everyday perspective of the instinct of workmanship such waste is deprecated.

divinities" (Veblen, 1899/1994:73). The members of the leisure class not only must consume these things, but must consume them in the "proper" manner, and they must become connoisseurs of them. Further, it is not enough to consume for oneself, but one must give expensive presents and throw lavish parties.

Those in other social classes seek to emulate the conspicuous consumption (and leisure) of the leisure class. However, in the lower classes the head of the household cannot afford not to work. The obligation then falls upon the wife to demonstrate conspicuous leisure by performing household tasks that indicate that it is not necessary for her to be gainfully employed. The housewife also tends to obtain those things that are signs of conspicuous consumption in this social class. She consumes such things in order to enhance the reputation of her spouse.

More generally, the leisure classes stand on the pinnacle of the stratification system and it is incumbent on all classes that rank below them, including even the very lowest classes, to emulate the way they live. However, the influence of the leisure class is not direct, except on the class immediately below it in the hierarchy. In Veblen's view, each class tends to emulate the one in the stratum immediately above. It is rare to compare oneself to those in strata that are far above or those that rank below. The ways that the leisure class lives and thinks ultimately determine the ways of life and modes of thought of the entire community. However, this effect takes place gradually over time as the process of emulation works its way through the stratification system. Thus, the leisure class cannot bring about an abrupt revolution that dramatically alters the way the community thinks and consumes.

To the degree that they can, all social classes engage in conspicuous consumption and conspicuous leisure. Thus, Veblen (1899/1994:85) contends: "no class of society, not even the abjectly poor, foregos all customary conspicuous consumption. The last items of this category of consumption are not given up except under stress of the direst necessity. Very much of squalor and discomfort will be endured before the last trinket or the last pretence of pecuniary decency is put away."

Waste

Veblen makes it clear that, although all social classes engage in waste, most people do not intentionally seek to waste money or time. Rather, they do so as a result of "a wish to conform to established usage, to avoid unfavourable notice and comment, to live up to the accepted canons of decency in the kind, amount, and grade of goods consumed, as well as in the decorous employment of . . . time and effort" (Veblen, 1899/1994:115).

It is not just that this principle of waste affects consumption; it affects habits of thought more generally, including "the sense of duty, the sense of beauty, the sense of utility, the sense of devotional or ritualistic fitness, and the scientific sense of truth" (Veblen, 1899/1994:116). Thus, for example, churches are constructed with an eye to demonstrating at least some degree of wasteful expenditure. Clerical clothing is often costly, ornate, and quite uncomfortable. Clerics are not expected to engage in work that is productive from an industrial point of view. Things that we consider to be beautiful tend also to be expensive; if they are not expensive, they are not likely to be deemed beautiful. We consider useless household pets like dogs beautiful, whereas the barnyard animals like hogs and cattle are useful and, as result, not considered beautiful. The dog comes under particular merciless (and humorous) attack: "He is the filthiest of the domestic animals in his person and the nastiest in his habits. For this he makes up in servile, fawning attitude towards his master, and a readiness to inflict damage and discomfort on all else . . . he is also an item of expense, and commonly serves no industrial purpose" (Veblen, 1899/1994:141). Thus, it can easily be argued that we conspicuously consume in the domestic animals we choose to purchase and maintain (to say nothing of the way in which we maintain them). Veblen makes a similar argument about fast horses, which are also expensive to maintain; they are wasteful and useless, except in that they can be used to win races and thereby satisfy the owner's need for aggression and dominance.

Veblen looks at female beauty in much the same way. For example, such beauty is associated with small hands and a narrow waist. However, from the point of view of doing most types of productive work, these are structural faults that "show that the person so affected is incapable of useful effort and must therefore be supported in idleness by her owner. She is useless and expensive, and she is consequently valuable as evidence of pecuniary strength" (Veblen, 1899/1994:149). He makes the same point about the propensity of the Chinese to bind and mutilate women's feet. Similarly, clothing, especially women's clothing, is considered desirable and beautiful if it demonstrates that the wearer is unable to work. The high heel is one example, as is the skirt, which women persist in wearing even though "it is expensive and hampers the wearer at every turn and incapacitates her for all useful exertion" (Veblen, 1899/1994:171). The corset is a "mutilation" that is "undergone for the purpose of lowering the subject's vitality and rendering her permanently and obviously unfit for work" (Veblen, 1899/1994:172).

Veblen offers a hilarious discussion of our preference for handmade over industrially produced products. It is clear that the industrial product is the more perfect product. Handmade products tend to be full of imperfections and irregularities. The process of handmaking things is far more wasteful than making them industrially. Nonetheless, we prefer the handmade product because it demonstrates more honorific waste.

Strikingly, Veblen goes further to argue that we engage in conspicuous consumption not only in those things that are seen publicly, but even in those things that are consumed in total privacy. Thus, the habit of mind associated with conspicuous consumption has pervaded virtually every domain.

Other Characteristics of the Leisure Class

Veblen associates a number of other characteristics with the leisure class; these characteristics are modern survivals of demonstrations of prowess in an earlier stage of barbarian society associated with a predatory instinct and an animistic habit of mind. All of these have tended to outlive their usefulness.

- Religiosity is another characteristic of the leisure class and Veblen (1899/1994:295) sees the religious temperament as related to sporting and gambling temperaments in that all involve "the belief in an inscrutable propensity or a preternatural interposition in the sequence of events."

- A propensity to fight, duel, to have a martial spirit, to be patriotic. Here, as elsewhere, Veblen sees a similarity between the frames of mind of the leisure class and lower-class delinquents. He sees this as a case of "arrested spiritual development" that the industrial classes have, to a large degree, been able to overcome.
- Sport, which is related to aggression, and is ultimately futile, or purposeless. In contrast, "the instinct of workmanship demands purposeful action" (Veblen, 1899/1994:259) with the result that sporting activity is much more occasional among the industrial classes.
- Gambling is enjoyed by the leisure class because it involves a belief in luck and it offers the opportunity of gaining at the advantage of the loser. However, like everything else about the leisure class, it "is recognised to be a hindrance to the highest industrial efficiency" (Veblen, 1899/1994:276). The notion of luck stands in contradiction to the industrial concern with causal sequences.

Overall, the leisure class, and its pecuniary orientation, are associated with "waste, futility, and ferocity" (Veblen, 1899/1994:351). In encouraging such things, the leisure class tends to stand in opposition to the needs of modern, industrial society: "In this as in other relations, the institution of a leisure class acts to conserve, and even to rehabilitate, that archaic type of human nature and those elements of the archaic culture which the industrial evolution of society in its later stages acts to eliminate" (Veblen, 1899/1994:331).

Business versus Industry

In the course of his discussion of the leisure class, Veblen introduces the distinction between "business" and "industry" (see the preceding discussion of his model of social change) that informs virtually all his life's work. To our way of thinking these terms seem closely related, but to Veblen there is a stark contrast, in fact an inherent conflict, between them: "The material interest of the underlying population [largely those associated with industry] is best served by maximum output at a low cost, while the business interests of the industry's owners ["business"] may best be served by a moderate output at an enhanced price." Veblen (1923:249) takes the United States as the "exemplar" of the conflict between business and industry, as well as of the predominance of business.

Business

Veblen details a historic change in the nature of business and business leaders. The early leaders tended to be entrepreneurs who were designers, builders, shop managers, and financial managers. They were more likely to have earned their income because, at least in part, it was derived from their direct contribution to production (industry). Today's business leaders are almost exclusively concerned with financial matters, and therefore, at least in Veblen's view, they are not earning their income since finance makes no direct contribution to industry. (In fact, if anything, as we will see, finance inhibits industry rather than enhancing it.) A further development involved the routinization of financial matters and the resulting handling of them by large financial organizations (for example, investment bankers). As a result, the business leader is left as an intermediary between industry and finance, with little concrete knowledge of either one.

Business tends to define the world of Veblen's day, especially the interests of the upper classes. A business orientation is defined by a pecuniary approach to economic processes; that is, the dominant interest is money. The focus is not on the interest of the larger community but rather on the profitability of the organization. Relatedly, it is oriented to acquisition, not production, and it serves the interest of invidious rather than noninvidious interests. The occupations of those with a business interest tend to relate to ownership and acquisition. It is the leisure class that tends to occupy these positions. Thus, the "captains of industry"[7] as well as the "captains of solvency" (the investment bankers, financiers who come eventually to control the captains of industry) have a business orientation. Because it is nonproductive, Veblen sees a business orientation as parasitic and exploitative: "the chances are that the owner has contributed less than his per-capita quota, if anything, to that common fund of knowledge on the product of which he draws by virtue of his ownership, because he is likely to be fully occupied with other things,—such things as lucrative business transaction, e.g., or the decent consumption of superfluities" (Veblen, 1919/1964:69). Instead of production, business leaders focus on "sharp practice," "cornering the market," and "sitting tight" (Veblen, 1923:34). He sees such a system as a holdover from earlier, predatory societies and one that is not well adapted to the new realities.

Veblen gives the business leader credit for increasing productive capacity, but as we will see, Veblen's (1904) most distinctive contribution here is to see such leaders as being at least as much involved in "disturbing" production and in restricting capacity as they are in increasing it. Veblen associates business leaders not only with the waste of material resources, equipment, and manpower as a result of the restriction of capacity, but with other ills as well. Businesspeople are responsible for the unproductive and wasteful expansion of "salesmanship" and the attendant sales costs that are passed on to the consumer. Veblen (1923:78) sees salesmanship as meaning "little else than prevarication." In addition, Veblen attributes to businesspeople the production of unnecessary and useless products and the dislocation of industrial processes through sabotage.

Veblen sees the modern corporation as a type of business. As such, its interests are in financial matters like profit and in sales and not in production and workmanship. As he puts it, "the corporation is always a business concern, not an industrial appliance. It is a means of making money, not of making goods" (Veblen, 1923:85).

Industry

Industry has to do with "the apprehension and coordination of mechanical facts and sequences, and to their appreciation and utilisation for the purposes of human life" (Veblen, 1899/1994:232). An industrial orientation is associated with those involved in workmanship and production. It is the working classes that are most likely to be involved in these activities and to have such an orientation. Unlike business's pecuniary orientation, which leads to a personal standpoint, the industrial orientation leads to an

[7]Another term favored by Veblen (1923), especially in his later writings, is *absentee ownership.*

"impersonal standpoint, of sequence, quantitative relations, mechanical efficiency, or use" (Veblen, 1899/1994:239).

Unfortunately, industry is controlled by the captains of industry who have little or no understanding of it and only understand the "higgling of the market" and "financial intrigue" (Veblen, 1919/1964:89). In fact, the main interest of those leaders is to restrict production—restrict the free operation of the industrial system—in order to keep prices (and therefore profits) high. The result is that the main task of the business leader to Veblen is to obstruct, retard, and sabotage[8] the operation of the industrial system. Without such obstructions, the extraordinary productivity of the industrial system would drive prices and profits progressively lower.

Veblen also calls those associated with a business orientation "vested interests," or those with the "marketable right to get something for nothing" (Veblen, 1919/1964:100). While they may be getting something for nothing, they cost the larger society a great deal. These costs stem from three business activities aimed at increasing profit—limitation of the supply of products, obstruction of their traffic, and publicity. All these are aimed at salesmanship, not workmanship. They add nothing to production and, as a result, are viewed by Veblen as waste.[9] He argues that although it may benefit the pecuniary interests of the captains of industry, the work that salesmen and accountants perform "is, on the whole, useless or detrimental to the community at large" (Veblen, 1904:63). To the costs associated with these activities, Veblen adds illegal business activities such as fraud. Not only are the captains of industry parasites, but Veblen (1904:64) describes entire industries—advertising, military equipment, and those involved in "turning out goods for conspicuously wasteful consumption"—as parasitic.

The increasingly tightly interlocking industrial system lends itself to cooperative undertakings, but this characteristic makes it increasingly vulnerable to the efforts of business and national leaders to sabotage it. This may be done consciously or as a result of the business leader's increasing ignorance of industrial operations (Veblen [1921:64] writes of the "one-eyed captains of industry"). In either case, it results in hardship to the community in the form of unemployment, idle factories, and wasted resources. Veblen (1904:213–214) even goes so far as to imply that business leaders are consciously responsible for depressions; they reduce production because under certain market conditions they feel they cannot derive what they emotionally consider to be a "reasonable" profit from their goods.[10]

> Industrial depression means that the business men engaged do not see their way to derive a satisfactory gain from letting the industrial process go forward on the lines and in the volume for which the material equipment of industry is designed. It is not worth their while, and it might even work them pecuniary harm. Commonly their apprehension of the discrepancy which forbids an aggressive pursuit of industrial business is expressed by the phrase "overproduction."
>
> (Veblen, 1904:213–214)

---

[8]Veblen also saw most labor unions, especially the American Federation of Labor, as engaged in such sabotage.

[9]Riesman (1953/1995) argues that one of the ways to look at the basic conflict in Veblen's work is the conflict between workmanship and wastemanship.

[10]It is this that leads Veblen (1904:241) to argue: "Depression is primarily a malady of the affections of the business men."

To Veblen, from the point of view of the larger community, there is no such thing as overproduction. However, even with the activities of the business leaders, including the creation of depressions, the industrial system is still so effective and efficient that it allows business leaders and their investors huge profits.

Free Income

The modern industrial system—"mechanical, specialised, standardised, drawn on a large scale"—is highly productive. In fact, it is so productive that it yields returns far beyond those required to cover costs and to give reasonable returns to owners and investors. These additional returns are the source of what Veblen calls "free income." Most generally, free income is that "income for which no equivalent in useful work is given" (Veblen, 1923:126). This free income is attributed by business leaders to intangible assets of the firm such as possession of a trade secret, a trademark, a patent, and a monopoly. The problem is that these intangibles produce nothing. Rather, the free income that goes to the captains of industry and their investors is the result of the constraints that these intangible assets place on the free operation of the industrial system. In addition to harming industrial efficiency, these intangibles also adversely affect the entire community because far less is produced than could be. Veblen (1919/1964:76) sees an analogy between the operations of business leaders and "blackmail, ransom, and any similar enterprise that aims to get something for nothing." (Immediately following this assertion, Veblen [1919/1964:76] offers one of his snide caveats contending that the analogy should "not be taken to cast any shadow of suspicion on the legitimacy of all the businesslike sabotage that underlies this immaterial corporate capital and its earning capacity.")

The free income earned by the captains of industry has been capitalized by the firm and this results in pressure on the firm to keep prices and profits high. The following is a good summary of Veblen's (1921:15) thinking on this issue:

> these large earnings (free income) have been capitalized; their capitalized value has been added to the corporate capital and covered with securities bearing a fixed income-charge; this income-charge, representing free income, has thereby become a liability on the earnings of the corporation; this liability cannot be met in case the concern's net aggregate earnings fall off in any degree; therefore prices must be kept up to such a figure as will bring the largest net aggregate return.
>
> (Veblen, 1921:15)

This, of course, leads the captain of industry in the direction of restriction of output and other means of sabotage.

Capitalization of the firm is no longer just the cost of the plant, but also the "good will" of the organization including "established customary business relations, reputation for upright dealing, franchises and privileges, trade-marks, brands, patent rights, copyrights, exclusive use of special processes guarded by law or by secrecy, exclusive control of particular sources of materials" (Veblen, 1904:139). The problem with all of these things is that they "give a differential advantage to their owners, but they are of no aggregate advantage to the community. They are wealth to the individuals concerned—differential wealth; but they make no part of the wealth of nations" (Veblen, 1904:139–140).

The Price System

Veblen traces many of the problems within the economy to the operation of the price system. For example, he argues that the nature of the price system and the need to maintain prices so that a reasonable profit may be earned and business recession prevented make it necessary for the captains of industry to sabotage production through "peaceable or surreptitious restriction, delay, withdrawal, or obstruction" (Veblen, 1921:4). The "problem," again, is that the industrial system is so productive that business leaders must sabotage it to some degree or else prices and profits will plunge.

Veblen sees the relationship between the price system and business leaders in much the same way that Marx sees the relationship between the capitalist system and the capitalists. That is, both are seen as structures that are constraining on actors. Thus, in Veblen's case, even if a business leader wanted to ignore profits and concentrate on producing more goods so that the larger community might benefit, that business leader would quickly be pushed to the brink of bankruptcy. More generally, Veblen (1921:14) sees businesspeople as "creatures and agents" of the price system.

Who Should Be in Charge?

In Veblen's view, the industrial system should be run by "production engineers" (industrial experts, skilled technologists, etc.), but because business leaders do not understand them, they have been employed "only reluctantly, tardily, sparingly, and with shrewd circumspection" (Veblen, 1921:64). The industrial system forms an interlocking network that not only is vulnerable to the meddling of business leaders, but requires production engineers throughout the system to work together, or at least not to work at cross-purposes. In this sense, it is in the interest of companies, communities, and even nations to work together to enhance the operation of the industrial system to their mutual benefit. As Veblen (1921:52) puts it, "In point of material welfare, all the civilized peoples have been drawn together by the state of the industrial arts into a single going concern." Of course, such a view is anathema to the vested interests in specific companies and nations. Thus, Veblen believes that control should be wrested away from these vested interests and put in the hands of the engineers who are presumed to be interested solely in increasing the efficiency of industry. Here, Veblen is operating with the questionable view that engineers have no personal, professional, or commercial biases that will, themselves, have a negative effect on industry.

Employing Marxian terminology, Veblen (1921:71) argues that "these technologists have begun to become uneasily 'class-conscious.'" They are recognizing both their indispensability and the waste that exists under the regime of the captains of industry. It is these technologists who can become the solution to the problem created by the opposition between business and industry. Thus, Veblen, unlike Marx, sees no hope in the working class, especially in representatives such as the AFL (although workers might well follow the leadership of a revolution undertaken by the technologists). The technologists have a common purpose, the elimination of the pervasive confusion, obstructionism, and wastefulness that is so characteristic of a business orientation. And they have the possibility of coming together to accomplish this end: "So slight are their numbers, and so sharply defined and homogeneous is their class, that a sufficiently compact and inclusive organization of their forces should arrange itself almost as a matter of course, so soon as any appreciable proportion of them shall be moved by any common purpose" (Veblen, 1921:80). Veblen (1921:82) is optimistic about their chances of success: "a general strike of the technological specialists in industry need involve no more than a minute fraction of one percent of the population; yet it would swiftly bring a collapse of the old order and sweep the timeworn fabric of finance and absentee sabotage into the discard for good and all."

Veblen deemed the Russian Revolution reasonably successful, and taking it at least in part as a model, he discussed a "Soviet of technicians," although he felt that the opposition of business leaders made such a development highly unlikely (Veblen, 1921:134). Such a soviet would include technical people from productive industry, transportation, and distribution, as well as consulting "production economists," but there would be no place in it for the current business leaders or even those trained in business. In spite of hopeful comments about a general strike of technologists, Veblen sees no immediate possibility of a revolution led by such soviets, especially because vested interests oppose it, there is no evidence that technologists want it, and in any case the mind-set of the American public is to prefer businesspeople as leaders and to distrust technicians.

The Impact of Industry and the Machine on Society

Veblen (1904:323) sees the machine and its ubiquity as the "unequivocal mark of the Western culture of to-day as contrasted with the culture of other times and places." As such, it has a powerful impact on other institutions in society, such as the state, law, and "matter-of-fact" science, which come to operate in a machinelike manner. Machines affect all classes, although their most direct impact is on those who work most directly with them. Most generally, the machine affects the habits of thought, the ways of thinking, within society as a whole. And Veblen (1904:372–373) sees this as spreading:

> The machine discipline, however, touches wider and wider circles of the population, and touches them in an increasingly intimate and coercive manner. In the nature of the case, therefore, the resistance opposed to this cultural trend given by the machine discipline on grounds of received conventions weakens with the passage of time. The spread of materialistic, matter-of-fact preconceptions takes place at a cumulatively accelerating rate.
>
> (Veblen, 1904:372–373)

The only thing that can impede its spread is some other cultural factor such as business interests, which may, as we have seen, at times see the proliferation of industry and the machine as contrary to its pecuniary interests. However, in the long run Veblen (1904) is certain that the machine and industry will win out. One of the reasons that the machine process and industry will emerge victorious is that "it touches larger classes of the community and inculcates its characteristic habits of thought more unremittingly" (Veblen, 1904:381).

Trained Incapacity

The idea of "trained incapacity" plays a minor role in Veblen's work, but it has received an inordinate amount of attention from sociologists and other social scientists. One of the places that Veblen (1919/1964) raises it is in the context of a discussion of the role played by owners, bankers, and workers in modern industry. His basic point is that all of these focus, in their own way, on pecuniary matters, with the result that the most important task—the efficient and effective operation of industry—suffers. As Veblen (1919/1964:347) puts it, the problems of modern industry are at least in part traceable to the "trained incapacity on the part of the several contestants to appreciate large and general requirements of the industrial situation." In being socialized to look after their own interests, the members of each of these groups are unable to understand the larger picture and especially what is of utmost importance in the modern world. The term "trained incapacity" is now often used more generally to describe any situation in which a particular type of training serves to incapacitate, at least in some way, those who have undergone such socialization.

Politics

Veblen tends to approach politics in much the same way he does the economy. The reason for this, at least in part, is that political leaders are seen as being the tools of the "vested interests" and the "captains of industry." He sees the national government as being "charged with the general care of the country's business interests" (Veblen, 1921:19). He views the nation with its legal and military powers negatively as something that is needed by business "to enforce the claims of its business men abroad" (Veblen, 1919/1964:155). The warlike nature of relationships between businesses is reflected in warlike relationships between nations. According to Veblen (1904:398): "The quest of profits leads to a predatory national policy."

Although the nation may be operated in the interest of business, it retards industry that is inherently international in scope. National boundaries serve only to retard international industrial exchanges and the international development of industrial processes. Tariffs are a specific example of a national act that operates against the interests of industry, which require free passage in order to operate most effectively. Thus, tariffs are an example of "sabotage," this time being practiced at the level of the nation rather than the business enterprise. Nations are oriented to self-aggrandizement and stand in opposition to the principle of "live and let live" that Veblen thinks should govern international (and all other) relationships. Like businesses, nations operate with what they perceive to be the right "to seek their own advantage at the cost of the rest" (Veblen, 1919/1964:120). Thus, the nation is "a predatory organism, in practical effect an association of persons moved by a community interest in getting something for nothing by force and fraud" (Veblen, 1923:442). Wars are fought and nations engage in imperialism in order to strengthen their own positions and fortify the economic positions of their business interests.

Summary

Thorstein Veblen's ideas were shaped, both positively and negatively, by a variety of theoretical inputs, especially those from evolutionary theory, Marxian theory, and economics. Much of his theory is based on a series of assumptions about human nature, especially the instinct of workmanship, the parental bent, idle curiosity, and emulation. Although such instincts are important, they are shaped and affected by larger social and cultural factors. Also basic to his theory is the notion of industrial arts, or the stock of knowledge, especially technology, that is common to the community. He operates with the view that there is a tendency for cultural lag, with changes in law and custom particularly likely to lag behind changes in the industrial arts.

The theory of the leisure class is undoubtedly Veblen's first and most lasting contribution to contemporary social theory. Particularly notable is his thinking on invidious distinctions, emulation, and conspicuous leisure and conspicuous consumption. Although best known today for that theory, Veblen was most concerned throughout much of his career with the conflict between business and industry. Industry was capable of almost unlimited production in the modern world and this high level of productivity would greatly benefit the entire community. However, the resulting flood of goods would serve to lower prices and profits. As a result, it is in the interest of business, indeed it is necessary for business, given the price system, to sabotage industry so that it is not nearly as productive as it could be. Much else that business does relates to salesmanship rather than workmanship and in that sense not only contributes nothing to the common welfare, but is a drag on it. Because it contributes nothing to industry, business obtains "free income" and that income is attributed to, and is capitalized in the firm as, such nonmaterial assets as "good will." Once capitalized, things like good will become a liability against the firm, which can be met only by keeping the income and profits high, and that is done by sabotaging industry. Veblen argues for a system run not by business leaders, but by engineers who understand the way industry really works. In any case, because they would not be dominated by the profit motive, engineers would have no interest in undermining industry. Industry and the machine technology have a wide range of effects on society, including the matter-of-fact way in which people in general, and scientists in particular, think.

Veblen's thinking about politics is affected by the business–industry conflict. Business seeks to control the state and to use the state to sabotage (by tariffs, for example) the free trade between nations. This adversely affects industry around the world as well as the lives of people in the affected nations. Nations themselves, as well as the politicians that lead them, develop a similar interest in self-aggrandizement (for example, nationalism) that adversely affects international industrial processes.

Thorstein Veblen has been the subject of more than his share of criticisms. Tilman (1992) has demonstrated that his work has been attacked from a wide range of positions on the political spectrum—conservative (for example, business is more important than Veblen indicates), liberal (he is too radical a critic of modern society), and radical (Veblen underestimated the importance of the working class). More generally, he has been criticized for his pessimism and for his tendency to criticize contemporary society without offering a blueprint for an alternative society (Dowd, 1966). Among other major criticisms are his adoption of an outmoded evolutionary perspective, a lack of clarity, a tendency to conceal his true views and motivations (often behind irony), a need to be humorous, which served to alienate the serious audience for his work, his technological determinism (given the centrality of the industrial arts dominated by technology), and his technical elitism (as reflected in his thinking on a soviet of engineers). In spite of these and many other criticisms, Veblen's legacy continues and is even growing with the increasing relevance of his work to the emerging consumer society.

C H A P T E R 13

Joseph Schumpeter[1]

Chapter Outline

Like Karl Marx (Chapter 6) and Thorstein Veblen (Chapter 12), Joseph Schumpeter (1883–1950) was long thought of as an economist. However, also like those predecessors, Schumpeter has over the years come to be less accepted in economics, but to have developed a wider audience in sociology. His economic theories (especially his famous idea of creative destruction) have great relevance to sociology, and later in his career he moved explicitly in the direction of making his theories more sociological. As a result, he has attracted increasing attention from sociologists, especially those associated with the growing field of economic sociology (Swedberg, 1993). It is also the case that Schumpeter's thinking has much in common with the work of perhaps the two most important thinkers in the history of sociology: Marx and Max Weber (Chapter 8). He even taught a course at Harvard with another eminent classical sociological theorist, Talcott Parsons (Chapter 17).

Creative Destruction

Schumpeter's most famous idea is that of creative destruction. He used this concept to highlight the process by which capitalism continuously revolutionizes itself as new products and business processes are created that render obsolete (i.e., destroy) those that exist (Schumpeter, 1942/1975). Examples include the creation of the automobile and of the automobile industry leading to the destruction of the horse and buggy and the industry that preceded it, as well as the destruction of the typewriter industry with the advent of the personal computer (PC) industry. For Schumpeter, this process of creative destruction is "the essential fact about capitalism" as waves of creation and destruction

[1]This chapter is co-authored by Craig Lair.

are constantly sweeping over the economy. The result of this "perennial gale" of creative destruction is that capitalism is a highly dynamic and revolutionary system where "[a]ny existing structures and all the conditions of doing business are always in a process of change" (Schumpeter, 1942/1947/1950:31). In other words, the "capitalist economy is not and cannot be stationary" because the process of creative destruction is constantly changing it (Schumpeter, 1942/1947/1950:31).

Two important aspects of the dynamic of creative destruction in capitalism need to be emphasized. The first is that the source of creative destruction comes *from within* the economic system itself as entrepreneurs and businesses create new goods, technologies, organizations, and practices that replace, and destroy, that which already exists. While Schumpeter (1942/1975:82) acknowledges that various non-economic (i.e., climatological, demographic, sociological) factors such as global warming, population growth, and social conflict can, to a degree, affect economic operations, these are not the "prime movers" of capitalism. Rather, the dynamism of capitalism is traceable to factors inherent in the economy and not to those outside it. This is a very important point for Schumpeter since one of his goals, at least early in his career, was to create a purely economic theory of economic development and change (this, as we will see, was to change later in his career). Only by finding a mechanism that is internal to the economy is such a theory possible. The idea of creative destruction can be seen as the culmination of this quest.

The second aspect of creative destruction to be highlighted is that the type of change involved in the process of creative destruction is *qualitative* in nature. That is, Schumpeter's prime concern was not with minor, quantitative, or incremental changes to products or economic processes already in place (e.g., how the creation of a computer that is ten percent faster than those already in existence might affect business operations). Rather, he would be much more interested in how the computer, as an entirely new and different product, affected existing products (e.g., the typewriter) and business operations. The type of change that Schumpeter (1911–34/2007:64) had in mind can be seen, at least in a negative sense, in one of his most famous lines: "Add successively as many mail coaches as you please, you will never get a railway thereby." This also implies that the changes brought about by processes of creative destruction do not take place in a linear or orderly fashion as existing organizations adapt to changing conditions in an incremental manner. Rather, the history of capitalism is a "history of revolutions" spurred by waves of economic creation and littered with the remains of economic destruction.

The idea of creative destruction has come to be associated, almost entirely, with Schumpeter (Auerswald, 2007:125). It was in *Capitalism, Socialism and Democracy* (first published in 1942) that Schumpeter introduced "his famous term 'creative destruction'" (McCraw, 2007:351). The notoriety of this idea, and Schumpeter's association with it, is somewhat ironic since Schumpeter used the term only in that one book published late in his career. Moreover, the discussion of this concept was confined mostly to a brief (approximately five-page) section entitled "The Process of Creative Destruction" with a scattering of references to it throughout the book's remaining four-hundred-plus pages.

Furthermore, the idea that creation and destruction are intertwined predates Schumpeter by eons. This is particularly the case in "[t]he idea that the birth of something new is founded on the destruction of previous existence" (Reinert and Reinert, 2006).

Examples include the Egyptian and Greek myth of the Phoenix, the Hindu view that "[c]reation is always re-creation . . . part of a cycle that has no beginning and no end" (Rosenberg, 1994:327), and Nietzsche's thinking on "man" going beyond what he currently is by developing himself into something new, different, and better (Nietzsche, 2007:76). Schumpeter was not even the first to introduce the idea of creative destruction into economics. Rather, it was the German economist (and sociologist) Werner Sombart who linked the destruction of forests in Europe to the development of a "creative spirit" that eventually led to the development of nineteenth century capitalism (Reinert and Reinert, 2006:72).

This idea is also evident in the work of Karl Marx who had a profound, though unlikely, influence upon Schumpeter's thinking. As Schumpeter (1942/1975:32) notes, "Marx saw this [dynamic] process of industrial change more clearly and he realized its pivotal importance more fully than any other economist of his time." He gave Marx a great deal of credit for recognizing the dynamic nature of economic development. However, Schumpeter also thought that many errors in Marxian theory were the result of Marx not taking the implications of capitalism's dynamism far enough. Marx's (and Engels's) dynamic vision of capitalism is captured in his famous portrayal of the revolutionary nature of the bourgeoisie from *The Communist Manifesto* that "all that is solid melts into air" (Marx and Engels, 1848/1969:38).

Marshall Berman (1982:99) has expanded upon this theme arguing that all the concrete achievements of capitalism "are made to be broken tomorrow, smashed or shredded or pulverized or dissolved, so they can be recycled or replaced next week, and the whole process can go on again and again, hopefully forever, in ever more profitable forms."

While the idea of creative destruction is not original to Schumpeter, he brought the concept to academic (and popular) attention and it was his thinking on it that had the most profound effect on later thinking in the area. It also represents the crystallization and culmination of the most important and most unique elements of Schumpeter's thoughts on economic development and change. As Andersen (2004:1) notes, though Schumpeter only used this term explicitly in a very limited fashion, this "expression could have been used throughout his work" because it "clearly reflects core elements of Schumpeter's vision of economic evolution."

Perhaps the best sense of what Schumpeter means by creative destruction can be gleaned from his view of it as involving the

> process of industrial mutation—if I may use that biological term—that incessantly revolutionizes the economic structure *from within*, incessantly destroying the old one, incessantly creating a new one. This process of Creative Destruction is the essential fact of about capitalism. It is what capitalism consists in and what every capitalist concern has got to live in (Schumpeter, 1942/1947/1950:83).

Thus, capitalism would not exist without creative destruction; capitalism would simply not *be* capitalism without creative destruction. This means that the system must be allowed to evolve on its own (contra the Keynesian view that government involvement in the economy is necessary at times, a view that continues to have many adherents to this day) and ordinarily nothing should be done that would hamper the evolution of capitalism and the process of creative destruction. In short, Schumpeter thought that capitalism, through the process of creative destruction, was dynamic enough to manage its own problems.

To Schumpeter, creative destruction is a generally positive phenomenon producing many beneficial economic (e.g., a higher standard of living) and non-economic (e.g., modern culture) outcomes. As Schumpeter (1942/1975:125) put it, "not only the modern mechanized plant and the volume of the output that pours from it, not only modern technology and economic organization, but all the features and achievements of modern civilization are, directly or indirectly, the products of the capitalist process." In addition, the destruction of the old is viewed as a positive development since it is seen as standing in the way of the creation of the new and must therefore be destroyed in order to make room for the new (Baumol 2001:21)

The concept of creative destruction becomes somewhat clearer when it is placed within the broader context of Schumpeter's thinking on capitalism. The basic logic of his argument is as follows:

- Following Adam Smith, David Ricardo, and others (and contra Marx), capitalism is seen as a desirable system (though this did not deter Schumpeter from serving as an economic advisor in a communist government and seeming to prophesize capitalism's downfall to socialism).
- Creative destruction is a positive process; that is, to move forward, to progress, capitalism *must* engage in creative destruction.
- Progress means invention and innovation, the creation of the "new."
- Invention, innovation, the new, creative destruction, and ultimately capitalism are threatened in various ways, especially by rationalization.
- All of this is encompassed by a broad view of capitalism as a system that is constantly in motion and ever-changing. Contrary to the views of most economists, to Schumpeter capitalism cannot be stable, stationary, in equilibrium.

Is Creative Destruction a Good Thing?

Schumpeter clearly sees that economic growth and development must take place through the process of creative destruction. However, he is agnostic as to whether the changes that result from this process are necessarily positive or beneficial. Thus, Schumpeter (1942/1975:68) can argue "that the capitalist process, not by coincidence but by virtue of its mechanism, raises the standard of life of the masses" without necessarily equating this economic growth with social or economic "progress." Nevertheless, the overall thrust of his analysis of capitalism and creative destruction is positive in nature and therefore tends to overlook the negatives associated with this.

For example, it is clear that the new is not always desirable; there can be undesirable new developments. Similarly, that which is old is not necessarily undesirable; at least some of the old should be retained. This all cries out for a subtler discussion of the positive and negative aspects of both the old and the new and their relationship to creative destruction.

A potential model for such analysis of creative destruction, and its relationship to the old and the new, is Robert Merton's (1968) famous functional paradigm in which he

Joseph Schumpeter

A Biographical Sketch (1883–1950)

Born and educated in Austria-Hungary, Joseph Schumpeter's life was filled with a mixture of success, paradox, and tragedy. He received his Ph.D. in 1906 from the University of Vienna and, after practicing law in Egypt for a year, earned early success as a promising young economist. However, his academic career was interrupted by WWI. After the war, he served as Minister of Finance in Austria's only socialist government between World War I and World War II, and later became President of a bank. However, by 1924 that bank collapsed when the Vienna stock market crashed, bankrupting Schumpeter. In spite of this personal disaster, Schumpeter gained invaluable practical insight into capitalism and its ever-present "gales." He gained a position at the University of Bonn (Germany) in 1925, but began visiting Harvard in the late 1920s and with the rise of Nazism in Germany, he moved to Harvard on a permanent basis in 1932. He taught there until his death in 1950.

Schumpeter carried himself in an aristocratic manner with much time and effort devoted to his appearance and dress (he told the wife of one colleague that it took him an hour to get dressed in the morning) (Allen, 1991a:134). He also liked to tell his students that as a young man he had three ambitions in life: to be the world's greatest economist, the world's greatest horseman, and the world's greatest lover (Swedberg, 1991:12). But despite all of his bravado and his escapades, Schumpeter's personal life was also filled with tragedy. It appears that Schumpeter had two great loves in his life. The first was his mother who doted on him and took great pains to ensure that he had a proper upbringing even to the point of marrying a minor noble to ensure that Schumpeter could attend the best schools (Allen, 1991a:18). The other was his second wife whom Schumpeter married in 1925. In June of 1926 Schumpeter's mother died; in August of the same year so, too, did his wife and son during childbirth. Although Schumpeter was able to recover from these tragedies, he often characterized his life as one of peace but not joy (Allen, 1991b). In the fall of 1926 he began recopying his dead wife's diary, eventually inserting his own comments and contemporary thoughts into it. Schumpeter also began to elevate his dead wife and mother into his own personal deities from whom he would ask for advice and protection (Allen, 1991a:225–229).

Known primarily as an economist, Schumpeter was a multidisciplinary thinker who "knew that law, mathematics, and history mattered mightily, as did the newer fields of *sociology*, psychology, and political science" (McCraw, 2007:55; italics added). Integrating insights from various disciplines, and focusing on the big economic issues of his day, Schumpeter, like many of the other theorists dealt with in this book, "was following a long European tradition aimed at constructing *grand social theory*" (McCraw, 2007:156).

seeks to enumerate both the functions and dysfunctions of structures and to come up with a sense of their net balance. One would have liked to have seen Schumpeter do a similar kind of analysis enumerating the positive and negative aspects of that which is created—the new that results from the process of creative destruction in capitalism. More important, especially for our purposes, there is a similar lack of nuance in his discussion of that which is destroyed in the process of creative destruction. Clearly, the destruction of the old is often a positive development, although even here one would want a lot more specificity about those benefits, as well as which parts of society gain (and lose). More importantly, what is almost totally ignored, at least in this formulation by Schumpeter, are the negative aspects associated with the destruction of the old. Furthermore, Schumpeter's conceptualization is completely devoid of any indication that creative destruction can in some overall sense be a negative process with negative results for most, if not all, involved. Creative destruction is assumed to be good for capitalism, the economy, and for all of society.

Schumpeter's Broader Economic Theory

While Schumpeter's thinking on creative destruction is embedded in his theories of capitalism, both are part of his broader work in economics; he devoted a great deal of his life to defining and advancing this discipline. In the history of economic thinking, Schumpeter undoubtedly offered one of the boldest and most innovative visions of how the economy operates. This vision was formed early and a significant portion of his later career was devoted to the working out, and refining, the implications of his views on economics (Allen, 1991a:51–52). The strongest and most unique elements of Schumpeter's thinking on economics are his theory of economic development and the distinction between static and dynamic economics, which Swedberg (1991a:29) argues "is absolutely crucial to [Schumpeter's] whole economic theory."

For Schumpeter (1911–34/2007:63), economic development refers to "changes in economic life as are not forced upon it from without but arise by its own initiative, from within." In other words, it refers to situations where forces internal to the economy cause it to change. The problem for Schumpeter was that most economic thought offered no mechanism to account for economic development in this sense and, as such, could only view the economy as adapting to external influences (e.g., to a declaration of war or to a substantial increase in population). Schumpeter (1939:14) attributed this to the *static* conception of economic operations that he saw at the foundation of most economic thought. Given the importance of this conception in the history of economic thought, Schumpeter takes great pains to lay bare the fundamental propositions of static economics not only in order to evaluate their strengths and limitations, but also to contrast them with his very different vision of the economics he was seeking to develop.

Static economics has a number of distinguishing features. The first is that static economics "*considers economic phenomena, essentially and as a matter of principle, without taking into account their variations in time*" (Kondratief, 1925:576; emphasis in original). That is, it seeks to understand economic relations at a specific point in time without regard to how these conditions might change over time. The classic example of this type of analysis is supply and demand since "it relates demand, supply, and price as they are supposed to be at any moment of observation" and with "nothing else [being] taken into consideration" (Schumpeter, 1954/1994:963). Not taken into consideration is how these variables might change as a result of future developments in the economy (e.g., because of major social changes, the supply and demand curve for horse and buggies today looks very different than it did in the 1800s).

It should be noted that the word static is not meant to imply a situation where all economic activity is frozen and unmoving (i.e., a state where economic agents do not act), but rather one where the *pattern* of economic activity is assumed to remain the same over time. Schumpeter sees the human circulatory system as an example, outside of economics, of a static system. Although blood is continually flowing through this system, the pathways through which the blood moves are fixed. In a similar manner, static economics assumes that the pattern of the actions of economic agents (e.g., what, how, and how much they produce and consume) remains essentially the same over time. This does not mean that this method of analysis necessarily assumes that the economy is always the same or that it precludes all forms of economic change; it does allow for certain forms of economic change. However, they are *not* the ones Schumpeter thought were important in accounting for economic development.

One type of change of concern in mainstream economics involves continuous processes that unfold in a more or less uniform manner over time (e.g., the economy increasing by a certain percentage each year). Schumpeter (1911–34/2007) did not consider such changes to be significant since they require only an "adaptive response" on the part of the economy. That is, they do not require the economy to do anything that is qualitatively different from the way it previously operated because the difference is merely of a quantitative nature consisting in "small variations at the margins" (Schumpeter, 1911–34/2007:81). This type of change resembles adding a constant to all the variables in an equation. Although this value affects the outcome, it does not fundamentally alter the relationship among the variables.

A second type of change is that which results from extra-economic factors. If this was the only type of change possible, then the economy would simply be passively reacting to outside influences. And if this were the case, there would be no economic development in Schumpeter's sense of the term (i.e., changes in the economy resulting from economic forces). As was mentioned earlier, and as will be addressed in more detail later, Schumpeter thought that a focus on the kinds of changes mentioned earlier overlooked the most important characteristic of the capitalist economy: its ability to change from within.

Static economics also assumes that economic conditions tend to move toward equilibrium, a state where conditions are in balance with one another. For example, if the market leads to a situation where the supply of, and the demand for, a product are in perfect proportion to one another, then this system is in a state of equilibrium assuming that no outside forces are disturbing it (Allen, 1991a:77). More generally, this can be thought of as the tendency of the economic system to "stabilize itself" and relationships between its variables (i.e., supply, demand, and price) (Swedberg, 1991a:28).

The model of static economics that Schumpeter addresses does not simply look at how the market for certain goods comes to be in a balanced state, what is known as "partial equilibrium," but also how the entire economic system can come to be stabilized in this manner, i.e., a state of "general equilibrium." That such a state is possible is based on the assumption that specific economic quantities are part of an overall system where the value of any one quantity is related to all others. The implication of this assumption is that economic quantities are in "a state of mutual dependence [so] that a change in one of them, leads to a change in all of them" (Schumpeter, cited in Swedberg, 1991a:28). For example, if the price of one commodity (e.g., oil) increases, others (e.g., gasoline, air fares) will as well, and this, in turn, can affect the decisions of various economic actors (e.g., consumers may drive or fly less in response to increased fuel costs or the price of airline tickets). If an economy achieves general equilibrium under static conditions, the result is a state of "static-equilibrium." As will be seen, the idea of static-equilibrium, and the assumption that the economy is moving toward such a state, has played a very important role in the history of economic thought. Schumpeter, however, believed there were other, more powerful, forces operating in the economy that either prevented the economy from remaining in this state for long, or from achieving it in the first place.

The view that the economy tended to move toward a general state of static-equilibrium is largely the result of another feature of static analysis: the assumption that the market operates on the basis of "perfect competition" without any barriers to prevent businesses from producing any goods or services they wish. This idea implies, first, that there are no advantages that favor one firm over another. Second, it assumes that goods and services are produced in a more or less uniform manner by a number of different producers. Third, businesses can easily and freely move from producing one good or service to another if this is seen as being more profitable. Such a state is generally seen as being good for the consumer since it prevents any one firm from keeping prices artificially high as would be the case if it had a monopoly on a particular product.

Schumpeter thought that this thinking on perfect competition was all wrong and that a different, and much more *imperfect*, form of competition was what mattered in economic development. To show the limitations of perfect competition and the static-equilibrium model more generally, Schumpeter created an ideal type of an economy operating under the conditions of this model. He referred to this as the "stationary" or "circular flow of economic life."

A stationary economy has a number of distinguishing features, especially that no economic development would take place in it. That is, it offers no means by which economic factors can introduce new and different elements into the economy. As a result, it is forced to assume that economic variables (e.g., the supply and demand for labor, goods, raw materials, etc.) are more or less stable over time. Also, since this economy would be in a state of general equilibrium, or would quickly move there if any outside influence disturbed it, Schumpeter argues that all economic variables would necessarily be in balance. This means that production and consumption would be so balanced that, over time, the same types of goods, and in the same quantities, would be produced and consumed by the same people in a regular and repeating pattern. The result of this would be self-repeating loops of economic activity that Schumpeter (1911–34/2007:150) refers to as the circular, or stationary, *flow*. Under these conditions, competition would reduce the price of all goods and services to the value of their costs. That is, since businesses cannot offer anything new and/or different, and since perfect competition assumes that any business can easily and effectively provide any specific good or service offered in the economy, the only way that businesses can compete is on the basis of price, in particular by underselling their competition. But since no business is exempt from this situation because of perfect competition, any business that enjoys large, or even any, profits, would eventually be undersold by another business. This process of underselling will continue to chip away at profit margins until there is nothing from which to cut both for specific goods and for the economy as a whole. Once this point has been reached, "production must flow on endlessly profitless" (Schumpeter (1911–34/2007:31). This does not mean that people would not make money and not have their needs met, or that enterprises would go bankrupt, but it does mean that what is often considered the central feature of capitalism—profit and the profit motive—would vanish under these conditions. In fact, the implication of this is that profit, far from being the heart of normal capitalist operations, is actually something that occurs only under anomalous conditions. As Collins (1992:174) puts it, Schumpeter's theory shows "that the general equilibrium model of neoclassical theory has room in it neither for change nor for profit; these come exogenously in the form of disturbances or for arbitrarily given resources." This is because "[t]he pure working of the market . . . implies that the unimpeded flow of capital and labor to the areas of greatest return should quickly equalize everyone's returns. In the pure market, no one can make a profit, since competition will drive everything down to its cost" (Collins, 1992:174). That the economy working "in its most perfect condition should operate without profit" is both a paradox of static theory and a position that the theory cannot overcome (Schumpeter 1911–34/2007:31).

Although the preceding description may seem like an unrealistic picture of how the economy actually operates, the image of a static economy moving in a circular manner does, in fact, stand at the heart of much classical economic thinking (Allen, 1991b:213) and even some more contemporary work in the field (Lazonick, 1994:249). Schumpeter (1908) took this type of economics so seriously that his first book was devoted largely to an analysis of it. In it, he showed the importance of static economics to the study of such issues as price formation, exchange, savings, and the process of distribution (Swedberg, 1991a:28). On a more general level, Schumpeter (2003:66) thought that this type of analysis was an important first step in the study of economics because it allowed the discipline to develop as a science of the economy.

However much static analysis can reveal, and however important it was to the development of economics as a science, Schumpeter was also quick to point out that there is much that this perspective does not, and indeed cannot, address. Its most important limitation is that it cannot deal with how the economy develops and changes over time. Schumpeter (2003:66) thought that a static analysis was like "a frame for a picture" where "the picture itself still has [yet] to be painted." Moreover, because of its assumptions and its views of the world, this was a picture that static analysis simply could not paint. Even if it could, it would be like taking a snapshot of a motion picture: while certainly some, perhaps important, information would be captured in this image, much more would necessarily be missed. (Schumpeter [1954/1994:964] argues that in all fields of study, static analyses are developed prior to dynamic analyses because they are simpler to work out and their propositions are easier to prove. Talcott Parsons [see Chapter 17] had a similar view.) As a result, in his first book, Schumpeter called for the development of a new, and very different, form of economics that would try to capture all the movement found in capitalist economies. However, it was not until his second book that he began painting the picture that static economics could not.

Toward a More Dynamic Theory of the Economy

What are the economic factors *within* capitalism that cause it to change and thereby serve as an engine of economic development? Schumpeter traces capitalism's dynamism to entrepreneurs (as agents) and their creative economic actions. He saw entrepreneurs as "the Carusos of big business" (McCraw, 2007:72). In particular, entrepreneurs are responsible for the development of what Schumpeter calls "new combinations," or the combining of existing resources, materials, and/or means of production in novel ways. In Schumpeter's (1911–34/2007:31) words, "[t]o produce other things, or the same things by a different method, means to combine these materials and forces differently." However, later in his career Schumpeter (1939:59) offered a much broader definition of new combinations as simply any instance of "doing things differently" in the realm of economic life.

In either case, an example can be seen in Henry Ford's combining of the assembly-line production method he saw at slaughter houses with the production of automobiles. For Schumpeter, new combinations like these are produced by entrepreneurs (like Ford) with vision, insight, and desire. In fact, Schumpeter (1911–34/2007:74) actually defines entrepreneurs as those who create new combinations: "The carrying out of new combinations we call 'enterprise'; the individuals whose function it is to carry them out we call 'entrepreneurs.'" (It should be noted that entrepreneurs are not necessarily inventors and vice versa. While it is true that both entrepreneurs and inventors are innovative, it is entrepreneurs who introduce inventors' innovations and creations into the economic system, thereby allowing for economic development. Any invention, no matter how novel and important, if not introduced into the economy by an entrepreneur, cannot be the basis for economic development. Similarly, an entrepreneur may not invent anything at all but simply combine existing elements in an economically novel manner.)

Thus, economic development is ultimately the result of economic agents seeking to do things differently in the economy. Where does this vision come from? Schumpeter's initial answer, which is sometimes referred to as Mark I, attributed this to three *psychological* traits of entrepreneurs: "the dream and the will to found a private kingdom"; "the will to conquer"; and "the joy of creating, of getting things done, or simply of exercising one's energy or ingenuity" (Schumpeter, 1911–34/2007:93). These were very heroic conceptions of entrepreneurs. Schumpeter (1951/1989:65) believes that their creative ability has less to do with intellect than it does with will. In other words, entrepreneurship is primarily a question of leadership as entrepreneurs carry through on their bold new visions in the face of the majority who are content to leave things as they are. However, this ability is not widely distributed in the population so that "the carrying out of new combinations is a special function, and the privilege of a type of people who are much less numerous than all those who have the 'objective' possibility of doing it" (Schumpeter, 1911–34/2007:81). In short, entrepreneurs "are a special type," few in number despite being responsible for most economic development (Schumpeter, 1911–34/2007:81).

Creative actions lead to the introduction of qualitatively new and different elements into the economy so that the change inherent in capitalism is not continuous or linear, but rather discontinuous and non-linear. This means that, as a result of such change, things become somehow different in economic life; there are new products, new production techniques, new systems of distribution, and the like, which simply cannot be reduced to what came before (e.g., the iPod cannot be reduced to the Walkman, while automation cannot be reduced to the assembly line). These changes also have a disequilibrating effect so that while market forces may act to stabilize economic relations once a change has been introduced, *no general or permanent state of equilibrium can ever be maintained since changes of this type are continually occurring.*

This is similar to a rock thrown into a still pond. The rock initially creates waves, but they dissipate over time and the pond becomes still again. Schumpeter's point is that even though this dissipation occurs for any single new combination introduced into the economy, entrepreneurs are continually throwing new rocks into the pool agitating economic relations with their creations so that the economy is never in a state of rest.

Profit is a particularly important result of the creative actions of entrepreneurs. For example, if a company discovers a new source of raw material that it uses in its product that is dramatically cheaper than the materials it currently uses, and if the company employs this new raw material, a dramatic cost savings will result that can be translated into higher profits for the company. Thus, according to Schumpeter, new combinations are the mechanism by which profit is generated in capitalism. But it is also the case that once the success of these new combinations is recognized by others, they will also use them (e.g., integrate the new raw material), thereby creating competition in this area. The result of this is that over time, and without the addition of other new combinations, newly generated profits will vanish. Profit is therefore ephemeral for Schumpeter (1911–34/2007:153–154), something that "slips from the entrepreneur's grasp as soon as the entrepreneurial function is performed." But it is also something that is inexorably intertwined with economic development: quite simply, "[w]ithout development there is no profit, without profit no development" (Schumpeter, 1911–34/2007:154).

We can now see that what is normally considered economic success—profit—is the product of the creative actions of entrepreneurs and the introduction of qualitatively new elements into the economy. These also lead to capitalism's dynamism and are the foundation of the ability of the economy to develop from within. There is, however, a flipside to this process. While Schumpeter does not pay as much attention to it as he does to the introduction of the new, it is nevertheless of central importance to his theory. That is, while new elements are continually being introduced into the economy, it is also the case that old elements are being eliminated from it as a result of these innovations. As Schumpeter (1911–34/2007:67) puts it, in a competitive economy the introduction of new elements "mean the competitive elimination of the old"; the competition created by doing things differently in economic life can lead to the elimination of that which already exists.

While it is true that throughout his career Schumpeter placed more "emphasis on the creative rather than destructive aspects of the process of economic evolution" (Andersen, 2004:1), he did give at least some attention to the role destruction plays in this process. In particular, Schumpeter (1942/1947/1950:85) notes that destruction is important because of the motivating role it plays in capitalism. The mere possibility of elimination or destruction by the creations of others presents "an ever-present threat" to existing businesses. The result of this threat is that it "disciplines before it attacks. The businessman [sic] feels himself to be in a competitive situation even if he is alone in his field or . . . any effective competition between him and any other firms in the same or a neighboring field" (Schumpeter 1942/1975:85). Schumpeter's point is that the threat of destruction by the innovations of others motivates existing entrepreneurs to not rest on their laurels but instead to innovate as a means of staving off actual, or possible, competition from the creations of others. If businesses do not do this, they could see their enterprise, or even entire industry, rendered obsolete by the innovative efforts of others. This ever-present threat of destruction was also the reason that Schumpeter, unlike others, did not fear monopolies. If they were to become stagnant in their operations, monopolies too could easily be eliminated by the creations of a new, more innovative, firm.

While the threat of destruction is ever-present for businesses, in reality Schumpeter thought that major waves of creation, innovation, and ultimately destruction tended to occur in clusters with one innovation sparking the development of a number of others. While creative destruction can happen at any time, it tends to occur in cycles or waves centered on a key innovation (e.g., the computer, the Internet, or earlier, the railroad).

Schumpeter's Sociology

As we saw, in many of his works Schumpeter attempted to develop a strictly economic theory of economic activity, but it is also the case that at many other times in his career he branched out to address issues not purely economic in nature. In fact, for Schumpeter (1911–34/2007:3) there *were no purely economic facts*: "The social process is really one indivisible whole. Out of its great stream the classifying hand of the investigator artificially extracts economic facts . . . A fact is never exclusively or purely economic; other—and often more important—aspects always exist." Schumpeter (1911–34/2007:3) did think that it was possible to "speak of economic facts in science just as in ordinary life." This can be done in much the same way "with which we may write a history of literature even though the literature of a people is inseparably connected with all the other elements of its existence" (Schumpeter, 1911–34/2007:3). Schumpeter recognized that perspectives other than economics were both possible and needed for investigations into the operations of the social whole. This was particularly the case for sociology. Over his career, Schumpeter did address sociological topics (e.g., imperialism, class, the role of the state) while also outlining the relationship between economics, sociology, and the other social sciences.

As Schumpeter (1949:167) once put it,

> [t]here is nothing surprising in the habit of economists to invade the sociological field. A large part of their work—practically the whole of what they have to say on institutions and on the forces that shape economic behavior–inevitably overlaps the sociologist's preserves. In consequence, a no-man's land or everyman's land has developed that might conveniently be called economic sociology.

Schumpeter even included economic sociology as one of the "fundamental fields" that comprises the field of economics.

In general, what Schumpeter (1954/1994:21) means by *economic sociology* is the study of how "not only actions and motives and propensities [of people] but also social institutions that are relevant to economic behavior such as government, property inheritance, contract, and so on" affect economic action. For example, the introduction of the institution of free contracts, or of government regulations, means that social facts have been introduced into the economic equation, and that a purely economic analysis cannot account for these factors. Although the contract is essential to the operation of the capitalist economy, economics can say nothing about how or why contracts became the central, socially sanctioned means for organizing economic relations. This is a more general way of saying that economic action is often embedded in social processes and that without an understanding of such processes, one's picture of economics is necessarily limited. While Schumpeter thought that limiting one's focus was often necessary in order to get a very thorough and detailed understanding of economic action, he also saw the need at times to venture into economic sociology and beyond to explore how economic action was affected by changes in social structures and institutions.

Capitalism, Socialism, and Democracy is Schumpeter's best-known venture into the area of economic sociology. There, Schumpeter made the bold prediction that the capitalist system would come to an end and be replaced by a socialist order. This, however, would not be the result of purely economic factors (e.g., that the market can no longer grow and/or there are no longer any opportunities for economic investment), but rather because capitalism comes to undermine its own institutional foundations (Swedberg, 1991a:156). The general contours of this prediction regarding the fate of capitalism are the same as those of Marx, though the root cause is very different.

Schumpeter (1942/1975:167) defines socialism as "an institutional pattern in which the control over the means of production and over production itself is vested with a central authority." This involves a situation where the private sphere of the economy belongs to, and is controlled by, the public sphere of the state. Capitalism and entrepreneurialism would vanish under socialism since all economic matters would be centrally planned and performed by the government. The inclusion of the state, government, and central planning illustrate going beyond economic factors to include more sociological variables.

Schumpeter's Relationship to Other Classical Sociological Theorists. What we saw earlier is the fact that Schumpeter vacillated between being a "pure" economic theorist and a more sociological theorist. We can get a better sense of him as a sociological theorist by looking at his work in the context of that of other theorists discussed in this book, especially Marx and Weber.

Schumpeter clearly read Marx's work and was a sophisticated commentator on, and critic of, that work. Indeed, he was a far better student of Marx's work than was Weber whose comments on Marx are largely marginal and superficial. Weber did not take Marx seriously as a social theorist, but Schumpeter certainly did. This may be traceable to the fact that while he was a wide-ranging thinker, Schumpeter remained more embedded in the field of economics than Weber did in any single field (although he came to be increasingly identified with sociology and to see himself as a sociologist). As broad a thinker as Schumpeter was, Weber was the much more wide-ranging intellectual of the two.

As a theoretically oriented economist trained in Europe in the late nineteenth century, and one who came of intellectual age there in the early twentieth century, Schumpeter could have hardly escaped an engagement with Marx. However, Schumpeter did manage to avoid the pitfalls of becoming either a "true believer" in Marxian theory or one who dismissed the theory in its entirety, often without reading it seriously. Thus, Schumpeter, like Weber, developed his theoretical orientation in a dialogue with Marx's ideas. In Schumpeter's case, that dialogue was quite direct and explicit, while in Weber's case the dialogue was largely elliptical and implicit. In this sense, Schumpeter's thinking on Marx's theory is far superior to that of Weber.

In making this argument, we are positioning Schumpeter in the same league as Weber as a social theorist. This is a big step for Schumpeter who, while he has long been thought of as an important theorist in the history of economics (at least today by non-economists), is generally not accorded a similar status as a social theorist. Thus, one is highly unlikely to find Schumpeter's work dealt with in works on social theory (Ritzer, 2003), but the ideas of Weber (and Marx) are *always* dealt with in such works. Schumpeter came to be associated with Talcott Parsons in his later career at Harvard, and while Parsons became part of the canon, Schumpeter has not (yet) been accorded that status.

Schumpeter knew Weber personally and even once had an argument with him over the Russian Revolution that so frustrated Weber that he jumped out of his chair and stormed out of the coffeehouse where the argument occurred (Jaspers, cited in Swedberg, 1991a:93). Nevertheless, these thinkers respected each other and appreciated the other's work. Weber, for example, commissioned Schumpeter to write a history of economic theory for a handbook in economics that he edited (*Grundriss der Sozialökonomik*) as well as write a letter of support for Schumpeter's appointment to the University of Vienna. Also, one can still find an annotated copy of Schumpeter's *Theory of Economic Development* in Weber's library. For his part, Schumpeter wrote a powerful and moving obituary for Weber that outlined what Schumpeter thought were Weber's major intellectual contributions (Schumpeter, 1991:220–229; Swedberg, 1991a:92–93). Also, during his years at Harvard, Schumpeter had much contact with Talcott Parsons who was the major American translator and interpreter of Weber's work, and was intimately familiar with Weber's work in general, and on rationalization in particular. Schumpeter and Parsons even taught a seminar, beginning in 1939, on "rationality" that "flourished" with Schumpeter presenting the initial paper in that seminar (McCraw, 2007:301).

Yet, despite this familiarity with each other's work, the influence of Schumpeter and Weber on one another was limited and this was undoubtedly unfortunate for both of them. For example, had they been more influenced by each other's ideas, Weber might have developed a deeper appreciation for Marx as a scholar and Schumpeter would have gained a greater, and certainly an even more sociological, sense of the economy, capitalism, and especially rationalization.

Rationalization and Schumpeter's Later Theorizing

Schumpeter's (1911–34/2007:57) interest was largely restricted to the rationalization of capitalism, while Weber (1904–05/1958; 1927/1981) was very much interested in that, but also in the rationalization of much else including the economy in general, religion, political structures, the city, and so on (Weber, 1921/1968). Further, Weber developed what has come to be seen as the most important general theory of rationalization (Kalberg, 1980; Levine, 1981a; Ritzer, 2008) and there is no question that Schumpeter's thinking on the rationalization of capitalism would have benefited from greater exposure to Weber's far broader theory of rationalization. Not only did Schumpeter stand to gain much from that theory, but also from Weber's criticisms of the rationalization process, especially the "irrationality of rationality." Schumpeter was not a dispassionate analyst of capitalism. While he generally wrote approvingly about it, he was also a critic of the way in which it was growing increasing rationalized.

Schumpeter, as we've seen, agrees with Marx about the ultimate destruction of capitalism. However, while Marx welcomes that destruction because of his hatred of capitalism, Schumpeter (1942/1975:155) fears it because he is a great admirer of the capitalist system, at least in its pure form. While Marx sees the source of this destruction as inherent in the structures of capitalism, Schumpeter sees those structures as, in the main, quite sound. To Schumpeter, capitalism is being destroyed both by internal processes unleashed by it (especially the rationalization of the capitalist system) and by external changes that are also being affected, in part, by rationalization and that are adversely affecting capitalism.

Schumpeter, like Weber, sees rationalization as an ever-expanding process. Also like Weber, Schumpeter worries about this trend and its negative effects. Weber's concern is characteristically broad with a focus on the development of an iron cage of rationalization that would adversely affect the individual, especially the "charismatic" individual. More narrowly, Schumpeter is concerned with a future in which capitalism is increasingly rationalized leaving little room for the initiative and creativity of the entrepreneur. In this sense, Schumpeter's theory can be seen as a more specific version of Weber's larger theory of rationalization (although there is, as we have seen, much more to Schumpeter's theory [and Weber's] than this).

Schumpeter contends that rationalized business organizations operate against the "heroic" individuals, those who have the will to produce something new in the economic system, who are needed for innovation. Here is the way he expresses his critique of rationalized business organizations:

> economic progress tends to become depersonalized and automatized. Bureau and committee work tends to replace individual action . . . Rationalized and specialized office work will eventually blot out personality, the calculable result, the "vision." The leading man no longer has the opportunity to fling himself into the fray. He is

> becoming just another office worker—and one who is not always difficult to replace (Schumpeter, 1942/1975:133).

In this context Schumpeter is discussing, implicitly, the death of the entrepreneur in big business.

Schumpeter's argument here is very close to Weber's more general argument about charisma and its loss as a result of the routinization of charisma. In the early history of capitalism, in Schumpeter's (1939) view, charismatic inventors, innovators, entrepreneurs played a much more important role. However, as capitalism came to be dominated by highly rationalized big businesses, there was less and less of a role for such charismatic figures. Specialists within those firms do produce new ideas and one gets the sense that Schumpeter has almost as little regard for such specialists as does Weber (1904–05/1958:182).

In spite of his regret for the demise of the "heroic" entrepreneur, there is a tendency for Schumpeter, especially in his later work such as *Capitalism, Socialism and Democracy*, to reify his thinking about capitalism in the sense that he saw economic action being propelled less by individual actors and more by institutional processes, especially what he called the "capitalist engine." Such an engine can be seen as a reified phenomenon since once it is turned "on," it runs without human intervention. We have encountered the concept of reification previously in both the chapters on Marx (5) and Simmel (8). It is an idea associated mainly with Marx ("fetishism of commodities") and neo-Marxists (especially Georg Lukács). It involves "thingification"; the fact that when people treat various phenomena as things, they are likely to become things that are not only beyond people's control, but control people.

What does the capitalist engine "do" when it is "on," when it is continually "moving forward"? When it is on, the capitalist engine is producing and when it is moving forward, it is producing what is essential to Schumpeter's view of capitalism–that which is "new." Thus, of great importance to capitalism, in Schumpeter's view, is innovation since that is the process that yields that which is new: "The fundamental impulse that sets and keeps the capitalist engine in motion comes from the *new* consumer goods, the *new* methods of production or transportation, the *new* markets, the *new* forms of industrial organization that capitalist enterprise creates" (Schumpeter, 1942/1975:83; italics added).

Such a reified perspective tends to leave little or no place for a heroic, charismatic figure like an entrepreneur. The "capitalist engine" is a reified entity, and it is animated by an equally reified impulse to move forward. To put this another way, it is the capitalist engine, animated by this impulse, that "acts" by creating that which is new. In his later (Mark II) work, Schumpeter appears to endow capitalism, especially the capitalist engine, with a life of its own apart from the actors who are involved in, or even lead, it. Thus, the emphasis is on capital*ism* and not on the capital*ist*. Schumpeter argues that the innovative role of entrepreneurs has been, and will, as a result of a widespread process of social rationalization, continue to be displaced by a more standardized and bureaucratic form of innovation (Dahms, 1995). This is another way of saying that Schumpeter thought that innovation was increasingly being routinized as the entrepreneurial function was taken over by large-scale enterprises (such as big business) with their research and development divisions.

This reified conceptualization contradicts Schumpeter's previously discussed thinking on the *entrepreneur*. In his early work, the entrepreneur is a human actor and, in fact, he mentions people like Richard Arkwright, Josiah Wedgewood, and James Watt as specific examples of the entrepreneur. However, what makes them entrepreneurs is *not* their role in invention, innovation, or in creating anything new. As Schumpeter (1942/1975:132; italics added) puts it, "the function of entrepreneurs is to reform or revolutionize the pattern of production by *exploiting an invention*, or more generally, an untried technological possibility for producing a new commodity or producing an old one in a new way, by opening up a new supply of materials or a new outlet for products, by reorganizing an industry and so on." Thus, the entrepreneurial function does not consist in creation and or invention; rather, it is to take what has been created and invented and doing something with them in the realm of the economy (e.g., creating a new market for an invention, using an invention to produce goods in a new manner, etc.). Schumpeter (1942/1975:132; italics added) is more explicit slightly later: "This [entrepreneurial] function *does not essentially consist in either inventing anything or otherwise creating* the conditions which the enterprise exploits. It consists in *getting things done*." (Getting things done undoubtedly involves creating the "new combinations" discussed earlier.) But because he gets things done, the entrepreneur is, in Schumpeter's view, *more* important to the capitalist system than inventors, innovators, and even the capitalists (and their economic capital), Without them these innovations would remain outside of the economic system and therefore would have no impact on it.

Given his emphasis on creativity, it is somewhat surprising that Schumpeter is so little interested in, and devotes so little attention to, invention. Inventors (Richard Arkwright was both an inventor and entrepreneur) are mentioned in his work, but, in fact, Schumpeter is little interested in either the inventor or the invention; he simply assumes that there will be those who invent. Instead, his focus is on what happens to the invention *after* it is created, what happens to it once it finds its way into the capitalist engine and/or into the hands of the entrepreneur for, as just mentioned, inventions are only economically important when they enter the economy and it is the function of entrepreneurs to introduce innovations into the economic system.

Even if we accord importance to the individual (the inventor, but especially the entrepreneur), such an actor played a more creative role in the early history of capitalism. Schumpeter saw this role declining, especially in large corporations, as capitalism has moved forward. Thus, there are two Schumpeters: Schumpeter I strongly endorses entrepreneurs. Schumpeter II sees their downfall with the rise of a new type of constantly innovative corporate organization" (Carayannis, Ziemnowicz and Spillan, 2007:24). Thus, in the later Schumpeter it is the reified (and rationalized) organization that creates, not the individual. The innovative entrepreneur remains important in Schumpeter's later work in small start-up businesses. However, the "giant firm," itself an important innovation from Schumpeter's perspective (and a product of the creative destruction of the small firm), operates against creativity on the part of the entrepreneur, and puts it in the hands of the organization as a whole. Large firms become key components of the capitalist engine in advanced capitalism.

It is interesting to note that what Schumpeter actually fears about the future of capitalism is that it will become even more (too) reified, further reducing the crucial role played by the entrepreneur (and perhaps the inventor). This is because Schumpeter believed that as capitalism developed, it spawned bigger and bigger businesses that both centralized and rationalized their operations to an increasing degree. This process of rationalization is particularly important for Schumpeter because of the way it operates against the entrepreneur by making what were once "heroic" acts of economic creation (e.g., the introduction of a new product into the market by the will of an individual entrepreneur) something seemingly almost automatic. The "social function" of the entrepreneur is "losing importance and is bound to lose it at an accelerating rate in the future even if the economic process itself of which entrepreneurship was the prime mover went on unabated" because resistance to change is diminishing as people become accustomed to it (Schumpeter, 1942/1975:132). Innovation "is being reduced to routine. Technological progress is increasingly becoming the business of teams of trained specialists who turn out what is required and make it work in predictable ways. The romance of earlier commercial adventure is rapidly wearing away, because so many more things can be strictly calculated that had of old to be visualized in a flash of genius" (Schumpeter, 1942/1975:132). When this happens, the nature of economic development changes: instead of the explosive periods of growth brought about by the innovations of individual entrepreneurs, there will be the slow and steady "development" of specialized economic planners who will "routinely produce growth, but not real change" (Allen, 1991b:124). In other words, the economic development of the entrepreneur will be displaced by the economic management of the planned economy where innovation and development happen in a routine, rationalized, and seemingly reified manner.

Like Weber, Schumpeter thought that capitalism and the spread of rationality were processes that went hand in hand. However, Schumpeter (1942/1975:122) notes that "the rational attitude presumably forced itself on the human mind primarily from economic necessity; it is the everyday economic task to which we as a race owe our elementary training in rational thought and behavior." Nevertheless, for Schumpeter (1942/1975:124), "capitalism . . . has after all been the propelling force of the rationalization of human behavior." However, the process of social rationalization is not limited to the economy and one area of sociological concern where Schumpeter saw rationalization proceeding quite rapidly was in the family. For example, Schumpeter (1942/1975:157) thinks that the "disintegration of the bourgeois family" is "wholly attributable to the rationalization of everything in life, which we have seen is one of the effects of capitalist evolution. In fact, it is but one of the results of the spread of that rationalization to the sphere of private life." Schumpeter (1942/1975:157) thinks that the rationalization of family life entails the incorporation of "a sort of inarticulate system of cost accounting" into private life which allows one "to become aware of the heavy personal sacrifices that family ties and especially parenthood entail under modern conditions. . ." He argues that this fosters an attitude that focuses their attention "on ascertainable details of immediate utilitarian relevance" as opposed to the less tangible benefits of family life which "almost invariably [escape] the rational searchlight of modern individuals" (Schumpeter 1942/1975:158). Schumpeter thinks that one of the reflections of this trend is the increase in childless, or one-child, families.

So while capitalism was the initial impetus for rationalization by helping in both its development and spread, Schumpeter believes that over time rationalization begins to undermine this economic system by destroying the institutional framework within which capitalism operates. One example of this for Schumpeter was just seen in the discussion of how rationalization is leading to the disintegration of the traditional bourgeois family. A similar example within capitalism is the way it comes to undermine increasingly the standing of lower-level capitalists, as small producers and traders face competition from big businesses that will, over time, force them out of business. Thus, Schumpeter agrees with Marx that the future of industry will be dominated by a small number of very large firms that have driven out their smaller competitors.

The Future

Schumpeter believes that rationalization is the ultimate gravedigger of capitalism. However, as rationalization undermines the institutional foundations of capitalism, it also lays the foundations for socialism, or the centralized planning and operation of the economy. This is because, far from entailing the demise of rationalization, "the socialist blueprint is [actually] drawn at a higher level of rationality" (Schumpeter 1942/1975:196). In other words, Schumpeter thought that socialism would continue, although at a higher degree, the process of "social rationalization" that capitalism had helped to nourish and support (Dahms, 1995). In fact, Schumpeter (1942/1975:188) believed it could very well be that a socialist economy is more economically efficient than its capitalist counterpart. Thus, in summarizing his argument, Schumpeter notes that

> the whole of our argument might be put in a nutshell by saying that socialization means a stride beyond big business on the way that has been chalked out by it or, what amounts to the same thing, that socialist management may conceivably prove as superior to big-business capitalism as big-business capitalism has proved to be to the kind of competitive capitalism of which the English industry of a hundred years ago was the prototype (Schumpeter, 1942/1975:195–196).

Of course, this prediction has not come to pass—capitalism has not transitioned into socialism—and Schumpeter's venture into prophecy, much like Marx's, was not a success. In many ways this is because Schumpeter overestimated the effects of rationalization on social life as a whole, including economic matters, as well as underestimating the ability of capitalism to creatively destroy the developments on which he based his predictions (such as many big businesses; see the following). In fact, Schumpeter's prediction regarding the transformation of capitalism to socialism is based, somewhat ironically, on a static conception of rationality. That is, Schumpeter thought that economic rationality would only manifest itself in the rise of big business and that these businesses, because of their size and their superior rationalization, would come to dominate the economy. Rationality, however, is not static; instead, it is a very dynamic phenomenon that is transformed over time and in different contexts. For example, while Weber focused on the disenchanting nature of rationalization, both Campbell (2005) and Ritzer (2005) have shown how rationality can also be used as a means of enchantment, especially in consumer settings. Even Weber (1904–05/1958:78), who thought that life as a whole was increasingly being rationalized, cautioned that "[r]ationalism is an historical concept which covers a whole world of different things" and that every study of rationalism should begin with the proposition that "one may . . . rationalize life from fundamentally different basic points of view and in very different directions." Thus, what is rational in one place and one point in time may not be rational in another, so that even if capitalist organizations are becoming increasingly rationalized, how this manifests itself will change over time (in much the same way that while capitalist firms might always be guided by the profit motive, how they go about trying to obtain this will, because of creative destruction, change over the course of time). For example, it might have been rational for businesses to increase their size and scope (i.e., to develop into big businesses) under conditions of Fordism (Harvey, 1990). However, beginning in the early 1970s Fordism began to face a number of crises (Glyn, 2006) that challenged its entire operational base, many of which centered around a trait that was both the key to Fordism's success and ultimately to its demise: rigidity (Harvey, 1990:142). As a result, we have seen the near-demise of the ultimate big businesses—the Big Three of the American automobile industry—GM, Ford, and Chrysler. That Schumpeter did not recognize that capitalism could develop in a manner other than through the rise of big businesses highlights that he, the thinker who most stressed the dynamic nature of capitalism, held a very static of idea of what rationalism was and how it would affect economic development.

As can be seen, Schumpeter was not good at forecasting the future of capitalism, and there is a certain irony to the fact that Schumpeter's work is today experiencing a revival even though current circumstances look nothing like Schumpeter's predictions. It should, however, be pointed out that Schumpeter also felt that Marx got a great deal wrong in his prophecy in particular, and in his theory more generally, but he and his followers were nevertheless able to develop many important ideas and to build upon them. The same can be done with many of Schumpeter's ideas, especially creative destruction.

In spite of some poor forecasts, Schumpeter's thinking remains highly relevant today in a variety of ways and at various levels. For example, in terms of contemporary theory, he offers a kind of agency-structure theory dealing with the relationship between the entrepreneur and the capitalist engine. Turning to the real world, his emphasis on innovation and the new is highly relevant with the global economy in recession beginning in late 2007. Further, his view that the government should not bail out the companies mired in old methods of operation runs counter to, for example, the efforts of the American government to bail out the automobile industry and its increasingly obsolete automobiles and the technology used to produce them (although this is in accord with Schumpeter's prediction that private economic functions would increasingly be controlled by public and governmental regulation).

Summary

Joseph Schumpeter is usually thought of as an economic theorist, but there is clearly a strong sociological theory embedded in his economic theory. He offers a dynamic model of the economy that contrasts with the static models that tended to dominate economic thinking. Of particular interest to sociology is his dynamic model of capitalism and the key role accorded to innovation in a capitalistic economy. In his early work, he saw the entrepreneur as the agent most responsible for innovation in capitalism. In his later work, his focus shifted dramatically to the structures of capitalism where he saw the "capitalist engine," rather than the entrepreneur as agent, as the key force in innovation in particular and in the dynamism of capitalism more generally.

Schumpeter is best-known today for his ideas on creative destruction. While he had relatively little to say about this concept, it has proven highly attractive to many academicians (including sociologists) and businesspeople. In many ways it is the most essential process within capitalism and, in its extreme, may be seen as synonymous with capitalism. That is, a capitalist system is defined by the creation of the new which is often associated with, if not leading to, the destruction of the old, especially that which stands in the way of the new.

Schumpeter's thinking has much in common with the work of classical sociological theorists, especially Marx and Weber. Like Marx, he has a dynamic theory of capitalism and believes that there is ongoing movement in the direction of socialism. In Schumpeter's view, this movement is associated with the development of large-scale, highly rational organizations that are supplanting the entrepreneur. Such organizations, with their centralized structures and planning, have much in common with socialized organizations and represent movement in the direction of socialism. This also serves to indicate Schumpeter's interest in rationality and the process of rationalization. He shares such an interest with Weber, and both worried about the threats posed by rationalization. Schumpeter's concerns about the fate of the entrepreneur parallel Weber's worry over the fate of charisma in a rationalized world.

CHAPTER 14

Karl Mannheim

Chapter Outline

In some ways, Karl Mannheim is an unusual figure to deal with in a book on classical sociological theory. For example, unlike many others, Mannheim is not viewed by most observers as having created a "grand theory" that has stood the test of time.[1] As Longhurst put it, "Mannheim did not attempt to produce a completely closed and unified theory or system" (1988:24). Furthermore, whereas all the other classical theorists discussed in this book have created many memorable theoretical ideas, it is hard to associate more than a few such ideas with Mannheim. Mannheim was an essayist who wrote no great tomes like Marx's *Capital* or Weber's *Economy and Society.* Finally, unlike the other classic theorists discussed here, Mannheim's critics have far outnumbered his adherents. Even Robert Merton, an early and sympathetic analyst of Mannheim's work, ends his famous essay on that work on a highly critical note: It "is by no means definitive—a term which strikes a harsh discord when applied to any work of science" (1941/1957:508).

Because, in part, his work is spread across many essays written over several decades, it tends to be repetitious and disjointed. Many ideas are raised but never completely and fully developed. At innumerable points in Mannheim's work, one encounters phrases such as, "but I do not have time to deal with this issue now." There are also many inconsistencies in the body of Mannheim's work, and although he was well aware of them, he never undertook a comprehensive and systematic effort to reconcile them.[2] Said Mannheim:

> I use this method [essays] because I think that in a marginal field of human knowledge we should not conceal inconsistencies, so to speak covering up our wounds, but our duty is to show the sore spots in human thinking at its present stage. . . . These inconsistencies are the thorn in the flesh from which we have to start.
>
> (Mannheim, cited in Kettler, Meja, and Stehr, 1982:26–27)

[1]At the close of this chapter we will argue that perhaps one can see the outlines of a grand theory in Mannheim's work.
[2]Although a posthumous book misleadingly titled *Systematic Sociology: An Introduction to the Study of Society* (Mannheim, 1957) was published, this book was based on Mannheim's lectures and did not offer an overarching theoretical perspective.

Further complicating matters is the fact that in 1933, Mannheim was forced to move from Germany to England as a result of the Nazis' ascent to power. His work in Germany (and prior to that in Hungary) was very different from the essays he wrote in England, and this difference contributed to the impression that his work is disjointed.

Given all this, the obvious question is: Why bother writing (to say nothing of reading) a chapter devoted to the work of Karl Mannheim? The answer is that Mannheim was *the* major figure in the invention of a field, the *sociology of knowledge (Wissenssoziologie),* that has been, and is, of great interest to sociologists in general and sociological theorists in particular (McCarthy, 1996; Pels, 1996). Furthermore, it was Mannheim's intellectual efforts over a period of many years that played *the* key role in institutionalizing the field. Few individual thinkers can be credited with the central role in the "invention" of a field, as well as with successfully nurturing it into becoming an established subfield within sociology. Today the sociology of knowledge is such a field, and those who work within it owe a great debt to the ideas of Karl Mannheim. In spite of his critical orientation toward Mannheim's work, Merton makes this clear:

> Mannheim has sketched the broad contours of the sociology of knowledge with remarkable skill and insight. . . . Mannheim's procedures and substantive findings clarify relations between knowledge and social structure which have hitherto remained obscure. . . . We may await considerable enlightenment from further explorations of the territory in which he pioneered.
>
> (Merton, 1941/1957:508)

Given this introduction, we turn immediately to the heart of Mannheim's legacy to sociological theory (and sociology more generally)—the sociology of knowledge.

The Sociology of Knowledge

Although there are many other forerunners, Mannheim makes it quite explicit that "the sociology of knowledge emerged from Marx" (1931/1936:309).

The Sociology of Knowledge and the Theory of Ideology

Mannheim argues that Marx created the prototype of the sociology of knowledge, the "theory of ideology." As we saw in Chapter 6, Marx sees ideologies as distortions of reality that reflect the interests of the ruling class (the capitalists). Mannheim argues that such ideologies are seen by Marxists as "more or less conscious deceptions and disguises" (1931/1936:265). To the followers of Marx, the goal of the study of ideologies is to unmask these conscious distortions.

Although Mannheim acknowledges the importance of the theory of ideology as a starting point, he also believes that it has great limitations. For one thing, ideologies need *not,* in his view, involve the *conscious* intention to distort reality. Rather, distortions are more likely to occur simply because ideas emerge from specific sectors of the social world and are therefore *inherently* limited, one-sided, and *distorted.* Thus, whereas Marx uses the term ideology in a negative sense, to Mannheim ideology "has no moral or denunciatory intent" (Mannheim, 1931/1936:266). Ideologies are almost inevitable because ideas emerge from specific and circumscribed areas of the social world.

For another thing, ideologies are not, as the Marxists suggested, simply the product of social classes, especially the ruling class, but can emerge from any and all sectors of the social world, including "generations, status groups, sects, occupational groups, schools, etc." (Mannheim, 1931/1936:276). In spite of these multiple sources, Mannheim concludes that "*class stratification is the most significant,* since in the final analysis all the other social groups arise from and are transformed as parts of the more basic conditions of production and domination"[3] (1931/1936:276; italics added). Nonetheless, Mannheim defines the sociology of knowledge, far more broadly than would a Marxist, as the study of "the relationship between human thought and the conditions of existence in general" (1931/1936:277).

In differentiating between ideological and sociological analyses of knowledge, Mannheim distinguishes between intrinsic and extrinsic perspectives. If one peers out from within one's own group, one tends to believe that it produces "ideas," whereas all other groups produce "ideologies." However, adopting the extrinsic perspective of the sociologist, one is able to see that *all* systems of ideas, including those emanating from one's own group, are ideologies. "The sociological consideration of intellectual phenomena is a special class of extrinsic interpretation of ideas" (Mannheim, 1926/1971:119).

Generations

Mannheim's (1928–29/1952) discussion of the relationship between generations and knowledge illustrates well the difference between his orientation and that of Marx. The position of a person's generation vis-à-vis other generations is clearly not economic in nature, but it nonetheless has a profound effect on the thinking of those associated with it. The members of a generation are not a "concrete group" in the sense that they do not interact with one another in a patterned and repetitive manner. However, they can be considered as a kind of a group by virtue of the fact that they share a particular social *location.* A generation has this characteristic in common with a social class. However, the nature of their social locations is different. Social classes are defined by their location in the political-economic system, whereas generations "share the same year of birth, are endowed, to that extent, with a common location in the historical dimension of the social process" (Mannheim, 1928–29/1952:290). (Another group of people that Mannheim [1932/1993] describes as sharing a social location is women [Kettler and Meja, 1993].) The key to a generation is not the biological fact of the common year of birth, but the sociological implications of that biological fact (Pilcher, 1994). For example, what is crucial is the fact that the members of each generation share in a distinctive phase of the collective historical process. They experience a common set of events, a set that is different from that experienced by all generations that have come before or will come after (Cherrington, 1997; Turner and Edmunds, 2005).

---

[3]Here Mannheim is anticipating the view of the structural Marxists that the economy is, in the end, the most important social institution.

KARL MANNHEIM

A Biographical Sketch

Two major facts defined a good portion of the life of Karl Mannheim: ill health and refugee status.

Mannheim was born in Budapest, Hungary, on March 27, 1893. A heart defect made him sickly from birth; he had a slight heart attack when he was only twenty and he died prematurely from a heart attack on January 9, 1947, at the age of 53 (Woldring, 1986). Although he accomplished much during his life, one wonders what he might have accomplished had he been blessed with better health and a longer life.

Mannheim was born into a middle-class Jewish family. He attended the University of Budapest (as well as the University of Berlin, where he frequented lectures by Georg Simmel), from which he received a doctorate in philosophy in 1918. He encountered the leading Hungarian scholar of the time, Georg Lukács, and participated in the circle that surrounded him. In fact, Lukács became his early mentor, and Mannheim declared himself a "respectful follower" of Lukács (Loader, 1985:13).

In 1918, Hungary experienced a revolution in which a bourgeois-socialist regime under Mihály Károlyi came to power. However, it was short-lived and was replaced in early 1919 by Béla Kun's communist regime. Lukács had become a communist in late 1918 and became a government official under Kun. Although Mannheim had remained largely apolitical, Lukács appointed him lecturer in philosophy in the College of Education at the University of Budapest. By mid-1919, however, Kun had been replaced by a counterrevolutionary, fascist, anti-Semitic regime headed by Admiral Miklós Horthy. (Interestingly, much of Mannheim's later thinking was to be affected by the relationship among the three ideologies—bourgeois, communist, fascist—he encountered in his intellectually formative years in Hungary.) Given his linkages to Lukács, and thereby indirectly to communism, and the fact that he was Jewish, Mannheim was forced to flee Hungary by the end of 1919 and became a refugee for the first time (Karacsony, 2008).

After several intermediate stops, Mannheim ended up in Heidelberg, Germany, in March, 1921. In that same month, he married Juliska Lang, the daughter of a very prosperous Budapest family. The latter disapproved of their daughter's marriage to a relatively impoverished academic. Juliska Lang was an intellectual herself, with a Ph.D. in psychology, and she later held a professorship at the University of Amsterdam. The marriage was childless. Juliska was to play a key role in Mannheim's work, especially in the posthumous publication of many of his essays.

In Heidelberg, Mannheim became a member of the "Weber group." Although Max Weber had died the preceding year, the group continued on, headed by his wife, Marianne, and his brother, Alfred, himself a noted scholar. It was Alfred Weber who succeeded Georg Lukács as Mannheim's mentor.

Over the next several years, Mannheim lived as a private scholar in Heidelberg. Finally, in mid-1926 Mannheim became a privatdocent (the same marginal position occupied by Simmel for much of his academic life) at Heidelberg. After his appointment, Mannheim applied for German citizenship and was naturalized. It appeared as if his days as a refugee were over. In 1930 Mannheim stepped up to the position of professor and director of the College of Sociology at Goethe University in Frankfurt.

However, Mannheim now found himself deeply affected by two ideologies of which he disapproved—communism and Nazism. His disapproval of communism served to distance him from the famous Institute of Social Research in Frankfurt (the so-called Frankfurt school), even though the Institute was housed in the same building as the sociology department (Pels, 1993). This school produced a number of famous sociologists (Max Horkheimer, Theodor Adorno, and others) as well as a theoretical orientation, "critical theory," that was to play an important role in the future of sociology. Although he was put off by its communist orientation, Mannheim did share with the Frankfurt school an opposition to Nazism. For their part, the critical theorists were angered by Mannheim's lack of interest in practical and political matters (Wiggershaus, 1994).

In January 1933, Adolph Hitler came to power, and as a Jew, Mannheim was almost immediately given a "leave of absence" from the university. Sensing imminent grave danger, Mannheim left Germany within a few months and eventually arrived in London in May, 1933, as a result of an invitation from the London School of Economics. He was again a refugee, a position he was to occupy until 1940, when he became a naturalized British citizen.

For many years Mannheim held temporary lectureships in England, and it was not until 1945 that he was awarded a full-time professorship (in sociology *and* education) at the University of London. After the war, Mannheim was invited to return to the University of Budapest as professor of sociology, but he refused.

Mannheim's work went through a variety of stages that reflected changes in his personal life and in the society and world in which he lived (Remmling, 1975). His earliest work, 1918 to 1924, was highly philosophical. In Germany between 1925 and 1932, his work became largely sociological, with his most notable, albeit controversial, contribution (Kettler and Meja, 1994, 1995; Shils, 1995) in this period being *Ideology and Utopia* (1929/1936). After 1933 and his move to England, Mannheim grew more interested in applying sociological ideas to a variety of issues, especially the planning of society. His most important book during this period was *Man and Society in an Age of Reconstruction* (1935/1940).

Mannheim lived much of his life as a refugee from Hungary, first in Germany and then in England. This marginality, and others (for example, his position vis-à-vis Marxist revolutionaries), led him to become a member of what became a central idea in his work, the "socially unattached intelligentsia." Living in a variety of social and cultural settings, the intelligentsia is in a unique position to have a diverse set of experiences. But Mannheim went beyond simply relishing this diversity; he used it to synthesize a variety of antithetical ideas and social forces (Kettler, Meja, and Stehr, 1984). It was Mannheim's unique, "unattached" position, as well as his desire to use that position to synthesize a wide variety of ideas, that helped to give his work its unique qualities.

Although they occupy different locations, classes and generations "both endow the individuals sharing in them with a common location in the social and historical process, and thereby limit them to a specific range of potential experience, predisposing them for a certain characteristic mode of thought and experience, and a characteristic type of historically relevant action" (Mannheim, 1928–29/1952:290).

Mannheim refines his notion of generation by arguing that a *generation as actuality* emerges when members of a generation begin to orient themselves to one another, both positively and negatively, on the basis of larger ideas and their interpretation of them. Then there are *generation units,* or members of a generation who share common ideas and develop a much more concrete bond with one another. Any generation may be made up of a number of different generation units.

Thus, Mannheim's use of the concept of generations is useful in allowing us to begin to get a better sociological understanding of intra- and intergenerational differences in thought and action. That is, a given generation can be made up of a number of generation units that may differ, and even conflict, with one another. It is even more likely that different generations will have conflicting viewpoints.

Politics

In contrast to the Marxian perspective, the major goal of the sociology of knowledge to Mannheim is not the unmasking of distortions, but rather the careful *study* of the social sources of distorted thinking. Thus, while for Marx the theory of ideology is primarily political in orientation, Mannheim's sociology of knowledge is more academic and scientific in its approach. As Simonds puts it, "Throughout his work, the sociology of knowledge is recommended not as a means for discrediting, undermining, or devaluing knowledge, but as a tool of *understanding*" (1978:30).

This is not to say, however, that Mannheim's sociology of knowledge is apolitical. We will deal with the political implications of Mannheim's thinking toward the close of this chapter. Anticipating that discussion, Mannheim believed that the problems of his day, especially the rise of fascism, were a result of the fact that thought had grown out of control. The sociology of knowledge promised to regain control over knowledge by uncovering its unconscious motivations, presuppositions, and roots. After these were uncovered, they could be controlled. Conversely, they could not be controlled as long as we are unaware of them. Thus, in Mannheim's view, the sociology of knowledge can lead to the "scientific guidance of political life" (1929/1936:5). In other words, it can help the political system prevent knowledge systems from spiraling out of control.

Thus, Mannheim wants his approach to be *both* political *and* scientific. As a result, Pels writes of the "obvious tensions between involvement and detachment which seem to ravage Mannheim's work from beginning to end" (1993:49).

A Sociological Approach

Although his work is divided on the issue of politics and science, there is no ambiguity over the fact that it is sociological in orientation. For example, Mannheim describes the sociology of knowledge as "one of the youngest branches of sociology" (1931/1936:264). Mannheim took as his goal the institutionalization of the sociology of knowledge as a subfield within sociology: "The sociological analysis of thought, undertaken thus far only in a fragmentary and casual fashion, now becomes the object of a comprehensive scientific programme" (1925/1971:105).

Mannheim sometimes describes the sociology of knowledge as a theory, and at other times as a method, but it is certainly *empirical* because it is oriented to the study, description, and (theoretical) analysis of the ways in which social relationships influence thought. One of the most common ways in which Mannheim describes the sociology of knowledge is in terms of its concern with "existential determination of knowledge." In other words, knowledge is determined by social existence (with the individual actor standing between, or mediating, the relationship between the social world and knowledge). However, even though he uses the word "determines," unlike some Marxists (but not Marx himself), Mannheim is *not* a determinist: "this does not mean to say that mind and thought are nothing but the expression and reflex of various 'locations' in the social fabric, and that there exist[s] . . . no potentiality or 'freedom' granted in mind" (Mannheim, 1952/1971b:260–261). He means, rather, that there is always some sort of relationship between existence and knowledge, but the precise nature of that relationship varies and can be determined only by empirical study.

Although knowledge is amenable to a variety of types of empirical research, Mannheim is most interested in historical-sociological research tracing the forms taken by the relationship between knowledge and existence over time:

> The most important task of the sociology of knowledge at present is to demonstrate its capacity in actual research in the historical-sociological realm. In this realm it must work out criteria for exactness for establishing empirical truths and for assuring their control. It must emerge from the stage where it engages in casual intuitions and gross generalizations.
>
> (Mannheim, 1931/1936:306)

Positivism

Mannheim's interest in "exact" empirical research might lead one to believe that he was a positivist. While Mannheim (1953b:195) clearly wanted the sociology of knowledge to be scientific (as opposed to philosophical), and more generally a "science of society," he regarded positivism as a "deluded school" because it emphasizes only one type of empiricism (the collection of data in the manner that it is done in the natural sciences) and because it sees no role for philosophical and theoretical orientations. Thus, Mannheim (1953) criticized the American sociology of his day on these grounds by, for example, attacking its "exactitude complex" and its lack of concern for the great theoretical problems of the day. The natural science approach was not deemed useful for analyzing the most important factors in social life.

Mannheim, like Weber,[4] sees many advantages in the human sciences over the positivistic natural sciences, especially their ability to "understand" and interpret the phenomena (knowledge, the human mind, and its products) they are studying. For example, Mannheim argues that "by the use of the technique of understanding, the functional

---

[4]More generally, both Weber and Mannheim were part of the German hermeneutic tradition known as *Geisteswissenschaften.*

interpenetration of psychic experiences and social situations . . . can . . . be much more intensively penetrated in their essential character than if coefficients of correlation were established between the various factors" (1929/1936:44–45). Furthermore, although Mannheim wanted the sociology of knowledge to be empirical, he also wanted it to involve the theoretical (even philosophical) interpretation of its results.

However, the greatest weakness of positivism in Mannheim's view is its focus on reality that is experienced as real and material. As a result, "its methods are entirely inadequate especially in treating intellectual-spiritualistic reality" (Mannheim, 1925/1971:76). The natural science model is well suited to the study of material realities (Durkheim's material social facts), but not to immaterial realities such as ideas (Durkheim's nonmaterial social facts) that are the concern of the sociology of knowledge. Similarly, positivism is inadequate from a phenomenological perspective (see Chapter 15, on Alfred Schutz) because it is "blind to the fact that perception and knowledge of meaningful objects as such involves interpretation and understanding" (Mannheim, 1925/1971:76).

In spite of the fact that he was not a positivist and was highly critical of positivism, this viewpoint was important to Mannheim for three reasons. First, Mannheim (controversially) saw Marx as a positivist and it was Marx who, as we have seen, was considered by Mannheim to be the founder of the modern study of the sociology of knowledge. Second, positivism shifted the center of experience to the economic-social sphere, and it is in this existential realm that Mannheim embeds knowledge. Finally, positivism led to the granting of primacy to empirical reality and to empirical research. As such, it helped to end the predominance of pure speculation in the study of ideas. As a result, one could no longer merely philosophize and theorize about knowledge, but had to go out and collect empirical data on knowledge. Theory was possible, but only on the basis of empirical results. Mannheim did not want to do natural science, but he did want to do a kind of "science" that was suitable to the study of knowledge: "Mannheim's sociology of knowledge represented an attempt to do justice to the meaningful nature of social thought without thereby surrendering the aspiration to establish 'objective' (in the sense of intersubjectively communicable) knowledge about social phenomena" (Simonds, 1978:20).

Phenomenology

Another important input into Mannheim's sociology of knowledge was phenomenology, especially the work of Max Scheler (Dürrschmidt, 2005). The phenomenologist points to the importance of the mental, something that the (Marxian) materialist either overlooks or subordinates in importance and sees as an epiphenomenon. However, the phenomenologist operates purely within the realm of the mental, accepting the idea that the mental world has an immanent logic of its own. While accepting the phenomenologist's emphasis on mental phenomena, Mannheim seeks the integration of "the real and the mental," arguing that "there is something true in the materialist conception of history" (1925/1971:85, 86). In other words, Mannheim seeks to integrate Marxian theory and phenomenology.

In addition to criticizing phenomenology for ignoring the real, material world, Mannheim is dissatisfied with its belief in "supratemporally valid truths," such as the "transcendental ego" (1925/1971:80). In contrast, Mannheim is a *historicist.* Historicism leads to the view that there are no supratemporal truths, but rather "various essential meanings come into being together with the epochs to which they belong" (Mannheim, 1925/1971:96). This historicism means that Mannheim is committed to the study of the social roots of knowledge in specific historical settings, as well as to the study of the changing relationship over time between ideas and their social sources.

Other Approaches

A similar contrast is drawn with another field, the history of ideas. As its name suggests, the history of ideas is concerned with the relationships among ideas over time. In this sense, it focuses on ideas themselves and ignores the social roots of those ideas. In contrast, according to Mannheim, we need to look at "how the various intellectual standpoints and 'styles of thought' are rooted in an underlying historico-social reality" (1925/1971:107).

By focusing on the empirical study of the effect of the social world on knowledge, or more generally the relationship between being and thought, Mannheim is distinguishing the sociology of knowledge from other, more philosophical fields that are interested in the way in which the development of knowledge is affected by factors internal to knowledge itself.

A Sociology of the Sociology of Knowledge

Mannheim even does a sociology-of-knowledge analysis of the rise of the sociology of knowledge. For example, he argues that the sociology of knowledge could not have arisen during a historical period (say, the Middle Ages) when there was social stability and substantial agreement, even unity, over worldviews. However, in more recent years this belief in unity has been destroyed, largely by the increase in social mobility. What increased mobility has done is "to reveal the multiplicity of styles of thought" (Mannheim, 1929/1936:7). Mannheim distinguishes between horizontal and vertical mobility. Horizontal mobility leads people to see that other people think differently, but it does not lead them to question their own group's knowledge system. Because people are moving horizontally, no group is "better" than any other. As a result, no thought system is seen as preferable to any other. However, vertical mobility leads people not only to see that others think differently, but also to be uncertain, even skeptical of their own group's mode of thought. This uncertainty is especially likely to occur when one encounters different thought systems in groups that stand higher in the stratification system than one's own. Vertical mobility also tends to lead to a "democratization" of thought whereby the ideas of the lower strata can come to confront those of the upper strata on more equal footing. More generally, all of this leads to the following questions:

> How is it possible that identical human thought-processes concerned with the same world produce different conceptions of that world? And from this point it is only a step further to ask: Is it not possible that the thought processes which are involved here are not at all identical? May it not be found . . . that there are numerous alternative paths which can be followed?
>
> (Mannheim, 1929/1936:9)

These questions lead to a crisis in society in which there seems to be nothing to believe in, all ideas appear equal, and everything seems to be up for grabs. But in Mannheim's view, this crisis, and the questions that led to it, also lead dialectically to the development of the field—the sociology of knowledge—that offers potential solutions to the crisis. However, Mannheim believes that there is some urgency for those interested in doing a sociology of knowledge in order to help cope with the crisis because "the opportunity may be lost, and the world will once again present a static, uniform, and inflexible countenance" (Mannheim, 1929/1936:85).

Relativism and Relationism

Mannheim contrasts the "relationism" that he prefers to see as characteristic of the sociology of knowledge with the "relativism" that he fears because it leads people to feel that there is nothing to believe in, that truth is *"socially and historically conditioned"* (Remmling, 1967:45; Goldman, 1994). *Relativism* leads to the viewpoint that there are no absolute standards by which one can judge right or wrong, good or bad, and so on. *Relationism,* on the other hand, is simply the idea that there is a relationship among specific ideas, the larger system of ideas of which they are part, and the social system in which they are found. To the relationist, the effort to discover truth independent of historical and social meanings is a "vain hope" (Mannheim, 1929/1936:80). Instead of searching for fixed, immutable ideas, Mannheim urges that we "learn to think dynamically and relationally rather than statically" (1929/1936:87). However, there *are* criteria of right and wrong, good and bad, but they cannot be formulated absolutely, once and for all. Such criteria can be defined for a given social situation and must be redefined anew with each change in social reality; "there *is* a moral obligation, but . . . this obligation *is derived from the concrete situation to which it is related*" (Mannheim, 1953:212). Says Mannheim, "The dynamic relationism for which I stand has nothing to do with nihilism. . . . It . . . does not despair of the solubility of the crisis of our existence and thought" (1929/1971:267).

The sociology of knowledge can be used nonevaluatively or evaluatively. It can be used nonevaluatively simply to analyze the relationship between a social situation and ideas, or it can be used evaluatively: "A theory . . . is wrong if in a given practical situation it uses concepts and categories which, if taken seriously, would prevent man from adjusting himself at that historical stage" (Mannheim, 1929/1936:95). Mannheim enumerates three examples of idea systems that could cause such maladjustment. The first is the continued existence of antiquated norms. The second is living by absolutes that may have applied to one social setting but that no longer apply to the changed social setting. Finally, there is the use of forms of knowledge that are no longer capable of comprehending present realities. This leads Mannheim to a new definition of the Marxian concept of false consciousness: "Knowledge is distorted and ideological when it fails to take account of the new realities applying to a situation, and when it attempts to conceal them by thinking of them in categories which are inappropriate" (Mannheim, 1929/1936:96).

Relatedly, Mannheim asks how knowledge and objectivity are possible after it is recognized that any "given finding should contain the traces of the position of the knower" (1931/1936:296). Mannheim responds that this reality should not be denied, but rather we should ask, "How, granted these perspectives, knowledge and objectivity are still possible" (Mannheim, 1931/1936:296). He responds with the argument that we need to juxtapose a series of partial perspectives in order to achieve a new level of objectivity. In so doing, we need to reject the positivistic idea that there is some detached, impersonal, ideal realm of truth, some "sphere of perfection" (Mannheim, 1931/1936:297). Rather, we must strive to constantly enlarge our knowledge of what we are studying through the juxtaposition of a number of all-too-human partial perspectives. Furthermore, we can compare points of view and determine which one "gives evidence of the greatest comprehensiveness and the greatest fruitfulness in dealing with empirical material" (Mannheim, 1931/1936:301).

The Intelligentsia

The changing nature of society produces a dramatic change in what Mannheim calls the "intelligentsia,"[5] or the "social groups whose special task it is to provide an interpretation of the world for that society" (Mannheim, 1929/1936:10; 1932/1993). In previous, static societies, the intelligentsia tended to be not only well defined, but also "static and lifeless." The members of the intelligentsia are oriented more by their own need to systematize ideas than by the need to use those ideas to deal with life's concrete problems. In the modern world this closed intelligentsia has been replaced by what Mannheim calls *socially unattached (or free) intelligentsia* (Loader, 1997). Today's intelligentsia is derived from a number of different social strata, and its members are no longer rigidly organized or constrained by such an organization. As a result, "the intellectual's illusion that there is only one way of thinking disappears" (Mannheim, 1929/1936:12). Thus, various groups of the intelligentsia, buying into different sets of ideas, openly compete with one another for the attention of the larger world.

The appearance and spread of a socially unattached intelligentsia has mixed implications. On the one hand, the intelligentsia has helped to produce the "profound disquietude" of Mannheim's (1929/1936:13) day. That is, intellectuals, and people in general, no longer accept one system of ideas; society is a buzzing confusion of competing idea systems. On the other hand, it is the intelligentsia that is able to rise above the limitations of a restricted vision to find truth.[6] It is from this new intelligentsia that the sociologist of knowledge emerged, and it is this sociologist who is in a distinctive position to offer a solution to the world's intellectual chaos. According to Simonds:

> Mannheim's faith in the intellectuals is, then, a faith in the powers of the intellect to overcome the limitations of this or that personal experience as a ground of knowledge, to expand the self by engaging in authentic communication with others, to aspire to a more comprehensive view of our shared human condition by virtue of the communicative ability to gain access to contexts of thought other than the one into which we are born.
>
> (Simonds, 1978:131)

---

[5]Mannheim took this idea from the work of Max Weber's brother, Alfred, himself a noted scholar of his day.

[6]Remmling finds the creation of the intelligentsia as a solution to the problem of truth to be a "dubious construction" (1967:45).

Before it created the sociology of knowledge, this new intelligentsia created two other methods of thought and investigation. One was *epistemology,* an immanent theory of knowledge that emerged out of a process of pure contemplation. The other was *psychology,* which focused on such things as the genesis of meaning within the individual. In different ways, both of these approaches were, from Mannheim's point of view, guilty of separating the individual mind from the larger community. It is this error that the sociology of knowledge serves to correct. As Mannheim put it, "Knowledge is from the beginning a cooperative process of group life, in which everyone unfolds his knowledge within the framework of a common fate, a common activity, and the overcoming of common difficulties" (1929/1936:29).

The modern world has led not only to the realization that there is a multitude of views, but also to the desire, linked to Marx's theory of ideology, to "unmask" the unconscious motivations that lie behind systems of ideas. This desire to see what lies behind idea systems has led to the sense that there is a "collective unconscious" that is the irrational foundation of systems of ideas. Intellectuals are not the only ones involved in the unmasking of these irrational foundations; members of all groups are involved in the unmasking of the ideas of those in other, often competing, groups. The result of all of this questioning is, again, the undermining of "man's confidence in human thought in general" (Mannheim, 1929/1936:41). As a result of this inability to believe in anything, "more and more people took flight into skepticism and irrationalism" (Mannheim, 1929/1936:41). This is one of the ways that Mannheim links the intellectual and social crises of his day, especially the irrationalism associated with the rise of fascism. Hungry for something to believe in, people were vulnerable to the irrational idea systems put forth by the fascists.

Yet, dialectically, this process of unmasking not only creates a crisis, but again provides the basis for the resolution of that crisis. As Mannheim puts it, "What seems so unbearable in life itself, namely, to continue to live with the unconscious uncovered, is the historical prerequisite of scientific critical self-awareness" (1929/1936:47). That is, it allows for greater insight into the social determination of knowledge, and such knowledge can provide the basis for emancipation from such social determination.

Weltanschauung

In his sociology of knowledge, Mannheim (1952/1971a) is generally not interested in isolated ideas and beliefs, but rather in getting at the *Weltanschauung,* or systematic totality of ideas of an epoch or group which, in turn, is composed of a series of mutually interdependent parts. The *Weltanschauung* is more than the sum of its parts, but each of the parts can be studied to give us a sense of the *Weltanschauung.* But there is a dialectical relationship between the *Weltanschauung* and its parts: "We understand the whole from the part, and the part from the whole. We derive the 'spirit of the epoch' from its individual *documentary* manifestations on the basis of what we know about the spirit of the epoch" (Mannheim, 1952/1971a:49; italics added).

Mannheim sees three levels of meaning in cultural products such as knowledge. The objective level of meaning is that which is inherent in the product itself. The expressive level of meaning is what the actor intended in producing the product. Finally, and most important to Mannheim, the documentary meaning is that the product serves as a "document," or allows us to get a sense, of the *Weltanschauung*. Mannheim is generally not interested in specific cultural products, but what they allow him to deduce about the *Weltanschauung* in which they exist. And he is not so much interested in unmasking individual ideas as he is in "determining the functional role of any thought whatever" within the *Weltanschauung* (Mannheim, 1925/1971:69).

Functional analysis is key to Mannheim. He is interested not only in the functional relationship between specific ideas and the *Weltanschauung,* but also in the functional relationship between ideas and the larger social setting. One of Mannheim's more important definitions of the sociology of knowledge is "a discipline which explores the functional dependence of each intellectual standpoint on the differentiated social group reality standing behind it, and which sets itself the task of retracing the evolution of the various standpoints" (Mannheim, 1925/1971:115). In doing a sociology of knowledge, Mannheim is doing a *functional* analysis; that is, he is viewing knowledge as a function of the social world from which it emanates and of the *Weltanschauung* of which it is part.

Steps in Practicing the Sociology of Knowledge

This definition leads Mannheim to identify a series of steps involved in the practice of the sociology of knowledge. First, it is necessary to specify, for each historical period under study, "the various systematic intellectual standpoints on which the thinking of creative individuals and groups was based" (Mannheim, 1925/1971:114). Second, the sociologist is to explore the "non-theoretical, vital roots" of these standpoints by uncovering "the hidden metaphysical premises of the various systematic positions; then we must ask further which of the 'world postulates' coexisting in a given epoch are the correlates of a given style of thought" (Mannheim, 1925/1971:114). Third, in uncovering the latter we will, in the process, have identified the various intellectual strata at work at a given point in time. It is Mannheim's view that these intellectual strata will be in conflict with one another in an effort to gain preeminence for a particular *Weltanschauung*. Finally, there is what Mannheim considers the sociological task proper:

> finding the social strata making up the intellectual strata in question. It is only in terms of these latter strata within the overall process, in terms of their attitudes toward the emerging new reality, that we can define the fundamental aspirations and world postulates existing at a given time which can absorb already existing ideas and methods and subject them to a change of function—not to speak of new created forms.
>
> (Mannheim, 1925/1971:114)

In other words, the basic task of the sociology of knowledge is getting at the nature of the social group that lies at the base of the intelligentsia as well as the idea systems under consideration.

As we have seen, for a variety of reasons Mannheim sees his era as being in the midst of an intellectual crisis. It is in the context of this crisis that Mannheim deals with two of his most important ideas—ideology and utopia. Mannheim sees them as characterizing the "final intensification of the intellectual crisis" (1929/1936:39–40). Let us look now in some detail at what Mannheim has to say about these two idea systems.

Ideology and Utopia

Mannheim's most systematic thoughts on the concepts of ideology and utopia are to be found, not surprisingly, in his best-known work, *Ideology and Utopia* (Mannheim, 1929/1936; Kettler and Meja, 1994; B. Turner, 1995).

Ideology

We have already encountered a few of Mannheim's thoughts on ideology in our discussion of the roots of the sociology of knowledge in Marx's theory of ideology. An ideology, as well as a utopia, is a system of ideas, a *Weltanschauung.* An *ideology* is a set of ideas that "conceals the present by attempting to comprehend it in terms of the past" (Mannheim, 1929/1936:97). A *utopia,* in contrast, is a set of ideas that "transcends the present and is oriented to the future" (Mannheim, 1929/1936:97). Those who use ideologies are attempting to defend the status quo by obscuring certain things about it, whereas those who use utopias are endeavoring to overthrow the status quo by emphasizing the advantages of an alternative social form. Those who adopt a utopia are seeking a goal "which seems to be unrealizable only from the point of view of a given social order which is already in existence" (Mannheim, 1929/1936:196). Thus, there is always a fundamental conflict of interest between those accepting a utopia and those buying into an ideology.

In fact, it is usually the opposing group that labels a set of ideas as either an ideology or a utopia: "It is always the dominant group which is in full accord with the existing order that determines what is to be regarded as utopian, while the ascendant group which is in conflict with things as they are is the one that determines what is regarded as ideological" (Mannheim, 1929/1936:203). In this sense, "ideology" and "utopia" are labels that one group places on the ideas of an opposing group.

In order for him to be able to judge whether ideas are ideological or utopian, Mannheim needs a more objective base point, and that is provided by his concept of *adequate* ideas: "Ideas which correspond to the concretely existing and *de facto* order are designated as 'adequate' and situationally congruous. These are relatively rare and only a state of mind that has been sociologically fully clarified operates with situationally congruous ideas and motives" (Mannheim, 1929/1936:194). In contrast to those ideas that are "properly" rooted in the present, there are ideas that are anchored in the past (ideologies) and in the future (utopias). It can be very difficult to judge what category a specific complex of ideas fits into, but Mannheim feels that it can be done by an external observer. But Mannheim is forced to admit, "To determine concretely, however, what in a given case is ideological and what utopian [as well as 'adequate'] is extremely difficult" (1929/1936:196).

One of the complicating factors in making this judgment is the fact that in historical reality, the two are not clearly separated from one another. For example, "The utopias of ascendant classes are often, to a large extent, permeated with ideological elements" (Mannheim, 1929/1936:203). Another is that the noise of partisan conflict serves to make it unclear which ideas are utopian and which are ideological. As a result, Mannheim is forced to conclude that the only way one can really tell whether one is dealing with an ideology or with a utopia is with the hindsight of history: "Ideas which later turned out to have been only distorted representations of a past or potential social order were ideological, while those which were adequately realized in the succeeding social order were relative utopias" (Mannheim, 1929/1936:204).

Judged from the point of view of adequate ideas, *both* ideologies and utopias are distorted mental structures. One task of the sociologist of knowledge is to unmask the distortions in the two idea systems. More important, the objective is the uncovering of their social sources. Most generally, the goal of the sociologist of knowledge is to "attempt to escape ideological and utopian distortions . . . a quest for reality" (Mannheim, 1929/1936:98). Only the external observer, the socially unattached intellectual, the sociologist of knowledge, is able to discover this undistorted social reality.

Mannheim distinguishes between the particular and the total conception of ideology (Kettler and Meja, 2001). *Particular* ideologies refer to the ideas of our opponents and are typically seen as conscious distortions. *Total* ideologies are the ideas of a concrete sociohistorical group, or even of an entire age or epoch, and are not typically viewed as involving conscious distortions. Mannheim draws three other distinctions between particular and total ideologies. First, in the case of a particular ideology, only a portion of an opponent's idea system is considered ideological, whereas in a total ideology, an opponent's entire *Weltanschauung* is thought to be ideological. Second, in the case of a particular ideology, opposing groups continue to share some ideas, such as the basic standards of validity. In contrast, the total ideologies of opposing groups differ on everything; they are "fundamentally divergent thought-systems" (Mannheim, 1929/1936:57). Third, the study of particular ideologies involves a psychological analysis of the interests of those involved with the idea system. The study of total ideologies involves a functional (or sociological) analysis in which there is a study of the "correspondence between a given social situation and a given perspective" (Mannheim, 1929/1936:58). Thus, a particular ideology is in line with the way Marxists use the term ideology, whereas total ideology reflects the orientation of the sociology of knowledge.[7]

The Marxists, of course, used the idea of ideology to critique and discredit the views of the capitalists. However, as Weber pointed out, those same tools can be used to analyze Marxian thinking: "The materialist conception of history is not to be compared to a cab that one can enter or alight from at will, for once they enter it, even revolutionaries themselves are not free to leave it" (Weber, cited in Mannheim, 1929/1936:74). Or, in Mannheim's terms, "Nothing was to prevent the opponents of Marxism from availing themselves of the weapon and applying it to Marxism itself" (Mannheim, 1929/1936:75). Ultimately, of course, everyone could use the total conception of ideology and apply it to any and all idea systems. Crucial in Mannheim's eyes is the willingness and the ability to apply the total conception of ideology not only to other idea systems, but to one's own idea system as well.

---

[7]However, Mannheim (1929/1936:74) does give Marxian theory credit for discovering the total conception of ideology and fusing it with the psychological (particular) approach.

Utopia

While Mannheim's thinking on ideology is deeply tied to its Marxian roots, he is more original in his thinking on utopia, as well as on its relationship to ideology. A utopia, like an ideology, is incongruous with reality. However, what distinguishes a utopia is the fact that it not only "transcends reality," but also "breaks the bond of the existing reality" (Mannheim, 1929/1936:192). Although utopias are revolutionary *ideas,* they can affect action, which will "tend to shatter either partially or wholly, the order of things prevailing at the time" (Mannheim, 1929/1936:192).

Mannheim has a dialectical view of utopias (and most other things). An existing order tends to give birth to a series of "unrealized and unfulfilled tendencies which represent the needs of each age" (Mannheim, 1929/1936:199). That is, dialectically, a given social order has within it the seeds of its own destruction. Mannheim sees these ideas as "explosive material" capable of overturning the extant order. When these revolutionary ideas are transformed into action, they are capable of breaking "the bonds of the existing order, leaving it free to develop in the direction of the next order of existence" (Mannheim, 1929/1936:199). When that "next" order of existence comes into being, the stage is presumably set for the process to begin again with the rise of the next set of utopian ideas.

Of course, all utopian ideas must overcome the opposition of countervailing ideologies. Ideologies serve to protect the existing social order, while utopias perform "the function of bursting the bonds of the existing order" (Mannheim, 1929/1936:206). The group espousing a utopia may, in fact, achieve power and come to be the dominant group within society. In that case, the utopian mentality can reach its end point; that is, it becomes "completely infused into every aspect of the dominating mentality of the time" (Mannheim, 1929/1936:209). However, because the group carrying the idea has come into power, the utopia is gradually transformed into an ideology that sooner or later gives birth to one or more counter-utopias.

Where does a utopia come from? Mannheim makes it clear that a utopia can emerge from a single individual: "It happens very often that the dominant utopia first arises as the wish-fantasy of a single individual and does not until later become imported into the political aims of a more inclusive group" (Mannheim, 1929/1936:209). Following Weber, Mannheim sees such an individual as "charismatic." However, the utopian ideas of the charismatic individual must, in order to survive and succeed, be in touch with the collective problems of the day and be linked in various ways with some group. For one thing, the ideas of the individual must be in accord with the collective impulse of a larger group. In other words, the individual must be giving expression to sentiments that are already present as currents within a collectivity. For another, more important thing, in order for the utopia to be effective in tearing asunder the existing order, the ideas must be taken up by some group and translated by it into action. In other words, individuals are not capable of social revolution; only a group can bring about such a revolution. Although, as we saw earlier, many groups can espouse utopias and bring about social revolutions, in the last resort social classes are the most important of these groups. In spite of the centrality of social classes, we should not lose sight of the fact that utopias can be produced by other social groups. As Mannheim puts it, "the key to the intelligibility of utopias is the structural situation of the social stratum which at any given time espouses them" (1929/1936:208).

Mannheim identifies four historical ideal types of utopias. The first is *orgiastic chiliasm.*[8] Chiliasts tend to be irrational, unreflective, ecstatic-orgiastic, and like all utopians, oriented to transcending the existing world. The carriers of this utopia were members of the lowest strata within society. The second type is the *liberal-humanitarian* utopia carried by the middle strata of bourgeoisie and intellectuals. The utopian image here is of a more rational future toward which we are gradually moving. Third is the *conservative* utopia (discussed later in this chapter) that develops in reaction to the liberal-humanistic and chiliastic utopias. The utopian goal here is a world in which everything that does exist continues to exist. Great value is placed on things that are derived from the past and that continue to exist in the present. Conservative utopian ideas tend to be carried by those groups that have made it in society and are interested in protecting their position. Finally, there is the *socialist-communist* utopia. The goal of this type is the overthrow of the present society and the creation of a classless society. The carrier is the proletariat, or other ascendant social groups.

When he looks at the contemporary world, Mannheim tends to see the demise of utopias, and he seems to regret their disappearance greatly. Why do utopias tend to disappear? For one thing, as we have seen, when a group espousing a utopia moves into established positions, it tends to adapt its ideas to the existing reality. A second factor is the warfare among utopias and the fact that "different coexistent forms of utopian mentality are destroying one another in reciprocal conflict" (Mannheim, 1929/1936:250). Finally, out of this conflict of utopias, and the propensity toward critical examination of one another's idea systems, is the more general tendency toward critical analysis of the historical and social roots of all ideas, including utopian ideas.

The result of all this is that our earlier utopias have come to be nothing more than a number of different points of view. We are left with a series of atomistic viewpoints; we are left without a comprehensive view of the world. To put it another way, with the demise of utopias comes the disappearance of total points of view.

Disenchantment

Mannheim goes further and, in another viewpoint that resembles Weberian theory, tends to see a progressive disenchantment of the world. In this case, we are seeing the disappearance of *both* utopias *and* ideologies; we are moving toward a world in which "all ideas have been discredited and all utopias have been destroyed" (Mannheim, 1929/1936:256). In an excellent description of the disenchantment of the world, Mannheim describes the movement toward the "complete destruction of all spiritual elements, the utopian as well as the ideological . . . emergence of a 'matter of factness' . . . in sexual life, art, and architecture, and the expression of the natural impulses in sports" (Mannheim, 1929/1936:256).

In spite of this progressive disenchantment of the world, Mannheim argues that this disenchantment is to be regretted because people need utopias (and ideologies). As Mannheim puts it:

> It is possible, therefore, that in the future, in a world in which there is never anything new, in which all is finished and each moment is a repetition of the past, there can

---

[8]This type of utopia is usually associated with the Anabaptists, a religious sect.

> exist a condition in which thought will be utterly devoid of all ideological and utopian elements. But the complete elimination of reality-transcending elements from our world would lead us to a "matter-of-factness" which ultimately would mean the decay of the human will.
>
> (Mannheim, 1929/1936:262)

Yet, although Mannheim regrets the progressive disappearance of both ideologies and utopias, it is the demise of the latter that is the far greater problem. The reason is that although the death of an ideology would pose a crisis for the social strata espousing it, the disappearance of utopias would have a profoundly negative effect on human nature and human development as a whole:

> The disappearance of utopia brings about a static state of affairs in which man himself becomes no more than a thing. We would be faced then with the greatest paradox imaginable, namely that man, who has achieved the highest degree of rational mastery of existence, left without any ideals, becomes a mere creature of impulses. Thus, after a long tortuous, but heroic development, just at the highest stage of awareness, when history is ceasing to be blind fate, and is becoming more and more man's own creation, with the relinquishment of utopias, man would lose his will to shape history and therewith his ability to understand it.
>
> (Mannheim, 1929/1936:262–263)

Hope for the Future

The hope for the future lies in the fact that there are still two groups that are capable of instilling the world with tension. First, there are the "strata whose aspirations are not yet fulfilled" and the fact that they "will always cause the counter-utopias to rekindle and flare up again" (Mannheim, 1929/1936:257). Mannheim associates the strata whose aspirations are unfulfilled with the proletariat and its communist utopia, and the major counter-utopia with conservatism. However, when looked at from the vantage point of the world of the century, although there are certainly still strata whose aspirations remain unfulfilled, there is little or no faith in communism or socialism as viable alternatives to the extant system. It seems clear that the strata are still there, but at the moment they are lacking a utopian vision.

The other group that offers some hope as far as Mannheim is concerned is his favored "socially unattached intellectuals." This group of intellectuals, which has always existed to some degree, is seen by Mannheim as expanding. They are being drawn from all strata of society not just the privileged classes; they are increasingly separated from the rest of society and are increasingly dependent on their own resources. Four alternatives are open to such intellectuals. First, they can affiliate themselves with radical socialists and communists. Second, they can become skeptics dedicated to the elimination of all ideology. Third, they can orient themselves romantically to the past and attempt to "revive religious feeling, idealism, symbols, and myths" (Mannheim, 1929/1936:259). Finally, they can renounce the world, as well as any interest in radical politics. However, in choosing the latter alternative, intellectuals become part of the problem rather than a potential solution, because they then come to "take part in the great historical process of disillusionment" (Mannheim, 1929/1936:259–260). It seems clear that Mannheim prefers the second alternative as the course to be taken by the intelligentsia.

Rationality and the Irrationality of the Times

Mannheim, very much influenced by the work of Weber (and Simmel), developed a theory of rationality which, among other things, allowed him to deal with many of the problems of his day under the heading of irrationality. In *Ideology and Utopia* (1929/1936), Mannheim offered a gross differentiation between rationality and irrationality, which he refined later in his work. In that early work, the *rational* sphere of society was defined as "consisting of settled and routinized procedures in dealing with situations that recur in an orderly fashion" (Mannheim, 1929/1936:113). The *irrational* sphere was defined residually, although Mannheim made it clear that it continued to be more prevalent than the rational sectors of society: "Rationalized as our life may seem to have become, all the rationalizations that have taken place so far are merely partial since the most important realms of our social life are even now anchored in the irrational" (1929/1936:115). The economy, for example, was still dominated by irrational free competition rather than having become a more rational planned economy. Similarly, in the stratification system, one's place was still determined by competition and struggle, not by objective tests that decided one's position within that system. And in politics, planning had not yet been able to eliminate the struggle for dominance at the national and international levels.

Although the irrational continues to predominate, Mannheim seems to imply that rationalization is a process that has invaded various sectors of society and that others are likely to come under its sway in the future. In other words, the irrational is likely to retreat in the face of the forward march of the rational. As Mannheim puts it, "The chief characteristic of modern culture is the tendency to include as much as possible in the realm of the rational and to bring it under administrative control—and, on the other hand, to reduce the 'irrational' element to the vanishing point" (1929/1936:114).

Mannheim was forced to back away from this optimistic view in his later work in the face of the increasing prevalence of such irrationalities as economic depression, war, fascism, and so on. It became increasingly hard in Mannheim's day to argue that irrationalities were in the process of disappearing. If anything, the opposite seemed to be the case. As we will see, Mannheim came to feel that rationality could not be left to advance on its own but had to be helped along through planning. Furthermore, as he came to refine his sense of rationality, he came to see that the forward march of at least one type of rationality may in fact be a major *cause* of at least some of these irrationalities (more on this shortly).

Rationalization, for Mannheim, involves behavior that is in accord with some rational structure or framework. Rational actors follow definite prescriptions "entailing no personal decision whatsoever" (Mannheim, 1929/1936:115). The image is of the actor following the dictates of some larger, bureaucratically organized structure, and this image is supported by the examples offered by Mannheim—petty officials, judges, factory workers, and so on. Rational action is contrasted to *conduct,* which begins "where rationalization has not yet penetrated, and where we are forced to make decisions in situations which have *as yet* not been subjected to regulation" (Mannheim, 1929/1936:115; italics added). In this early work, conduct is clearly associated with the irrational realm. It is also clear that Mannheim holds the view that conduct, like irrationality more generally, will sooner or later come to be limited or even eliminated by the process of rationalization.

Mannheim is ambivalent on this process of rationalization. On the one hand, he clearly favors the progressive rationalization of sectors that have heretofore been dominated by the irrational. Because they will come to be controlled by administrative dictates, irrational decisions and actions will be reduced or eliminated. On the other hand, Mannheim cannot really want a world in which all decisions are controlled—in which there is no personal decision making, no personal freedom, whatsoever. We will return to this issue when we discuss Mannheim's view on planning, but before we do we need to discuss his later and more sophisticated delineation of the difference between the rational and the irrational.

Types of Rationality and Irrationality

Mannheim had much more to say about rationality and irrationality in one of the essays included in *Man and Society in an Age of Reconstruction* (1935/1940). Here he argues that both rationality and irrationality can be subdivided into the substantial and the functional. Substantial rationality and irrationality deal with *thinking,* whereas functional rationality and irrationality are concerned with *action. Substantial rationality,* then, is defined as "an act of thought which reveals intelligent insight into the inter-relations of events in a given situation" (Mannheim, 1935/1940:53). Adopting again a residual notion of irrationality, Mannheim defines *substantial irrationality* as "everything else which either is false or not an act of thought at all (as for example drives, impulses, wishes and feelings, both conscious and unconscious)" (Mannheim, 1935/1940:53). This clearly is a very different sense of the distinction between rational and irrational, since previously Mannheim had associated rationality with the lack of thought, while here substantial irrationality involves a lack of thought. However, previously the lack of thought had been associated with administrative control, while in the case of substantial irrationality it is linked to drives, impulses, wishes, and feelings.

Mannheim comes closer to his earlier sense of rationality in his definition of *functional rationality* as "a series of actions . . . organized in such a way that it leads to a previously defined goal, every element in this series of actions receiving a functional position and role" (Mannheim, 1935/1940:53). The series of actions is functionally rational in that each has a role to play in the achievement of the ultimate goal, although the goal itself can be either rational or irrational. Thus, for example, salvation is defined as an irrational goal, but it can be sought through a series of functionally rational actions.

Mannheim's concept of functional rationality has much in common with Weber's sense of formal rationality. For example, efficiency is a central characteristic of rationality from Weber's point of view, and Mannheim argues that a "functional organization of a series of actions will, moreover, be at its best when, in order to attain the given goal, it coordinates the means most efficiently" (1935/1940:53).

Interestingly, to Mannheim functional and substantive rationality may be substitutes for, or even in conflict with, one another. For example, a soldier may act in accord with the functional organization of the military without thinking through his or her action. In fact, a functional organization like the military often wants its members to act in accord with its dictates and *not* to think things through on their own.

Finally, *functional irrationality* is defined, once again residually, as "everything which breaks through and disrupts functional ordering" (Mannheim, 1935/1940:54). Violence committed by unruly individuals is an example of functional irrationality. The functionally rational actions of those in one organization can also be functionally irrational from the point of view of those in another organization. For example, when state officials raise taxes on corporations, those taxes may be seen as functionally irrational from the perspective of those in such businesses. Thus, "'functional irrationality' never characterizes an act itself but only with reference to its position in the entire complex of conduct of which it is part" (Mannheim, 1935/1940:55).

Weber was most interested in the spread of formal rationality in the West, and Mannheim has a similar level of concern for, and offers a similar hypothesis about, the spread of functional rationality:

> The more industrialized a society is and the more advanced its division of labour and organization, the greater will be the number of spheres of human activity which will be functionally rational and hence also calculable in advance. Whereas the individual in earlier societies acted only occasionally and in limited spheres in a functionally rational manner, in contemporary society he is *compelled* to act in this way in more and more spheres of life.
>
> (Mannheim, 1935/1940:55; italics added)

Mannheim goes beyond functional rationalization to posit the intimately related phenomenon of *self-rationalization,* or "the individual's systematic control of his impulses" (Mannheim, 1935/1940:55). In fact, self-rationalization is sometimes described as a type of functional rationalization, and in any case the two are closely linked—"the functional rationalization of objective activities ultimately evokes self-rationalization" (Mannheim, 1935/1940:56). There is a high level of rationalization when functional rationalization and self-rationalization occur together. This situation is most likely to arise in the administrative staff of large organizations. Here the external control of the organization's rules and regulations is supplemented by self-rationalization, especially in the case of staff members and their careers. In Mannheim's words, the career prescribes "not only the actual processes of work but also the prescriptive regulation both of the ideas and feelings one is permitted to have and of one's leisure time" (1935/1940:56). Thus, self-regulation exerts control over matters (ideas, feelings, leisure time) that functional rationalization cannot reach.

However, self-rationalization is *not* the highest and most extreme form of rationalization. That honor goes to what Mannheim calls *self-observation.* Self-rationalization involves a

> process of mental training, subordinating my inner motives to an external aim. Self-observation, on the other hand, is more than such form of mental training. Self-observation aims primarily at inner *self-transformation.* Man reflects about himself and his actions mostly for the sake of remoulding or transforming himself more radically.
>
> (Mannheim, 1935/1940:57)

Mannheim thus seems to envision a hierarchy running from substantial rationalization to functional rationalization, self-rationalization, and ultimately self-observation.

Although in the earlier stages of modernity, society may have been able to rely on functional rationalization, more complex and rapidly changing modern societies require self-rationalization and especially self-observation, which control people better and more efficiently and enable them to adapt more readily to complex new situations.

Returning to his central concepts, Mannheim argues that industrialization has led to an increase in functional rationalization, but not necessarily substantial rationalization. In fact, Mannheim goes further by arguing that functional rationalization has tended to "paralyze" substantial rationalization by leaving people less and less room to utilize their independent judgment. This idea seems to be Mannheim's version of Weber's irrationality of rationality. That is, the irrational consequence of the spread of functional rationality is the decline of substantial rationality. Here Mannheim differentiates between those at the top of the organization and those below them. Those at the top tend to retain substantial rationality, whereas the substantial rationality of those below them declines as the responsibility for decision making is turned over to those at the top. This process has disastrous consequences for a person who does not occupy a high-level, decision-making position:

> He becomes increasingly accustomed to being led by others and gradually gives up his own interpretation of events for those others give him. When the rationalized mechanism of social life collapses in terms of crisis, the individual cannot repair it by his own insight. Instead his own impotence reduces him to a state of terrified helplessness.
>
> (Mannheim, 1935/1940:59)

Another irrationality of rationality stems from the fact that because of industrialization, great masses of people are crowded together in large cities. In other words, industrialization brings with it the creation of what has come to be called "mass society." Thus, paradoxically, as large-scale industrial society produces increases in functional rationality, self-rationalization, and self-observation, it also creates the conditions in mass society for irrational threats to that rational system:

> It produces all the irrationalities and emotional outbreaks which are characteristic of amorphous human agglomerations. As an industrial society, it so refines the social mechanism that the slightest irrational disturbance can have the most far-reaching effects, and as a mass society it favors a great number of irrational impulses and suggestions and produces an accumulation of unsublimated psychic energies which, at every moment, threatens to smash the whole subtle machinery of social life.
>
> (Mannheim, 1935/1940:61)

Although Mannheim retains the view that irrationality is not always a problem, in the modern world irrationalities are finding their way into places where rational planning and control are indispensable.

Thus, in Mannheim's view, the basic sources of the irrational in modern life are the *same* as the sources of the formally rational. In other words, Mannheim has offered a *sociological,* not a psychological, theory of the origins of both rationality and irrationality. He sees the sources of *both* as being built into the structure of modern society:

> They are driven, now in one direction, now in another by the dual nature of the social structure that certain human beings are now calculating creatures who work out their

actions to the very last detail, and now volcanic ones who think it right that at a given time they should reveal the worst depths of human brutality and sadism.

(Mannheim, 1935/1940:66)

There is another dialectical aspect to Mannheim's thinking. That is, increasing formal rationality leads not only to an increase in certain irrationalities, but also to the beginning of a rational sense that *planning* is needed to deal with these problems; not just piecemeal planning, but rather planning at the level of the whole of society. The rationalization of society, as well as its growing irrationality, has made planning inevitable, but the issue is: Who will do that planning? Those who represent narrow interest groups? Or those who have the interests of society as a whole in mind? Clearly, Mannheim prefers that the latter do the planning, and they are either sociologists, or they have the kind of totalistic perspective that only sociology can offer.

A Critical Analysis of Mannheim's Work

Mannheim's reputation is based on the fact that he is credited with inventing a subfield of sociology that remains viable to this day. However, much of the work that he did under that heading has come under severe attack (Meja and Stehr, 1990). Although, as we will see, there is much of merit in those critiques, the critiques also have often been too harsh and have ignored a number of Mannheim's more specific contributions. For example, although it is derived from the work of Simmel and Weber, Mannheim's theory of rationality is in many ways clearer than those of Simmel and Weber, and it is more clearly linked to his diagnosis of the problems—the irrationalities—of his day. However, there are a number of important criticisms of Mannheim's approach that must be dealt with here.

Merton (1941/1957) got to the heart of the matter with two devastating criticisms of Mannheim's work. The first is that in a body of work designed to create and legitimize the sociology of *knowledge,* Mannheim never offered a clear-cut definition of what he meant by knowledge. As Merton put it, "Knowledge is at times regarded so broadly as to include every type of assertion and every mode of thought from folkloristic maxims to rigorous positive science" (1941/1957:497). Among those things dealt with as knowledge in Mannheim's work are "ethical convictions, epistemological postulates, material predications, synthetic judgments, political beliefs, the categories of thought, eschatological doxies, moral norms, ontological assumptions and observations of empirical fact" (Merton, 1941/1957:497).

Along the same lines, Mannheim sometimes uses other terms to describe his field of concern. For example, he writes about the "sociology of the mind," defined as the "study of mental functions in the context of action" (Mannheim, 1953). The mind and knowledge are hardly coterminous. We can conceive of the mind in a micro sense as belonging to an individual actor or in a macro sense as a collective mind. In either case, the mind is a process, and one of the results of that process is the creation of knowledge. Further complicating matters, at other times Mannheim writes about the sociology of thought and the sociology of cognition as if they were coterminous with the sociology of knowledge (and mind).

Unclear about knowledge, Mannheim was also obscure on the *relationship* between knowledge and society. According to Merton, Mannheim is guilty of a "failure to specify the *type* or *mode* of relations between social structure and knowledge" (1941/1957:498). Merton reviews Mannheim's work on this relationship and finds in it arguments that knowledge is *in accord with* industrial society or with the time, that social structures are the *causal determinants* of ideological errors, that ideas are *bound up with* a given social setting, that ideas *grow out of* such a setting, that ideas change *in harmony with* social changes, that changes in ideas are *closely connected* to structural realities, that ideas change *in close conjunction with* social forces, and so on. The point is that a wide range of relationships between knowledge and society are discussed in Mannheim's work. He does not clearly differentiate one from the others, nor does he show how all of these diverse relationships might be combined under a single broad heading.

Because of its vagueness about what knowledge is and its ambiguity about the relationship between knowledge and society, Mannheim's sociology of knowledge is, not surprisingly, riddled with gaping holes. Given these holes, one wonders why the sociology of knowledge caught on as it did, why it has had staying power, and why Mannheim occupies such a dominant place in the history of that subfield. Part of the answer lies, perhaps, in Thomas Kuhn's (1962, 1970) notion of a paradigm. To Kuhn, a successful new paradigm must *both* offer a new way of looking at the world *and* leave open many questions to be answered by those who were later to become attracted to working on the paradigm. Mannheim's sociology of knowledge fits the paradigm concept very well, at least in these senses of the term. It *did* offer an attractive new way of looking at a part of the social world (knowledge), and it certainly left open many issues for those who were to follow in Mannheim's footsteps.

Merton offers another criticism, one that most analysts of Mannheim's work make. This criticism is that, in spite of various efforts, Mannheim never did solve the problem of relativism (Goldman, 1994). It does appear that a consequence of Mannheim's approach is that it is impossible to believe in anything fully, including Mannheim's own views, because all ideas emanate from inherently limited positions in society.

Mannheim's later, more political, work is even easier to criticize. In that work, Mannheim was writing for a more general audience, not other academics, as had been the case in his earlier writings in Hungary and Germany. The result is a considerable discontinuity in the two bodies of work.[9] Much of the earlier work is dense, at times impenetrable, whereas the later work is much easier to read. The problem is that after reading it, one is left feeling that there is not much of substance there. The later work contains relatively little sociology, and the sociology that is there yields relatively few striking insights.

The later work also suffers from being timely. This seems like a strange problem because sociologists, especially sociological theorists, are generally criticized for doing work that is irrelevant to the concerns of the day. (Indeed, much of Mannheim's early

---

[9]Longhurst disagrees: "*Ideology and Utopia* represents the high point of Mannheim's development of a detailed sociology of knowledge and after this he increasingly concerned himself with more general problems of sociology and society, though these had, of course, always been present in the sociology of knowledge" (1988:16). Of *Man and Society in an Age of Reconstruction* (Mannheim, 1935/1940), Longhurst says, "The basic tenets of a sociology of knowledge are accepted as given."

work has this character.) In his later work, Mannheim was struggling with the problems of his day and was trying to offer timely solutions to those problems. Thus, for example, Mannheim was struggling with the threat posed by fascism, especially Nazism. Although certainly a problem for England in the late 1930s and early 1940s, fascism in general and Nazism in particular inspire little fear these days. More generally, Mannheim often described cataclysmic threats to society, threats that would destroy society unless there was a dramatic response of the type he described. However, from today's vantage point, the threats described by Mannheim did not pose anywhere near the danger he forecast. Furthermore, society did not implement his suggestions, and it does not seem to have suffered for it. Read from today's vantage point, Mannheim's fears seem overdrawn and his reforms Pollyannish.

There is an interesting parallel between the work of Mannheim and that of Comte. In both cases, the early work was serious and scholarly and constitutes their lasting contribution to sociology. In addition, later in life both men turned to more practical, political writings that seem unfortunate when examined from today's vantage point. In fact, Mannheim came close to elevating sociology to a Comtian vision of the "queen of the sciences" by defining "*sociology* as the basic discipline of the social sciences" (1953:203). More specifically, "it is only structural sociology which is capable of a comprehensive synthesis of all these facts which are the outcome of the separate social sciences" (Mannheim, 1953:208). Both Comte and Mannheim also came to a kind of religious orientation late in their careers, although Mannheim, unlike Comte, never envisioned himself as the "pope" of a new religion. More specifically, both came to see Catholicism as offering a model for the new world.

There is a troublesome elitism and conservatism about Mannheim's ideas. He seemed to have little regard for the masses and saw them as a potential threat to modern society. He saw the need for elites to run society. For example, he argued that "democracy is characterized, not by the absence of elite strata, but rather by a new mode of elite selection and a new self-interpretation of the elite" (Mannheim, 1956/1971:300). Later, he saw the need for elite planners to come up with designs for society so that it could avoid the looming disasters. However, all this requires trust in the elites and the planners. How is society to control them? What is to prevent them from forming the kind of fascistic regime that Mannheim so feared and detested?

We might close this chapter with some thoughts on the point with which we began—that Mannheim was not a grand theorist in the tradition of Weber or Marx. That is, Mannheim's contributions have been restricted largely to the sociology of knowledge and did not involve a grand theory of society. Although there is much truth in this position, it can be argued that the sociology of knowledge is about more than just knowledge, but is relevant to all sociocultural phenomena. That is, all cultural products can, indeed must, be analyzed in the same way that knowledge is analyzed by Mannheim. In fact, Mannheim defines cultural sociology as the "science of the embeddedness of cultural formations within social life" (1982:55). In other words, as Simonds puts it, "the sciences of men are themselves hermeneutical" (1978:136). The fact is that there is increasing support these days in many quarters of sociological theory for the idea that some sort of hermeneutic approach is preferable to one inspired by positivism. In this sense, Mannheim can be seen as a pioneer of the hermeneutic approach in sociology.

More specifically, his work on knowledge can be seen as an exemplar for similar work on the full panoply of cultural phenomena.

There is another sense in which it can be argued that Mannheim had a more general, if not a "grand," theory—that is, his effort to develop a theory of the relationship between the individual and society, which in today's terms is called micro-macro or agency-structure integration. For example, Mannheim concerns himself with the "unceasing interplay between our primary impulses which seek for satisfaction" and social institutions, or the "network of already established relationships," which remakes and remolds those impulses (1953:240).

More generally, Mannheim sought to develop a synthetic theory, a "sociological psychology," which synthesized insights from the disciplines of psychology and sociology, as well as other social sciences. Both disciplines look at the same material, but the sociologist looks at attitudes and behaviors with reference to the social context, whereas the psychologist tends to concentrate on the individual. What is needed is a sociological psychology that fuses the insights provided by these two disciplines and in the process provides the kind of integrative perspective so valued by Mannheim. The effort to synthesize various theories is another characteristic of modern sociological theory, one that was clearly anticipated by Mannheim in his ideas on sociological psychology.

Thus, while Mannheim's work certainly has its weaknesses, it *did* lead to the development of the sociology of knowledge and it *may* have embedded in it the kind of integrative and synthetic theory that is very much in line with the latest developments in sociological theory. Although many have followed up on Mannheim's ideas on the sociology of knowledge, at least until recently, few have explored the possibilities inherent in his broader theoretical perspective.

Summary

Karl Mannheim's theoretical work does not have the broad sweep of most of the other theorists covered in this book. However, his work did lead to the creation and development of an important field in contemporary sociology—the sociology of knowledge, or the study of the "existential determination of knowledge."

In creating the sociology of knowledge, Mannheim drew on a number of sources—most important, Karl Marx's ideas on ideologies. However, unlike Marx, Mannheim did not see ideologies as necessarily involving conscious distortions or emanating from social classes. Mannheim demonstrated that ideologies could emanate from generations (and other social sources) just as they could from social classes.

Mannheim focused on knowledge, approaching it from a sociological point of view. He was interested in studying knowledge empirically, especially using historical methods. Although he was interested in empirical research, Mannheim rejected the excesses of positivism. Among other things, he did not think that positivism was well suited to the study of ideas. Mannheim accepted much of the phenomenological approach, although he criticized phenomenology for ignoring material reality and for its search for ahistorical truths.

Mannheim sees a crisis in his time—relativism—in which all ideas seem to be equal and there appears to be nothing to believe in. However, he sees the sociology of knowledge arising out of this milieu and offering solutions to the problems associated with relativism. In contrast to the lack of absolute standards to make judgments associated with relativism, Mannheim sees the sociology of knowledge as characterized by relationism, or the idea that there is a relationship among specific ideas, larger idea systems, and the social system. Although this idea leads to the view that there are no eternal standards, there are standards specific to a given context that allow one to judge right and wrong. The intelligentsia, which plays a key role in Mannheim's thinking, is the group best able to make these kinds of judgments because it is the most capable of rising above a specific, limited viewpoint.

In his sociology of knowledge, Mannheim is generally not interested in specific ideas, but rather in the *Weltanschauung*—the systematic totality of ideas of an epoch or group. Much of this chapter focuses on three examples of a *Weltanschauung* that are of central importance to Mannheim—ideology, utopia, and conservatism. An ideology is a set of ideas that conceals the present by attempting to understand it in terms of the past, whereas a utopia is an idea system that endeavors to transcend the present and is oriented to the future. Mannheim emphasizes the fundamental conflict of interest among these two idea systems. Ideology and utopia are treated more generically, but conservatism is dealt with mainly in terms of its development in the first half of the nineteenth century. The confrontation of ideas is as important in Mannheim's thinking about conservatism as it is in the relationship between ideology and utopia.

Mannheim offered a number of important insights into the idea of rationality. Most important is his distinction between substantive and functional rationality and irrationality. He places great importance on the increase in functional rationalization, and its extension in the form of self-rationalization, and ultimately, self-observation. The chief irrationality of the increase in functional rationality is that it tends to paralyze substantive rationality. Mannheim also worries about the irrationalities associated with mass society.

C H A P T E R 15

George Herbert Mead

Chapter Outline

Intellectual Roots

The Priority of the Social

The Act

Mental Processes and the Mind

Self

Society

As we will see throughout this chapter, the social-psychological theories of George Herbert Mead were shaped by a variety of intellectual sources (Joas, 1985; 2001), but of great importance was the influence of psychological behaviorism.[1]

Intellectual Roots

Behaviorism

Mead defines *behaviorism* in its broadest sense as "simply an approach to the study of the experience of the individual from the point of view of his *conduct*" (1934/1962:2; italics added). (*Conduct* is used here as another word for behavior.) Mead has no trouble with this approach to behaviorism, but he does have difficulty with the way in which behaviorism came to be defined and practiced by the most prominent behaviorist of Mead's day, John B. Watson (Buckley, 1989).

The behaviorism of Mead's time, as practiced by Watson and most others and then applied to humans, had been imported from animal psychology, where it worked quite well. There it was based on the premise that it is impossible through introspection to get at the private, mental experiences (assuming they exist) of lower animals and therefore all that can and should be done is to focus on animal behavior. Rather than seek to adapt behaviorism to the fact that there are obvious mental differences between animals and humans, Watson simply applied the principles of animal behavior to humans. To Watson, people are little more than "organic machines" (Buckley, 1989:x). Given this view of

[1]For a critique of this position, see Natanson (1973b).

people and the analogy between humans and animals, Watson rejected the idea of the study of human consciousness by introspection or any other method. As Mead puts it, in colorful fashion, "John B. Watson's attitude was that of the Queen in *Alice in Wonderland*—'Off with their heads!' " (1934/1962:2–3).

In Mead's view, Watson seeks to use behavior (conduct) to explain individual experience, without a concern for inner experience, consciousness, and mental imagery. In contrast, Mead believes that even inner experience can be studied from the point of view of the behaviorist, as long as this viewpoint is *not* narrowly conceived. Thus, Mead *is* a behaviorist, albeit what he calls a "social" behaviorist. However, this seemingly slight extension makes an enormous theoretical difference. The symbolic-interactionist theory that emerged, in significant part from Mead's theory, is very different from behaviorist theories (such as early exchange theory), and indeed they exist in different sociological paradigms (Ritzer, 1975a).[2]

Although Mead wants to include what goes on within the mind as part of social behaviorism, he is as opposed as is Watson to the use of introspection to study mental processes. Mead wants to study the mind behavioristically, rather than introspectively:

> The opposition of the behaviorist to *introspection* is justified. It is *not* a *fruitful* undertaking from the point of view of psychological study. . . . What the behaviorist is occupied with, and what we have to come back to, is the actual reaction itself, and it is only in so far as we can translate the content of introspection over into response that we can get any satisfactory psychological doctrine.
>
> (Mead, 1934/1962:105; italics added)

Instead of studying the mind introspectively, Mead focuses on the *act* or, if other people are involved, the *social* act. Acts are behaviors defined in part in terms of the behaviorists' notions of stimulus and response. That is, some external stimulus causes the person to respond with an act. Mead's extension here is to argue that "part of the act lies within the organism and only comes to expression later; it is that side of behavior which I think Watson has passed over" (1934/1962:6). Mead does not ignore the inner experience of the individual, because that inner experience is *part,* indeed a crucial part, of the act (we will have much more to say about the act shortly). It is in this sense that Mead contends that "the existence as such of mind or consciousness, in some sense or other, must be admitted" (1934/1962:10). Mead is aware that the mind cannot be reduced solely to behaviors, but he argues that it is possible to explain it in behavioral terms without denying its existence.

Mead defines the mind in *functional* rather than idealist terms. That is, the mind is viewed in terms of what it does, the role it plays in the act, rather than as some transcendental, subjective phenomenon. The mind is a part, the key part, of the central nervous system, and Mead seeks to extend the analysis of the act, especially the social act, to what transpires in the central nervous system: "What I am insisting upon is that the patterns which one finds in the central nervous system are patterns of action—not of

---

[2]However, there are those (for example, Lewis and Smith, 1980) who argue that this difference has more to do with the way Mead's work was interpreted by his successors, especially Herbert Blumer, than with Mead's theories themselves (see also McPhail and Rexroat, 1979).

George Herbert Mead

A Biographical Sketch

Most of the important theorists discussed throughout this book achieved their greatest recognition in their lifetimes for their published work. George Herbert Mead, however, was at least as important, at least during his lifetime, for his teaching as for his writing. His words had a powerful impact on many people who were to become important sociologists in the twentieth century. As one of his students said, "Conversation was his best medium; writing was a poor second" (T. V. Smith, 1931:369). Let us have another of his students, himself a well-known sociologist—Leonard Cottrell—describe what Mead was like as a teacher:

> For me, the course with Professor Mead was a unique and unforgettable experience. . . . Professor Mead was a large, amiable-looking man who wore a magnificent mustache and a Vandyke beard. He characteristically had a benign, rather shy smile matched with a twinkle in his eyes as if he were enjoying a secret joke he was playing on the audience. . . .
>
> As he lectured—always without notes—Professor Mead would manipulate the piece of chalk and watch it intently. . . . When he made a particularly subtle point in his lecture he would glance up and throw a shy, almost apologetic smile over our heads—never looking directly at anyone. His lecture flowed and we soon learned that questions or comments from the class were not welcome. Indeed, when someone was bold enough to raise a question there was a murmur of disapproval from the students. They objected to any interruption of the golden flow. . . .
>
> His expectations of students were modest. He never gave exams. The main task for each of us students was to write as learned a paper as one could. These Professor Mead read with great care, and what he thought of your paper was your grade in the course. One might suppose that students would read materials for the paper rather than attend his lectures but that was not the case. Students always came. They couldn't get enough of Mead.
>
> (Cottrell, 1980:49–50)

Mead had enormous difficulty writing and this troubled him a great deal. "I am vastly depressed by my inability to write what I want to" (cited in G. Cook, 1993:xiii). However, over the years, many of Mead's ideas came to be published, especially in *Mind, Self and Society* (a book based on students' notes from a course taught by Mead). This book and others of Mead's works had a powerful influence on the development of contemporary sociology, especially symbolic interactionism.

Born in South Hadley, Massachusetts, on February 27, 1863, Mead was trained mainly in philosophy and its application to social psychology. He received a bachelor's degree from Oberlin College (where his father was a professor) in 1883, and after a few years as a secondary-school teacher, surveyor for railroad companies, and private tutor, Mead began graduate study at Harvard in 1887. After a few years of study at Harvard, as well as at the Universities of Leipzig and Berlin, Mead was offered an instructorship at the University of Michigan in 1891. It is interesting to note that Mead *never* received any graduate degrees. In 1894, at the invitation of John Dewey, he moved to the University of Chicago and remained there for the rest of his life.

As Mead makes clear in the following excerpt from a letter, he was heavily influenced by Dewey: "Mr. Dewey is a man of not only great originality and profound thought but the most appreciative thinker I have ever met. I have gained more from him than from any one man I ever met" (cited in Cook, 1993:32). This was especially true of Mead's early work at Chicago and he even followed Dewey into educational theory (Dewey left Chicago in 1904). However, Mead's thinking quickly diverged from Dewey's and led him in the direction of his famous social psychological theories of mind, self, and society. He began teaching a course on social psychology in 1900. In 1916–1917 it was transformed into an advanced course (the stenographic student notes from the 1928 course became the basis of *Mind, Self and Society*) that followed a course in elementary social psychology that was taught after 1919 by Ellsworth Faris of the sociology department. It was through this course that Mead had such a powerful influence on students in sociology (as well as psychology and education).

In addition to his scholarly pursuits, Mead became involved in social reform. He believed that science could be used to deal with social problems. For example, he was heavily involved as a fund raiser and policy maker at the University of Chicago Settlement House, which had been inspired by Jane Addams's Hull House. Perhaps most importantly, he played a key role in social research conducted by the settlement house.

Although eligible for retirement in 1928, he continued to teach at the invitation of the university and in the summer of 1930 became chair of the philosophy department. Unfortunately, he became embroiled in a bitter conflict between the department and the president of the university. This led in early 1931 to a letter of resignation from Mead written from his hospital bed. He was released from the hospital in late April, but died from heart failure the following day. Of him, John Dewey said he was "the most original mind in philosophy in the America of the last generations" (Cook, 1993:194).

contemplation" (1934/1962:26). Furthermore, what goes on in the central nervous system is not really separable from the act; it is an integral part of the act. Thus, Mead does not want to think of the mind in subjective terms but rather as something that is part of an objective process.

Pragmatism

Another important intellectual input into Mead's thinking was *pragmatism;* indeed, Mead was one of the key figures in the development of pragmatic philosophy (others were John Dewey and Charles Pierce) (Halton, 2005; Lewis and Smith, 1980; Lo Conto and Arrington, 2007; Wiley, 2006). Mead (1938/1972) regarded pragmatism as a "natural American outgrowth." Pragmatism reflected the triumph of science and the scientific method within American society and their extension into the study of the social world (Baldwin, 1986). Instead of being contemplative and otherworldly, as were previous philosophical systems, pragmatism adopted a focus on this world, on empirical reality. Pragmatists believe in the superiority of scientific data over philosophical dogma and all other types of knowledge. As John Baldwin summarizes, "Science is superior to trial-and-error learning, introspection, a priori logic, religious dogma, idealism, speculative philosophy, and all other nonempirical sources of knowledge" (1986:16). Science is seen as the optimum means not only for obtaining knowledge but also for analyzing and solving social problems. Scientific theories, as well as ideas in general, are to be tested using the full array of scientific procedures. The ideas that survive are those that are likely to provide knowledge that is useful and that solves problems. Pragmatists reject the idea of absolute truths. Rather, following the scientific model, they regard all ideas as provisional and subject to change in light of future research.

Pragmatism also involves a series of ideas that relate more directly to Mead's sociological theory (Charon, 2000). First, to pragmatists, truth and reality do not exist "out there" in the real world; they are "actively created as we act in and toward the world" (Hewitt, 1984:8; see also Shalin, 1986). Second, people remember the past and base their knowledge of the world on what has proved useful to them. They are likely to alter what no longer "works." Third, people define the social and physical "objects" that they encounter in the world according to their use for them. Finally, if we want to understand actors, we must base our understanding on what they actually do in the world. Given these viewpoints, we can understand John Baldwin's contention that pragmatism is "rooted in a 'rough and ready' American ethic developed by the settlers who had faced the challenges of new frontiers and dealt with the practical problems of taming a new land" (1986:22). In sum, pragmatism is a "pragmatic" philosophy in several senses, including the fact that it adopts the scientists' focus on the here and now as well as scientific methods; it is concerned with what people actually do, and it is interested in generating practical ideas that can help us cope with society's problems.

Lewis and Smith (1980) differentiate between two strands of pragmatism—*nominalist pragmatism* (associated with John Dewey and William James) and *philosophical realism* (associated with Mead). The nominalist position is that although societal phenomena exist, they do not exist independently of people and do not have a determining effect upon individual consciousness and behavior (in contrast to Durkheim's social facts and the reified worlds of Marx, Weber, and Simmel). More positively, this view "conceives of the individuals themselves as existentially free agents who accept, reject, modify, or otherwise 'define' the community's norms, roles, beliefs, and so forth, according to their own personal interests and plans of the moment" (Lewis and Smith, 1980:24). In contrast, to social realists the emphasis is on society and how it constitutes and controls individual mental processes. Rather than being free agents, actors and their cognitions and behaviors are controlled by the larger community.[3]

Given this distinction, Lewis and Smith conclude that Mead's work fits better into the realist camp. There is much of merit in this position, and it will inform some of the ensuing discussion (especially on the priority Mead accords to the social). However, to classify Mead as a realist would be to include him in the same category as Durkheim, and this is unacceptable because there are clearly important differences between their theories. In fact, Mead's theory cannot be forced into either of these categories. There are elements of *both* nominalism and realism in Mead's thinking. To put it more concretely, in most of Mead's work, social processes and consciousness mutually inform one another and cannot be clearly distinguished. In other words, there is a dialectic between realism and nominalism in Mead's work.

Dialectics

This brings us to another important source of Mead's thinking—the philosophy of Hegel, especially his dialectical approach. We have already encountered the dialectic, especially in Chapter 6 on Marx, and many of the ideas expressed there apply to Mead's thinking. We will return to this issue later in the chapter because, as we will see, dialectical thinking makes it almost impossible to separate Mead's many theoretical ideas; they are dialectically related to one another. However, adopting the strategy followed by Mead himself, we will differentiate among various concepts for the sake of clarity of discussion. Bear in mind (and occasionally the reader will be reminded) through each of the specific discussions that there is a dialectical interrelationship among the various concepts.

The Priority of the Social

In his review of Mead's best-known work, *Mind, Self and Society,* Ellsworth Faris argued that "not mind and then society; but society first and then minds arising with that society . . . would probably have been [Mead's] preference" (cited in Miller, 1982a:2). Faris's inversion of the title of this book reflects the widely acknowledged fact, recognized by Mead himself, that society, or more broadly the social, is accorded priority in Mead's analysis.

In Mead's view, traditional social psychology began with the psychology of the individual in an effort to explain social experience; in contrast, Mead always gives priority to the social world in understanding social experience. Mead explains his focus in this way:

---

[3]For a criticism of this distinction, see D. Miller (1982b, 1985).

> We are not, in social psychology, building up the behavior of the social group in terms of the behavior of separate individuals composing it; rather, we are *starting out with a given social whole* of complex group activity, into which we analyze (as elements) the behavior of each of the separate individuals composing it. . . . We attempt, that is, to explain the conduct of the social group, rather than to account for the organized conduct of the social group in terms of the conduct of the separate individuals belonging to it. For social psychology, the *whole (society) is prior to the part (the individual),* not the part to the whole; and the part is explained in terms of the whole, not the whole in terms of the part or parts.
>
> (Mead, 1934/1962:7; italics added)

To Mead, the social whole precedes the individual mind both logically and temporally. A thinking, self-conscious individual is, as we will see later, logically impossible in Mead's theory without a prior social group. The social group comes first, and it leads to the development of self-conscious mental states.

The Act

Mead considers the act to be the most "primitive unit" in his theory (1982:27). In analyzing the act, Mead comes closest to the behaviorist's approach and focuses on stimulus and response. However, even here the stimulus does not elicit an automatic, unthinking response from the human actor. As Mead says, "We conceive of the stimulus as an occasion or opportunity for the act, not as a compulsion or a mandate" (1982:28).

Stages

Mead (1938/1972) identified four basic and interrelated stages in the act (Schmitt and Schmitt, 1996); the four stages represent an organic whole (in other words, they are dialectically interrelated). Both lower animals and humans act, and Mead is interested in the similarities, and especially the differences, between the two.

Impulse

The first stage is that of the *impulse,* which involves an "immediate sensuous stimulation" and the actor's reaction to the stimulation, the need to do something about it. Hunger is a good example of an impulse. The actor (both nonhuman and human) may respond immediately and unthinkingly to the impulse, but more likely, the human actor will think about the appropriate response (for example, eat now or later). In thinking about a response, the person will consider not only the immediate situation but also past experiences and anticipated future results of the act.

Hunger may come from an inner state of the actor or may be elicited by the presence of food in the environment, or, most likely, it may arise from some combination of the two. Furthermore, the hungry person must find a way of satisfying the impulse in an environment in which food may not be immediately available or plentiful. This impulse, like all others, may be related to a problem in the environment (that is, the lack of immediately available food), a problem that must be overcome by the actor. Indeed, although an impulse like hunger may come largely from the individual (although even here hunger can be induced by an external stimulus, and there are also social definitions of when it is appropriate to be hungry), it is usually related to the existence of a problem in the environment (for example, the lack of food). Overall, the impulse, like all other elements of Mead's theory, involves both the actor and the environment.

Perception

The second stage of the act is *perception,* in which the actor searches for, and reacts to, stimuli that relate to the impulse, in this case hunger as well as the various means available to satisfy it. People have the capacity to sense or perceive stimuli through hearing, smell, taste, and so on. Perception involves incoming stimuli, as well as the mental images they create. People do not simply respond immediately to external stimuli but rather think about, and assess them through mental imagery. People are not simply subject to external stimulation; they also actively select characteristics of a stimulus and choose among sets of stimuli. That is, a stimulus may have several dimensions, and the actor is able to select among them. Furthermore, people are usually confronted with many stimuli, and they have the capacity to choose which to attend to and which to ignore. Mead refuses to separate people from the objects that they perceive. It is the act of perceiving an object that makes it an object to a person; perception and object cannot be separated from (are dialectically related to) one another.

Manipulation

The third stage is *manipulation.* After the impulse has manifested itself and the object has been perceived, the next step is manipulating the object or, more generally, taking action with regard to it. In addition to their mental advantages, people have another advantage over lower animals. People have hands (with opposable thumbs) that allow them to manipulate objects far more subtly than can lower animals. The manipulation phase constitutes, for Mead, an important temporary pause in the process so that a response is not manifested immediately. A hungry human being sees a mushroom, but before eating it, he or she is likely to pick it up first, examine it, and perhaps check in a guidebook to see whether that particular variety is edible. The lower animal, on the other hand, is likely to eat the mushroom without handling and examining it (and certainly without reading about it). The pause afforded by handling the object allows humans to contemplate various responses. In thinking about whether to eat the mushroom, both the past and the future are involved. People may think about past experiences in which they ate certain mushrooms that made them ill, and they may think about the future sickness, or even death, that might accompany eating a poisonous mushroom. The manipulation of the mushroom becomes a kind of experimental method in which the actor mentally tries out various hypotheses about what would happen if the mushroom were consumed.

Consummation

On the basis of these deliberations, the actor may decide to eat the mushroom (or not), and this constitutes the last phase of the act, *consummation,* or more generally the taking of action that satisfies the original impulse. Both humans and lower animals may consume the mushroom, but the human is less likely to eat a bad mushroom because of his or her ability to manipulate the mushroom and to think (and read) about the implications of eating it. The lower animal must rely on a trial-and-error method, and this is a less-efficient technique than the capacity of humans to think through their actions.[4] Trial-and-error in this situation is quite dangerous; as a result, it seems likely that lower animals are more prone to die from consuming poisonous mushrooms than are humans.

For ease of discussion, the four stages of the act have been separated from one another in sequential order; however, the fact is that Mead sees a dialectical relationship among the four stages. John Baldwin expresses this idea in the following way: "Although the four parts of the act sometimes *appear* to be linked in linear order, they actually interpenetrate to form one organic process: Facets of each part are present at all times from the beginning of the act to the end, such that each part affects the other" (1986:55–56). Thus, the later stages of the act may lead to the emergence of earlier stages. For example, manipulating food may lead the individual to the impulse of hunger and the perception that one is hungry and that food is available to satisfy the need.

Gestures

Whereas the act involves only one person, the *social act* involves two or more persons. The *gesture* is in Mead's view the basic mechanism in the social act and in the social process more generally. As he defines them, "gestures are movements of the first organism which act as specific stimuli calling forth the (socially) appropriate responses of the second organism" (Mead, 1934/1962:14; see also Mead, 1959:187). Lower animals and humans both are capable of gestures in the sense that the action of one individual mindlessly and automatically elicits a reaction by another individual. The following is Mead's famous example of a dogfight in terms of gestures:

> The act of each dog becomes the stimulus to the other dog for his response. . . . The very fact that the dog is ready to attack another becomes a stimulus to the other dog to change his own position or his own attitude. He has no sooner done this than the change of attitude in the second dog in turn causes the first dog to change his attitude.
>
> (Mead, 1934/1962:42–43)

Mead labels what is taking place in this situation a "conversation of gestures." One dog's gesture automatically elicits a gesture from the second; there are no thought processes taking place on the part of the dogs.

Humans sometimes engage in mindless conversations of gestures. Mead gives as examples many of the actions and reactions that take place in boxing and fencing matches, when one combatant adjusts "instinctively" to the actions of the second. Mead labels such unconscious actions "nonsignificant" gestures; what distinguishes humans is their ability to employ "significant" gestures, or those that require thought on the part of the actor before a reaction.

The vocal gesture is particularly important in the development of significant gestures. However, not all vocal gestures are significant. The bark of one dog to another is not significant; even some human vocal gestures (for example, a mindless grunt) may

---

[4]For a critique of Mead's thinking on the differences between humans and lower animals, see Alger and Alger, 1997.

not be significant. However, it is the development of vocal gestures, especially in the form of language, which is the most important factor in making possible the distinctive development of human life: "The specialization of the human animal within this field of the gesture has been responsible, ultimately, for the origin and growth of present human society and knowledge, with all the control over nature and over the human environment which science makes possible" (Mead, 1934/1962:14).

This development is related to a distinctive characteristic of the vocal gesture. When we make a physical gesture, such as a facial grimace, we cannot see what we are doing (unless we happen to be looking in the mirror). On the other hand, when we utter a vocal gesture, we hear ourselves just as others do. One result is that the vocal gesture can affect the speaker in much the same way that it affects the listeners. Another is that we are far better able to stop ourselves in vocal gestures than we are able to do in physical gestures. In other words, we have far better control over vocal gestures than physical ones. This ability to control oneself and one's reactions is critical, as we will see, to the other distinctive capabilities of humans. More generally, "it has been the vocal gesture that has preeminently provided the medium of social organization in human society" (Mead, 1959:188).

Significant Symbols

A significant symbol is a kind of gesture, one which only humans can make. Gestures become *significant symbols* when they arouse in the individual who is making them the same kind of response (it need not be identical) as they are supposed to elicit from those to whom the gestures are addressed. Only when we have significant symbols can we truly have communication; communication in the full sense of the term is not possible among ants, bees, and so on. Physical gestures can be significant symbols, but as we have seen, they are not ideally suited to be significant symbols because people cannot easily see or hear their own physical gestures. Thus, it is vocal utterances that are most likely to become significant symbols, although not all vocalizations are such symbols. The set of vocal gestures most likely to become significant symbols is *language:* "a symbol which answers to a meaning in that experience of the first individual and which also calls out the meaning in the second individual. Where the gesture reaches that situation it has become what we call 'language.' It is now a significant symbol and it signifies a certain meaning" (Mead, 1934/1962:46). In a conversation of gestures, only the gestures themselves are communicated. However, with language the gestures and their meanings are communicated.

One of the things that language, or significant symbols more generally, does is call out the same response in the individual who is speaking as it does in others. The word *dog* or *cat* elicits the same mental image in the person uttering the word as it does in those to whom it is addressed. Another effect of language is that it stimulates the person speaking as it does others. The person yelling "fire" in a crowded theater is at least as motivated to leave the theater as are those to whom the shout is addressed. Thus, significant symbols allow people to be the stimulators of their own actions.

Adopting his pragmatist orientation, Mead also looks at the "functions" of gestures in general and of significant symbols in particular. The function of the gesture "is to make adjustment possible among the individuals implicated in any given social act with reference to the object or objects with which that act is concerned" (Mead, 1934/1962:46). Thus, an involuntary facial grimace may be made in order to prevent a child from going too close to the edge of a precipice and thereby prevent him or her from being in a potentially dangerous situation. Although the nonsignificant gesture works, the "significant symbol affords far greater facilities for such adjustment and readjustment than does the nonsignificant gesture, because it calls out in the individual making it the same attitude toward it . . . and enables him to adjust his subsequent behavior to theirs in the light of that attitude" (Mead, 1934/1962:46). From a pragmatic point of view, a significant symbol works better in the social world than does a non-significant gesture. In other words, in communicating our displeasure to others, an angry verbal rebuke works far better than contorted body language. The individual who is manifesting displeasure is not usually conscious of body language and therefore is unlikely to be able to consciously adjust later actions in light of how the other person reacts to the body language. On the other hand, a speaker is conscious of uttering an angry rebuke and reacts to it in much the same way (and at about the same time) as the person to whom it is aimed reacts. Thus, the speaker can think about how the other person might react and can prepare his or her reaction to that reaction.

Of crucial importance in Mead's theory is another function of significant symbols—that they make the mind, mental processes, and so on, possible. It is only through significant symbols, especially language, that human *thinking* is possible (lower animals cannot think, in Mead's terms). Mead defines *thinking* as "simply an internalized or implicit conversation of the individual with himself by means of such gestures" (1934/1962:47). Even more strongly, Mead argues: "Thinking is the same as talking to other people" (1982:155). In other words, thinking involves talking to oneself. Thus, we can see clearly here how Mead defines thinking in behaviorist terms. Conversations involve behavior (talking), and that behavior also occurs within the individual; when it does, thinking is taking place. This is not a mentalistic definition of thinking; it is decidedly behavioristic.

Significant symbols also make possible *symbolic interaction.*[5] That is, people can interact with one another not just through gestures but also through significant symbols. This ability, of course, makes a world of difference and makes possible much more complex interaction patterns and forms of social organization than would be possible through gestures alone.

The significant symbol obviously plays a central role in Mead's thinking. In fact, David Miller (1982a:10–11) accords the significant symbol *the* central role in Mead's theory.

Mental Processes and the Mind

Mead uses a number of similar-sounding concepts when discussing mental *processes,* and it is important to sort out the most important of them. Before we do, the point should

---

[5]This is the label that was ultimately affixed (by Herbert Blumer) to the sociological theory derived, in significant part, from Mead's ideas.

be made that Mead is always inclined to think in terms of processes rather than structures or contents. In fact, Mead is often labeled a "process philosopher" (Cronk, 1987; D. Miller, 1982a).

Intelligence

One term that sounds as though it belongs under the heading of "mental processes" but actually does not in Mead's thinking is *intelligence.*[6] Mead defines *intelligence* most broadly as the mutual adjustment of the acts of organisms. By this definition, lower animals clearly have "intelligence," because in a conversation of gestures they adapt to one another. Similarly, humans can adapt to one another through the use of nonsignificant symbols (for example, involuntary grimaces). However, what distinguishes humans is that they can also exhibit intelligence, or mutual adaptation, through the use of significant symbols. Thus, a bloodhound has intelligence, but the intelligence of the detective is distinguished from that of the bloodhound by the capacity to use significant symbols.

Mead argues that animals have "unreasoning intelligence." In contrast, humans have "reason," which Mead defines in a characteristically behavioristic manner: "When you are reasoning you are indicating to yourself the characters that call out certain responses—and that is all you are doing" (1934/1962:93). In other words, individuals are carrying on conversations with themselves.

What is crucial to the reflective intelligence of humans is their ability to inhibit action temporarily, to delay their reactions to a stimulus (Mead, 1959:84). In the case of lower animals, a stimulus leads immediately and inevitably to a reaction; lower animals lack the capacity to inhibit their reactions temporarily. As Mead puts it, "Delayed reaction is necessary to intelligent[7] conduct. The organization, implicit testing, and final selection . . . would be impossible if his overt responses or reactions could not in such situations be delayed" (1934/1962:99). There are three components here. First, humans, because of their ability to delay reactions, are able to organize in their own minds the array of possible responses to a situation. Humans possess in their minds the alternative ways of completing a social act in which they are involved. Second, people are able to test out mentally, again through an internal conversation with themselves, the various courses of action. In contrast, lower animals lack this capacity and therefore must try out reactions in the real world in trial-and-error fashion. The ability to try out responses mentally, as we saw in the case of the poison mushroom, is much more effective than the trial-and-error method. There is no social cost involved in mentally trying out a poorly adapted response. However, when a lower animal actually uses such a response in the real world (for example, when a dog approaches a poisonous snake), the results can be costly, even disastrous. Finally, humans are able to pick out one stimulus among a set of stimuli rather than simply reacting to the first or strongest stimulus. In addition, humans can select among a range of alternative actions, whereas lower animals simply act. As Mead says:

> It is the entrance of the alternative possibilities of future response into the determination of present conduct in any given environmental situation, and their

---

[6]Although, as we will see later, Mead uses this term inconsistently; sometimes it includes mental processes.

[7]Here is one place where Mead is using *intelligence* in a different sense from that employed in the previous discussion.

> operation, through the mechanism of the central nervous system, as part of the factors or conditions determining present behavior, which *decisively* contrasts intelligent conduct or behavior with reflex, instinctive, and habitual conduct or behavior-delayed reaction with immediate reaction.
>
> (Mead, 1934/1962:98; italics added)

The ability to choose among a range of actions means that the choices of humans are likely to be better adapted to the situation than are the immediate and mindless reactions of lower animals. As Mead contends, "Intelligence is largely a matter of selectivity" (1934/1962:99).

Consciousness

Mead also discusses *consciousness,* which he sees as having two distinguishable meanings (1938/1972:75). The first is that to which the actor alone has access, that which is entirely subjective. Mead is less interested in this sense of consciousness than the second, which basically involves reflective intelligence. Thus, Mead is less interested in the way in which we experience immediate pain or pleasure than he is in the way in which we think about the social world.

Consciousness is to be explained or accounted for within the social process. That is, in contrast to most analysts, Mead believes that consciousness is *not* lodged in the brain: "Consciousness is functional not substantive; and in either of the main senses of the term it must be located in the objective world rather than in the brain—it belongs to, or is a characteristic of, the environment in which we find ourselves. What is located, what does take place, in the brain, however, is the physiological process whereby we lose and regain consciousness" (1934/1962:112).

In a similar manner, Mead (1934/1962:332) refuses to position *mental images* in the brain, but sees them as social phenomena: "What we term 'mental images' . . . can exist in their relation to the organism without being lodged in a substantial consciousness. The mental image is a memory image. Such images which, as symbols, play so large a part in thinking, belong to the environment."

Meaning is yet another related concept that Mead addresses behavioristically. Characteristically, Mead rejects the idea that meaning lies in consciousness: "Awareness or consciousness is not necessary to the presence of meaning in the process of social experience" (1934/1962:77). Similarly, Mead rejects the idea that meaning is a "psychical" phenomenon or an "idea." Rather, *meaning* lies squarely within the social act: "Meaning arises and lies within the field of the relation between the gesture of a given human organism and the subsequent behavior of this organism as indicated to another human organism by that gesture. If that gesture does so indicate to another organism the subsequent (or resultant) behavior of the given organism, then it has meaning" (Mead, 1934/1962:75–76). It is the adjustive response of the second organism that gives meaning to the gesture of the first organism. The meaning of a gesture can be seen as the "ability to predict the behavior that is likely to occur next" (Baldwin, 1986:72).

While meaning is to be found in behavior, it becomes conscious when meaning is associated with symbols. However, although meaning can become conscious among humans, it is present in the social act *prior* to the emergence of consciousness and the awareness of meaning. Thus, in these terms, lower animals (and humans) can engage in meaningful behavior even though they are not aware of the meaning.

Mind

Like consciousness, the *mind,* which is defined by Mead as a process and not a thing, as an inner conversation with one's self, is not found within the individual; it is not intracranial but is a social phenomenon. It arises and develops within the social process and is an integral part of that process. The social process precedes the mind; it is not, as many believe, a product of the mind. Thus, the mind, too, is defined functionally rather than substantively. Given these similarities to ideas like consciousness, is there anything distinctive about the mind? We have already seen that humans have the peculiar capacity to call out in themselves the response they are seeking to elicit from others. A distinctive characteristic of the mind is the ability of the individual "to call out in himself not simply a single response of the other but the response, so to speak, of the community as a whole. That is what gives to an individual what we term 'mind.' To do anything now means a certain organized response; and if one has in himself that response, he has what we term 'mind'" (Mead, 1934/1962:267). Thus, the mind can be distinguished from other like-sounding concepts in Mead's work by its ability to respond to the overall community and put forth an organized response.

Mead also looks at the mind in another, pragmatic way. That is, the mind involves thought processes oriented toward problem solving. The real world is rife with problems, and it is the function of the mind to try to solve those problems and permit people to operate more effectively in the world.

Self

Much of Mead's thinking in general, and especially on the mind, involves his ideas on the critically important concept of the *self,* basically the ability to take oneself as an object; the self is the peculiar ability to be both subject and object. As is true of all Mead's major concepts, the self presupposes a social process: communication among humans. Lower animals do not have selves, nor do human infants at birth. The self arises with development and through social activity and social relationships. To Mead, it is impossible to imagine a self arising in the absence of social experiences. However, after a self has developed, it is possible for it to continue to exist without social contact. Thus, Robinson Crusoe developed a self while he was in civilization, and he continued to have it when he was living alone on what he thought for a while was a deserted island. In other words, he continued to have the ability to take himself as an object. After a self is developed, people usually, but not always, manifest it. For example, the self is not involved in habitual actions or in immediate physiological experiences of pleasure or pain.

The self is dialectically related to the mind (we will have more to say shortly about the dialectic in Mead's thought). That is, on the one hand, Mead argues that the body is not a self and becomes a self only when a mind has developed. On the other hand, the self, and its reflexiveness, is essential to the development of the mind. Of course, it is impossible to separate mind and self because the self is a mental process. However, even though we may think of it as a mental process, the self is a social process. In his discussion of the self, as we have seen in regard to all other mental phenomena, Mead resists the idea of lodging it in consciousness and instead embeds it in social experience and social processes. In this way, Mead seeks to give a behavioristic sense of the self: "But it is where one does respond to that which he addresses to another and where that response of his own becomes a part of his conduct, where he not only hears himself but responds to himself, talks and replies to himself as truly as the other person replies to him, that we have *behavior* in which the individuals become objects to themselves" (1934/1962:139; italics added). The self, then, is simply another aspect of the overall social process of which the individual is a part.

The general mechanism for the development of the self is reflexivity, or the ability to put ourselves unconsciously into others' places and to act as they act. As a result, people are able to examine themselves as others would examine them. As Mead says:

> It is by means of reflexiveness—the turning-back of the experience of the individual upon himself—that the whole social process is thus brought into the experience of the individuals involved in it; it is by such means, which enable the individual to take the attitude of the other toward himself, that the individual is able consciously to adjust himself to that process, and to modify the resultant process in any given social act in terms of his adjustment to it.
>
> (Mead, 1934/1962:134)

The self also allows people to take part in their conversations with others. That is, one is aware of what one is saying and as a result is able to monitor what is being said and to determine what is going to be said next.

In order to have selves, individuals must be able to get "outside themselves" so that they can evaluate themselves, so they can become objects to themselves. To do this, people basically put themselves in the same experiential field as they put everyone else (Schwalbe, 2005). Everyone is an important part of that experiential situation, and people must take themselves into account if they are to be able to act rationally in a given situation. Having done this, they seek to examine themselves impersonally, objectively, and without emotion.

However, people cannot experience themselves directly. They can do so only indirectly by putting themselves in the position of others and viewing themselves from that standpoint. The standpoint from which one views one's self can be that of a particular individual or that of the social group as a whole. As Mead puts it, most generally, "It is only by taking the roles of others that we have been able to come back to ourselves" (1959:184–185).

Child Development

Mead is very interested in the genesis of the self. He sees the conversation of gestures as the background for the self, but it does not involve a self, because in such a conversation the people are not taking themselves as objects. Mead traces the genesis of the self through two stages in childhood development.

Play Stage

The first stage is the *play stage;* it is during this stage that children learn to take the attitude of particular others to themselves. Although lower animals also play, only human beings "play at being someone else" (Aboulafia, 1986:9). Mead gives the example of a child playing (American) "Indian": "This means that the child has a certain set of stimuli which call out in itself the responses they would call out in others, and which answer to an Indian" (Mead, 1934/1962:150). As a result of such play, the child learns to become both subject and object and begins to become able to build a self. However, it is a limited self because the child can take only the role of distinct and separate others. Children may play at being "mommy" and "daddy" and in the process develop the ability to evaluate themselves as their parents, and other specific individuals, do. However, they lack a more general and organized sense of themselves.

Game Stage

It is the next stage, the *game stage,* that is required if the person is to develop a self in the full sense of the term. Whereas in the play stage the child takes the role of discrete others, in the game stage the child must take the role of everyone else involved in the game. Furthermore, these different roles must have a definite relationship to one another. In illustrating the game stage, Mead gives his famous example of a baseball (or, as he calls it, "ball nine") game:

> But in a game where a number of individuals are involved, then the child taking one role must be ready to take the role of everyone else. If he gets in a ball nine he must have the responses of each position involved in his own position. He must know what everyone else is going to do in order to carry out his own play. He has to take all of these roles. They do not all have to be present in consciousness at the same time, but at some moments he has to have three or four individuals present in his own attitude, such as the one who is going to throw the ball, the one who is going to catch it, and so on. These responses must be, in some degree, present in his own make-up. In the game, then, there is a set of responses of such others so organized that the attitude of one calls out the appropriate attitudes of the other.
>
> (Mead, 1934/1962:151)

In the play stage, children are not organized wholes because they play at a series of discrete roles. As a result, in Mead's view they lack definite personalities. However, in the game stage,[8] such organization begins and a definite personality starts to emerge. Children begin to become able to function in organized groups and, most important, to determine what they will do within a specific group.

Generalized Other

The game stage yields one of Mead's (1959:87) best-known concepts, the *generalized other.* The generalized other is the attitude of the entire community or, in the example of the baseball game, the attitude of the entire team. The ability to take the role of the generalized other is essential to the self: "Only in so far as he takes the attitudes of the organized social group to which he belongs toward the organized, co-operative social

---

[8]Although Mead uses the term "games," it is clear, as Aboulafia (1986:198) points out, that he means any system of organized responses (for example, the family).

activity or set of such activities in which that group is engaged, does he develop a complete self" (Mead, 1934/1962:155). It is also crucial that people be able to evaluate themselves from the point of view of the generalized other and not merely from the viewpoint of discrete others. Taking the role of the generalized other, rather than that of discrete others, allows for the possibility of abstract thinking and objectivity (Mead, 1959:190). Here is the way Mead describes the full development of the self:

> So the self reaches its full development by organizing these individual attitudes of others into the organized social or group attitudes, and by thus becoming an individual reflection of the general systematic pattern of social or group behavior in which it and others are involved—a pattern which enters as a whole into the individual's experience in terms of these organized group attitudes which, through the mechanism of the central nervous system, he takes toward himself, just as he takes the individual attitudes of others.
>
> (Mead, 1934/1962:158)

In other words, to have a self, one must be a member of a community and be directed by the attitudes common to the community. Whereas play requires only pieces of selves, the game requires a coherent self.

Not only is taking the role of the generalized other essential to the self, but it is also crucial for the development of organized group activities. A group requires that individuals direct their activities in accord with the attitudes of the generalized other. The generalized other also represents Mead's familiar propensity to give priority to the social, because it is through the generalized other that the group influences the behavior of individuals.

Mead also looks at the self from a pragmatic point of view. At the individual level, the self allows the individual to be a more efficient member of the larger society. Because of the self, people are more likely to do what is expected of them in a given situation. Because people often try to live up to group expectations, they are more likely to avoid the inefficiencies that come from failing to do what the group expects. Furthermore, the self allows for greater coordination in society as a whole. Because individuals can be counted on to do what is expected of them, the group can operate more effectively.

The preceding, as well as the overall discussion of the self, might lead us to believe that Mead's actors are little more than conformists and that there is little individuality because everyone is busy conforming to the expectations of the generalized other. But Mead is clear that each self is different from all others. Selves share a common structure, but each self receives unique biographical articulation. In addition, it is clear that there is not simply one grand generalized other but that there are many generalized others in society because there are many groups in society. People, therefore, have multiple generalized others and, as a result, multiple selves. Each person's unique set of selves makes him or her different from everyone else. Furthermore, people need not accept the community as it is; they can reform things and seek to make them better. We are able to change the community because of our capacity to think. But Mead is forced to put this issue of individual creativity in familiar, behavioristic terms: "The only way in which we can react against the disapproval of the entire community is by setting up a higher sort of community which in a certain sense out-votes the one we find . . . he may stand out by himself over against it. But to do that he has to comprehend the voices of the past and of the future. That is the only way the self can get a voice which is more than the voice of the community" (1934/1962:167–168). In other words, to stand up to the generalized other, the individual must construct a still larger generalized other, composed not only from the present but also from the past and the future, and then respond to it.

Mead identifies two aspects, or phases, of the self, which he labels the "I" and the "me" (for a critique of this distinction, see Athens, 1995). As Mead puts it, "The self is essentially a social process going on with these two distinguishable phases" (1934/1962:178). It is important to bear in mind that the "I" and "me" are processes within the larger process of the self; they are not "things."

"I" and "Me"

The "I" is the immediate response of an individual to others. It is the incalculable, unpredictable, and creative aspect of the self. People do not know in advance what the action of the "I" will be: "But what that response will be he does not know and nobody else knows. Perhaps he will make a brilliant play or an error. The response to that situation as it appears in his immediate experience is uncertain" (Mead, 1934/1962:175). We are never totally aware of the "I," and through it we surprise ourselves with our actions. We know the "I" only after the act has been carried out. Thus, we know the "I" only in our memories. Mead lays great stress on the "I" for four reasons. First, it is a key source of novelty in the social process. Second, Mead believes that it is in the "I" that our most important values are located. Third, the "I" constitutes something that we all seek—the realization of the self. It is the "I" that permits us to develop a "definite personality." Finally, Mead sees an evolutionary process in history in which people in primitive societies are dominated more by "me," whereas in modern societies there is a greater component of "I."

The "I" gives Mead's theoretical system some much-needed dynamism and creativity. Without it, Mead's actors would be totally dominated by external and internal controls. With it, Mead is able to deal with the changes brought about not only by the great figures in history (for example, Einstein) but also by individuals on a day-to-day basis. It is the "I" that makes these changes possible. Because every personality is a mix of "I" and "me," the great historical figures are seen as having a larger proportion of "I" than most others have. But in day-to-day situations, anyone's "I" may assert itself and lead to change in the social situation. Uniqueness is also brought into Mead's system through the biographical articulation of each individual's "I" and "me." That is, the specific exigencies of each person's life give him or her a unique mix of "I" and "me."

The "I" reacts against the "me," which is the "organized set of attitudes of others which one himself assumes" (Mead, 1934/1962:175). In other words, the "me" is the adoption of the generalized other. In contrast to the "I," people are conscious of the "me"; the "me" involves conscious responsibility. As Mead says, "The 'me' is a conventional, habitual individual" (1934/1962:197). Conformists are dominated by "me," although everyone—whatever his or her degree of conformity—has, and must have, substantial "me." It is through the "me" that society dominates the individual. Indeed, Mead defines the idea of *social control* as the dominance of the expression of the "me" over the expression of the "I." Later in *Mind, Self and Society,* Mead elaborates on his ideas on social control:

> Social control, as operating in terms of self-criticism, exerts itself so intimately and extensively over individual behavior or conduct, serving to integrate the individual and his actions with reference to the organized social process of experience and behavior in which he is implicated. . . . Social control over individual behavior or conduct operates by virtue of the social origin and basis of such [self-] criticism. That is to say, self-criticism is essentially social criticism, and behavior controlled socially. Hence social control, so far from tending to crush out the human individual or to obliterate his self-conscious individuality, is, on the contrary, actually constitutive of and inextricably associated with that individuality.
>
> (Mead, 1934/1962:255)

Mead also looks at the "I" and "me" in pragmatic terms. The "me" allows the individual to live comfortably in the social world, whereas the "I" makes the change of society possible. Society gets enough conformity to allow it to function, and it gets a steady infusion of new developments to prevent it from stagnating. The "I" and the "me" are thus part of the whole social process and allow both individuals and society to function more effectively.

Society

At the most general level, Mead uses the term *society* to mean the ongoing social process that precedes both the mind and the self. Given its importance in shaping the mind and self, society is clearly of central importance to Mead. At another level, society to Mead represents the organized set of responses that are taken over by the individual in the form of the "me." Thus, in this sense, individuals carry society around with them, giving them the ability, through self-criticism, to control themselves. Mead also, as we will see, deals with the evolution of society. But Mead has relatively little to say explicitly about society, in spite of its centrality in his theoretical system (Athens, 2005). His most important contributions lie in his thoughts on mind and self. Even John Baldwin, who sees a much more societal (macro) component in Mead's thinking, is forced to admit: "The macro components of Mead's theoretical system are not as well developed as the micro" (1986:123).

At a more specific societal level, Mead does have a number of things to say about social *institutions.* Mead broadly defines an *institution* as the "common response in the community" or "the life habits of the community" (1934/1962:261, 264; see also Mead, 1936:376). More specifically, he says that "the whole community acts toward the individual under certain circumstances in an identical way . . . there is an identical response on the part of the whole community under these conditions. We call that the formation of the institution" (Mead, 1934/1962:167). We carry this organized set of attitudes around with us, and it serves to control our actions, largely through the "me."

Education is the process by which the common habits of the community (the institution) are "internalized" in the actor. This is an essential process because, in Mead's view, people neither have selves nor are genuine members of the community until they can respond to themselves as the larger community does. To do so, people must have internalized the common attitudes of the community.

But again Mead is careful to point out that institutions need not destroy individuality or stifle creativity. Mead recognizes that there are "oppressive, stereotyped, and ultra-conservative social institutions—like the church—which by their more or less rigid and inflexible unprogressiveness crush or blot out individuality" (1934/1962:262). However, he is quick to add: "There is no necessary or inevitable reason why social institutions should be oppressive or rigidly conservative, or why they should not rather be, as many are, flexible and progressive, fostering individuality rather than discouraging it" (Mead, 1934/1962:262). To Mead, institutions should define what people ought to do only in a very broad and general sense and should allow plenty of room for individuality and creativity. Mead here demonstrates a very modern conception of social institutions as both constraining individuals *and* enabling them to be creative individuals (see Giddens, 1984). Mead was distinct from the other classical theorists in emphasizing the enabling character of society—arguably disregarding society's constraining power (Athens, 2002).

What Mead lacks in his analysis of society in general, and institutions in particular,[9] is a true macro sense of them in the way that theorists such as Comte, Spencer, Marx, Weber, and Durkheim dealt with this level of analysis. This is true in spite of the fact that Mead does have a notion of *emergence* in the sense that the whole is seen as more than the sum of its parts. More specifically, "Emergence involves a reorganization, but the reorganization brings in something that was not there before. The first time oxygen and hydrogen come together, water appears. Now water is a combination of hydrogen and oxygen, but water was not there before in the separate elements" (Mead, 1934/1962:198). However, Mead is much more prone to apply the idea of emergence to consciousness than to apply it to the larger society. That is, mind and self are seen as emergent from the social process. Moreover, Mead is inclined to use the term *emergence* merely to mean the coming into existence of something new or novel (D. Miller, 1973:41).

Summary

George Herbert Mead developed his sociological theory out of the confluence of a number of intellectual inputs, the most important of which was behaviorism. Basically, Mead accepted the behavioristic approach and its focus on conduct but sought to extend it to a concern for mental processes. He was also a creator of, and influenced by, pragmatism. Pragmatism gave Mead a powerful faith in science and, more generally, in

[9]There are at least two places where Mead offers a more macro sense of society. At one point he defines *social institutions* as "organized forms of group or social activity" (Mead, 1934/1962:261). Earlier, in an argument reminiscent of Comte, he offers a view of the family as the fundamental unit within society and as the base of such larger units as the clan and state.

conduct motivated by reflective intelligence. It, like behaviorism, led Mead to focus on what people actually "do" in the social world. He was also strongly influenced by Hegel, and this is manifest in a number of places (for example, his focus on evolution), especially in his dialectical approach to the social world.

Substantively, Mead's theory accorded primacy and priority to the social world. That is, it is out of the social world that consciousness, the mind, the self, and so on emerge. The most basic unit in his social theory is the act, which includes four dialectically related stages—impulse, perception, manipulation, and consummation. Even in his thoughts on the act, Mead does not emphasize external stimuli (as a behaviorist would); rather, he holds that a stimulus is an opportunity, not a compulsion, to act. A *social* act involves two or more persons, and the basic mechanism of the social act is the gesture. Whereas lower animals and humans are capable of having a conversation of gestures, only humans can communicate the conscious meaning of their gestures.

Humans are peculiarly able to create vocal gestures, and this capacity leads to the distinctive human ability to develop and use significant symbols. Significant symbols lead to the development of language and the distinctive capacity of humans to communicate, in the full sense of the term, with one another. Significant symbols also make possible thinking as well as symbolic interaction.

Mead looks at an array of mental processes as part of the larger social process; such mental processes include reflective intelligence, consciousness, mental images, meaning, and, most generally, the mind. Humans have the distinctive capacity to carry on an inner conversation with themselves. All the mental processes, in Mead's view, are lodged not in the brain but rather in the social process.

The self is the ability to take oneself as an object. Again, the self arises within the social process. The general mechanism of the self is the ability of people to put themselves in the place of others and to act as others act and to see themselves as others see them. Mead traces the genesis of the self through the play and game stages of childhood. Especially important in the latter stage is the emergence of the generalized other. The ability to see oneself from the viewpoint of the community is essential to the emergence of the self as well as of organized group activities. The self also has two phases—the "I," which is the unpredictable and creative aspect of the self, and the "me," which is the organized set of attitudes of others assumed by the actor. Social control is manifest through the "me," whereas the "I" is the source of innovation in society.

Mead has relatively little to say about society, which he sees most generally as the ongoing social processes that precede mind and self. Mead largely lacks a macro sense of society. Institutions are defined as little more than collective habits. Mead does have a strong sense of evolution, especially of reflective intelligence as well as of science, the latter being merely a concrete and formalized manifestation of that intelligence. Finally, Mead manifests dialectical thinking throughout his theoretical system.

Mead's theory is not as broad as those of most of the other theorists examined in this book. Nevertheless, it continues to be influential in contemporary symbolic interactionism, social psychology, and sociology more generally. Work continues to emerge in sociology (as well as in philosophy), building upon Mead's theories (for example, Collins, 1989b). Mead's work still attracts theorists both in the United States and in the rest of the world (for example, Habermas, 1984). This is the case in spite of a number of notable weaknesses in his theory. The greatest weakness, one that has been mentioned several times in this chapter, is that he has little to offer to our understanding of the macro-societal level. Other weaknesses include some vague and fuzzy concepts; an inconsistent definition of concepts (especially intelligence); the difficulty in clearly differentiating one of his concepts from the others; his lack of concern, in spite of his focus on the micro level, for emotional and unconscious aspects of human conduct; and the fact that about the only source of social change in his theoretical system appears to be the individual, especially through the "I." In spite of these and other weaknesses, Mead offers a powerful and important theory that is likely to be influential in sociology for many years to come.

C H A P T E R 16

Alfred Schutz

Chapter Outline

Of all the theorists discussed in this book, Alfred Schutz is the most controversial inclusion. Schutz is not often included in the pantheon of classical sociological theorists because his work only recently has come to be widely influential in sociology, especially in the contemporary theories of phenomenological sociology and ethnomethodology. However, because of its recently expanding influence, as well as the fact that it offers a profound, wide-ranging, and distinctive perspective (Rogers, 2000), Schutzian theory warrants full-chapter treatment in this text on classical sociological theory. It is thought of as *classical* theory because of its nature and scope, as well as the time of its development. Schutz's most important theoretical statement, *The Phenomenology of the Social World* (1932/1967), was published in the 1930s—the same decade that witnessed the publication of other now-classical theoretical works such as Mead's *Mind, Self and Society* and Parsons's *The Structure of Social Action.*

Interpretations of Schutz's Work

We can divide traditional interpretations of Schutz's work into several camps. First, ethnomethodologists and phenomenologists saw in Schutz the source of their interest in the way actors create or construct social reality. Among the ethnomethodologists, for example, Hugh Mehan and Houston Wood argued that the focus of their approach was on the way actors "create situations and rules, and so at once create themselves and their social realities" (1975:115). They went on to say that "ethnomethodologists adopted this research program from Schutz" (Mehan and Wood, 1975:115). Monica Morris, in her book on creative sociology, came to a similar conclusion: "For Schutz, the subject matter of sociology is the manner in which human beings constitute, or create, the world of everyday life" (1977:15). These commentators, as well as many others, generally have seen Schutz as focusing on the way actors create social reality, and they have lauded him for this micro orientation.

Other commentators have taken a similar view of the substance of his work but have come to very different conclusions about it. A good example is Robert Bierstedt, who criticized Schutz for his focus on the way actors construct social reality and his corresponding lack of concern with the reality of the larger structures of society:

> The phenomenological reduction . . . has consequences of a . . . rather serious kind for sociology. . . . Society itself, as an objective phenomenon, tends to disappear in the realm of the intersubjective. That is, society itself . . . comes to be a creation of the mind in intersubjectivity and something that is wholly exhausted in the common-place affairs of daily living.
>
> (Bierstedt, 1963:91)

Thus, Bierstedt criticized Schutz for precisely the same thing for which Mehan and Wood, Morris, and others praised him.

Although these two camps came to very different conclusions about Schutz's work, they did at least agree on its micro focus. A third school of thought, however, views Schutz in an almost diametrically opposite way, as a cultural determinist. For example, Robert Gorman (1975a, 1975b, 1977) suggested that, contrary to the interpretations of the ethnomethodological and sociological establishments, Schutz emphasized the constraints imposed on the actor by society. Actors do not freely choose beliefs or courses of action, nor do they freely construct a sense of social reality. Rather, as members of society, they are free only to obey.

> Socially determined action patterns are adhered to by free actors. Each actor bases his action on his stock of knowledge at hand, and this knowledge consists of these socially determined action patterns. Each of us chooses, for himself, to act as these patterns prescribe, even though they have been imposed from outside.
>
> (Gorman, 1975a:11)

Gorman concluded that for Schutz "social behavior is apparently caused by factors independent of the subject [actor]" (1977:71).

As we review Schutz's theory, we will see that the most legitimate perspective involves a combination of the first and third views of his work. That is, Schutz's actors do create social reality, but that creation takes place in, and is constrained by, socially determined action patterns (Thomason, 1982). We will also see that the second position, articulated by Bierstedt, is erroneous and ignores the constraining reality of culture and society in Schutz's theory.

The Ideas of Edmund Husserl

Before turning to the theories of Alfred Schutz, we need to deal with the ideas of his most important intellectual predecessor, the philosopher Edmund Husserl. Although other thinkers (for example, Henri Bergson and Max Weber) had a strong impact on Schutz, the influence of Husserl stands above that of all the others.

Husserl's highly complicated philosophy is not easily translated into sociological concepts; indeed, a good portion of it is not directly relevant to sociology (Srubar, 1984). We discuss here a few of his ideas that proved useful to Alfred Schutz as well as to other phenomenological sociologists.

In general, Husserl believed that people view the world as a highly ordered place; actors are always engaged in the active and highly complex process of ordering the world. However, people are unaware that they are patterning the world; hence, they do not question the process by which this is accomplished. Actors see the social world as naturally ordered, not structured by them. Unlike people in the everyday world, phenomenologists are acutely aware that patterning is taking place, and that ordering process becomes for them an important subject of phenomenological investigation (Freeman, 1980).

Husserl's scientific phenomenology involves a commitment to penetrate the various layers constructed by actors in the social world in order to get to the essential structure of consciousness, the transcendental ego. Schutz defines the *transcendental ego* as "the universe of our conscious life, the stream of thought in its integrity, with all its activities and with all its cogitations and experiences" (1973:105).

The idea of the transcendental ego reflects Husserl's interest in the basic and invariant properties of human consciousness. As Schutz says, "According to Husserl, phenomenology aims to be an eidetical science, dealing not with existence but with essence" (1973:113), especially the essence of consciousness—the transcendental ego.

Although he is often misinterpreted on this point, Husserl did not have a mentalistic, metaphysical conception of consciousness. For him, consciousness is not a thing or a place, but a process. Consciousness is found not in the head of the actor but in the relationship between the actor and objects in the world. Husserl expressed this in the idea of *intentionality.* For him, consciousness is always consciousness of something, some object. Consciousness is found in this relationship; consciousness is not interior to the actor. Heap and Roth argue simply that "consciousness *is* intentional" (1973:355). Furthermore, meaning inheres not in objects but in the relationship of actors to objects. This conception of consciousness as a process that gives meaning to objects is at the heart of Husserl's phenomenology and is the starting point for Schutzian theory.

Another key to Husserl's work was his orientation to the *scientific* study of the basic structures of consciousness. Husserl sought to develop "philosophy as a rigorous science" (Kockelmans, 1967b:26). However, to Husserl, science did not mean empiricism and statistical analysis of empirical data. In fact, he feared that such a science would reject consciousness as an object of scientific scrutiny and that consciousness would be found either to be too metaphysical or to have been turned into something physical.

What Husserl did mean by science was a philosophy that was methodologically rigorous, systematic, and critical. In using science in this way, Husserl believed that phenomenologists ultimately could arrive at absolutely valid knowledge of the basic structures of actors' "lived experience" (especially that which is conscious). This orientation to science has had two effects on later phenomenologists, including Alfred Schutz. First, phenomenologists continue to eschew the tools of modern social-science research (although they do research; see Psathas, 1989)—standardized methods, high-powered statistics, and computerized results. They prefer, as did Husserl, attention to, and description of, all social phenomena—including social situations, events, activities, interaction, and social objects—as *experienced* by human beings. Second, phenomenologists continue to oppose vague, "soft" intuitionism. In other words, they are opposed to "subjectivism" that is not concerned with discovering the basic structures of phenomena as experienced by people. Philosophizing about consciousness is a rigorous and systematic enterprise.

Husserl conceived of actors' natural standpoint, or their "natural attitude," as the major obstacle to the scientific discovery of phenomenological processes. Because of actors' natural attitude, conscious-ordering processes are hidden to them. These processes will remain hidden to phenomenologists unless they are able to overcome their own natural attitudes. Phenomenologists must be able to accomplish the very difficult task of "disconnecting," or "setting aside" ("bracketing"), the natural attitude so that they will be able to get at the most basic aspects of consciousness involved in the ordering of the world (Freeman, 1980). In Husserl's view, the natural attitude is a source of bias and distortion to the phenomenologist.

After the natural attitude is set aside, or "bracketed," the phenomenologist can begin to examine the invariant properties of consciousness that govern all people. Here is the way Schutz describes Husserl's orientation on this issue:

> The phenomenologist does not deny the existence of the outer world, but for his analytical purpose he makes up his mind to suspend belief in its existence—that is, to refrain intentionally and systematically from all judgments related directly or indirectly to the existence of the outer world. . . . Husserl called this procedure "putting the world in brackets" or "performing the phenomenological reduction" . . . [to] go beyond the natural attitude of man living within the world he accepts, be it reality or mere appearance . . . to disclose the pure field of consciousness.
>
> (Schutz, 1973:104)

The phenomenologist also must set aside the incidental experiences of life that tend to dominate consciousness. Husserl's ultimate objective was to get at the pure form of consciousness, stripped of all empirical content.

Ilja Srubar (1984) argues that Husserl not only did a rigorous philosophy of consciousness but also laid the groundwork for a phenomenological sociology. That is, Husserl found it necessary to extend his work to the world of interpersonal relations, the "life-world." Thus Husserl's work helps point to the position that "phenomenology must become a science of the life world" (Srubar, 1984:70). However, Schutz concluded that "the least satisfactory part of [Husserl's] analysis is that dealing with sociality and social groups" (1975:38). As a result, whereas Husserl's work largely turned inward to the transcendental ego, Schutz's work turned outward to intersubjectivity, the social world, and the life-world. Here is the way Wagner explained the task confronting Schutz:

> The phenomenological method, by definition, serves the exploration of the solitary consciousness. It can procure access to the social realm of human experience only if it offers a solution for what Husserl called the problem of intersubjectivity. A viable theory of intersubjectivity, in turn, would be the strongest, albeit indirect, support for the sociology of understanding that phenomenology could supply. . . . Schutz placed the

ALFRED SCHUTZ

A Biographical Sketch

Alfred Schutz was not widely known during his lifetime, and only in recent years has his work attracted the attention of large numbers of sociologists. Although his obscurity was in part a result of his intellectual orientation—his then highly unusual interest in phenomenology—a more important cause was his very unusual career as a sociologist.

Born in Vienna, Austria, in 1899, Schutz received his academic training at the University of Vienna (Wagner, 1983). Soon after completing his law examination, he embarked on a lifelong career in banking. Although rewarding economically, banking did not satisfy his need for deeper meaning in his life. Schutz found that meaning in his work on phenomenological sociology. He was not an academician in the 1920s, but many of his friends were, and he participated in a number of informal lecture and discussion circles (Prendergast, 1986). Schutz was drawn to Weberian theory, especially Weber's work on action and the ideal type. Although impressed with Weber's work, Schutz sought to overcome its weaknesses by integrating ideas from the philosophers Edmund Husserl and Henri Bergson. According to Christopher Prendergast (1986), Schutz was motivated to provide the Austrian School of Economics with a scientific, subjective theory of action. These influences led to the publication by Schutz in 1932 of what was to become a very important book in sociology, *The Phenomenology of the Social World.* It was not translated into English until 1967, so a wide appreciation of Schutz's work in the United States was delayed thirty-five years.

As World War II approached, Schutz emigrated, with an intervening period in Paris, to the United States, where for many years he divided his time between serving as legal counsel to a number of banks and writing about and teaching phenomenological sociology. Simultaneously with his work in banking, Schutz began teaching courses in 1943 at the New School for Social Research in New York

> whole problem on the level of mundanity, that of everyday life. Here, he was confident, a phenomenological-psychological bridge between ego and alter could be found.
>
> (Wagner, 1983:43)

We will have much more to say about intersubjectivity and the life-world later, but before we do, we need to discuss Schutz's ideas on science and typifications.

Science and the Social World

As was true of Husserl, Schutz sees phenomenology as a rigorous science. He explicitly counters many of the critics of phenomenology by arguing that it is *not* based on "a kind of uncontrollable intuition or metaphysical revelation" (Schutz, 1973:101). Also in

City (Prendergast, 2005). As Richard Grathoff points out, the result was that "the social theorist for whom scientific thought and everyday life defined two rather distinct and separate realms of experience upheld a similar division in his personal life" (1978:112). Not until 1956 did Schutz give up his dual career and concentrate entirely on teaching and writing phenomenological sociology. Because of his interest in phenomenology, his dual career, and his teaching at the then avant-garde New School, Schutz remained on the periphery of sociology during his lifetime. Nevertheless, Schutz's work and his influence on students (for example, Peter Berger, Thomas Luckmann, Harold Garfinkel) moved him to the center of sociological theory.

Another factor in Schutz's marginal position in sociological theory was that his theory seemed highly abstract and irrelevant to the mundane social world. Although Schutz did separate theory from reality, he did not feel that his work was irrelevant to the world in which he lived. To put it in terms of his phenomenology, he saw a relationship between the everyday construction of reality and the pregiven historical and cultural world. To think otherwise is to think that the man who fled National Socialism (Nazism) regarded his academic work as irrelevant. The following quotation from one of his letters indicates that although Schutz was not optimistic, he was not prepared to accept the irrelevance of his theorizing and, more generally, the social construction of reality to the world as a whole:

> You are still optimist enough to believe that phenomenology may save itself among the ruins of this world—as the *philosophica aera perennis?* I do not believe so. More likely the African natives must prepare themselves for the ideas of national socialism. This shall not prevent us from dying the way we have lived; and we must try, therefore, to build . . . order into *our* world, which we must find lacking in—our *world.* The whole conflict is hidden in this shift of emphasis.
>
> (Schutz, cited in Grathoff, 1978:130)

In short, although the ability of people to affect the larger society is restricted by such phenomena as Nazism, they must continue to strive to build a social and cultural reality that is *not* beyond their reach and control.

Alfred Schutz died in 1959.

accord with Husserl, Schutz sees science as a theoretical and conceptual endeavor. The science of sociology, from Schutz's point of view, is not merely about describing the social world but involves the construction of rigorous conceptual and theoretical models of that world. As Schutz put it:

> We should certainly be surprised if we found a cartographer in mapping a town restricting himself to collecting information from natives. Nevertheless, social scientists frequently choose this strange method. They forget that their scientific work is done on a level of [theoretical] interpretation and understanding different from the naive attitudes of orientation and interpretation peculiar to people in daily life.
>
> (Schutz, 1976:67)

We gain considerable insight into Schutz's views on science when we understand that he considers science to be one of a multitude of "realities." To Schutz there are a number of different realities, including the worlds of dreams, art, religion, and the insane. The *paramount reality,* however, is the intersubjective world of everyday life (the life-world) because it is "the archetype of our experience of reality. All the other provinces of meaning may be considered as its modifications" (Schutz, 1973:xlii). As we will see, Schutz is focally concerned in his phenomenological sociology with the life-world, but our interest here is with the relationship of the life-world to another reality, that of science.

Life-World versus Science

There are several key differences between the life-world and the world of science, especially social science. First, the commonsense actor in the life-world is oriented toward dealing pragmatically with the mundane problems of everyday life. The social scientist, in contrast, is "aloof," a "disinterested observer" who is not pragmatically involved in the life-world of the actors being studied and their mundane problems. Second, the stock of knowledge of the commonsense actor is derived from the everyday world, whereas the scientist works with the stock of knowledge that belongs to the body of science. The social scientist exists in a world of problems stated, solutions suggested, methods worked out, and results obtained by other social scientists. Third, in their theorizing, as we have already discussed, social scientists must detach themselves from (must "bracket") their own biographical situations in the life-world and operate in that province of meaning labeled "the world of science." Commonsense actors, in contrast, are enmeshed in their biographical situations and operate in the life-world. These three differences not only help us define the world of science, but furthermore the social scientist who fulfills these criteria can be seen as having attained the scientific attitude needed to study the life-world. To have the proper scientific attitude, social scientists must be detached from (that is, have a nonpragmatic interest in) the life-world of those they are studying, enmeshed in the world of science, and must bracket their own biographical situation within the life-world.

Although the world of everyday life is populated by people who act sensibly or reasonably, scientists must create a model of that world which is composed of people who act rationally. In the everyday world people act *sensibly,* that is, their actions are in accord with socially approved rules for dealing with typical problems using typical means to achieve typical ends. People may also act *reasonably* in making "judicious" choices of means to ends, even if they merely follow traditional or habitual patterns. Although people may act sensibly or reasonably in the everyday world, it is only in the theoretical models created by social scientists that they act *rationally* in the full sense of the term, possessing "clear and distinct insight into the ends, the means, and the secondary results" (Schutz, 1973:28). (Here Schutz is using rationality in the same way that Weber used means-ends rationality.) Schutz makes it quite clear that rationality is a theoretical construct in his work: "Thus, the concept of rationality in the strict sense already defined does not refer to actions within the common-sense experience of everyday life in the social world; it is the expression for a *particular* type of construct of certain *specific* models of the social world made by the social scientist for certain methodological purposes" (1973:42). Action in everyday life is, at best, only partly rational. People who act sensibly or reasonably are rational only to some degree; they are far from fully rational. Thus, it is the task of the social scientist to construct rational theoretical models of the largely less-than-fully-rational everyday social world. This need to construct such models is premised on the belief that the social scientist can, indeed must, use rational models to analyze the less-than-rational behavior that is found in the life-world. (Again, this is similar to Weber and his development and use of ideal types.)

But the everyday social world is "meaningful" to the actors in it, and the social scientist is confronted with the problem of constructing fully rational systems of knowledge of the subjective-meaning structures of everyday life. Schutz found himself in the paradoxical position of attempting to develop a subjective sociology in the tradition of Max Weber while also meeting the demands of a rigorous conception of science. As Schutz put the question (the answer to which lies at the heart of his theoretical system): "How is it, then, possible to grasp by a system of objective knowledge subjective meaning structures?" (1973:35). Schutz's response is that "it is possible to construct a model of a sector of the social world consisting of typical human interaction and to analyze this typical interaction pattern as to the meaning it might have for the personal types of actors" (1973:36).

Constructing Ideal Types

The ability to accomplish this is based on the fact that both in the world of everyday life and in science we rely on constructs (ideal types) in order to interpret reality and grasp the part of reality that is relevant to us. The constructs that we use in the life-world are first-order constructs ("typifications"; see the next section), and the social scientist develops second-order constructs on the basis of these first-order constructs. It is this building of scientific constructs on everyday constructs that makes an objective, rational science of subjectivity possible. However, to meet the demands of science, the meaning of the world from the actor's perspective must be captured in abstraction from its unique and unpredictable expression within immediate reality. Schutz is not concerned with specific, unique actors but with typical actors and typical actions. All observers in the life-world develop constructs that allow them to understand what is going on there, but the ability to understand the life-world is increased in science because the (scientific) observer systematically creates much more abstract and standardized constructs with which to understand everyday life.

The key to Schutz's scientific approach is the construction of these second-order constructs or, in more conventional sociological terms, ideal types of social actors and social action. (Good examples are set forth in Schutz's essays on the "stranger" and the "homecomer.") Developing second-order constructs involves the theoretical replacement of human beings in the life-world with puppets (or as Schutz often calls them, "homunculi") created by the social scientist. The scientific model of the life-world is "not peopled with human beings in their full humanity, but with puppets, with *types;* they are constructed as though they could perform working actions and reactions"

(Schutz, 1973:255). Schutz thinks in terms of types of people as well as types of courses of action that actors might take.

Social scientists restrict the puppets' consciousness to what is necessary to perform the typical course of action relevant to the scientific problem under consideration. The puppets are not able to selectively perceive objects in their environment that may be relevant for the solution of problems at hand. They exist in situations created not by them but by the social scientist. The puppets do not choose, nor do they have knowledge outside of the typical knowledge granted them by the social scientist. The following is one of Schutz's most complete articulations of the nature of the social scientist's puppets:

> A merely specious consciousness is imputed to them by the scientist, which is constructed in such a way that its presupposed stock of knowledge at hand (including the ascribed set of invariant motives) would make actions originating from it subjectively understandable, provided that these actions were performed by real actors within the social world. But the puppet and his artificial consciousness is not subjected to the ontological conditions of human beings. The homunculus was not born, he does not grow old, and he will not die. He has no hopes and fears; he does not know anxiety as the chief motive of all of his deeds. He is not free in the sense that his acting could transgress the limits his creator, the social scientist, has predetermined. He cannot, therefore, have other conflicts of interest and motives than those the social scientist has imputed to him. He cannot err, if to err is not his typical destiny. He cannot choose, except among the alternatives the social scientist has put before him as standing to his choice . . . the homunculus, placed into a social relationship is involved therein in his totality. He is nothing else but the originator of his typical function because the artificial consciousness imputed to him contains merely those elements which are necessary to make such functions subjectively meaningful.
>
> (Schutz, 1973:41)

Thus, through the construction of ideal-typical actors and actions, the social scientist develops the tools needed to analyze the social world.

The construction of these puppets (or ideal types, more generally) is not an arbitrary process. To adequately reflect the subjective reality of the life-world and the demands of a rigorous science, ideal types must meet the following criteria:

1. *Postulate of relevance:* Following Weber, Schutz asserted that the topic being investigated in the social world should determine what is to be studied and how it is to be approached. In other words, what the social scientist does must be relevant to the topic being investigated in the life-world.
2. *Postulate of adequacy:* According to this principle, ideal types should be constructed by the social scientist so that the typifications of the actors' behavior in the life-world would make sense to the actors themselves as well as to their contemporaries.
3. *Postulate of logical consistency:* Types must be constructed with a high degree of consistency, clarity, and distinctness and must be compatible with the principles of formal logic. Fulfillment of this postulate "warrants the objective validity of the thought objects constructed by the social scientist" (Schutz, 1973:43).

4. *Postulate of compatibility:* The types constructed by the social scientist must be compatible with the extant body of scientific knowledge or must demonstrate why at least part of this body of knowledge is inadequate.
5. *Postulate of subjective interpretation:* The scientific types, as well as the more general model of the social world, must be based on, and be compatible with, the subjective meaning that action has for real actors in the world of everyday life.

In Schutz's view, the social scientist who adheres to these five postulates will create types and models that meet the need to be true both to the subjective meaning of actors in the life-world and to the demands of a rigorous science.

Typifications and Recipes

In the preceding section, we discussed Schutz's use of ideal types (second-order constructs)[1] to analyze the social world scientifically. However, as we have already mentioned, people also develop and use *typifications* (first-order constructs) in the social world. In any given situation in the world of everyday life an action is determined "by means of a type constituted in earlier experiences" (Schutz and Luckmann, 1973:229). Typifications ignore individual, unique features and focus on only generic and homogeneous characteristics.

While we routinely typify others, it is also possible for people to engage in self-typification: "Man typifies to a certain extent his own situation within the social world and the various relations he has to his fellow-men and cultural objects" (Schutz, 1976:233).

Typification takes many forms. When we label something (for example, a man, a dog), we are engaging in typification. More generally, anytime we are using language, we are typifying, that is, we are applying, linguistic types. Indeed, Schutz calls language "the typifying medium *par excellence*" (1973:75). Language can be thought of as a "treasure house" of types that we use to make sense of the social world. Although we routinely typify others, it is also possible for people to engage in self-typification. "Man typifies to a certain extent his own situation within the social world and the various relations he has to his fellow-men and cultural objects" (Schutz, 1976:233).

The linking of typifications to language makes it clear that typifications exist in the larger society and that people acquire and store typifications throughout the socialization process, indeed throughout their lives. The types that we use are largely socially derived and socially approved. They have stood the test of time and have come to be institutionalized as traditional and habitual tools for dealing with social life. Although the individual may create some typifications, most of them are preconstituted and derived from the larger society.

Schutz sometimes talks of *recipes,* which, like typifications, "serve as techniques for understanding or at least controlling aspects of . . . experience" (Natanson, 1973a:xxix). People use recipes to handle the myriad routine situations that they

---

[1]While people use first-order constructs on a day-to-day basis, social scientists use second-order constructs (Schutz's "stranger," for example) in their work.

encounter each day. Thus, when someone greets us with the recipe "How are you?" we respond with the recipe "Fine, and you?" Continuing the cooking analogy, Schutz argues that we function with "cook-book knowledge . . . recipes . . . to deal with the routine matters of daily life. . . . Most of our daily activities from rising to going to bed are of this kind. They are performed by following recipes reduced to cultural habits of unquestioned platitudes" (1976:73–74). Even when we encounter unusual or problematic situations, we first try to use our recipes. Only when it is abundantly clear that our recipes won't work do we abandon them and seek to create, to work out mentally, new ways of dealing with situations.

Schutz and Luckmann (1973:231) outline conditions under which situations become problematic and people must create new ways of dealing with them (new recipes or typifications). If there is no recipe available to handle a novel situation, or if a recipe does not allow one to handle the situation it is supposed to deal with, a new one must be created. In other words, when the stock of knowledge currently available is inadequate, the person must add to it by creating new recipes (or typifications).

Because of the recurrent existence of problematic situations, people cannot rely totally on recipes and typifications. They must be adaptive enough to deal with unforeseen circumstances. People need "practical intelligence" in order to deal with unpredictable situations by assessing alternative courses of action and devising new ways of handling situations.

The Life-World

The *life-world* (or *Lebenswelt*) is Schutz's term (derived from Husserl) for the world in which the taken-for-granted, the mundane, takes place. Schutz uses many terms to communicate his sense of this world, including "common-sense world," "world of everyday life," "everyday working world," "mundane reality," "the paramount reality of common-sense life," and so on (Natanson, 1973a:xxv). It is in this world that people operate in the "natural attitude"; that is, they take the world for granted and do not doubt its typifications and recipes until a problematic situation arises.

Schutz defines six basic characteristics of the life-world. First, there is a special tension of consciousness, which Schutz labels "wide-awakeness" (1973:213), in which the actor gives "full attention to life and its requirements." Second, the actor suspends doubt in the existence of this world. Third, it is in the life-world that people engage in working; that is, they engage in "action in the outer world, based upon a project and characterized by the intention to bring about the projected state of affairs by bodily movement" (Schutz, 1973:212). It is work that lies at the heart of the life-world:

> The core region of the life-world is the world of working. . . . Specifically, it is a sphere of activities directed upon objects, animals, and persons "within our actual reach." Typically, operations in it follow "tested recipes of action": it is "my world of routine activities." . . . Such working is planful physical acting upon tangible objects in order to shape and use them for tangible purposes.
>
> (Wagner, 1983:290)

Fourth, there is a specific form of experiencing one's self in which the working self is experienced as the total self. Fifth, the life-world is characterized by a specific form of sociality involving the "common intersubjective world of communication and social action" (Schutz, 1973:230). Obviously, the worlds of dreams and fantasies are not intersubjective worlds. Finally, in the life-world there is a specific time perspective that involves the intersection of the person's own flow of time and the flow of time in the larger society. By contrast, in dreams or fantasies the person's flow of time is usually out of touch with the flow of time in the larger society. That is, one may fantasize, for example, about life in the Middle Ages while one is living in the twentieth century.

Although Schutz writes often as if there is only one life-world, the fact is that each of us has his or her own life-world; however, there are many common elements in all of them. Thus, others belong to our life-world and we belong to the life-worlds of many others.

The life-world is an intersubjective world, but it is one that existed long before our birth; it was created by our predecessors. It (particularly typifications and recipes, but also social institutions and so on) is given to us to experience and to interpret. Thus, in experiencing the life-world, we are experiencing an obdurate world that constrains what we do (Ho, 2008). However, we are not simply dominated by the preexisting structure of the life-world:

> We have to dominate it and we have to change it in order to realize the purposes which we pursue within it among our fellow-men . . . these objects offer resistance to our acts which we have either to overcome or to which we have to yield . . . a pragmatic motive governs our natural attitude toward the world of everyday life. World, in this sense, is something that we have to modify by our actions or that modifies our actions.
>
> (Schutz, 1973:209)

Here we begin to get a sense of Schutz's thinking as dialectical, with actors and structures mutually affecting one another. Wagner takes such a dialectical position when he argues that Schutz's ideas on the life-world blend individual experience "not only with those of social interaction and therefore with the life-worlds of others but also with the socially pregiven interpretive schemes and prescriptions [typifications and recipes] for practical conduct" (1983:289).

This dialectic is even clearer in Schutz's thinking about the cultural world. On the one hand, it is clear that the cultural world was created by people in the past as well as in the present because it "originates in and has been instituted by human actions, our own and our fellow-men's, contemporaries and predecessors. All cultural objects—tools, symbols, language systems, works of art, social institutions, etc.—point back by their very origin and meaning to the activities of human subjects" (Schutz, 1973:329). On the other hand, this cultural world is external and coercive of actors: "I find myself in my everyday life within a world not of my own making . . . I was born into a pre-organized social world which will survive me, a world shared from the outset with fellow-men who are organized in groups" (Schutz, 1973:329).

In his analysis of the life-world, Schutz was concerned mainly with the shared social stock of knowledge that leads to more or less habitual action. We have already discussed *knowledge of typifications and recipes,* which is a major component of the stock of knowledge. Schutz views such knowledge as the most variable element in our stock of knowledge because, in a problematic situation, we are able to come up with innovative ways of handling the situation. Less likely to become problematic are the other two aspects of our stock of knowledge. *Knowledge of skills* (for example, how to walk) is the most basic form of knowledge in that it rarely becomes problematic (an exception in the case of walking would be temporary paralysis) and thus is accorded a high degree of certainty. *Useful knowledge* (for example, driving a car or playing the piano) is a definite solution to a situation that was once problematic. Useful knowledge is more problematic (for example, needing to think about one's driving in an emergency situation) than knowledge of skills, but it is not as likely to become problematic as recipes and typifications.

Intersubjectivity

Most broadly, Schutz's phenomenological sociology focuses on intersubjectivity not only because intersubjectivity was largely ignored by Husserl, but also because Schutz believed it to be taken for granted and unexplored by any other science. The study of intersubjectivity seeks to answer questions such as these: How do we know other motives, interests, and meanings? Other selves? How is a reciprocity of perspectives possible? How is mutual understanding and communication possible?

An intersubjective world is not a private world; it is common to all. It exists "because we live in it as men among other men, bound to them through common influence and work, understanding others and being understood by them" (Schutz, 1973:10). Intersubjectivity exists in the "vivid present" in which we speak and listen to each other. We share the same time and space with others. "This simultaneity is the essence of intersubjectivity, for it means that *I grasp the subjectivity of the alter ego at the same time as I live in my own stream of consciousness.* . . . And this grasp in simultaneity of the other as well as his reciprocal grasp of me makes possible *our* being in the world together" (Natanson, 1973a:xxxii–xxxiii; italics added).

The italicized portion of the last quotation gets to the essence of Schutz's thinking on intersubjectivity. Schutz was interested in interaction, but mainly as the vehicle whereby people grasp each other's consciousnesses, the manner in which they relate to one another intersubjectively.

Knowledge

Schutz also uses the idea of intersubjectivity in a broader sense to mean anything that is social. He argues that knowledge is intersubjective (or social) in three senses. First, there is a *reciprocity of perspectives* in which we assume that other people exist and objects are known or knowable by all. In spite of this reciprocity of perspectives, it is clear that the same object may mean somewhat different things to different people. This difficulty is overcome in the social world by the existence of two "idealizations." The idealization of the *interchangeability of standpoints* assumes that if we stood in the place of others, we would see things as they do. The idealization of the *congruency of the system of relevance* assumes that we can ignore our differences and that objects are defined sufficiently alike to allow us to proceed on a practical basis as if the definitions were identical. (Schutz calls these two idealizations the "general thesis of reciprocal perspectives.")

The second sense in which knowledge is intersubjective (or social) is in the *social origin of knowledge.* Individuals create a very small part of their own knowledge; most of it exists in shared stocks of knowledge and is acquired through social interaction with parents, teachers, and peers.

Third, knowledge is intersubjective in that there is a *social distribution of knowledge.* That is, the knowledge people possess varies according to their position in the social structure. In our commonsense thinking we take into account the fact that the stock of actual knowledge varies from individual to individual according to their social positions.

Thus, whereas Husserl identified the transcendental ego as his primary focus, Schutz turned phenomenology outward to a concern for the intersubjective, social world. (Although this is an important difference, we should not lose sight of the fact that both thinkers focused on subjectivity—Husserl within the realm of consciousness and Schutz in the social world.)

Private Components of Knowledge

Schutz also was aware that all the elements of the cultural realm can and often do vary from individual to individual[2] because personal experience differs. The stock of knowledge is "biographically articulated":

> That means that I "know" more or less adequately that it is the "result" of prior situations. And further, I "know" that this, my situation, is in that respect absolutely "unique." Indeed, the stock of knowledge, through which I determine the present situation, has its "unique" biographical articulation. This refers not only to the content, the "meaning" of all the prior experiences sedimented in it, in situations. It refers also to the intensity, . . . duration, and sequence of these experiences. This circumstance is of singular importance, since it really constitutes the individual stock of knowledge.
>
> (Schutz and Luckmann, 1973:111–112)

Thus, according to Schutz, the stock of knowledge always has a private component. However, even this unique and private component of the stock of knowledge is not solely of the actor's own making: "It must be stressed . . . that sequence, experiential depth and nearness, and even the duration of experiences and the acquisition of knowledge, are socially objectivated and determined. In other words, there are social categories of biographical articulation" (Schutz and Luckmann, 1973:113).

Because of their source in individual biography, private stocks of knowledge are not part of the life-world. Because they are biographical in nature, Schutz felt that the unique and private components of knowledge are not amenable to scientific study. They are, in Schutz's view, nonetheless important components of the everyday life of actual actors.

Realms of the Social World

Schutz identified four distinct realms of social reality. Each is an abstraction of the social world and is distinguished by its degree of immediacy (the degree to which situations are within reach of the actor) and determinability (the degree to which they can be

---

[2]And from group to group because the social stock of knowledge is stratified.

controlled by the actor). The four realms are *umwelt,* the realm of directly experienced social reality; *mitwelt,* the realm of indirectly experienced social reality; *folgewelt,* the realm of successors; and *vorwelt,* the realm of predecessors. The realms of successors and predecessors (*folgewelt* and *vorwelt*) were of peripheral interest to Schutz. However, we shall deal with them briefly because the contrast between them illustrates some of the characteristics of Schutz's major focus—the *umwelt* and the *mitwelt.*

Folgewelt and *Vorwelt*

The future (*folgewelt*) is a purely residual category in Schutz's work (in contrast to Marx's, for example, where it plays a crucial role in his dialectic). It is a totally free and completely indeterminant world. It can be anticipated by the social scientist only in a very general way and cannot be depicted in any great detail. One could not place great stock in the ideal types and models of the future constructed by the social scientist. Thus, there is little that Schutz's phenomenological science has to offer to the conventional scientist seeking to understand or predict the future.[3]

The past (*vorwelt*), on the other hand, is somewhat more amenable to analysis by the social scientist. The action of those who lived in the past is totally determined; there is no element of freedom, because the causes of their actions, the actions themselves, and their outcomes have already occurred. Despite its determinacy, the study of predecessors presents difficulties for a subjective sociology. It is difficult to interpret the actions of people who lived in an earlier time because we would probably have to use contemporary categories of thought in the historical glance back rather than the categories that prevailed at the time. The interpretation of contemporaries is likely to be more accurate because sociologists share interpretive categories with those whose action they seek to understand. Thus, although a subjective sociology of the past is possible, the probability of misinterpretation is great.

The essential point here is that the objective for Schutz was to develop a sociology based on the interpretations of the social world made by the actors being studied. It is difficult to know the interpretations of predecessors and impossible to understand those of successors. However, it is possible to understand contemporaries (*mitwelt*) and the interpretations of those with whom we are in immediate face-to-face contact (*umwelt*).

Umwelt and We Relations

The *umwelt* involves what Schutz calls "consociates," or people involved in face-to-face relationships with one another. Thus, the idea of the *umwelt* is "equally applicable to an intimate talk between friends and the co-presence of strangers in a railroad car" (Schutz, 1973:16). Being in face-to-face contact is all that is required to be considered part of the *umwelt.* There is a unique character and intensity in the *umwelt:*

> Each partner participates in the on-rolling life of the other, can grasp in a vivid present the other's thoughts as they are built up step by step. They may thus share one

---

[3]We can study what contemporaries *expect* of the future, but we cannot study the future itself.

> another's anticipations of the future as plans, or hopes or anxieties. In brief, consociates are mutually involved in one another's biography; they are growing older together; they live, as we may call it, in a pure we-relationship.
>
> (Schutz, 1973:16–17)

We relations are defined by a relatively high degree of intimacy, which is determined by the extent to which the actors are acquainted with one another's personal biographies. The pure we relation is a face-to-face relationship "in which the partners are aware of each other and sympathetically participate in each other's lives for however short a time" (Schutz, 1932/1967:164). The we relation encompasses the consciousness of the participants as well as the patterns of action and interaction that characterize face-to-face interaction. The we relation is characterized by a "thou orientation," which "is the universal form in which the other is experienced 'in person'" (Schutz and Luckmann, 1973:62). In other words, we relations are highly personal and immediate.

The immediacy of interaction has two implications for social relations. First, in a we relation, unlike in a they relation, there are abundant indicators of the other's subjective experience. Immediacy allows each actor to enter into the consciousness of the other. Second, when entering any social relation, an individual has only typical knowledge of the other. However, in the continuing process of a face-to-face interaction, typifications of the other are tested, revised, reenacted, and modified. That is, interaction with others necessarily modifies typologies.

Schutz not only offered a number of insights into we relations per se but also linked these relationships to cultural phenomena in the real world. For example, in we relations actors learn the typifications that allow them to survive socially. People not only learn recipes in we relations but use them there as well—trying them out, altering them when they prove ineffective or inappropriate.

Schutz was aware that there is considerable give-and-take among actors in we relations. People try out different courses of action on other people. They may quickly abandon those that elicit hostile reactions and continue to use those that are accepted. People also may find themselves in situations where recipes do not work at all, and they must create appropriate and workable sets of actions. In other words, in we relations people constantly adjust their actions with regard to those with whom they interact.

People also adjust their conceptions of others. They enter a given relationship with certain assumptions about what the other actors are thinking. In general, people assume that the thinking of others is of the same order as their own. Sometimes this is confirmed by what they find, but in other circumstances the facial expressions, the movements, the words, and the actions of others are inconsistent with people's sense of what others are thinking. People then must revise their view of others' thought processes and then adjust their responses on the basis of this new image of what others are thinking. This is an indirect process because people cannot actually know what others are thinking. Thus, they may tentatively change their actions in the hope that this will elicit responses consistent with what they now think is going on in others' minds. People may be forced to revise their conception of others' thought processes and their actions a number of times before they are able to understand why others are acting in a particular way. It is even conceivable that in some instances people cannot make an adequate number of adjustments, with the result that they are likely to flee the particular interaction, completely confused. In such a case, they may seek more comfortable situations where familiar recipes can be applied.

Even within we relations in everyday life, most action is guided by recipes. People do not *usually* reflect on what they do or on what others do. However, when they encounter problems, inappropriate thoughts and actions, they must abandon their recipes and reflect on what is going on to create an appropriate response. This departure from recipes is psychologically costly, because people prefer to act and interact in accord with recipes.

Because of the freedom of actors within it, the *umwelt* is clearly difficult to deal with from a scientific point of view. In the *umwelt,* people and their actions are often not typified. However, people in the *umwelt* do employ typifications of other people and their courses of action. The result is that the social scientist can, albeit with some difficulty, construct typifications of the *umwelt.* In other words, rational models of this often nonrational world can be constructed, and these models can be used to understand life in the *umwelt* better. At the minimum, they can be used to assess differences between the rational models and the way people actually behave. In this approach, Schutz (1976:81) is using typifications in much the same way that Weber used his ideal types.

Before we turn to the *mitwelt,* it should be pointed out that it is in the *umwelt* that the typifications used in daily life (first-order constructs) are created. Thus, to Schutz the *umwelt* is the crucial source of first-order constructs (in contrast to the second-order constructs used in the social sciences), and it is an important, albeit difficult, arena of scientific study. Although it is difficult to analyze the *umwelt* scientifically, it is far easier to study the *mitwelt* in this manner. However, although it may be easier to study the *mitwelt,* such study is not likely to be as rewarding as a study of the *umwelt* because of the latter's key role in the creation of typifications and its central role in the social lives of people in the life-world.

Mitwelt and They Relations

The *mitwelt* is that aspect of the social world in which people deal only with types of people or with larger social structures rather than with actual actors. People do fill these types and these structures, but in this world of "contemporaries," these people are not experienced directly. Because actors are dealing with types rather than with actual people, their knowledge of people is not subject to constant revision on the basis of face-to-face interaction. This relatively constant knowledge of general types of subjective experience can be studied scientifically and can shed light on the general process by which people deal with the social world. A number of specific examples of the *mitwelt* will be discussed a little later in this chapter.

Whereas in the *umwelt,* people coexist in the same time and space, in the *mitwelt,* spatial distances make it impossible to interact on a face-to-face basis. If the spatial situation changes and the people draw closer to each other, then face-to-face interaction becomes possible, but if it occurs, we have returned to the *umwelt.* People who were once in my *umwelt* may draw away from me and ultimately, because of spatial distances, become part of the *mitwelt.* Thus, there is a gradual transition from *umwelt* to *mitwelt* as people grow apart from one another. Here is the way Schutz describes this gradual transition:

> Now we are face-to-face, saying good-bye, shaking hands; now he is walking away. Now he calls back to me; now I see him waving to me; now he has disappeared around the corner. It is impossible to say at which precise moment the face-to-face situation ended and my partner became a mere contemporary of whom I have knowledge (he has, probably, arrived home) but no direct experience.
>
> (Schutz, 1976:37)

Similarly, there are no clear dividing lines among the various levels of the *mitwelt* discussed next.

The *mitwelt* is a stratified world with levels arranged by degree of anonymity. The more anonymous the level, the more people's relationships are amenable to scientific study. Some of the major levels within the *mitwelt,* beginning with the least anonymous, are:

1. Those whom actors encountered face-to-face in the past and could meet again. Actors are likely to have fairly current knowledge of them because they have been met before and could be met again. Although there is a relatively low level of anonymity here, such a relationship does not involve ongoing face-to-face interaction. If these people were to be met personally at a later date, this relationship would become part of the *umwelt* and no longer be part of the *mitwelt.*
2. Those once encountered not by us but by people whom we deal with. Because this level is based on secondhand knowledge of others, it involves more anonymity than the level of relationships with people we have encountered in the past. If we were ever to meet people at this level, the relationship would become part of the *umwelt.*
3. Those whom we are on the way to meet. As long as we have not yet met them, we relate to them as types, but when we actually meet them, the situation again becomes part of the *umwelt.*
4. Those whom we know not as concrete individuals but simply as positions and roles. For example, we know that there are people who sort our mail or process our checks, but although we have attitudes about them as types, we never encounter them personally.
5. Collectivities whose function we may know without knowing any of the individuals who exist within them. For example, we know about the Senate, but few people actually know any of the individuals in it, although we do have the possibility of meeting those people.
6. Collectivities that are so anonymous that we have little chance of ever encountering people in them. For most people, the Mafia would be an example of such a collectivity.
7. Objective structures of meaning that have been created by contemporaries with whom actors do not have and have not had face-to-face interaction. The rules of English grammar would be an example of such a structure of meaning.
8. Physical artifacts that have been produced by a person we have not met and whom we are not likely to meet. For example, people would have a highly anonymous relationship with a museum painting.

As we move further into the *mitwelt* relationships, they become more impersonal and anonymous. People do not have face-to-face interaction with others and thus cannot know what goes on in others' minds. Their knowledge is therefore restricted to "general types of subjective experience" (Schutz, 1932/1967:181).

They relations, which are found in the *mitwelt,* are characterized by interaction with impersonal contemporaries (for example, the unseen postal employee who sorts our mail) rather than consociates (for example, a personal friend). In they relations, the thoughts and actions of people are dominated by anonymous typifications.

In the "pure" they relation, the typical schemes of knowledge used to define other actors are not available for modification. Because we do not interact with actual people but with impersonal contemporaries, information that varies from our typifications is not provided to us. In other words, new experiences are not constituted in they relations. Cultural typifications determine action, and they cannot be altered by the thoughts and actions of actors in a they relationship. Thus, whereas we relations are subject to negotiation, they relations are not.

In spite of the distinction between we and they relations, the typifications used in they relations have their historical roots in we relations: "The first and originally objective solution of a problem was still largely dependent on the subjective relevance awareness of the individual" (Schutz and Luckmann, 1973:225). However, these solutions ultimately become more typified and anonymous—in short, more and more a part of the cultural realm.

Consciousness, Meanings, and Motives

Whereas Husserl had focused on consciousness, especially the universal structures of consciousness, Schutz turned away from consciousness and toward the direction of intersubjectivity, the life-world, and we and they relations. Thus, consciousness is not of focal concern to Schutz; rather, it constitutes the point of departure for his science of intersubjectivity (Etzrodt, 2008).

Schutz believed that in the everyday world, as long as things are running smoothly in accord with recipes, reflective consciousness is relatively unimportant, and actors pay little attention to what is going on in their minds or in the minds of others. Similarly, Schutz (1932/1967:190) believed that in the science of phenomenological sociology, one could ignore individual consciousness. In fact, because Schutz found the mind impervious to scientific study, and because he wanted to focus on intersubjectivity, he admitted in his own work that he was going to abandon the traditional phenomenological focus on mental processes (1932/1967:97). We thus have the seemingly paradoxical situation of a sociologist who is the field's most famous phenomenologist abandoning the approach for which phenomenology is best known. However, the paradox is resolved when we realize that Schutz does carry on the traditional phenomenological concern with subjectivity. Instead of focusing on individual subjectivity (as Husserl did), Schutz focuses, as we have seen throughout this chapter, on intersubjectivity.

Despite Schutz's avowed focus on intersubjectivity, he offered many insights into consciousness. In fact, Schutz argued that the base of all his sociological concerns lay in the "processes of meaning establishment and understanding occurring within individuals, processes of interpretation of the behavior of other people and processes of self-interpretation" (1932/1967:11).

The philosophical basis of Schutz's image of the social world, albeit a basis that is, for him, not amenable to scientific study, is deep consciousness (*durée*), in which is found the process of meaning establishment, understanding, interpretation, and self-interpretation. A phenomenological sociology must be based on "the way meaning is constituted in the individual experience of the solitary Ego. In so doing we shall track meaning to its very point of origin in the inner time consciousness in the duration of the ego as it lives through its experience" (Schutz, 1932/1967:13). This is the domain that was of central concern to Schutz's philosophical predecessors, Henri Bergson and Edmund Husserl. They were interested in philosophizing about what went on in the mind, but a central question to Schutz was how to turn this interest into a scientific sociological concern.

Schutz was drawn to the work of Max Weber, particularly that part of Weber's work concerned with social action, because it reflected, he thought, both an interest in consciousness and a concern for a scientific sociology. As we saw in Chapter 8, the interest in individual action was only a minor and secondary concern for Weber, who was more concerned with the impact of social structures on action than with the bases of action in consciousness. According to Prendergast, Schutz had "no apparent interest in Weber's theory of bureaucracy, sociology of religion, political sociology, or general economic history" (1986:15). Schutz, therefore, was concerned with only a small and peripheral portion of Weber's sociology. But even in that, Weber was a less-than-satisfying model for Schutz but not for the reasons implied here. To Schutz, the problem with Weber's work was that there were inadequacies in his conception of consciousness. Weber failed to distinguish among types of meanings, and he failed to distinguish meanings from motives. In clarifying what Weber failed to do, Schutz told us much about his own conception of consciousness.

Schutz argued that we must distinguish meanings from motives. In the process, he differentiated between two subtypes of both meanings and motives. Although he did not always succeed in keeping them neatly separated, for Schutz *meanings* concern how actors determine what aspects of the social world are important to them, whereas *motives* involve the reasons that actors do what they do. One type of meaning is the *subjective* meaning context. That is, through our own independent mental construction of reality, we define certain components of reality as meaningful. However, although this process is important in the everyday life-world, Schutz did not see it as amenable to scientific study, because it is too idiosyncratic.

Of concern to scientific sociology is the second type of meaning, the *objective* meaning context, the sets of meanings that exist in the culture as a whole and that are the shared possession of the collectivity of actors. In that these sets of meanings are shared rather than idiosyncratic, they are as accessible to sociologists as to anyone else. In that they have an objective existence, they can be studied scientifically by the sociologist, and they were one of Schutz's main concerns. Schutz was critical of Weber for failing to differentiate between subjective and objective meaning and for failing to make it clear that objective meaning contexts can be most easily scrutinized in scientific sociology.

Schutz also differentiated between two types of motives—"in-order-to" and "because" motives. Both involve reasons for an individual's actions, but only because motives are accessible to both the person acting and the sociologist. *In-order-to motives* are the reasons that an actor undertakes certain actions; actions are undertaken to bring about some future objective or occurrence. They exist only when action is taking place. In-order-to motives are "subjective." They are private and can be known by the actor but are inaccessible to others. In-order-to motives can be grasped only retrospectively by the actor, after the action is completed and the objective is (or is not) achieved. Sociology is little concerned with in-order-to motives because they are difficult to study scientifically. But sociology can study *because motives,* or retrospective glances at the past factors (for example, personal background, individual psyche, environment) that caused individuals to behave as they did. Because motives are "objective"; they can be studied retrospectively using scientific methods. Since the actions have already occurred, the reasons for them are accessible to both the actor and the social scientist. However, neither other actors nor social scientists can know others' motives, even because motives, fully. Both actors and scientists must be satisfied with being able to deal with typical motives.

In spite of their greater accessibility to the social scientist, because motives were of little more interest to Schutz than were in-order-to motives. They represented a Husserlian return to a concern for consciousness, but Schutz, as we have seen many times, was interested in moving on to the intersubjective world. However, Schutz believed that all social interaction is founded on a reciprocity of motives: "[T]he actor's in-order-to motives will become because-motives of his partner and vice versa" (1976:23).

Schutz embeds his most basic sociological concepts in consciousness. *Action,* for example, is "conduct self-consciously projected by the actor" (Natanson, 1973a:xxxiv), "conduct devised by the actor in advance" (Schutz, 1973:19). More explicitly, Natanson argues: "The crucial feature of action in every case is its purposive and projective character. Action has its source in the *consciousness* of the actor" (1973a:xxxiv; italics added). *Social action* is "action which involves the attitudes and actions of others and is oriented to them in its course" (Schutz, 1976:13).

One other point should be made about Schutz's thoughts on consciousness. Schutz sees within consciousness a fundamental human anxiety that lies at the base of his intersubjective world:

> I know that I shall die and I fear to die. This basic experience we suggest calling the *fundamental anxiety.* It is the primordial anticipation from which all the others originate. From the fundamental anxiety spring the many interrelated systems of hopes and fears, of wants and satisfactions, of chances and risks which incite man within the natural attitude to attempt the mastery of the world; to overcome obstacles, to draft projects and to realize them.
>
> (Schutz, 1973:228)

Interpreting Schutzian Theory

In many ways, Schutzian theory is more difficult to interpret than the work of any other major theorist discussed thus far in this book. First, Schutz (along with, perhaps, Mead) is probably the most single-mindedly abstract theorist whom we have encountered. Others have been much more deeply involved in the empirical world. Weber, for example, offered us his theory embedded in a great deal of historical detail. Marx moved back and forth between theoretical abstraction and the real-world evils of capitalism. Even Parsons, whom we encounter in the next chapter and who was a highly abstract thinker, touched base now and again with the real world. As close as Schutz (1976) ever came to the real world were his abstract essays on social types such as the stranger and the homecomer.

Second, Schutz's theory is embedded in a philosophical tradition that is foreign to sociology and translates only with great difficulty into sociological terms. James Heap and Phillip Roth (1973) argue that it is highly questionable whether Husserl's phenomenology, which is one of the main roots of Schutzian theory, can be translated into sociology. We can characterize Schutz's work as an effort to do just that. The success of Schutz's efforts is illustrated by the popularity of theories derived from his work—particularly ethnomethodology. Nevertheless, his roots in phenomenological philosophy make it difficult for us to grasp his sociology adequately.

Thus, we return to the debate with which we began this chapter. First, some commentators praise Schutz for his micro focus on how actors create the social world. Others criticize him for this focus. Still others see Schutz as having a large-scale, cultural focus. The view developed in this chapter constitutes a rejection of the second position and an integration of the first and third positions. That is, Schutz was dialectically concerned with how actors create the social world and with the impact on actors of the large-scale social and cultural world that they create. Although Schutz shares this dialectic with many classical theorists, what distinguishes his approach is that it is purely and exclusively subjective.

Summary

Alfred Schutz took the phenomenological philosophy of Edmund Husserl, which was aimed inward toward an understanding of the transcendental ego, and turned it outward toward a concern for intersubjectivity, the life-world, and the social world.

The key to understanding Schutz's approach is a comprehension of his sense of science. Science was one of a number of worlds examined by Schutz—others included the worlds of dreams, fantasies, insanity, and especially the "paramount reality" of the everyday world. Scientists are not pragmatically involved in the everyday world of the subjects they study or, while they are doing science, their own everyday world. Instead, they are involved in the world of science and rely on its stock of knowledge rather than on the stock of knowledge associated with life in the everyday world.

While in the everyday world, people may behave sensibly or reasonably; only in the theoretical models of the social scientist can they behave in a fully rational manner. The rational models and (second-order) constructs of the social scientists (that is, the "ideal types") are based upon the first-order constructs that people must use to function in their daily lives. The social scientists' analyses result in constructed ideal types of fully rational actors (puppets, or "homunculi") and their courses of action. The construction of these ideal types must meet the demands of a rigorous science. It is this type of theorizing, says Schutz, that makes an objective rational science of subjectivity possible.

Implied in much of the preceding discussion is the centrality of typifications to both social scientists and people in the everyday world. Typifications are usually socially derived and socially approved and allow people to function on a daily basis. It is only in problematic situations that people (reluctantly) abandon their typifications (and recipes) and create new ways of dealing with the social world.

As mentioned earlier, Schutz was focally concerned with intersubjectivity, or the way in which people grasp the consciousness of others while they live within their own streams of consciousness. Much of Schutz's work focuses on the life-world, or the world of everyday life. This is an intersubjective world in which people both create social reality and are constrained by the preexisting social and cultural structures created by their predecessors. Although much of the life-world is shared, there are also private (biographically articulated) aspects of that world.

There are four realms of the social world—the future (*folgewelt*); the past (*vorwelt*); the present world of consociates with whom we have face-to-face contact (*umwelt*); and the present world of contemporaries whom we know only as types (*mitwelt*). First-order constructs are created in the *umwelt;* the social scientists' second-order constructs can be applied most easily to the *mitwelt,* although they are most importantly applied to the *umwelt.* Intimate we relations are found in the *umwelt,* and typified they relations characterize the *mitwelt.*

Although Schutz had turned away from consciousness, he did offer insights into it, especially in his thoughts on meaning and motives.

Controversy exists over whether Schutz offers a micro or a macro theory; however, the view in this chapter is that his theory is concerned with the dialectical relationship between the way people construct social reality and the already present, obdurate cultural reality that others have constructed and are continuing to construct. People are influenced by these realities, but they are also capable of "making sense" of, interpreting, and even reconstructing the cultural world.

C H A P T E R 17

Talcott Parsons

Chapter Outline

Parsons's Integrative Efforts

General Principles

The Action System

Change and Dynamism in Parsonsian Theory

We come now to the last, and most contemporary, of the classical theorists to be discussed in this book, Talcott Parsons (1902–1979). Although Parsons died only a relatively short time ago, it is appropriate to discuss his work in this book for two major reasons. For one thing, it was Parsons, in *The Structure of Social Action* (1937), who brought European classical theory, especially the work of Weber and Durkheim, to the attention of American sociology (Camic, 1989). For another, Parsons created his own distinctive "grand" (or classical) theory. Parsons's theory rivals in scope and grandeur the classical theories discussed in the preceding chapters of this book.

Parsons was undoubtedly the most important American sociological theorist. His written work was widely cited and used by sociologists. Even more important, he shaped the structure of a large portion of American sociological theory, as well as sociology in general, from his position as professor at Harvard University. Many of the most important American theorists were his students, and they went on to endow their own departments, and their own students, with Parsonsian-style theory. Among the many theorists who worked with Parsons at Harvard were Robert Merton, Kingsley Davis, Robin Williams, Wilbert Moore, Marion Levy, and Neil Smelser.

Parsons's Integrative Efforts

Of all the sociological theorists discussed in this book, Parsons was the most explicit in his intention to develop an integrated approach to sociological theory. There are a number of manifestations of this. First, Parsons founded the Department of Social Relations at Harvard University with the intention of unifying the various social sciences. Included in his integrative goal were such fields as clinical psychology, behavioral psychology, anthropology, and sociology. Second, in his own theorizing Parsons developed a clear sense of levels of social analysis, best exemplified in his notion of four action systems—behavioral organism, personality, social system, and cultural system. Finally,

Talcott Parsons

A Biographical Sketch

Talcott Parsons was born in 1902 in Colorado Springs, Colorado. He came from a religious and intellectual background; his father was a Congregational minister, a professor, and ultimately president of a small college. Parsons got an undergraduate degree from Amherst College in 1924 and set out to do graduate work at the London School of Economics. In the next year, he moved on to Heidelberg, Germany. Max Weber had spent a large portion of his career at Heidelberg, and although he had died five years before Parsons arrived, Weber's influence survived and his widow continued to hold meetings in her home, meetings that Parsons attended. Parsons was greatly affected by Weber's work and ultimately wrote his doctoral thesis at Heidelberg, dealing, in part, with Weber's work.

Parsons became an instructor at Harvard in 1927, and although he switched departments several times, Parsons remained at Harvard until his death in 1979. His career progress was not rapid; he did not obtain a tenured position until 1939. Two years previously, he had published *The Structure of Social Action,* a book that not only introduced major sociological theorists such as Weber to large numbers of sociologists, but also laid the groundwork for Parsons's own developing theory.

After that, Parsons made rapid academic progress. He was made chairman of the Harvard sociology department in 1944, and two years later he set up and chaired the innovative Department of Social Relations, which included not only sociologists but a variety of other social scientists. By 1949, he had been elected president of the American Sociological Association. In the 1950s and into the 1960s, with the publication of such books as *The Social System* (1951), Parsons became the dominant figure in American sociology.

However, by the late 1960s, Parsons came under attack from the emerging radical wing of American sociology. Parsons was seen as being a political conservative, and his theory was considered highly conservative and little more than an elaborate categorization scheme. But in the 1980s, there was a resurgence in interest in Parsonsian theory, not only in the United States but around the world (Alexander, 1982–1983; Buxton, 1985; Camic, 1990; Holton and Turner, 1986; Sciulli and Gerstein, 1985). Holton and Turner have perhaps gone the furthest, arguing that "Parsons' work . . . represents a more powerful contribution to sociological theory than that of Marx, Weber, Durkheim or any of their contemporary followers" (1986:13). Furthermore, Parsons's ideas influenced not only conservative thinkers but neo-Marxian theorists as well, especially Jurgen Habermas.

Upon Parsons's death, a number of his former students, themselves sociologists of considerable note, reflected on his theory, as well as on the man behind the theory (for a more recent, and highly personal, reminiscence, see Fox, 1997). In their musings, these sociologists offered some interesting insights into Parsons and his work. The few glimpses of Parsons reproduced here do not add up to a coherent picture, but they do offer some provocative glimpses of the man and his work.

Robert Merton was one of his students when Parsons was just beginning his teaching career at Harvard. Merton, who became a noted theorist in his own right, makes it clear that graduate students came to Harvard in those years to study not with Parsons but rather with Pitirim Sorokin, the senior member of the department, who was to become Parsons's archenemy (Zafirovski, 2001):

> Of the very first generation of graduate students coming to Harvard . . . precisely none came to study with Talcott. They could scarcely have done so for the simplest of reasons: in 1931, he had no public identity whatever as a sociologist.
>
> Although we students came to study with the renowned Sorokin, a subset of us stayed to work with the unknown Parsons.
>
> (Merton, 1980:69)

Merton's reflections on Parsons's first course in theory are interesting, too, especially because the material provided the basis for one of the most influential theory books in the history of sociology:

> Long before Talcott Parsons became one of the Grand Old Men of world sociology, he was for an early few of us its Grand Young Man. This began with his first course in theory. . . . [It] would provide him with the core of his masterwork, *The Structure of Social Action* which . . . did not appear in print until five years after its first oral publication.
>
> (Merton, 1980:69–70)

Although all would not share Merton's positive evaluation of Parsons, they would acknowledge the following:

> The death of Talcott Parsons marks the end of an era in sociology. When [a new era] does begin . . . it will surely be fortified by the great tradition of sociological thought which he has left to us.
>
> (Merton, 1980:71)

Parsons argued in one of his most important works, *The Social System,* that the integration of levels of social analysis is of central importance in the social world:

> This *integration* of a set of common value patterns with the internalized need-disposition structure of the constituent personalities is the core phenomenon of the dynamics of social systems. That the stability of any social system except the most evanescent interaction process is dependent on a degree of such integration may be said to be the *fundamental dynamic theorem of sociology.*
>
> (Parsons, 1951:42; italics added)

Parsons made a similar point when he argued that the key issue to him was "the problem of theoretical formulation of the relations between the *social system* and the *personality* of the individual" (1970:1; italics added).

This integrative goal, which runs through a large portion of Parsons's work, is to be lauded and indeed has been applauded by some; however, others (for example, Alexander, 1978; Menzies, 1977) came to see it as "muddled" and "confused." These critics argued that Parsons began *The Structure of Social Action* as a micro-oriented action theorist but that even before he finished that work, and progressively as the years passed, he moved more and more in the direction of a macro-oriented structural-functional theory. Some of the confusion in Parsons's work resulted from his inability to give up older theoretical positions or to integrate them adequately with newer ones. As early as the preface to the second edition of *The Structure of Social Action,* Parsons spoke of his shift

> from the analysis of the structure of social action as such to the structural-functional analysis of social systems. They are, of course, in the last analysis, systems of social action. But the structure of such systems is, in the newer version, treated not directly in action terms, but as "institutionalized patterns."
>
> (Parsons, 1949:D)

One view (Menzies, 1977), shared by this author, is that a basic problem of Parsons's work stems from his never having completed the shift from action theory to structural functionalism, with the result that the two theories are interrelated in a muddled fashion throughout his work. It is not that the integration of action theory and structural functionalism is impossible or undesirable; rather, it is that Parsons never did reconcile them adequately. They often stand side by side in his work rather than being intertwined.

Parsons's frequent use of two different definitions of many key concepts reflects the continuing duality of his theoretical orientation. For example, Ken Menzies (1977) said that in defining *deviance,* Parsons used both a structural-functional approach, emphasizing the larger system's failure to socialize the actor adequately, and an action-theory approach, defining *deviance* as a "motivated tendency for an actor to behave in contravention of one or more institutionalized normative patterns" (Parsons, 1951:250).

In part, Parsons's integrative work is muddled because he never reconciled his Weberian action theory (as he interpreted Weber) with his Durkheimian structural functionalism. It is this duality, along with other factors we will discuss as we proceed, that mars, but does not destroy, Parsons's theoretical approach.[1]

[1]As will be seen throughout this chapter, the authors tend to adopt an admiring, but critical, stance toward Parsons's work. For an even more positive analysis, see Richard Münch (1981, 1982).

General Principles

A starting point for getting at the substance of Parsons's theoretical orientation is the general principles behind his theory building (Devereux, 1961). Parsons set as his goal the construction of an adequate general theory, a grand theory[2] that was to be analytical, systematic, complete, and elegant. First, such a theory must, from his point of view, be an action theory in which "the central mechanism must always be some notion of actors orienting themselves to situations, with various sorts of goals, values, and normative standards, and behaving accordingly" (Devereux, 1961:19). Second, such a theory must be based on the principle of *voluntarism,* that is, an actor's "choice among alternative values and courses of action must remain at least potentially free" (Devereux, 1961:20). Third, such cultural phenomena as ideas, ideals, goals, and norms must be considered causally relevant factors. Fourth, Parsons adopted the idea of *emergence*—the notion that higher-order systems emerge out of lower-order systems. Such higher-order systems, he felt, must not be able to be inferred from, or explained in terms of, component parts. Finally, the emergent systems must never become wholly detached from their component parts. We will have numerous occasions in this chapter to question how well Parsons actually carried through on these principles in the course of his theoretical work. Although Parsons moved away from this base as his career progressed, the principles are those upon which he built his entire theory.

Philosophical and Theoretical Roots

The source of these ideas on theory can be found in Parsons's 1937 analysis of the roots of modern sociology. Here, and in other works, Parsons always gave the impression that he felt the whole of recent intellectual history was converging in him and his work. He analyzed and criticized utilitarianism and classical economics for dealing with isolated individuals, for assuming individual rationality, and for holding the view that social order came either from the pursuit of individual self-interest or from externally imposed sanctions. Parsons believed that we need to analyze nonrational as well as rational action and that we need to look toward institutionalized common values for the source of social order. He attacked positivism for its view of the world as a closed, deterministic system leaving no room for such critical notions as mind, consciousness, values, ends, and norms. Finally, Parsons lauded idealism for accepting the very ideas rejected by positivism, but he rejected the view that all the social world could be explained by such cultural factors.

The bulk of *The Structure of Social Action* is devoted to a discussion of Alfred Marshall, Vilfredo Pareto, Emile Durkheim, and Max Weber, who developed ideas that were converging on what Parsons called the "voluntaristic theory of action." Parsons's work on these four thinkers is largely a summary of their work, and there is little that is new in it. However, it has been criticized severely for being highly biased and deceptive.

---

[2]Ironically, Parsons praised Durkheim for *not* doing grand theory, for doing what many critics felt Parsons never did, that is, integrating theory and reality: "Durkheim was a scientific theorist in the best sense of one who never theorized 'in the air,' never indulged in 'idle speculation' but was always seeking the solution of crucially important empirical problems" (1937:302).

What is significant is that Parsons used their work to derive a number of ideas that proved crucial to him, including the nonrational, action, voluntarism, norms, and values. Basically, Parsons was saying that these thinkers had freed themselves from their theoretical roots (such as utilitarianism, positivism) and by so doing provided *him* with the tools *he* needed to construct a voluntaristic theory of action.

Action Theory

As a result of these influences and interpretations, Parsons's early work is heavily oriented to action theory. Not too many years ago, a book on sociological theory would have devoted a great deal of attention to action theorists (MacIver, 1931, 1942; Parsons, 1937; Znaniecki, 1934). Today, however, interest in action theory has faded, although some more recent work (Coleman, 1986; Sciulli, 1986) has helped resuscitate it to some degree.

Action theory had its origin in Max Weber's work on social action (see Chapter 8). Although Weber embedded his work in assumptions on actors and action, his real interest was in the cultural and structural constraints on them. Instead of focusing on this aspect of Weber's work, action theory operated at the level of individual thought and action, as is clear from Roscoe Hinkle's summary of the tenets of action theory:

1. Men's social activities arise from their consciousnesses of themselves (as subjects) and of others and the external situations (as objects).
2. As subjects, men act to achieve their (subjective) intentions, purposes, aims, ends, objectives, or goals.
3. They use appropriate means, techniques, procedures, methods, and instruments.
4. Their courses of action are limited by unmodifiable conditions or circumstances.
5. Exercising will or judgment, they choose, assess, and evaluate what they will do, are doing, and have done.
6. Standards, rules, or moral principles are invoked in arriving at decisions.
7. Any study of social relationships requires the researcher to use subjective investigative techniques such as "*verstehen,*" imaginative or sympathetic reconstruction, or vicarious experience.

(Hinkle, 1963:706–707)

There is some evidence that such a micro-level action approach was anticipated by pre-World War I sociologists such as Lester Ward, E. A. Ross, Franklin Giddings, Albion Small, and Charles H. Cooley, although their link to modern action theory is tenuous. Most of these early sociologists were preoccupied with the large-scale question of societal evolution. They discussed an active, creative view of the individual but tended to give society coercive power over the individual.

The exception to this tendency was Cooley. Although he accepted some of the tenets of his contemporaries, and their interest in evolution, "what became ultimately significant in social life [were] subjective consciousness and personal feelings, sentiments, ideas, or ideals in terms of which men initiate and terminate their actions toward one another" (Hinkle, 1963:709).

Sociologists who worked between the end of World War I and the Depression exhibited a far greater connection with later action theory. Among the more important of these sociologists were Robert Park, Ellsworth Faris, W. I. Thomas, George Herbert Mead, and Talcott Parsons. Parsons was the major inheritor of the Weberian orientation, and his use of action theory in his early work gave that approach its widest audience.

Parsons's Action Theory

Parsons was eager to differentiate action theory from behaviorism. In fact, he chose the term *action* because it had a different connotation from that of *behavior. Behavior* implies mechanical response to stimuli, whereas *action* implies an active, creative, "mental" process. As Parsons put it, "A theory which, like behaviorism, insists on treating human beings in terms which exclude his subjective aspect, is not a theory of action" (1937:77–78).

Three concepts lie at the heart of Parsons's action theory—the unit act, voluntarism, and *verstehen.* The most basic phenomenon in Parsons's action theory is what he called the *unit act,* which he defined in terms of four components. First, it implies the existence of an *actor.* Second, the unit act involves an *end,* or a future state toward which action is oriented. Third, the action takes place in a *situation* that involves two elements: things the actor cannot control *(conditions)* and those over which the actor can exert control *(means).* Finally, *norms* and *values* serve to shape the actor's choice of means to ends (Parsons, 1937). Parsons said that there is "no such thing as action except as effort to conform to norms" (1937:76–77). Already in the unit act we see the integrative concerns that were to dominate Parsons throughout his life. Although he began with an interest in actors and their actions, he implied an interest in consciousness in terms of the voluntary choice of means to ends. But that choice is not free, which implies an interest on Parsons's part in the social structures that constrain action. Cultural entities such as norms and values play a key role here, as they do throughout Parsons's work. Intimately related to the unit act is Parsons's concept of voluntarism. *Voluntarism* pertains to actors who are seen as making choices in social situations (Procter, 1978). This is not to say that the actors are totally free in those choices; voluntarism is not equivalent to "free will." Nevertheless, the concept of voluntarism clearly implies a mind, consciousness, and individuals making decisions. Finally, there is the concept of *verstehen,* or the need to analyze action from the subjective perspective.

The Turn Away from Action Theory

In our view, although Parsons never abandoned the idea of individual choice constrained by external forces, he did abandon the focus on consciousness and action implied strongly in *The Structure of Social Action.* This is reflected in the degree to which Parsons backed off from three central concepts in his early work—the unit act, voluntarism, and *verstehen* (which he interpreted as a method largely oriented to the study of consciousness and action).

The unit act lay at the very core of the theoretical contribution of *The Structure of Social Action,* but it progressively disappeared as Parsons's theories developed. In *The Social System* (1951) the unit act is cited only three times in a book that runs close to 600 pages. When it is cited, the impression is that Parsons simply used it to legitimize his earlier work and that it has no relevance to the project at hand. In *The Social System,* Parsons perfunctorily remarked that the unit act is still the basic unit, but

> for most purposes of the more macroscopic analysis of social systems . . . it is convenient to make use of a higher order unit than the act, namely the status-role. . . . It is the structure of the *relations* between the actors as involved in the interactive process which is essentially the structure of the social system. . . . It is the *participation* of an actor in a patterned interactive relationship which is for many purposes the most significant unit of the social system.
>
> (Parsons, 1951:25)

The unit act and the status-role are very different phenomena, as far as we are concerned. Whereas the unit act refers to actor and action, the *status-role* refers to position within a structure of interaction. In his later work, Parsons developed the concept of need-disposition as the most significant unit at the personality level; value orientations occupy the same position in the cultural system. As we will see later, *need-dispositions* are biological needs shaped by external forces, and *value orientations* are internalized cultural standards. The issue here is whether these three new concepts have "emerged" from the unit act or whether they are entirely new concepts. Only the value orientation is traceable directly to the unit act and Parsons's thinking in 1937. Status-role and need-disposition are entirely new, arising out of Parsons's later thought. In his preface to the second edition of *The Structure of Social Action* (1949), Parsons admitted that in the 1937 edition he did not include two critical influences—those of Sigmund Freud on the psychological side and those of anthropologists such as Franz Boas. It is from these sources that Parsons's concepts of need-disposition and status-role undoubtedly came. Clearly, we do not need the unit act to understand the three later concepts. Furthermore, Parsons did not need (or use) the unit act to analyze the social, cultural, and personality systems. As he became, in turn, a structural functionalist, a functionalist, and an evolutionist, the unit act became increasingly extraneous. In his basic work on evolution, *Societies* (1966), the unit act disappears completely.

Finally, there is the disappearance of *verstehen* from Parsons's theory. As Parsons put it: "Contrary to the point of view held by the author in *The Structure of Social Action,* it now appears that this postulate [the subjective point of view] is not essential to the frame of reference of action in its most elementary form" (1951:543). Thus *verstehen* followed the unit act and voluntarism into Parsonsian oblivion. In fact, the subjective perspective had to go when Parsons deserted the unit act and voluntarism. It was because he was looking at a voluntaristic unit act that Parsons needed a subjective methodology. According to Scott, it was the influence of behaviorism that helped to move Parsons away from *verstehen.* Finally, a sociologist need not use *verstehen* to study need-dispositions, status-roles, or value orientations, concepts that characterized the next phase of Parsons's work (see the next section).

Need-Dispositions

In work published in the early 1950s, Parsons's interest in the individual level took a new turn. Parsons moved from the unit act, voluntarism, and *verstehen* to need-dispositions and the orientations of actors to situations. There is a concern with consciousness here, albeit a constrained one, one devoid of virtually all creativity. Actors are depicted as being driven by need-dispositions to seek the optimization of gratification; that is, they are impelled by innate needs that are shaped and molded by external forces into dispositions. Within this context, Parsons dealt with the motivational and value orientations of actors.

Motivational Orientations

Actors use the framework of motivational orientations to analyze social phenomena that are of interest to them. Of major concern is the degree to which the phenomena represent actual or potential satisfaction of their need-dispositions. This process involves three dimensions. First, actors must analyze the situation *cognitively.* That is, they must:

1. Locate social phenomena (individuals, collectivities, physical culture objects).
2. Differentiate them from other social phenomena.
3. Relate them to general classes of objects.
4. Determine the social phenomenon's properties.
5. Determine the social phenomenon's actual or potential functions.

Simultaneously, the actors must assess the *cathectic* significance of the social phenomenon: they must decide how much affect, or emotion, to invest in each phenomenon they perceive. That determination is influenced by the degree to which a phenomenon is likely to gratify or deprive actors in terms of their need-dispositions. Then actors go through an *evaluative* process in which they determine how to allocate their energies in order to optimize gratification and minimize deprivation.

This discussion of motivational orientation relates to consciousness to some extent. However, it is not the conscious process but the norms and values that shape this process that were of prime significance to Parsons.

Value Orientations

It is in the context of norms and values that Parsons dealt with value orientations, or the cultural standards for judging solutions to each of the three motivational issues discussed in the previous section. Through the socialization process, actors internalize these standards, which become aspects of the actors' orientations, and commit them to the observance of certain norms, standards, and criteria of selection whenever they must make *choices.* Parsons described three value orientations that parallel the three modes of motivational orientation.

First, the actors acquire a set of *cognitive* standards. Among other things, these standards help the actors decide whether the data they are receiving are important, whether their observations are useful, and the relative importance of various situations and problems. In other words, cognitive standards handle informational problems associated with a motivational decision. Then there are *appreciative* standards that allow actors to assess the appropriateness and the consistency of the amount of cathectic energy they have invested in various social phenomena. These are the social rules that help us determine whether a given social entity will satisfy our need-dispositions. Finally, there are *moral* standards that permit actors to assess the consequences of their actions for the integrity of and relationship between the personality and social systems. Overall, the existence of these three sets of standards in Parsons's work, and the sense that they guide (to a large extent even determine) actors' choices, leads us to doubt that Parsons retained very much of a sense of voluntarism.

Types of Action Parsons used the three modes of motivational and value orientation to develop four basic types of action. *Intellectual action* involves cognitive motivational interests and cognitive value standards; *expressive action* combines cathectic interests and appreciative standards; and *moral action* involves evaluative interests and moral standards. *Instrumental action,* the fourth type, is more complex. It involves future goals determined by cathectic interests and appreciative standards and means to those goals determined by cognitive standards.[3]

Although Parsons was willing to offer us a static typology of action, there is in fact very little sense of dynamic individual action in his work. He based his model of a social system on the interaction of ego and alter ego, but he had very little to say about this, using it only as a base on which to build his large-scale sense of the social system. This lack of action in Parsons's model, even when he was supposedly an action theorist, led William F. Whyte to argue that "in the world of Talcott Parsons, actors are constantly orienting themselves to situations and very rarely, if ever, acting" (1961:255).

Pattern Variables

Returning to Parsons's work on action and consciousness, we encounter the famous, or infamous, pattern variables, which reflect Parsons's overwhelming penchant for parallelisms and conceptual neatness. At the most basic level, the *pattern variables* are a conceptual set of five dichotomous choices of action that actors must make in every situation. At this level they are tools for analyzing conscious processes. The pattern variables are universal choices an actor must make before a situation will have determinate meaning; they address the fundamental problem of orienting oneself to a situation (Parsons, 1951:60). The pattern variables are:

1. *Affectivity–affective neutrality:* The attitudinal problem of how we feel toward a social phenomenon—how much emotion, affect, to invest in it. For example, should physicians develop emotional ties to patients or should physicians keep patients at a distance?
2. *Specificity–diffuseness:* The attitudinal problem of whether to orient ourselves to part or all of the social phenomenon. Should patients accept advice from physicians on all kinds of problems or only on those within the physicians' area of expertise?
3. *Universalism–particularism:* The problem of how to categorize social phenomena. Are we to judge them in terms of general standards that apply universally to all such entities, or are we to use more specific, more emotional standards in such judgments? For example, we are likely to judge potential

[3]As a matter of fact, this is a good definition of Weber's "value-rational action."

physicians with universal standards, but we are likely to assess our own children with more particular standards.

4. *Ascription–achievement:* The problem of whether we characterize social phenomena by what they are endowed with or by what they acquire. Are people born with the ability to become physicians, or are such abilities learned?
5. *Self–collectivity:* The dilemma of whether we should pursue our own private interests or those shared with other members of the collectivity. Is the physicians' desire to earn a good living incompatible with their stated goal of helping humankind?

Parsons went on to use the pattern variables to analyze other aspects of his theoretical system. They can be used to differentiate habits of choice within the personality system, to examine the different role expectations within the social system, and to differentiate among the various normative patterns in the cultural system. This tendency to use the same conceptual scheme at different levels of social analysis gives Parsons's work an orderly feel, but it also created problems for him. There is no obvious reason why the same concepts should fit such diverse levels. As Alfred Baldwin said: "The problem of integrating motives within the person bears only a slight resemblance to that of integrating people in society" (1961:185). In general, there is no persuasive reason to believe that all systems, no matter what their level of complexity, have the same set of dilemmas.

AGIL

As has been pointed out previously in this chapter, over the course of his career Parsons moved from action theory to structural functionalism. We will encounter some of Parsons's thoughts on structures and systems shortly, but first we will discuss some of his ideas on functionalism. A *function* is "a complex of activities directed towards meeting a need or needs of the system" (Rocher, 1975:40). Using this definition, Parsons believed that there are four functional imperatives that are necessary for (characteristic of) all systems—adaptation (A), goal attainment (G), integration (I), and latency (L). Together, these four functional imperatives are known as the AGIL scheme. To survive, a system must perform these four functions:

1. *Adaptation:* A system must cope with external situational exigencies. It must adapt to its environment and adapt the environment to its needs.
2. *Goal attainment:* A system must define and achieve its primary goals.
3. *Integration:* A system must regulate the interrelationship of its component parts. It also must manage the relationship among the other three functional imperatives (A, G, L).
4. *Latency (pattern maintenance):* A system must furnish, maintain, and renew both the motivation of individuals and the cultural patterns that create and sustain the motivation.

As with the pattern variables, Parsons designed the AGIL scheme to be used at *all* levels in his theoretical system (for one example, see Paulsen and Feldman, 1995). As Chandler Morse noted:

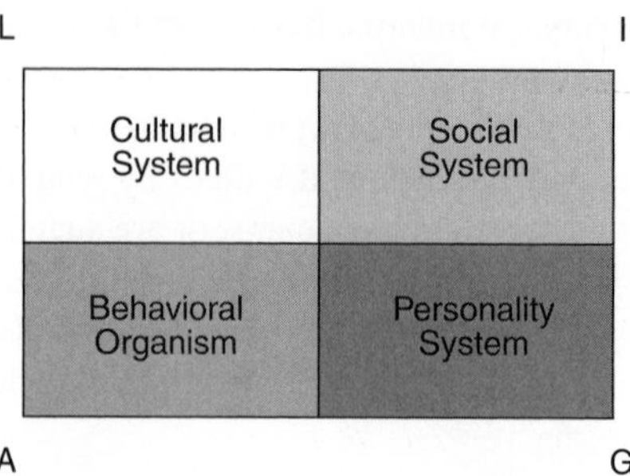

FIGURE 17.1 ***Structure of the General Action System***

> The four functional imperatives, or problems, operate at both a micro-analytic and a macro-analytic level in the Parsonian model. At the micro-level they purport to specify the phases through which *individual actors* in a small action system and the action system as a whole must progress during an action cycle. At the macro-level the imperatives provide a means of (a) allocating roles analytically among four functional sub-systems of any given system, and of (b) sorting out the input-output flows among those sub-systems.
>
> (Morse, 1961:116)

In the discussion that follows on the four action systems, we will illustrate how Parsons uses the AGIL system; later, we will show how he applies it to society.

At their most general level, the four functional imperatives are linked to the four action systems (discussed in detail shortly). The *behavioral organism* is the action system that handles the adaptation function by adjusting to and transforming the external world. The *personality system* performs the goal-attainment function by defining system goals and mobilizing resources to attain them. The *social system* copes with the integration function by controlling its component parts. Finally, the *cultural system* performs the latency function by providing actors with the norms and values that motivate them for action. Figure 17.1 summarizes the structure of the action system in terms of the AGIL schema.

Consistency in Parsonsian Theory: Integration and Order

We have been stressing some of the changes in Parsonsian theory but have, if anything, understated them, because Parsonsian theory takes many other twists and turns. For example, in his later work, Parsons came to think of his approach not so much as action, structural functional, or functional, but as cybernetic. His concern was with communication among action systems as well as control of lower-order systems by higher-order ones. In spite of all these dramatic changes, there were consistent elements in Parsonsian theory. Parsons himself, while he came to admit certain shifts, emphasized his "essential continuity over the forty-year period since *The Structure of Social Action*" (1977a:2).

One of Parsons's most important concerns from the beginning was the question of order in society (Burger, 1977; Chen, 2004; Münch, 2005). Given a modern, complex society, the question arises of how a "war of all against all," rampant social conflict, is avoided. Throughout his career, Parsons argued that power is not the force that prevents such social warfare. In his view, power is not a sound means of maintaining order in society. Although exercises of power may work in the short run, in the long run they are only likely to bring about more disorder. The use of power evokes negative reactions that lead to further disintegration in society. Furthermore, constant vigilance is required for the exercise of power to work. It is difficult, time-consuming, and expensive to maintain order in society on the basis of power. In short, power is an inadequate and inefficient method of maintaining order in society. This antipower position was a consistent theme of Parsons from his earliest works.

Another consistent idea of Parsons was his alternative solution to the problem of order. To Parsons, the ideal way for a society to maintain order is to develop a cultural system that emphasizes cooperation and then have that set of ideas internalized in the actors through socialization. This idea relates to Parsons's fundamental theorem, which involves the integration of "common value patterns" (culture) and "need-dispositions" (personality). Put somewhat crudely, order in society is best maintained when people are put in the position of constraining themselves. Because people carry common value patterns around in their heads, they are able to determine for themselves if they are out of line and are able to realign themselves with the cultural value system. Ideally, no external power source is needed to maintain order in society; the society that governs least governs best. Of course, in some instances power is necessary, but these should be few and far between. If the authorities are forced to use power too often, then a society is in deep trouble, perhaps even in danger of disintegration.

This issue of order, power, and integration was an essential theme of Parsons throughout his career. At the end of *The Structure of Social Action* (1937), Parsons considered the solution of the power question to be in value integration. The integration of values and need-dispositions lies at the heart of *The Social System* (1951) and is central to many of Parsons's books and essays after that time. For example, in a well-known essay on organizations, Parsons argued that his "main point of reference for analyzing the [organization] . . . is its value pattern" (1960:20). Although he did discuss power, his primary interest was in cultural dimensions that provide organizational integration. Thus, whereas most people conceive of organizations as arenas of power and power struggles, Parsons emphasized the values that held organizations together. This kind of thinking over the years earned Parsons the title of "consensus" theorist. We will have occasion to return to this theme in the next section.

The Action System

We are now ready to discuss the overall shape of Parsons's action system. Figure 17.2 is an outline of the major levels of Parsons's schema.

It is obvious that Parsons had a clear notion of "levels" of social analysis as well as their interrelationship. The hierarchical arrangement is clear, and the levels are integrated in Parsons's system in two ways. First, each of the lower levels provides the conditions, the energy, needed for the higher levels. Second, the higher levels control those below them in the hierarchy.

In terms of the environments of the action system, the lowest level, the physical and organic environment, involves the nonsymbolic aspects of the human body, its

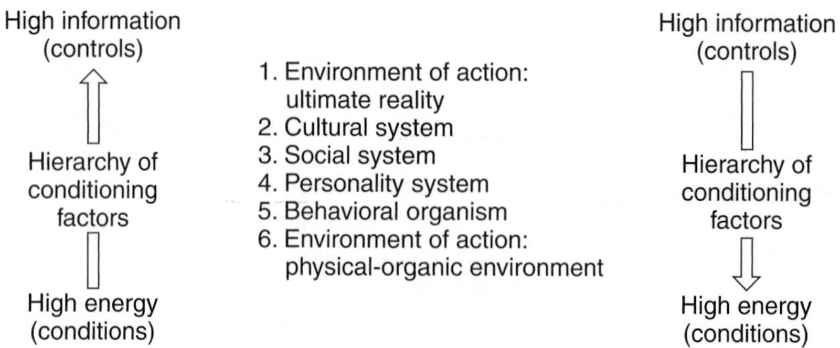

FIGURE 17.2 ***Parsons's Action Schema***

anatomy and physiology. The highest level, ultimate reality, has, as Jackson Toby suggests, "a metaphysical flavor," but Toby also argues that Parsons "is not referring to the supernatural so much as to the universal tendency for societies to address symbolically the uncertainties, concerns, and tragedies of human existence that challenge the meaningfulness of social organization" (1977:3).

The heart of Parsons's work is found in his four action systems. In discussing these systems and their interrelationships, Parsons moved away from his earlier action theory and in the direction of structural functionalism (this move is also clear in the earlier discussion of AGIL). In the assumptions that Parsons made regarding his action systems, we encounter again the problem of order that was his overwhelming concern and that has become a major source of criticism of his work (Schwanenberg, 1971). The Hobbesian problem of order—what prevents a social war of all against all—was not answered to Parsons's (1937) satisfaction by the earlier philosophers. Parsons found his answer to the problem of order in structural functionalism, which operates in his view with the following set of assumptions:

1. Systems have the property of order and interdependence of parts.
2. Systems tend toward self-maintaining order, or equilibrium.[4]
3. The system may be static or involved in an ordered process of change.
4. The nature of one part of the system has an impact on the form that the other parts can take.
5. Systems maintain boundaries with their environments.
6. Allocation and integration are two fundamental processes necessary for a given state of equilibrium of a system.
7. Systems tend toward self-maintenance involving the maintenance of boundaries and of the relationships of parts to the whole, control of environmental variations, and control of tendencies to change the system from within.

---

[4]Most often, to Parsons, the problem of order related to the issue of why action was nonrandom or patterned. The issue of equilibrium was a more empirical question to Parsons. Nonetheless, Parsons himself often conflated the issues of order and equilibrium.

These assumptions led Parsons to make the analysis of the *ordered* structure of society his first priority. In so doing, he did little with the issue of social change, at least until later in his career:

> We feel that it is uneconomical to describe changes in systems of variables before the variables themselves have been isolated and described; therefore, we have chosen to begin by studying particular combinations of variables and to move toward description of how these combinations change only when a firm foundation for such has been laid.
>
> (Parsons and Shils, 1951:6)

Parsons was so heavily criticized for his static orientation that he devoted more and more attention to change; in fact, as we will see, he eventually focused on the evolution of societies. However, in the view of most observers, even his work on social change tended to be highly static and structured.

In reading about the four action systems, the reader should keep in mind that they do not exist in the real world but are, rather, analytical tools for analyzing the real world.

Social System

Parsons's conception of the social system begins at the micro level with interaction between ego and alter ego, defined as the most elementary form of the social system. He spent little time analyzing this level, although he did argue that features of this interaction system are present in the more complex forms taken by the social system. Parsons defined a *social system* thus:

> A social system consists in a plurality of individual actors *interacting* with each other in a situation which has at least a physical or environmental aspect, actors who are motivated in terms of a tendency to the "optimization of gratification" and whose relation to their situations, including each other, is defined and mediated in terms of a system of culturally structured and shared symbols.
>
> (Parsons, 1951:5–6)

This definition seeks to define a social system in terms of many of the key concepts in Parsons's work—actors, interaction, environment, optimization of gratification, and culture.

Despite his commitment to viewing the social system as a system of interaction, Parsons did not take interaction as his fundamental unit in the study of the social system. Rather, he used the *status-role* complex as the basic unit of the system. As mentioned earlier, this is neither an aspect of actors nor an aspect of interaction, but rather a *structural* component of the social system. *Status* refers to a structural position within the social system, and *role* is what the actor does in such a position, seen in the context of its functional significance for the larger system. The actor is viewed not in terms of thoughts and actions, but instead (at least in terms of position in the social system) as nothing more than a bundle of statuses and roles.

In his analysis of the social system, Parsons was interested primarily in its structural components. In addition to a concern with the status-role, Parsons (1966:11) was interested in such large-scale components of social systems as collectivities, norms, and values. In his analysis of the social system, however, Parsons was not simply a structuralist but also a functionalist. He thus delineated a number of the functional prerequisites of a social system. First, social systems must be structured so that they operate compatibly with other systems. Second, to survive, the social system must have the requisite support from other systems. Third, the system must meet a significant proportion of the needs of its actors. Fourth, the system must elicit adequate participation from its members. Fifth, it must have at least a minimum of control over potentially disruptive behavior. Sixth, if conflict becomes sufficiently disruptive, it must be controlled. Finally, a social system requires a language in order to survive.

It is clear in Parsons's discussion of the functional prerequisites of the social system that his focus was large-scale systems and their relationship to one another (societal functionalism). Even when he talked about actors, it was from the point of view of the system. Also, the discussion reflects Parsons's concern with the maintenance of order within the social system.

Actors and the Social System

However, Parsons did not completely ignore the issue of the relationship between actors and social structures in his discussion of the social system. In fact, as we saw earlier, he called the integration of value patterns and need-dispositions "the fundamental dynamic theorem of sociology" (Parsons, 1951:42). Given his central concern with the social system, of key importance in this integration are the processes of internalization and socialization. That is, Parsons was interested in the ways that the norms and values of a system are transferred to the actors within the system. In a successful socialization process, these norms and values are internalized; that is, they become part of the actors' "consciences." As a result, in pursuing their own interests, the actors are in fact serving the interests of the system as a whole. As Parsons put it, "The combination of value-orientation patterns which is acquired [by the actor in socialization] *must in a very important degree be a function of the fundamental role structure and dominant values of the social system*" (1951:227).

In general, Parsons assumed that actors usually are passive recipients in the socialization process.[5] Children learn not only how to act but also the norms and values, the morality, of society. Socialization is conceptualized as a conservative process in which need-dispositions (which are themselves largely molded by society) bind children to the social system, and it provides the means by which the need-dispositions can be satisfied. There is little or no room for creativity; the need for gratification ties children to the system as it exists. Parsons sees socialization as a lifelong experience. Because the norms and values inculcated in childhood tend to be very general, they do not prepare children for the various specific situations that they encounter in adulthood. Thus, socialization must be supplemented throughout the life cycle with a series of more specific socializing experiences. Despite this need later in life, the norms and values learned in childhood tend to be stable and, with a little gentle reinforcement, tend to remain in force throughout life.

Despite the conformity induced by lifelong socialization, there is a wide range of individual variation in the system. The question is: Why is this normally not a major problem for the social system, given its need for order? For one thing, a number of

---

[5]This is a controversial interpretation of Parsons's work with which many disagree. François Bourricaud, for example, talks of "the dialectics of socialization" (1981:108) in Parsons's work and not of passive recipients of socialization.

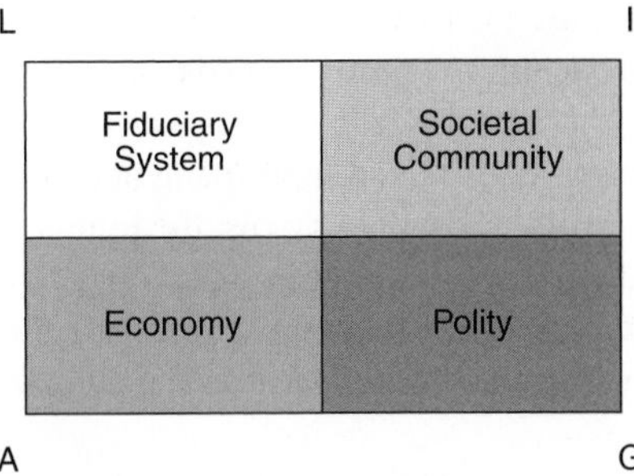

FIGURE 17.3 ***Society, Its Subsystems, and the Functional Imperatives***

social control mechanisms can be employed to induce conformity. However, as far as Parsons was concerned, social control is strictly a second line of defense. A system runs best when social control is used only sparingly. For another thing, the system must be able to tolerate some variation, some deviance. A flexible social system is stronger than a brittle one that accepts no deviation. Finally, the social system should provide a wide range of role opportunities that allow different personalities to express themselves without threatening the integrity of the system.

Socialization and social control are the main mechanisms that allow the social system to maintain its equilibrium. Modest amounts of individuality and deviance are accommodated, but more extreme forms must be met by reequilibrating mechanisms. Thus, social order is built into the structure of Parsons's social system:

> Without deliberate planning on anyone's part there have developed in our type of social system, and correspondingly in others, mechanisms which, within limits, are capable of forestalling and reversing the deep-lying tendencies for deviance to get into the vicious circle phase which puts it beyond the control of ordinary approval-disapproval and reward-punishment sanctions.
>
> (Parsons, 1951:319)

Again, Parsons's main interest was the system as a whole rather than the actor in the system—how the system controls the actor, not how the actor creates and maintains the system. This reflects Parsons's commitment on this issue to a structural-functional orientation.

Society Although the idea of a social system encompasses all types of collectivities, one specific and particularly important social system is *society,* "a relatively self-sufficient collectivity the members of which are able to satisfy all their individual and collective needs and to live entirely within its framework" (Rocher, 1975:60).[6] As a structural functionalist, Parsons distinguished among four structures, or subsystems, in society in terms of the functions (AGIL) they perform (see Figure 17.3). The *economy* is the subsystem that performs the function for society of adapting to the environment through

[6]Barber (1993, 1994) argues that although there is considerable terminological confusion in Parsons's work, the idea of a social system should be restricted to inclusive, total systems such as societies.

labor, production, and allocation (Moss and Savchenko, 2006). Through such work, the economy adapts the environment to society's needs, and it helps society adapt to these external realities. The *polity* (or political system) performs the function of goal attainment by pursuing societal objectives and mobilizing actors and resources to that end. The *fiduciary system* (for example, in the schools, the family) handles the latency function by transmitting culture (norms and values) to actors and allowing it to be internalized by them. Finally, the integration function is performed by the *societal community* (for example, the law), which coordinates the various components of society (Parsons and Platt, 1973).

As important as the structures of the social system were to Parsons, the cultural system was more important. In fact, as we saw earlier, the cultural system stood at the top of Parsons's action system,[7] and Parsons (1966) labeled himself a "cultural determinist."

Cultural System

Parsons conceived of culture as the major force binding the various elements of the social world, or, in his terms, the action system. Culture mediates interaction among actors and integrates the personality and the social systems. Culture has the peculiar capacity to become, at least in part, a component of the other systems. Thus, in the social system, culture is embodied in norms and values, and in the personality system, it is internalized by the actor. But the cultural system is not simply a part of other systems; it also has a separate existence in the form of the social stock of knowledge, symbols, and ideas. These aspects of the cultural system are available to the social and personality systems, but they do not become part of them (Morse, 1961:105; Parsons and Shils, 1951:6).

Parsons defined the cultural system, as he did his other systems, in terms of its relationship to the other action systems. Thus, *culture* is seen as a patterned, ordered system of symbols that are objects of orientation to actors, internalized aspects of the personality system, and institutionalized patterns (Parsons, 1990) in the social system. Because it is largely symbolic and subjective, culture is readily transmitted from one system to another. Culture can move from one social system to another through diffusion and from one personality system to another through learning and socialization. However, the symbolic (subjective) character of culture also gives it another characteristic, the ability to control Parsons's other action systems. This is one of the reasons that Parsons came to view himself as a cultural determinist.

Again establishing parallelism and orderliness in his thinking, Parsons argued that the cultural system has three components that parallel the three modes of motivational orientation discussed earlier. The *cognitive* motivational orientation is paralleled in culture by systems of beliefs and idea systems that represent guidelines to the solution of motivational problems. The *cathectic* motivational orientation has its parallel in culture in systems of expressive symbols, means of expressing a cathectic attachment to a social object. Finally, the *evaluative* motivational orientation is paralleled by similar cultural

---

[7]Interestingly, Alexander and Smith (2001:13a) see Parsons as "insufficiently cultural," lacking a "thick description" of culture.

guidelines—systems of value orientations. (Each component can be subdivided in precisely the same way. Thus, for example, as discussed earlier, the system of value orientations can be broken down into cognitive, appreciative, and moral standards.) Parsons came to the conclusion that the moral standards are "the superordinate integrative techniques of a system of action" (Parsons and Shils, 1951:170). This conclusion reflects the crucial idea in Parsons's theory—that the cultural system is preeminent. But if culture is preeminent, Parsons's integrative work is questionable, for any kind of determinism is suspect from the point of view of an integrated sociology. (For a more integrated conception of Parsons's work, see Camic, 1990). This problem is exacerbated when we look at the personality system and see how weakly it is developed in Parsons's work.

Personality System

The personality system is controlled not only by the cultural system but also by the social system. Parsons's early conception of consciousness and action, in terms of his work on the unit act, voluntarism, and so forth, was reviewed earlier and found wanting. Parsons seemed to be aware of the charge that he had given up his earlier emphasis on voluntarism, and he sought to salvage his position by according some independence to the personality system:

> My view will be that, while the main content of the structure of the personality is derived from social systems and culture through socialization, the personality becomes an independent system through its relations to its own organism and through the uniqueness of its own life experience; it is not a mere epiphenomenon.
>
> (Parsons, 1970:82)

We get the feeling here that Parsons is protesting too much. If the personality system is not an epiphenomenon, it is certainly reduced to secondary or dependent status in his theoretical system.

The *personality* is defined as the organized system of orientation and motivation of action of the individual actor. The basic component of the personality is the need-disposition, a concept we discussed earlier but which now needs further explication. Parsons and Shils defined need-*dispositions* as the "most significant units of motivation of action" (1951:113). They differentiated need-dispositions from drives, which are innate tendencies—"physiological energy that makes action possible" (Parsons and Shils, 1951:111). In other words, drives are better seen as part of the biological organism. Need-dispositions are then defined as "these same tendencies when they are not innate but acquired through the process of action itself" (Parsons and Shils, 1951:111). In other words, need-dispositions are drives that are shaped by the social setting.

Need-dispositions impel actors to accept or reject objects presented in the environment or to seek out new objects if the ones that are available do not adequately satisfy need-dispositions. Parsons differentiated among three basic types of need-dispositions. The first type impels actors to seek love, approval, and so forth from their social relationships. The second type includes internalized values that lead actors to observe various cultural standards. Finally, there are the role expectations that lead actors to give and get appropriate responses.

This gives a very passive image of actors. They seem to be either impelled by drives, dominated by the culture, or, more usually, shaped by a combination of drives and culture (that is, by need-dispositions). A passive personality system is clearly a weak link in an integrated theory, and Parsons seemed to be aware of it. On various occasions, he tried to endow the personality with some creativity. For example, he said: "We do not mean . . . to imply that a person's values are entirely 'internalized culture' or mere adherence to rules and laws. The person makes creative modifications as he internalizes culture; but the novel aspect is not the culture aspect" (Parsons and Shils, 1951:72). Despite claims such as these, the dominant impression that emerges from Parsons's work is one of a passive personality system.

Parsons's emphasis on need-dispositions creates other problems. Because it leaves out so many other important aspects of personality, his system becomes a largely impoverished one. Alfred Baldwin, a psychologist, makes precisely this point:

> It seems fair to say that Parsons fails in his theory to provide the personality with a reasonable set of properties or mechanisms aside from need-dispositions, and gets himself into trouble by not endowing the personality with enough characteristics and enough different kinds of mechanisms for it to be able to function.
>
> (A. Baldwin, 1961:186)

Baldwin makes another telling point about Parsons's personality system, arguing that even when Parsons analyzed the personality system, he was really not focally interested in it: "Even when he is writing chapters on personality structure, Parsons spends many more pages talking about social systems than he does about personality" (1961:180). This is reflected in the various ways that Parsons linked the personality to the social system. First, actors must learn to see themselves in a way that fits with the place they occupy in society (Parsons and Shils, 1951:147). Second, role expectations are attached to each of the roles occupied by individual actors. Then there is the learning of self-discipline, internalization of value orientations, identification, and so forth. All these forces point toward the integration of the personality system with the social system, which Parsons emphasized. However, he also pointed out the possible malintegration, which is a problem for the system that needs to be overcome.

Another aspect of Parsons's work—his interest in internalization as the personality system's side of the socialization process—reflects the passivity of the personality system. Parsons (1970:2) derived this interest from Durkheim's work on internalization, as well as from Freud's work, primarily that on the superego. In emphasizing internalization and the superego, Parsons again manifested his conception of the personality system as passive and externally controlled.

Although Parsons was willing to talk about the subjective aspects of personality in his early work, he progressively abandoned that perspective. In so doing, he limited his possible insights into the personality system. Parsons at one point stated clearly that he was shifting his attention away from the internal meanings that the actions of people may have: "The organization of observational data in terms of the theory of action is quite possible and fruitful in modified behavioristic terms, and such formulation avoids many of the difficult questions of introspection or empathy" (Parsons and Shils, 1951:64).

Behavioral Organism

Though he included the behavioral organism as one of the four action systems, Parsons had very little to say about it. It is included because it is the source of energy for the rest of the systems. Although it is based on genetic constitution, its organization is affected by the processes of conditioning and learning that occur during the individual's life.[8] The behavioral organism is clearly a residual system in Parsons's work, but at the minimum, Parsons is to be lauded for including it as a part of his sociology, if for no other reason than that he anticipated the interest in sociobiology and the sociology of the body (B. Turner, 1985) among at least a few sociologists.

Change and Dynamism in Parsonsian Theory

Evolutionary Theory

Parsons's work with conceptual tools such as the pattern variables, the functional imperatives, and the four action systems led to the accusation that he offered a structural theory that was unable to deal with social change. Parsons had long been sensitive to this charge, arguing that although a study of change was necessary, it must be preceded by a study of structure. But by the 1960s he could resist the charges no longer and made another major shift in his work, this time to the study of social change,[9] particularly the study of social evolution. By Parsons's (1977b:50) own testimony, that interest was first stimulated by a seminar on social evolution held in 1963.

Parsons's (1966) general orientation to the study of social change was shaped by biology. To deal with this process, Parsons developed what he called "a paradigm of evolutionary change."

The first component of that paradigm is the process of *differentiation.* Parsons assumed that any society is composed of a series of subsystems that differ in terms of both their *structure* and their *functional* significance for the larger society. As society evolves, new subsystems are differentiated. This is not enough, however; they also must be more adaptive than earlier subsystems. Thus, the essential aspect of Parsons's evolutionary paradigm was the idea of *adaptive upgrading.* Parsons described this process:

> If differentiation is to yield a balanced, more evolved system, each newly differentiated substructure . . . must have increased adaptive capacity for performing its *primary* function, as compared to the performance of *that* function in the previous, more diffuse structure. . . . We may call this process the *adaptive upgrading* aspect of the evolutionary change cycle.
>
> (Parsons, 1966:22)

This is a highly positive model of social change (although Parsons certainly had a sense of its darker side). It assumes that as society evolves, it grows generally better able

---

[8]Because of this social element, in his later work Parsons developed the word *organism* and labeled this the "behavioral system" (1975:104).

[9]To be fair, we must report that Parsons had done some earlier work on social change, but it did not become a paramount concern, and his contributions were minimal, until the 1960s (see Parsons, 1942, 1947; see also Alexander, 1981; Baum and Lechner, 1981).

to cope with its problems. In contrast, in Marxian theory, social change leads to the eventual destruction of capitalist society. For this reason, among others, Parsons is often thought of as a very conservative sociological theorist. In addition, although he did deal with change, he tended to focus on the positive aspects of social change in the modern world rather than on modernity's negative side.

Next, Parsons argued that the process of differentiation leads to a new set of problems of *integration* for society. As subsystems proliferate, the society is confronted with new problems in coordinating the operations of these units.

A society undergoing evolution must move from a system of ascription to one of achievement. A wider array of skills and abilities is needed to handle the more diffuse subsystems. The generalized abilities of people must be freed from their ascriptive bonds so that they can be utilized by society. Most generally, this means that groups formerly excluded from contributing to the system must be freed for inclusion as full members of the society.

Finally, the *value* system of the society as a whole must undergo change as social structures and functions grow increasingly differentiated. However, because the new system is more diverse, it is harder for the value system to encompass it. Thus a more differentiated society requires a value system that is "couched at a higher level of generality in order to legitimize the wider variety of goals and functions of its subunits" (Parsons, 1966:23). However, this process of generalization of values often does not proceed smoothly as it meets resistance from groups committed to their own narrow value systems.

Evolution proceeds through a variety of cycles, but no general process affects all societies equally. Some societies may foster evolution, whereas others may "be so beset with internal conflicts or other handicaps" that they impede the process of evolution, or they may even "deteriorate" (Parsons, 1966:23). What most interested Parsons were those societies in which developmental "breakthroughs" occur, because he believed that once they occurred, the process of evolution would follow his general evolutionary model.

Although Parsons conceived of evolution as occurring in stages, he was careful to avoid a unilinear evolutionary theory: "We do not conceive societal evolution to be either a continuous or a simple linear process, but we can distinguish between broad levels of advancement without overlooking the considerable variability found in each" (1966:26). Making it clear that he was simplifying matters, Parsons distinguished three broad evolutionary stages—primitive, intermediate, and modern. Characteristically, he differentiated among these stages primarily on the basis of cultural dimensions. The crucial development in the transition from primitive to intermediate is the development of language, primarily written language. The key development in the shift from intermediate to modern is "the institutionalized codes of normative order," or law (Parsons, 1966:26).

Parsons next proceeded to analyze a series of specific societies in the context of the evolution from primitive to modern society. One particular point is worth underscoring here: Parsons turned to evolutionary theory, at least in part, because he was accused of being unable to deal with social change. However, his analysis of evolution is *not* in terms of process; rather, it is an attempt to "order structural types and relate them sequentially" (Parsons, 1966:111). This is comparative *structural* analysis, not really a study of the processes of social change. Thus, even when he was supposed to be looking at change, Parsons remained committed to the study of structures and functions.

Generalized Media of Interchange

One of the ways in which Parsons introduces some dynamism, some fluidity (Alexander, 1983:115) into his theoretical system is through his ideas on the generalized media of interchange within and among the four action systems (especially within the social system) discussed previously. The model for the generalized media of interchange is money, which operates as such a medium within the economy. But instead of focusing on material phenomena such as money, Parsons focuses on *symbolic* media of exchange. Even when Parsons does discuss money as a medium of interchange within the social system, he focuses on its symbolic rather than its material qualities. In addition to money, and more clearly symbolic, are other generalized media of interchange—political power, influence, and value commitments. Parsons makes it quite clear why he is focusing on symbolic media of interchange: "The introduction of a theory of media into the kind of structural perspective I have in mind goes far, it seems to me, to refute the frequent allegations that this type of structural analysis is inherently plagued with a static bias, which makes it impossible to do justice to dynamic problems" (1975:98–99).

Symbolic media of interchange have the capacity, like money, to be created and to circulate in the larger society. Thus, within the social system, those in the political system are able to create political power. More importantly, they can expend that power, thereby allowing it to circulate freely in, and have influence over, the social system. Through such an expenditure of power, leaders presumably strengthen the political system as well as the society as a whole. More generally, it is the generalized media that circulate between the four action systems and within the structures of each of those systems. It is their existence and movement that gives dynamism to Parsons's largely structural analyses.

As Alexander (1983:115) points out, generalized media of interchange lend dynamism to Parsons's theory in another sense. They allow for the existence of "media entrepreneurs" (for example, politicians) who do not simply accept the system of exchange as it is. That is, they can be creative and resourceful and in this way alter not only the quantity of the generalized media, but also the manner and direction in which the media flow.

Summary

In a few short years, Talcott Parsons went from being the dominant figure in sociological theory to being, in some quarters, nearly a theoretical outcast. Neither extreme status is deserved. Parsons's theoretical system always had serious weaknesses, but it is certainly not without major significance.

To his credit, Parsons articulated early in his work an interest in integrating the diverse levels of social analysis, and he maintained that interest, despite basic changes in his theoretical system, throughout his life. Most basically, Parsons was interested in integrating the social and personality systems. Despite such a laudable goal, his work has been marred by some basic confusions, specifically the uncomfortable mix of action theory and structural functionalism. On the basis of his analyses of the people whom he considered to be the major thinkers in the history of sociology, Parsons initially articulated what seemed to be a micro orientation in his action theory. This orientation is particularly clear in his emphasis on the unit act and voluntarism in his early work. However, over the years the unit act and voluntarism tended to disappear from Parsons's theory, as did action theory. In its place, there evolved a structural-functional theory in which actors were seen not as acting in a voluntaristic manner but as constrained primarily by social structures and culture. In the 1940s and 1950s, Parsons developed new concepts such as need-dispositions, motivational orientations, and value orientations. They all reflected Parsons's increasing tendency to see actors as constrained by external structures rather than as voluntaristic actors. Other well-known Parsonsian concepts were developed in this period, including the pattern variables and later the AGIL system. Through these changes, Parsons retained a lifelong interest in order and a preference for cultural rather than power solutions to the problem of order.

The heart of Parsons's theory lies in his sense of the major levels of social analysis, especially the four action systems. Although Parsons is probably best known for his work on the social system, the most important level in his theory is the cultural system. It stands at the pinnacle of the four action systems and exercises control over the other three (the social, personality, and behavioral organism systems). Although the other levels are not completely controlled by the cultural system, Parsons described himself as a "cultural determinist." Parsons retained an interest in the actor in his later work, but he talked of the personality system, not voluntaristic actors. The problem here is that Parsons tended to see the personality system as determined by the systems that stand above it, the social system and, particularly, the cultural system.

In his later work, Parsons sought to give his perspective more of a change orientation. This is reflected in his work on the evolution of societies. However, despite an apparent focus on change, Parsons's ideas on evolution remained more structural and functional than change-oriented. Also in his later work, Parsons sought to give his approach more dynamism through his ideas on the generalized media of interchange.

References

Abbott, Edith

1906 "Harriet Martineau and the Employment of Women in 1836." *Journal of Political Economy* 14:611–626.

1910 *Women in Industry.* New York: Appleton.

1936/1970 *The Tenements of Chicago 1908–1935.* New York: Arno.

Abel, Theodore

1948 "The Operation Called Verstehen." *American Journal of Sociology* 54:211–218.

Aboulafia, Mitchell

1986 *The Mediating Self: Mead, Sartre, and Self-Determination.* New Haven: Yale University Press.

Abraham, Gary A.

1992 *Max Weber and the Jewish Question: A Study of the Social Outlook of His Sociology.* Urbana: University of Illinois Press.

Abrams, Philip

1968 *The Origins of British Sociology: 1834–1914.* Chicago: University of Chicago Press.

Abrams, Philip, Deem, Rosemary, Finch, Janet, and Rock, Paul

1981 *Practice and Progress: British Sociology 1950–1980.* London: Allen and Unwin.

Acevedo, Gabriel A.

2005 "Turning Anomie on Its Head: Fatalism as Durkheim's Concealed and Multidimensional Alienation Theory." *Sociological Theory* 23:75–85.

Adair-Toteff, Christopher

2005 "Max Weber's Charisma." *Journal of Classical Sociology* 5:189–204.

Adams, Bert N.

2005 "Pareto, Vilfredo." In George Ritzer (ed.), *Encyclopedia of Social Theory.* Thousand Oaks, Calif.: 544–547.

Addams, Jane

1895 "The Settlement as a Factor in the Labor Movement" in *Hull-House Maps and Papers,* by Residents of Hull-House, Boston: Thomas Crowell, pp. 183–204.

1902/1907 *Democracy and Social Ethics.* New York: Macmillan.

1905 "Problems of Municipal Administration." *American Journal of Sociology* 10:425–444.

1907 *Newer Ideals of Peace.* New York: Macmillan.

1910/1990 *Twenty Years at Hull-House.* James Hurt (ed.), Urbana: University of Illinois Press.

1916 *The Long Road of Women's Memory.* New York: Macmillan.

1922 *Peace and Bread in Times of War.* New York: Macmillan.
1930 *The Second Twenty Years at Hull-House.* New York: Macmillan.

Agger, Ben
1998 *Critical Social Theories: An Introduction.* Boulder, Colo.: Westview.

Albrow, Martin
1996 *The Global Age*. Cambridge: Polity.

Albrow, Martin, and King, Elizabeth
1990 *Globalization, Knowledge and Society.* London: Sage.

Alexander, Elizabeth
1995 "'We Must Be about Our Father's Business': Anna Julia Cooper and the Incorporation of the Nineteenth Century African-American Woman Intellectual." *Signs* 20:336–356.

Alexander, Jeffrey
1978 "Formal and Substantive Voluntarism in the Work of Talcott Parsons: A Theoretical and Ideological Reinterpretation." *American Sociological Review* 43:177–198.
1981 "Revolution, Reaction, and Reform: The Change Theory of Parsons's Middle Period." *Sociological Inquiry* 51:267–280.
1982–1983 *Theoretical Logic in Sociology.* 4 vols. Berkeley: University of California Press.
1983 *Theoretical Logic in Sociology.* Vol. 4, *The Modern Reconstruction of Classical Thought: Talcott Parsons.* Berkeley: University of California Press.
1988a "Culture and Political Crisis: 'Watergate' and Durkheimian Sociology." In J. C. Alexander (ed.), *Durkheimian Sociology: Cultural Studies.* Cambridge, Eng.: Cambridge University Press: 187–224.
1988b "Introduction: Durkheimian Sociology and Cultural Studies Today." In J. C. Alexander (ed.), *Durkheimian Sociology: Cultural Studies.* Cambridge, Eng.: Cambridge University Press: 1–21.

Alexander, Jeffrey, and Smith, Philip
2001 "The Strong Program in Cultural Theory: Elements of a Structural Hermeneutics." In Jonathan Turner (ed.), *Handbook of Sociological Theory.* New York: Kluwer Academic/Plenum Publishers: 135–150.

Alger, Janet M., and Alger, Steven F.
1997 "Beyond Mead: Symbolic Interaction between Humans and Felines." *Society and Animals* 5:65–81.

Alieva, Dilbar
2008 "'Catcher in the Rye' of Everyday Life." *Czech Sociological Review* 44:889–922.

Allen, Robert Loring
1991a *Opening Doors: The Life and Work of Joseph Schumpeter: Europe (Volume 1).* New Brunswick, NJ: Transaction Publishers.
1991b *Opening Doors: The Life and Work of Joseph Schumpeter: America (Volume 2).* New Brunswick, NJ: Transaction Press.

Alpert, Harry
1939 *Emile Durkheim and His Sociology.* New York, London: Columbia University Press; P. S. King & Son, Ltd.

Alt, John
1985–1986 "Reclaiming C. Wright Mills." *Telos* 66:6–43.

Althusser, Louis
1969 *For Marx.* Harmondsworth, Eng.: Penguin.

Alway, Joan
1995 "The Trouble with Gender: Tales of the Still Missing Feminist Revolution in Sociological Theory." *Sociological Theory* 13:209–226.

Andersen, Esben Sloth
2004 "The Process of Creative Destruction: From Vision to Measurement and Evolutionary Explanation." Paper presented at the DRUID Summer Conference 2004 on Industrial Dynamics, Innovation and Development, June 14–16, Elsinore, Denmark.

Anderson, Elijah
1996 "Introduction to the 1996 edition of *The Philadelphia Negro.*" In *The Philadelphia Negro: A Social Study.* Philadelphia: University of Pennsylvania Press: ix–xxvi.
1999 *Code of the Street: Decency, Violence, and the Moral Life of the Inner City.* New York: W. W. Norton.

Andrews, Howard F.
1993 "Durkheim and Social Morphology." In S. P. Turner (ed.), *Emile Durkheim: Sociologist and Moralist.* London: Routledge: 111–135.

Annandale, Ellen.
2007 "Assembing Harriet Martineau's Gender and Health Jigsaw." *Women's Studies International Forum* 30:355–366.

Antonio, Robert J.
1985 "Values, History and Science: The Metatheoretic Foundations of the Weber-Marx Dialogues." In R. J. Antonio and R. M. Glassman (eds.), *A Weber-Marx Dialogue.* Lawrence: University Press of Kansas: 20–43.
2000 "Karl Marx." In George Ritzer (ed.), *The Blackwell Companion to Major Social Theorists.* Malden, Mass.: Blackwell.
2001 "Nietzsche: Social Theory in the Twilight of the Millennium." In George Ritzer and Barry Smart (eds.), *Handbook of Social Theory.* London: Sage: 163–178.
Forthcoming "The Cultural Construction of Neoliberal Globalization: 'Honey . . . I Think I Shrunk the Kids.'" In G. Ritzer (ed.), *The Blackwell Companion to Globalization.* Oxford: Blackwell.

Antonio, Robert J., and Glassman, Ronald M. (eds.)
1985 *A Weber-Marx Dialogue.* Lawrence: University Press of Kansas.

Appadurai, Arjun
1996 *Modernity at Large, Cultural Dimensions of Globalization.* Minneapolis, London: University of Minnesota Press.

Archer, Margaret S.
1982 "Morphogenesis versus Structuration: On Combining Structure and Action." *British Journal of Sociology* 33:455–483.
1988 *Culture and Agency: The Place of Culture in Social Theory.* Cambridge, Eng.: Cambridge University Press.
1995 *Realist Social Theory: The Morphogenetic Approach.* Cambridge, Eng.: Cambridge University Press.

Arditi, Jorge
1996 "Simmel's Theory of Alienation and the Decline of the Nonrational." *Sociological Theory* 14:93–108.

Arendt, Hannah
2002 "Karl Marx and the Tradition of Western Political Thought." *Social Research* 69:273–361.

Arnia, Caroline, and Mueller, Charlotte
2004 "More Sociological than the Sociologists? Undisciplined and Undisciplinary Thinking about Society and Modernity in the Nineteenth Century." In Barbara L. Marshall and Ann Witz (eds.), *Engendering the Social: Feminist Encounters with Sociological Theory.* Berkshire, Eng.: Open University Press: 71–97.

Aron, Raymond
1965 *Main Currents in Sociological Thought,* Vol. 1. New York: Basic Books.
1979/2005 "Tocqueville Reconsidered." *The Tocqueville Review* 26:25–46.

Aronowitz, Stanley
1994 "The Simmel Revival: A Challenge to American Social Science." *Sociological Quarterly* 35:397–414.

Aronson, Ronald
1995 *After Marxism.* New York: Guilford Press.

Asante, Molefi Kete
1996 "The Afrocentric Metatheory and Disciplinary Implications." In Mary F. Rogers (ed.), *Multicultural Experiences, Multicultural Theories.* New York: McGraw-Hill: 61–73.

Athens, Lonnie
1995 "Mead's Vision of the Self: A Pair of 'Flawed Diamonds.'" *Studies in Symbolic Interaction* 18:245–261.
2002 "'Domination': The Blind Spot in Mead's Analysis of the Social Act." *Journal of Classical Sociology* 2:25–42.
2005 "Mead's Lost Conception of Society." *Symbolic Interaction* 28:305–325.

Auerswald, Philip
2007 "Retroview: Schumpeter's Century." *The American Interest* 2:124–134.

Avino, Elvira del Pozo
2006 *Integralism, Altruism and Reconstruction: Essays in Honor of Pitirim A. Sorokin.* Valencia, Spain: PUV.

Ayres, C. E.
1958 "Veblen's Theory of Instincts Reconsidered." In Douglas F. Dowd (ed.), *Thorstein Veblen: A Critical Reappraisal.* Ithaca, N.Y.: Cornell University: 25–37.

Bailey, Cathryn
1997 "Making Waves and Drawing Lines: The Politics of Defining the Vicissitudes of Feminism." *Hypatia* 12:16–28.
2004 "Anna Julia Cooper: 'Dedicated in the Name of My Slave Mother to the Education of Colored Working People'" *Hypatia* 19:56–73.

Bakker, Hans
2007 "Economic Determinism." In George Ritzer (ed.), *Encyclopedia of Sociology.* Oxford: Blackwell: 1293–1294.

Balch, Emily Greene
1941/1972 *Beyond Nationalism: The Social Thought of Emily Balch Greene.* New York: Twayne.

Baldwin, Alfred
1961 "The Parsonian Theory of Personality." In M. Black (ed.), *The Social Theories of Talcott Parsons.* Englewood Cliffs, N.J.: Prentice-Hall: 153–190.

Baldwin, John
1986 *George Herbert Mead: A Unifying Theory for Sociology.* Newbury Park, Calif.: Sage.

Ball, Richard A.
1979 "The Dialectical Method: Its Application to Social Theory." *Social Forces* 57:785–798.

Ball, Terence
1991 "History: Critique and Irony." In T. Carver (ed.), *The Cambridge Companion to Marx.* Cambridge, Eng.: Cambridge University Press: 124–142.

Banks, Alan, Billings, Dwight, and Tice, Karen
1996 "Appalachian Studies and Postmodernism." In Mary F. Rogers (ed.), *Multicultural Experiences, Multicultural Theories.* New York: McGraw-Hill: 81–90.

Baran, Paul, and Sweezy, Paul M.
1966 *Monopoly Capital: An Essay on the American Economic and Social Order.* New York: Monthly Review Press.

Barbalet, J. M.
1983 *Marx's Construction of Social Theory.* London: Routledge and Kegan Paul.

Barber, Bernard
1993 *Constructing the Social System.* New Brunswick, N.J.: Transaction Publishers.
1994 "Talcott Parsons on the Social System: An Essay in Clarification and Elaboration." *Sociological Theory* 12:101–105.

Bar-Haim, Gabriel
1997 "The Dispersed Sacred: Anomie and the Crisis of Ritual." In Stewart M. Hoover and Knut Lundby (eds.), *Rethinking Media, Religion, and Culture.* Thousand Oaks, Calif.: Sage: 133–145.

Barnes, Barry
2001 "The Macro/Micro Problem and the Problem of Structure and Agency." In George Ritzer and Barry Smart (eds.), *Handbook of Social Theory.* London: Sage: 339–352.

Baudrillard, Jean
1970/1998 *The Consumer Society.* London: Sage.
1972/1981 *For a Critique of the Political Economy of the Sign.* St. Louis: Telos Press.

Baum, Rainer C., and Lechner, Frank J.
1981 "National Socialism: Toward an Action-Theoretical Perspective." *Sociological Inquiry* 51:281–308.

Bauman, Zygmunt
1976 *Towards a Critical Sociology: An Essay on Commonsense and Emancipation.* London: Routledge and Kegan Paul.
1998 *Globalization: The Human Consequences.* New York: Columbia University Press.
2000 *Liquid Modernity.* Cambridge: Polity Press.
2003 *Liquid Love: On the Frailty of Human Bonds.* Cambridge: Polity Press.

2005 *Liquid Life*. Cambridge: Polity Press.
2006 *Liquid Fear*. Cambridge: Polity Press.
2007 *Liquid Times: Living in an Age of Uncertainty*. Cambridge: Polity Press.

Baumol, William
2001 "Innovation and Creative Destruction." In by L. W. McKnight, P. M. Vaaler, and R. L. Katz (eds.) *Creative Destruction: Business Survival Strategies in the Global Internet Economy*. Cambridge, MA: The MIT Press: 21–38.

Beamish, Rob
2007 "Dialectical Materialism." In George Ritzer (ed.), *Encyclopedia of Sociology.* Oxford: Blackwell: 1150–1151.

Beck, Ulrich
1992 *Risk Society: Towards a New Modernity.* London: Sage.
2000 *What Is Globalization?* Cambridge, Eng.: Polity.
2005 *Power in the Global Age.* Cambridge: Polity.

Beck, Ulrich, and Beck-Gersheim, Elizabeth
2002 *Individualization: Institutionalized Individualism and Its Social and Political Consequences.* London: Sage.

Beilharz, Peter
1996 "Negation and Ambivalence: Marx, Simmel and Bolshevism on Money." *Thesis Eleven* 47:21–32.
2005a "Alienation." In George Ritzer (ed.), *Encyclopedia of Social Theory.* Thousand Oaks, Calif.: Sage: 9–10.
2005b "Marx, Karl." In George Ritzer (ed.), *Encyclopedia of Social Theory.* Thousand Oaks, Calif.: Sage: 475–478.
2005c "Marxism." In George Ritzer (ed.), *Encyclopedia of Social Theory.* Thousand Oaks, Calif.: Sage: 479–483.
2005d "Socialism." In George Ritzer (ed.), *Encyclopedia of Social Theory.* Thousand Oaks, Calif.: Sage: 769–772.

Beland, Daniel
2008 *States of Global Insecurity: Policy, Politics and Society.* New York: Worth.

Bell, Daniel
1992 "George C. Homans (11 August 1910–29 May 1989)." *Proceedings of the American Philosophical Society* 136:587–593.

Bellah, Robert N.
1973 "Introduction" in R. Bellah (ed.), *Emile Durkheim: On Morality and Society.* Chicago: University of Chicago Press: ix–lv.

Bellah, Robert N., et al.
1985 *Habits of the Heart: Individualism and Commitment in American Life.* New York: Harper and Row.

Bender, Frederick (ed.)
1970 *Karl Marx: The Essential Writings.* New York: Harper.

Benjamin, Jessica
1988 *The Bonds of Love: Psychoanalysis, Feminism, and the Problem of Domination.* New York: Pantheon.

Berger, Peter, and Luckmann, Thomas
1967 *The Social Construction of Reality.* Garden City, N.Y.: Anchor.

Berk, Bernard
2006 "Macro-Micro Relationships in Durkheim's Analysis of Egoistic Suicide." *Sociological Theory* 24:58–80.

Berlin, Isaiah
1954 *Historical Inevitability.* London: Oxford University Press.

Berman, Marshall
1982 All that is Solid Melts into Air: *The Experience of Modernity.* NY: Simon and Schuster.

Besnard, Philippe
1983 "The 'Année Sociologique' Team." In P. Besnard (ed.), *The Sociological Domain.* Cambridge, Eng.: Cambridge University Press: 11–39.
1993 "Anomie and Fatalism in Durkheim's Theory of Regulation." In S. P. Turner (ed.), *Emile Durkheim: Sociologist and Moralist.* London: Routledge: 169–190.

Best, Steven, and Kellner, Douglas
1991 *Postmodern Theory: Critical Interrogations.* New York: Guilford Press.

Biernacki, Richard
2007 "Practice." In George Ritzer (ed.), *Encyclopedia of Sociology.* Oxford: Blackwell: 3607–3609.

Bierstedt, Robert
1963 "The Common Sense World of Alfred Schutz." *Social Research* 30:116–121.

Biggart, Nicole Woolsey
1991 "Explaining Asian Economic Organization: Toward a Weberian Institutional Perspective." *Theory and Society* 20:199–232.

Birnbaum, Pierre
2008 *Geography of Hope: Exile, the Enlightenment, Disassimilation.* Stanford, CA: Stanford University Press.

Birnbaum, Pierre, and Todd, Jane Marie
1995 "French Jewish Sociologists between Reason and Faith: The Impact of the Dreyfus Affair." *Jewish Social Studies* 2:1–35.

Blankenship, Ralph L. (ed.)
1977 *Colleagues in Organization: The Social Construction of Professional Work.* New York: Wiley.

Blau, Peter
1960 "Structural Effects." *American Sociological Review* 25:178–193.
1964 *Exchange and Power in Social Life.* New York: Wiley.

Bleicher, Josef
1980 *Contemporary Hermeneutics: Hermeneutics as Method, Philosophy and Critique.* London: Routledge and Kegan Paul.

Blumer, Herbert
1969 *Symbolic Interaction: Perspective and Method.* Englewood Cliffs, N.J.: Prentice-Hall.

Boli, John, and Lechner, Frank
2005 *World Culture: Origins and Consequences*. Oxford: Blackwell.

Bonilla-Silva, Eduardo
2003 *Racism without Racists: Color-Blind Racism and the Persistence of Racial Inequality in the United States*. Lanham, Md.: Rowman & Littlefield.

Bookman, Ann, and Morgen, Sandra (eds.)
1988 *Women and the Politics of Empowerment.* Philadelphia: Temple University Press.

Booth, Charles
1892–1902 *The Life and Labour of the People of London.* 17 volumes. London: Macmillan.

Boswell, Terry, and Dixon, William J.
1993 "Marx's Theory of Rebellion: A Cross-National Analysis of Class Exploitation, Economic Development, and Violent Revolt." *American Sociological Review* 58:681–702.

Bottomore, Tom, and Frisby, David
1978 "Introduction to the translation of Georg Simmel, *The Philosophy of Money*" (orig. 1907). London: Routledge and Kegan Paul: 1–49.

Boucher, Daniella
2006 "Small Victories, Lasting Change: Harriet Martineau, Slavery, and Woman's Rights." *Human Architecture: Journal of Sociology of Self-Knowledge* 4:321–329.

Boudon, Raymond
1995 "Should One Still Read Durkheim's Rules after One Hundred Years?" (Interview with Massimo Borlandi) *Schweizerische Zeitschrift fur Soziologie* 21:559–573.

Bourdieu, Pierre
1977 *Outline of a Theory of Practice.* London: Cambridge University Press.

Bourdieu, Pierre, and Wacquant, Loïc J. D.
1992 "The Purpose of Reflexive Sociology (The Chicago Workshop)." In P. Bourdieu and L.J.D. Wacquant (eds.), *An Invitation to Reflexive Sociology.* Chicago: University of Chicago Press: 61–215.

Bourricaud, François
1981 *The Sociology of Talcott Parsons.* Chicago: University of Chicago Press.

Boyd, Richard
2001 "Tocqueville's Algeria." *Society* 38(6):65–70.

Bradley, Owen
2005a "Bonald, Louis de." In George Ritzer (ed.), *Encyclopedia of Social Theory.* Thousand Oaks, Calif.: Sage: 65–66.
2005b "Maistre, Joseph de." In George Ritzer (ed.), *Encyclopedia of Social Theory.* Thousand Oaks, Calif.: Sage: 454–466.

Bramson, Leon
1961 *The Political Context of Sociology.* Princeton: Princeton University Press.

Braverman, Harry
1974 *Labor and Monopoly Capital: The Degradation of Work in the Twentieth Century.* New York: Monthly Review Press.

Breckinridge, Sophonisba

1921/1971 *New Homes for Old.* Montclair, N.J.: Patterson Smith.

Breiner, Peter

2005 "Weber's *The Protestant Ethic* as Hypothetical Narrative of Original Accumulation." *Journal of Classical Sociology* 5: 11–30.

Britton, Anne Camden

1979 "The Life and Thought of Marianne Weber." Master's thesis. San Francisco, Calif.: San Francisco State University.

Broschart, Kay

1991a "Beatrice Webb." In M. J. Deegan (ed.), *Women in Sociology: A Bio-Bibliographical Sourcebook.* Westport, Conn.: Greenwood Press: 425–431.

1991b "Ida B. Wells-Barnett." In M. J. Deegan (ed.), *Women in Sociology: A Bio-Bibliographical Sourcebook.* Westport, Conn.: Greenwood Press: 432–439.

Broschart, Kay Richards

2005 "Harriet Martineau and Beatrice Webb: A Comparison of Empirical Perspectives and Methods of Research." *Sociological Origins* 3:83–84.

Brown, Richard

2005 "Hermeneutics." In George Ritzer (ed.), *Encyclopedia of Social Theory.* Thousand Oaks, Calif.: Sage: 362–364.

Brubaker, Rogers

1984 *The Limits of Rationality: An Essay on the Social and Moral Thought of Max Weber.* London: George Allen and Unwin.

Brugger, Bill

1995 "Marxism, Asia, and the 1990s." *Positions* 3:630–641.

Bryant, Christopher G. A.

1985 *Positivism in Social Theory and Research.* New York: St. Martin's.

Buckley, Kerry W.

1989 *Mechanical Man: John Broadus Watson and the Beginnings of Behaviorism.* New York: Guilford Press.

Buffalohead, W. Roger

1996 "Reflections on Native American Cultural Rights and Resources." In Mary F. Rogers (ed.), *Multicultural Experiences, Multicultural Theories.* New York: McGraw-Hill: 154–156.

Bulmer, Martin

1984 *The Chicago School of Sociology: Institutionalization, Diversity, and the Rise of Sociological Research.* Chicago: University of Chicago Press.

1985 "The Chicago School of Sociology: What Made It a 'School'?" *The History of Sociology: An International Review* 5:62–77.

Bunzel, Dirk

2007 "Rational Legal Authority." In George Ritzer (ed.), *Encyclopedia of Sociology.* Oxford: Blackwell: 3805–3808.

Burawoy, Michael

1979 *Manufacturing Consent: Changes in the Labor Process under Monopoly Capitalism.* Chicago: University of Chicago Press.

Burger, Thomas
1976 *Max Weber's Theory of Concept Formation: History, Laws and Ideal Types.* Durham, N.C.: Duke University Press.
1977 "Talcott Parsons, the Problem of Order in Society, and the Program of an Analytical Sociology." *American Journal of Sociology* 83:320–334.
1993 "Weber's Sociology and Weber's Personality." *Theory and Society* 22:813–836.

Buttel, Frederick H. (ed.)
1990 "Symposium: Evolution and Social Change." *Sociological Forum* 5:153–212.

Buxton, William
1985 *Talcott Parsons and the Capitalist Nation-State: Political Sociology as a Strategic Vocation.* Toronto: University of Toronto Press.

Calhoun, Craig
1989 "Classical Social Theory and the French Revolution of 1848." *Sociological Theory* 7:210–225.

Calhoun, Craig, and Karaganis, Joseph
2001 "Critical Theory." In George Ritzer and Barry Smart (eds.), *Handbook of Social Theory.* London: Sage: 179–200.

Camic, Charles
1989 "Structure after 50 Years: The Anatomy of a Charter." *American Journal of Sociology* 95:38–107.
1990 "An Historical Prologue." *American Journal of Sociology* 55:313–319.

Camic, Charles (ed.)
1997 *Reclaiming the Sociological Classics: The State of Scholarship.* Oxford: Blackwell.

Campbell, Colin
2005 *Romantic Ethic and the Spirit of Modern Consumerism*. York: Alcuin Academics/Writers Printshop.

Campbell, J., and Pederson, O. K. (eds.)
2001 *The Rise of Neoliberalism and Institutional Analysis.* Princeton: Princeton University Press.

Canclini, Nestor Garcia
1995 *Hybrid Cultures: Strategies for Entering and Leaving Modernity.* Minneapolis: University of Minnesota Press.

Caplow, Theodore
1968 *Two against One: Coalition in Triads.* Englewood Cliffs, N.J.: Prentice Hall.

Carayannis, E. G., Ziemnowicz, C., and Spillan, J. E.
2007 "Economics and Joseph Schumpeter's Theory of Creative Destruction: Definition of Terms." In E. G. Carayannis and C. Ziemnowicz (eds.), *Rediscovering Schumpeter: Creative Destruction Evolving into "Mode 3."* New York, NY: Palgrave Macmillan: 23–45.

Carver, Terrell
1983 *Marx and Engels: The Intellectual Relationship.* Bloomington: Indiana University Press.

Castells, Manuel
1996 *The Rise of the Network Society, The Information Age: Economy, Society, and Culture,* Vol. I. Cambridge, Mass.: Blackwell.

Castillo, Juan Jose, and Castillo, Santiago
2004 "Los Webb de la democracia industrial a lo democracia politica." *Sociologia del Trabajo* 50:9–34.

Ceplair, Larry (ed.)
1991 *Charlotte Perkins Gilman: A Non-Fiction Reader.* New York: Columbia University Press.

Cerullo, John J.
1994 "The Epistemic Turn: Critical Sociology and the 'Generation of 68.'" *International Journal of Politics, Culture and Society* 8:169–181.

Chafetz, Janet Saltman
1997 "Feminist Theory and Sociology: Underutilized Contributions for Mainstream Theory." *Annual Review of Sociology* 23:97–190.

Chapoulie, Jean-Michel
1996 "Everett Hughes and the Chicago Tradition." *Sociological Theory* 14:3–29.

Charon, Joel
1995 *Symbolic Interaction: An Introduction, an Interpretation, an Integration.* 5th ed. Englewood Cliffs, N.J.: Prentice-Hall.
2000 *Symbolic Interaction: An Introduction, an Interpretation, an Integration.* 7th ed. Englewood Cliffs, N.J.: Prentice-Hall.

Chen, Hon-Fai
2004 "Self-Reference, Mutual Identification, and Affect." *Journal of Classical Sociology* 4:259–288.

Cherkaoui, Mohamed
2007 *Good Intentions: Max Weber and the Paradox of Unintended Consequences.* Oxford: The Bardwell Press.

Cherrington, Ruth
1997 "Generational Issues in China: A Case Study of the 1980s Generation of Young Intellectuals." *British Journal of Sociology* 48:302–320.

Chitnis, Anand C.
1976 *The Scottish Enlightenment: A Social History.* Totowa, N.J.: Rowman and Littlefield.

Chodorow, Nancy
1978 *The Reproduction of Mothering: Psychoanalysis and the Sociology of Gender.* Berkeley: University of California Press.
1999 *The Power of Feelings: Personal Meaning in Psychoanalysis, Gender and Culture.* London: Yale University Press.

Chriss, James J.
1993 "Durkheim's Cult of the Individual as Civil Religion: Its Appropriation by Erving Goffman." *Sociological Spectrum* 13:251–275.
2005a "Gouldner, Alvin." In George Ritzer (ed.), *Encyclopedia of Social Theory.* Thousand Oaks, Calif.: Sage: 340–342.

2005b "Mead, George Herbert." In George Ritzer (ed.), *Encyclopedia of Social Theory.* Thousand Oaks, Calif.: Sage: 486–491.
2006 "Giddings and the Social Mind." *Jouranl of Classical Sociology* 6:123–144.

Cladis, Mark Sydney
1992 *A Communitarian Defense of Liberalism: Emile Durkheim and Contemporary Social Theory.* Stanford, Calif.: Stanford University Press.

Clark, Brett and Bellamy Foster, John
2006 "Florence Kelley and the Struggle Against the Degradation of Life." *Organization and Environment* 19:251–263.

Cockerham, William C., Abel, Thomas and Luschen, Gunther
1993 "Max Weber, Formal Rationality, and Health Lifestyles." *Sociological Quarterly* 34:413–425.

Cohen, David
2001 *Chasing the Red, White, and Blue: A Journey in Tocqueville's Footsteps through Contemporary America.* New York: Picador.

Cohen, Ira
1981 "Introduction to the Transaction Edition." In M. Weber, *General Economic History.* New Brunswick, N.J.: Transaction Publishers: xv–lxxxiii.

Coleman, James
1986 "Social Theory, Social Research, and a Theory of Action." *American Journal of Sociology* 91:1309–1335.
1990 *Foundations of Social Theory.* Cambridge, Mass.: Belknap Press of Harvard University Press.

Collins, Patricia Hill
1990 *Black Feminist Thought: Knowledge, Consciousness and the Politics of Empowerment.* Boston: Unwin Hyman.
1998 *Fighting Words: Black Women and the Search for Justice.* Minneapolis: University of Minnesota Press.

Collins, Randall
1975 *Conflict Sociology: Toward an Explanatory Science.* New York: Academic Press.
1980 "Weber's Last Theory of Capitalism: A Systematization." *American Sociological Review* 45:925–942.
1981 "On the Microfoundations of Macrosociology." *American Journal of Sociology* 86:984–1014.
1985 *Weberian Sociological Theory.* Cambridge, Eng.: Cambridge University Press.
1989a "Sociology: Proscience or Antiscience?" *American Sociological Review* 54:124–139.
1989b "Toward a Neo-Meadian Sociology of Mind." *Symbolic Interaction* 12:1–32.
1990 "Conflict Theory and the Advance of Macro-Historical Sociology." In G. Ritzer (ed.), *Frontiers of Social Theory: The New Syntheses.* New York: Columbia University Press: 68–87.

Collins, Randall
1992 "Rediscovering Schumpeter." *Contemporary Sociology* 21:171–175.
1993 "Heroizing and Deheroizing Weber." *Theory and Society* 36:289–313.

1997a "An Asian Route to Capitalism: Religious Economy and the Origins of Self-Transforming Growth in Japan." *American Sociological Review* 62:843–865.

1997b "A Sociological Guilt Trip: Comment on Connell." *American Journal of Sociology* 102:1558–1564.

Collins, Randall, and Makowsky, Michael

1998 *The Discovery of Society,* 6th ed. New York: McGraw-Hill.

Comte, Auguste

1830–1842/1855 *The Positive Philosophy of Auguste Comte.* New York: Calvin Blanchard.

1851/1957 *A General View of Positivism.* New York: R. Speller.

1851/1968 *System of Positive Polity,* Vol. 1. New York: Burt Franklin.

1852/1968 *System of Positive Polity,* Vol. 2. New York: Burt Franklin.

1853/1968 *System of Positive Polity,* Vol. 3. New York: Burt Franklin.

1854/1968 *System of Positive Polity,* Vol. 4. New York: Burt Franklin.

1891/1973 *The Catechism of Positive Religion.* Clifton, N. J.: A. M. Kelley.

Connell, R. W.

1996 "Men and the Women's Movement." In Mary F. Rogers (ed.), *Multicultural Experiences, Multicultural Theories.* New York: McGraw-Hill: 409–415.

1997 "How Is Classical Theory Classical?" *American Journal of Sociology* 102:1511–1557.

Cook, Gary

1993 *George Herbert Mead: The Making of a Social Pragmatist.* Urbana: University of Illinois Press.

Cook, Karen, O'Brien, Jodi, and Kollock, Peter

1990 "Exchange Theory: A Blueprint for Structure and Process." In G. Ritzer (ed.), *Frontiers of Social Theory: The New Syntheses.* New York: Columbia University Press: 158–181.

Cook, Karen S., and Whitmeyer, J. M.

2000 "Richard Emerson." In George Ritzer (ed.), *The Blackwell Companion to Major Social Theorists.* Oxford, England, and Cambridge, Mass.: Blackwell: 486–512.

Cooper, Anna Julia

1892/1969 *A Voice from the South by a Black Woman from the South.* New York: Negro University Press.

1925/1988 "Equality of Races and the Democratic Movement." In Charles Lemert and Esme Bahn (eds.), *The Voice of Anna Julia Cooper.* Lanham, Md: Rowman and Littlefield: 291–298.

1925/1988 *Slavery and the French Revolutionists (1788–1805).* Frances Richardson Keller (trans.). Queenston, Ontario: Edwin-Mellen Press.

Cooper, Dereck

1991 "On the Concept of Alienation." *International Journal of Contemporary Sociology* 28:7–26.

Cortese, Anthony

1995 "The Rise, Hegemony, and Decline of the Chicago School of Sociology, 1892–1945." *Social Science Journal* 32:235–254.

Coser, Lewis

1956 *The Functions of Social Conflict.* New York: Free Press.

Coser, Lewis (ed.)
1965 *Georg Simmel.* Englewood Cliffs, N.J.: Prentice-Hall.

Costin, Lela
1983 *Two Sisters for Social Justice: A Biography of Edith and Grace Abbott.* Urbana: University of Illinois Press.

Cotterrell, Roger
1999 *Emile Durkheim: Law in a Moral Domain.* Stanford, Calif.: Stanford University Press.

Cottrell, Jr., Leonard S.
1980 "George Herbert Mead: The Legacy of Social Behaviorism." In R. K. Merton and M. W. Riley (eds.), *Sociological Traditions from Generation to Generation: Glimpses of the American Experience.* Norwood, N.J.: Ablex: 45–65.

Crippen, Timothy
1994 "Toward a Neo-Darwinian Sociology: Its Nomological Principles and Some Illustrative Applications." *Sociological Perspectives* 37:309–335.

Cronk, George
1987 *The Philosophical Anthropology of George Herbert Mead.* New York: Peter Lang.

Crook, Stephen
2001 "Social Theory and the Postmodern." In George Ritzer and Barry Smart (eds.), *Handbook of Social Theory.* London: Sage: 308–338.

Curtis, Bruce
1981 *William Graham Sumner.* Boston: Twayne.

Dahme, Heinz-Jurgen
1990 "On the Current Rediscovery of Georg Simmel's Sociology—A European Point of View." In M. Kaern, B. S. Phillips, and R. S. Cohen (eds.), *Georg Simmel and Contemporary Sociology.* Dordrecht, Netherlands: Kluwer: 13–37.

Dahms, Harry
1995 "From Creative Action to the Social Rationalization of the Economy: Joseph A. Schumpeter's Social Theory." *Sociological Theory* 13, 1:1–13.
1997 "Theory in Weberian Marxism: Patterns of Critical Social Theory in Lukács and Habermas." *Sociological Theory* 15:181–214.

Dahrendorf, Ralf
1959 *Class and Class Conflict in Industrial Society.* Stanford, Calif.: Stanford University Press.

Dandaneau, Steven
2007a "Marcuse, Herbert." In George Ritzer (ed.), *Encyclopedia of Sociology.* Oxford: Blackwell: 2759–2761.
2007b "Mills, C. Wright." In George Ritzer (ed.), *Encyclopedia of Sociology.* Oxford: Blackwell: 3050–3055.

Dant, Tim
1996 "Fetishism and the Social Value of Objects." *Sociological Review* 44:495–516.

Davies, Christie
1992 "The Protestant Ethic and the Comic Spirit of Capitalism." *British Journal of Sociology* 43:421–442.

Davis, Kingsley
1959 "The Myth of Functional Analysis as a Special Method in Sociology and Anthropology." *American Sociological Review* 24:757–772.

Dauder, Silvia Garcia
2008 "Annie Marion MacLean: "'The Mother of Contemporary Ethnography' and Pioneer in the Sociology of Distance Learning." *Athenae Digital* 13:237–246.

Dean, Mitchell
2001 "Michel Foucault: 'A Man in Danger.'" In George Ritzer and Barry Smart (eds.), *Handbook of Social Theory.* London: Sage: 324–338.

Deegan, Mary Jo
1988 *Jane Addams and the Men of the Chicago School 1892–1913.* New Brunswick, N.J.: Transaction Books.
2005 "Harriet Martineau and the Phenomenology of the Sickroom (1844)." *Sociological Origins* 3:86–92.
2008 "Harriet Martineau and the Sociology of Health: 'England and Her Soldiers' (1859) and 'Health, Husbandary, and Handicraft' (1881)." *Advances in Gender Research* 12:43–81.

Deegan, Mary Jo (ed.)
1991 *Women in Sociology: A Bio-Bibliographical Sourcebook.* Westport, Conn.: Greenwood Press.
2002a *The New Woman of Color: The Collected Writings of Fannie Barrier Williams, 1893–1918.* DeKalb, Ill.: Northern Illinois University Press.
2002b *Race, Hull-House, and the University of Chicago.* Westport, CT: Praeger.

Deegan, Mary Jo, and Rynbrandt, Linda
2002 "For God and Community: The Unitarian Female Ministers' Tradition and Chicago Sociology, 1892–1918." *Advances in Gender Research* 4:1–25.

Deflem, Matthieu
2003 "The Sociology of the Sociology of Money: Simmel and the Contemporary Battle of the Classics." *Journal of Classical Sociology* 3:67–96.

Delaney, Tim
2005a "Coser, Lewis." In George Ritzer (ed.), *Encyclopedia of Social Theory.* Thousand Oaks, Calif.: Sage: 155–157.
2005b "Sumner, William Graham." In George Ritzer (ed.), *Encyclopedia of Social Theory.* Thousand Oaks, Calif.: Sage: 814–815.

Delamont, Sarah
2003 *Feminist Sociology*. London: Sage Publications.

Delgado, R., and Stefancic, J.
2001 *Critical Race Theory: An Introduction*. New York: New York University Press.

Densimore, Dana
1973 "Independence from the Sexual Revolution." In A. Koedt et al. (eds.), *Radical Feminism.* New York: Quadrangle: 107–118.

Deutscher, Penelope
2004 "The Descent of Man and the Evolution of Woman." *Hypatia* 19:35–55.

Deutschmann, Christoph
1996 "Money as a Social Construction: On the Actuality of Marx and Simmel." *Thesis Eleven* 47:1–19.

Devereux, Edward C.

1961 "Parsons's Sociological Theory." In M. Black (ed.), *The Social Theories of Talcott Parsons.* Englewood Cliffs, N.J.: Prentice-Hall: 1–63.

Dickens, Peter

2005 "Social Darwinism." In George Ritzer (ed.), *Encyclopedia of Social Theory.* Thousand Oaks, Calif.: Sage: 729–731.

Dill, Jeffrey S.

2007 "Durkheim and Dewey and the Challenge of Contemporary Moral Education." Journal *of Moral Education* 36:221–237.

DiMaggio, Paul J., and Powell, Walter W.

1983 "The Iron Cage Revisited: Institutional Isomorphism and Collective Rationality in Organizational Fields." *American Sociological Review* 48:147–160.

DiMaggio, Paul J., and Powell, Walter W. (eds.)

1991 *The New Institutionalism in Organizational Analysis.* Chicago: University of Chicago Press.

Domhoff, G. William

2005 "Mills, C. Wright." In George Ritzer (ed.), *Encyclopedia of Social Theory.* Thousand Oaks, Calif.: Sage: 503–505.

Dorfman, Joseph

1966 *Thorstein Veblen and His America: With New Appendices.* New York: Augustus M. Kelley.

Douglas, Jack

1967 *The Social Meanings of Suicide.* Princeton, N.J.: Princeton University Press.

1980 "Introduction to the Sociologies of Everyday Life." In J. Douglas et al. (eds.), *Introduction to the Sociologies of Everyday Life.* Boston: Allyn and Bacon: 1–19.

Dowd, Douglas F.

1966 *Thorstein Veblen.* New York: Washington Square Press.

Drysdale, John

1996 "How Are Social-Scientific Concepts Formed? A Reconstruction of Max Weber's Theory of Concept Formation." *Sociological Theory* 14:71–88.

Du Bois, W.E.B.

1897/1995 "The Conservation of Races." In David Lewis Levering (ed.), *W.E.B. Du Bois: A Reader.* New York: Henry Holt and Co.: 20–27.

1898/1995 "The Negroes of Farmville, Virginia." In David Lewis Levering (ed.), *W.E.B. Du Bois: A Reader.* New York: Henry Holt and Co.: 231–236.

1899/1996 *The Philadelphia Negro: A Social Study.* Philadelphia: University of Pennsylvania Press.

1900/1995 "To the Nations of the World." In David Lewis Levering (ed.), *W.E.B. Du Bois: A Reader.* New York: Henry Holt and Co.: 639–641.

1903/1996 *The Souls of Black Folk.* New York: The Modern Library.

1904/1995 "The Parting of the Ways." In David Lewis Levering (ed.), *W.E.B. Du Bois: A Reader.* New York: Henry Holt and Co.: 329–332.

1915/1995 "The Negro Problems." In David Lewis Levering (ed.), *W.E.B. Du Bois: A Reader.* New York: Henry Holt and Co.: 48–53.

1920/1999 *Darkwater: Voices from Within the Veil.* Mineola, N.Y.: Dover.

1921/1995 "The Class Struggle." In David Lewis Levering (ed.), *W.E.B. Du Bois: A Reader.* New York: Henry Holt and Co.: 555–556.

1923/1995 "The Superior Race." In David Lewis Levering (ed.), *W.E.B. Du Bois: A Reader.* New York: Henry Holt and Co.: 470–477.

1926/1995a "Criteria of Negro Art." In David Lewis Levering (ed.), *W.E.B. Du Bois: A Reader.* New York: Henry Holt and Co.: 509–515.

1926/1995b "Russia, 1926." In David Lewis Levering (ed.), *W.E.B. Du Bois: A Reader.* New York: Henry Holt and Co.: 581–582.

1931/1995 "The Negro and Communism." In David Lewis Levering (ed.), *W.E.B. Du Bois: A Reader.* New York: Henry Holt and Co.: 583–593.

1933/1995a "The Negro College." In David Lewis Levering (ed.), *W.E.B. Du Bois: A Reader.* New York: Henry Holt and Co.: 69–75.

1933/1995b "Marxism and the Negro Problem." In David Lewis Levering (ed.), *W.E.B. Du Bois: A Reader.* New York: Henry Holt and Co.: 538–544.

1934/1995 "Segregation." In David Lewis Levering (ed.), *W.E.B. Du Bois: A Reader.* New York: Henry Holt and Co.: 557–558.

1935/1998 *Black Reconstruction in America: 1860–1880.* New York: Free Press.

1936/1995a "A Negro Nation Within the Nation" In David Lewis Levering (ed.), *W.E.B. Du Bois: A Reader.* New York: Henry Holt and Co.: 563–570.

1936/1995b "The Present Plight of the German Jew." In David Lewis Levering (ed.), *W.E.B. Du Bois: A Reader.* New York: Henry Holt and Co.: 81–82.

1937/1995 "Japanese Colonialism." In David Lewis Levering (ed.), *W.E.B. Du Bois: A Reader.* New York: Henry Holt and Co.: 83–84.

1940/1968 *Dusk of Dawn: An Essay Toward an Autobiography of a Race Concept.* New York: Schocken Books.

1940/1995 "Apology." In David Lewis Levering (ed.), *W.E.B. Du Bois: A Reader.* New York: Henry Holt and Co.: 215–217.

1944/1995 "My Evolving Program for Negro Freedom." In David Lewis Levering (ed.), *W.E.B. Du Bois: A Reader.* New York: Henry Holt and Co.: 610–618.

1945/1995 "Japan, Color, and Afro-Americans." In David Lewis Levering (ed.), *W.E.B. Du Bois: A Reader.* New York: Henry Holt and Co.: 86–87.

1947/1995 "Behold the Land." In David Lewis Levering (ed.), *W.E.B. Du Bois: A Reader.* New York: Henry Holt and Co.: 545–550.

1948/1995 "The Talented Tenth: Memorial Address." In David Lewis Levering (ed.), *W.E.B. Du Bois: A Reader.* New York: Henry Holt and Co.: 347–353.

1951/1995 "'There Must Come a Vast Social Change in the United States'." In David Lewis Levering (ed.), *W.E.B. Du Bois: A Reader.* New York: Henry Holt and Co.: 619–621.

1953/1995 "On Stalin." In David Lewis Levering (ed.), *W.E.B. Du Bois: A Reader.* New York: Henry Holt and Co.: 796–797.

1957/1995 "The Present Leadership of American Negroes." In David Lewis Levering (ed.), *W.E.B. Du Bois: A Reader.* New York: Henry Holt and Co.: 354–357.

1958/1995 "A Vista of Ninety Fruitful Years." In David Lewis Levering (ed.), *W.E.B. Du Bois: A Reader.* New York: Henry Holt and Co.: 143–147.

1961/1995 "Application for Membership in the Communist Party of the United States of America." In David Lewis Levering (ed.), *W.E.B. Du Bois: A Reader.* New York: Henry Holt and Co.: 631–633.

1968 *The Autobiography of W.E.B. Du Bois: A Soliloquy on Viewing My Life from the Last Decade of Its First Century.* New York: International Publishers.

Durkheim, Emile
1885/1978 "Review of Albert Schaeffle, *Bau und Leben des Sozialen Korpers: Erster Band.*" In Mark Traugott (ed.), *Emile Durkheim on Institutional Analysis.* Chicago: University of Chicago Press: 93–114.
1887/1993 *Ethics and the Sociology of Morals.* Buffalo: Prometheus Books.
1892/1997 *Montesquieu: Quid Secundatus Politicae Scientiae Instituendae Contulerit.* Oxford: Durkheim Press.
1893/1964 *The Division of Labor in Society.* New York: Free Press.
1895/1962 *The Rules of the Sociological Method.* New York: Free Press of Glencoe.
1895/1982 *The Rules of the Sociological Method.* New York: Free Press.
1897/1951 *Suicide.* New York: Free Press.
1898/1974 "Individual and Collective Representations." In E. Durkheim, *Sociology and Philosophy.* New York: Free Press: 1–34.
1900/1973a "Individualism and the Intellectuals." In R. Bellah (ed.), *Emile Durkheim: On Morality and Society.* Chicago: University of Chicago Press: 43–57.
1900/1973b "Sociology in France in the Nineteenth Century." In R. Bellah (ed.), *Emile Durkheim: On Morality and Society.* Chicago: University of Chicago Press: 3–32.
1906/1974 "Determination of Moral Facts." In E. Durkheim, *Sociology and Philosophy.* New York: Free Press: 35–62.
1912/1965 *The Elementary Forms of Religious Life.* New York: Free Press.
1914/1973 "The Dualism of Human Nature and Its Social Condition." In R. Bellah (ed.), *Emile Durkheim.* Chicago: University of Chicago Press: 149–163.
1922/1956 *Education and Sociology.* New York: Free Press.
1925/1961 *Moral Education: A Study in the Theory and Application of the Sociology of Education.* New York: Free Press.
1928/1962 *Socialism.* New York: Collier Books.
1938/1977 *The Evolution of Educational Thought.* London: Routledge and Kegan Paul.
1979 "Durkheim's Review of Georg Simmel's *Philosophie des Geldes.*" *Social Research* 46:321–328.

Durkheim, Emile, and Mauss, Marcel
1903/1963 *Primitive Classification.* Chicago: University of Chicago Press.

Dürrschmidt, Jorg
2005 "Scheler, Max." In George Ritzer (ed.), *Encyclopedia of Social Theory.* Thousand Oaks, Calif.: Sage: 672–673.

Eberts, Paul R., and Witton, Ronald A.
1970 "Recall from Anecdote: Alexis de Tocqueville and the Morphogenesis of America." *American Sociological Review* 35:1081–1097.

Edmunds, J., and Turner, B.
2002 *Generations, Culture and Society.* Open University Press.

Edwards, Jane
2007 "'Marriage is Sacred': The Religious Right's Arguments Against 'Gay Marriage' in Australia." *Culture Health and Sexuality* 9:247–261.

Ehrenreich, Barbara
2001 *Nickled and Dimed: On Not Getting By in America.* New York: Henry Holt.

Eisen, Arnold
1978 "The Meanings and Confusions of Weberian 'Rationality.'" *British Journal of Sociology* 29:57–70.

Eisenberg, Andrew

1998 "Weberian Patrimonialism and Imperial Chinese History." *Theory and Society* 27:83–102.

Eisenberg, Anne F.

2007 "Habitus/Field." In George Ritzer (ed.), *Encyclopedia of Sociology.* Oxford: Blackwell: 2045–2046.

Ekberg, Merryn

2007 "The Parameters of the Risk Society—A Review and Exploration." *Current Sociology* 55:343–366.

Eliaeson, Sven

2000 "Constitutional Caesarism: Weber's Politics in Their German Context." In S. Turner (ed.), *The Cambridge Companion to Weber.* Cambridge: Cambridge University Press: 131–150.

Elias, Norbert

1939/1994 *The Civilizing Process.* Oxford: Blackwell.

Elliott, Anthony

1992 *Social Theory and Psychoanalysis in Transition: Self and Society from Freud to Kristeva.* Oxford, England and Cambridge, Mass.: Blackwell.

Elshtain, Jean Bethke

2001 "Jane Addams and the Social Claim." *Public Interest* 145:82–92.

2002 *Jane Addams and the Dream of American Democracy.* New York: Basic Books.

2008 "Peace, Order, Justice: Competing Understandings." *Millenium: Journal of International Studies* 36:413–423.

Elshtain, Jean Bethke (ed.)

2002 *The Jane Addams Reader.* New York: Basic Books.

Emerson, Richard M.

1981 "Social Exchange Theory." In M. Rosenberg and R. H. Turner (eds.), *Social Psychology: Sociological Perspectives.* New York: Basic Books: 30–65.

Emirbayer, Mustafa

1996 "Useful Durkheim." *Sociological Theory* 14:109–130.

1997 "Manifesto for a Relational Sociology." *American Journal of Sociology* 103:281–317.

Engels, Friedrich

1884/1970 *The Origins of the Family, Private Property and the State.* New York: International.

Engerman, Stanley

2000 "Max Weber as Economist and Economic Historian." In Stephen Turner (ed.), *The Cambridge Companion to Weber.* Cambridge, Eng.: Cambridge University Press: 256–271.

Eriksson, Bjorn

1993 "The First Formulation of Sociology: A Discursive Innovation of the 18th Century." *Archives of European Sociology* 34:251–276.

Etzkorn, K. Peter (ed.)

1968 *Georg Simmel: The Conflict in Modern Culture and Other Essays.* New York: Teachers College Press, Columbia University.

Etzrodt, Christian
2008 "The Foundation of an Interpretive Sociology: A Critical Review of the Attempts of George H. Mead and Alfred Schutz." *Human Studies* 31:157–177.

Evans, Sara
1980 *Personal Politics: The Roots of the Women's Liberation Movement in the Civil Rights Movement and the New Left.* New York: Vintage.

Faghirzadeh, Saleh
1982 *Sociology of Sociology: In Search of . . . Ibn-Khaldun's Sociology Then and Now.* Teheran: Soroush Press.

Faia, Michael A.
1986 *Dynamic Functionalism: Strategy and Tactics.* Cambridge, Eng.: Cambridge University Press.

Faris, R.E.L.
1970 *Chicago Sociology: 1920–1932.* Chicago: University of Chicago Press.

Farrell, Chad R.
1997 "Durkheim, Moral Individualism and the Dreyfus Affair." *Current Perspectives in Social Theory* 17:313–330.

Fauconnet, Paul
1922/1958. "Introduction to the Original Edition." In E. Durkheim, *Education and Sociology.* New York: Free Press: 27–57.

Featherstone, Mike
1991 "Georg Simmel: An Introduction." *Theory, Culture and Society* 8:1–16.

Femia, Joseph
1995 "Pareto's Concept of Demagogic Plutocracy." *Government and Opposition* 30:370–392.

Fenton, Steve
1984 *Durkheim and Modern Sociology.* Cambridge, Eng.: Cambridge University Press.

Ferguson, Harvie
2001 "Phenomenology and Social Theory." In George Ritzer and Barry Smart (eds.), *Handbook of Social Theory.* London: Sage: 232–248.

Ferguson, Kathy E.
1980 *Self, Society and Womankind: The Dialectic of Liberation.* Westport, Conn.: Greenwood Press.

Ferry, Luc, and Renaut, Alain
1985/1990 *French Philosophy of the Sixties: An Essay on Antihumanism.* Amherst: University of Massachusetts Press.

Fine, Gary Alan, and Manning, Philip
2000 "Erving Goffman." In George Ritzer (ed.), *The Blackwell Companion to Major Social Theorists.* Malden, Mass.: Blackwell.

Fine, William F.
1979 *Progressive Evolutionism and American Sociology, 1890–1920.* UMI Research Press (*n.p.*).

Fischer, Norman
1984 "Hegelian Marxism and Ethics." *Canadian Journal of Political and Social Theory* 8:112–138.

Fish, Virginia Kemp
1981 "Annie Marion MacLean: A Neglected Part of the Chicago School." *Journal of the History of Sociology* 3:43–62.
1985 "Hull House: Pioneer in Urban Research During Its Creative Years." *Journal of the History of Sociology* 6:1:33–54.

Fitzpatrick, Ellen
1990 *Endless Crusade: Women Social Scientists and Progressive Reform.* New York: Oxford University Press.

Foley, Michael W., and Edwards, Bob (eds.)
1998 "Beyond Tocqueville: Civil Society and Social Capital in Comparative Perspective." *American Behavioral Scientist* 42: entire issue.

Fontana, Andrea
2005 "Sociologies of Everyday Life." In George Ritzer (ed.), *Encyclopedia of Social Theory.* Thousand Oaks, Calif.: Sage: 773–775.

Form, William
2007 "Memories of C. Wright Mills—Social Structure and Biography." *Work and Occupations* 34:148–173.

Forte, James
2003 "Applied Symbolic Interactionism: Meanings, Memberships, and Social Work." In Larry T. Reynolds and Nancy J. Herman-Kinney (eds.), *Handbook of Symbolic Interactionism.* Walnut Creek, Calif.: AltaMira Press: 915–936.

Foster, John B.
2000 *Marx's Ecology: Materialism and Nature.* New York: Monthly Review Press.

Foucault, Michel
1965 *Madness and Civilization: A History of Insanity in the Age of Reason.* New York: Vintage.
1979 *Discipline and Punish: The Birth of the Prison.* New York: Vintage.
1980a *The History of Sexuality.* Vol. 1, *An Introduction.* New York: Vintage.
1980b "Questions on Geography." In C. Gordon (ed.), *Power/Knowledge: Selected Interviews and Other Writings, 1972–1977.* New York: Pantheon: 63–77.
1986 "Of Other Spaces." *Diacritics* 16:22–27.

Fox, Renee C.
1997 "Talcott Parsons, My Teacher." *American Scholar* 66:395–410.

Francis, M.
2007 *Herbert Spencer and the Invention of Modern Life*. Stockfield: Acumen Publishing.

Frank, R. I.
1976 Translator's Introduction to Max Weber, *The Agrarian Sociology of Ancient Civilizations.* London: NLB: 7–33.

Franklin, Adrian
2007 "Posthumanism." In George Ritzer (ed.), *Encyclopedia of Sociology*. Oxford: Blackwell: 3548–3550.

Fraser, Nancy

1989 *Unruly Practices: Power, Discourse and Gender in Contemporary Social Theory.* Minneapolis: University of Minnesota Press.

Freeman, C. Robert

1980 "Phenomenological Sociology and Ethnomethodology." In J. D. Douglas et al. (eds.), *Introduction to the Sociologies of Everyday Life.* Boston: Allyn and Bacon: 113–154.

Freund, Julian

1968 *The Sociology of Max Weber.* New York: Vintage.

Friedman, Thomas

2000 *The Lexus and the Olive Tree: Understanding Globalization*. New York: Anchor Books.

2005 *The World Is Flat: A Brief History of the Twenty-First Century.* New York: Farrar, Straus, Reese, and Giroux.

Friedrichs, Robert

1970 *A Sociology of Sociology.* New York: Free Press.

1972 "Dialectical Sociology: Toward a Resolution of Current 'Crises' in Western Sociology." *British Journal of Sociology* 13:263–274.

Frisby, David

1981 *Sociological Impressionism: A Reassessment of Georg Simmel's Social Theory.* London: Heinemann.

1984 *Georg Simmel.* Chichester, Eng.: Ellis Horwood.

1992 *Simmel and Since: Essays on Georg Simmel's Social Theory.* London: Routledge.

Frisby, David (ed.)

1994 *Georg Simmel: Critical Assessments.* 3 vols. London: Routledge.

Fuhrman, Ellsworth R.

1980 *The Sociology of Knowledge in America: 1883–1915.* Charlottesville: University Press of Virginia.

Fulbrook, Mary

1978 "Max Weber's 'Interpretive Sociology.'" *British Journal of Sociology* 29:71–82.

Gadamer, Hans Georg

1989 *Truth and Method.* 2nd rev. ed. New York: Crossroad.

Gandy, D. Ross

1979 *Marx and History: From Primitive Society to the Communist Future.* Austin: University of Texas Press.

Gane, Mike

1988 *On Durkheim's Rules of the Sociological Method.* London: Routledge.

2001 "Durkheim's Project for a Sociological Science." In George Ritzer and Barry Smart (eds.), *Handbook of Social Theory.* London: Sage: 79–88.

2003 *French Social Theory.* London: Sage.

Gane, Mike (ed.)

1992 *The Radical Sociology of Durkheim and Mauss.* London: Routledge.

Gane, Nicholas

1997 "Max Weber on the Ethical Irrationality of Political Leadership." *Sociology* 31:549–564.

Gannett, Jr., Robert T.
2003 *Tocqueville Unveiled: The Historian and His Sources for* The Old Regime and the Revolution. Chicago: University of Chicago Press.

Ganobcsik-Williams, Lisa
1999 "The Intellectualism of Charlotte Perkins Gilman: Evolutionary Perspectives on Race, Ethnicity, and Class," In *Charlotte Perkins Gilman: Optimist Reformer,* edited by Jill Rudd and Val Gough, University of Iowa Press, 1999, pp. 16–41.

Garland, Anne Witte
1988 *Women Activists: Challenging the Abuse of Power.* New York: Feminist Press.

Gaziano, Emanuel
1996 "Ecological Metaphors as Scientific Boundary Work: Innovation and Authority in Interwar Sociology and Biology." *American Journal of Sociology* 101: 874–907.

Gellner, David
1982 "Max Weber, Capitalism and the Religion of India." *Sociology* 16:526–543.

Geras, Norman
1983 *Marx and Human Nature: Refutation of a Legend.* London: NLB.

Gerstein, Dean R.
1983 "Durkeim's Paradigm: Reconstructing a Social Theory." *Sociological Theory* 1:234–258.

Gerth, Hans, and Mills, C. Wright
1953 *Character and Social Structure.* New York: Harcourt, Brace and World.

Gerth, Hans, and Mills, C. Wright (eds.)
1958 *From Max Weber.* New York: Oxford University Press.

Gerth, Nobuko
1993 "Hans H. Gerth and C. Wright Mills: Partnership and Partisanship." *International Journal of Politics, Culture and Society* 7:133–154.

Gibbs, Jack P.
2003 "A Formal Restatement of Durkheim's 'Division of Labor' Theory." *Sociological Theory* 21:103–127.

Giddens, Anthony
1972 "Introduction: Durkheim's Writings in Sociology and Social Philosophy." In A. Giddens (ed.), *Emile Durkheim: Selected Writings.* Cambridge, Eng.: Cambridge University Press: 1–50.
1984 *The Constitution of Society: Outline of the Theory of Structuration.* Berkeley: University of California Press.
1990 *The Consequences of Modernity.* Stanford, Calif.: Stanford University Press.
1991 *Modernity and Self-Identity: Self and Society in the Late Modern Age.* Stanford, Calif.: Stanford University Press.
1992 *The Transformation of Intimacy: Sexuality, Love and Eroticism in Modern Societies.* Stanford, Calif.: Stanford University Press.
2000 *Runaway World: How Globalization Is Reshaping Our Lives.* New York: Routledge.

Giddings, Paula
1984 *When and Where I Enter: The Impact of Black Women on Race and Sex in America.* New York: William Morrow.

Gilbert, Margaret
1994 "Durkheim and Social Facts." In W.S.F. Pickering and H. Martins (eds.), *Debating Durkheim.* London: Routledge: 86–109.

Gil-Juarez, Adriana
2008 "Claiming a Political Ethics for Consuption: Florence Kelley and the Consumers' League." *Athenae Digital* 13:311–316.

Gilman, Charlotte Perkins
1892/1973 *The Yellow Wall-Paper.* New York: Feminist Press.
1898/1966 *Women and Economics: A Study of the Economic Relation between Men and Women as a Factor in Social Evolution.* New York: Harper and Row.
1900 *Concerning Children.* Boston: Small and Maynard.
1903 *The Home: Its Work and Influences.* New York: Macmillan.
1904 *Human Work.* New York: McClure and Phillips.
1911 *The Man-Made World.* London: Fisher Unwin.
1923 *His Religion and Hers: A Study of the Faith of Our Fathers and the Work of Our Mothers.* New York: Century.

Glatzer, Wolfgang
1998 "The German Sociological Association: Origins and Developments." Paper presented at the meetings of the International Sociological Association, Montreal, Canada.

Glass, Kathy L.
2005 Ending the Roots: Anna Julia Cooper's Sociolopolitical Thought and Activism." *Meridians: Feminism, Race, and Transnationalism.* 6:23–55.

Glyn, Andrew
2006 *Capitalism Unleashed: Finance, Globalization, and Welfare*. New York, NY: Oxford University Press.

Goffman, Erving
1959 *Presentation of Self in Everyday Life.* Garden City, N.Y.: Anchor.

Goldberg, Chad A.
2008 "Introduction to Emile Durkheim's 'Anti Semitism and Social Crisis.'" *Australian and New Zealand Journal of Criminology* 41:333–344.

Goldberg, Chad Alan
2001 "Social Citizenship and a Reconstructed Tocqueville." *American Sociological Review* 66:289–315.

Goldman, Harvey
1993 "Contemporary Sociology and the Interpretation of Weber." *Theory and Society* 22:853–860.
1994 "From Social Theory to Sociology of Knowledge and Back: Karl Mannheim and the Sociology of Intellectual Knowledge Production." *Sociological Theory* 12:266–278.

Gordon, Linda
1994 *Pitied but Not Entitled: Single Mothers and the History of Welfare.* New York: Free Press.

Gorman, Robert A.
1975a "Alfred Schutz: An Exposition and Critique." *British Journal of Sociology* 26:1–19.
1975b "The Phenomenological 'Humanization' of Social Science: A Critique." *British Journal of Sociology* 26:389–405.

1977 *The Dual Vision: Alfred Schutz and the Myth of Phenomenological Social Science.* London: Routledge and Kegan Paul.

Gouldner, Alvin

1958 "Introduction." In E. Durkheim, *Socialism and Saint-Simon.* Yellow Springs, Ohio: Antioch Press.

1959/1967 "Reciprocity and Autonomy in Functional Theory." In N. Demerath and R. Peterson (eds.), *System, Change and Conflict.* New York: Free Press: 141–169.

1962 "Introduction." In E. Durkheim, *Socialism.* New York: Collier Books: 7–31.

1970 *The Coming Crisis of Western Sociology.* New York: Basic Books.

Graham, Keith

1992 *Karl Marx, Our Contemporary.* Toronto: University of Toronto Press.

Grant, Linda, Stalp, Marybeth C., and Ward, Kathryn B.

2002 "Women's Sociological Research and Writing in the AJS in the Pre-World War II Era." *American Sociologist* 33:69–91.

Grathoff, Richard (ed.)

1978 *The Theory of Social Action: The Correspondence of Alfred Schutz and Talcott Parsons.* Bloomington: Indiana University Press.

Gronow, Jukka

1997 *The Sociology of Taste.* London: Routledge.

Gross, Matthias

2009 "Collaborative Experiments: Jane Addams, Hull House and Experimental Social Work." *Social Science Information* 48:81–95.

Gurney, Patrick J.

1981 "Historical Origins of Ideological Denial: The Case of Marx in American Sociology." *American Sociologist* 16:196–201.

Habermas, Jurgen

1981 "Modernity versus Postmodernity." *New German Critique* 22:3–14.

1984 *The Theory of Communicative Action.* Vol. 1, *Reason and the Rationalization of Society.* Boston: Beacon Press.

1987a *The Theory of Communicative Action.* Vol. 2, *Lifeworld and System: A Critique of Functionalist Reason.* Boston: Beacon Press.

1987b *The Philosophical Discourse of Modernity: Twelve Lectures.* Cambridge, Mass.: MIT Press.

Hackett, Amy

1976 "Feminism and Liberalism in Wilhelmine Germany 1890–1918." In B. Carroll (ed.), *Liberating Woman's History.* Urbana: University of Illinois Press: 127–136.

Hadari, Saguiv

1989 *Theory in Practice: Tocqueville's New Science of Politics.* Stanford, Calif.: Stanford University Press.

Haines, Valerie

1988 "Is Spencer's Theory an Evolutionary Theory?" *American Journal of Sociology* 93:1200–1223.

1992 "Spencer's Philosophy of Science." *British Journal of Sociology* 43:155–172.

1997 "Spencer and His Critics." In Charles Camic (ed.), *Reclaiming the Sociological Classics: The State of the Scholarship.* Malden, Mass.: Blackwell.

2005 "Spencer, Herbert." In George Ritzer (ed.), *Encyclopedia of Social Theory.* Thousand Oaks, Calif.: Sage: 781–787.

Halfpenny, Peter

1982 *Positivism and Sociology: Explaining Social Life.* London: Allen and Unwin.

2001 "Positivism in the Twentieth Century." In George Ritzer and Barry Smart (eds.), *Handbook of Social Theory.* London: Sage: 371–385.

2005 "Positivism." In George Ritzer (ed.), *Encyclopedia of Social Theory.* Thousand Oaks, Calif.: Sage: 571–575.

Halas, Elzbieta

2005 "Znaniecki, Florian Witold." In George Ritzer (ed.), *Encyclopedia of Social Theory.* Thousand Oaks, Calif.: Sage: 896–898.

Hall, John R.

2007 "Schutz, Alfred (1899–1959)." In George Ritzer (ed.), *Encyclopedia of Sociology.* Malden, MA: Blackwell: 4061–4064.

Hall, Robert T.

1987 *Emile Durkheim: Ethics and the Sociology of Morals.* New York: Greenwood Press.

Hallett, Tim and Greg Jeffers

2008 "A Long-Neglected Mother of Contemporary Ethnography." *Journal of Contemporary Ethnography* 37:3–37.

Halls, W. D.

1996 "The Cultural and Educational Influences of Durkheim, 1900–1945." *Durkheimian Studies* 2:122–132.

Halton, Eugene

2005 "Pragmatism." In George Ritzer (ed.), *Encyclopedia of Social Theory.* Thousand Oaks, Calif.: Sage: 595–599.

Hamlin, Cynthia L., and Brym, Robert J.

2006 "Return of the Native: A Cultural and Social Psychological Critique of Durkheim's *Suicide* Based on the Guarani-Kaiowa of Southwestern Brazil." *Sociological Theory* 24:42–57.

Hannerz, Ulf

1987 "The World in Creolisation." *Africa* 57:546–559.

Hardt, Michael, and Negri, Antonio

2000 *Empire.* Cambridge, Mass.: Harvard University Press.

2004 *Multitude: War and Democracy in the Age of Empire.* New York: Penguin.

Harley, Sharon

1978 "Anna J. Cooper: A Voice for Black Women." In S. Harley and R. Terborg-Penn (eds.), *The Afro-American Woman: Struggles and Images.* Port Washington, N.Y.: Kennikat Press.

1990 *The Condition of Postmodernity: An Inquiry into the Origins of Cultural Change.* Malden, MA: Blackwell.

Harvey, David

2000 *Spaces of Hope.* Berkeley: University of California Press.

2005 *A Brief History of NeoLiberalism.* Oxford: Oxford University Press.

Hawthorn, Geoffrey

1976 *Enlightenment and Despair.* Cambridge, Eng.: Cambridge University Press.

Hayden, Tom
2006 *Radical Nomad: C. Wright Mills and His Times.* Boulder, CO: Paradigm Publishers.

Heap, James L., and Roth, Phillip A.
1973 "On Phenomenological Sociology." *American Sociological Review* 38:354–367.

Heberle, Rudolph
1965 "Simmel's Methods." In L. Coser (ed.), *Georg Simmel.* Englewood Cliffs, N.J.: Prentice-Hall: 116–121.

Heckathorn, Douglas D.
2005 "Rational Choice." In George Ritzer (ed.), *Encyclopedia of Social Theory.* Thousand Oaks, Calif.: Sage: 620–624.

Hegel, G.W.F.
1807/1967 *The Phenomenology of Mind.* New York: Harper Colophon.
1821/1967 *The Philosophy of Right.* Oxford: Clarendon Press.

Heilbron, Johan
1990 "Auguste Comte and Epistemology." *Sociological Theory* 8:153–162.
1995 *The Rise of Social Theory.* London: Polity.

Heins, Volker
1993 "Weber's Ethic and the Spirit of Anti-Capitalism." *Political Studies* 41:269–283.

Hekman, Susan
1983 *Weber, the Ideal Type, and Contemporary Social Theory.* Notre Dame, Ind.: University of Notre Dame Press.

Helle, Horst Jurgen
2005 "Simmel, Georg." In George Ritzer (ed.), *Encyclopedia of Social Theory.* Thousand Oaks, Calif.: Sage: 698–703.

Hennis, Wilhelm
1994 "The Meaning of *'Wertfreiheit':* On the Background and Motives of Max Weber's 'Postulate.'" *Sociological Theory* 12:113–125.

Hereth, Michael
2003 *Alexis de Tocqueville: Threats to Freedom in Democracy.* Durham, N.C.: Duke University Press.

Heritage, John
1984 *Garfinkel and Ethnomethodology.* Cambridge, Eng.: Polity Press.

Herva, Soma
1988 "The Genesis of Max Weber's *Verstehende Sociologie.*" *Acta Sociologica* 31:143–156.

Hewitt, John P.
1984 *Self and Society: A Symbolic Interactionist Social Psychology.* 3rd ed. Boston: Allyn and Bacon.

Hewitt, Regina
2008 "Identities and Involutes: Some Reflections on Narrative Ethics." *Studies in Symbolic Interaction* 30:105–130.

Heyl, John D., and Heyl, Barbara S.
1976 "The Sumner-Porter Controversy at Yale: Pre-Paradigmatic Sociology and Institutional Crisis." *Sociological Inquiry* 46:41–49.

Hiatt, L. R.
1996 *Arguments about Aborigines: Australia and the Evolution of Social Anthropology.* Cambridge, Eng.: Cambridge University Press.

Hilbert, Richard A.
1986 "Anomie and Moral Regulation of Reality: The Durkheimian Tradition in Modern Relief." *Sociological Theory* 4:1–19.

Hill, Forrest
1958 "Veblen and Marx." In Douglas F. Dowd (ed.), *Thorstein Veblen: A Critical Reappraisal.* Ithaca, N.Y.: Cornell University: 129–149.

Hill, Lisa
1996 "Anticipations of Nineteenth and Twentieth Century Social Thought in the Work of Adam Ferguson." *Archives Europeenes de Sociologie* 37:203–228.

Hill, Michael R.
1989 "Empiricism and Reason in Harriet Martineau's Sociology." Introduction to M. Hill (ed.), *How to Observe Morals and Manners* by Harriet Martineau. New Brunswick, N.J.: Transaction Books.
2005 "Sociological Thought Experiments: Five Examples from the History of Sociology." *Sociological Origins* 3:3–19.
2007 "Ward, Lester Frank." In George Ritzer (ed.), *Encyclopedia of Sociology.* Oxford: Backwell: 5216.

Hill, Michael R., and Deegan, Mary Jo
2004 "Introduction: Charlotte Perkins Gilman's Sociological Perspective on Ethics and Society." In Michael R. Hill and Mary Jo Deegan (eds.), *Social Ethics: Sociology and the Future of Society.* Westport, Conn.: Greenwood Press: i–ix.

Hill, Michael R., and Hoecker-Drysdale, Susan
2000 *Harriet Martineau: Theoretical and Methodological Perspectives.* New York: Garland.

Hill, Michael R., and Hoecker-Drysdale, Susan (eds.)
2001 *Harriet Martineau: Theoretical and Methodological Perspectives.* New York: Routledge.

Hinkle, Roscoe
1963 "Antecedents of the Action Orientation in American Sociology before 1935." *American Sociological Review* 28:705–715.
1980 *Founding Theory of American Sociology: 1881–1915.* London: Routledge and Kegan Paul.
1994 *Developments in American Sociological Theory, 1915–1950.* Albany: State University of New York Press.

Hinkle, Roscoe, and Hinkle, Gisela
1954 *The Development of American Sociology.* New York: Random House.

Ho, Wing-Chung
2008 "The Transcendence and Non-Discursivity of the Lifeworld." *Human Studies* 31:323–342.

Hoecker-Drysdale, Susan
1994 *Harriet Martineau: First Woman Sociologist.* New York: Berg.
2000 "Harriet Martineau." In George Ritzer (ed.), *The Blackwell Companion to Major Social Theorists.* Malden, Mass.: Blackwell: 53–80.

2002 "Harriet Martineau: The Theory and Practice of Early Critical Social Research." In M. A. Romano (ed.), *Lost Sociologists Rediscovered.* Lewiston, New York: Edwin Mellen: 67–98.

2005 "The 'Nobleness of Labor' and the Instinct of Workmanship: Gender, Work, and Class in Harriet Martineau and Thorstein Veblen." *Sociological Origins*: 3:81–82.

Hofstadter, Richard

1959 *Social Darwinism in American Thought.* New York: Braziller.

Holmwood, John, and Stewart, Alexander

1994 "Synthesis and Fragmentation in Social Theory: A Progressive Solution." *Sociological Theory* 12:83–100.

Holton, Robert J.

2001 "Talcott Parsons: Conservative Apologist or Irreplaceable Icon?" In George Ritzer and Barry Smart (eds.), *Handbook of Social Theory.* London: Sage: 152–162.

Holton, Robert J., and Turner, Bryan S.

1986 "Reading Talcott Parsons: Introductory Remarks." In R. J. Holton and B. S. Turner (eds.), *Talcott Parsons on Economy and Society.* London: Routledge and Kegan Paul: 1–24.

Homans, George, and Curtis, Charles

1934 *An Introduction to Pareto, His Sociology.* New York: Knopf.

Homans, George C.

1961 *Social Behavior: Its Elementary Forms.* New York: Harcourt, Brace and World.

1962 *Sentiments and Activities.* New York: Free Press.

1984 *Coming to My Senses: The Autobiography of a Sociologist.* New Brunswick, N.J.: Transaction Books.

Hook, Sidney

1965 "Pareto's Sociological System." In J. H. Meisel (ed.), *Pareto and Mosca.* Englewood Cliffs, N.J.: Prentice-Hall: 57–61.

Horowitz, Irving L.

1962/1967 "Consensus, Conflict, and Cooperation." In N. Demerath and R. Peterson (eds.), *System, Change and Conflict.* New York: Free Press: 265–279.

1983 *C. Wright Mills: An American Utopian.* New York: Free Press.

Howard, Michael C., and King, John E.

2005 "Political Economy." In George Ritzer (ed.), *Encyclopedia of Social Theory.* Thousand Oaks, Calif.: Sage: 563–568.

Huaco, George

1986 "Ideology and General Theory: The Case of Sociological Functionalism." *Comparative Studies in Society and History* 28:34–54.

Hudelson, Richard

1993 "Has History Refuted Marxism?" *Philosophy of the Social Sciences* 23:180–198.

Hughes, John A., Martin, Peter J., and Sharrock, W. W.

1995 *Understanding Classical Sociology: Marx, Weber and Durkheim.* London: Sage.

Humphery, Kim

1998 *Shelf Life: Supermarkets and the Changing Cultures of Consumption.* Cambridge, Eng.: Cambridge University Press.

Huntington, Samuel P.
1996 *The Clash of Civilizations and the Remaking of World Order*. New York: Simon and Schuster.

Israel, Joachim
1971 *Alienation: From Marx to Modern Sociology.* Boston: Allyn and Bacon.

Jacobs, Glenn
2006 *Charles Horton Cooley: Imagining Social Reality.* Amherst: University of Massachusetts Press.

Jameson, Fredric
1984 "Postmodernism, or the Cultural Logic of Late Capitalism." *New Left Review* 146:53–93.
1991 *Postmodernism, or, The Cultural Logic of Late Capitalism.* Durham, N.C.: Duke University Press.

Janara, Laura
2002 *Democracy Growing Up: Authority, Autonomy, and Passion in Tocqueville's Democracy in America.* Albany: State University of New York Press.

Jasso, Guillermina
2001 "Formal Theory." In Jonathan Turner (ed.), *Handbook of Sociological Theory.* New York: Kluwer Academic/Plenum Publishers: 37–68.

Jaworski, Gary Dean
1991 "The Historical and Contemporary Importance of Coser's *Functions.*" *Sociological Theory* 9:116–123.
1995 "Simmel in Early American Sociology: Translation as Social Action." *International Journal of Politics, Culture and Society* 8:389–417.
1997 *Georg Simmel and the American Prospect.* Albany: State University of New York Press.

Jay, Martin
1973 *The Dialectical Imagination.* Boston: Little, Brown.
1984 *Marxism and Totality: The Adventures of a Concept from Lukács to Habermas.* Berkeley: University of California Press.

Jedlowski, Paolo
1990 "Simmel on Memory." In M. Kaern, B. S. Phillips, and R. S. Cohen (eds.), *Georg Simmel and Contemporary Sociology.* Dordrecht, Neth.: Kluwer: 131–154.

Jeffries, Vincent
2005 "Sorokin, Pitirim." In George Ritzer (ed.), *Encyclopedia of Social Theory.* Thousand Oaks, Calif.: Sage: 777–781.

Jenkins, Thomas H.
1996 "The Sociologist as Public Planner: American, German and British Examples." *Sociological Imagination* 33:18–36.

Jensen, Mette, and Blok, Anders
2008 "Pesticides in the Risk Society: The View from Everyday Life." *Current Sociology* 56:757–778.

Joas, Hans
1985 *G. H. Mead: A Contemporary Re-examination of His Thought.* Cambridge, Mass.: MIT Press.
1996 *The Creativity of Action.* Chicago: The University of Chicago Press.
2001 "The Emergence of the New: Mead's Theory and Its Contemporary Potential." In George Ritzer and Barry Smart (eds.), *Handbook of Social Theory.* London: Sage: 89–99.

Johnston, Barry V.
1995 *Pitirim Sorokin: An Intellectual Biography.* Lawrence: University Press of Kansas.

Jones, Greta
1980 *Social Darwinism and English Thought: The Interaction between Biological and Social Theory.* Atlantic Highlands, N.J.: Humanities Press.

Jones, Harold B.
1997 "The Protestant Ethic: Weber's Model and the Empirical Literature." *Human Relations* 50:757–778.

Jones, Robert Alun
1994 "The Positive Science of Ethics in France: German Influences in *De la Division du Travail Social.*" *Sociological Forum* 9:37–57.
2000 "Emile Durkheim." In George Ritzer (ed.), *The Blackwell Companion to Major Social Theorists.* Malden, Mass.: Blackwell: 205–250.

Jones, Susan Stedman
1996 "What Does Durkheim Mean by 'Thing'?" *Durkheimian Studies* 2:43–59.

Kaern, Michael, Phillips, Bernard S., and Cohen, Robert S. (eds.)
1990 *Georg Simmel and Contemporary Sociology.* Dordrecht, Neth.: Kluwer.

Kalberg, Stephen
1980 "Max Weber's Types of Rationality: Cornerstones for the Analysis of Rationalization Processes in History." *American Journal of Sociology* 85:1145–1179.
1985 "The Role of Ideal Interests in Max Weber's Comparative Historical Sociology." In R. J. Antonio and R. M. Glassman (eds.), *A Weber-Marx Dialogue.* Lawrence: University Press of Kansas: 46–67.
1990 "The Rationalization of Action in Max Weber's Sociology of Religion." *Sociological Theory* 8:58–84.
1994 *Max Weber's Comparative-Historical Sociology.* Chicago: University of Chicago Press.
1996 "On the Neglect of Weber's *Protestant Ethic* as a Theoretical Treatise: Demarcating the Parameters of Postwar American Sociological Theory." *Sociological Theory* 14:49–70.
1997 "Max Weber's Sociology: Research Strategies and Modes of Analysis." In Charles Camic (ed.), *Reclaiming the Sociological Classics: The State of Scholarship.* Oxford: Blackwell: 208–241.
2000 "Max Weber." In George Ritzer (ed.), *The Blackwell Companion to Major Social Theorists.* Malden, Mass.: Blackwell: 144–204.
2001 "Should the 'Dynamic Autonomy' of Ideas Matter to Sociologists? Max Weber on the Origin of Other-Worldly Salvation Religions and the Constitution of Groups in American Society Today." *Journal of Classical Sociology* 1:291–327.

Kamolnick, Paul

2001 "Simmel's Legacy for Contemporary Value Theory: A Critical Assessment." *Sociological Theory* 19:65–85.

Kandal, Terry R.

1988 *The Woman Question in Classical Sociological Theory.* Miami: International Universities Press.

Kaplan, Norman

1958 "Idle Curiosity," in Douglas F. Dowd (ed.), *Thorstein Veblen: A Critical Reappraisal.* Ithaca, N.Y.: Cornell University: 39–55.

Karacsony, Andras

2008 "Soul-Life-Knowledge: The Young Mannheim's Way to Sociology." *Studies in East European Thought* 60:97–111.

Karady, Victor

1983 "The Durkheimians in Academe: A Reconsideration." In P. Besnard (ed.), *The Sociological Domain.* Cambridge, Eng.: Cambridge University Press: 71–89.

Kasler, Dirk

1985 "Jewishness as a Central Formation-Milieu of Early German Sociology." *History of Sociology: An International Review* 6:69–86.

Kaye, Howard L.

1991 "A False Convergence: Freud and the Hobbesian Problem of Order." *Sociological Theory* 9:87–105.

2003 "Was Freud a Medical Scientist or a Social Theorist? The Mysterious 'Development of the Hero.'" *Sociological Theory* 21:375–397.

Keith, Bruce

1991 "Charlotte Perkins Gilman 1860–1935." In Mary Jo Deegan (ed.), *Women in Sociology: A Bio-Bibliographical Sourcebook.* Westport, Conn.: Greenwood Press: 149–156.

Kelley, Florence (ed.)

1887/1986 "The Need for Theoretical Preparation for Philanthropic Work." In K. K. Sklar (ed.), *Notes of Sixty Years—The Autobiography of Florence Kelley.* Chicago: Charles H. Kerr: 91–104.

1895 *Hull-House Maps and Papers.* Boston: Crowell.

1899 "Aims and Principles of the Consumers League." *American Journal of Sociology* 5:289–304.

1905/1969 *Some Ethical Gains through Legislation.* New York: Arno.

Kellner, Douglas

1993 "Critical Theory Today: Revisiting the Classics." *Theory, Culture and Society* 10:43–60.

1995 "Marxism, the Information Superhighway, and the Struggle for the Future." *Humanity and Society* 19:41–56.

Kellner, Douglas (ed.)

1989 *Postmodernism, Jameson, Critique.* Washington, D.C.: Maisonneuve Press.

Kellor, Frances

1904/1915 *Out of Work.* New York: G.P. Putnam.

Kendhammer, Brandon

2007 "DuBois the Pan-Africanist and the Development of African Nationalism." *Ethnic and Racial Studies* 30:51–71.

Kettler, David, and Meja, Volker
1993 "Their 'Own Peculiar Way': Karl Mannheim and the Rise of Women." *International Sociology* 8:5–55.
1994 "'That Typically German Kind of Sociology Which Verges towards Philosophy': The Dispute about Ideology and Utopia in the United States." *Sociological Theory* 12:279–303.
1995 *Karl Mannheim and the Crisis of Liberalism.* New Brunswick, N.J.: Transaction Publishers.
2001 "Karl Mannheim and the Sociology of Knowledge." In George Ritzer and Barry Smart (eds.), *Handbook of Social Theory.* London: Sage: 100–111.

Kettler, David, Meja, Volker, and Stehr, Nico
1982 "Introduction: Karl Mannheim's Early Writings on Cultural Sociology." In K. Mannheim, *Structures of Thinking.* London: Routledge and Kegan Paul.
1984 *Karl Mannheim.* Chichester, Eng.: Ellis Horwood; London: Tavistock.

Kilminster, Richard, and Mennell, Stephen
2000 "Norbert Elias." In George Ritzer (ed.), *The Blackwell Companion to Major Social Theorists.* Malden, Mass.: Blackwell: 601–629.

Kimmel, Michael
1996 *Manhood in America: A Cultural History.* New York: Free Press.

Kippenberg, Hans
2005 "Religious Communities and the Path to Disenchantment: The Origins, Sources and Theoretical Core of the Religion Section." In Hans Kippenberg (ed.), *Max Weber's Economy and Society.* Stanford, Calif.: Stanford University Press: 164–182.

Klagge, Jay
1997 "Approaches to the Iron Cage: Reconstructing the Bars of Weber's Metaphor." *Administration and Society* 29:63–77.

Kleiner, Marcus S.
2005 "German Idealism." In George Ritzer (ed.), *Encyclopedia of Social Theory.* Thousand Oaks, Calif.: Sage: 316–321.

Knight, L.W.
2006 *Citizen: Jane Addams and the Struggle for Democracy.* Chicago: University of Chicago Press.

Knorr-Cetina, Karin
1981 "Introduction: The Micro-Sociological Challenge to Macro-Sociology: Towards a Reconstruction of Social Theory and Methodology." In K. Knorr-Cetina and A. Cicourel (eds.), *Advances in Social Theory and Methodology.* New York: Methuen: 1–47.
2001 "Postsocial Relations: Theorizing Sociality in a Postsocial Environment." In G. Ritzer and B. Smart (eds.), *Handbook of Social Theory.* London: Sage.
2007 "Postsocial." In George Ritzer (ed.), *Encyclopedia of Sociology.* Oxford: Blackwell: 3578–3580.

Kockelmans, Joseph J.
1967a *Phenomenology: The Philosophy of Edmund Husserl and Its Interpretations.* Garden City, N.Y.: Anchor.
1967b "Some Fundamental Themes of Husserl's Phenomenology." In J. Kockelmans (ed.), *Phenomenology: The Philosophy of Edmund Husserl and Its Interpretations.* Garden City, N.Y.: Anchor.

Kohn, Melvin L.
1976 "Occupational Structure and Alienation." *American Journal of Sociology* 82:111–127.

Kondratieff, N. D.
1925 "The Static and the Dynamic View of Economics." *The Quarterly Journal of Economics* 39:575–583.

Koritansky, John C.
1986 *Alexis de Tocqueville and the New Science of Politics: An Interpretation of* Democracy in America. Durham, N.C.: Carolina Academic Press.

Korllos, Thomas S.
1994 "Uncovering Simmel's Forms and Social Types." *International Social Science Review* 69:17–22.

Kripke, Saul A.
1982 *Wittgenstein on Rules and Private Language: An Elementary Exposition.* Cambridge, Mass.: Harvard University Press.

Kronman, Anthony
1983 *Max Weber.* Stanford, Calif.: Stanford University Press.

Kuhn, Thomas
1962 *The Structure of Scientific Revolutions.* Chicago: University of Chicago Press.
1970 *The Structure of Scientific Revolutions.* 2nd ed. Chicago: University of Chicago Press.

Kurzweil, Edith
1995 *Freudians and Feminists.* Boulder, Colo.: Westview Press.

Lachman, L. M.
1971 *The Legacy of Max Weber.* Berkeley, Calif.: Glendessary Press.

Langsdorf, Lenore
1995 "Treating Method and Form as Phenomena: An Appreciation of Garfinkel's Phenomenology of Social Action." *Human Studies* 18:177–188.

Larrain, Jorge
1979 *The Concept of Ideology.* London: Hutchinson.

Lash, Scott, and Lury, Celia
2007 *Global Culture Industry*. Cambridge: Polity Press.

Lassman, Peter, and Velody, Irving
1989 "Max Weber on Science: Disenchantment and the Search for Meaning." In P. Lassman, I. Velody, with H. Martins (eds.), *Max Weber's "Science as a Vocation."* London: Unwin Hyman: 159–204.

Latour, Bruno
2007 *Reassembling the Social: An Introduction to Actor Network Theory.* Oxford: Oxford University Press.

Law, John, and Hetherington, Kevin
2002 "Materialities, Spatialities, Globalities." In Michael J. Dear and Steven Flusty (eds.), *The Spaces of Postmodernity: Readings in Human Geography.* Oxford: Blackwell: 390–401.

Lazonick, W.
1994 "The Integration of Theory and History: Methodology and Ideology in Schumpeter's Economics." In L. Magnusson (ed.), *Evolutionary and neo-Schumpeterian Approaches to Economics.* NY: Springer: 245–264.

Leck, Ralph Matthew
2000 *Georg Simmel and Avant-Garde Sociology: The Birth of Modernity, 1880–1920.* Amherst, N.Y.: Humanity Books.

Lefebvre, Henri
1968 *The Sociology of Marx.* New York: Vintage.
1974/1991 *The Production of Space.* Oxford: Blackwell.

Leggewie, Claus
2005 "Herrschaft (Rule)." In George Ritzer (ed.), *Encyclopedia of Social Theory.* Thousand Oaks, Calif.: Sage: 364–369.

Lehmann, Jennifer M.
1993a *Deconstructing Durkheim: A Post-Post-Structuralist Critique.* London: Routledge.
1993b *Durkheim and Women: The Problematic Relationship.* Lincoln: University of Nebraska Press.

Lemert, Charles
1990 "The Uses of French Structuralisms in Sociology." In G. Ritzer (ed.), *Frontiers of Social Theory: The New Syntheses.* New York: Columbia University Press: 230–254.
1994a "The Canonical Limits of Durkheim's First Classic." *Sociological Forum* 9:87–92.
1994b "Social Theory at the Early End of a Short Century." *Sociological Theory* 12:140–152.
1995 *Sociology after the Crisis.* Boulder, Colo.: Westview.
2000 "W.E.B. Du Bois." In George Ritzer (ed.), *The Blackwell Companion to Major Social Theorists.* Malden, Mass.: 345–366.
2001 "Multiculturalism." In George Ritzer and Barry Smart (eds.), *Handbook of Social Theory.* London: Sage: 297–307.
2002 *Dark Thoughts: Race and the Eclipse of Society.* New York: Routledge.
2005 "Du Bois, William Edward Burghardt (W. E. B.)." In George Ritzer (ed.), *Encyclopedia of Social Theory.* Thousand Oaks, Calif.: Sage: 213–218.

Lemert, Charles (ed.)
1999 *Social Theory: The Multicultural and Classical Readings.* Boulder, Colo.: Westview Press.

Lemert, Charles, and Bahn, Esme (eds.)
1998 *The Voice of Anna Julia Cooper.* Lanham, Md.: Rowman and Littlefield.

Lengermann, Patricia M.
1979 "The Founding of the *American Sociological Review.*" *American Sociological Review* 44:185–198.

Lengermann, Patricia and Niebrugge, Gillian
1998/2007 *The Women Founders: Sociology and Social Theory*, 1830–1930. Long Grove, IL: Waveland Press.

Lengermann, Patricia M., and Niebrugge, Jill
1995 "Intersubjectivity and Domination: A Feminist Investigation of the Sociology of Alfred Schutz." *Sociological Theory* 13:25–37.

Lengermann, Patricia, and Niebrugge-Brantley, Jill
1998 *The Women Founders: Sociology and Social Theory, 1830–1930.* New York: McGraw-Hill.
2001a "Classical Feminist Social Theory." In George Ritzer and Barry Smart (eds.), *Handbook of Social Theory.* London: Sage: 125–137.
2001b "The Meaning of 'THINGS': Theory and Method in Harriet Martineau's *How to Observe Morals and Manners* (1838) and Emile Durkheim's *The Rules of Sociological Method* (1895)." In Michael R. Hill and Susan Hoecker-Drysdale (eds.), *Harriet Martineau: Theoretical and Methodological Perspectives.* New York: Routledge: 75–98.
2002 "Back to the Future: Settlement Sociology, 1885–1930." *American Sociologist* 33:3:5–22.
2005 "Harriet Martineau's Sociology of Race Relations." *Sociological Origins* 3: 84–85.
2006 "Thrice-Told: Narratives of the Relation between Sociology and Social Work." In Craig Calhoun (ed.), *Sociology in America.* Chicago: University of Chicago Press: 87–134.

Lenin, Vladimir Ilich
1972 *Collected Works.* Moscow: Progress Publishers.

Lenzer, Gertrud (ed.)
1975 *Auguste Comte and Positivism: The Essential Writings.* Magnolia, Mass.: Peter Smith.

Lepenies, Wolf
1988 *Between Literature and Science: The Rise of Sociology.* Cambridge, Eng.: Cambridge University Press.

Lerner, Gerda
1993 *The Creation of Feminist Consciousness.* New York: Oxford.

Lerner, Max
1969/1994 *Tocqueville and American Civilization.* New Brunswick, N.J.: Transaction Publishers.

Lester, David (ed.)
1994 *Emile Durkheim,* Le Suicide: *One Hundred Years Later.* Philadelphia: Charles Press.

Levine, Donald
1971 "Introduction." In D. Levine (ed.), *Georg Simmel: Individuality and Social Forms.* Chicago: University of Chicago Press: ix–xiv.
1981a "Rationality and Freedom: Weber and Beyond." *Sociological Inquiry* 51:5–25.
1981b "Sociology's Quest for the Classics: The Case of Simmel." In B. Rhea (ed.), *The Future of the Sociological Classics.* London: Allen and Unwin: 60–80.
1985 "Ambivalent Encounters: Disavowals of Simmel by Durkheim, Weber, Lukács, Park and Parsons." In D. Levine (ed.), *The Flight from Ambiguity: Essays in Social and Cultural Theory.* Chicago: University of Chicago Press: 89–141.
1989 "Simmel as a Resource for Sociological Metatheory." *Sociological Theory* 7:161–174.
1991a "Simmel and Parsons Reconsidered." *American Journal of Sociology* 96:1097–1116.
1991b "Simmel as Educator: On Individuality and Modern Culture." *Theory, Culture and Society* 8:99–118.
1995a *Visions of the Sociological Tradition.* Chicago: University of Chicago Press.
1995b "The Organism Metaphor in Sociology." *Social Research* 62:239–265.
1997 "Simmel Reappraised: Old Images, New Scholarship." In Charles Camic (ed.), *Reclaiming the Sociological Classics: The State of Scholarship.* Oxford: Blackwell: 173–207.

2000 "On the Critique of 'Utilitarian' Theories of Action: Newly Identified Convergences among Simmel, Weber and Parsons." *Theory, Culture and Society* 17:63–78.

Levine, Donald, Carter, Ellwood B., and Gorman, Eleanor Miller

1976a "Simmel's Influence on American Sociology—I." *American Journal of Sociology* 81:813–845.

1976b "Simmel's Influence on American Sociology—II." *American Journal of Sociology* 81:1112–1132.

Levine, Rhonda

2005 *Enriching the Sociological Imagination: How Radical Sociology Changed the Discipline.* Boulder, CO: Paradigm Publishers.

Levy-Bruhl, Lucien

1903/1973 *The Philosophy of Auguste Comte.* Clifton, N.J.: A. M. Kelley.

Lewis, David Levering

1993 *W.E.B. Du Bois: Biography of a Race, 1869–1919.* New York: Holt.

2000 *W.E.B. DuBois: The Fight for Equality and the American Century, 1919–1963.* New York: Holt.

Lewis, David Levering (ed.)

1995 *W.E.B. Du Bois: A Reader.* New York: Henry Holt and Co.

Lewis, J. David, and Smith, Richard L.

1980 *American Sociology and Pragmatism: Mead, Chicago Sociology, and Symbolic Interaction.* Chicago: University of Chicago Press.

Lewis, Reba Rowe

1991 "Forging New Syntheses: Theories and Theorists." *American Sociologist* Fall/Winter:221–230.

Lichtblau, Klaus, and Ritter, Mark

1991 "Causality or Interaction? Simmel, Weber and Interpretive Sociology." *Theory, Culture and Society* 8:33–62.

Lichterman, Paul

2006 "Social Capital or Group Style? Rescuing Tocqueville's Insights on Civic Engagement." *Theory and Society* 35:529–563.

Lidz, Victor

2000 "Talcott Parsons." In George Ritzer (ed.), *The Blackwell Companion to Major Social Theorists.* Malden, Mass.: Blackwell: 388–431.

Lilla, Mark

1994 "The Legitimacy of the Liberal Age." In M. Lilla (ed.), *New French Thought: Political Philosophy.* Princeton, N.J.: Princeton University Press: 3–34.

Lindbekk, Tore

1992 "The Weberian Ideal-Type: Development and Continuities." *Acta Sociologica* 35:285–297.

Lindner, Rolf

1996 *The Reportage of Urban Culture: Robert Park and the Chicago School.* Cambridge, Eng.: Cambridge University Press.

Lipovetsky, Gilles

1987/1994 *The Empire of Fashion: Dressing Modern Democracy.* Princeton, N.J.: Princeton University Press.

Liska, Allen E.
1990 "The Significance of Aggregate Dependent Variables and Contextual Independent Variables for Linking Macro and Micro Theories." *Social Psychology Quarterly* 53:292–301.

Lively, Jack
1962 *The Social and Political Thought of Alexis de Tocqueville.* Oxford: Clarendon Press.

Loader, Colin
1985 *The Intellectual Development of Karl Mannheim.* Cambridge, Eng.: Cambridge University Press.
1997 "Free Floating: The Intelligentsia in the Work of Alfred Weber and Karl Mannheim." *German Studies Review* 20:217–234.

Loader, Colin, and Alexander, Jeffrey C.
1985 "Max Weber on Churches and Sects in North America: An Alternative Path toward Rationalization." *Sociological Theory* 3:1–6.

Loader, Colin, and Kettler, David
2002 *Karl Mannheim's Sociology as Political Education.* New Brunswick, N.J.: Transaction Publishers.

Lockwood, David
1956 "Some Remarks on *The Social System.*" *British Journal of Sociology* 7:134–146.

LoConto, David G., and Arrington, Paige R.
2007 "Pragmatism and Grieving: Incorporating Mead and Dewey to Understand the Grieving of People with Mental Retardation. *Sociological Spectrum* 27:537–553.

Lodge, Peter
1986 "Connections: W. I. Thomas, European Social Thought and American Sociology." In R. C. Monk (ed.), *Structures of Knowing.* Lanham, Md.: University Press of America: 135–160.

Lohmann, Georg, and Wilkes, Geoff
1996 "The Adaptation of Inner Life to the Inner Infinity of the Metropolis: Forms of Individualization in Simmel." *Thesis Eleven* 44:1–11.

Longhurst, Brian
1988 *Karl Mannheim and the Contemporary Sociology of Knowledge.* New York: St. Martin's.

Love, John
2000 "Max Weber's Orient." In Stephen Turner (ed.), *The Cambridge Companion to Weber.* Cambridge, Eng.: Cambridge University Press: 172–199.

Lovell, David W.
1992 "Socialism, Utopianism and the 'Utopian Socialists.'" *History of European Ideas* 14:185–201.

Low, Jacqueline
2008 "Structure, Agency, and Social Reality in Blumerian Symbolic Interactionism: The influence of Georg Simmel." *Symbolic Interaction* 31:325–343.

Lowy, Michael
1996 "Figures of Weberian Marxism." *Theory and Society* 25:431–446.

Luhmann, Niklas
1982 *The Differentiation of Society.* New York: Columbia University Press.
1984/1995 *Soziale Systeme. Grundreiner allgemeinen Theorie/Social Systems: Outline of a General Theory.* Frankfurt am Main: Suhrkamp/Stanford, Calif.: Stanford University Press.

Lukács, Georg
1922/1968 *History and Class Consciousness.* Cambridge, Mass.: MIT Press.
1991 "Georg Simmel." *Theory, Culture and Society* 8:145–150.

Lukes, Steven
1972 *Emile Durkheim: His Life and Work.* New York: Harper & Row.

MacIver, Robert
1931 *Society: Its Structure and Changes.* New York: Long and Smith.
1942 *Social Causation.* Boston: Ginn.

Mackinnon, Malcolm H.
2001 "Max Weber's Disenchantment: Lineages of Kant and Channing." *Journal of Classical Sociology* 1:329–351.

MacLean, Annie Marion
1899 "Two Weeks in Department Stores." *American Journal of Sociology* 21:721–741.

MacRae, Donald G.
1974 *Max Weber.* Harmondsworth, Eng.: Penguin.

Maines, David R.
2005 "Blumer, Herbert." In George Ritzer (ed.), *Encyclopedia of Social Theory.* Thousand Oaks, Calif.: Sage: 58–62.

Maines, David, Bridger, Jeffrey C., and Ulmer, Jeffery T.
1996 "Mythic Facts and Park's Pragmatism: On Predecessor-Selection and Theorizing in Human Ecology." *Sociological Quarterly* 37:521–549.

MacPherson, C. B.
1962 *The Political Theory of Possessive Individualism.* Oxford: Clarendon Press.

Maletz, Donald J.
2005 "Tocqueville on Mores and the Preservation of Republics." *American Journal of Political Science* 49:1–15.

Mancini, Matthew
1994 *Alexis de Tocqueville.* New York: Twayne Publishers.

Manent, Pierre
1994/1998 *The City of Man.* Princeton, N.J.: Princeton University Press.

Mann, Michael
1986 *The Sources of Social Power,* Vol. 1. New York: Cambridge University Press.

Mannheim, Karl
1925/1971 "The Problem of a Sociology of Knowledge." In K. H. Wolff (ed.), *From Karl Mannheim.* New York: Oxford University Press: 59–115.
1926/1971 "The Ideological and the Sociological Interpretation of Intellectual Phenomena." In K. H. Wolff (ed.), *From Karl Mannheim.* New York: Oxford University Press: 116–131.

1928–1929/ 1952 "The Problem of Generations." In Karl Mannheim, *Essays on the Sociology of Knowledge.* New York: Oxford University Press: 276–320.

1929/1936 *Ideology and Utopia.* New York: Harcourt, Brace and World.

1929/1971 "Problems of Sociology in Germany." In K. H. Wolff (ed.), *From Karl Mannheim.* New York: Oxford University Press: 262–270.

1931/1936 "The Sociology of Knowledge." In K. Mannheim, *Ideology and Utopia.* New York: Harcourt, Brace and World: 264–311.

1932/1993 "The Sociology of Intellectuals." *Theory, Culture and Society* 10:69–80.

1935/1940 *Man and Society in an Age of Reconstruction.* New York: Harcourt, Brace and World.

1943 *Diagnosis of Our Time: Wartime Essays of a Sociologist.* London: Routledge and Kegan Paul.

1944/1971 "Education, Sociology and the Problem of Social Awareness." In K. H. Wolff (ed.), *From Karl Mannheim.* New York: Oxford University Press: 367–384.

1950 *Freedom, Power and Democratic Planning,* H. Gerth and E. K. Bramstedt (eds.). London: Routledge and Kegan Paul.

1952/1971a "On the Interpretation of *Weltanschauung.*" In K. H. Wolff (ed.), *From Karl Mannheim.* New York: Oxford University Press: 8–58.

1952/1971b "Competition as Cultural Phenomenon." In K. H. Wolff (ed.), *From Karl Mannheim.* New York: Oxford University Press: 223–261.

1953 *Essays on Sociology and Social Psychology.* London: Routledge and Kegan Paul.

1953/1971 "Conservative Thought." In K. H. Wolff (ed.), *From Karl Mannheim.* New York: Oxford University Press: 132–222.

1956/1971 "The Democratization of Culture." In K. H. Wolff (ed.), *From Karl Mannheim.* New York: Oxford University Press: 271–346.

1957 *Systematic Sociology: An Introduction to the Study of Society.* J. S. Eros and W.A.C. Stewart (eds.). New York: Philosophical Library.

1982 *Structures of Thinking.* David Kettler, Volker Meja, and Nico Stehr (eds. and trans.). London: Routledge and Kegan Paul.

Mannheim, Karl, and Stewart, W.A.C.

1962 *An Introduction to the Sociology of Education.* London: Routledge and Kegan Paul.

Manning, Philip

1991 "Drama as Life: The Significance of Goffman's Changing Use of the Theatrical Metaphor." *Sociological Theory* 9:70–86.

1992 *Erving Goffman and Modern Sociology.* Stanford, Calif.: Stanford University Press.

2005a "Dramaturgy." In George Ritzer (ed.), *Encyclopedia of Social Theory.* Thousand Oaks, Calif.: Sage: 210–213.

2005b "Goffman, Erving." In George Ritzer (ed.), *Encyclopedia of Social Theory.* Thousand Oaks, Calif.: Sage: 333–339.

2005c "Impression Management." In George Ritzer (ed.), *Encyclopedia of Social Theory.* Thousand Oaks, Calif.: Sage: 397–399.

2007 "Dramaturgy." In George Ritzer (ed.), *Encyclopedia of Sociology.* Oxford: Blackwell: 1226–1229.

Manuel, Frank E.

1962 *The Prophets of Paris.* Cambridge, Mass.: University Press.

1992 "A Requiem for Karl Marx." *Daedalus* 121:1–19.

Marcuse, Herbert

1971 "Industrialization and Capitalism." In O. Stammer (ed.), *Max Weber and Sociology Today.* New York: Harper & Row.

Markus, Gyorgy

2005 "Lukacs, Gyorgy." In George Ritzer (ed.), *Encyclopedia of Social Theory.* Thousand Oaks, Calif.: Sage: 458–460.

Martin, Michael

2000 *Verstehen: The Uses of Understanding in Social Science.* New Brunswick, N.J.: Transaction Publishers.

Martineau, Harriet

1822 "Female Writers on Practical Divinity." *Monthly Repository* 17:593–596.

1830/1836 "Letter to the Deaf." In H. Martineau, *Miscellanies,* Vol. 1. Boston: Hilliard Gray: 248–265.

1832 "Demerara." In H. Martineau, *Illustrations of Political Economy.* London: Charles Fox: 1–129.

1832/1836 "Essays on the Art of Thinking." In H. Martineau, *Miscellanies,* Vol. 1. Boston: Hilliard Gray: 122–179.

1832–1834 *Illustrations of Political Economy.* London: Charles Fox.

1836 *Miscellanies.* Boston: Hilliard Gray.

1836/1837 *Society in America.* 2 vols. New York: Saunders and Otley.

1837/1962 *Society in America.* Garden City, N.Y.: Doubleday Anchor.

1838a "Domestic Service." *London and Westminster Review* 29:405–432.

1838b *How to Observe Morals and Manners.* London: Charles Knight.

1838/1989 *How to Observe Manners and Morals.* New Brunswick, N.J.: Transaction Books.

1848 *Eastern Life: Present and Past.* London: Edward Moxon.

1853 *The Positive Philosophy of Auguste Comte, freely translated and condensed by Harriet Martineau.* London: John Chapman.

Marx, Karl

1842/1977 "Communism and the *Augsburger Allegemeine Zeitung.*" In D. McLellan (ed.), *Karl Marx: Selected Writings.* New York: Oxford University Press: 20.

1843/1970 "A Contribution to the Critique of Hegel's Philosophy of Right" In *Marx/Engels Collected Works Vol. 3.* New York: International Publishers: 3–129.

1847/1963 *The Poverty of Philosophy.* New York: International Publishers.

Marx, Karl, and Engels, Frederick

1848/1969 *Karl Marx and Frederick Engels: Selected Works in One Volume.* New York, NY: International Publishers.

1852/1963 *The Eighteenth Brumaire of Louis Bonaparte.* New York: International Publishers.

1857–1858/1964 *Pre-Capitalist Economic Foundations,* Eric J. Hobsbawm (ed.). New York: International Publishers.

1857–1858/1974 *The Grundrisse: Foundations of the Critique of Political Economy.* New York: Random House.

1859/1970 *A Contribution to the Critique of Political Economy.* New York: International Publishers.

1867/1967 *Capital: A Critique of Political Economy,* Vol. 1. New York: International Publishers.

1932/1964 *The Economic and Philosophic Manuscripts of 1844,* Dirk J. Struik (ed.). New York: International Publishers.

1964 *The Class Struggles in France, 1848–1850.* New York: International Publishers.

Marx, Karl, and Engels, Friedrich

1845/1956 *The Holy Family.* Moscow: Foreign Language Publishing House.

1845–1846/1970 *The German Ideology,* Part 1, C. J. Arthur (ed.). New York: International Publishers.

1848/1948 *Manifesto of the Communist Party.* New York: International Publishers.

Maryanski, A. R.
2005 "Evolutionary Theory." In George Ritzer (ed.), *Encyclopedia of Social Theory.* Thousand Oaks, Calif.: Sage: 257–263.

Maryanski, Alexandra, and Turner, Jonathan H.
1992 *The Social Cage: Human Nature and the Evolution of Society.* Stanford, Calif.: Stanford University Press.

Matthews, Fred H.
1977 *Quest for an American Sociology: Robert E. Park and the Chicago School.* Montreal: McGill University Press.

May, Vivian M.
2004 "Thinking from the Margins, Acting at the Intersections: Anna Julia Cooper's *A Voice from the South.*" *Hypatia* 19:74–91.

Mayall, Margery
2007 "Attached to Their Style: Traders, Technical Analysis and Postsocial Relationships." *Journal of Sociology* 43:421–437.

Mayer, J. P.
1966 *Alexis de Tocqueville: A Biographical Study in Political Science*. Gloucester, Mass.: Peter Smith.

McCann, Stewart J. H.
1997 "Threatening Times and the Election of Charismatic U.S. Presidents: With and Without FDR." *Journal of Psychology* 131:393–400.

McCarthy, E. Doyle
1996 *Knowledge as Culture: The New Sociology of Knowledge.* New York: Routledge.
2007 "Sociology of Knowledge." In George Ritzer (ed.), *Encyclopedia of Sociology.* Oxford: Blackwell: 2482–2485.

McCormick, Charles
2007 "Poststructuralism." In George Ritzer (ed.), *Encyclopedia of Sociology.* Oxford: Blackwell: 3580–3584.

McCraw, Thomas K.
2007 *Prophet of Innovation: Joseph Schumpeter and Creative Destruction*. Cambridge, MA: Belknap Press of Harvard University Press.

McDonald, Lynne
1994 *The Women Founders of the Social Sciences.* Ottawa, Canada: Carleton University Press.
1998 *Women Theorists on Society and Politics.* Waterloo, Ontario: Wilfred Laurier University Press.

McFalls, Laurence H.
2007 *Max Weber's 'Objectivity' Reconsidered.* Toronto, CN: University of Toronto Press.

McKinney, John C.
1966 *Constructive Typology and Social Theory.* New York: Appleton-Century-Crofts.

McLaughlin, Neil
2007 "Fromm, Erich." In George Ritzer (ed.), *Encyclopedia of Sociology*. Oxford: Blackwell:1804–1808.

McLellan, David
1973 *Karl Marx: His Life and Thought.* New York: Harper Colophon.

McLennan, Gregor
2001 "Maintaining Marx." In George Ritzer and Barry Smart (eds.), *Handbook of Social Theory.* London: Sage: 43–53.

McMurty, John
1978 *The Structure of Marx's World-View.* Princeton, N.J.: Princeton University Press.

McPhail, Clark, and Rexroat, Cynthia
1979 "Mead vs. Blumer." *American Sociological Review* 44:449–467.

McVeigh, Rory, and Sikkink, David
2005 "Organized Racism and the Stranger." *Sociological Forum* 20:497–522.

Mead, George H.
1907/1964 "Concerning Animal Perception." In A. J. Reck (ed.), *Selected Writings.* Indianapolis: Bobbs-Merrill.
1934/1962 *Mind, Self and Society: From the Standpoint of a Social Behaviorist.* Chicago: University of Chicago Press.
1936 *Movements of Thought in the Nineteenth Century.* Chicago: University of Chicago Press.
1938/1972 *The Philosophy of the Act.* Chicago: University of Chicago Press.
1959 *The Philosophy of the Present.* LaSalle, Ill.: Open Court Publishing.
1982 *The Individual and the Social Self: Unpublished Work of George Herbert Mead.* Chicago: University of Chicago Press.

Mehan, Hugh, and Wood, Houston
1975 *The Reality of Ethnomethodology.* New York: Wiley.

Meisenhelder, Tom
1991 "Toward a Marxist Analysis of Subjectivity." *Nature, Society, and Thought* 4:103–125.

Meja, Volker, and Stehr, Nico (eds.)
1990 *Knowledge and Politics: The Sociology of Knowledge Dispute.* London: Routledge.

Melonio, Francoise
1993/1998 *Tocqueville and the French.* Charlottesville: University Press of Virginia.

Menzies, Ken
1977 *Talcott Parsons and the Social Image of Man.* London: Routledge and Kegan Paul.

Merton, Robert
1941/1957 "Karl Mannheim and the Sociology of Knowledge." In R. Merton (ed.), *Social Theory and Social Structure.* Rev. and enl. ed. New York: Free Press: 489–508.
1968 *Social Theory and Social Structure.* New York: Free Press.
1980 "Remembering the Young Talcott Parsons." *American Sociologist* 15:68–71.

Mestrovic, Stjepan G.
1988 *Emile Durkheim and the Reformation of Sociology.* Totowa, N.J.: Rowman and Littlefield.
1992 *Durkheim and Postmodern Culture.* New York: Aldine de Gruyter.
1998 *Anthony Giddens: The Last Modernist.* London: Routledge.

Mèszáros, István
1970 *Marx's Theory of Alienation.* New York: Harper Torchbooks.

Meyer, Hans-Dieter
2003 "Tocqueville's Cultural Institutionalism." *Journal of Classical Sociology* 3: 197–220.

Meyer, John W., Boli, John, Thomas, George M., and Ramirez, Francisco O.
1997 "World Society and the Nation-State." *American Journal of Sociology* 103: 144–181.

Mill, John Stuart
1961 *Auguste Comte and Positivism.* Ann Arbor: University of Michigan Press.

Miller, David
1973 *George Herbert Mead: Self, Language and the World.* Austin: University of Texas Press.
1982a "Introduction." In G. H. Mead, *The Individual and the Social Self: Unpublished Work of George Herbert Mead.* Chicago: University of Chicago Press: 1–26.
1982b Review of J. David Lewis and Richard L. Smith, *American Sociology and Pragmatism. Journal of the History of Sociology* 4:108–114.
1985 "Concerning J. David Lewis' Response to My Review of *American Sociology and Pragmatism.*" *Journal of the History of Sociology* 5:131–133.

Miller, James
1993 *The Passion of Michel Foucault.* New York: Anchor Books.

Miller, Richard
1991 "Social and Political Theory: Class, State, Revolution." In Terrell Carver (ed.), *The Cambridge Companion to Marx.* Cambridge Eng.: Cambridge University Press: 55–105.

Miller, W. Watts
1993 "Durkheim's Montesquieu." *British Journal of Sociology* 44:693–712.

Mills, C. Wright
1951 *White Collar.* New York: Oxford University Press.
1956 *The Power Elite.* New York: Oxford University Press.
1959 *The Sociological Imagination.* New York: Oxford University Press.

Mills, Kartryn, with Mills, Pamela
2000 *C. Wright Mills: Letters and Autobiographical Writings.* Berkeley: University of California Press.

Mitroff, Ian
1974 "Norms and Counter-Norms in a Select Group of the Apollo Moon Scientists: A Case Study of the Ambivalence of Scientists." *American Sociological Review* 39:579–595.

Mitzman, Arthur
1969/1971 *The Iron Cage: An Historical Interpretation of Max Weber.* New York: Grosset and Dunlap.

Miyahara, Kojiro
1983 "Charisma: From Weber to Contemporary Sociology." *Sociological Inquiry* 55:368–388.

Mizruchi, Mark S.
2005 "Network Society." In George Ritzer (ed.), *Encyclopedia of Social Theory.* Thousand Oaks, Calif.: Sage: 534–540.

Molm, Linda D.
2001 "Theories of Social Exchange and Exchange Networks." In George Ritzer and Barry Smart (eds.), *Handbook of Social Theory.* London: Sage: 260–272.

Mommsen, Wolfgang J.
1974 *The Age of Bureaucracy.* New York: Harper & Row.

Morgan, Robin (ed.)
1970 *Sisterhood Is Powerful: An Anthology of Writings from the Women's Liberation Movement.* New York: Vintage.

Morris, Monica B.
1977 *Excursion into Creative Sociology.* New York: Columbia University Press.

Morrow, Raymond A.
1994 "Critical Theory, Poststructuralism, and Critical Theory." *Current Perspectives in Social Theory* 14:27–51.

Morse, Chandler
1961 "The Functional Imperatives." In M. Black (ed.), *The Social Theories of Talcott Parsons.* Englewood Cliffs, N.J.: Prentice-Hall: 100–152.

Morton, Donald
1996 "The Politics of Queer Theory in the (Post)Modern Moment." In Mary F. Rogers (ed.), *Multicultural Experiences, Multicultural Theories.* New York: McGraw-Hill: 90–98.

Moss, Laurence S., and Savchenko, Andrew
2006 *Talcott Parsons: Economic Sociologist of the 20th Century.* Maiden, MA: Blackwell Publishing.

Mouzelis, Nicos
1997 "In Defence of the Sociological Canon: A Reply to David Parker." *Sociological Review* 97:244–253.

Movahedi, Siamak
2007 "Psychoanalysis." In George Ritzer (ed.), *Encyclopedia of Sociology.* Oxford: Blackwell: 3694–3696.

Moyers, Imogene L.
2003 "Jane Addams: Pioneer in Criminology." *Women and Criminal Justice* 14:2–3, 1–14.

Mozetic, Gerald, and Weiler, Bernd
2007 "Pareto, Vilfredo." In George Ritzer (ed.), *Encyclopedia of Sociology.* Oxford: Blackwell: 3360–3362.

Muller, Hans-Peter
1994 "Social Differentiation and Organic Solidarity: The *Division of Labor* Revisited." *Sociological Forum* 9:73–86.

Münch, P. A.
1975 "'Sense' and 'Intention' in Max Weber's Theory of Action." *Sociological Inquiry* 45:59–65.

Münch, Richard
1981 "Talcott Parsons and the Theory of Action. I. The Structure of the Kantian Core." *American Journal of Sociology* 86:709–739.
1982 "Talcott Parsons and the Theory of Action. II. The Continuity of the Development." *American Journal of Sociology* 87:771–826.

2005 "Parsons, Talcott." In George Ritzer (ed.), *Encyclopedia of Social Theory.* Thousand Oaks, Calif.: Sage: 550–555.

Muncy, Robyn
1991 *Creating a Female Dominion of Reform.* New York: Oxford University Press.

Nafassi, Mohammed R.
1998 "Reframing Orientalism: Weber and Islam." *Economy and Society* 27:97–118.

Nass, Clifford I.
1986 "Bureaucracy, Technical Expertise, and Professionals: A Weberian Approach." *Sociological Theory* 4:61–70.

Natanson, Maurice
1973a "Introduction." In A. Schutz, *Collected Papers I: The Problem of Social Reality.* The Hague: Martinus Nijhoff: xxv–xlvii.
1973b *The Social Dynamics of George H. Mead.* The Hague: Martinus Nijhoff.

Nedelmann, Birgitta
1990 "Georg Simmel as an Analyst of Autonomous Dynamics: The Merry-Go-Round of Fashion." In M. Kaern, B. S. Phillips, and R. S. Cohen (eds.), *Georg Simmel and Contemporary Sociology.* Dordrecht, Neth.: Kluwer: 225–241.
1991 "Individualization, Exaggeration and Paralysation: Simmel's Three Problems of Culture." *Theory, Culture and Society* 8:169–194.
2001 "The Continuing Relevance of Georg Simmel: Staking out Anew the Field of Sociology." In George Ritzer and Barry Smart (eds.), *Handbook of Social Theory.* London: Sage: 66–78.

Nedelmann, Birgitta, and Sztompka, Piotr
1993 "Introduction." In B. Nedelmann and P. Sztompka (eds.), *Sociology in Europe: In Search of Identity.* Berlin: Walter de Gruyter: 1–23.

Nemedi, Denes
1995 "Collective Consciousness, Morphology, and Collective Representations: Durkheim's Sociology of Knowledge, 1894–1900." *Sociological Perspectives* 38:41–56.

Nettl, J. P., and Robertson, Roland
1968 *International Systems and the Modernization of Societies.* New York: Basic Books.

Nielsen, Donald A.
1999 *Three Faces of God: Society, Religion, and the Categories of Totality in the Philosophy of Emile Durkheim.* Albany: State University of New York Press.
2005 "Annales School." In George Ritzer (ed.), *Encyclopedia of Social Theory.* Thousand Oaks, Calif.: Sage: 12–16.

Nietzsche, Friedrich
2007 *Ecce Homo: How One Becomes What One Is.* New York, NY: Oxford University Press.

Nisbet, Robert
1953 *Community and Power.* New York: Galaxy Books.
1959 "Comment." *American Sociological Review* 24:479–481.
1966 "Many Tocquevilles." *The American Scholar* 59–75.

1967 *The Sociological Tradition.* New York: Basic Books.

1976 *The Social Philosophers*. Paladin, Frogmore.

Norkus, Zenonas

2000 "Max Weber's Interpretive Sociology and Rational Choice Approach." *Rationality and Society* 12:259–282.

Oakes, Guy (ed.)

1984 *Georg Simmel on Women, Sexuality and Love.* New Haven: Yale University Press.

Oakes, Len

1997 *Prophetic Charisma: The Psychology of Revolutionary Religious Personalities.* Syracuse: N.Y.: Syracuse University Press.

Offe, Claus

2005 *Reflections on America: Tocqueville, Weber, and Adorno in the United States.* Cambridge, Mass.: Polity.

Offer, John

1999 "Spencer's Vision of Welfare: A Vision Eclipsed." *Sociological Review* 47:136–162.

Ogburn, William Fielding

1922/1964 *Social Change.* New York: Viking.

Oliver, Ivan

1983 "The 'Old' and the 'New' Hermeneutic in Sociological Theory." *British Journal of Sociology* 34:519–553.

Ollman, Bertell

1976 *Alienation.* 2nd ed. Cambridge, Eng.: Cambridge University Press.

Olson, Richard

1993 *The Emergence of the Social Sciences, 1642–1792.* New York: Twayne.

Ono, Michikuni

1996 "Collective Effervescence and Symbolism." *Durkheimian Studies* 2:79–98.

Orr, Catherine M.

1997 "Charting the Currents of the Third Wave." *Hypatia* 12:29–43.

Outhwaite, William

1994 *Habermas: A Critical Introduction.* Stanford, Calif.: Stanford University Press.

Owen, David (ed.)

1997 *Sociology after Postmodernism.* London: Sage.

Pareto, Vilfredo

1935 *A Treatise on General Sociology.* 4 vols. New York: Dover.

Park, Robert E.

1927/1973 "Life History." *American Journal of Sociology* 79:251–260.

Park, Robert, and Burgess, Ernest

1921 *Introduction to the Science of Sociology.* Chicago: University of Chicago Press.

Parker, David

1997 "Why Bother with Durkheim?" *Sociological Review* 45:122–146.

Parsons, Talcott
1937 *The Structure of Social Action.* New York: McGraw-Hill.
1942 "Some Sociological Aspects of the Fascist Movements." *Social Forces* 21:138–147.
1947 "Certain Primary Sources and Patterns of Aggression in the Social Structure of the Western World." *Psychiatry* 10:167–181.
1949 *The Structure of Social Action.* 2nd ed. New York: McGraw-Hill.
1951 *The Social System.* Glencoe, Ill.: Free Press.
1960 "A Sociological Approach to the Theory of Organizations." In T. Parsons (ed.), *Structure and Process in Modern Societies.* New York: Free Press: 16–58.
1961 "Some Considerations on the Theory of Social Change." *Rural Sociology* 26:219–239.
1966 *Societies.* Englewood Cliffs, N.J.: Prentice-Hall.
1970 *Social Structure and Personality.* New York: Free Press.
1971 *The System of Modern Societies.* Englewood Cliffs, N.J.: Prentice-Hall.
1975 "Social Structure and the Symbolic Media of Interchange." In P. Blau (ed.), *Approaches to the Study of Social Structure.* New York: Free Press: 94–100.
1977a "General Introduction." In T. Parsons (ed.), *Social Systems and the Evolution of Action Theory.* New York: Free Press: 1–13.
1977b "On Building Social System Theory: A Personal History." In T. Parsons (ed.), *Social Systems and the Evolution of Action Theory.* New York: Free Press: 22–76.
1990 "Prolegomena to a Theory of Social Institutions." *American Sociological Review* 55:319–333.

Parsons, Talcott, and Platt, Gerald
1973 *The American University.* Cambridge, Mass.: Harvard University Press.

Parsons, Talcott, and Shils, Edward A. (eds.)
1951 *Toward a General Theory of Action.* Cambridge, Mass.: Harvard University Press.

Paulsen, Michael B., and Feldman, Kenneth A.
1995 "Toward a Reconceptualization of Scholarship: A Human Action System with Functional Imperatives." *Journal of Higher Education* 66:615–640.

Pearce, Frank
1989 *The Radical Durkheim.* London: Unwin Hyman.
2005 "Durkheim, Emile." In George Ritzer (ed.), *Encyclopedia of Social Theory.* Thousand Oaks, Calif.: Sage: 218–223.

Peel, J.D.Y.
1971 *Herbert Spencer: The Evolution of a Sociologist.* New York: Basic Books.

Pels, Dick
1993 "Missionary Sociology between Left and Right. A Critical Introduction to Mannheim." *Theory, Culture and Society* 10:45–68.
1996 "Karl Mannheim and the Sociology of Scientific Knowledge: Towards a New Agenda." *Sociological Theory* 14:30–48.

Perrin, Robert
1976 "Herbert Spencer's Four Theories of Social Evolution." *American Journal of Sociology* 81:1339–1359.
1995 "Emile Durkheim's Division of Labor and the Shadow of Herbert Spencer." *Sociological Quarterly* 36:791–808.

Perry, Wilhelmia E., Abbott, James R., and Hutter, Mark
1997 "The Symbolic Interactionist Paradigm and Urban Sociology." *Research in Urban Sociology* 4:59–92.

Pickering, Mary
1993 *Auguste Comte: An Intellectual Biography.* Vol. 1. Cambridge, Eng.: Cambridge University Press.
1997 "A New Look at Auguste Comte." In Charles Camic (ed.), *Reclaiming the Sociological Classics: The State of Scholarship.* Oxford: Blackwell: 11–44.
2000 "Auguste Comte." In George Ritzer (ed.), *The Blackwell Companion to Major Social Theorists.* Malden, Mass.: Blackwell: 25–52.

Pieterse, Jan Nederveen
2004 *Globalization and Culture: Global Melange.* Lanham, Md.: Rowman and Littlefield.

Pilcher, Jane
1994 "Mannheim's Sociology of Generations: An Undervalued Legacy." *British Journal of Sociology* 45:481–495.

Poggi, Gianfranco
1972 *Images of Society: Essays on the Sociological Theories of Tocqueville, Marx and Durkheim.* Stanford, Calif.: Stanford University Press.
1993 *Money and the Modern Mind: Georg Simmel's Philosophy of Money.* Berkeley: University of California Press.
1996 "Three Aspects of Modernity in Simmel's *Philosophie des Geldes:* Its Epiphanic Significance, the Centrality of Money and the Prevalence of Alienation." In Richard Kilminster and Ian Varcoe (eds.), *Culture, Modernity and Revolution: Essays in Honour of Zygmunt Bauman.* London: Routledge: 42–65.

Pope, Whitney
1976 *Durkheim's Suicide: A Classic Analyzed.* Chicago: University of Chicago Press.
1986 *Alexis de Tocqueville: His Social and Political Theory.* Beverly Hills: Sage.

Pope, Whitney, and Cohen, Jere
1978 "On R. Stephen Warner's 'Toward a Redefinition of Action Theory: Paying the Cognitive Element Its Due.'" *American Journal of Sociology* 83:1359–1367.

Postone, Moishe
1993 *Time, Labor, and Social Domination: A Reinterpretation of Marx's Critical Theory.* Cambridge, Eng.: Cambridge University Press.

Powell, Jason, and Owen, Tim (eds.)
2007 *Reconstructing Postmodernism.* New York: Nova Science Publishers.

Powers, Charles H.
1986 *Vilfredo Pareto.* Newbury Park, Calif.: Sage.
2005 "Veblen, Thorstein." In George Ritzer (ed.), *Encyclopedia of Social Theory.* Thousand Oaks, Calif.: Sage: 863–864.

Prendergast, Christopher
1986 "Alfred Schutz and the Austrian School of Economics." *American Journal of Sociology* 92:1–26.
2005 "Schutz, Alfred." In George Ritzer (ed.), *Encyclopedia of Social Theory.* Thousand Oaks, Calif.: Sage: 674–675.

Pressler, Charles A., and Dasilva, Fabio
1996 *Sociology and Interpretation: From Weber to Habermas.* Albany: State University of New York Press.

Procter, Ian
1978 "Parsons's Early Voluntarism." *Sociological Inquiry* 48:37–48.

Prus, Robert
1996 *Symbolic Interaction and Ethnographic Research: Intersubjectivity and the Study of Human Lived Experience.* Albany: State University of New York Press.

Psathas, George
1989 *Phenomenology and Sociology: Theory and Research.* Lanham, Md.: University Press of America.

Putnam, Robert
2001 *Bowling Alone: The Collapse and Revival of American Community.* New York: Simon and Schuster.

Quine, W. V.
1972 "Methodological Reflections On Current Linguistic Theory." In Donald Davidson and Gilbert Harman (eds.), *Semantics of Natural Language.* Dordrecht, Neth.: Reidel: 442–454.

Rabaka, Reiland
2006 "The Souls of Black Radical Folk: W.E.B. DuBois, Critical Social Theory, and the State of Africana Studies." *Journal of Black Studies* 36:732–763.
2007 *Critical Theory.* New York: Lexington Books.

Ramet, Sabrina P.
1991 *Social Currents in Eastern Europe: The Sources and Meaning of the Great Transformation.* Durham, N.C.: Duke University Press.

Rammstedt, Otthein
1991 "On Simmel's Aesthetics: Argumentation in the Journal *Jugend,* 1897–1906." *Theory, Culture and Society* 8:125–144.

Rattansi, Ali
1982 *Marx and the Division of Labour.* London: Macmillan.

Rawls, Anne Warfield
1996 "Durkheim's Epistemology: The Neglected Argument." *American Journal of Sociology* 102:430–482.
2001 "Durkheim's Treatment of Practice: Concrete Practice vs Representations as the Foundation of Reason." *Journal of Classical Sociology* 1:33–68.
2007 "Durkheim, Emile." In George Ritzer (ed.), *Encyclopedia of Sociology.* Oxford: Blackwell: 1250–1261.

Reedy, W. Jay
1994 "The Historical Imaginary of Social Science in Post-Revolutionary France: Bonald, Saint-Simon, Comte." *History of the Human Sciences* 7:1–26.

Reich, Robert
2000 *The Future of Success.* New York: Knopf.

Reinert, Hugo and Erik Reinert.
2006 "Creative Destruction in Economics: Nietzsche, Sombart, Schumpeter." In J. Backhaus and W. Drechsler (eds.), *Friedrich Nietzsche (1844–1900): Economy and Society*. NY: Springer: 55–86.

Reinharz, Shulamit
1992 *Feminist Methods in Social Research.* New York: Oxford University Press.

Reinharz, Shulamit (ed.)
1993 *A Contextualized Chronology of Women's Sociological Work.* Waltham, Mass.: Brandeis University Press.

Remmling, Gunter
1967 *Road to Suspicion: A Study of Modern Mentality and the Sociology of Knowledge.* New York: Appleton-Century-Crofts.
1975 *The Sociology of Karl Mannheim.* Atlantic Highlands. N.J.: Humanities Press.

Rhoades, Lawrence J.
1981 *A History of the American Sociological Association.* Washington, D.C.: American Sociological Association.

Riesman, David
1950 *The Lonely Crowd.* New Haven: Yale University Press.
1953/1995 *Thorstein Veblen.* New Brunswick, N.J.: Transaction Publishers.

Ringer, Fritz
1997 *Max Weber's Methodology: The Unification of the Cultural and Social Sciences.* Cambridge, Mass.: Harvard University Press.

Ritzer, George
1975a *Sociology: A Multiple Paradigm Science.* Boston: Allyn and Bacon.
1975b "Sociology: A Multiple Paradigm Science." *American Sociologist* 19:156–167.
1975c "Professionalization, Bureaucratization and Rationalization: The Views of Max Weber." *Social Forces* 53:627–634.
1979 "Toward an Integrated Sociological Paradigm." In W. Snizek et al. (eds.), *Contemporary Issues in Theory and Research.* Westport, Conn.: Greenwood Press: 25–46.
1980 *Sociology: A Multiple Paradigm Science.* Rev. ed. Boston: Allyn and Bacon.
1981 *Toward an Integrated Sociological Paradigm: The Search for an Exemplar and an Image of the Subject Matter.* Boston: Allyn and Bacon.
1983 "The McDonaldization of Society." *Journal of American Culture* 6:100–107.
1985 "The Rise of Micro-Sociological Theory." *Sociological Theory* 3:88–98.
1989 "Of Levels and 'Intellectual Amnesia.'" *Sociological Theory* 7:226–229.
1990 "Micro-Macro Linkage in Sociological Theory: Applying a Metatheoretical Tool." In G. Ritzer (ed.), *Frontiers of Social Theory: The New Syntheses.* New York: Columbia University Press: 347–370.
1991 *Metatheorizing in Sociology.* Lexington, Mass.: Lexington Books.
1995 *Expressing America: A Critique of the Global Credit Card Society.* Thousand Oaks, Calif.: Pine Forge Press.
1996 *The McDonaldization of Society.* Revised ed. Thousand Oaks, Calif.: Pine Forge Press.
1997 *Postmodern Social Theory.* New York: McGraw-Hill.
1998 *The McDonaldization Thesis.* London: Sage.

2001a *Explorations in the Sociology of Consumption: Fast Food, Credit Cards, and Casinos.* London: Sage.

2001b *Explorations in Socal Theory: From Metatheorizing to Rationalization.* London: Sage.

2003 *The Blackwell Companion to Major Contemporary Social Theorists.* Malden, MA: Oxford: Blackwell.

2004a *The McDonaldization of Society: Revised New Century Edition.* Thousand Oaks, Calif.: Pine Forge Press.

2004b *The Globalization of Nothing.* Thousand Oaks, Calif.: Pine Forge Press.

2005 *Enchanting a Disenchanted World: Revolutionizing the Means of Consumption.* 2nd ed. Thousand Oaks, Calif.: Pine Forge Press.

2008 *The McDonaldization of Society 5.* Thousand Oaks, CA: Pine Forge Press.

2009 "Focusing on the Prosumer: On Correcting an Error in the History of Social Theory." Paper Presented at Conference on the Prosumer, Frankfurt, April.

2010 *Globalization: A Basic Text.* Oxford: Wiley-Blackwell.

Ritzer, George (ed.)

2000b *The Blackwell Companion to Major Social Theorists.* Malden, Mass.: Blackwell.

2002 *McDonaldization: The Reader.* Thousand Oaks, Calif.: Pine Forge Press.

2005 *Encyclopedia of Social Theory.* 2 vols. Thousand Oaks, Calif.: Sage.

2007 *Encyclopedia of Sociology.* 11 vols. Oxford: Blackwell.

Ritzer, George, and Gindoff, Pamela

1992 "Methodological Relationism: Lessons for and from Social Psychology." *Social Psychology Quarterly* 55:128–140.

1994 "Agency-Structure, Micro-Macro, Individualism-Holism-Relationism: A Metatheoretical Explanation of Theoretical Convergence between the United States and Europe." In P. Sztompka (ed.), *Agency and Structure: Reorienting Social Theory.* Amsterdam: Gordon and Breach: 3–23.

Ritzer, George, and Goodman, Douglas

2001 "Postmodern Social Theory." In Jonathan Turner (ed.), *Handbook of Sociological Theory.* New York: Kluwer Academic/Plenum: 151–169.

Ritzer, George, Goodman, Douglas, and Wiedenhoft, Wendy

2001 "Theories of Consumption." In George Ritzer and Barry Smart (eds.), *Handbook of Social Theory.* London: Sage: 410–427.

Ritzer, George, and LeMoyne, Terri

1991 "Hyperrationality: An Extension of Weberian and Neo-Weberian Theory." In G. Ritzer, *Metatheorizing in Sociology.* Lexington, Mass.: Lexington Books: 93–115.

Ritzer, George, and Smart, Barry (eds.)

2001 *Handbook of Social Theory.* London: Sage.

Ritzer, George, and Walczak, David

1988 "Rationalization and the Deprofessionalization of Physicians." *Social Forces* 67:1–22.

Robbins, Richard H.

2005 *Global Problems and the Culture of Capitalism,* 3rd ed. Boston: Pearson.

Robertson, Roland

1992 *Globalization: Social Theory and Global Culture.* London: Sage.

Robinson, W. I.

2004 *A Theory of Global Capitalism.* Baltimore: Johns Hopkins University Press.

Forthcoming "Theories of Globalization." In George Ritzer (ed.), *The Blackwell Companion to Globalization*. Oxford: Blackwell.

Rocher, Guy
1975 *Talcott Parsons and American Sociology.* New York: Barnes and Noble.

Rock, Paul
1979 *The Making of Symbolic Interactionism.* Totowa, N.J.: Rowman and Littlefield.

Rockmore, Tom
2002 *Marx after Marxism: The Philosophy of Karl Marx.* Malden, Mass.: Blackwell Publishers.

Rogers, Mary
1996b "Theory—What? Why? How?" In Mary F. Rogers (ed.), *Multicultural Experiences, Multicultural Theories.* New York: McGraw-Hill: 11–16.
2000 "Alfred Schutz." In George Ritzer (ed.), *The Blackwell Companion to Major Social Theorists.* Malden, Mass.: Blackwell: 367–387.
2001 "Contemporary Feminist Theory." In George Ritzer and Barry Smart (eds.), *Handbook of Social Theory.* London: Sage: 285–296.

Rogers, Mary (ed.)
1996a *Multicultural Experiences, Multicultural Theories.* New York: McGraw-Hill.
1998 *Contemporary Feminist Theory.* New York: McGraw-Hill.

Rojek, Chris
1995 "Veblen, Leisure and Human Need." *Leisure Studies* 14:73–86.

Rosenau, James N.
2003 *Distant Proximities: Dynamics beyond Globalization.* Princeton, N.J.: Princeton University Press.

Rosenau, Pauline Marie
1992 *Post-Modernism and the Social Sciences: Insights, Inroads, and Intrusions.* Princeton, N.J.: Princeton University Press.

Rosenberg, Bernard
1956 *The Values of Veblen: A Critical Appraisal.* Washington, D.C.: Public Affairs Press.
1963 "Introduction." In Bernard Rosenberg (ed.), *Thorstein Veblen.* New York: Crowell: 1–14.

Rosenberg, Donna
1994 *World Mythology*. New York, NY: McGraw-Hill.

Rosenberg, Julius
2005 "Globalization Theory: A Post Mortem." *International Politics* 42:2–74.

Rosenberg, Rosalind
1982 *Beyond Separate Spheres: Intellectual Roots of Modern Feminism.* New Haven: Yale University Press.

Ross, Dorothy
1991 *The Origins of American Social Science.* Cambridge, Eng.: Cambridge University Press.

1998 "Gendered Social Knowledge: Domestic Discourse, Jane Addams, and the Possibilities of Social Science." In Helene Silverberg (ed.) *Gender and American Social Science: The Formative Years.* Princeton: Princeton University Press: 235–264.

Rossi, Alice
1974 *The Feminist Papers: From Adams to de Beauvoir.* New York: Bantam.

Rossi, Alice (ed.)
1973 *The Feminist Papers.* New York: Bantam.

Roth, Guenther
1968 "Introduction." In G. Roth and C. Wittich (eds.), *Max Weber, Economy and Society,* Vol. 1. Totowa, N.J.: Bedminster Press: xxvii–civ.
1971 "Sociological Typology and Historical Explanations." In G. Roth and R. Bendix (eds.), *Scholarship and Partisanship: Essays on Max Weber.* Berkeley: University of California Press: 109–128.
1976 "History and Sociology in the Work of Max Weber." *British Journal of Sociology* 27:306–318.
1990 "Marianne Weber and Her Circle." *Society* 127:63–70.
2000 "Global Capitalism and Multi-ethnicity: Max Weber Then and Now." In S. Turner (ed.), *The Cambridge Companion to Weber.* Cambridge, Eng.: Cambridge University Press: 117–130.
2005 "Transatlantic Connections: A Cosmopolitan Context for Max and Marianne Weber's New York Visit 1904." *Max Weber Studies* 5:81–112.

Ruef, Martin
2007 "Mannheim, Karl." In George Ritzer (ed.), *Encyclopedia of Sociology.* Oxford: Blackwell: 2756–2759.

Rueschemeyer, Dietrich
1994 "Variations on Two Themes in Durkheim's *Division du Travail:* Power, Solidarity, and Meaning in Division of Labor." *Sociological Forum* 9:59–71.

Runciman, W. G.
1972 *A Critique of Max Weber's Philosophy of Social Science.* London: Cambridge University Press.

Rundell, John
2001 "Modernity, Enlightenment, Revolution and Romanticism: Creating Social Theory." In George Ritzer and Barry Smart (eds.), *Handbook of Social Theory.* London: Sage: 13–29.

Ryan, Michael
2005 "Queer Theory." In George Ritzer (ed.), *Encyclopedia of Social Theory.* Thousand Oaks, Calif.: Sage: 615–618.

Ryan, William
1971 *Blaming the Victim.* New York: Pantheon.

Ryndbrandt, Lynne
1999 *Caroline Bartlett Crane and Progressive Reform: Social Housekeeping and Sociology.* New York: Garland.

Sadri, Ahmad
1992 *Max Weber's Sociology of Intellectuals.* New York: Oxford University Press.

Salinas, Haley
2004 "A Sociological Analysis of Charlotte Perkins Gilman's *Herland* and *With Her in Ourland.*" *The Discourse of Sociological Practice* 6:127–135.

Salomon, A.
1945 "German Sociology." In G. Gurvitch and W. F. Moore (eds.), *Twentieth Century Sociology.* New York: Philosophical Library: 586–614.
1963/1997 "Georg Simmel Reconsidered." In Gary D. Jaworski, *Georg Simmel and the American Prospect.* Albany: State University of New York Press: 91–108.

Sanderson, Stephen K.
2001 "Evolutionary Theorizing." In Jonathan Turner (ed.), *Handbook of Sociological Theory.* New York: Kluwer Academic/Plenum Publishers: 439–455.

Sandstrom, Kent L., and Kleinman, Sherryll
2005 "Symbolic Interaction." In George Ritzer (ed.), *Encyclopedia of Social Theory.* Thousand Oaks, Calif.: Sage: 821–826.

Sandstrom, Kent L., Martin, Daniel D., and Fine, Gary Alan
2001 "Symbolic Interactionism at the End of the Century." In George Ritzer and Barry Smart (eds.), *Handbook of Social Theory.* London: Sage: 217–231.

Sawyer, R. Keith
2002 "Durkheim's Dilemma: Toward a Sociology of Emergence." *Sociological Theory* 20:227–247.
2005 "Emergence." In George Ritzer (ed.), *Encyclopedia of Social Theory.* Thousand Oaks, Calif.: Sage: 245–246.

Sayer, Derek
1991 *Capitalism and Modernity: An Excursus on Marx and Weber.* New York: Routledge.

Sayers, Sean
2007 "The Concept of Labor: Marx and His Critics." *Science and Society* 71:431–454.

Scaff, Lawrence A.
1988 "Weber, Simmel, and the Sociology of Culture." *Sociological Review* 36:1–30.
1989 *Fleeing the Iron Cage: Culture, Politics, and Modernity in the Thought of Max Weber.* Berkeley: University of California Press.
2000 "Georg Simmel." In George Ritzer (ed.), *The Blackwell Companion to Major Social Theorists.* Malden, Mass.: Blackwell: 251–278.
2005 "Rationalization." In George Ritzer (ed.), *Encyclopedia of Social Theory.* Thousand Oaks, Calif.: Sage: 624–628.

Schaefer, Emmett
2004 "Transformations of the Self: Pedagogies from the Margins." *The Discourse on Sociological Practice* 6:197–201.

Scharff, Robert C.
1995 *Comte after Positivism.* New York: Cambridge.

Scharnhorst, Gary
1985 *Charlotte Perkins Gilman: A Bibliography.* Metuchen, N.J.: Scarecrow Press.

Schechter, Patricia
2001 *Ida B. Wells-Barnett and American Reform, 1880–1930.* Chapel-Hill, N.C.: University of North Carolina Press.

Scheff, Thomas

2006 *Goffman Unbound! A New Paradigm for Social Science.* Boulder, CO: Paradigm Publishers.

Schluchter, Wolfgang

1981 *The Rise of Western Rationalism: Max Weber's Developmental History.* Berkeley: University of California Press.

1996 *Paradoxes of Modernity: Culture and Conduct in the Theory of Max Weber.* Stanford, Calif.: Stanford University Press.

Schmaus, Warren

1994 *Durkheim's Philosophy of Science and the Sociology of Knowledge: Creating an Intellectual Niche.* Chicago: University of Chicago Press.

Schmitt, Raymond L., and Schmitt, Tiffani Mari

1996 "Community Fear of AIDS as Enacted Emotion: A Comparative Investigation of Mead's Concept of the Social Act." *Studies in Symbolic Interaction* 20:91–119.

Schneider, Louis

1967 *The Scottish Moralists: On Human Nature and Society.* Chicago: University of Chicago Press.

1971 "Dialectic in Sociology." *American Sociological Review* 36:667–678.

Schneider, Mark A.

1993 *Culture and Disenchantment.* Chicago: University of Chicago Press.

Schroeter, Gerd

1985 "Dialogue, Debate, or Dissent? The Difficulties of Assessing Max Weber's Relation to Marx." In R. J. Antonio and R. M. Glassman (eds.), *A Weber-Marx Dialogue.* Lawrence: University Press of Kansas: 2–19.

Schubert, Hans-Joachim

2005 "Cooley, Charles Horton." In George Ritzer (ed.), *Encyclopedia of Social Theory.* Thousand Oaks, Calif.: Sage: 150–155.

2007 "Cooley, Charles Horton." In George Ritzer (ed.), *Encyclopedia of Sociology.* Oxford: Blackwell: 798–801.

Schulz, Markus S.

2007a "Horkheimer, Max." In George Ritzer (ed.), *Encyclopedia of Sociology.* Oxford: Blackwell: 2163–2165.

2007b "Adorno, Theodor W." In George Ritzer (ed.), *Encyclopedia of Sociology.* Oxford: Blackwell: 27–30.

Schumpeter, Joseph Alois

1908 *Das Wesen und der Hauptinhalt der Theoretischen Nationalokonomie.* Leipzig: Duncker and Humbolt.

1911/1934/2007 *The Theory of Economic Development: An Inquiry into Profits, Capital, Credit, Interest, and the Business Cycle.* New Brunswick, N.J.: Transaction Publishers.

1939 *Business Cycles: A Theoretical, Historical and Statistical Analysis of the Capitalist Process.* New York, NY: McGraw-Hill.

1942/1947/1950 *Capitalism, Socialism, and Democracy.* New York.: Harper and Brothers.

1949 "Vilfredo Pareto." *The Quarterly Journal of Economics* 63:147–173.

1951/1989 "The Instability of Capitalism." In R.V. Clemence (ed.) *Essays: On Entrepreneurs, Innovations, Business Cycles, and the Evolution of Capitalism.* New Brunswick, N.J.: Transaction Publishers: 47–72.

1954/1994 *History of Economic Analysis*. New York: Oxford University Press.

1976 *Capitalism, Socialism and Democracy.* 5th ed. London: George Allen and Unwin.

1991 "Max Weber's Work." In R. Swedberg (ed.), *The Economics and Sociology of Capitalism*. Princeton, N.J.: Princeton University Press: 220–229.

2003 "The Theory of Economic Development." In J. Backhaus (ed.), *Joseph Alois Schumpeter: Entrepreneurship, Style and Vision*. New York.: Springer: 61–116.

Schutte, Gerhard

2007 "Phenomenology." In George Ritzer (ed.), *Encyclopedia of Sociology.* Oxford: Blackwell: 3401–3404.

Schutz, Alfred

1932/1967 *The Phenomenology of the Social World.* Evanston, Ill.: Northwestern University Press.

1973 *Collected Papers I: The Problem of Social Reality.* The Hague: Martinus Nijhoff.

1975 *Collected Papers III: Studies in Phenomenological Philosophy.* The Hague: Martinus Nijhoff.

1976 *Collected Papers II: Studies in Social Theory.* The Hague: Martinus Nijhoff.

Schutz, Alfred, and Luckmann, Thomas

1973 *The Structure of the Life World.* Evanston, Ill.: Northwestern University Press.

Schwalbe, Michael

2005 "Self and Self-Concept." In George Ritzer (ed.), *Encyclopedia of Social Theory.* Thousand Oaks, Calif.: Sage: 684–687.

Schwanenberg, Enno

1971 "The Two Problems of Order in Parsons' Theory: An Analysis from Within." *Social Forces* 49:569–581.

Schwartz, Barry

1998 "Postmodernity and Historical Reputation: Abraham Lincoln in Late Twentieth-Century American Memory." *Social Forces* 77:63–103.

Schwartz, Robert M., and Robert A. Schneider

2003 *Tocqueville and Beyond: Essays on the Old Regime.* Newark: University of Delaware Press.

Schweber, Silvan S.

1991 "Auguste Comte and the Nebular Hypothesis." In R. T. Bienvenu and M. Feingold (eds.), *In the Presence of the Past: Essays in Honor of Frank Manuel.* Dordrecht, Neth.: Kluwer: 131–191.

Schwendinger, Julia, and Schwendinger, Herman

1974 *Sociologists of the Chair.* New York: Basic Books.

Scimecca, Joseph

1977 *The Sociological Theory of C. Wright Mills.* Port Washington, N.Y.: Kennikat Press.

Sciulli, David

1986 "Voluntaristic Action as a Distinct Concept: Theoretical Foundations of Societal Constitutionalism." *American Sociological Review* 51:743–766.

Sciulli, David, and Gerstein, Dean
1985 "Social Theory and Talcott Parsons in the 1980s." *Annual Review of Sociology* 11:369–387.

Scott, Joan Firor
1964 "Introduction to *Democracy and Social Ethics* by Jane Addams." Cambridge, Mass.: Harvard University Press.

Scott, John Finley
1963 "The Changing Foundations of the Parsonian Action Schema." *American Sociological Review* 28:716–735.

Seckler, David
1975 *Thorstein Veblen and the Institutionalists.* Boulder, Colo.: Colorado Associated University Press.

Seidman, Steven
1983 *Liberalism and the Origins of European Social Theory.* Berkeley: University of California Press.
1994 "Symposium: Queer Theory/Sociology: A Dialogue." *Sociological Theory* 12:166–177.

Seigel, Jerrold E.
1978 *Marx's Fate: The Shape of a Life.* Princeton, N.J.: Princeton University Press.

Seigfried, Charlene Haddock
1996 *Pragmatism and Feminism: Reweaving the Social Fabric.* Chicago: University of Chicago Press.
1999 "Socializing Democracy: Jane Addams and John Dewey." *Philosophy of the Social Sciences* 29:207–230.

Seligman, Adam B.
1993 "The Representation of Society and the Privatization of Charisma." *Praxis International* 13:68–84.

Sellerberg, Ann-Mari
1994 *A Blend of Contradictions: Georg Simmel in Theory and Practice.* New Brunswick, N.J.: Transaction Publishers.

Shalin, Dmitri
1986 "Pragmatism and Social Interactionism." *American Sociological Review* 51: 9–29.
2000 "George Herbert Mead." In George Ritzer (ed.), *The Blackwell Companion to Major Social Theorists.* Malden, Mass.: Blackwell: 302–344.

Shamir, Ronen
1993 "Formal and Substantive Rationality in American Law: A Weberian Perspective." *Social and Legal Studies* 2:45–72.

Sharrock, Wes
2001 "Fundamentals of Ethnomethodology." In George Ritzer and Barry Smart (eds.), *Handbook of Social Theory.* London: Sage: 249–259.

Sherlock, Steve
1997 "The Future of Commodity Fetishism." *Sociological Focus* 30:61–78.

Shields, Rob

1996 "Meeting or Mis-Meeting? The Dialogical Challenge to Verstehen." *British Journal of Sociology* 47:275–294.

Shils, Edward

1995 "Karl Mannheim." *American Scholar* 64:221–235.

1996 "The Sociology of Robert E. Park." *American Sociologist* 27:88–106.

Shreve, Anita

1989 *Women Together, Women Alone: The Legacy of the Consciousness Raising Movement.* New York: Viking.

Shweder, Richard A., and Fiske, Donald W.

1986 "Introduction: Uneasy Social Science." In D. W. Fiske and R. A. Shweder (eds.), *Metatheory in Social Science.* Chicago: University of Chicago Press: 1–18.

Sica, Alan

1986 "Hermeneutics and Axiology: The Ethical Content of Interpretation." In M. L. Wardell and S. P. Turner (eds.), *Sociological Theory in Transition.* Boston: Allen and Unwin: 142–157.

1988 *Weber, Irrationality and Social Order.* Berkeley: University of California Press.

2001 "Weberian Theory Today: The Public Face." In Jonathan Turner (ed.), *Handbook of Sociological Theory.* New York: Kluwer Academic/Plenum Publishers: 487–507.

2005 "Modernity." In George Ritzer (ed.), *Encyclopedia of Social Theory.* Thousand Oaks, Calif.: Sage: 505–511.

Silber, Ilana Friedrich

1993 "Monasticism and the 'Protestant Ethic': Asceticism, Rationality and Wealth in the Medieval West." *British Journal of Sociology* 44:103–123.

Simmel, Georg

1903/1971 "The Metropolis and Mental Life." In D. Levine (ed.), *Georg Simmel.* Chicago: University of Chicago Press: 324–339.

1904/1971 "Fashion." In D. Levine (ed.), *Georg Simmel.* Chicago: University of Chicago Press: 294–323.

1906/1950 "The Secret and the Secret Society." In K. Wolff (ed. and trans.), *The Sociology of Georg Simmel.* New York: Free Press: 307–376.

1907/1978 *The Philosophy of Money,* Tom Bottomore and David Frisby (eds. and trans.). London: Routledge and Kegan Paul.

1908/1950a "Subordination under a Principle." In K. Wolff (ed. and trans.), *The Sociology of Georg Simmel.* New York: Free Press: 250–267.

1908/1950b "Types of Social Relationships by Degrees of Reciprocal Knowledge of the Participants." In K. Wolff (ed. and trans.), *The Sociology of Georg Simmel.* New York: Free Press: 317–329.

1908/1955 *Conflict and the Web of Group Affiliations.* New York: Free Press.

1908/1959a "How Is Society Possible?" In K. Wolff (ed.), *Essays in Sociology, Philosophy and Aesthetics.* New York: Harper Torchbooks: 337–356.

1908/1959b "The Problem of Sociology." In K. Wolff (ed.), *Essays in Sociology, Philosophy and Aesthetics.* New York: Harper Torchbooks: 310–336.

1908/1971a "Group Expansions and the Development of Individuality." In D. Levine (ed.), *Georg Simmel.* Chicago: University of Chicago Press: 251–293.

1908/1971b "The Stranger." In D. Levine (ed.), *Georg Simmel.* Chicago: University of Chicago Press: 143–149.
1908/1971c "The Poor." In D. Levine (ed.), *Georg Simmel.* Chicago: University of Chicago Press: 150–178.
1908/1971d "Domination." In D. Levine (ed.), *Georg Simmel.* Chicago: University of Chicago Press: 96–120.
1917/1950 "The Problem Areas of Sociology." In K. H. Wolff (ed.), *The Sociology of Georg Simmel.* New York: Free Press: 16–25.
1918/1971 "The Transcendent Character of Life." In D. Levine (ed.), *Georg Simmel.* Chicago: University of Chicago Press: 353–374.
1921/1968 "The Conflict in Modern Culture." In K. P. Etzkorn (ed.), *Georg Simmel.* New York: Teachers College Press, Columbia University: 11–25.
1950 *The Sociology of Georg Simmel,* Kurt Wolff (ed. and trans.). New York: Free Press.
1984 *On Women, Sexuality and Love,* Guy Oakes (trans.). New Haven: Yale University Press.
1991 "Money in Modern Culture." *Theory, Culture and Society* 8:17–31.

Simonds, A. P.
1978 *Karl Mannheim's Sociology of Knowledge.* Oxford: Clarendon Press.

Simpson, Brent
2007 "Rational Choice Theories." In George Ritzer (ed.), *Encyclopedia of Sociology.* Oxford: Blackwell: 3794–3799.

Singer, Brian C. J.
2004 "Montesquieu, Adam Smith, and the Discovery of the Social." *Journal of Classical Sociology* 4:31–57.
2005a "Rousseau, Jean-Jacques." In George Ritzer (ed.), *Encyclopedia of Social Theory.* Thousand Oaks, Calif.: Sage: 656–658.
2005b "Montesquieu, Charles Louis De Secondat." In George Ritzer (ed.), *Encyclopedia of Social Theory.* Thousand Oaks, Calif.: Sage: 512–515.

Singer, Peter
1980 *Marx.* Oxford; New York: Oxford University Press.

Sklar, Kathryn Kish
1995 *Florence Kelley and the Nation's Work 1830–1900.* New Haven, Conn.: Yale University Press.

Skocpol, Theda
1979 *States and Social Revolutions.* Cambridge, Eng.: Cambridge University Press.
1997 "The Tocqueville Problem." *Social Science History* 21:455–479.

Skog, Ole-Jorgen
1991 "Alcohol and Suicide—Durkheim Revisited." *Acta Sociologica* 34:193–206.

Slater, Don
1997 *Consumer Culture and Modernity.* Cambridge, Eng.: Polity Press.
2005 "Consumer Culture." In George Ritzer (ed.), *Encyclopedia of Social Theory.* Thousand Oaks, Calif.: Sage: 139–145.

Smith, Cyril
1997 "Friedrich Engels and Marx's Critique of Political Economy." *Capital and Class* 62:123–142.

Smith, David Norman
1998 "Faith, Reason, and Charisma: Rodolf Sohm, Max Weber, and the Theology of Grace." *Sociological Inquiry* 68:32–60.

Smith, Dorothy
1987 *The Everyday World as Problematic: A Feminist Sociology.* Boston: Northeastern University Press.

Smith, Greg
2006 *Erving Goffman.* NY: Routledge.

Smith, Ken
2007 "Operationalizing Max Weber's Probability Concept of Class Situation: The Concept of Social Class." *British Journal of Sociology* 58:87–104.

Smith, Norman Erik
1979 "William Graham Sumner as an Anti-Social Darwinist." *Pacific Sociological Review* 22:332–347.

Smith, Philip
2008 "Durkheim and Criminology: Reconstructing the Legacy." *Australian and New Zealand Journal of Criminology* 26:299–323.

Smith, T. V.
1931 "The Social Philosophy of George Herbert Mead." *American Journal of Sociology* 37:368–385.

So, Alvin Y., and Suwarsono
1990 "Class Theory or Class Analysis? A Reexamination of Marx's Unfinished Chapter on Class." *Critical Sociology* 17:35–55.

Sociological Perspectives
1995 Vol. 38. (Special edition)

Soeffner, Hans-Georg
2005 "Verstehen." In George Ritzer (ed.), *Encyclopedia of Social Theory.* Thousand Oaks, Calif.: Sage: 864–868.

Soja, Edward W.
1989 *Postmodern Geographies: The Reassertion of Space in Critical Theory.* London: Verso.

Spencer, Herbert
1850/1954 *Social Statics.* New York: Robert Schalkenbach Foundation.
1864/1883/1968 *Reasons for Dissenting from the Philosophy of M. Comte and Other Essays.* Berkeley, Calif.: Glendessary Press.
1873/1961 *The Study of Sociology.* Ann Arbor: University of Michigan Press.
1883 *Recent Discussions in Science, Philosophy and Morals.* New York: Appleton.
1892/1965 *The Man versus the State.* Caldwell, Idaho: Caxton.
1897/1978 *The Principles of Ethics.* 2 vols. Indianapolis: Liberty Classics.
1902/1958 *First Principles.* New York: DeWitt Revolving Fund.
1904a *An Autobiography,* Vol. 1. New York: Appleton.
1904b *An Autobiography,* Vol. 2. New York: Appleton.
1908a *The Principles of Sociology,* Vol. 1. New York: Appleton.
1908b *The Principles of Sociology,* Vol. 2. New York: Appleton.
1908c *The Principles of Sociology,* Vol. 3. New York: Appleton.

Spykman, Nicholas
1925/1966 *Social Theory of Georg Simmel.* Chicago: Aldine.

Squier, Susan
2007 "Wayward Reproductions: Genealogies of Race and Nation in Transatlantic Modern Thought." *Hypatia* 122:194–196.

Srubar, Ilja
1984 "On the Origin of 'Phenomenological' Sociology." In K. H. Wolff (ed.), *Alfred Schutz: Appraisals and Developments.* Dordrecht, Neth.: Martinus Nijhoff: 57–83.
1985 "The Missing Feminist Revolution in Sociology." *Social Problems* 32:301–316.
2005 "Phenomenology." In George Ritzer (ed.), *Encyclopedia of Social Theory.* Thousand Oaks, Calif.: Sage: 557–562.

Stacey, Judith, and Thorne, Barrie
1996 "Is Sociology Still Missing the Feminist Revolution?" *Perspectives* 18:1–3.

Standley, Arline R.
1981 *Auguste Comte.* Boston: Twayne.

Staples, Clifford
2007 "Feuerbach, Ludwig." In George Ritzer (ed.), *Encyclopedia of Sociology.* Oxford: Blackwell: 1747–1749.

Starosta, Guido
2008 "The Commodity-Form and the Dialectical Method: On the Structure of Marx's Exposition in Chapter 1 of *Capital.*" *Science and Society* 72:295–318.

Stebbins, Robert
2007a "Thomas, W. I." In George Ritzer (ed.), *Encyclopedia of Sociology.* Oxford: Blackwell: 5000.
2007b "Znaniecki, Florian." In George Ritzer (ed.), *Encyclopedia of Sociology.* Oxford: Blackwell: 5316–5317.

Stehr, Nico
2001 "Modern Societies as Knowledge Societies." In George Ritzer and Barry Smart (eds.), *Handbook of Social Theory.* London: Sage: 494–508.

Steinmetz, George
2007 "Marxism and Sociology." In George Ritzer (ed.), *Encyclopedia of Sociology.* Oxford: Blackwell: 2815–2818.

Stiglitz, Joseph E.
2002 *Globalization and Its Discontents.* New York: W.W. Norton.

Stokoe, Elizabeth
2006 "On Ethnomethodology, Feminism, and the Analysis of Categorical Reference to Gender in Talk-in-Interaction." *Sociological Review* 54:467–494.

Stones, Rob
2005 *Structuration Theory.* Cambridge: Palgrave McMillan.

Strauss, Anselm
1996 "Everett Hughes: Sociology's Mission." *Symbolic Interaction* 19:271–283.

Strenski, Ivan
1997 *Durkheim and the Jews of France.* Chicago: University of Chicago.

Strydom, Piet
2005 "The Scottish Enlightenment." In George Ritzer (ed.), *Encyclopedia of Social Theory*. Thousand Oaks, Calif.: Sage: 675–680.

Swartz, David
1997 *Culture and Power: The Sociology of Pierre Bourdieu*. Chicago: University of Chicago Press.

Swedberg, Richard
1991 "Introduction: The Man and His Work." In R. Swedberg (ed.), *The Economics and Sociology of Capitalism*. Princeton, N.J.: Princeton University Press: 3–98.
1991a *Schumpeter: A Biography*. Princeton, N.J.: Princeton University Press.
1993 "On the Relationship between Economic Theory and Economic Sociology in the Work of Joseph Schumpeter." In R. Swedberg (ed.), *Explorations in Economic* Sociology. New York: Russell Sage Foundation: 42–61.

Swedberg, Richard
1998 *Max Weber and the Idea of Economic Sociology*. Princeton: Princeton University Press.

Sweezy, Paul
1958 "Veblen on American Capitalism." In Douglas F. Dowd (ed.), *Thorstein Veblen: A Critical Reappraisal*. Ithaca, N.Y.: Cornell University: 177–197.

Symbolic Interaction
1988 Special issue on Herbert Blumer's legacy. 11:1–160.

Szmatka, Jacek, and Mazur, Joanna
1996 "Theoretical Research Programs in Social Exchange Theory." *Polish Sociological Review* 3:265–288.

Sztompka, Piotr (ed.)
1994 *Agency and Structure: Reorienting Social Theory*. Amsterdam: Gordon and Breach.

Tabboni, Simonetta
1995 "The Stranger and Modernity: From Equality of Rights to Recognition of Difference." *Thesis Eleven* 43:17–27.

Takayama, K. Peter
1998 "Rationalization of State and Society: A Weberian View of Early Japan." *Sociology of Religion* 59:65–88.

Takla, Tendzin, and Pope, Whitney
1985 "The Force Imagery in Durkheim: The Integration of Theory, Metatheory and Method." *Sociological Theory* 3:74–88.

Tenbruck, F. H.
1959 "Formal Sociology." In K. Wolff (ed.), *Essays on Sociology, Philosophy and Aesthetics*. New York: Harper Torchbooks: 61–99.

Terkel, Studs
1974 *Working*. New York: Pantheon.

Then, Gabe
2007 "Reappraising the Risk Society Thesis: Telescopic Sight or Myopic Vision?" *Current Sociology* 55:793–813.

Thistle, Susan
2000 "The Trouble with Modernity: Gender and the Remaking of Social Theory." *Sociological Theory* 18(2):275–288.

Thomas, J.J.R.
1985 "Rationalization and the Status of Gender Divisions." *Sociology* 19:409–420.

Thomas, Jan E., and Kukulan, Annis
2004 "'Why Don't I Know These Women?': The Integration of Early Women Sociologists in Classical Theory Courses." *Teaching Sociology* 32:252–263.

Thomas, William, and Znaniecki, Florian
1918/1958 *The Polish Peasant in Europe and America.* New York: Dover Publications.

Thomas, William I., and Thomas, Dorothy S.
1928 *The Child in America: Behavior Problems and Programs.* New York: Knopf.

Thomason, Burke C.
1982 *Making Sense of Reification: Alfred Schutz and Constructionist Theory.* Atlantic Highlands, N.J.: Humanities Press.

Thompson, Kenneth
1975 *Auguste Comte: The Foundation of Sociology.* New York: Halstead Press.

Thomson, Ernie
1994 "The Sparks That Dazzle Rather than Illuminate: A New Look at Marx's 'Theses on Feuerbach.'" *Nature, Society and Thought* 7:299–323.

Tijssen, Lietake van Vucht
1991 "Women and Objective Culture: George Simmel and Marianne Weber." *Theory, Culture and Society* 8:203–218.

Tilman, Rick
1984 *C. Wright Mills: A Native Radical and His American Intellectual Roots.* University Park: Pennsylvania State University Press.
1992 *Thorstein Veblen and His Critics, 1891–1963: Conservative, Liberal, and Radical Perspectives.* Princeton, N.J.: Princeton University Press, 1992.

Tilman, Rick
2007 *Thorstein Veblen and the Enrichment of Evolutionary Naturalism.* Columbia, MO: University of Missouri Press.

Timming, Andrew
2004 "Florence Kelley: A Recognition of Her Contributions to Sociology." *Journal of Classical Sociology* 4:283–309.

Tiryakian, Edward A.
1974 "Review of *Emile Durkheim on Morality and Society." American Journal of Sociology* 80:769–771
1979 "The Significance of Schools in the Development of Sociology." In W. Snizek, E. Fuhrman, and M. Miller (eds.), *Contemporary Issues in Theory and Research.* Westport, Conn.: Greenwood Press: 211–233.
1981 "The Sociological Import of Metaphor." *Sociological Inquiry* 51:27–33.
1986 "Hegemonic Schools and the Development of Sociology: Rethinking the History of the Discipline." In R. C. Monk (ed.), *Structures of Knowing.* Lanham, Md.: University Press of America: 417–441.

1994 "Revisiting Sociology's First Classic: *The Division of Labor in Society* and Its Actuality." *Sociological Forum* 9:3–16.
1995 "Collective Effervescence, Social Change and Charisma: Durkheim, Weber and 1989." *International Sociology* 10:269–281.
2007 "Pitirim A. Sorokin and Social Change." In George Ritzer (ed.), *Encyclopedia of Sociology.* Oxford: Blackwell: 4619–4623.

Tiryakian, Edward
2009 *For Durkheim: Essays in Historical and Cultural Sociology*. Burlington, VT: Ashgate.

Titunik, Regina F.
1997 "A Continuation of History: Max Weber and the Advent of a New Aristocracy." *The Journal of Politics* 59:680–700.

Toby, Jackson
1966 "The Intellectual Debt that Deviance Theory Owes Talcott Parsons." *Journal of Classical Sociology* 5:349–364.

Tocqueville, Alexis de
1835–1840/1969 *Democracy in America*. Garden City, N.Y.: Doubleday.
1856/1983 *The Old Regime and the French Revolution*. New York: Doubleday.
1893/1959 *The Recollections of Alexis de Tocqueville*. New York: Meridian Books.

Tole, Lise Ann
1993 "Durkheim on Religion and Moral Community in Modernity." *Sociological Inquiry* 63:1–29.

Touraine, Alain
1995 *Critique of Modernity.* Cambridge, Mass.: Blackwell.

Travers, Andrew
1992 "The Conversion of Self in Everyday Life." *Human Studies* 15:169–238.

Trevino, A. Javier
2005 "Parsons's Action-System Requisite Model and Weber's Elective Affinity." *Journal of Classical Sociology* 5:319–348.

Tribe, Keith
1989 "Introduction." In K. Tribe (ed.), *Reading Weber.* London: Routledge: 1–14.

Tseelon, Efrat
1992 "Is the Presented Self Sincere? Goffman, Impression Management and the Postmodern Self." *Theory, Culture and Society* 9:115–128.

Tucker, Robert C. (ed.)
1970 *The Marx-Engels Reader.* New York: Norton.

Turner, Brian
1991 *Religion and Social Theory.* Thousand Oaks, Calif.: Sage.

Turner, Bryan S.
1974 *Weber and Islam: A Critical Study.* London: Routledge and Kegan Paul.
1981 *For Weber: Essays in the Sociology of Fate.* Boston: Routledge and Kegan Paul.
1985 *The Body and Society: Explorations in Social Theory.* Oxford: Blackwell.

1986 "Simmel, Rationalization and the Sociology of Money." *Sociological Review* 34:93–114.

1995 "Karl Mannheim's *Ideology and Utopia.*" *Political Studies* 43:718–727.

Turner, Bryan S., and Edmunds, June

2005 "Global Generations: Social Change in the Twentieth Century." *British Journal of Sociology* 56:559–577.

Turner, Jonathan

1985a "In Defense of Positivism." *Sociological Theory* 3:24–30.

1985b *Herbert Spencer: A Renewed Appreciation.* Beverly Hills, Calif.: Sage.

1990 "The Past, Present, and Future of Theory in American Sociology." In G. Ritzer (ed.), *Frontiers of Social Theory: The New Syntheses.* New York: Columbia University Press: 371–391.

2000 "Herbert Spencer." In George Ritzer (ed.), *The Blackwell Companion to Major Social Theorists.* Malden, Mass.: Blackwell: 81–104.

2001a "The Origins of Positivism: The Contributions of Auguste Comte and Herbert Spencer." In George Ritzer and Barry Smart (eds.), *Handbook of Social Theory.* London: Sage: 30–42.

2007 "Spencer, Herbert." In George Ritzer (ed.), *Encyclopedia of Sociology.* Oxford: Blackwell: 4638–4641.

Turner, Jonathan (ed.)

2001b *Handbook of Sociological Theory.* New York: Kluwer Academic/Plenum Publishers.

Turner, Jonathan, and Beeghley, Leonard

1974 "Current Folklore in the Criticisms of Parsonsian Action Theory." *Sociological Inquiry* 44:47–63.

Turner, Jonathan, and Maryanski, A. Z.

1988 "Is 'Neofunctionalism' Really Functional?" *Sociological Theory* 6:110–121.

Turner, Jonathan H., and Boyns, David E.

2001 "The Return of Grand Theory." In Jonathan Turner (ed.), *Handbook of Sociological Theory.* New York: Kluwer Academic/Plenum: 353–378.

Turner, Stephen Park

1983 "Weber on Action." *American Sociological Review* 48:506–519.

1993 "Introduction: Reconnecting the Sociologist to the Moralist." In S. P. Turner (ed.), *Emile Durkheim: Sociologist and Moralist.* London: Routledge: 1–22.

1998 "Who's Afraid of the History of Sociology?" *Schwezerische Zeistschrift fur Soziologie* 24:3–10.

2003 "Charisma Reconsidered." *Journal of Classical Sociology* 3:5–26.

Turner, Stephen Park, and Factor, Regis A.

1994 *Max Weber: The Lawyer as Social Thinker.* London: Routledge.

Udehn, Lars

1981 "The Conflict between Methodology and Rationalization in the Work of Max Weber." *Acta Sociologica* 24:131–147.

Ullmann-Margalit, Edna

1997 "The Invisible Hand and the Cunning of Reason." *Social Research* 64:181–198.

Urry, John
1995 *Consuming Places.* London: Routledge.

van Krieken, Robert
2001 "Norbert Elias and Process Sociology." In George Ritzer and Barry Smart (eds.), *Handbook of Social Theory.* London: Sage: 353–367.

Van Staveren, Irene
2003 "Feminist Fiction and Feminist Economics: Charlotte Perkins Gilman on Efficiency." In Drucilla K. Barker and Edith Kuiper (eds.), *Toward a Feminist Philosophy of Economics.* London and New York: Routledge: 56–69.

Vandenberghe, Frederic
2005 "Historical Materialism." In George Ritzer (ed.), *Encyclopedia of Social Theory.* Thousand Oaks, Calif.: Sage: 373–375.

Varga, Ivan
2006 "Social Morals, the Sacred and State Regulation in Durkheim's Sociology." *Social Compass* 53:457–466.

Varul, Matthias Zick
2007 "Thorstein Veblen." In George Ritzer (ed.), *Encyclopedia of Sociology.* Oxford: Blackwell: 5186.

Veblen, Thorstein
1899/1994 *The Theory of the Leisure Class.* New York: Penguin Books.
1899/1900/1964 "The Preconceptions of Economic Science." In Wesley Mitchell (ed.), *What Veblen Taught: Selected Writings of Thorstein Veblen.* New York: Augustus M. Kelley: 39–150.
1904 *The Theory of the Business Enterprise.* New York: Charles Scribner's Sons.
1906/1963 "The Socialist Economics of Karl Marx and His Followers." In Bernard Rosenberg (ed.), *Thorstein Veblen.* New York: Crowell: 58–73.
1909/1964 "The Limitations of Marginal Utility." In Wesley Mitchell (ed.), *What Veblen Taught: Selected Writings of Thorstein Veblen.* New York: Augustus M. Kelley: 151–175.
1915/1942 *Imperial Germany and the Industrial Revolution.* New York: Viking.
1918/1965 *The Higher Learning in America: A Memorandum on the Conduct of Universities by Business Men.* New York: Augustus M. Kelley.
1919/1964 *The Vested Interests and the Common Man.* New York: Augustus M. Kelley.
1921 *The Engineers and the Price System.* New York: Viking.
1922/1964 *The Instinct of Workmanship and the State of the Industrial Arts.* New York: Augustus M. Kelley.
1923 *Absentee Ownership and Business Enterprise in Recent Times: The Case of America.* New York: Viking.

Venkatesh, Alladi
2007 "Postmodern Consumption." In George Ritzer (ed.), *Encyclopedia of Sociology.* Oxford: Blackwell: 3552–3556.

Vetter, Lisa P.
2008 "Harriet Martineau on the Theory and Practice of Democracy in America." *Political Theory* 36:424–455.

Vidich, Arthur J., and Lyman, Stanford M.
1985 *American Sociology: Worldly Rejections of Religion and Their Directions.* New Haven, Conn.: Yale University Press.

Vidler, Anthony
1991 "Agoraphobia: Spatial Estrangement in Georg Simmel and Siegfried Kracauer." *New German Critique* 54:31–45.

Wagner, Helmut
1983 *Alfred Schutz: An Intellectual Biography.* Chicago: University of Chicago Press.

Wallerstein, Immanuel
1974 *The Modern World-System: Capitalist Agriculture and the Origins of the European World Economy in the 16th Century.* New York: Academic Press.
1980 *The Modern World-System II: Mercantilism and the Consolidation of the European World-Economy, 1600–1750.* New York: Academic Press.
1986 "Marxisms as Utopias: Evolving Ideologies." *American Journal of Sociology* 91:1295–1308.
1989 *The Modern World-System III: The Second Era of Great Expansion of the Capitalist World-Economy, 1730–1840.* New York: Academic Press.

Wallimann, Isidor
1981 *Estrangement: Marx's Conception of Human Nature and the Division of Labor.* Westport, Conn.: Greenwood Press.

Warde, Alan
2005 "Consumption and Theories of Practice." *Journal of Consumer Culture* 5: 131–153.

Warner, Michael (ed.)
1993 *Fear of a Queer Planet: Queer Politics and Social Theory.* Minneapolis: University of Minnesota Press.

Warriner, Charles
1969 "Social Action, Behavior and Verstehen." *Sociological Quarterly* 10:501–511.

Wartenberg, Thomas E.
1982 "'Species-Being' and 'Human Nature' in Marx." *Human Studies* 5:77–95.

Wax, Murray
1967 "On Misunderstanding Verstehen: A Reply to Abel." *Sociology and Social Research* 51:323–333.

Webb, Beatrice Potter
1887 "The Dock Life of East London." *Nineteenth Century* 22:301–314.
1891 *The Co-operative Movement in Great Britain.* London: Swan, Sonnenschein and Company.
1926 *My Apprenticeship.* New York: Longman, Green.

Weber, Marianne
1905/1919 "Jobs and Marriage." In M. Weber, *Frauenfrage und Frauengedanke.* Tübingen, Ger.: J.C.B. Mohr: 20–37.
1907 *Ehefrau und Mutter in der Rechtsentwicklung.* Tübingen: J.C.B. Mohr.
1912/1919a "Authority and Autonomy in Marriage." In M. Weber, *Frauenfrage und Frauengedanke.* Tübingen, Ger.: J.C.B. Mohr: 67–79.

1912/1919b "The Valuation of Housework." In M. Weber, *Frauenfrage und Frauengedanke.* Tübingen, Ger.: J.C.B. Mohr: 80–94.

1912a/1919/1998 "Authority and Autonomy in Marriage." Elizabeth Kirchen (trans.) in Patricia Lengermann and Jill Niebrugge-Brantley, *The Women Founders: Sociology and Social Theory, 1830–1930.* New York: McGraw-Hill. (Originally published in *Frauenfragen und Frauengedanken.* Tübingen: J.C.B. Mohr: 67–79.)

1913/1919 "Women and Objective Culture." In M. Weber, *Frauenfrage und Frauengedanke.* Tübingen, Ger.: J.C.B. Mohr: 95–134.

1918/1919/1998 "Women's Special Cultural Tasks." Elizabeth Kirchen (trans.) in Patricia Lengermann and Jill Niebrugge-Brantley, *The Women Founders: Sociology and Social Theory, 1830–1930.* New York: McGraw-Hill. (Originally published in *Frauenfragen und Frauengedanken.* Tübingen, Ger.: J.C.B. Mohr: 238–261.)

1926/1975 *Max Weber: A Biography*. New York: Wiley

1935 *Frauen und Liebe* ("Women and Love"). Koonigestein in Taunus, Ger.: K. B. Langewissche.

1975 *Max Weber: A Biography,* Harry Zohn (ed. and trans.). New York: Wiley.

Weber, Max

1896–1906/1976 *The Agrarian Sociology of Ancient Civilizations.* London: NLB.

1903–1906/1975 *Roscher and Knies: The Logical Problems of Historical Economics.* New York: Free Press.

1903–1917/1949 *The Methodology of the Social Sciences,* Edward Shils and Henry Finch (eds.). New York: Free Press.

1904–1905/1958 *The Protestant Ethic and the Spirit of Capitalism.* New York: Scribner's.

1906/1985 "'Churches' and 'Sects' in North America: An Ecclesiastical Socio-Political Sketch." *Sociological Theory* 3:7–13.

1915/1958 "Religious Rejections of the World and Their Directions." In H. H. Gerth and C. W. Mills (eds.), *From Max Weber: Essays in Sociology.* New York: Oxford University Press: 323–359.

1916/1964 *The Religion of China: Confucianism and Taoism.* New York: Macmillan.

1916–1917/1958 *The Religion of India: The Sociology of Hinduism and Buddhism.* Glencoe, Ill.: Free Press.

1921/1958 *The Rational and Social Foundations of Music.* Carbondale: Southern Illinois University Press.

1921/1963 *The Sociology of Religion.* Boston: Beacon Press.

1921/1968 *Economy and Society.* 3 vols. Totowa, N.J.: Bedminster Press.

1922–1923/1958 "The Social Psychology of the World Religions." In H. H. Gerth and C. W. Mills (eds.), *From Max Weber: Essays in Sociology.* New York: Oxford University Press: 267–301.

1927/1981 *General Economic History.* New Brunswick, N.J.: Transaction Books.

Weigert, Andrew

1981 *Sociology of Everyday Life.* New York: Longman.

Weiler, Bernd

2007a "Social Darwinism." In George Ritzer (ed.), *Encyclopedia of Sociology.* Oxford: Blackwell: 4390–4392.

2007b "Sumner, William Graham." In George Ritzer (ed.), *Encyclopedia of Sociology.* Oxford: Blackwell: 4884–4886.

Weingartner, Rudolph H.
1959 "Form and Content in Simmel's Philosophy of Life." In K. Wolff (ed.), *Essays on Sociology, Philosophy and Aesthetics.* New York: Harper Torchbooks: 33–60.

Weinstein, Deena, and Weinstein, Michael A.
1993 *Postmodern(ized) Simmel.* London: Routledge.
1998 "Simmel-Eco vs. Simmel-Marx: Ironized Alienation." *Current Perspectives in Social Theory* 18:63–77.

Weiss, Johannes
1987 "On the Irreversibility of Western Rationalization and Max Weber's Alleged Fatalism." In S. Whimster and S. Lash (eds.), *Max Weber, Rationality and Modernity.* London: Allen & Unwyn.

Wells, Gordon C., and Baehr, Peter
1995 "Editors' Introduction." In Max Weber, *The Russian Revolutions.* Ithaca, N.Y.: Cornell University Press.

Wells-Barnett, Ida B.
1894/1969 *On Lynchings.* New York: Arno.
1970 *Crusade for Justice: The Autobiography of Ida B. Wells,* Alfreda M. Duster (ed.). Chicago: University of Chicago Press.

Werbner, Pnina, and Basu, Helene
1998 *Embodying Charisma: Modernity, Locality and the Performance of Emotion in Sufi Cults.* London: Routledge.

Wernick, Andrew
2005 "Comte, Auguste." In George Ritzer (ed.), *Encyclopedia of Social Theory.* Thousand Oaks, Calif.: Sage: 128–134.

West, Cornell
1994 *Race Matters.* New York: Vintage.

Wheatland, Thomas
2009 *The Frankfurt School in Exile.* Minneapolis, Minn.: University of Minnesota Press.

Whimster, Sam
2001 "Max Weber: Work and Interpretation." In George Ritzer and Barry Smart (eds.), *Handbook of Social Theory.* London: Sage: 54–65.
2005a "Weber, Max." In George Ritzer (ed.), *Encyclopedia of Social Theory.* Thousand Oaks, Calif.: Sage: 877–882.
2005b "Marianne Weber: Contributing to Work and Person." *Max Weber Studies* 5:131.

Whipps, Judy D.
2004 "Jane Addams's Social Thought as a Model for a Pragmatist-Feminist Communitarianism." *Hypatia* 19:118–133.

White, Everett
1961 "Introduction." In E. Durkheim, *Moral Education.* New York: Free Press: ix–xxviii.

Whitehead, Alfred North
1917/1974 *The Organization of Thought, Educational and Scientific.* Westport, Conn.: Greenwood Press.

Whyte, William F.
1961 "Parsons' Theory Applied to Organizations." In M. Black (ed.), *The Social Theories of Talcott Parsons.* Englewood Cliffs, N.J.: Prentice-Hall: 250–267.

Wiggershaus, Rolf
1994 *The Frankfurt School: Its History, Theories, and Political Significance.* Cambridge, Mass.: MIT Press.

Wilde, Lawrence
1991 "Logic: Dialectic and Contradiction." In T. Carver (ed.), *The Cambridge Companion to Marx.* Cambridge, Eng.: Cambridge University Press: 275–295.

Wiley, Norbert
1979 "The Rise and Fall of Dominating Theories in American Sociology." In W. Snizek, E. Fuhrman, and M. Miller (eds.), *Contemporary Issues in Theory and Research.* Westport, Conn.: Greenwood Press: 47–79.
1986 "Early American Sociology and *The Polish Peasant.*" *Sociological Theory* 4:20–40.
2006 "Peirce and the Founding of American Sociology." *Journal of Classical Sociology* 6:23–50.
2007 "Znaniecki's Key Insight: The Merger of Pragmatism and Neo-Kantianism." *Polish Sociological Review* 158:133–143.

Williams, Joyce
2007 "Albion W. Small." In George Ritzer (ed.), *Encyclopedia of Sociology.* Oxford: Blackwell: 4341–4342.

Williamson, J.
1990 "What Washington Means by Policy Reform." In J. Williamson (ed.), *Latin American Adjustment: How Much Has Happened?* Washington, D.C.: Institute for International Economics, 7–20.
1997 "The Washington Consensus Reassessed." In L. Emmerij (ed.), *Economic and Social Development into the XXI Century.* Washington, D.C.: Inter-American Development Bank, 48–61.

Wiltshire, David
1978 *The Social and Political Thought of Herbert Spencer.* London: Oxford University Press.

Winant, Howard
2001 *The World Is a Ghetto: Race and Democracy since World War II.* New York: Basic Books.

Winterer, Caroline
1994 "A Happy Medium: The Sociology of Charles Horton Cooley." *Journal of the History of the Behavioral Sciences* 30:19–27.

Wittgenstein, Ludwig
1953 *Philosophical Investigations.* Oxford: B. Blackwell.

Wobbe, Theresa
2004 "Elective Affinities: Georg Simmel and Marianne Weber on Gender and Moderntiy" pp. 54–68 In Barbara L. Marshall and Anne Witz (eds.), *Engendering the Social.* Berkshire, England: Open University Press.

Woldring, Henk E. S.
1986 *Karl Mannheim: The Development of His Thought.* Assen/Maastricht, Neth.: Van Gorcum.

Wolf, Harald
2005a "Capital." In George Ritzer (ed.), *Encyclopedia of Social Theory.* Thousand Oaks, Calif.: Sage: 75–76.
2005b "Capitalism." In George Ritzer (ed.), *Encyclopedia of Social Theory.* Thousand Oaks, Calif.: Sage: 76–80.

Wolosky, Shira
2003 "Public Women, Private Men: American Women Poets and the Common Good." *Signs* 28:665–694.

Wood, Ellen M.
1995 *Democracy Against Capitalism: Renewing Historical Materialism.* Cambridge, Eng.: Cambridge University Press.

Wortmann, Susan
2007a "Praxis." In George Ritzer (ed.), *Encyclopedia of Sociology.* Oxford: Blackwell: 3612–3613.
2007b "Collective Conscience." In George Ritzer (ed.), *Encyclopedia of Sociology.* Oxford: Blackwell: 581–583.

Wrong, Dennis
1994 *The Problem of Order: What Unites and Divides Society.* New York: Free Press.

Yates, Gayle Graham
1985 *Harriet Martineau on Women.* New Brunswick, N.J.: Rutgers University Press.

Zafirovski, Milan
2001 "Parsons and Sorokin: A Comparison of the Founding of American Sociological Theory Schools." *Journal of Classical Sociology* 1:227–256.

Zeitlin, Irving M.
1996 *Ideology and the Development of Sociological Theory.* 6th ed. Englewood Cliffs, N.J.: Prentice-Hall.

Zijderveld, Anton C.
2005 "Ideal Type." In George Ritzer (ed.), *Encyclopedia of Social Theory.* Thousand Oaks, Calif.: Sage: 389–390.

Znaniecki, Florian
1934 *Method of Sociology.* New York: Farrar and Rhinehart.

Zunz, Olivier, and Kahan, Alan S. (eds.)
2002 *The Tocqueville Reader: A Life in Letters and Politics.* Oxford: Blackwell.

Zweigenhaft, Richard L., and Domhoff, G. William
2006 *Diversity in the Power Elite: How It Happened, Why It Matters.* Lanham, MD: Bowman and Littlefield.

Credits

Chapter 3 Alexis de Tocqueville, excerpts from *Democracy in America,* edited by J. P. Mayer, translated by George Lawrence. Copyright © 1969 by Harper and Row. Reprinted with the permission of Doubleday, a division of Random House, Inc. • Alexis de Tocqueville, excerpts from *The Old Regime and the French Revolution,* translated by Stuart Gilbert. Copyright © 1955 by Stuart Gilbert. Reprinted with the permission of Doubleday, a division of Random House, Inc.
Chapter 4 Auguste Comte, excerpts from *A General View of Positivism,* translated by J. H. Bridges. Copyright © 1957. Reprinted with the permission of Robert Speller & Sons, Publishers.
Chapter 6 Karl Marx, excerpts from Capital: A Critique of Political Economy, Volume I. Reprinted with the permission of International Publishers.
Chapter 7 Barry Schwartz, excerpt from "Postmodernity and Historical Reputation: Abraham Lincoln in Late Twentieth-Century American Memory" from *Social Forces* 77:1 (September 1998). Copyright © 1998 by Social Forces, University of North Carolina Press. Reprinted with the permission of the publisher. • Lisa Ann Tole, excerpt from "Durkheim on Religion and Moral Community in Modernity" from *Sociological Inquiry* 63 (1993). Copyright © 1993 by the University of Texas Press. Reprinted with the permission of Blackwell Publishers, Inc.
Chapter 8 Max Weber, excerpts from *Economy and Society,* 2 volumes edited by Guenther Roth and Claus Wittich, translated by the editors and others. Copyright © 1978 by The Regents of the University of California. Reprinted with the permission of the University of California Press.
Chapter 9 Georg Simmel, excerpts from *The Philosophy of Money,* edited and translated by Tom Bottomore and David Frisby. Copyright © 1978 by Routledge & Kegan Paul, Ltd. Reprinted with the permission of Routledge.
Chapter 13 Karl Mannheim, excerpts from *Ideology and Utopia,* translated by Louis Wirth and Edward Shils (New York: Harcourt Brace, 1936). Reprinted with the permission of Routledge. • Karl Mannheim, excerpts from *Man and Society in an Age of Reconstruction,* translated by Edward Shils. Reprinted with the permission of Routledge.
Chapter 14 George Herbert Mead, excerpts from *Mind, Self and Society: From the Standpoint of a Social Behaviorist.* Copyright © 1934 by The University of Chicago, renewed © 1962 by Charles W. Morris. Reprinted with the permission of The University of Chicago Press.
Chapter 15 Alfred Schutz, excerpts from *Collected Papers I: The Problems of Social Reality,* edited by Maurice Natanson. Reprinted with the permission of Kluwer Academic Publishers, The Netherlands.
Chapter 16 Figures 16.1 and 16.3: "Structure of the General Action System" and "Society, Its Subsystems and the Functional Imperatives" from Talcott Parsons and Gerald Platt, *The American University.* Copyright © 1973 by The President and Fellows of Harvard College. Reprinted with the permission of the Harvard University Press. • Figure 16.2: "Parson's Action Schema" adapted from Talcott Parsons, *Societies: Evolutionary and Comparative Perspectives.* Copyright © 1966. Adapted with the permission of Pearson Education, Upper Saddle River, NJ.

Photo Credits Page 30: Courtesy of the Library of Congress; p. 48: Courtesy of American Sociological Association; p. 61: © Fritz Goro/Time Life Pictures/Getty Images; p. 84: © Time Life Pictures/Getty Images; p. 110: © Apic/Getty Images; p. 130: © Edward Gooch/Getty Images; p. 154: Courtesy of the Library of Congress; p. 186: © Bettmann/Corbis; p. 220: © Hulton Archive/Getty Images; p. 264: © INTERFOTO/Alamy; p. 294: © Spencer Arnold/Getty Images; p. 300: Courtesy of the Library of Congress; p. 308: Courtesy of the Library of Congress; p. 316 top: Courtesy of Oberlin College Archives; p. 316 bottom: Courtesy of the Library of Congress; p. 330: Courtesy of the Library of Congress; p. 352: © Bettmann/Corbis; p. 374: © Imagno/Getty Images; p. 394: Courtesy of Mrs. J. Molncar Piliszanska; p. 420: Courtesy of the University of Chicago; p. 444: Courtesy of the Estate of Alfred Schutz; p. 464: Courtesy of American Sociological Association

Name Index

[Note: Page numbers followed by *f* and *n* refer to figures and footnotes.]

Subject Index

[Note: Page numbers followed by *f* or *n* refer to figures or footnotes.]